MADE IN AMERICA

Made in America

A Social History of American Culture and Character

CLAUDE S. FISCHER

The University of Chicago Press CHICAGO & LONDON

CLAUDE S. FISCHER is professor of sociology at the University of California, Berkeley. He is the author or coauthor of several books, including *To Dwell Among Friends* (1982), *America Calling* (1992), *Inequality by Design* (1996), and *Century of Difference* (2006). He is also the founding editor of *Contexts* magazine.

The University of Chicago Press, Chicago 60637
The University of Chicago Press, Ltd., London
© 2010 by The University of Chicago
All rights reserved. Published 2010
Printed in the United States of America

20 19 18 17 16 15 14 13 12 11 10   2 3 4 5

ISBN-13: 978-0-226-25143-1 (cloth)
ISBN-10: 0-226-25143-8 (cloth)

Library of Congress Cataloging-in-Publication Data

Fischer, Claude S., 1948–
    Made in America : a social history of American culture and character / Claude S. Fischer.
        p. cm.
    Includes bibliographical references and index.
    ISBN-13: 978-0-226-25143-1 (cloth : alk. paper)
    ISBN-10: 0-226-25143-8 (cloth : alk. paper) 1. National characteristics, American.
2. United States—Civilization. 3. United States—Social life and customs. I. Title.
    E169.1.F538 2010
    973—dc22   2009024798

To Avi and Leah,
who will help build the American future

Contents

Preface and Acknowledgments

I have spent much of the last twenty years immersed in American social history, reading a trove of detailed yet evocative studies of ordinary people's everyday lives in times long ago. Partly it was just fascination with the stories, learning about the routines, challenges, and outlooks of early tobacco growers fighting disease in the Chesapeake region, farm girls going to work in the mills of antebellum Massachusetts, businessmen striving to make a go of it in new Midwestern towns, young brides trying to fashion a domestic home on the barren Western frontier, and myriad other players in the American experience. Immersion in this literature has been a pleasure, not only an education.

But I also wanted to use this rich scholarship to address the classic issue of "modernity." What has modern life, the coming of industry, technology, metropolises, and wealth, meant for the experiences and personalities of average people? Are there distinctively modern individuals, and if so, what are the culture and character of such individuals? Sociology, my profession, arose in response to these questions, and sociologists remain entranced by them.

This book applies what I learned from social historians—and from other scholars as well—to a few facets of the modernity question, American version. It starts with the basics that condition culture and character: life, health, security, and assets. Modern Americans gained much more of each; did those gains translate into greater confidence or perhaps a greater pursuit of goods? The book then turns to Americans' personal relationships, describing the proliferation of small groups, public activities, and social choices in modern life. Strikingly, the *voluntarism* that distinguished the culture of colonial America—a melding of individualism *with* community—seems to have strengthened and expanded over time. Modern life allowed more Americans to become more typically "American," to be independent persons in voluntary communities. The book finally turns to character, asking whether modern Americans think or feel differently than their ancestors did; are they, for example, more skeptical or more anxious? Strikingly, the answer is, much less than one might imagine. Yet more Americans gained cognitive skills and developed emotional habits which enabled them to more fully participate in the voluntaristic culture that characterizes America.

*

I must first acknowledge the social historians upon whose findings this book is built. Their efforts to uncover the lived past were long and hard work. Having done some historical research myself (*America Calling: A Social History of the Telephone*), I can testify that working the archives requires serious discipline. I hope I have been faithful to their scholarship.

Research support for this book has been slim but steady, small annual grants from University of California, Berkeley's Committee on Research. It has funded, over much of two decades, many students to help me sift through the voluminous literature: John Chan, Cristina Cielo, Christine Getz, Graham Hill, Steven Kerr, Benjamin Moodie, Michael Pelton, Jon Pennington, Tom Pessah, Amy Schalet, Lisa Stampnitzky, Charles Stephens, Jennifer Utrata, Ann Wood, and Richard Wood. Avi Fischer and Leah Fischer provided a bit of help, too.

As this project matured into a book, I benefited from partial readings by Michael Hout, John Levi Martin, Peter Stromberg, Viviana Zelizer, and Sharon Zukin, and by sociology editors Karl Bakeman and Tim Sullivan. James T. Sparrow read and commented on the whole book; Paul DiMaggio did the same with such intensity and thoroughness that he could have asked for coauthorship.

Working with the University of Chicago Press team, led by legendary and exuberant editor Doug Mitchell and his assistant Tim McGovern, has once again been a delight. Mary Gehl edited a complex manuscript with diligence. Matt Avery gets credit for the design and Levi Stahl for the marketing campaign (and book naming).

Finally and fulsomely, I thank my family. My children, Avi and Leah, patiently watched me disappear into the study to work on this project from their toddler years to their adulthood. Ann Swidler played two roles. It will be clear to many sociologists that I have engaged and appropriated some of her ideas without giving full credit; you can learn something over one-third of a century of marriage. And she has unstintingly, enthusiastically sympathized with and supported all my efforts, small and large, from rooting for the Giants to this lengthy project. "A woman of worth . . . The heart her husband safely trusts in her, and he shall have no lack of gain."

1 The Stories We Tell

The former drover George C. Duffield, whose memoir of a cattle drive inspired the television series *Rawhide*, recalled his mother's life on the Iowa frontier in the 1820s and '30s. She cared for the babies, cleaned the floors, made the beds, cultivated a garden, dressed turkeys, cured meat, made candles, preserved fruit, spun and knitted to make clothing, cut the children's hair, taught them to spell, and "did the thousand things for us a mother only finds to do." Hall of Fame ballplayer Cal Ripken Jr., whose Iron Man career inspired thousands of little leaguers, recalled his mother's life during the 1960s and '70s. Because his father was also a ballplayer, she did some of both parents' duties. She kept score at his games, coached his hitting, and bucked him up when he lost. When Cal Sr. was home, she joined in family basketball games (she "had a really good two-handed set shot"). On the road, she packed and unpacked, set up housekeeping, did the laundry, handled the family budget, and settled the children's quarrels. Ripken did not mention, as Duffield had, the food, clothing, barbering, and schooling that his mother took care of—that went without saying. He noted instead the emotional support and companionship she provided.[1]

Such contrasting memoirs illustrate how greatly Americans' everyday lives changed over a century and a half—both in the mundane details of life and in their personal nature. This book asks how Americans' *culture and character* developed over the nation's history. The long answer to that question is complex, partial, and sometimes surprising. The short answer is that centuries of material and social expansion enabled more people to become more characteristically "American," meaning—among other things—insistently independent but still sociable, striving, and sentimental. Answering this question calls for a history that is not focused on presidents and politics but on ordinary people living ordinary lives, a *social* history. The question generates many detailed inquiries pursued in the chapters that follow. How have longer life spans affected Americans' sense of control over their lives? How has greater wealth affected Americans' taste for luxury? Have more city living and faster communications enriched or depleted individuals' social ties? Have Americans become increasingly satisfied or more discontent?

Understanding the cultural and psychological path Americans have taken not only satisfies our curiosity, it helps us think about the path Americans should take. Historians, for example, have intensely debated the mindset of farmers in the colonial era. Did they try to shrewdly maximize their families' wealth, or did they simply follow traditional, local practices? Behind this question lies a broader one: were American farmers individualists from the earliest colonial days or did they become so only in the nineteenth century? Energizing this debate is the feeling that if early Americans subordinated their individual interests to those of the community, then more collective arrangements could work in America "again." If, on the other hand, early Americans calculatingly pursued their private interests, that would seem to imply—incorrectly perhaps—that Americans are self-interested by nature and suggest—incorrectly perhaps—that communitarian reforms are futile. What historians discover in, say, farmers' ledgers from the 1700s does not *logically* imply taking one political position versus another. But history is psychologically, rhetorically compelling. That is why political combatants wheel out their own versions of history: as artillery in battles for public opinion. As to this example, the historical record suggests that Americans' degree of self-interestedness has changed little over the centuries. In other ways, however, Americans' character did change; they seemed, for example, to become more sentimental.

The fundamental contrast between early Americans and today's Americans in their circumstances of life, the material and social conditions that influence culture and character, can be captured by the word "more." Modern Americans have more of almost everything: more time on Earth, more wealth, more things, more information, more power, more acquaintances, and so many more choices. Not more of absolutely everything—twenty-first-century Americans, for example, have fewer siblings and cousins—but generally, more Americans gained more access to more things material, social, and personal. Americans began as a "people of plenty," in historian David Potter's words, but became even more so. And, over the generations, more of those who had been outside the circle of plenty and outside the culture of independence which that plenty sustained—a culture which I will describe shortly—joined it. In this sense, more Americans became more American.

Before elaborating on these ideas, I need to address some conventional misunderstandings of American social history. I discuss several specific myths of the American past and a few habits of thought that currently cloud our views of that past.

MYTHS OF AMERICAN SOCIAL HISTORY

Much of what we "know"—and I include many sociologists such as myself in the "we"—is mythical. Some myths are mere folktales easily and often debunked, like the story that the Pilgrims landed at Plymouth Rock. Other myths are more subtle. For example, the familiar lament that families no longer take dinner together assumes that typical Americans had until recently shared such meals. However, this supposedly timeless tradition arose only among the middle class in the late nineteenth century. Similarly, people often regret that religious holidays are no longer sacred holy days. But such holidays, too, are often recent inventions or reinventions. Over two hundred years ago, for example, the American Christmas was more a carnival of excess than a religious experience. It was only around the end of the nineteenth century that the family-and-church Christmas that modern Americans consider to be traditional developed, thanks in some measure to *A Christmas Carol* and "'Twas the Night Before Christmas."[2]

More important than these sorts of misconceptions is the deeper, conventional wisdom about American history that academics, politicians, journalists, and writers of all sorts regularly invoke. Hardworking historians have in recent decades mined rich veins of archives, bringing to the surface stories of how Americans of the past really lived, revealing how much those conventional assumptions turn out to be myths or half-truths. Here are five illustrations.

✻ *Myth: over the generations Americans moved around more.* The belief that residential mobility increased is one of my favorite myths, because it is so widespread, so contrary to fact, and yet so resistant to correction. Many learned essayists speak of "our increasingly mobile society" and the disorientation all this modern moving around supposedly creates. In 2001, for example, the editorial page of the *New York Times* attributed recent changes in American family life in part to "the ever-growing mobility of Americans." In 2008, an eminent psychiatrist explained a spurt in suicides by Americans' "more frequent moves away from friends and relatives." In fact, Americans moved around *less and less* in those very years and less and less over recent decades. Furthermore, modern Americans change homes and neighborhoods less often than Americans did in the mid-twentieth century and less often than Americans did in the early nineteenth century, the years of George Duffield's childhood.[3]

* *Myth: Americans turned away from religion.* Sage commentators sometimes mourn, sometimes celebrate, the decline of religion and the rise of existential doubt. In fact, proportionately *more* twentieth-century Americans belonged to churches than belonged in prior centuries. Rates of membership fell a bit after the 1950s, but participation in churches still remained more widespread than in earlier eras. Whether modern churchgoers remained believers or became skeptics is hard to determine, but evidence suggests that Americans have generally kept the faith.[4]

* *Myth: Americans became more violent.* The specter of violent crime haunts contemporary Americans and they typically believe that life was safer in earlier days. This perception is basically wrong. Criminal violence fluctuates sharply in the short term—historically low in the 1950s, rising rapidly in the 1960s through 1980s, and then declining almost to 1950s levels by 2000. In a longer view, early-twenty-first-century Americans run a notably *lower* risk of being assaulted or killed than Americans ran in the nineteenth century or before. The general culture of violence—including bar brawls; gang attacks; wife, child, and animal abuse; eye-gouging fights; and the like—dissipated.[5]

* *Myth: Americans became increasingly alienated from their work.* Many commentators assume that modern industry forced workers who had been independent craftsmen into specialized, repetitive, subservient, and disheartening jobs, pointing to, say, the unemployed artisanal carriage-maker forced to work on the automobile assembly line. This certainly happened to many individuals. But if we consider American workers as a whole, far more of them and their children gladly left the drudgery of farming or labor, such as stevedoring, to move into more stimulating jobs, such as industrial and clerical work, however imperfect those were. Americans' labor became less alienating.[6]

* *Myth: Americans became indifferent to the needy.* "We once took care of one another," some people say to indict modern selfishness and others say to indict the modern "nanny state." In fact, earlier generations did at best a mediocre job of caring for the needy. In the eighteenth and nineteenth centuries, Americans gave some assistance to longtime neighbors who were widowed, orphaned, or disabled through no fault of their own. However, the destitute who were strangers, newcomers, or morally sus-

pect instead received directions to leave town. In the twentieth century, growing affluence and a variety of government programs virtually eliminated starvation and radically reduced poverty. These and other signs indicate growing—not lessening—sympathy over the generations.[7]

Such mythic misunderstandings of American social and cultural history persist. Sometimes, they even determine public policy, say, about crime or poverty. The myths in part follow from the systematic ways that we—both scholars and the general public—think about history, about how we tell stories.

Habitual Stories

Nostalgia contributes to mythologizing the past. As individuals, we draw on the gauzy memories of our own childhoods; as a culture, we share a millennia-long grief about the loss of Eden. Scholars, even secular ones, are not immune. Polemicists of both the Right and Left share the yearning for a mythic past. Nineteenth-century continental writers who bemoaned the loss of *gemeinschaft*—the small and intimate community yet untainted by modernity—accepted the romantic images of rural life in that era's fiction and painting. Longing for a "world we have lost" spurs both reactionaries to call for a return to the past and radicals to call for a revolution against the present.[8]

We also have a habit of seeing our specific moment in history as an epochal turning point. Judeo-Christian tradition invests historical events with great import; each drives us closer to the End of Days. Here, too, secular thinkers share this inclination. Hegel and Marx, for example, "were convinced that the novelties of any particular era represented the fulfillment of some hidden purpose implicit throughout earlier historical progression." Such thinking leads us to exaggerate change, to read our time as the best of times or the worst of times, or even both at the same time (as Dickens labeled both the age of the French Revolution and his own era, about seventy years later). But this habit of thought misleads us. Most generations live, by definition, in ordinary times. Why not us?[9]

Another habit is to view the past as normal, natural, and eternal, thereby making today seem abnormal, unnatural, and changeable. Many traditions, like the family Christmas or mothers' spiritual role in the family, seem "immemorial" only because people cannot remember when those practices started. Many supposedly timeless folkways turn out to be recent developments, including the Zambian bride-wealth system, Maori creation myths, celebrations of birthdays, and Americans' renderings of customs from the "old country."[10]

We weave stories, creating the past perhaps as much as remembering it. Precolonial New England was a "forest primeval," for example, only in the romantic stories of nineteenth-century authors. (The natives had already heavily worked over the land.) Holidays, statues, and television docudramas are all about constructing what historians call collective memory. Intense struggles break out over how those memories ought to be constructed. For several years after 1968, partisans fought over whether Americans would remember Martin Luther King Jr. as a liberator, or as a troublemaker, or not at all. The institution of a national holiday settled that argument. It is no wonder that noisy disputes break out over school history books, for example, over how to best describe the lives of women or the conditions of slaves in the past.[11]

It is no wonder, as well, that Americans of differing backgrounds remember the nation's history differently. In a survey conducted in the 1990s, almost all white respondents asked to describe "the American past" answered largely in terms of their own families' histories. Black respondents, in contrast, more commonly described the past in collective, *racial* terms. Ironically, although the black interviewees often talked about slavery and oppression, most of them said that the nation was making progress. White respondents, on the other hand, overwhelmingly said that their own families were doing fine but the nation was in decline.[12]

We typically tell and understand history as a set of stories ("narratives," academics say) rather than as just one thing happening after another. Stories provide coherence, plot, and dramatic tension; they tell us why things happened and what the moral is. The Civil War, for example, tested the proposition "that all men are created equal" and provided "a new birth of freedom," according to master storyteller Abraham Lincoln. One grand story about America is triumphal and romantic: Americans built a "shining city on the hill" by pioneering, gumption, democracy, welcoming immigrants, and so on. Disenchanted historians of the 1960s recast the American story as bitter and tragic: Americans' hopes were dashed by heroes undone, Indians murdered, Africans enslaved, workers repressed, immigrants deracinated, environments befouled, and so on. During the early 1990s, essayists dueled in the journals of opinion about a set of "national historical standards" that a team of historians had developed for teaching of fifth- through twelfth-grade history. Conservative critics saw the proposed content as too tragic, too critical. One of them wrote, "A nation grown cynical about its own history soon ceases to be a nation at all."[13]

The romantic and tragic versions of American history derive in part from greater epics of Western history. One epic is utopian: modern society is the summit of, or at least a station on the way to, Progress. The other is dystopian: modern society is a pit into which we have fallen. Other possible sagas, such as seeing history as an endless cycle of pretty much the same thing over and over, make little sense to Westerners. Most Americans tacitly believe both stories, the optimistic and the pessimistic. (Regular people are not ideologically consistent—and why should they be?) Depending on the events of a particular day, we see progress or decline. In the last several decades, Americans seem to have increasingly seen decline.[14]

The Modernization Story

Many scholars have long held onto a specific story called "modernization theory": once, Western societies were "traditional"—small, simple, and intimate—and then sometime between the sixteenth and mid-twentieth centuries, material conditions, social arrangements, and cultural ideas changed radically, bringing forth "modern" society—large, complex, and impersonal. The many variants of this story all presume that a social revolution occurred—for example, the rise of manufacturing or the development of science—which had cascading effects. Societies are so tightly woven that changes in one domain radiated through others and eventually altered how people think and feel. The result, goes the theory, was a shift from tradition to "modernity."[15]

Criticisms of modernization theory fill the pages of academic journals. Critics attack, for example, its assumption that societies are tightly knit, or its image of earlier communities as simple and orderly. Of particular interest to us is the charge that modernization theory generally depicts twentieth-century America as the quintessential modern society, but America does not really fit the theory. Typically, the modernization thesis assumes that a people have had a feudal past, peasantry, and common heritage—think of a remote Alpine village. But none of these existed in early America. Often, critics imagined that they had buried modernization theory—only to see its ghost soon again roaming the halls of academe. It rises from the dead because it provides a powerful, all-encompassing story, one which corresponds to popular understandings and one which can tie together many historical strands.[16]

Indeed, historians bemoan all the loose threads that comprise the study of American social history. Especially since the 1960s, researchers have uncovered a treasure of detailed information about the past— about family patterns, neighborhoods, work, leisure, immigrants, slaves, farmers, homemakers, and the new middle class, each in particular communities and years. But this fortune became burdensome. "We were— and still are," wrote one historian in 1992, "snowed under by an avalanche of information, much of it unassimilable into a coherent national narrative." And so historians ask: "how do we develop larger frameworks of meaning that help to grasp the . . . long-run historical change and continuity?" Modernization theory remains, mainly by default, the most common framework.[17]

Perhaps historians should be guided by no grand story at all and just tell what happened, one thing after another. But this is not really possible. No one is an unfocused lens; we all fix on certain issues, attend to some themes and not others. Similarly, try as we might to avoid reading some coherence, plot, or moral into history, eventually we must sum it all up and try to make sense of what happened. In the next two sections of this introduction, I outline the topics in American social history I have selected to explore and the summary story I have extracted.

THEMES AND THESIS

My purpose is to sketch how American culture and character changed— or did not change—over the course of the nation's history from the colonial era to the turn of the twenty-first century. This is, of course, an outrageously vast and absurdly ambitious goal. By necessity, therefore, I focus on only a handful of themes and give only brief attention to many other worthy topics, such as Americans' work lives and how they dealt with race. I am struck that underlying most social trends is the vast expansion, between the years shortly before George Duffield's childhood and the years of Cal Ripken Jr.'s childhood, in how much more Americans had gained materially, socially, and culturally. How did having so much *more* in so many realms—more clothes, more comfort, more clubs, more religions, more acquaintances, and so on—alter how Americans thought, felt, and behaved?[18] The specific themes are as follows.

✱ *Security.* By the middle of the twentieth century more Americans were freer from physical and economic threats than ever before. This development was uneven; for example, young Americans faced increased economic vulnerabilities at the turn of the twenty-first century. Still, the long span of American history brought average Americans a level of material security that even wealthy Americans in earlier periods could not achieve. How much that reality translated into feeling secure is less certain.

✱ *Goods.* From the start, Americans were a "people of plenty," and their collection of goods only accelerated. Observers have long said that all this buying and owning corroded American character and may have turned

Americans into a "consumerist" nation. The evidence suggests that in this respect, however, American character did not change. Americans today may be entranced by consumer glitter, but so were Americans centuries ago. Critically, mass production, mass distribution, and mass credit meant that more Americans could attain the goods that were part of the good life. Security and goods together created a foundation for the expansion of middle-class American culture.

* *Groups.* America began as an unusually individualistic society—more precisely, a *voluntaristic* society, as I explain below—and only became more so. More Americans participated in more groups of more kinds, including relatively new kinds of groups, such as clubs, work teams, and free-floating friendships. They not only took advantage of these social options to form new sorts of bonds, they also used them to maintain independence from and voice in each group. The broadest example is how women gained greater power in American households.

* *Public spaces.* American culture emphasizes the small, voluntary group, and the sparseness of early American settlement encouraged private life. But through roughly the nineteenth century, more Americans discovered and joined in a vibrant public life on city streets, in department stores, at amusement parks, and in movie houses. Then, as the twentieth century unrolled, Americans moved back into their private homes and parochial social groups. Americans' participation in politics followed a similar arc of greater and then lesser involvement in the public space.

* *Mentality.* For centuries, middle-class Americans worked on their "selves"—their characters—whether they were colonial landowners copying the British gentry or religious enthusiasts preparing their souls for salvation. As America became materially and socially richer, more people engaged in such self-perfecting. Americans became no smarter nor more rational than their ancestors, but they gained a set of cognitive and practical tools to operate in the world, tools that gave them greater command of their lives and themselves. Americans learned to restrain their disruptive emotions and cultivate their socially useful ones, like sympathy and sentimentality. The end result was probably somewhat better mental health and a bit more happiness.

What runs through these seemingly disparate themes is an argument: the availability and expansion of material security and comfort enabled early American social patterns and culture to expand and solidify, to both delineate and spread an American national character. With growth, more people could participate in that distinctive culture more fully and could become "more American."

This claim is somewhat unusual among grand narratives about Americans. Writers more commonly describe modern American culture and character as a break with or even a reversal of the past—and usually for the worse. Many, usually in the mid-twentieth century, depicted modern Americans as having lost their ancestors' individuality, as having become sheep in a mass society. Others, usually in the late twentieth century, described modern Americans as self-absorbed, even selfish individualists who have torn apart the tight-knit communities of their ancestors. I am unpersuaded by assertions of revolutionary change in either direction and am more impressed by continuity over the centuries. (This, perhaps, is why Tocqueville's 1836 classic, *Democracy in America*, still speaks to us.) Americans came to live, think, and feel more intensely in ways distinctive to mainstream, middle-class American culture; they became more "American."

But what do I mean by mainstream American culture and character? By culture, I refer to the collection of shared, loosely connected, taken-for-granted rules, symbols, and beliefs that characterize a people. That culture is declared, sustained, and enforced by what sociologists call institutions, such as family, law, arts, and religion. By national character, I refer to ways of thinking, feeling, and behaving that individuals typically share with others in their nation. A central feature of American culture and character is *voluntarism*.

Voluntarism

The first key element of voluntarism is believing and behaving *as if* each person is a sovereign individual: unique, independent, self-reliant, self-governing, and ultimately self-responsible. Free men of early America stressed the importance of attaining what they called "competency" or "virtue," the independence that came with having enough property to support a household on one's own. The second key element of voluntarism is believing and behaving *as if* individuals succeed through fellowship—not in egoistic isolation but in sustaining, voluntary communities. I describe American voluntarism in more detail in chapter 4, but here I point out a few of its implications and address some objections.[19]

In a voluntaristic culture, people assume that they control their own fates and are responsible for themselves. Contrast that notion to what most cultures have historically presumed, that individuals are only parts of a social whole, acting out roles determined by God or fate and by those who rank above them (think, for example, of the medieval serf). A voluntaristic culture encourages people to examine and improve themselves, because they can and because their individuality is key to their fortunes. A voluntaristic culture implies procedural equality; each person is free in principle to join or leave the group and none can coerce another. Because success means doing well in voluntary groups, a voluntaristic culture also encourages individuals to strive for status. In several ways, then, many traits that outside observers have for generations described as particularly American—such as self-absorption, "can-do" confidence, egalitarianism, conformism, and status-striving—derive from a voluntaristic culture.[20]

To be sure, observers have described many other ways that Americans stand apart, such as their intense faith, moralism, violence, and cheeriness. These distinctive traits may derive from sources other than voluntarism and may in some ways contradict voluntarism. It may be hard, for example, to square belief in a God who has a plan for everyone with belief that each individual is responsible for his or her own destiny, but people do. Cultures, as well as individuals, need not be and are not logically consistent. The core distinction of American culture, I am arguing, is its voluntarism.

Even in the eighteenth century, more Americans than Europeans participated in a voluntaristic culture. Visiting European gentry often complained in particular about all the equality they saw in America. Yet most Americans of that era were still not fully part of this culture. Most did *not* see themselves as autonomous self-creators nor as free to join or leave social groups; they saw the world more the way members of the subservient classes in feudal Europe did. They were dependents without "competency": servants, slaves and descendants of slaves, subjugated natives, wives, children, the poor, the ill, the uneducated, and the newly arrived. Over the centuries, however, servitude nearly disappeared, and more Americans in these categories became part of the now-majority, middle-class or bourgeois culture of voluntarism.*

Voluntarism provides a frame for weaving together many threads in the story of American social change, but loose strands still remain. Other

---

* A note on language: this culture has been labeled "bourgeois," "middle class," "liberal," "individualistic," and "modern." There is certainly some overlap in these terms. I occasionally use the labels "bourgeois" or "middle class," because the bourgeois and the middle class—rather than the gentry or those people too subjugated to have "competency"—lived this culture the most and they promoted it to other Americans. The terms "liberal" and "individualistic" do not fit American culture quite as well, because they both fail to acknowledge the critical role of community. The term "modern" is often entangled with debates around modernization theory. When I use "modern," I simply mean "these days" rather than in earlier times.

things happened, ranging from the construction of a racial caste system to the multiplication of television sets, that shaped American culture and character. The expansion of voluntarism is a central story I tell, but it is not the only one that needs to be told.

Objections and Responses

After the 1960s, many American scholars, now focused by civil rights movements on diversity, objected to studies of national character. One historian wrote in 1988: "The concept of a national character has been shattered by the historical pluralism of the past two decades; like Humpty Dumpty it is beyond saving." Americans are too varied to have *a* national character or *a* common history. How, they asked, can one lump the experiences of men and women, black and white and Latino, worker and farmer, and so forth into one box? True: most societies are complex, pluralistic, and often conflicting, including that of early America. Nonetheless, out of this variety emerged a dominant social character, which I describe as voluntarist, which originated among Northeastern Protestants and then spread and gained power over time. Increasing proportions of women, youth, ethnic minorities, and the working class adopted that culture, even after sometimes resisting it. (Nineteenth-century Catholic institutions, for instance, tried to protect their immigrant members from the American culture's insistence on free thinking.) While many scholars emphasize the survival of ethnic diversity into the twenty-first century, what is sociologically striking is the extent to which the American mainstream has overflowed and washed away that diversity, leaving behind little but food variety and self-conscious celebrations of multiculturalism.[21]

Those skeptical about national character can point, for example, to the fact that homicide rates in Louisiana run about nine times higher than those in North Dakota, as large as a gap as that between the Ukraine and Iceland. They can also point to how much is shared across national borders, for example, the political similarities of English-speaking societies. Both arguments—that the United States is internally diverse and that it is in some ways similar to other nations—are valid challenges to the idea of a national culture. Nonetheless, important distinctions do coincide with national borders. All but a few small American states have homicide rates higher than those of other Western nations; so we can say that the United States *is* distinctively violent among affluent, Western societies. And American voting rates run substantially below those of comparable English societies; so we can say that Americans are distinctive that way, too. Discussing distinctive national character does make sense.[22]

A different challenge to my description of American national character points out that voluntarism hardly applies to the extremely involuntary experience of slaves and their descendants unto this day. Does this not negate the claim of *a* singular, national character? No. All national cultures are complex and contradictory. The centrality in American life of this particular contradiction is precisely what earned its racial caste system the label of *The* American Dilemma. Nonetheless, in the centuries-old contest between the Northeastern culture of voluntarism and Southern hierarchical culture, it is clear which side has had history—and armies and wealth and ideological power—on its side, which side has long claimed national dominance. The victims of the defeated system, which was finally defeated only about a generation ago, are now and only too-slowly benefitting.

Skepticism about national character leads many scholars to also reject the common description of America as an "exceptional" society. For over a century, many historians influenced by Frederick Jackson Turner have sought to explain American history in terms its special traits, such as an open frontier. Sociologists have wondered why the United States avoided the socialism of Europe and speculated that its wealth or ethnic diversity explains its distinction. But the notion of exceptionalism is now "in ill repute," according to an historian writing in 1995. The ill repute rests in part on linguistic confusion. "Exceptional" can mean "unusually good" or, in some renderings, being immune to the general laws of history. Both implications rankle many scholars. The common meaning of exceptional, however, is simply "unusual." In many ways, America is in fact noticeably unusual among major Western countries. Americans, for example, are the most accepting of economic inequality, the most religious, the most patriotic, and the most voluntarist of Westerners. All societies, of course, are exceptional in some fashion—not better, not worse, but distinct in their own particular ways. Much of America's history broadened and strengthened its distinctiveness.[23]

Saying that American social history moved in the direction of deepening its national culture risks implying some sort of inevitability, of suggesting that history unfolded in some destined fashion. In truth, that social history involved starts and stalls and reversals, such as economic depressions and civil disorders. Some events stymied the widening of the American mainstream—the rise of Jim Crow, for example—and others accelerated it—like the economic boom after World War II. Moreover, Americans fought over these cultural patterns, in apocalyptic fashion on the battlefields of Antietam and Gettysburg, but also in more mundane ways, over issues such as public schooling, alcohol, and women's rights. There was no inevitability. Still, the general trends toward greater security, increasing wealth, and more social groups meant that, in the long run, American voluntarism expanded.

EVIDENCE, CAVEATS, AND AUDIENCE

How do we *know* how American culture and character changed over the centuries? Too often, one picks up a book addressing this topic only to discover the author intently describing changes in how intellectuals *talked about* American culture and character. Ideas do matter, but typically the winds of intellectual ferment hardly disturb the deep currents of social transformations. (Can we, for example, take seriously the claim made by one author that quantum theory unsettled Americans' sense of security, given that most Americans do not believe in evolution, much less invisible quanta?) Difficult as it is, we must search for direct evidence of how average Americans thought, felt, and acted.[24]

There is so-called hard evidence: the censuses, surveys, and administrative records that measure Americans' behavior and sometimes their opinions and feelings as well. But the farther back we go, before World War II and certainly before 1900, the more we must rely on so-called soft evidence, such as diaries, letters, memoirs, and news accounts. We must also infer people's thoughts, feelings, and behavior from the material aspects of their lives. For example, historians surmise that early Americans rarely invited guests into their homes, because those homes rarely had chairs. Others infer from tiny tombstones carved with only the word "Baby" that early American parents were emotionally distant from their newborns. Whether using a survey result from 2005, a young girl's diary of 1835, or kitchenware from 1685, researchers must be skeptical of all evidence, search for confirmation, compare it to others, and place it within a larger set of such data. With such an approach, historians have learned a great deal about how ordinary people lived — and even thought and felt — in the distant past. I have constructed this book largely from many of their richly detailed studies.[25]

The sheer volume of what scholars have learned poses another complexity. The wide scope of this book necessitates compromises in depth. Each topic has an almost bottomless literature to which I cannot do justice; to be complete would require an encyclopedia. To charges that I have missed important pieces of scholarship, I plead no contest. But I hope that the literature which I have sampled fairly represents what historians know of these topics.[26]

Such limitations also partly explain my focus on the American "mainstream." Because I am trying to describe changes in average Americans' lives, I devote less attention to those whose experiences diverged from the average. The working and middle classes get more attention than either the elites or the destitute, Protestants get more attention than Catholics and Jews, Northerners more than Southerners, the native-born more than immigrants, and whites more than nonwhites. This necessarily means that readers can challenge some of my summaries as insufficiently attentive to class, regional, religious, racial, or ethnic variations.

My focus on the mainstream is not, however, just a practical expedient; there are also substantive reasons. First, the American middle class lives and promulgates the distinctive and dominant character of the society. To see national change, we need to look at these people. Second, much of this book's story is precisely about the widening of the mainstream, about the ways more Americans joined the broadening center. Few American adults, for example, held voting and property rights in the early 1800s; eventually most did. By the twentieth century, to take another example, far more Americans than ever before followed a common life course: attending school through late adolescence, taking a first full-time job, marrying, having children, seeing the children leave home, living as an empty-nest couple, and then retiring. Different categories of Americans varied greatly in how much and when they moved into the mainstream. Most notably, far fewer African Americans than European Americans could share this lifestyle. Nonetheless, clearly more and more Americans joined the mainstream culture.[27]

These topics raise moral and political implications. Too often, grand narratives of American history serve political commitments. Sometimes, even matters of minute detail, such as how colonists dressed or how tall Civil War enlistees were, seem to signal the author's position on twenty-first century politics. One observer has remarked that "all of American history today is a plain where contestants for the soul of the United States quite openly wage war." The dispute is commonly not about the facts in question but how to label or "spin" them. For instance, middle-class women in the early twentieth century had more sexual experiences at a younger age than their mothers had had. Is that sexual "liberation" or sexual "licentiousness"? Was this empowering of or harmful to women? In the end, history does not unfold according to a political or moral logic that lines up all the changes into neat moral phalanxes. I hope to avoid entangling this historical account with political strings. In previous books, I have not hesitated to focus on the class and caste inequalities of modern America. While such themes also emerge in this book, the focus is elsewhere, on the expanding circle of American culture and character. There *is* an American cultural center; its assimilative pull is powerful; and it is distinctive—or "exceptional." The historical record speaks.[28]

And to whom does it speak? This book addresses a few kinds of readers. I hope it informs nonhistorians, like my fellow sociologists, about the magnificent research trove unearthed by American social historians; we can benefit from an historical perspective. I also hope that historians will find an outsider's view of their research and the application of material from other social sciences useful. Most ambitiously, I hope that this book will brief general readers about the evolution of American culture and character and its implications. Because that general audience is so important, I have written the book for readers who have a basic familiarity with American history and a curiosity about the questions addressed here, but little time or patience for scholastic argument or detailed documentation. (Those, like me, who love the argument and the details can consult the endnotes.)

For all the focus on mentality and lifestyles, we must start with the basic material conditions of life. For example, Mrs. Ripken, busy as she was, could still be baseball coach, basketball playmate, and emotional guide to her children in ways that Mrs. Duffield, caught up with basic feeding and clothing of her children, could not. The next chapter addresses the fundamental question of how Americans' survival and security changed over our history.

2 Security

In early 1865, Abraham Lincoln was the most powerful man in the Western Hemisphere. He was also a man whose grandfather had been killed by Indians. He saw his infant brother die, he lost his mother when he was ten and his older sister when he was nineteen, and he grieved when Ann Rutledge—perhaps his sweetheart, perhaps just a friend—died of typhoid. He buried two of his four sons before they had reached the age of twelve and a third when he reached eighteen. He had a wife who was emotionally unstable, suffered depression himself, and would die prematurely and violently. This Job-like litany was perhaps severe even in the nineteenth century, but its like was familiar to Lincoln's contemporaries. For example, most parents of that era buried at least one child, an experience that mercifully few American parents faced a century later. Life was precarious.[1]

Over the centuries, American life became much less precarious. The threat of arbitrary and unpredictable calamities from illness or injury or economic misfortune abated. Being able to count on food, shelter, and safety from one day to the next helped more Americans gain confidence in their own power and a sense of self-reliance. More Americans made plans, charted their careers, scheduled their childbearing, designed their children's education, arranged their retirements. Greater physical and economic security probably lowered Americans' feelings of anxiety. In myth, the past appears to be seemingly unproblematic, but the prospect of, for example, a crop-destroying blight probably once frightened Americans more than the specter of a job layoff does today.

Security grew neither smoothly nor without interruption. In some periods, during domestic wars, for example, it stalled or even slipped back. The early twenty-first century seems to be such a period. "A new insecurity has entered every mind, regardless of wealth or status," said United

Nations secretary general Kofi Annan in December 2001. He was alluding, of course, to the 9/11 terrorist attacks, which took nearly three thousand lives. Foreign threats loomed again. But of probably deeper, more everyday, consequence was the growing economic insecurity that average Americans experienced from the 1970s into the financial crisis of the late 2000s.[2]

The historical expansion of security was unevenly distributed. In some eras, for example, when medicine began to seriously improve, richer Americans gained much more than poorer ones did. In other eras, for example, when public health measures took effect, the poorer gained the most, because their conditions had been so bad. Such qualifications in mind, we can still say that modern Americans lived with far more security and predictability than their ancestors did, even than their presidents did. Whether Americans' *feelings* of security kept pace is a more complex question.

SECURITY FROM DEATH AND DISEASE

Several cold numbers describe the context of Abraham Lincoln's miseries. In 1850, when his son Willie was born, a typical, white baby boy had only a 75 percent chance of making it to his first birthday and could expect to live only to thirty-eight. (Willie did not make it past ten.) One hundred and fifty years later, a white baby boy had a better than 99 percent chance of surviving his first year with a life expectancy of seventy-five years. Black babies have notably shorter life expectancies, albeit they are still longer than ever before. In the nineteenth century, even young men who had made it through infancy and childhood ran great risks. About one of every four men who turned twenty in 1880 failed to reach forty-five; a century later, only one of every fourteen died that early. Americans of the early generations faced—and feared—death regularly. The average woman of the revolutionary era would have already buried both of her parents and four of her children by the time she reached middle age. The diaries and letters of American mothers show that "the experience of infant death formed a constant backdrop . . . [of their] experiences and emotions." It was not until after World War I that the typical mother would live to see all her children grow up. And because chronic injuries and illnesses diminished, she could expect to see them grow up healthy. This improvement did not, however, follow a smooth upward course; the generation of Lincoln's ill-fated sons may have been one of the most short-lived in the nation's history. And, while America was once an especially healthy nation, by 2000 it had lost that distinction.[3]

Perhaps a Paradise

The first generations of European settlers in America discovered abundant wildlife, dense forests, rivers teeming with fish, and endless acres of fertile soil. This profusion meant that after the first difficult decades, the newcomers could count on living relatively well. By the mid-eighteenth century, they had discovered the most efficient crops for the new land and, through expanding trade, brought yearlong variety into their diets. Colonists of the 1700s ate as much meat as Europeans did two centuries later, avoided the periodic famines that afflicted Europe, and probably toiled less for better fare than Europeans did. Largely dispersed across the countryside, Americans also evaded many of the epidemics that devastated Europeans, who were typically crowded into villages and cities. New Englanders enjoyed the best health in the colonies, thanks in part to freezing winters, which eliminated many pathogens. (So healthy and fertile were the Puritans that, although originally relatively few in number, their descendants dominated the North two hundred years later.) Elsewhere, especially in the humid South, death took many adults and left behind many young orphans. Still, colonists generally could view their land as blessed by Providence. White Americans were born in greater numbers and grew ever taller, healthier, and longer-lived than their cousins back home. We can understand why European observers tended to describe early America as both an Arcadian garden of plenty and as a land of upstarts and braggarts.[4]

Life for others in the New World, however, worsened. Old-World diseases arriving from Europe, often in the veins of young children, effectively annihilated many Indian tribes in the early 1600s. A settler's journal refers to a plague "which swept away most of the inhabitants all along the sea coast, and in some places utterly consumed man, woman, and childe, so that there is no person left to claim the soyle which they possessed." Infections, displacement, wars, and a psychological malaise that depressed their will to bear children shrank the Northeast Indian population by perhaps 80 percent within a century. African slaves, too, paid a price for opening up the New World. Those who survived the "middle passage" faced new diseases, grueling work, and often brutal treatment. In the early 1700s, one-fourth of imported slaves in the Chesapeake region died within their first year. On average, slaves lived only five years after arrival. (And yet these conditions were better than in the West Indies!) It was not until the later 1700s that Africans in North America lived well enough to enlarge their numbers by childbearing. Many Europeans who arrived as servants faced similarly harsh conditions. In the early 1600s, about 80 percent of white indentured servants died of illness or maltreatment.[5]

As healthy as they were by comparison to Europeans, Indians, and servants, colonial freemen of "competence" typically led brief and hazardous lives. They struggled with accidents, Indian attacks, unsanitary homes, nutritional deficiencies, the perils of childbirth, and occasional plagues. In many communities, well-off families evacuated low-lying areas for higher ground during the pestilential summer months. Still, chronic pain and debilitation were commonplace. Historian Robert Darnton, reflecting on George Washington's ruined teeth, ruminated that "it seems incongruous, but having read thousands of letters from the eighteenth century, I often think of the dread of rotting teeth, the horror of the itinerant tooth puller, the sheer pain in jaws everywhere in the early modern world." Diarists of the era recorded months of continuous affliction. Benjamin Franklin cast about for some redeeming virtue in chronic pain. He decided that it spurred people on. "We are first mov'd by *Pain*, and the whole succeeding course of our Lives is but one continu'd Series of Action with a View to be freed from it." Nighttime commonly brought even more sensitivity and desperation. A well-known New England minister applied a "mixture of cow manure and hog fat on his face at night" in search of some palliative. Alcohol provided temporary relief, but many who were pain-ridden—and their families—often welcomed permanent relief in death. The people who lived in such a world of chronic physical pain probably endured their torments more stoically than modern Americans, with their bathroom cabinets of painkillers, do, but nonetheless, their affliction surely increased their distress, depression, and irritability.[6]

Emotional pain, especially the sort prompted by loved ones' agonies and deaths, also pervaded everyday life. Early Americans responded with religious hopes, but often felt only fatalism and resignation. Many avoided sorrow by avoiding emotional commitments. Parents commonly restrained their ardor for their newly born. A woman who lost eight of twelve infants recorded the brief life of one daughter so:

> Sept. 5, 1767. I was brought to bed about 2 o'clock AM of a daughter.
> Sept. 6. The Child Baptized Mary.
> Sept. 7. The Baby very well till ten o'clock in the evening & then taken with fits.
> Sept. 8. The Baby remained ill all day.
> Sept. 9. It died about 8 o'clock in the morning.
> Sept. 10. Was buried.

Another eighteenth-century woman bore a son in July and barely mentioned him again in her diary until two months later and not by name until yet six months later, when she was more certain of his survival. The diary of Jacob Hiltzheimer, a successful German immigrant who came to Philadelphia shortly before the Revolution, similarly suggests an effort—not always successful—to temper grief. On July 6, 1766, he wrote, "My wife gave birth to a son at three o'clock this morning." Hiltzheimer gave no name and made no further mention of the son for the rest of the year. He noted the deaths of grandchildren in passing, rarely naming them. On October 1, 1794: "Last night in returning from Thomas Fisher's, who gave a permit for the burial of my son Thomas's child in Friend's ground, I sprained my foot so badly. . . . At four o'clock my son's child was buried." But, Hiltzheimer does report attending to adult deaths—at the deathbed of his forty-nine-year-old wife in 1790, holding his dying thirty-one-year-old son in his arms in 1793, and recalling the "sweet smile" of his twenty-one-year-old daughter upon her death in 1794. In early America, such emotional pain was common, as was the "emotion work"—defensive coolness, seeking religious solace—to blunt it.[7]

Colonial Americans understood the precariousness of life. Puritan ministers stressed death's whim and the need to stay religiously prepared. Many could recite the saying, as Reverend Cotton Mather did, "If an old man has death before his face, a young man has death behind his back; the Deadly Blow may be as near to one as 'tis the other." Similarly, a 1776 gravestone in Schenectady, New York, reads: "The soul prepared needs no delay / The summon comes the saint obeys." Over the eighteenth century, Americans confronted their grief more directly, increasingly, survivors placed tombstone epitaphs on more graves, including those of women and children, and in those epitaphs wrote of their sorrow. We get hints here that a less resigned (and more sentimental) attitude to death was coming, but even in 1800 Americans lived not with the cloud of death on the horizon, but directly under its shadow.[8]

For all the briefness and harshness of life, even for the privileged like Hiltzheimer, the land was sufficiently bountiful to instill among a growing number of Americans a sense of optimism and even entitlement. It took a century or more to significantly expand the circle of the self-confident. More difficult times intervened.

No Garden of Eden

The nineteenth century brought dramatic economic growth: farms took over forests and grassland, canals joined rivers and lakes, factories drew power from waterways, and cities expanded. As the economy prospered, however, average Americans' health deteriorated. Bio-historians have established that adult height is a good indicator of people's fitness, particularly of how well they eat and of how healthy they were in childhood. American men who were born after 1830 were, on average, shorter than those born earlier. Average life expectancy declined as well. A twenty-year-old man in 1800 could expect to live to forty-seven, but a twenty-year-old man in 1850 could expect to live to only forty-one.[9]

This "antebellum puzzle," that the economy grew but Americans shrank, provokes many explanations. Some scholars stress disease: more immigrants from abroad, more travel within, more crowding into the cities, and more Americans working in factories and going to school spread infections farther and faster. Toxic byproducts of industrialization, such as coal smoke, contributed. Disease stunts growth and, of course, raises death rates. (European countries that industrialized before the development of modern public health systems seemed also to suffer increased mortality.) Other scholars addressing the "antebellum puzzle" stress nutrition: rapid population growth, especially in cities, strained food supplies and raised prices. Customers replaced expensive and nourishing foods with cheaper and simply filling foods. American diets shifted from milk and cheese to bread and sugar, perhaps because livestock became harder to keep in towns. Even on the farm, children born in the midcentury grew up shorter, perhaps because their fathers used more of their land for cash crops. Both the exponents of the disease and of the diet explanations also point to widening economic inequality in antebellum America. Average incomes increased, but differences in wealth widened as well, as did differences in height and longevity. Industrialization left increasing numbers of poor children with less to eat and more susceptibility to disease, while sons of the elite, such as Harvard students, suffered no or little reduction in height. Ironically, male slaves also showed little or no reduction in height, as slave owners protected their financial investments. Average Americans seemed to have become worse off.[10]

Townsfolk feared the specter of plague—the First Horseman of the Apocalypse—which rode in regularly. In 1832, residents of Schenectady noted reports of cholera in England and then tracked its advance through upstate New York. Civic leaders mobilized citizens to clean the streets, experiment with chlorine or vinegar disinfectants, reform their personal habits, and join in prayer. In the end, there was little to do that summer but endure more than forty deaths in a town of five thousand people. New York City, further south, suffered far worse. Tens of thousands of the well-to-do fled Manhattan. "The roads, in all directions, were lined with well-filled stagecoaches, livery coaches, private vehicles, and equestrians, all panic-struck, fleeing the city" and filling up farm homes for miles around. Over 3,500 of those who did not or could not flee, largely poor, immigrant, and black New Yorkers, died. In some neighborhoods death arrived so quickly that bodies remained lying in the gutter. On the Illinois frontier, federal troops carried the cholera into communities which were already beset by seasonal epidemics. Cholera lasted there into 1834; deaths mounted so rapidly that sometimes two bodies shared a blanket for a coffin.[11]

The seemingly chance course of disease made for painful ironies. While the children of the emerging middle-class grew taller and stronger than the children of the poor, they remained, in this age of scientific ignorance, almost as vulnerable to water-borne germs and contagious infections. Parents in well-appointed homes as well as in shacks experienced losses much as Lincoln did when his Willie died: "My poor boy. He was too good for this earth. God has called him home. I know that he is much better off in heaven, but then we loved him so. It is hard, hard to have him die!"[12]

Lincoln's cry, like that of many other parents in the emerging antebellum middle class, invoked God's hidden motives as some form of explanation but also expressed a growing intensity of loss. The decline in the number of children women bore, making each one that more special, probably amplified parents' anguish. The passionate response may also have reflected the newly spreading idea that babies were born angelic rather than damned. As we shall see in chapter 6, middle-class Americans increasingly immersed themselves in, rather than retreated from, the experience of grieving. Romantic sensibilities flourished in the antebellum years and deaths occasioned many such expressions, often in new, park-like cemeteries designed to deepen the poignancy of loss. Thus, in sharp contrast to the matter-of-fact report of Child Mary's death in 1767, a bereaved mother wrote in 1801, "At bedtime, instead of my charming boy, my lovely babe . . . instead of my laughing cherub to receive the caresses of a tender mother—I found a lifeless corpse—laid out in the white robes of innocence and death." Sarah Connell Ayer, a middle-class New Englander whose teenage diary I will quote later in this book, returned to diary-writing in 1815 with this entry: "Since closing my last journal, I have been the mother of four children, which now lay side by side in the graveyard. . . . [The] last was a sweet, interesting boy, and lived to be six months old. He was a lovely flower, and I trust he is now transplanted in the garden of Heaven. Though the death of this child was a great trial, yet I hope I was made to bow submissive to the will of my Heavenly Father."[13]

Even when spared from death, nineteenth-century Americans suffered chronic ailments, disfigurement from diseases such as smallpox, and disabilities from accidents. Those in the West suffered, in particular, from malaria. Survivors lived with periodic attacks of chills, chronic fatigue, and susceptibility to other diseases. Many treatments, such as bleeding and opium, often left people worse off still. Accidents, especially on farms, were common. (Lincoln himself, at age nine, was kicked in the head by a horse so hard that neighbors called his father to the presumed deathbed.) Workers in industrial shops endured burns, having fingers trapped in equipment, and occasional explosions. Even later in the century, mortality risks remained high. Historian Peter Knights traced the records of over two thousand native-born Boston men between 1860 and 1870 and found that many fell off scaffolds, got caught in machinery, or died in other accidents. Immigrant workers in large factories led particularly hazardous lives. In the Pittsburgh mills, "molten metal spattered the millhands. Unstable piles of iron billets stood everywhere. Hot floors burned feet through wooden-soled shoes. Molds and furnaces exploded. . . . The noise deafened or impaired millworkers' hearing." The coming of trains and streetcars in the second half of the century added accidents for pedestrians, passengers, and even conductors. One conductor noted that every time he collected fares along the outside seats of the trolley car, he was "liable to collide with a brick pile or lime kiln." Yet farm life, with its cantankerous animals and crude machinery, remained even more dangerous.[14]

For all the danger and debilitation, physical security improved greatly in the late nineteenth and early twentieth centuries. Helped by an emerging understanding of disease, local governments developed public sanitation. They built or expanded water-delivery systems, sewer complexes, and waste-treatment facilities; purified drinking water; drained stagnant pools; and rid streets of offal and ordure. As always, some benefitted before others. Even into the 1900s, residents of working-class neighborhoods drew water from streams contaminated by cesspool overruns. Eventually, however, government projects vastly reduced water- and waste-borne bacteria for virtually all townspeople. Spurred by disasters such as the Great Chicago Fire, cities augmented their firefighting resources. New building codes improved safety by limiting crowding and requiring minimal ventilation. Food regulation, particularly prosecuting dairy deliverers who watered their milk, also curtailed disease. In the 1890s alone, New York City cut its death rate by about one-fourth, in part thanks to over three hundred sanitary inspectors; Boston cut its death rate by about one-seventh, in part by examining thousands of milk samples a year.[15]

Individual Americans intensified their personal sanitation. Early in the nineteenth century, most Americans, according to reformer Catharine Beecher, regularly washed only their faces, necks, hands, and feet. Some believed that dirt was healthy and frequent washing dangerous. Given the lack of running water, most Americans could not wash regularly anyway. By midcentury, however, middle-class Americans increasingly had running water and had also accepted the new idea that bathing could improve health and beauty. They added indoor toilets as well as bathtubs to their homes and taught their children habits of cleanliness. Some evangelized cleanliness to immigrants and the working class, sponsoring public baths and teaching hygiene in settlement houses.[16]

These public and private initiatives sharply reduced the toll of epidemics. In 1892, another cholera epidemic arrived in New York City; it had already killed many thousands in Europe and dozens of passengers on arriving ships. The city's health authorities quickly diagnosed the disease, quarantined the ill, disinfected homes, and cleaned the streets. In the end, only nine New Yorkers died. Epidemics did not disappear—the 1918–19 influenza pandemic took about five hundred lives in Schenectady alone—but death rates, especially for the youngest, dropped substantially. More generally, Americans' health improved and their average heights rose. These advancements, as usual, first reached the middle classes so that, at the turn of the twentieth century, the affluent were notably healthier and taller than the poor; it took another generation or two for other Americans to catch up.[17]

Extending Life

One might wonder how our health could be so much better than our ancestors', given the flood of scary reports about food additives, lack of exercise, sunburn, and the like. Ironically, these obsessions emerged because many more people are living long enough to encounter diseases of aging (such as Alzheimer's), because more plentiful food is leading to diseases of obesity, and because more Americans expect to stay vigorous longer (case in point: the popularity of sexual invigoration drugs).

The life expectancy of an American newborn lengthened by about thirty years over the twentieth century—for white women, from dying at about fifty to dying at about eighty. The change was most dramatic for poor infants who had in earlier generations been fated for short lives. The causes of death have changed. Nineteenth-century Americans died largely from infectious diseases; late-twentieth-century Americans succumbed to ailments of old age like heart disease and to social causes like auto accidents. A host of killing maladies disappeared or contracted significantly, such as smallpox, cholera, tuberculosis, typhoid, and rickets. Even the terrible AIDS epidemic of the late twentieth century was, by historical standards, a minor killer. In 1900, about one of every five hundred Americans died of tuberculosis; by the end of the century only about one of every six thousand Americans was even *diagnosed* with AIDS. Accidents, notably those resulting from hazards of farm life, declined. After 1930, rates of serious injuries in manufacturing dropped by over half. General well-being improved. Americans matured physically at earlier ages, grew taller, and suffered fewer disabling handicaps. Long-term changes in parasites and human immunities account for some of this improvement, and growing wealth in the twentieth century accounts for yet more, but social intervention accounts for much of it.[18]

The health initiatives that governments began at the turn of the twentieth century, such as clean water, broadened into further programs, such as safety regulation, nutritional supplements, vaccination, and pest eradication. Most major city governments began sweeping streets and collecting trash. City dwellers came to expect public health measures that once were private responsibilities; in 1920, several residents sued the city of Schenectady because family members had contracted typhoid from polluted water. In parallel, Victorian-era admonitions for personal hygiene and clean homes intensified, urged on by home economists, doctors, and teachers, as well as businessmen eager to sell products such as disinfectant. Later public initiatives contributed: Medicare, work safety and consumer product regulations, sponsored medical research, food oversight, and so on. Death rates plunged and, dramatically, because infections were under control, urban Americans no longer ran a higher risk of death than rural Americans.[19]

Twentieth-century Americans also ate better than their ancestors — not more calories, but more nutritious calories. Technological improvements in agricultural productivity, processing, canning, transportation, and refrigeration brought Americans everywhere relatively fresh fruit, vegetables, meat, and dairy products. And they brought cheaper food: a dozen eggs in 1919 cost the average worker eighty minutes of labor; in 1997, it cost five minutes. In 1901, urban white-collar workers devoted 46 percent of their total spending to food; in 1986, it was only 19 percent. Technology and productivity, together with the provision of vitamins and of government programs to enrich food, teach nutrition, and provide food subsidies to the poor, profoundly improved the American diet. That became apparent during the 1930s and '40s: despite the severity of the Great Depression and the shortages of World War II, Americans did not starve, and their health generally continued to improve.[20]

While nutritional and public health measures accounted for most of the improvement early in the century, later on new drugs, such as penicillin and antibiotics, and medical care, such as neonatology for the youngest and heart attack treatments for the oldest, added the most years of life. A shift in spending testifies to the dramatic change; in 1900, Americans spent about twice as much on funerals as on medicine; by 1990, they spent about ten times as much on medicine as on funerals.[21]

Less privileged Americans—minorities, the elderly, Southerners, and the poor—gained the most from the twentieth-century developments and joined the mainstream. Nobel Prize–winning economist Robert Fogel commented that if "anything sets [the twentieth] century apart from the past, it is this huge increase in the longevity of the lower classes." This convergence in life chances occurred largely in the early to mid-twentieth century. Life spans continued to lengthen for Americans in general afterwards, but the gaps no longer closed. Important differences in infant mortality and overall death rates remained between social classes and most dramatically between blacks and whites. At the start of the new millennium, African Americans faced overall death rates 60 percent higher than whites did. (Hispanics, however, actually had better health prospects than non-Hispanic whites.) Nonetheless, even black-white differences narrowed considerably over the entire twentieth century.[22]

A new and surprising gap did open up, however, in both height and life expectancy. For generations, Americans grew taller and lived longer than Europeans, but by 1900 Europeans had roughly caught up. And by the twenty-first century, while health had improved on both sides of the Atlantic, Europeans living in comparable circumstances grew taller and lived longer than Americans. The reasons are unclear but might be attributed to America's greater economic inequality and—despite all the programs of the century—its weaker government health programs.[23]

At the same time that the twentieth-century cornucopia extended Americans' lives and heights (albeit not as much as Europeans'), it brought Americans new ways to disable themselves—notably by driving, smoking, overeating, and under-exercising. Between 1919 and 1926, for instance, the extension of rural highways in North Dakota multiplied the number of automobile accident fatalities from eleven to seventy-seven annually. The national death rate by motor vehicle peaked at thirty-one per hundred thousand in 1937, but was still around fifteen in the 2000s. Cancer death rates zoomed from sixty-four to nearly two hundred per hundred thousand during the same period. In the later decades of the century, medical experts pointed with alarm to rising weight and its health consequences, such as asthma and diabetes. Americans recognized the weight problem as a personal one, telling poll takers that they would like to lose weight; in the 1950s, one of three respondents said that, but in the early 2000s, most Americans did. Illnesses of abundance had replaced illnesses of scarcity.[24]

Implications

The great extensions of life and improvements in health had profound implications. As late as 1870, people sixty-five years or older were only one of every thirty-three Americans; in the early 2000s, they composed about one in *eight* Americans; in 2050, they will probably be one in *five.* The ratio ballooned mainly because parents had many fewer children over the generations (discussed in chapter 4). One reason Americans had fewer children was that so many of their offspring survived. The combination of longer lives and fewer children meant that most modern Americans passed through a stage in life that had once been experienced by few: "empty nest"—a married couple living apart from their adult children. In 1900, only 15 percent of elderly Americans lived in an empty nest; most of the others lived with their children, as dependent widows or widowers. In 2000, by stunning contrast, about half of the elderly lived in independent couples; most of the rest lived as singles. Within families, the elderly increasingly supported their adult children, rather than vice versa. Outside families, increasing numbers, better health and greater wealth gave the elderly growing social, economic, political, and cultural clout. Their interests and tastes increasingly shaped those of wider America.[25]

Americans encountered death and serious disability less often. They came to see illness or the premature loss of a loved one less fatalistically, less as bad luck or the will of God, and more as avoidable and controllable. Historians Nancy Dye and Daniel Blake Smith traced this changing worldview in the letters and diaries of middle-class mothers whose infants had died. Fatalism in the eighteenth century gave way to a sense of personal responsibility in the nineteenth century and then in the twentieth century to a conviction that the wider society may also be to blame—say, in poor food inspections. Now, human action, alone or collectively, could delay the Angel of Death. In 1910, for example, the administrator of New York City's Milk Commission declared: "In the last analysis, infant mortality is to be solved not by philanthropy or by institutions . . . but by intelligent motherhood." That sense of responsibility and control, together with healthier children, contributed, some scholars persuasively argue, to Americans limiting the size of their families; they could count on their children surviving. Similarly, as death became increasingly an experience of only old people, it became more unremarkable and routine. People and their survivors could plan for death. In these ways, both forestalling and planning for death, more Americans gained that control and sense of capacity that is part of voluntarism.[26]

Conversely, less fear of death and its seeming capriciousness, some argue, reduced Americans' need to find comfort in religion. Faith should have declined—but it did not (see chapter 6). Instead, perhaps, the nature of Americans' faith changed, from accepting the mysterious edicts of a fickle god to celebrating the steadfast beneficence of a loving god.[27]

Reductions in premature death might have also led Americans to invest themselves more firmly in the lives of loved ones. Parents seemed to permit themselves greater emotional attachment to their infants and children as survival became increasingly certain. Similarly, Americans seemed to value life increasingly more. Think of the growing public expectations for government action, for legal guarantees, for insurance, and for compensation (such as the Schenectady mourners who sued the city over typhoid deaths in 1920). Life was not as cheap as it used to be.[28]

Finally, we might speculate that fewer encounters with "too-early" deaths and with debilitating illness or injury diminished the emotional pain Americans regularly suffered. Or perhaps not. Americans in the colonial era had to face what one historian called "the sheer normality of death." Perhaps, in the modern context, the occasional experience of a loved ones' dying or debility became all that much scarier and more painful for being so much rarer.[29]

SECURITY FROM ONE ANOTHER

Among the cases that the young lawyer Abraham Lincoln took to subsidize his political ambitions were run-of-the-mill murders typical of the nineteenth century: the aftermaths of heavy drinking, domestic spats, or brooding grudges. In one well-known trial, Lincoln gained the acquittal of a man who had confessed to a killing. Lincoln argued self-defense on the grounds that his client had been warned that the victim was going to attack him. Casual violence often flared up both on Lincoln's frontier and in the frontier-like, lawless districts of large cities where young transients congregated. Americans also often used violence to control violence—or even to just enforce local norms. In his first major public address in 1838, Lincoln responded to "accounts of outrages committed by mobs, [which] form the every-day news of the times. They have pervaded the country, from New England to Louisiana." He listed lynchings in Mississippi of gamblers, slaves suspected of plotting insurrection, suspected abolitionists, and just strangers; he noted a mob's burning of a black man in St. Louis; and he did not need to remind his Springfield audience that an abolitionist editor had been lynched in Alton, Illinois, the previous fall. This culture of violence waned over the generations, but Americans remained anxious about being attacked through the end of the twentieth century. In 1995, survey respondents considered crime as the arena of life in which the nation had "experienced the greatest decline," another example of systematic misremembering. While victimization rose and fell over American history, the age of Lincoln was far more violent than the modern age.[30]

For centuries before 1800, both Europeans and Americans ran much higher risks than they do today of being victims of all sorts of violence, Europeans perhaps even more than the colonists. People calculated their daily rounds to avoid highwaymen, city toughs, drunks, irate neighbors, and enraged spouses. People often settled their disputes violently. The play-ending bloodbaths in Shakespearian tragedies resonated with his audiences' experiences in the premodern era. After the early nineteenth century, rates of everyday violence dropped substantially in Western nations. But it did not recede nearly as much or as fast in the United States. In the twentieth century, America stood out as distinctively violent among affluent Western nations. (Americans were not particularly *criminal*; their rates of crimes such as burglary and purse-snatching ranked around the middle among Western nations.) By the early 2000s, even though the homicide rate in the United States nearly reached a forty-year low, at about 5.6 per 100,000 residents, it remained triple or more the rates of the European Union, Canada, and Australia. America's dubious badge of distinction seems to reflect exceptionally high violence rates in specific populations and also a culture that calls upon men to defend unto the death their "honor" from, say, a romantic competitor or a scowling stranger.[31]

A Violent Heritage

Violence and fear had special features in colonial North America. Centuries of skirmishes between the settlers and the indigenous peoples occasionally led to massacres on both sides. Daniel Drake, who grew up to be a noted medical professor, recalled a routine of his Kentucky childhood in the 1780s: the family kept axes and scythes "under the bed as weapons of defense, in case the Indians should make an attack. In the morning, the first duty was to ascend, by a ladder which always stood leaning against the door, to the loft, and look out through the cracks for the Indians, lest they might have planted themselves near the door, to rush in when the cross-bar should be removed." Periodically, Indian wars and wars between England and France swept up yeoman farmers into militias, long marches, and battles. Over five thousand colonial militia died or suffered injury in the Seven Years' War. (The Revolution itself, of course, provoked bloody clashes among neighbors in various corners of the new nation.) Violence was common among masters, slaves, indentured servants, transported English convicts, and freed bondsmen. What passed for a criminal justice system relied on civilians to be both watchmen and justices. Victims of crime had to find and prosecute their assailants themselves. Courts, especially in New England, focused more on moral than on personal crimes; they handed out death penalties for adultery and buggery in the 1600s. Typically, the authorities stood aside when people settled their quarrels by violence, dismissed attacks on women as inconsequential, and ignored infanticides. Because of their dispersion, mobility, and economic independence, early Americans could avoid the sorts of intercommunal warfare, such as blood feuds, which plagued much of Europe. Nonetheless, individual, interpersonal violence was never too far away.[32]

Violence probably grew even more common in the nineteenth century. Much of the country was a weakly regulated frontier society populated by transients. Historian Elliot Gorn describes how in parts of rural America men regularly engaged in "honor fights" highlighted by the gouging out of eyes and the severing of ears. Belligerency was not restricted to the West. Gorn also describes how men in New York City saloons fought savagely to defend their personal or ethnic groups' honor. City youth formed gangs and contested control of the streets. Much nineteenth-century violence surged on the torrents of liquor that saturated male life. An historian of the Illinois frontier noted that "not all men drank themselves into oblivion or fought like dogs, of course, but male culture generally accepted such conduct as a regular occurrence of public life." Male violence also spilled onto others. One St. Louis citizen wrote, "the town's only night watch were prowlers who stole everything in sight and, worse still, terrorized women and children." Women took great risks if they went onto the streets unaccompanied. Sexual assaults, notably on unmarried women, were underreported and often ignored. Women also faced risks at home. In one upper New York State case, a master turned away his maid's complaints that a house guest was molesting her and left her to be raped. As with street assaults, we know only about the domestic violence that made it to court. Neighbors who for years heard men beating their wives reported the incidents only when the attackers were arrested for murder. A "normal" level of wife beating was acceptable. Both rapes and domestic attacks apparently increased in the antebellum years. Women, too, engaged in more violence, at least in the form of infanticide. Interpersonal violence was, as one historian notes, "part of the daily fabric of family life," in child rearing, schooling, recreation, and certainly as the way to resolve disputes.[33]

Antebellum criminal justice, where present, remained lackadaisical. Watchmen and constables were often ineffective, courts were passive, and juries went easy on assaulters and murderers when they heard any honorable justification for the violence (such as Lincoln's defense). A drinking buddy's insult, a wife's harping, or a slave's defiance would suffice to excuse an assault. In 1858, in Chesterfield, Massachusetts, Charles Gibson deliberately and brutally killed his wife Isabella, whom he had often beaten before. The jury found him guilty of only manslaughter in light her history of drunkenness and disobedience. Historian Eric Monkkonen estimated, from close examination of court records and newspaper stories, that in nineteenth-century New York City, half to three-quarters of killers avoided any punishment at all and many others received only token penalties.[34]

Group violence also grew in the nineteenth century. European immigrants, notably the Irish, and native whites often brawled in city neighborhoods like New York's Five Points; whites assaulted free blacks in Northern cities; nativists attacked Catholics; and political clubs mauled one another on election days. In many cities, young men got together in workers' fraternities or voluntary fire companies and, well-lubricated with spirits, fought one another over jobs, water hoses, or simply bragging rights. Vigilantes attacked brothels, abolitionists, and others who offended propriety (recall Lincoln's 1838 speech). War with the Indians, now that they had been pushed much farther West, affected relatively few white Americans, but its savagery probably only grew. In 1855, a column in the *New York Daily Times* entitled "The Indians—A War of Extermination" reported that all over the far West, Indian tribes were rising up, "murdering and scalping [white] man, woman, and child." The author noted sadly and almost sympathetically that the native people were "only striking for their Fatherland, their homes, and their rights," that the "proud and passionate savages will waylay and murder, as they always have; and the revengeful frontiersmen *will* . . . kill the 'Indian devils' like so many dogs," and concluded that the natives' historical destiny was to perish before the advance of the "Anglo-Saxon race." Most pervasive and fateful was the chronic violence slave owners exacted on slaves and the episodic attacks of slaves on Southern whites. Slaves experienced the habitual abuse of kicks and smacks and the threat of the whip; whites worried about retribution ("We have a wolf by the ears," warned Jefferson). The violence ingrained in slavery combined with a culture of manly honor to beget chronic violence in the South, a tradition which characterized the region for generations.[35]

Effective government control of individual and group violence emerged only slowly. Large cities began forming professional police departments in the mid-nineteenth century, largely to rein in insurrectionary mobs. States also professionalized the justice system; for example, attorneys for the public, for the "district," took over prosecutions. The authorities slowly began to contain daily, interpersonal violence as well as mob violence. The new procedures, first developed in the larger cities, helped make cities safer than rural regions for the next few generations.[36]

Fuller control over violence was delayed by the vast and bloody struggles over slavery, secession, and race before, during, and after the Civil War. The Blue and the Gray together conscripted a higher proportion of the population than for any other war in Western history, and that war killed more soldiers than all of America's other wars combined. One of every eight white men of fighting age died during the war—one of every four from the South—altering American demography for a generation and leaving a pall of death over the nation. The war dislocated many men, brutalized them, trained and equipped them to kill, all of which contributed to high levels of violence long after Appomattox.[37]

In the Reconstruction South, whites used lethal threats and acts—most notoriously, lynchings—to keep freed blacks working, to suppress their claims for equality, and to retake political power. On Easter Day 1873, in Colfax, Louisiana, whites contesting the installation of Republican officials murdered over one hundred blacks, leaving bodies, throats cut, lying on an open field. In other instances, anti-Reconstruction insurgents also killed white Republicans. The West experienced both organized violence, in the sometimes-genocidal Indian wars, and disorganized violence among settlers in places such as mining camps and cattle towns. A Tucson, Arizona, saloonkeeper recounted in his diary of the 1870s how one man was hanged for stealing a mule and how another was paid to leave town after killing a black. (The keep's diary also notes many suicides by poisoning, drugs, and gunfire.) The Northern cities had their danger zones, too: low-income, often immigrant or black neighborhoods in which the person-to-person street and saloon violence of the prewar era continued and continued to be accepted. In 1883, a Chicago jury acquitted Jerry Dunn of murdering prizefighter James Elliott. The accused had tracked the pugilist down in a restaurant and shot him. As with Abraham Lincoln's client decades earlier, the jury ruled the act self-defense because Dunn had heard that Elliott had threatened him. An editor of *The Nation* magazine decried the verdict as "of course tantamount to notice to all the dangerous and brutal class of the city that the law will not meddle with their quarrels, and that they may fight each other with deadly weapons and butcher each other with impunity." He complained that in many parts of the nation citizens were forced, by uncaring authorities, to arm themselves for protection.[38]

All this bloodshed notwithstanding, interpersonal violence generally abated in the latter half of the nineteenth century. A militant labor movement did spark strikes, boycotts, attacks on scabs, and fierce crackdowns by public and private police. Men besotted by liquor, manly pride, or both still accounted for most of the violence, but several social changes started to bridle them. Government, as noted earlier, shifted from haphazard to professional policing and administration. In families, bourgeois ideals stigmatized brutishness and encouraged domestic habits such as bypassing the saloon on the way home after work. At work, industrial, team jobs with regular hours and supervision forced discipline on working-class men. And the spreading middle-class culture—taught, for example, to working-class children in schools that they were increasingly forced to attend—increasingly emphasized self-control.[39]

Twentieth-Century Cycles

Violence—most dramatically, lynching and riots—continued, but during the first half of the twentieth century it slowly subsided. Homicide rates, the most reliable indicators of violence generally, dropped to what was probably their lowest ever of about 4.5 per 100,000 people in the 1950s. Attacks that did not result in deaths were less well recorded, but the rates of such violence probably declined even more steeply. Americans in the late 1950s lived in what was most likely the era of greatest safety from violence.[40]

Scholars offer several reasons for the abatement of criminal violence. Quieting trends of the late nineteenth century continued into the twentieth, such as increasing school attendance, more factory work, waning of saloons, development of the justice system, sanctification of life, and declines in the number of single men on the loose. (The percentage of men aged twenty-five to forty-four living outside of a family declined from a peak of 22 percent in 1920 to 10 percent in 1950.) Person-to-person violence had generally subsided over about a century. Yet violence subsided less in America than in Europe, and the decrease turned out not to be permanent.[41]

Then came the 1960s. In 1960, murder took the lives of about five of every hundred thousand Americans; in 1980 and again in 1991, it took eleven of every hundred thousand, a rate that approached that of the nineteenth century. Police recorded multifold increases in other crimes as well, including assaults and robberies. As late as 1968, fewer than one-third of Americans told a Gallup poll that there was somewhere within a mile of their homes where they were afraid to walk alone at night; by 1981, almost half said they were afraid.[42]

Trying to explain the explosion of criminal violence after 1960 has occupied many criminologists—with uncertain results. In part, the babies of the baby boom grew up to be an unusually large cohort of teenagers, and teenage boys are especially likely to commit crimes. What else drove the surge of violence is greatly debated. Some say that the loss of blue-collar jobs in the major cities left many black men unemployed; others say that an increase in unmarried mothers and working mothers left teens unsupervised and homes unguarded during the day; and some say that racial tensions spurred the violence, which was heavily concentrated in black ghettos. Others blame cultural changes: that the Vietnam War brewed up an atmosphere of violence; alternatively, that opposition to the war and other rebellions undermined authority; or perhaps it was television—this was the first generation reared in front of the screen. An explanation beyond the teen boom remains elusive.[43]

The homicide rate sagged in the early 1980s and then surged again a few years later, this latter wave clearly rising with gang wars over the "crack" cocaine trade. Then, the official rates of plunged—suddenly, unexpectedly, and rapidly. Homicides fell from about 10 per 100,000 in 1991 to about 5.5 in the early 2000s. The dive occurred in part because crack use subsided and along with it firefights among drug dealers, but the sudden drop in homicides made visible a longer, more general reduction in crime and violence. Homicide rates for Americans twenty-five and older had been falling since the mid-1970s, and fewer Americans were telling survey takers that they had been crime victims. By one estimate, the decline in murder added two years to the life expectancy of black men. (The 1990s plunge may indicate that the historical "quieting" had finally reached America's most dangerous neighborhoods.) Criminologists suggested that the "great crime decline" resulted from the aging of baby boomers, stronger law enforcement, merciless imprisonment, more jobs in the 1990s, and perhaps a cultural shift.* Yet an explanation for the 1990s decline remains as clouded as the explanation for the 1960s rise.[44]

In 1990, *Time* magazine could say, with only moderate exaggeration, that New Yorkers—and, by extension, Americans generally—increasingly believed "that deadly violence, once mostly confined to crime-ridden ghetto neighborhoods ... is now lashing out randomly at anyone, anytime, even in areas once considered relatively safe." The satirical television show "Saturday Night Live" would open its show announcing that it came "from the most dangerous city in America." Yet by 2000, calm was returning and the public began feeling more secure. The proportion of survey respondents who said that they were afraid to walk alone at night in their neighborhoods descended to its lowest levels since the 1960s. New York City became one of the safest big cities in the nation. And for the first time in a generation, more Americans said that crime

* A gradual but similar drop in crime occurred in Canada.

was decreasing in their areas than said it was increasing. Still, in the early 2000s, about one-sixth of Americans said that they worried at least occasionally about getting murdered and about one-fourth about getting mugged; about one-fifth said they had a gun for protection. We cannot tell how those numbers would compare to ones decades earlier, but it appears that Americans at the end of the century had not reclaimed the tranquility of the 1950s, nor could they assume the beneficent trend would continue.[45]

*

Waves of violence throughout American history make any simple before-and-after comparison difficult. Certainly, Americans at the start of the twenty-first century still ran high risks; a significant proportion of them either have experienced or will experience a violent crime sometime in their lives. Perhaps a quarter or more of women, for example, will experience a sexual assault. Nonetheless, personal violence—both the violence that came to the attention of officials and the commonplace violence that usually did not, such as brawls, sexual attacks, wife beating, child slapping, caning, and mugging—diminished. It diminished for a few interconnected reasons. One certainly is increasing state power; more governments became more effective in policing violence in more corners of the nation. The casual "outrages by mobs" that Lincoln complained about in 1838 became rare. Governments also instituted mass schooling, which kept boys off the streets and forced discipline upon them. The modern economy provided regular and regimented jobs and also a comfortable standard of living which fewer men were willing to endanger. And then so-called civilizing changes—expanded feelings of sympathy toward more people, more revulsion to blood and gore, more self-discipline (matters examined in chapter 6)—also probably curbed more Americans' inclination to use violence. To be sure, residents of many twenty-first century American neighborhoods felt surrounded by the threat of violence; in 2000, black teenage boys were ten times likelier to be victims of violent crime than were middle-aged white women. However, in the long run, Americans overall had become safer from attack.[46]

Feeling safer is another matter. The decline in highway banditry and gang attacks over the centuries probably increased, as did better health, Americans' sense of controlling their lives—but probably not proportionately. People are frightened by news reports of dramatic crimes, especially ones reported in the local media, and they fear crime when they see ethnically different "others" around them. To the extent that modern Americans lived in more diverse communities and learned of more violent incidents than their ancestors did, they feared assault at rates beyond the true risks. Perceptions of danger can outrun reality.[47]

SECURITY FROM PRIVATION

Poverty, too, created chronic insecurity in early America. Latham Clarke was born in 1700 in Newport, Rhode Island, to parents of means. In his twenties, as a blacksmith of middling income, Clarke moved through a few different communities, migrating as far away as New Jersey. In his fifties, he sold his land and moved back to Hopkington, one of the Rhode Island towns in which he had once lived, settling in with his son Stephen's family. In a few years, the money from the land sale ran out. He tried to work again as a blacksmith but no longer owned the expensive tools the job required and ended up seeking public support. Hopkington officials turned him down and sent Clarke to his birthplace, Newport. (Clarke's son Stephen eventually also fell into poverty when his wife contracted smallpox. Stephen himself died shortly afterwards.) Newport officials contested Latham Clarke's claims for relief in court but lost, so they placed him, destitute and in his sixties, in the town workhouse.[48]

The story of Latham and Stephen Clarke was not typical, but it was common enough to illustrate the risks people of that era faced. In the roughly 250 years since, economic growth and public policy brought basic material security—food, shelter, clothing, and more—to increasing numbers of Americans. But not to all. Progress was irregular, periods of enrichment alternating with periods of such impoverishment that millions went tramping the roads for work. Even twenty-first-century affluence did not eliminate stomach-churning drops in economic fortunes.

Born to Advantage

By the Revolution, white Americans were probably the wealthiest people in the world, although in a world of privation, that may not say much. Compared to Europeans, who often starved and fled famine, colonial Americans were settled and assured. There was land to farm for those free men who would clear it. It was so bountiful that farmers could afford to be wasteful, repeatedly planting the same crops on the same acreage until the soil was depleted, and then moving on to new soil. Regional variations shade this rosy picture. The Northeast best fit the model of tidy and (almost) self-sufficient farm households. Hessian mercenaries fighting for the British during the Revolution composed songs about the well-off colonists, including the verse, "Everything that man seeks in the

world/All that a man seeks there/Is in America." Southern land was divided between large plantations and small, ramshackle holdings; both
rich and poor depended greatly on raising high-risk export crops, such as
tobacco and rice. One observer described the homes of small Southern
farmers as "not half so good as the houses which judicious planters provide for their slaves . . . made of mere sticks, or small poles notched, or
rather thatched together, and filled with mud, mixed with leaves." Farms
on the Western frontier were small, surrounded by woods, and barely
sustainable. Nonetheless, this rural economy, together with urban commerce and the first "manufactures," grew at a world-leading pace in the
colonial years.[49]

As elsewhere in the world, some reaped bounty from the labor of others. In the seventeenth century, white indentured servants typically provided that labor. In Middlesex County, Virginia, in 1668, they comprised
almost half of the total population. Selling oneself or one's children into
bondage to pay for transport to America continued into the nineteenth
century. But the indentured provided an insecure supply of labor; American employers depended on bad times in England or Germany to draw
help, and the indentured typically worked off their debts in several years.
Some colonists tried instead to enslave Indians, but the natives proved
unsatisfactory. African slavery was more efficient than either Indian slavery or white servitude. African slaves cost less to support than white servants, especially because owners fed them less; Africans rarely demanded
an Englishman's rights; and far fewer became free to compete with whites
for jobs. Africans' high death rates seemed to matter little; the steady arrival of slaving ships made them cheap. By 1700, African slaves greatly
outnumbered white servants in the Chesapeake region. Conveniently,
whites convinced themselves that some work could be done only by Africans. A visitor to Georgia wrote in 1735 that "the Work is too labori-
ous, the heat very intent, and the Whites can't work in the wett of that
Season of the year as Negrs do to weed the Rice." In the eighteenth and
early nineteenth centuries, landowners expanded the plantation system
to meet world demand for tobacco, rice, and most notably cotton; this
radically changed slaves' lives. The earliest African bondsmen were jacks
of all trades, general helpers working next to their masters; many lived
in towns and some bought their freedom. Increasingly, however, African slaves toiled in large work gangs doing repetitive, grueling labor on
sprawling plantations, with little prospect of freedom but great prospects
of sale, injury, and death. By the Revolution, African slaves outnumbered
all whites in the lower South. Slave-based agriculture came to define the
Southern economy, to the long-run detriment of the region's whites, as
well as blacks.[50]

Even free colonists, however better their circumstances compared to those in the English midlands, Scottish hills, or cramped cities they had left behind, faced grave economic insecurities: droughts and freezes, the vagaries of international trade and, for those on the frontier, periodic wars. In the South, having depleted the soil with tobacco farming and losing the competition with slave-owning planters, small-scale farmers pushed into the hilly "back country." In the Northeast, growing families forced many heirs to wait longer to inherit and to inherit evermore subdivided farms. A hundred-acre farm for the first generation could be a twenty-five-acre farm for the third generation, often not enough for "competency." Many farmers' younger sons—such as Abraham Lincoln's father, Thomas—had to move west or into town upon the deaths of their fathers.[51]

Thus, inequality widened over the eighteenth century. Some lineages thrived—because of skill, birth control, or simply good luck—and others struggled; the successful bought out the failures. Frontier land started to fill up, making it harder for the poor or the disinherited to simply move a little further west (at least until the new nation permitted settlers to invade Indian lands west of the Appalachian mountains). Displaced farmers became tenants for their richer neighbors or laborers in the growing towns. Some colonists fell into abject poverty, usually because the man of the house fell ill, got injured, became too old, drank too much, or died or, in the case of women, because they became pregnant out of wedlock, or for everyone, simply because of bad luck, such as recessions.[52]

These unfortunates could barely count on public assistance. Town authorities first demanded that kin support the destitute, and, absent kin, they provided limited charity to those deemed "deserving," such as families only temporarily down on their luck or widows with children. In Philadelphia, even the families of employed artisans often skirted the edge of hunger and dispossession. During the winter of 1783–84, a private charity fund helped about 1,600 families, or about one of every seven Philadelphians. But getting help was difficult; we've already seen the experience of Latham Clarke in Rhode Island. Towns often placed poor adults or their children in local households as indentured servants. An orphanage in Charleston, South Carolina, in the late 1700s, for example, bound out their charges, largely children of poor single parents, once they reached adolescence. The most efficient strategy for fiscally cautious officials was to send released servants and slaves, single pregnant women, alcoholics, and the uncared-for elderly back to where they came from. Towns "warned out" thousands of the "vicious," as they were termed, declaring, as colonial law allowed them to do, that these people were not their responsibility. In 1785, a blind man was transferred twenty-four times from one town to another as the authorities of Eastchester, New York, sent him back to his official home of Providence, Rhode Island. Over the eighteenth century, as the numbers and the mobility of the destitute increased, so did warning out. In the first half of the 1760s, communities in Essex County, Massachusetts, warned out about nine hundred households. In 1770, Charleston banned the following from receiving assistance: immigrants from France, Ireland, Germany, or neighboring colonies; migrants from other Carolina towns who would not go home; and families of men who had left to join the army. Moreover, resentment toward the poor generally seemed to grow as Americans increasingly faulted them rather than their bad luck or God's mysterious will for their poverty and as the poor increasingly spoke up. In small communities, rich and poor clashed on issues such as paying taxes for ministers' salaries and laws regulating commercial activities. Poor residents in larger towns took to the streets to demand redress, calling on the government to control the price of food. Class tensions rose, fed the national Revolution, and stirred the social revolutions to come.[53]

The Turmoil of Industrialization

Immense economic growth in the nineteenth century raised up a middle class and its bourgeois culture. It eventually brought growing comfort to many. But it also brought great insecurity to many people—often the same ones. In 1800, four of five American adults farmed; they reaped the benefits of new lands, products, and markets. Governments stoked the economic expansion by building roads, subsidizing canals, selling public land, displacing Indians, providing postal service, dredging harbors, circulating cash, facilitating credit, and providing legal cover for investors. Many families simply took unclaimed land, paying for it only later. Thomas Lincoln squatted a plot in Indiana for almost a year before he was able to pay for even half of it. In 1817, Zachariah and Nancy Peter and their five children took over an empty cabin in Sugar Creek, Illinois. When the cabin's owners returned over a year later, the Peters moved out and built a home a few miles away. In Illinois in 1828, two-thirds of farmers were squatters. Many failed and moved on. Others, such as Zachariah Peter, succeeded; he eventually rose from squatter to justice of the peace.[54]

Most farmers thrived as new transportation technologies cut the cost of shipping from dollars to nickels and dimes, allowing Western wheat growers, for example, to serve European demand spurred by the Napoleonic Wars. In the South, plantation owners shifted from rice and tobacco to cotton, now made exceedingly lucrative by Eli Whitney's gin. Between 1800 and 1820 alone, cotton production increased tenfold; by

1830, cotton comprised over half the value of all American exports. Slavery, which in the 1700s had seemed increasingly unprofitable, revived and flourished. New industrial forms of production reduced the prices of hard goods as well as food.[55]

By grasping onto national and international markets, however, farmers increasingly rode their ups and downs; not all could hang on. The Panic of 1819 and subsequent depression shocked Americans, who now realized that their fortunes could depend on decisions made in Washington and overseas. Eastern farmers struggled to coax more out of often depleted lands while facing growing competition from Western produce. In upstate New York, the competition turned many wheat farmers to sheep-raising, dairying, and harvesting forests for barrel staves. Farm consolidation and population growth forced yet more farmers' sons to become tenants or laborers. In the South, expanding cotton production favored plantations and thus slave owners—about one-fourth of all freemen—over the hardscrabble small-holders who had to work harder, become tenants, or move on. North, South, and West, Americans moved around rapidly in response to the opportunities that they saw beckoning over the horizon; even more moved in reaction to economic disruptions. Lincoln's father left a long track of failures at addresses across Kentucky, Indiana, and Illinois. Four of every five families living in 1840 in Sangamon County, Illinois—one of both Thomas Lincoln's and Zachariah Peter's addresses—were gone by1850.[56]

Increasing commerce enticed farmers' wives and daughters to work at home on commission ("outwork"), making hats and brooms and finishing shoes, for example. Many daughters briefly worked in the new textile factories built along New England's rivers. Four of New Hampshire farmer Samuel Fowler's five daughters spent part of the their teens in the 1830s and early 1840s working in the mills of Lowell, Massachusetts. Two of the four eventually settled back home as married women; only the fifth, the stay-at-home daughter, became a farmer's wife. Mill work was a regular stage of life for many New England women, but within a few decades, immigrants, particularly from Ireland and French Canada, replaced the Yankee girls. The newcomers provided employers a more stable and pliable work force.[57]

Antebellum cities fed on the expanding national and world trade and the building of factories. Land speculators platted new towns in the Midwest. Many of those towns never moved from drawings to reality, but other plans grew into brick-and-mortar oases on the plains. Master craftsmen, capitalizing on their experience and contacts, became small manufacturers of furniture, tools, and clothing. They gave up the lathe or awl for the ledger book, hired wage laborers for routinized tasks, and moved their families out of the workshops they had shared with apprentices. Asa Bragg of Providence, Rhode Island, for example, used income from a side job to pay off his indenture to a shoemaker, then started peddling his own shoes, and finally scraped together enough cash to employ a houseful of cobblers to produce cheap footwear for Southern slaves. Micajah Pratt, a Lynn, Massachusetts, Quaker, followed a probably more common route to success. The son of an affluent shoe dealer, Pratt sold sturdy shoes to Western settlers, eventually building a large, steam-powered factory and employing five hundred people at a time.[58]

Entrepreneurs such as Bragg and Pratt joined a growing, increasingly well-off, and increasingly well-defined class in towns and cities. These men ranked socially below the wealthy landlords and merchants but above manual workers; they formed a "middle" class. Economic expansion generated, at least in the North, many thousands of new, nonmanual occupations, in business—as owners, managers, office workers, and salesmen—and in the professions—teachers, doctors, and lawyers. Abraham Lincoln, a small-town lawyer with railroad companies for clients and an ambitious woman for a wife, exemplified the aspiring bourgeoisie. Members of the new middle class built a distinctive culture. They moved to particular neighborhoods and joined particular clubs and churches. They committed themselves to faith, sobriety, restraint, and the pursuit of gentility. They taught these views and disciplines to their children. This emerging bourgeois way of life would become the template for modern America.[59]

Mass production lowered prices for consumers and thus raised Americans' standard of living. But it also displaced craftsmen. A "Country Tailor" wrote to a New York newspaper that "the wholesale clothing establishments . . . are forcing their work [product] into the villages, along the rivers, canals, and railroads, absorbing the business of the country; and thus casting many an honest and hardworking man out of employment, or drawing them to your city by taking work there." Uprooted rural artisans, farmers' landless sons, and Irish and German immigrants composed a growing, distinct class of free wage earners. Unlike peasants, serfs, servants, and apprentices, they could sell their labor to the highest bidder. But propertyless and powerless, they hardly fit the new nation's image of the freeman; their "competency" was at best marginal. Militant members of this class, generally the more skilled journeymen and artisans, armed with the labor theory of value (the idea that a product was solely worth the work put into it), charged their employers with exploitation and "wage slavery," organized their cadres, and went on strike. In the end, however, the relatively few militants among the wage earners could not repel industrial capitalism.[60]

Wage earners had escaped the constraints of authoritarian fathers and masters, but also lost the security that fathers and masters provided. They faced competition from eager immigrants and emancipated slaves. When the business cycle turned down, as it did in the panics of 1819 and 1837, urban workingmen faced spells of unemployment and depressed wages with little to fall back on—not even a backyard patch for garden produce. They had to borrow from kin or fraternal societies, remove children from school, take in boarders, beg for charity, or, typically, move on. In antebellum Philadelphia, more than three-fourths of families left town or their neighborhoods within ten years. As in rural America, urban America experienced widening gap between the new economy's winners and losers.[61]

Several types of workers—farm laborers, sailors, dockhands, house builders, factory employees—faced long stretches of idleness, particularly in winter. Others suffered deprivation, because, having aged, they were unable to work and lacked wealth or nearby children. To insure against a desperate old age, many still-able farmers signed over their farms to their sons in return for stipulated guarantees of support for themselves and their widows. In an era still marked by early death, widows and orphans formed a large portion of the chronically poor. Clockmaker Chauncey Jerome recalled the death of his father, a blacksmith, in Connecticut in 1804:

> The day of his death was a sad one for me, for I knew I would lose my happy home, and be obliged [at age 11] to leave it to seek work for my support. . . . [P]oor boys were obliged to let themselves to the farmers, and it was extremely difficult to find a place to live where they would treat a poor boy like a human being. . . . I knew that the rest of the family had got to leave soon, and I perhaps never to see any of them again.

Jerome was bound out to a farmer and then to a carpenter until he turned twenty-one. Robert Percifull, an affluent Virginian, died in 1817 owing a neighbor $200. After his entire estate was sold to pay off his debts, his family was left impoverished and his two children ended up on the county relief rolls for several years. As in the colonial era, the "deserving" poor gained some community sympathy and some meager relief. Towns began building almshouses as one alternative to "warning out" the poor; many of them evolved into old age homes. Authorities preferred to bind out the able-bodied, like Chauncey Jerome, as boarding workers for local families. The "undeserving"—the strangers, foreigners, or elderly slaves cut loose by their owners, for example—often drifted from place to place.[62]

No free American, whether employed or vagabond, faced the existential insecurity that slaves did, who could be sold or destroyed on whim.

Day to day, however, conditions varied greatly. Most slaves, although heavily worked, had, as Southern apologists claimed, security of employment, meals, and shelter so long as their masters lived and the estates were intact. On smaller farms, slave and slave owner might work side by side, with the master gaining some feeling of paternalistic responsibility for his bondsman. Less fortunate slaves had brutal overseers and owners with few qualms about selling them. An elderly couple interviewed in the 1930s about their slave years had contrasting memories. As a child, Jack Maddox had to sleep with his "brothers and sisters . . . on the floor in the cabin, huddled together in cold weather so we wouldn't freeze to death. Our life was a misery. I hate the white man every time I think of us being no more than animals." Maddox also recalled hunger and beatings and sexual exploitation. His wife, Rosa, however, remembered a childhood in "good little cabins. . . . And we had cotton mattresses and blankets. We had enough to eat, too . . . syrup, meal, flour and meat, potatoes, and plenty of milk." Of her master, Rosa said, "I never heard of him bothering any women." A third interviewee, Charlie Moses, recalled conditions that may have been more common, especially for field workers on large plantations: "Master would beat, knock, kick, kill. He did everything he could except eat us. We were worked to death. . . . I know it ain't right to have hate in the heart, but—God Almighty—it's hard to be forgiving when I think of old man Rankin. . . . Hungry—hungry—we were so hungry!" Brutalized and hungry, but alive and not starving. Slave owners generally kept care of their property, providing them, for example, with more medical care than poor whites received. Food rations were thin but regular, often supplemented by gardening and hunting. None of this minimal security could, despite the protestations of slavery's propagandists, make up for the ultimate insecurity of being someone's chattel.[63]

Members of the antebellum middle class also encountered economic shocks. Chauncey Jerome (the orphan bound out to farm work in 1804) became a major manufacturer of clocks, but suffered first a fire that destroyed much of his business; later, his business failed completely. Harriet Cooke ended up as a widow schoolteacher in New England in the 1830s, but took a torturous road to that respectable position. She was orphaned at age ten when her father died at sea; was "relatively" impoverished in 1813 when her merchant husband could not meet a promissory note he had cosigned for her own brother and went to debtors' prison; and was then widowed in Georgia, where her husband had tried to restart his career but died of the "fever." After weeks of nervous prostration, Cooke recalled, "the question presented itself, what shall I do?—in what business engage, in order to support myself and my children? . . . I determined to open a boarding-house, and . . . with my pecuniary resources reduced to *nine dollars* . . . I commenced my new life of widowhood and responsibility." America had an emerging—but still unsteady—middle class.[64]

Recovery

The Civil War devastated many lives (although relatively few of the Northern middle class, who could buy their way out of military service), but it did not radically alter the American economy. Economic development in the North slowed noticeably during the war, but picked up afterwards.[65]

The war, on the other hand, ravaged and effectively bankrupted much of the South. Thousands of slave owners had much of their "property" (valued at about $60 billion in 2008 dollars) confiscated and handed to ex-slaves in the form of their own bodies. Federal efforts to stake freedmen to land largely failed, but by 1890, a fifth of black farmers owned their own plots. Many of the freed slaves followed the paths of other free laborers, preferring autonomy over constraining arrangements such as wage contracts. One Georgia planter complained of this passion for freedom, asserting that freedmen "will almost starve and go naked before they will work for a white man." Jack Maddox ran away from his owners during the last days of the war and worked as a teamster in San Antonio and a rafter for a sawmill in Arkansas, generally succumbing to his "itching heel." He married and took up farming in 1870, only to learn a few years later that he did not really hold title to the land. Maddox and his wife Rosa ended up, like many freedmen, as tenant farmers under the thumb of landowners. Charlie Moses's family also moved about as he worked a variety of odd jobs in the lower Mississippi region. In 1870, he became an itinerant preacher, finally settling down in 1873. His words in the 1930s suggest that economic security was not the ultimate value he sought: "I didn't expect nothing out of freedom except peace and happiness and the right to go my way as I pleased. I pray to the Lord for us to be free, always." Sharecropping, however, became black men's major form of employment, and it operated much like indentured servitude, providing both limited freedom and limited security.[66]

Beyond the defeated South, the postbellum years combined rapid long-term economic growth—faster than that of Europe—broken up by frequent economic depressions and recessions. Urban industry expanded rapidly, drawing on dozens of technological innovations and aided by energetic government policies and court rulings which cut the fetters on entrepreneurs. (Legislators and judges, for example, eased incorporation laws, reduced barriers to interstate trade, and overruled worker-protection legislation.) America's open door allowed in millions of immigrants to work in the factories and on the construction crews of the booming cities. In 1860, farmers and farm workers outnumbered manufacturing workers by four to one, but in 1900, by only about two to one. An urban, industrial society was coming, but in 1900, America remained a predominantly rural country; in fact, agriculture expanded rapidly in the last decades of the nineteenth century.[67]

The railroads and government land grants helped hundreds of thousands to homestead the West. Farmers benefitted from easier access to growing national and world markets, improved production methods, and the maturation of rural communities. On the other hand, increased production and competition kept prices down and farmers on a financial roller coaster. As ever in farming, nature wiped out many. A long drought during the 1890s encouraged half the farmers of Haskell County, Kansas, to leave. In the long run, two-thirds of Western homesteaders failed, Southern sharecroppers struggled with depleted soil and ferocious pests, and youngsters everywhere left the land.[68]

Urban workers took a similar boom-and-bust ride during the late nineteenth century. As the Panic of 1893 hit, for example, about half of San Francisco's craftsmen lost their jobs. Open immigration and government support for employers undermined organized labor's efforts to soften the economic bumps. Spells of unemployment came as a result of the economic cycles, but they also followed seasonal layoffs and the uncertain fortunes of particular industries. In Pittsburgh's iron and steel mills, a third of working-class men might be unemployed sometime during the year. (In some cases, employers temporarily closed factories to forestall unionization.) In the shoe industry, the workforce might shrink by half in midsummer and midwinter. Each year between 1885 and 1895, according to one estimate, about one-third of Massachusetts workers were out of work for an average of three or four months, older men even longer. Fewer than half the workers in America's largest textile mill, the Amoskeag plant in Manchester, New Hampshire, held a job for a full year. Many industries relied on an army of "floaters," transient men who would come in for the peak production season and then drift on. As late as 1910, perhaps 3.5 million unskilled laborers (out of a total of 10.4 million such workers) floated from job to job. Absent public aid for the able-bodied, even those with relatively stable careers were compelled to fall back on savings or the income of family members when possible, and when not possible, to move out of town. Asmokeag workers, for example, often returned to their parents' farms in Quebec during slow times. In this era, unlike before the Civil War, far fewer industrial workers had other sources of income, such as a farm or craft skills; they depended totally on wages and had to roam in search of employment. Community leaders typically resented the burden of migrants and delegated their care and disposal to the police. These "tramps were," as one historian put it, "the ordinary working people of the United States on the move between jobs and residences."[69]

Americans coped with the uncertainties of the economy in a variety of ways. According to historian of unemployment Alexander Keyssar, one might even describe working-class life at the end of the nineteenth century as a design for handling economic insecurity:

> It was not merely poverty but insecurity . . . that led workers to send their children into the labor force, to take in boarders, to move from one place to another, to hoard their small savings while living in substandard conditions. It was not only sentiment but the need for mutual support that led working people to maintain close ties with their relatives and to cluster in ethnic communities. The structures of life in the working class were molded by the recurrent task of adjusting to unemployment . . . [and] being prepared to adjust to unemployment.[70]

Some families coped with the insecurity by sending mothers out to work, most commonly as maids, servants, or washerwomen, even in the face of the Victorian ideal that women should stay home. Yet more relied on unmarried daughters earning a wage, often in the same lines of work. Being "in service" was among the least desirable jobs. One woman recalled the reaction when she told her mother that she had no alternative but to work as a maid: mother "turned away from me, leaned against the wall and cried, 'Is this what I have come to America for, that my children should become servants?'" Women even preferred arduous factory jobs to the degradations and restrictions of service. Yet about half of employed women in 1870 were servants (declining to about one-third in 1900). Taking in lodgers and boarders was a wife's major alternative. In 1880, about half of working-class families in Pittsburgh had boarders who typically provided about a quarter of families' incomes. Immigrants and working-class Americans generally valued security more than enterprise—for example, buying a house rather than investing in a business or a child's education. A house, unlike a diploma years away, provided shelter, income from boarders, and sometimes a vegetable garden.[71]

When such strategies failed, when times were bad or physical disability prevented work, Americans of the late nineteenth century still found little formal help. If relatives' assistance or loans from ethnic associations no longer sufficed, families fell into dire poverty and men hit the road. As late as the early 1900s, about half of American families could be classified as poor, and they moved around frequently. For example, only one-fourth of Pittsburgh residents in 1900 were still there in 1905. This was the era when popularized Darwinism joined laissez-faire economics to define the poor as physically and morally unfit and label able-bodied men without income as "shirkers." Policy makers worried, as always, about saving money but now increasingly worried also about encouraging indolence. Some of the poor had options. Union Army veterans and their families earned the label of the "deserving poor" and received federal pensions; farmers in many places, including turn-of-the-century Illinois, would take in orphans as work hands; and in cities orphanages often cared for children of poor parents.* But most of the needy had to manage on their own or their relatives' resources or on the personal charity of neighbors—or else end up in the "poorhouse" alongside the aged, the infirm, and the mentally ill. An historian of rural New York noted that "people who were isolated from relatives by death or distance were particularly vulnerable"; they ended up homeless or institutionalized. Fear of the almshouse was common. In 1871, *Harper's Weekly* published a poem on its cover: "For I'm old and I'm helpless and feeble / The days of my youth have gone by / Then over the hill to the poor house / I wander lone there to die."[72]

For all the lurches and insecurities, the American economy nonetheless continued to accelerate, and average Americans' incomes rose. By the end of the nineteenth century, children once again were growing taller than their parents. The middle class expanded steadily. In 1850, about a half-million men held white-collar jobs; by 1900, nearly four million did, up from 10 to 17 percent of all employed men. The growing middle class literally altered the landscape by planting suburban homes in what had been the farmlands, woods, and plains of the city hinterlands—or in some cases, in what had been working-class villages. Winnetka, Illinois, Palo Alto, California, and other affluent enclaves emerged along commuter train lines or near ferry slips. Politically and culturally, as well, the middle class consolidated its position; it was not yet a majority, but a still-growing center.[73]

Nineteenth-century America offered economic opportunity everywhere, from open land on the Great Prairie to construction jobs in New York City. It drew tens of millions of immigrants who, tantalized by letters from relatives who had risked it all before them, scraped together their lira or rubles or krona for boat fare. Many of them or, more commonly, their children entered nonmanual occupations and the American middle class. At the same time, so many failed—on farms and in cities—that, lacking basic security, they kept on moving across the countryside or into town or even back across the Atlantic.[74]

* Noted sportswriter Jerome Holtzman and the influential sociologist Daniel Bell are among those who, even with a parent yet alive, were cared for in orphanages.

Finding Safe Harbor?

During the twentieth century, average Americans arrived—despite the severe tempest of the Great Depression—at widespread affluence and economic security. More of them worked at more secure jobs for better pay. The average full-time employee at the end of the century earned about four times the wages in real buying power than he or she would have in 1900. Around the beginning of the twentieth century, a pound of bread cost about a half-hour of work in a factory; at the end of the century, a pound of more nutritious, fresher bread cost about five minutes of work. In 1900, a couple had a one-in-two chance of being poor, but in 2000 a couple had about a one-in-twenty chance of being poor—and even if they were so unlucky, they usually had running water, central heating, and a television. Most American workers found nonmanual employment; by 2000, half of employed men and three-fifths of employed women were in white-collar, managerial, or professional jobs. In the mid-century, even those men who held manual jobs, if those jobs were in large, unionized companies, such as General Motors, earned incomes that permitted them to place their families into a middle-class lifestyle. Archetypal examples were the young couples who moved into new suburban tract housing built by Levitt & Sons around 1950, he a veteran with G.I. Bill benefits and an industrial job, she an aspiring housewife, moving from cramped working-class apartments they rented in the city to houses they owned in what seemed to be "the country." Critically, Americans in the postwar era rode much smoother waves of economic boom and bust and suffered much less from downward plunges—although the last decades of the century and the first decade of the new millenium brought significantly choppier seas.[75]

The growing industrial economy was one pillar of the new security. Greater productivity, new technologies, improving skills, and mass marketing brought unprecedented affluence to an unprecedented number of Americans. The economy democratized the "good life," as immigrants, women, blacks, the elderly, Southerners, rural residents, and others who had been in the rearguard moved up. Greater family wealth, thanks to greater economic productivity, cushioned economic shocks for many Americans in the twentieth century. (Few took in boarders any more.) It also permitted a shorter workweek and sufficient savings so that more workers could retire at increasingly early ages. A vast marketplace of goods and services enabled most Americans to invest their growing income in "securities," such as homes, mutual funds, health insurance, and private pension plans. The other great pillar of the new security, we shall see, was government management of the economy and insurance of citizens against severe losses. This propulsive industrial machine, however, occasionally lurched along the way and slowed in the last quarter of the twentieth century.[76]

For rural Americans, the twentieth century began with a golden age. Farmers transformed rising agricultural prices into cash to pay for goods they ordered out of Sears or Montgomery Ward catalogs and to buy Henry Ford's Model T. Even in these best of times, however, and despite much entreating and government studies of the "country problem," youngsters still fled the farms for better times in the cities. In some areas, agricultural land reverted to forest. Then, the end of World War I brought lower crop prices, an agricultural depression, the Great Depression, drought, and for many, life in the Dust Bowl. Often, what crops emerged were not worth harvesting and just rotted in the fields. The value of farmland in South Dakota dropped by half in the 1920s and by half again by 1935; nearby towns suffered similarly. Many farmers in the upper plains walked away from acreage which they had, responding to high prices, just started tilling. Windstorms blew the loose soil across the country—six tons landed in Chicago one night in 1934—and destroyed much of the remaining farmland (and the health of the farmers) in the lower plains. In rural Iowa around 1930, the lost farms, jobs, and dignity encouraged a wave of gruesome robberies, murders, and suicides. John Steinbeck's dispossessed farmers in *The Grapes of Wrath* were far from typical, but their story, like the iconic photographs of migrant workers by Dorothea Lange and Walker Evans, revealed the great insecurities of many rural people.[77]

The New Deal government responded with an array of aid, including direct assistance, public works jobs, and programs to reduce crop yields. By midcentury, those farmers who remained on the land depended on the federal government to sustain prices and living standards (and to fix the soil). Farming as a way of life succumbed to technology, particularly to the tractors and harvesters that created industrial farming and made most farmers redundant. By the end of the twentieth century, American farm families—now fewer than 2 percent of the population—earned only a small fraction of their income from the land. They were well-off and secure by any historical measure, but most descendants of rural America had moved on to the urban economy.[78]

The capsule story of the urban economy is of more, better, and more secure jobs. Yet the Great Depression is a critical part of that story, not only because of its duration and severity, but also because it, together with World War II, marked a new stage in Americans' economic security. In March 1933, more than a fourth of the labor force was officially unemployed; many more were underemployed. Those who held on to jobs saw their wages drop faster than consumer prices did. Half of American home mortgages were in default by 1933 (dwarfing the housing crisis of the late 2000s). In some corners of the nation, things were even worse. The Ford Motor Company, for example, laid off 70 percent of its work force by 1931; in 1932, nearly two-thirds of New York City construction workers were jobless. From everywhere came reports of desperation. (No surprise, then, that the suicide rate spiked around 1931.) In Oklahoma City, "thousands of people liv[ed] out of orange-crate shacks or inside the mildewed, rusted-out hulks of junk cars." Sixty-five percent of black children in Harlem were malnourished. Vagabonding increased; women and children joined the treks. Critically, the Great Depression, unlike several earlier downturns which had also sent many thousands of people tramping about the country, dislodged many from the new middle class who had held stable, well-paying jobs; some families responded by sending sons and mothers out to seek work. The usual sources of aid for the "deserving" poor—relatives, fraternal associations, charities, town governments—buckled under the burden. It was hard for many in the middle class to help when they themselves were needy.[79]

The federal government intervened in the industrial as well as agricultural economy: direct relief, food subsidies, housing assistance, regulation of securities, old-age pensions, minimum wage legislation, disability insurance, union protections, bank deposit insurance, and counter-cyclical spending policies. Republicans ended some of these programs in the later 1930s but also made many of them—notably, sustaining jobs and wages by manipulating the economy—permanent in the Eisenhower administration of the 1950s. The dominant concern that motivated the New Deal initiatives and protected many of them long after the Roosevelt years was, historian David Kennedy has emphasized, *security*. The nation sought, as Kennedy wrote, "freedom from fear." Across all realms of domestic policy, "the common objective was stability." Roosevelt wanted government "to sustain balance and equity and orderliness throughout American society," giving average Americans predictability in their lives. These initiatives had not yet ended economic insecurity by the eve of World War II. In 1939, unemployment was still at 17 percent. But, together, the economic boom that began with the war and the new arrangements largely succeeded in providing the predictability that Roosevelt sought.[80]

New macroeconomic tools enabled administrations and, notably, the Federal Reserve Board to influence the business cycle, extend periods of economic growth, and maneuver for "soft landings" during downturns. For individuals, being employed became surer: annual unemployment rates, which had exceeded 10 percent in fifteen of the fifty-five years before the end of World War II never reached 10 percent in the sixty-three years after the war. More workers could expect to hold a job for several more years than a generation or two earlier when bouncing from job to job was typical. The new employment stability contributed to the stereotype of the 1950s "organization man." Average Americans' jobs had become secure, well-paid, and accompanied by fringe benefits, such as health and retirement packages, so much so that they could afford to work fewer hours—perhaps 30 percent fewer hours a year for full-time workers in 1970 than in 1900—and to stop working long before the disabilities of old age forced them to stop.[81]

The New Deal also gave more Americans more security through unions and job protection legislation. As late as 1930, only 7 percent of American workers belonged to unions, but by the 1950s, 25 percent of American workers (35 percent outside of agriculture) did. Unions provided job and income security through long-term contracts, seniority rules, health benefits, pensions, discharge policies, and the like. Unions also aided nonmembers by setting both informal and legal benchmarks, so that, even as union membership fell to 14 percent by the end of the century, the major gains in economic security persisted. How much of the new security should be credited to the unions versus a productive economy is debated, but unionization contributed. At the same time, however, unionization may have helped divide American workers in two, a majority who held relatively secure jobs protected by union contracts or their bureaucratic equivalents and a minority who lacked such guarantees and moved from job to job in the "secondary labor market."[82]

Americans could further secure their families by buying insurance. In 1900, companies wrote only one life insurance policy for every five Americans, with an average value of about $3,000 (in 2008 dollars). Many Americans relied instead on financially shaky clubs and fraternal associations for insurance. By 2000, the insurance industry wrote more than one policy for each American, with an average value of about $75,000 (2008 dollars) per policy. In addition, 70 percent of Americans held private health insurance, most through their jobs. Add in car insurance, homeowner insurance, liability insurance, and so on, and one could describe at least middle-class Americans as ensconced in a cushioned nest of assurances.[83]

Yet for both the middle class and those less fortunate, the most critical development was government insurance. In the late nineteenth century, state and local officials made modest efforts to handle surges of unemployment, for example, by sponsoring hiring agencies and speeding up public works. In the early twentieth century, despite new ideas about the structural sources of joblessness, policy makers, and public opinion remained opposed to "handouts." Suspicions hardened when the federal government's largest system of income assistance, the Civil War pensions, came to be viewed as corrupt patronage. Even during the Great Depression, many local officeholders believed that New Deal support programs simply subsidized the indolent and the officials subverted their implementation. Harry Hopkins, Roosevelt's point man in this arena, wrote that such officials treated each recipient as "in some way morally deficient. He must be made to feel his pauperism. . . . to intensify his sense of shame." Even the successful programs often discriminated, notably against farm workers and servants, groups that were disproportionately African American. Southern landowners in particular made sure that the income support, such as the public works jobs, did not deprive them of cheap labor. Georgia governor Eugene Talmadge wrote to President Roosevelt: "I wouldn't plow nobody's mule for fifty cents a day when I could get $1.30 for pretending to work on a DITCH." Farmers, although especially dependent on New Deal programs, especially criticized them. By 1938, one-third of farmers' income came from government payments, but many rural Americans claimed that New Deal assistance undermined personal responsibility and created permanent dependency. For them and many other Americans, government aid was a necessary but hopefully temporary exception to voluntarism.[84]

Ultimately, many government insurance programs survived and expanded. Social Security and Medicare, together with growing affluence and private pension systems, revolutionized the experience of the elderly—and their children. They provided enough old-age assistance to shut down the almshouses and make the elderly, by the last quarter of the twentieth century, the age group *least* likely to be poor. The elderly had never been as destitute as often imagined; many had significant assets and could turn to their children. But Social Security pensions especially helped those who were destitute, and, significantly, they relieved adult children, including those in the middle class, of a major financial burden. More old people could live on their own. In 1900, five elderly widows lived with their children for each one who lived by herself; by 1950, the ratio was only two to one; and by the end of the century, elderly widows were over three times more likely to live alone as with their adult children. Elderly men experienced a less dramatic but similar increase in independent living. Social Security accelerated the advent of retirement as a normal stage in life. In 1900, three of five men over sixty-five years old were working; by 1980, fewer than one in five was.[85]

For middle-class Americans, the 1950s, when most Americans could be considered middle class, were the "good old days" of high marriage rates, large families, rising wages, good health and pension benefits, new suburban homes, low crime rates, active community participation, and a nation whose economy bestrode the world. The reverse side of that portrait was revealed late in the decade: pockets of poverty in places like Appalachia and Harlem, racial oppression, restlessness among suburban youths and even among suburban mothers. Nonetheless, the economic foundations of middle America remained firm through the turbulent '60s.

Rougher Times

Then the foundations fissured. Starting in the 1970s, the rising standard of living that Americans had come to take for granted slowed sharply. Although the top few percent of Americans did phenomenally well, wages for average men started to fall behind the cost of living and wages for poorly educated workers sank. Middle-class families sustained their lifestyles by increasing the hours that mothers worked, drawing down their savings, and borrowing on their homes. Families faced greater insecurity as employers weakened job guarantees and trimmed fringe benefits and as government support thinned. Proportionally fewer Americans, for example, had health insurance or qualified for unemployment insurance. Increasing numbers of middle-class families found themselves only a layoff or a major illness away from financial breakdown. Increasing homelessness signaled crises among poorer Americans. The new insecurity was greatest for workers who had started their careers in the post-1970s job market of low entry wages, conditional employment, and fewer fringe benefits.[86]

The twentieth-century rise of the middle class, at minimum, stalled. It was not stopped as suddenly as in the Depression, but it became apparent to researchers and to most Americans themselves that sustaining a middle-class standard of living was harder around the turn of the millennium than it had been since the end of the Depression. More Americans started describing their country as "divided into 'haves' and 'have-nots'" and themselves personally as "have-nots." Average Americans started falling behind Europeans—shorter and shorter-lived, as I noted earlier, but now also working more hours and with less opportunity to move up economically. The proportion of Americans who identified as middle class grew steadily after World War II, but that trend stalled after the early 1970s. American workers experienced growing job insecurity and increasingly expressed that feeling to survey takers. In 2008–9, as housing values fell and unemployment rose, the fewest middle-income Americans in nearly a half-century told poll takers that they were becoming "better off." And reports filtered in from a few places that some Americans were starting to look for boarders.[87]

The Long View

In the larger sweep of history, the travails of the children of the baby boom notwithstanding, the twentieth century brought dramatic gains in economic security. Even in slumping 2008, nearly two-thirds of American adults told a survey that their standard of living exceeded that of their parents at the same age. The wealth-creating engine that is American business certainly is one reason. The other is government action to support the economy and to compensate for its inevitable market failures and collateral damage—managing money and credit, tamping down business cycles, picking up some of the stranded, and so on. (In 1929, government redistribution accounted for one percent of the gross national product; by 1970, 8 percent.) Yet whether Americans at the turn of the twenty-first century *felt* more economically secure than their ancestors is another matter.[88]

Economic insecurity increases economic anxiety, which breeds stress, behavioral issues, and family problems. We cannot directly compare earlier Americans' worrying to that of modern Americans, but indirect signs suggest that it subsided, the woes of the late 2000s notwithstanding. One sign I have mentioned is the near-disappearance of the boarder; another is the near-disappearance of child labor. In 1910, about one-half of fifteen-year-old boys were employed; in 1930, one-sixth were; by 2000, the government did not even tabulate fifteen-year-olds' employment, and we can assume the bulk of it was part-time work for pocket change. (Families forewent their children's labor because the number of lucrative child-appropriate jobs shrank, schooling expanded, truancy was taken seriously, and families increasingly felt that they could afford to.) Another sign is the steady decline in residential turnover from the nineteenth to the end of the twentieth century. Despite many new stimulants to moving—cheap travel, college attendance, fast communications, relocation services, and so forth—Americans in the mid-2000s were probably the most sedentary generation in centuries. Moving, especially long-distance and repeated moving, is spurred by economic insecurity of job losses, farm failures, and other disasters, which had become less common.[89]

In the long run, more Americans had gained the economic security of middle-class life. And while they probably suffered middle-class anxieties—about paying the mortgage, funding college, affording a new car—those were less critical than the working-class anxieties of an earlier era—paying the rent, feeding the family, affording the undertaker. The financial malaise was certainly real—such as the downward spiral of house values in 2008–9—but Americans generally had attained the economic predictability Franklin Roosevelt sought.[90]

FEELING SECURE

Despite periods of setbacks, modern Americans lived longer, safer, healthier, and wealthier lives than their ancestors did. We can assume that Americans therefore became more confident and assertive. For example, increasingly sure both that their infants would grow to adulthood and that their own old age would be secure, couples reduced births. Even *trying* to control births required confidence that individuals could override nature. Similarly, more Americans could pursue the "standard" life-cycle path of school-to-job-to-marriage-to-children-to-empty nest-to-retirement; because they faced fewer disruptive traumas, such as the death of parents or sudden impoverishment, planning made sense. Some scholars contend that modern Americans have arrived at a "postmaterialist" age. Secure in body, they now focus on the soul—on higher personal goals, such as self-improvement, and higher social goals, such as saving the environment.[91]

Others would temper any celebrations about security in the modern era. Perhaps Americans became so confident that they succumbed to the "moral hazard" of taking on excessive risks. One conservative critic described government guarantees against insecurity as "a colossal lure tempting citizens to reckless behavior"—Americans had come to feel *so* safe that they acted unsafely, say, in taking on debt. Another concern is that as Americans benefitted from government guarantees, their reliance on their communities and associations waned, and those groups weakened, leaving Americans more socially isolated. Chapter 4 addresses the fate of such groups and generally finds the threat overblown.[92]

There is a yet more pessimistic view of modern Americans' sense of security. The "age of anxiety" was a popular catchphrase in the years after World War II. "Western man in the middle of the twentieth century is tense, uncertain, adrift. We look upon our epoch as a time of troubles, an age of anxiety," wrote historian Arthur Schlesinger Jr. in 1948—a statement that has remained prominent decades later.* At least three history textbooks covering the second half of the twentieth century link affluence and anxiety in their titles. Perhaps reducing the mundane risks of life made the remaining risks or emerging ones more fearsome. Will the

---

* "Age of anxiety" probably originated in W. H. Auden's extended poem of that name (1946), followed by a 1949 symphony by the young Leonard Bernstein and a 1951 ballet by the young Jerome Robbins . The *New York Times* printed the phrase over 650 times in the twentieth century—half of those instances between its first appearance in 1946 (by essayist Alfred Kazin) and 1963.

stock market fall? Will the plane crash? Will the glaciers melt? Mass media exacerbated worries. A child abduction anywhere in the nation or a report of trace carcinogens can frighten millions into whisking their children off the streets or tossing food out of their refrigerators. Some blame modern advertising for creating worry, making people anxious about their health, bad breath, or children's grades to sell more soap, mouthwash, and tutoring. As fewer young people died and old people died tucked away in hospitals, perhaps Americans anguished all the more about death—especially death in an institution. Material security, then, may have ironically produced an age of anxiety.[93]

Perhaps, as well, mundane security ironically increased existential anxiety by undermining traditional faith's assurances. Evocations of life everlasting might seem unpersuasive in the modern era and, if so, people are left suspended over the greatest chasm without a net. Science, wrote historian Henry Steele Commager in 1950, taught Americans that life and morality were not absolute, and that, in turn, led to "a transition from certainty to uncertainty, from faith to doubt, from security to insecurity." This argument, however logical, seems wrong, at least in the American case (see chapter 6). In 2006–8, 74 percent of a nationally representative survey's respondents told interviewers that they believed in life after death—even more than had said so in the 1970s.[94]

In the end, what are the reliable signs that modern Americans felt more or less secure than their ancestors? In chapter 6, we will look at some indicators of anxiety, such as alcohol use and psychiatric diagnoses, but there are some behavioral signs. I already mentioned a few: reducing childbirths and child labor and moving around less. More generally, Americans increasingly bet on the future by investing more of their time, money, and emotion in the future: they extended their schooling, borrowed to buy homes, parented intensively, planned retirement, and made other investments and expenditures that make sense only if the ground ahead is secure. In shaky conditions, it instead makes sense to either hoard resources for the likely catastrophe to come or live it up while one can. Consider the confidence middle-class parents must have in the future to put so much time, energy, and money into targeting their children toward a professional career that will pay off decades in the future. Americans were willing, for example, to pay much more to buy homes in school districts with high reading scores, and as of late 2007, Americans had set up over ten million accounts averaging over $12,000 each for their children's future college tuition. (Americans of earlier epochs also undertook big endeavors, such as migrating West, but their decisions more commonly reflected necessity—debt, drought, and disinheritance,

for example—rather than long-term plans.) The grounds for such investments trembled a bit early in the twenty-first century. But in the long run,
Americans came to feel more materially secure.[95]

Greater security, confidence, and control reinforced the self-reliance
theme of American voluntarism for many more Americans. When money
can be had at the corner bank, the twenty-four-hour supermarket is fully
stocked, and the police come if you call, it is easy to feel empowered—
even if some self-delusion is involved. For example, Dakotans who dis-
paraged federal aid in a recent study seemed to have forgotten how government agricultural programs in the 1930s saved tens of thousands from
total destitution. Many Americans overlook the ways that government
helped secure them by law enforcement, road construction, water projects, medical research, pensions, weather forecasts, food inspection, deposit insurance, and so on. In the 2000s (except right after 9/11), most
Gallup poll respondents agreed that "the government is trying to do too
many things that should be left to individuals and businesses" and they
endorsed voluntary groups as the best route to helping people in need.
Ironically, greater government-provided security may have reinforced
Americans' personal confidence and sense of independence.[96]

We should recall, nonetheless, that the path to that security has been
a jagged, often narrow one. In the mid-nineteenth century, strained living standards shrank Americans physically. In the 1920s and 1930s, an agricultural and then a general depression surrendered years of economic
gain. After the 1960s, rising rates of street crime frightened many Americans into staying home. Since the mid-1970s, unequal economic growth
pressed most Americans to work harder just to maintain the middle-class
lifestyle they expected. In the late 2000s, millions of new homeowners
lost their homes. Throughout, many Americans have fallen off the path
to security because of illness, poverty, and other risks. Many, particularly
the least educated, lived from partial paycheck to partial paycheck, always in danger that one injury or one recession would take back most of
the choices promised by the affluent society. Twenty-first-century Americans on the whole are more physically and economically secure than earlier generations, but remain reasonably anxious about the future.

3 Goods

In the 1990s, Northwest Airlines advertised "Shop 'til You Drop," a package of airfare and lodging to visit the largest shopping center in the United States, the Mall of America in Bloomington, Minnesota. While adults met the challenge of the tour's title, children enjoyed the mall's indoor amusement park. Shopping tourism was not new. Even during the Great Depression, Filene's of Boston attracted visitors from around the nation. And decades before that, the newly invented "department stores" provided a range of entertainment and services befitting destination sites. Each seasonal opening drew throngs of buyers and sightseers to gawk at the new fashions, especially "the crowning pleasure of a day's shopping," the hat department. And a century yet before that, country stores in colonial Virginia received visitors from miles around when word spread that a new shipment of merchandise had just arrived. Americans have always been enthusiastic about new goods, but over the generations they accumulated vastly more of them. In the nineteenth century, migrants crossed the Appalachians with a few worldly goods slung on their backs or packed into small wagons; around 2000, families moving across state lines with the Mayflower company crammed, on average, over three tons of possessions into eighteen-wheelers.[1]

The previous chapter addressed the question of whether and how greater security reshaped American culture and character. This chapter expands the inquiry: whether and how more possessions reshaped American culture and character. Like improving security, greater material wealth allowed more Americans to partake more fully in a voluntaristic society. But having more goods also raises its own issues, notably whether the cornucopia created, as many bemoan, a "consumerist" society, people, and national psyche. Have, as some fear, "worshiping money and conspicuous consumption . . . become the dominant American religion of the

twenty-first century"? The historical record suggests not. Widespread affluence allowed more Americans to aspire to and attain more goods; it
democratized luxury. Modern Americans are probably no more obsessed
with possessions than their ancestors were, but more Americans can aspire to and have more of them.[2]

This chapter approaches the topic from two directions. First, I describe the tremendous expansion of Americans' material culture, how so
many more Americans came to have so many more things. Second, I address the cultural and characterological issues: what does it mean to be
consumerist? Did average Americans become consumerist? How did having more possessions affect American character? But before the first step,
a few notes on context.

Consumption has long raised considerable ambivalence and even
contempt. Many eminent observers have worried that along with having
more goods comes an obsession with goods. In the 1850s, Henry David
Thoreau wrote, in a book later placed on thousands of high school reading lists, "I see young men, my townsmen, whose misfortune it is to have
inherited farms, houses, barns, cattle, and farming tools. . . . Better if they
had been born in the open pasture and suckled by a wolf. . . . Most of the
luxuries, and many of the so-called comforts of life, are . . . hindrances to
the elevation of mankind." In the 1990s, almost all Americans in a survey agreed that youths "today want too many material things." Some
postmodernist theorists, however, take an ironic stance and celebrate
shopping. They argue that people buy goods to express their identities,
to bond with like-minded others, and to resist the anomie of mass society. And still others, typically economists, simply assume that what people buy must, by definition, bring them satisfying "utility," and so all this
navel-gazing is beside the point. These contrasting views of consumption
fit into a larger, longer debate about capitalism itself: did it enrich or enslave people? Such concerns, of course, long predate capitalism. Ecclesi-
astes teaches, for example, that all the luxuries of life amount in the end
only to "vanity."[3]

Much writing on consumption reeks of moral judgment and snobbery—and sometimes reverse snobbery. The scholarly study of consumption, according to a leading anthropologist, is "becoming largely a site
where academics can demonstrate their stance towards the world." Western intellectuals criticize elephantine American cars, fast food, Hollywood blockbusters, and trips to Disneyland—but not pricey European
automobiles, well-aged wines, exhibitions of avant-garde paintings, and
excursions to Tuscany. One might share the critics' tastes (for the most
part, I do) without having to label other people's tastes as consumerist
and their choices as corrupt. Nor is the reverse, condescending fawn-

ing over the "authenticity" and "revolutionary potential" of Jell-O fruit molds, tractor pulls, or do-rags, particularly honest or useful either.[4]

Sociologist Viviana Zelizer reminds us that we err if we denigrate the material aspects of life, assuming that they corrupt people's more elevated sentiments (probably an idea inherited from the fiercely abstemious Puritans). Goods can matter in profound ways. People connect to memories of parents through the food and furnishings of their childhoods, worshipers connect to God through stained-glass windows and ritual objects, and lovers connect to one another through gifts and shared travel. ("We'll always have Paris," Humphrey said to Ingrid in *Casablanca*—$12.99 ordered online.) A purchased thing can be only a commodity, used and tossed away, perhaps a distraction from a deeper life, but it can also be deeply woven into life. And so more goods can sometimes mean a richer personal and community history.[5]

MORE GOODS

Colonial Extravagances

For several decades before the political revolution of 1776, observers in the colonies had noted what today's historians label a "consumer revolution": more people were buying considerably more manufactured, often imported, goods. Most colonists had grown up in the late 1600s in homes that lacked tables, lamps, or chamber pots; they had slept on floors, sat on stools, and eaten with their fingers. As the eighteenth century unfolded, however, increasing production and cheaper transport allowed householders of modest means to buy bedsteads and bed linens, chairs, utensils, and even to splurge on a mirror, mantle clock, art print, or special pot for brewing that new luxury, tea. In York County, Virginia, virtually no one in 1680 owned a watch or clock, a table fork, a tea service, or fine earthenware; about a century later, about one-fourth of York families owned a timepiece and about half owned each of those other goods. Objects that had once been the luxuries of the rich appeared in more and more common folks' homes. Aside from providing their owners with a display of their success, new goods such as chairs and teapots made domestic life more comfortable and entertaining guests easier. Spreading along with the luxuries was the cultural legitimation of "comfort," the notion that average people deserved small physical pleasures, such as a cup of hot tea, and relief from irritations of life, such as an umbrella to stay dry.[6]

Although American farmers produced many goods, such as food staples, rough clothes, and simple furniture for themselves or to exchange with neighbors, they also bartered or paid cash for many other items, including cloth, tools, utensils, candlesticks, dishware, guns, finer household furnishings, and sugar. As the settlements and their wealth grew, all sorts of tradesmen, from transatlantic merchants to backwoods peddlers, came around with merchandise to offer. They took over from local dealers, such as craftsmen and plantation masters, who had sold occasional goods on the side and brought new items—decorative clocks, paintings, and English imports—to eager rural customers, especially farm women.[7]

Each new shipment inspired community events. Merchants placed advertisements in the local press boasting of great choices and new fashions. ("A neat assortment of Indian China Ware . . . Much cheaper than they are usually sold," said one ad.) As I noted earlier, farmers came into town see the boxes of goods opened and to be captivated by the display. "When . . . rural Virginians stepped into the dim light of" John Hook's Bedford County store in 1772, "a world of color, fashion, and knowledge was also there: ruffles, ribbons, white kid gloves, and looking glasses to admire one's self." And they bought: "A woman . . . could buy her stays and other means of fashionable bondage of the figure. She could leave with fantails or hats of beaver, black satin, or colored silk . . . velvet bonnets or velvet hoods . . . large wax necklaces." As growth brought greater competition, city merchants huckstered yet harder, advertising their variety of goods (199 classes of merchandise in one 1773 Philadelphia ad) and easy credit plans. Men in colonial America made the routine store purchases, but women were beginning to shop and were the main targets for hawkers of new indulgences—not that men did not indulge as well, for example, in "quills, ink, sealing wax or wafers, inkpots, and penknives" for writing letters. Historian Richard Bushman describes the eighteenth century as an era when simple purchasing became a "shopping" experience.[8]

Almost from the beginning, men of high standing viewed much of this shopping with alarm. In the mid-1600s, Puritan minister Eleazar Mather chastised his audience for falling away from the founding generations' purity, from a time when there was "Less Trading, Buying, Selling, but more Praying." Over a century later, a commentator wrote that "all the world [is engaged in] an orgy of get and spend." Women in particular absorbed criticism for their "female extravagance." The affluent chastised the poor for splurging on tea sets, tea and sugar. One concern for those in the upper ranks was that those in the lower ranks would ape their dress and try to pass as gentry. Men in Benjamin Franklin's Philadelphia social circle, for example, paid great attention to clothing and appearance, seeing them as signs of character and social class. Just to make clear who was who, some towns passed sumptuary laws dictating who could wear what sorts of fabrics.[9]

On the eve of the Revolution, Americans' rush to buy what critics called the "baubles of Britain" merged with the rush of politics. On the one hand, patriots rallied colonists by assailing His Majesty's taxes and other English interferences with colonists' freedom to buy. On the other hand, they decried the buying of luxuries for undermining virtue, frugality, and simplicity. Consumer boycotts became a tool of the insurrection, a declaration of consumer independence. In the late 1760s, for example, Harvard and Yale graduates demonstrated against the British by attending their commencements in homemade clothing.[10]

While some colonials could choose between wearing their finery or wearing their patriotism on their sleeves, even more of them—frontier settlers, slaves, indentured servants, and urban laborers—still struggled for necessities. Philadelphia's poorest workers in the 1780s, for example, "dined like prisoners, dressed in the same fashion as almshouse inmates, and crowded into cramped quarters." Given one-room housing and minimal furniture, sexual partners sometimes shared a room or even a bed with others. Yet such abject poverty was old and familiar. What was new in the New World of the eighteenth century and worrisome to the elites was that so many common American folks had so much—compared to the settlers of the seventeenth century and also to common English folk. The elite critiqued "the great Extravagance that People . . . are fallen into beyond their Circumstances, in their Purchases, Buildings, Expenses, Apparel, and generally whole way of Living," in the words of one Massachusetts jurist.[11]

The New Republic of Buying

In the early 1800s, entrepreneurs organized workers into specialized, power-assisted, and disciplined factory teams that could mass produce, with the aid of new technologies like the inch ruler, cheaper versions of the goods that Americans imported from England or bought handmade from local artisans. Entrepreneurs also marshaled teams of salesmen to distribute those products in towns and villages along America's newly built or improved roads and waterways. Prices for both basic and "luxury" goods plummeted. By 1820, even "middling" households typically had mirrors and, if they were not too far from the manufacturer, stoves and mantle clocks, too. Chairs could be had for under fifty cents apiece, about a half-day's work for a laborer, allowing many more farm and labor families not only to eat at a table but also to invite others into their homes—homes that increasingly sported carpets on the floors and inexpensive prints on the walls. New technologies made it possible to build those homes both larger and cheaper; middle-class families could now have a separate bedroom for the parents. Industrialization revolutionized American clothing. By the 1850s, mass-produced garments had driven out much of the homespun. Most Americans were delighted to discard the scratchy shifts and trousers that mothers (such as George Duffield's, see p. 1) made for the finer, cheaper, brighter shirts and pants that stores sold. Wearing homespun increasingly became a sign of the "rube," and wearing readymade, the sign of a middle-class citizen in a new and sartorially egalitarian republic.[12]

All this bounty astonished European visitors and immigrants. In 1842, a recently arrived German farmer wrote home about the extravagance of his Indiana neighbors: "Twice as much is cooked or baked than is eaten and, when mealtime is over, the pigs, dogs and cats get all the leftovers — ham, baked goods, and so on." A young immigrant to Brooklyn, Edward Bok, who would become editor of a major nineteenth-century guide to consuming, the *Ladies' Home Journal*, recalled that "where the Dutchman saved, the American wasted. . . . The first time my mother saw the garbage pail of a family almost as poor as our own . . . she could scarcely believe her eyes. A half-pan of hominy lay in the pail next to a third of a loaf of bread."[13]

At the same time of course, many Americans, particularly those in poor urban districts and on the frontier, still did without. In 1820, at least one-fifth of Washington DC residents ate without utensils. When Sarah Johnston became Abraham Lincoln's stepmother in 1819, she brought into his rustic home some simple furnishings — bedding, a table, chairs, and utensils — that seemed so extraordinary that "the Lincoln children felt that they were joining in a world of unbelievable luxury." George Duffield recalled that as a child in the 1830s, "the youngest three or four of us were habitually sent into the woods on the approach of strangers, because of the lack of garments on our forms. For months, one old muskrat cap served the youngest three boys. The earliest riser wearing it, and the others going barehead."[14]

In the later decades of the nineteenth century and the early ones of the twentieth, major innovations in production and marketing accelerated the spread of goods even more. In cities, merchants experimented with new ways of presenting their merchandise. They consolidated small specialty shops into mammoth "department stores." The emporia arrayed large and varying stocks of goods at different levels of quality and cost, tagged items with no-haggling prices, and offered customers entertaining diversions. With attractive displays, solicitous salespeople, plentiful services — ladies' rooms, luncheonettes, nurseries, music, free delivery, credit plans, and eventually credit cards — Filene's, Macy's, Gimbels,

Marshall Field's, and their competitors made shopping a recreation for urban women. In response, small-town stores, typically places where men congregated to drink and sport, developed carnival-like sales and fairs to keep women customers from the big-city emporia. New forms of marketing came to rural customers, as well. Previously, farm families had picked items from the small and pricey inventories on the shelves of country stores, often paying with produce but more often relying on credit. Improved rail connections, the institution of rural free mail delivery in 1898 (purchases went directly to the home instead of to the nearest post office) and parcel post service in 1913 created the mail-order system. To the distress of the village merchant, rural Americans could choose from an immense selection of reasonably priced items in Sears, Roebuck or Montgomery Ward catalogs. For many rural people, these fat publications, especially Sears's, with its alluring photographs, became treasured entertainments and links to the outside world. Country hosts impressed their guests with the packaged foods they received by mail. Then, in the 1910s, Henry Ford's cheap Model T automobile arrived. Farmers were quick to buy them and then drive to the bigger towns for better deals. In both town and country, consumers encountered another new marketing development: national "brands." Instead of buying generic goods from merchants' bins, jars, and open shelves, Americans now bought prepackaged goods with well-advertised names. Branding came to many products, from flatware to bathtubs, but the most famous was Uneeda Biscuits. Its sealed and decorated packages pushed out the classic "cracker barrel."[15]

Advertising reached its modern form around 1900. Both national manufacturers and local merchants substantially increased their spending on ads; the profession of ad writing and the industry of advertising emerged; large-picture ads replaced small-print notices in newspapers; eventually new kinds of sales pitches appeared. Rather than simply describing a product's technical virtues, ads increasingly addressed consumers' deeper concerns. Instead of extolling the cleansing power of a particular soap, for example, the new ads emphasized the social embarrassment of body odor or the sex appeal of clean skin. Some scholars contend that the new advertising strategies actually created wants—that toothpaste ads taught Americans to want white teeth and detergent ads made housewives ashamed to send their children to school without perfectly clean clothes. This claim is debatable—for example, rural stores sold toothbrushes as early as 1820. Nonetheless, advertising in newspapers and magazines, on billboards and streetcars, and later, on the radio, became part of the twentieth-century environment—like the goods themselves.[16]

Mass production, mass marketing, and credit for the masses—buying goods "on time" or with a store "charge plate" instead of in cash or on informal credit—combined to deliver yet more goods to yet more Americans. Most families now had real beds for all (even if children shared one), tables, chairs, sets of utensils, canned food, dress shoes, clothing for different occasions, artificial lighting at night, packaged staples from coffee to soap powders, indulgences such as dime magazines and tobacco, and commercial entertainments like baseball and vaudeville. Middle-class American families had even more, stereotypically in overstuffed, over-decorated homes; good taste meant flock-papered walls hung with dozens of framed pictures and furniture so upholstered that it swallowed the sitter. By the eve of World War I, a bounty of consumer products and services had made, historian Thomas Schlereth wrote, the "good life" into the "goods life."[17]

As before, many Americans—although now proportionately fewer—remained outside that life looking in. Sharecropping families in the South, for example, still lived in one-room shacks with dirt floors and without running water. Newly arrived Russians and Sicilians crowded into dark tenement rooms, their misery displayed in the new art of muckraking photography. Nonetheless, the democratization of goods was well under way. Even struggling immigrant workers in New York City bought fashionable blouses, gas stoves, small pianos, and weekend trips to the "country." Social workers calculating lean budgets for their poor clients allocated money for separate bedrooms, lighting, indoor toilets, tobacco, club memberships, and newspapers—all luxury items only a few decades earlier.[18]

The Gilded Age was, of course, well-known for displays of opulence, which in turn encouraged denunciations of "conspicuous consumption." An American returning from Europe in 1897 wrote in the *New York Times*, "We are slow in putting up cathedrals, but with what alacrity do we not construct temples reaching to the skies, wherein we worship the modern gods of comfort and luxury!" Of widespread concern during the period was women's supposedly uncontrollable passion for goods. One common drama, often and fulsomely described in the press, played out in a courtroom: a woman of high position stands trial for shoplifting in a department store and pleads innocent on the grounds of irresistible urge. It was the fault of the goods for luring her so powerfully.[19]

The Twentieth-Century Spree

It is only around the start of the twentieth century that we can put some reliable numbers on Americans' accumulation of goods. Many more

Americans started spending much more on other than the bare necessities. Until the last quarter of the nineteenth century, urban residents spent about half of their money on food alone and perhaps 90 percent on food, shelter, and clothing combined. Afterwards, they spent steadily smaller proportions of their incomes on these items, especially on food, thanks to a sharp increase in agricultural productivity. As I noted in the previous chapter, workers in 2000 could buy with five minutes' work what took eighty minutes in 1919. The shrinking of food costs from about one-half to about one-seventh of all expenses, combined with growing incomes, left a lot more money to buy a lot more things.[20]

What twentieth-century Americans mainly purchased with that money were goods and services that had not existed or that were considered luxuries before: automobiles, life insurance, houses, and the facilities of the modern home, such as new furniture and telephone and electric service. Twentieth-century Americans contributed to churches and charities; they spent much more on entertainment, sporting goods, toys, radios, televisions and, especially after 1960, other audiovisual equipment. Although the well-off spent their money in different ways than the less well-off, their buying patterns changed in parallel; spending on automobiles, insurance, recreation, and gifts increased noticeably for both.[21]

Among the many new goods Americans bought, the automobile and the house loomed largest. In 1900, virtually no one owned a car; in 1918, fewer than one-third of middle-class Americans owned one; but by 1930, over half of *all* American families did. Purchases of automobiles accounted for over *two-thirds* of consumers' new spending on big-ticket items. Sociologists and consumer critics Robert and Helen Lynd were struck by the level of automobile expenditures in "Middletown" (Muncie, Indiana) in the 1920s; half of the working-class families had cars and they devoted about 9 percent of their budgets to them. The Lynds worried that automobiles had "unsettled the habit of careful saving." A 1927 study of University of California, Berkeley, professors noted that some had bought cars, "a relatively new type of expenditure that custom is rapidly ranging in the class of necessities though comfortable conservatives still regard it darkly as a luxury." In 2005, the average American household devoted 17 percent of its spending to buying, fueling, or maintaining vehicles, more than on food and second only to housing, at 33 percent.[22]

Spending on housing also increased proportionately over the twentieth century; it went for much larger, better-equipped, privately owned houses. In 1890, about one-third of America's nonfarm households owned the homes they lived in; by the end of the twentieth century, more than two-thirds of American households owned their homes and a much greater proportion owned a home at some point in their lives. The big

shift occurred during the 1940s and 1950s, when economic growth, easier mortgages, and New Deal programs spurred home ownership. Tastes,
or at least investment strategies, changed as well. In the nineteenth century, working-class families, seeing houses as sources of security and
sometimes of income from boarders, more often owned their homes than
middle-class families did. During the next century, middle-class Americans turned from renting to owning, perhaps because it became a wiser
investment and perhaps because of increasing interest in domestic life
(see also chapter 4).[23]

To finance these cars and homes, more Americans borrowed more. In
the 1920s many adopted credit as a lifestyle, not just an occasional necessity, borrowing not only to buy seed corn or children's shoes, but also
to buy consumer "durables" such as sofas and refrigerators. Even working-class borrowers now found that institutions would lend to them, replacing the pawnbrokers and loan sharks they had previously turned to.
During the 1920s, installment-plan buyers roughly doubled, from about
one-fifth to two-fifths of American households even though the terms
were by later standards onerous, with high down payments and high risk
of repossession. The average household owed legal lenders about $3,700
in 1920; that amount more than quadrupled over a decade to about
$19,000 in 1929 (both in 2008 dollars).[24]

Warnings about borrowing and spending were loud. In 1912, a federal
statistician criticized "unnecessary" expenditures by working families,
"which had increased enormously within the last generation," particularly for automobiles, telephone service, amusements, and "card parties
with prizes." In 1924, noted journalist Samuel Strauss denounced the rise
of "consumptionism," a philosophy which made "luxury and security and
comfort" the center of life.[25]

The Depression stopped the spending binge—but the Roosevelt administration tried to restart it. Some New Deal programs put money into
the hands of the consumers and other programs encouraged consumers to
spend it. For example, mortgage insurance expanded home loans, and rural electrification programs pressed farmers to buy appliances. The New
Deal committed the government to more than safeguarding Americans'
"freedom from want." As the influential, progressive editor Herbert Croly
put it, "What the wage-earner needs, and what it is to the interest of the
democratic state he should obtain, is a constantly higher standard of living." In an oft-repeated anecdote, FDR reputedly said that if he could put
one book in hands of a Russian Communist, it would be the Sears, Roebuck catalog. These efforts, combined with the acceptance of Keynesian
economics, officially legitimated consumer desires in ways that seemed
to break from the Puritanical tsk-tsking of an earlier America. Sustaining

Americans' ability to consume—to spur the economy and for its own sake—became an even more explicit agenda of government.[26]

The last half of the twentieth century extended the democratization of goods in America. Even laborers now spent the largest share of their income on things other than the basics of food, shelter, and clothing. Further production and distribution improvements and increasing importation from low-wage countries reduced the real cost of essentials, such as clothing, and what were once luxuries, such as washing machines. Wages for middle- and working-class Americans soared (until the 1970s). Middle-class consumers gained the financial clout to shape styles. Out went artsy Bauhaus touches and in came pastel-colored appliances, dismaying designers accustomed to more refined clients with cultured tastes. Home ownership spread to the lower middle class, and even working-class homes had microwaves, color televisions, and stereo systems. Although some of the very poorest Americans still lacked safe housing and basic diets, most American families had the goods.[27]

Class had not, of course, evaporated. Early in the twentieth century, the well-off had running water and telephone service and took car-camping vacations—goods less wealthy Americans lacked. In the last decades of the century, the well-off had enclosed shower stalls and broadband Internet connections and flew to ski vacations—goods less wealthy Americans lacked. Affluent Americans and average Americans also still differed in how many, how varied, and how stylish their possessions were. The home furnishings the affluent typically purchased were greater in quantity and of a different selection—antiques rather than Swedish modern, abstract rather than representational art. In these ways, class distinctions persisted. And then, as I noted in the last chapter, the convergence in living standards, just like trends toward income equality, stalled after 1970 (an issue to which I will return later in this chapter). Nonetheless, a far greater proportion of Americans shared the "goods way of life" in the early 2000s than in 1950, 1900, or 1800.[28]

This goods way of life stunned foreign visitors and they, like earlier witnesses, wondered about the mentality of the possessors. In 1934, a Chinese scholar, echoing Tocqueville a century earlier, remarked that American families had in their homes "all sorts of things. The mass of the American people have not yet acquired the art of appreciating a few good things. They haul in various articles *ad libitum* [as they wish] and are satisfied with nothing." In 1963, an Israeli journalist described his family's first spending binge in an American supermarket. "We realized that we too had been stricken by the great American plague. We shop. Not because we need something, but because . . . we shop." Homegrown intellectuals worried about the "rat race," the chase for the bigger house, greener lawn, and larger automobile. "The old thrift ethic had less meaning than ever," wrote noted historian Daniel Boorstin in 1973. "For the American Standard of Living had come to mean a habit of enjoying things before they were paid for." And as the survey cited at the top of this chapter showed, many Americans in the 1990s agreed. Now that the old constraints of privation and prudence had been loosened, now that countless choices had been laid out before them, Americans, many feared, had lost control of their acquisitive impulses.[29]

Where Do We Put It All?

If we understand a consumer society to be one in which many have and expect to have purchased goods, then the United States was certainly a consummate consumer society at the start of the twenty-first century. A striking illustration is one survey finding that 77 percent of American sixth-graders in 1999 had televisions in their own bedrooms. (The 77 percent may impress us; "own bedrooms" would stun our ancestors.) The more interesting definition of a consumer society is one in which average folks want and get what were once reserved for the few. Historians have nominated several moments for the turning point when the United States became in this specific sense—common people buy what had been luxuries—a consumer society: the mid-1700s, when new products and fashions came to America and found their way into the homes of "middling" folk (recall the statement that this was when the "shopping" experience emerged); the early 1800s, when such goods spread into the rural hinterland; the late 1800s, when mass production made many goods formerly considered opulent, like pianos, widely affordable; the early 1900s, when department stores, advertising, and commercial entertainments bloomed (recall the statement that this was when America adopted the "goods life"); the 1920s and '30s, when automobiles and electrical appliances spread widely; the 1950s and '60s, when swelling paychecks fueled mass suburbanization and television entered almost every home; and the 1980s, the decade of easy credit, greed, and "luxury fever." One historian has noted that his colleagues are continually discovering new consumer revolutions, going all the way back to at least 1650. Perhaps, then, no era was a turning point. With rare setbacks such as depressions and (some) wartimes, American history is one of ever-growing abundance. The issue of national character, however, concerns not when the threshold of a consumer society was crossed, but the social and psychological meanings of crossing that threshold. Did the deluge of goods give more Americans more personal confidence and freedom, or did it imbue them with a compulsive "consumerism"?[30]

CONSUMERISM?

Historian of department stores William Leach described modern American society as a "culture of desire that confuse[s] the good life with goods." He and others argue that Americans have become "consumed" by goods, defined by possessions, exhausted by pursuing them, trapped by their yearning. Novelist Theodore Dreiser gave "sister Carrie," a country girl corrupted in the big city, that sensation in 1900: As the title character walked through a department store, she found that "each separate counter was a showplace of dazzling interest and attraction. She could not help feeling the claim of each trinket and valuable upon her personally. . . . There was nothing there which she could not have used—nothing which she did not long to own." (Recall the shoplifter's courtroom defense: the call of the goods was irresistible.) The concern is, as sociologist George Ritzer put it, "Why have so many people come to want so much more?"[31]

Why Want So Much?

Why, indeed? Perhaps Americans succumbed to unquenchable desires; or perhaps there simply was more out there to want. In this section, I briefly address the psychology that explicitly or implicitly underlies ideas about consumption. In the subsequent section, I return to the historical question of whether Americans became "consumerist." Most commentators on this topic assert that a consumer society has a distinctive culture and produces a distinctive national character: individuals become mesmerized by goods, buy things, asserts one social historian, that they "clearly do not need," and come to see much of life, including their personal relations, as goods in a market. People overbuy, in most such analyses, for one or a combination of three reasons: to imitate others, to satisfy uncontrollable desires, or to announce who they are.[32]

Emulation is the desire to copy, impress, and join people of higher position. Over a century ago, economist Thorstein Veblen popularized the notion of "conspicuous consumption"; soon after, a cartoonist introduced the catchphrase "keeping up with the Joneses." Yet, as the history I summarized earlier shows, plenty of critics made similar points much earlier. A *Boston Gazette* contributor wrote in 1765: "They that are poorer . . . should and must give way to the Rich. Who but they should ordinarily buy the dearest and best of the kind?. . . . [W]e should be willing to live low, where God has set us, and . . . let us therewith be content." Around 1900, a young immigrant woman could say unselfconsciously, "I'm almost like an American, I have a rat [puff] for my hair." Around 2000, matrons in Beverly Hills told automobile dealers that they wanted to buy mammoth Hummer vehicles because they saw so many of them parked in their neighbors' driveways. Young children badger parents for clothes and toys that "everyone" in class has. Advertising, theorists of emulation argue, stimulates emulation by telling Americans that they are being judged on the whiteness of their teeth or the greenness of their lawns and then offering a toothpaste or plant food that will make them the envy of all.[33]

Explanations based on *uncontrollable desire* assume that overbuying results from an irresistible urge to possess and from the sensual, however fleeting, pleasure that comes from satisfying that urge—as with Dreiser's *Sister Carrie*. An essayist wrote in 1895: "It is not that we need so much more . . . but that we are not able to stand against the overwhelming temptations to buy which besiege us at every turn. . . . We look for a ribbon, a flower, a chiffon of some sort or other, and we find ourselves in a Paradise of ribbons, flowers, and chiffon, without which our life becomes impossible." Some charge that most of the things we buy have "now become addictive habits rather than necessities." Ritzer describes the shopping experience as a zombie-like trance. According to such arguments, where once American culture had instilled people with austere self-discipline—even a puritanical ethic—it later encouraged hedonism and unleashed consumerism. Buying was no longer a means to a practical end, but a sensual end in itself.[34]

One variation on this psychological analysis treats spending as "compensation." Buying and displaying goods is how Americans compensate for modern anxieties and frustrations, for tedium at work, soured relationships, or feeling powerless. The designer jeans or fifty-inch televisions provide ersatz—and ultimately unsatisfying—replacements for "real" rewards in life. Historians have often used the notion of compensation to explain the popularity of late-nineteenth-century entertainments. Watching professional sports, for example, allowed the "masses of people to blow off steam in a relatively harmless way." Others use the notion of compensation to explain how advertising works: ads make people anxious about possible deficiencies (do you look dowdy?) and then proffer products to compensate (this hair color will give you a burst of self-confidence).[35]

Self-expression moved to the forefront in recent decades as scholars found earlier theories of consumption unsatisfying and unacceptable, mainly because those explanations depict people as "cultural dopes," irrational and easily manipulated. Instead, scholars writing in a postmodern tone interpret buying as purposeful and thoughtful "signifying." "Consumption is a system of meaning, like language . . ."; goods convey messages. Whether it is the foppish wig of an eighteenth-century dandy, the

leather-bound Bible of a nineteenth-century family, or the kempt lawn of
a twentieth-century suburbanite, possessions tell other people and ourselves who we are as individuals—chic, pious, or hardworking—and to
which social groups we belong—the avant-garde, the faithful, or the respectable middle class. (Recall the distress of colonial gentlemen about
upstarts who dressed above their class.) Modern Americans in particular, the argument goes, do not try to emulate others but try to distinguish themselves in "self-creation" through goods. Men who demanded
that automobile dealers sell them the first Hummers on the lot were using the vehicles to announce their manly identities. African Americans
buy certain high-priced items more often than whites of comparable income do; marketing experts explain that blacks use such goods to assert
their self-worth in face of racial stigma and to signal other blacks of their
group identification. Even those Americans who disdain consumerism
announce their membership in the environmentalist community precisely by what they buy—organic foods, fair-trade coffee, and handmade
clothing, for example.[36]

All these analyses contend that people spend above and beyond some
economically rational or practical level, because the buying is about status, emotional release, or identity. Compounding the overspending, goes
the argument, consumers get caught up in competitive races to gain status, to experience yet greater thrills, or to keep refurbishing their identities.

Why Not Want So Much?

Dismissing these ideas, other analysts, mainly economists, argue that
we should simply take people's purchases on face value: people buy what
gives them pleasure, both functionally—a luxury car provides transportation—and psychically—a luxury car boosts pride. No outsider can presume to separate rational from irrational desire; those who try are merely
declaring their personal tastes. Indeed, many economists deride the very
notion of consumerism. Economic historian Jan de Vries gives the back
of his hand to the social historian I quoted earlier: "Who is he to say what
people 'clearly do not need'?"[37]

Efforts to separate "real needs" and from "false needs" have tangled
up social thinkers for generations. The easiest way to unravel the knot,
economists have argued, is to forget "needs" and just talk about tastes or
preferences; the whole issue of overbuying goes away. "The economist's
idea of the consumer suggests that the word 'need' is not needed," writes
economist Deirdre McCloskey, because the only real "need" is something for which people will pay any price, like oxygen. Everything else is

sensitive to price. From this point of view, pronouncing that a consumer society is one "in which the gratification of wants has come to displace the satisfaction of needs" makes no sense, because the pronouncer is arbitrarily separating wants from needs. Most economists also scoff at the idea that people were ever innocent of wanting luxuries. Premodern peoples long sought their own extravagances, even if only shells and feathers, and eagerly took up the Western goods they encountered. So, when over two-thirds of Americans polled in 2006 said that they "pretty much" thought of their clothes dryers, home air conditioning, and microwave ovens each "as a necessity," a culture critic might scoff, but there is no logic drawn from economics to separate those goods from virtually anything else people buy.[38]

And yet economists cannot so easily dismiss or define away the notion of overbuying; people do distinguish need from luxury and act accordingly. Needs may be socially defined, but are nonetheless real in their consequences. Over the years, charities and welfare agencies moved more items, such as hot water and telephone service, from the category of luxuries to the list of necessities that they would provide to poor families (see chapter 2). A mattress may have been a luxury in the nineteenth century, but it was a need in the twentieth. Both Adam Smith and Karl Marx understood necessities to include not just basic food, clothing, and shelter—items for which demand is least sensitive to price—but also goods that were common among the poor; today that includes mattresses. Similarly, social psychologists have long observed that people experience "relative deprivation"; they judge whether they are disadvantaged by what others like them have.[39]

People also recognize the possibility of overbuying. In 2006, four of five survey respondents admitted that there was something that they or their spouses spent too much on. And that is why people will try to discipline themselves, for example, by earmarking money for special purposes, perhaps in a Christmas gift fund. Some people see themselves as compulsive spenders; they can find twelve-step programs to break the habit.* Many less-driven consumers shop as entertainment. Distinguishing, then, buying out of necessity from other buying is common. And the distinction is *relative*. When survey researchers ask Americans how much money it takes for a family to just "get along" in their town, respondents typically suggest not some basic survival budget, but a dollar figure at

---

* One 2002 Web site identified symptoms of compulsive shopping such as "being unable to pass up a 'good deal'; making impulsive purchases; leaving price tags on clothes so they can be returned." Another listed the first step to recovery as: "We admitted we were powerless over spending and money."

about half of the median family income in their community. As median incomes rise, the amount people see as needed to "get along" rises. Thus, modern Americans *need*—in a social, lived sense—"extras" like attractive clothes, warm homes, transportation, schooling, and entertainment. At the same time, Americans also recognize that they and others often over-buy beyond even these socially defined needs.[40]

Denying the notion of overbuying assumes that people are provident and calculating consumers who maximize their preferences. Lately, how-ever, many psychologists and economists have undermined this assump-tion. They have shown how buyers often make choices that, in the long run, do not match their own explicit preferences. Often, consumers re-spond to subtle signals and circumstances they are unconscious of, unre-alistically presume that an item will please them tomorrow as much as it does today, and then adjust to a good, finding it less rewarding over time. (The shoes looked better under the store's lighting; I don't really have enough opportunities to wear them; and anyway they are starting to seem ordinary.) People could well conclude that, on reflection, they spent more than they should have.[41]

The *historical* issue dividing theorists of consumerism from skepti-cal economists is how to explain the spending of modern Americans. Overbuying—that is, buying beyond culturally defined needs—is a so-cial fact, so the issue then becomes whether more modern Americans overbuy more, and if so, why. There are several possible answers. One, overbuying did *not* increase; modern Americans overbuy no more than their ancestors did. Two, overbuying increased and did so because Amer-icans at some point mutated into consumerists, whether driven by em-ulation, desire, or signifying. Third, overbuying increased, not because a new consumerist psychology emerged, but because already existing con-sumerism *intensified*. That is, Americans always had the shopping bug, but more income, new products, marketing schemes, and easy credit height-ened that urge. Fourth, overbuying increased, not because Americans' psychology changed or intensified, but because Americans encountered much greater opportunities for buying. The simple combination of more goods out there—in store windows, in junk mail, on Web sites—and more money and credit cards in people's pockets means that more buy-ing, even more impulse buying, happens even with no change in psyche. Grandma had the same will to shop, but only the granddaughter had the way. (If you can afford it, *why not* visit Disneyland, *why not* purchase a leather-appointed car?) The last explanation is probably closest to accu-rate: overbuying increased in the long run mainly because more Ameri-cans had more *means*—and thus more could *aspire* more—to buy more things. Americans whose ancestors had been on the margins now joined the economic and cultural mainstream; they saw themselves as legitimate aspirants to a middle-class lifestyle. A closer look at the historical record might adjudicate among these various answers to George Ritzer's query, "Why have so many people come to want so much more?"

More Consumerism?

Answering the question of whether Americans became consumerist requires foraging through a variety of evidence. In this section, I review what we can learn from the histories of marketing, spending, debt, and work.

Modern marketing. No one needs to have a sharper understanding of American buyers than American sellers; their livelihoods depend on it. Seeing consumption through their eyes should be revealing, but since sellers often misunderstand the public, their views cannot be accepted on face value.

Marketing developed into a major industry in the last third of the nineteenth century: brand names, mail-order shopping, department stores, psychologically attuned advertising, and then later, radio, television, megamalls, and the Internet. Marketing's ever-expanding scale suggests the coming of ever-greater mesmerization and manipulation of the public. For example, the evolving art of department store window displays, contributed, claims William Leach, to "a new powerful universe of consumer enticements." Clever ad writers stoked readers' social anxieties. For example, ads in farmers' magazines for Listerine mouthwash warned that bad breath would doom their daughters to spinsterhood. In the twentieth century, ad designers read some psychology, reimagined their audience, and rewrote their copy accordingly. Previously, marketers commonly saw the consumer as a thrifty and skeptical bean counter who had to be persuaded by hard reason; modern marketers see the consumer as an improvident and gullible impulse buyer who can be manipulated by emotion. Between 1905 and 1975, the themes in magazine ads shifted from practicality ("this coat is durable") toward pleasure ("this coat makes you feel alluring").[42]

What do these developments in marketing tell us? Perhaps American consumers changed and became "suckers" during the twentieth century, and the marketing industry responded accordingly. Or perhaps twentieth-century advertisers *turned* American consumers into suckers. Or perhaps American consumers were *always* suckers and it took decades for marketers to realize it. (The success of "snake oil" salesmen in the nineteenth century makes one wonder about that era's image of the sharp-eyed buyer.) In any case, much of twentieth-century marketing assumed that the average consumer could be swept up, like sister Carrie, by dazzle.[43]

Drawing conclusions from the history of marketing, however, is premature. Historians have retrieved marketing campaigns, reproductions of advertisements, and chest-pounding boasts by ad executives, but they have gathered little evidence on how the public actually responded to such campaigns. We cannot take on face value assertions of display-case salesmen that glass showcases attract customers or those of copywriters that their slogans created new wants. Research suggests that advertising promotes demand for novel products, sways buyers toward one brand versus another, and captures young children. However, whether advertising significantly *creates* wants among adults—or accurately reflects their wants—remains an open question.[44]

We need to know whether Americans responded more to marketing over time. Did people increasingly buy the "sizzle" rather than the "steak," the sales pitch rather than the substance? The evidence is limited. Consider spending on marketing. Advertising expenditures, for store awnings to radio jingles, increased greatly in the twentieth century, from under $200 per American in 1900 to about $1,000 in 2005 (both in 2008 dollars). But proportion of the economy, both in labor and in money, devoted to retail trade and advertising declined. Early in the twentieth century, about 3 percent of the gross national product went to advertising; around the turn of the next century, about 2 percent did. The steak grew more than the sizzle. And whether twenty-first-century Americans succumbed to sizzle more than their predecessors did is not at all certain. Marketing had its triumphant moments in earlier times. Recall, for instance, the colonial Virginians flocking to see the new bonnets and bangles, and the nineteenth-century city folk jamming seasonal department store openings. Perhaps expanding marketing and advertising made Americans increasingly vulnerable to marketing, turning them into overconsuming suckers, as many culture critics assume. Or perhaps more marketing and advertising reflected sellers' growing desperation to be heard over their competitors' voices and to persuade adults who, increasingly educated and experienced, distrusted and resisted marketing.[45]

Luxury and indulgence. A better approach to understanding whether Americans became psychologically consumerist may be to look directly at what Americans bought. To what extent did Americans of different eras buy goods that they did not "need"? (Buying goods they could not afford will be discussed later.) Surely, modern Americans bought billions of dollars' worth of items that met no one's sense of "necessity," as a glance at an average child's room or at a mail-order catalog sufficiently illustrates. Economist Robert Frank diagnosed the economic ills of the 1980s and '90s as a case of "luxury fever," when average Americans lusted after the toys of the rich. But, aside from blatant examples, distinguishing a luxury from a necessity turns out to be difficult. In 1815, the federal government taxed dining tables and teapots as luxuries. In 2006, as I noted earlier, most Americans considered items such as microwave ovens and clothes dryers as necessities. And even these items changed position over the years; for example, only about one-quarter of Americans put air conditioning on the list of necessities in 1973, while 70 percent did in 2006—and then, in 2009, only about 50 percent did. The proportion of survey respondents calling clothes dryers and microwaves necessities also dropped sharply in 2009 as the deep recession led Americans to reweigh their desires. Evaluations of need are relative to time and place.[46]

If we use a relative definition of need, one that includes windows and forks in the nineteenth century and televisions and vacations in the twenty-first, the contrast in luxury spending between then and now is much less stark. Nonetheless, there is a contrast. As time passed, average Americans did buy more "extras"—the second and third television sets, the vacation in Hawaii rather than the Poconos. That is one consequence of moving from a society in which most people are in or near poverty to one in which most people live comfortably. The crux of the consumerism issue is whether buying more extras resulted simply from a greater ability to buy goods or a from deeper psychological change, from luxury fever. The most plausible answer is the former, a greater ability to buy.[47]

One reason for that conclusion is that luxury fever diagnoses were plentiful well before the late twentieth century. I presented a few examples in the first part of this chapter; there are more. In early 1900s, millions of affluent Americans bought and maintained expensive automobiles for recreation, most working-class families (at least in Massachusetts) owned or were paying off pianos, millions of immigrants bought clothes and parlor furniture to demonstrate that they had become "Yankees," and farmers across the country gave in to their wives' pleas for extras such as running water and electric lighting. Many young women, entering new factory and office jobs, spent their pay on fashion and "stepping out." Silk stockings, a wealthy woman's leg wear around 1900, was, within a couple of decades, a staple even for country women. Older middle-class women participated heavily in club-based cultural and artistic pursuits, each requiring "luxury" spending. In 1920, women suing for divorce in Los Angeles complained more often than women in the 1880s had that their husbands were not supporting them in an appropriate—escalating—lifestyle. Men, too, spilled much money on their pastimes, including fraternal associations, betting, sports, and especially drinking. Working-class families early in the twentieth century spent more of their income on alcohol than Americans did at the end of the century. Thus, observers in the early twentieth century saw much overbuying among the affluent and working-class alike.[48]

The same might be said of the early nineteenth century. An Englishman in 1807 claimed that "pride of wealth is as ostentatious in this country as ever the pride of birth has been elsewhere." Americans made similar observations, such as Thoreau's disdain for his neighbors' inheritances. Home economist Lydia Maria Child declared in 1832 that the "prevailing evil of our day is extravagance. . . . It is too plain that our present expensive habits are productive of much domestic unhappiness." Observers in Virginia complained that the young gentry were spending themselves into ruin. In New York, noted Reverend Henry Bellows in 1845 described the "excessive anxiety written in the American countenance. . . . It is the concentration of the faculties upon an object, which in its very nature is unattainable—the perpetual improvement of the outward condition."[49]

The Revolutionary era, a generation earlier, seems to have garnered the most commentary about luxuries—perhaps because this was when emerging democratic impulses stirred up the question of who was worthy enough to own what. Both contemporaries jotting down their observations and modern historians scrutinizing old estate records emphasized the extent to which Americans accumulated extras. The colonial man or woman of the gentry around 1750, wrote historian Kenneth Lockridge, was "a compulsive, consuming, display-oriented, other-directed personality, perpetually jockeying for position." But the rich complained about others: Samuel Adams, for example, wrote to John Adams in 1785 of the "fantastick Extravagance" indulged in by the poor. A journalist on the Kentucky frontier worried about imported goods like lace and fancy china: "There is no greater calamity can befall any people, than when luxury is introduced among them . . . [E]very individual is under some necessity of living beyond his fortune." An English traveler recorded his shock that women in rural North Carolina bought costly imported soap rather than make their own. Even back-country stores carried luxuries (recall the fantails and satin in Virginia). Middling-level Americans bought fancy treats like sugar and coffee; ornamental items, such as paintings and mantel clocks; toiletry articles, including dressing tables; and equipment for entertaining like ceramics. In 1774, at least 42 percent of *poor* householders' estates included tea services. As one historian put it, pungently: "For the pleasure of taking tea in the parlor, more than a few families were content to continue pissing in the barn." The 1815 federal luxury tax covered goods such as dining tables, chandeliers, pianofortes, and teapots;

it assessed *most* American families for at least $200 worth of such items (roughly the equivalent in work hours of over $37,000 in 2008). One might conclude that Americans have always thrilled to luxuries when they could afford them.[50]

One striking fact about modern American spending on extras is how much of it occurs during the Christmas season. "There are worlds of money wasted . . . in getting things that nobody wants, and nobody cares for after they are got," wrote one woman in 1850 who felt held hostage by the Christmas-buying frenzy — Harriet Beecher Stowe. The modern Christmas is becoming "a time for barter, for display, for acquisitiveness," complained the *New York Tribune* — in 1895. And a century later most American adults agreed. In the 1990s, four of five survey respondents complained that the holiday was too commercialized; most said they did not enjoy Christmas shopping; and about a third said they would just as soon do without exchanging gifts. Yet Americans complied — for generations. Gift buying around Christmastime, complete with Santa Claus and spoiled boys and girls, dates back to the early 1800s, as do organized movements to "put Christ back into Christmas." A profane Christmas of public carnival, drinking, and carousing preceded the spiritual, home-based American Christmas. Over the nineteenth century, the growing middle class sacralized and domesticated the holiday into a tame family event (as they did Thanksgiving and Independence Day) marked by major gift giving. At first, middle-class parents gave gifts only to their children, initially on New Year's Day and then in later generations on Christmas. By the middle of the twentieth century, everyone gave gifts to everyone. Merchants suggested yet more occasions to give gifts, most successfully Mother's and Father's days, and Americans went along. Indeed, much of what modern Americans spend on so-called luxuries — perhaps most purchases of toys, watches, and even toasters, for example — is for others. In the late twentieth century, about 3 percent of all consumer dollars, proportionately much more than before and equal in value to about one-fifth of food spending, went into gifts for someone outside the household. Many Americans consider some gift buying as less than discretionary (dare one forget Aunt Mary or the delivery boy at Christmas?), but to outside observers they are extras. Spending on these kinds of extras implies something about the spenders other than emulation, desire, or self-expression, something about their bonds to other people.[51]

Clearly, Americans have long sought what were the "luxuries" of their day. As thousands of goods eventually fell from exotic luxury to commonplaceness, new luxuries kept appearing. More Americans gained the means to buy the new luxuries and more Americans gained the confidence to *aspire* to those new luxuries as privilege gave way to the democratization of material life.

Debt. The history of debt gives us another view of whether and when Americans overspent. Expanding credit has been, most scholars would say, a great boon to raising American living standards. Credit enables people who lack wealth to invest for future wealth—say, with college loans—and to enjoy goods and services—such as a home or car—before they are wealthy enough to buy them outright. But people can borrow too much, and excessive borrowing can signal that the debtor is perhaps a "compulsive consumer." Sociologist Daniel Bell wrote in 1976 that "the single greatest engine in the destruction of the Protestant ethic [of self-discipline] was the invention of the installment plan. . . . With credit cards one could indulge in instant gratification." This sort of lament arises from what historian of consumer credit Lendol Calder calls the "myth of lost economic virtue," the fable that Americans were once debt free. It is a myth, because "a river of red ink runs through American history." And so does a river of black ink critiquing it.[52]

Debt funded the settling of America—literally. Before the Revolution, most Europeans arriving in America went into debt for the passage and then labored as indentured servants for years to pay off the loan. Farmers constantly borrowed from wealthy landowners, merchants, neighbors, and later, from banks to buy the land, livestock, seed, and tools they needed. Poor and rich farmers alike kept careful track of who owed whom how much in loaned goods or farm labor. Cargoes of goods, including those infamous tea sets, floated onto colonial shores on a tide of credit. Many of the elite, including numerous Southern planters, such as Thomas Jefferson, lived in splendor on the leniency of lenders as they delayed paying off their debts. Many Virginia planters bolted to Kentucky after the Revolution to avoid their English creditors coming to settle the books. Founding father and "financier of the American Revolution" Robert Morris ended up in debtors' prison for three years. Antebellum storekeepers placed ads in newspapers to publically remind customers to pay up but typically rolled over debts from one ledger to another. Planters, traders, and storekeepers themselves borrowed to finance their activities in a chain of debt reaching to London. In the cities, nineteenth-century working- and middle-class Americans increasingly turned to pawnbrokers for the cash that could carry them over between paydays or gaps in employment. By 1890, the average American household owed at least $880, about twice what the average worker earned in a year.[53]

Twentieth-century financiers developed new forms of credit, such as installment plans, credit cards, and easier home mortgages. In 1920,

Americans' outstanding consumer debt—money owed for cars and other installment purchases—amounted to about $1,250 (in 2008 dollars) per household; in 2008, consumer debt reached about $22,000 per household. Americans bought more cars, appliances, travel, more of everything on credit. And they especially borrowed more to buy homes. Mortgage debt grew from about $7,300 (2008 dollars) per nonfarm household in 1920 to about $89,000 in 2008. Americans could not have lived so well and accumulated so much without a way to have things in hand before they owned them in law.[54]

As noted, twentieth-century Americans' large debts were for housing. As government liberalized mortgages, made repayment terms easier, and kept mortgage rates low, more Americans became homeowners owing more in mortgages. Yet for most of the century, Americans' income and wealth grew faster than their debts. In 1890, the average household owed, including mortgage and consumer debts, about double the average household income; in 2007, even though credit was far easier to get, average debt was relatively lower, about 1.75 times average income. The debt-to-income burden grew heavier from 1980 into the 2000s, but that was almost totally due to more and larger home mortgages in an era of soaring house values; the ratio of general consumer debt to income remained roughly the same. These numbers suggest that Americans' debt became more, not less, affordable over most of the twentieth century. If so, why then did Americans file for bankruptcy at much higher rates in the last years of the century than they had in the previous decades? Bankruptcies soared in part because of changing laws, because banks increasingly loaned to low-earning Americans, and because of stagnant or declining earnings for most workers. The bankruptcies, however, like the run-up in debt around 2000, had less to do with any greater compulsion to buy and more to do with financial conditions, the availability of credit, and the insecurities of the job market.[55] *

The flip side of debt is savings, and observers at the turn of the millennium expressed much concern that spendthrift Americans were saving little. The official personal savings rate, which had increased through the postwar period, dropped from 9 percent in the 1980s to below zero in 2005; Americans spent more than they earned. However, saving patterns do not really say much about overbuying, either statistically or substantively. Some spending is itself a form of investment, such as repairing a house, paying for college, or buying a car to drive to work. Some of the

---

* Similarly, the subprime mortgage crisis starting in 2007, which threw many overly indebted homeowners into forfeiture, seemed the result of new policies and a deregulated mortgage system, not of citizens' increasing foolishness about debt.

decline in the official savings rate reflected well-to-do Americans moving their money from stagnant savings accounts into a great bull stock market. Some reflected average Americans investing in a booming real estate market (that turned out to be a bubble). Middle-class families increasingly borrowed and spent, confident that their portfolios and their appreciating homes would cover their debts — the "wealth effect," economists called it. To be sure, Americans still probably saved less than good planning would dictate. But the late-twentieth- and early-twenty-first-century savings trends seemed largely attributable to structural changes in markets, not to individual psychological change, such as growing, uncontrollable wants. The plunge in consumer spending and corresponding surge in household savings that followed the housing market collapse of 2008–9 testify to the wealth effect in reverse — and Americans' control of their buying impulses.[56]

In the twentieth century, access to reliable and affordable credit spread. Recall that expanding credit was part of the New Deal's efforts to re-energize the economy and broaden affluence; it helped Americans buy and modernize their homes, especially after World War II. For all the new debt Americans took on in the twentieth century, it did not, as a proportion of their assets, exceed the kinds of debt their ancestors bore. Nor were the risks of default, given insurance and bankruptcy protection, as great as in the days when farmers often lost their lands, merchants often lost their businesses, and Virginia plantation owners hightailed it to Kentucky. The history of debt thus does *not* tell a story of growing and overweening consumerism.[57]

To work or not to work? Another approach to understanding what economists might call a "taste" for goods examines the trade-off between goods and work. If people choose to work more hours — other things like wages, family situations, and cost of living staying the same — then it must be because their preferences have changed, that they have a growing taste for the things money can buy rather than for time off. (Of course, they might also work not for the money but for the joy of the labor, as ballplayers and professors claim they do.) The argument that Americans have increasingly foregone leisure to pursue the "almighty dollar" is a common part of the consumerism critique.[58]

Americans notoriously work longer than other people in well-off countries do, suggesting that their "taste" for money exceeds that of other people. Yet modern Americans work many fewer hours per day, weeks per year, and years over a lifetime than their ancestors did. Hours for poorly paid workers in particular declined over the decades. These trends are clear for the twentieth century. Nineteenth-century trends are much harder to assess, in part because most American men worked farms (and farm hours are hard to count), and also because most women's work combined the domestic and the commercial (for example, cooking meals for family and farmhands). Also, with the end of slavery, black workers' hours declined greatly, but it is difficult to say by how much. Nonetheless, we can safely assume that Americans in the 2000s generally worked many fewer hours than their ancestors. And if we were to count as "work" those hours spent on unpaid chores, such as cooking, cleaning, and fixing, then Americans of both sexes increasingly took more leisure time—implying that they developed *less* "taste" for money and for what money buys.[59]

Three particular controversies about work hours in the twentieth century touch on this trade-off. What deal did unions make in the interwar years? Did Americans work more in the last few decades? Why did married women go off to work? First, some scholars argue that modern Americans' comparatively long work hours derive from a Faustian bargain struck in the 1920s and '30s between unions and management. Organized labor surrendered control of working conditions, including schedules, in return for guaranteed higher wages. In effect, unions traded in leisure for goods. Though plausible, this story downplays the fact that the unions also extracted more vacation time and earlier retirement. In any case, the claim that these arrangements generated a new consumerism is tenuous.[60]

Second, some scholars argue that panting after consumer goods led Americans to work more hours starting in the 1970s and '80s. The titles of two companion books by economist-turned-sociologist Juliet Schor capture this argument: *The Overworked American* and *The Overspent American*. Counting and accounting for work hours is complex, but a fair summary of the research is this: in the last few decades, individual American workers did not work more hours, but American *couples* did. As more people joined the competitive ranks of professionals and managers and as more wives undertook such careers from the 1970s on, middle-class couples jointly worked more hours than middle-class couples had before (and they complained more about the time crunch). Meanwhile, working-class women worked more hours to make up for the dropping wages and shrinking hours of their male partners. Changes in work time thus had much more to do with changing gender roles and with the economic insecurities of the era than with consumer desires.[61]

Third, some scholars say that the twentieth-century movement of married women into the work force resulted from—and thereby reveals—growing consumerism. Wives wanted the new, alluring goods of the twentieth century: the refrigerators, cars, holidays, and the like. More American wives went to work in the twentieth century, however, for a variety of reasons, including changes in the nature of jobs and of house-work, dropping birth rates, and later, men's declining wages. Certainly, the vision of buying a new appliance or affording a car was part of the story, but a small part. In the long run, Americans traded work hours for more leisure hours, most dramatically in the form of earlier retirement. The history of work, like the histories of debt, luxuries, and marketing, does not support claims that Americans became increasingly driven by consumer urges.[62]

The Shopping Nation

A major long-term shift in Americans' trade-offs was, as I noted earlier, from spending on food to spending on other items. The plummeting cost of food probably suffices to explain that shift; we do not need to assume that Americans' "taste" for eating declined. Economic historian Carole Shammas has closely examined the broader trends in trade-offs, or elas-ticities of demand. She concluded that, by this measure, there was not much difference between the late twentieth century and the eighteenth century: "the relationship between income and consumer expenditures" among modern consumers pretty well fits that of consumers two hun-dred years before. In that sense, Americans' economic psychology did not change.[63]

For all the repeated claims that Americans became a distinctly con-sumerist people in the last century or so, we would have expected some clear indications in the historical record of some psychological or cultural transition or of a strong trend toward indulgent spending, reckless bor-rowing, or overwork. We do not see it. The best answer to George Ritzer's question, "Why have so many people come to want so much more?" may simply be that so many people could afford so much more.

But perhaps I have focused too much on buying; maybe the real is-sue is having.

MORE MATERIALISM?

Consumerism can be seen as one part of a larger psychological syndrome: *materialism*—giving "worldly possessions [a] central place" in one's life. Being materialist means more than having the shopping bug; it in-cludes hoarding, coveting, and judging others by their wealth. (Dickens's Scrooge was not much a shopper, but he was materialistic.) The charge that Americans are particularly materialistic has been around a long time. Tocqueville wrote in the 1830s that "the desire to acquire the good things of this world is the dominant passion among Americans. . . . Americans

cleave to the things of this world as if assured that they will never die."
Over a century later, an Egyptian civil servant, disgusted by what he saw
when he visited the United States, charged that "Americans measure man
by his income, according to his bank balance, and this wave of idolatry
is spreading from America to the rest of the world." (Sayyid Qutb would
later be the major intellectual source of Islamic militancy and Al Qaeda.)
Modern Americans also expressed concern; in a 1990s poll, nine of ten respondents concurred that "our society is much too materialistic." On the
other hand, Ronald Reagan is reputed to have once said that Americans'
drive for wealth "is not materialism; that is Americanism."[64]

Materialism would be consistent, as Reagan suggested, with the
American focus on personal success; goods provide both individual pleasure and signs of achievement. The question at hand is whether Americans' materialism increased. Most seem to think it did, even the editors of
Fortune magazine. In 1987, they featured an article entitled, "The Money
Society: Money Seems to be the Only Thing that Counts These Days."*
Others argue, however, that affluence brought Americans not materialism, but *post*materialism: enough security and confidence to focus on
higher things like self-development, fellowship, and spirituality (see earlier discussion, pp. 56–57).[65]

The historical picture, as one might expect, is fuzzy. We saw in the
first part of this chapter that in virtually every era, contemporary witnesses complained about Americans' materialism. But we also saw that
Americans' work hours declined; what happened to their passion for
goods? Two additional sorts of evidence might inform us about historical
changes in materialism. One consists of cultural artifacts, from high art
to low entertainment, which scholars "read" for what they say about the
values of an era. What do such artifacts say about materialism? The other
kind of evidence consists of studies seeking to measure materialism by
respondents' answers in mass surveys; these studies, however, can take us
back only to about the 1960s.

Images of Things

Any twenty-first century observer must believe that Americans are
swamped as never before by materialistic culture. Look at the magazine
ads, the lifestyle displays on television, and the logos people wear. Over
the centuries, Americans encountered vastly more media and therefore
vastly more images of every sort; the messages of every era include both
materialistic and non- or antimaterialistic themes. In the early nineteenth

---

* Only two years later, a *Fortune* headline read, "Is Greed Dead?"

century, Thoreau and the utopian romantics proclaimed the virtue of simplicity; in the Gilded Age, critics denounced conspicuous consumption; and advocates of "simple living" have carried the anticonsumerist credo into the twenty-first century. One couple told the *New York Times* in 2008 that they were hoping to rid themselves of all their possessions except "one personal carton per family member, plus bedding and kitchen utensils." Which kind of message—"flaunt it!" or "seek simplicity!"—characterizes each era? It is difficult to track, count, and weigh cultural motifs; it is harder still to interpret them and impute them to average people.[66]

Take painting. Art historian Simon Schama claims that no Western art is as obsessed with goods as Dutch still-life paintings of the seventeenth century. Colonial American portraits of roughly the same period also proclaim wealth and possessions in terms modern Americans would find shameless. The sitters wear finery, pose next to brocades, and point to tokens of their success. In the early 1770s, the Reverend Ebenezer Devotion of Windham, Connecticut, commissioned family portraits. He poses in front of his library of expensive books, most imported from England. In his wife's portrait, the Mrs. Reverend Devotion is shown in an expensive chair, self-assuredly showing a book to the viewer. Devotion's merchant son, Ebenezer Jr., stands at an elegant slant-top desk, pen poised above his account book. Devotion's daughter-in-law sits on a Chippendale side chair in a formal dress, ribboned cap, and black gloves. Possessions defined character in these sorts of portraits. Art historian Wayne Craven wrote, "It would be difficult to look upon the typical examples of mid-eighteenth-century American portraiture without sensing the power of materialism in them—both as cultural symbol and in artistic style." Twentieth-century portraits, in contrast, understate their subjects' wealth and emphasize other signs of character. Indeed, much of twentieth-century art seems to disdain goods; there are few warm-toned pictures of large estates, elegant vases, or plutocrats, but many sarcastic collages of consumer detritus. Contemporary portrait photographers, probably a better comparison to eighteenth-century oil-and-canvas portraitists, emphasize the informality, intimacy, and happiness of their subjects, only rarely their wealth—the dress code in these pictures seems to be denim. Perhaps a review of art, then, would suggest that materialism has actually declined.[67]

Or take novels. Late-nineteenth-century editor William Dean Howells once wrote, "novelists . . . really have charge of people's thinking these days." Many, if not most, novels of his era dealt with money concerns, often portraying people pursuing wealth and then succumbing to its corruption (as in Howells's own *The Rise of Silas Lapham*). Should we take that to mean that middle-class readers of the Gilded Age were especially materialistic—or the opposite, that they were horrified by greed? Reading the fine arts to measure popular opinion is dicey; our readings presume that artists accurately capture the preoccupations of the general public and that their respect or disdain for those preoccupations also reflects the public's values.[68]

Perhaps the popular art of home decoration better reveals popular values. Victorian-era middle-class women crammed their homes with decorative chairs and sofas, an abundance of paintings and statuary, and showcases full of glassware, souvenirs, and other tchotchkes—all designed at least in part to signal the taste of the residents. Victorians similarly decorated the outsides of houses with ornamental molding and gewgaws. It was more than simple display, however. This decorating style, argues historian Lori Merish, celebrated "the 'civilizing influence' of luxury and tasteful surroundings." The right objects could elevate residents' sensibilities and thus improve character. By the early decades of the twentieth century, however, this fashion was passé. Simplicity, naturalness, and understatement became the dominant themes in increasingly popular bungalows with spare Arts and Crafts furniture and low-profile ranch houses open to the outdoors. Both genres, of course, allowed the middle class to demonstrate their values. In the twentieth century, the style leaders said less flaunting is better, stepping ahead of working-class aspirants who often mimicked the out-of-date, overwrought furnishings of the nineteenth century.[69]

Cultural themes may also reveal themselves in the popular press. Historian Daniel Cohen, for example, finds the "birth of a consumer culture" in 1845, when the media frenzied over the case of Maria Bickford, a kept woman brutally murdered in Boston. Those who believed that her lover was guilty stressed Maria's virtues, pointing to the tasteful clothes and possessions in her room. The quality of her goods presumably testified to the high quality of her character. Those who claimed the lover was innocent or at least morally blameless pointed to Maria's extravagant wardrobe and disportment. The tawdriness of her goods and pastimes presumably testified to the baseness of her character. (In the end, the accused lover was acquitted, as was usual for rich young men.) Similarly, the popular media's stories of upper-crust scandals often pointed to their materialism. Reports of celebrities shoplifting, for example, helped fill tabloids of the late twentieth century, as did accounts of shoplifting by elite women in the late nineteenth century. The most constant theme here seems to be that money is the root of evil.[70]

We can look for materialistic themes in the advice literature, too. After the Revolution, authors of manners guides advised their readers to present themselves in Republican simplicity. Popular women advice writers of the nineteenth century depicted the home as a spiritual haven from a corrupt world; home economists taught frugality; and the boy scouting, urban park, and modern green movements extolled the "natural" life. About a century later, government agencies and consumer-rights spokespersons largely expressed skepticism toward commercial products. In 1937, Consumers Union published its first annual "Confidential Buying Guide," which told readers, for example, that Quaker Oats' Aunt Jemima–brand pancake flour was "not acceptable."[71]

Advice on child rearing seems, however, to have moved in a different direction. In the nineteenth century, advice books and books written for children emphasized restraining material desire; children should suppress envy and resign themselves to what they have. By the 1920s, however, such books encouraged children to strive for the good things in life and advised parents to reward and comfort children with toys. By the end of the twentieth century, affluence, marketing, and parental sentimentality had joined to make toy-buying a yearlong activity. Virtually all Americans felt that "children today"—although usually not *their own* children— "want too many material things."[72]

We could make more such explorations into aspects of American culture. In the 2000s, for example, one stream of popular music extolled, almost to parody, the accumulation of wealth. Hip-hop performers boasted of "fifty-dollar socks, a hundred thousand dollar shoes," declared "I got the price of a mansion 'round my neck and wrist," and sang that "It's all about the Benjamins!" Around the same time, ministers of "prosperity theology" found parishioners eager to hear that faith was a route to big cars and fancy clothes. (Both expressions of materialism, it is worth noting, emerged from deprived communities, not from privileged ones.) But pointing to such examples is being selective, focusing on the dramatic and the contemporary. Trying to interpret the entire cultural record, including the oysters Rockefeller of the Gilded Age and prideful portraits of the colonial one, yields a complex picture of American materialism.[73]

When, for example, Puritan ministers decried Mammon in their sermons, were they reflecting their congregants' disdain for things of this world, or were they addressing the chronic tensions in their communities over material issues? When romantic novelists of the Victorian era described the business world as corrupt, did they give voice to their readers' encounters with rampaging materialism, or did they ride a growing cultural movement that disdained materialism? As always, class condescension colors these discussions. (Is pride in buying spinning rims for your car more materialistic than pride in buying a rare art print?) Moreover, other cultural developments—in particular, the rise of sentimentality and love marriages (see chapters 4 and 6)—seem to imply declining materialism. Certainly the nature of materialism changed. It is one thing for an antebellum farm wife, George Duffield's mother, for instance, to be preoccupied with assuring food, clothes, and shelter for her children— perhaps splurging on a ribbon for herself—and another for a twenty-first-century professional woman to be preoccupied with which video game system she should buy her child for Christmas. But we can assume that the level of preoccupation in the second case, while more indulgent than in the first, hardly matched its intensity. As affluence spread, more Americans could obsess less about material *survival* and more about material *extras* the same way that the Devotion family did about their fine books and chairs. The best conclusion from the cultural record, however murky, is that more Americans enjoyed more possessions, but that they did *not*, in the long run, give "worldly possessions [a more] central place" in their emotional lives.[74]

Questioning Materialism Since the '60s

The psychometric approach to this question, so different than the cultural analysis, is to ask samples of Americans about their desires and to see how the answers changed over the years. In general, when interviewers have asked Americans what success meant to them or what would make them personally happy, respondents have listed family, friends, intimacy, and spirituality far more often than wealth or possessions. They have also reported that *other* Americans were driven by materialism. In any event, what we need to focus on are *changes* in these sorts of answers. Americans increasingly gave materialistic answers from about 1970 into the 1990s.[75]

One study, for example, annually asked high school seniors around the country how important fourteen various life goals were to them. The seniors ranked making "lots of money" higher and higher from 1976 to 1990, and then lower afterwards. In a similar survey, college freshmen were about twice as likely to rate being "very well off financially" highly after 1990 than they were in the early 1970s. (Students' choice of majors moved in rough parallel, with business concentrations rising from 1970 to 1990.) Starting in 1975, the Roper organization asked adult Americans what out of list of about twenty items they would like to have as part of the "good life." Over the next two decades, up to about 1990, respondents increasingly checked off answers such as high pay, lots of money, a swimming pool, and a vacation home; the selection of those answers leveled off or dropped a bit from the mid-1990s through 2003.[76]

Three explanations for more materialistic responses over the last years of the twentieth century are plausible. One, the trend is part of a long-term rise of materialism, but that explanation seems to contradict the longer history. Two, the trend reflects something specific to the 1970s and 1980s, probably the struggle with stagnant real wages, especially for young men. Some evidence supports this suggestion, notably the leveling out and decline in materialistic answers after the early 1990s when employment picked up. Three, the trend demonstrates instead the uniqueness of the 1960s, when young Americans seemed unusually idealistic. Bits of evidence point to this explanation, too, notably hints that materialistic responses were low during the 1960s. The paucity of surveys before 1970, however, makes deciding among these alternative explanations difficult.[77]

Materialism, as best as we can assess it from evidence such as paintings, Christmas celebrations, furnishings, and polls, has been with Americans for centuries—as have complaints about it. (Let us remember, by the way, that waking before dawn to do backbreaking farm chores and devoting evenings in dimly lit cabins to darning socks are spiritual experiences only for those who have a choice not to do them; for those compelled to do them, they are definitely material preoccupations.) Materialism may well have waxed and waned, perhaps in response to economic insecurity or cultural shifts. The end of the twentieth century may have been one era of swelling materialism, the Gilded Age and the years leading up to the American Revolution other such eras, while materialism may have receded during each of the Great Awakenings and during the 1960s, for example. What is certain is that, over time, there were far more material goods and far more widespread ownership of them. Freed from the material drudgery of earlier epochs and empowered with more time and wealth, more Americans furnished their lives with more, bigger, and better goods. Sociologist Viviana Zelizer concluded a review of "our most careful studies . . . inside and outside of sociology" and concluded that they "challenge the idea that consumers in general are increasingly leading impoverished lives as a consequence of growth in consumption." So we can conclude with regard to materialism, too.[78]

Perhaps Americans responded to surveys in more materialistic terms after the 1970s, because public conversations increasingly used the language of the market. Sociologist Robert Wuthnow and others charge that American opinion leaders turned to discussing social issues—say, education, or health care—in terms of costs and benefits, rates of return, and profitability. Such talk may assume Americans to be more materialistic than they really are. (Recall how survey respondents commonly claim spiritual values for themselves, but see materialism in others.) Ironically, such discussions may also lead more Americans to think more materialistically.[79]

Other Ways of Being Possessed

I have mainly addressed the psychological dimension of the question, have Americans became possessed by their possessions? There are more mundane ways that things might control us. One is simply a practical consideration: owned goods are "sunk costs" that entail guarding and maintaining. Cars must be repaired, clothes cleaned, houses painted, and furniture dusted. Ironically, cheap and disposable products, however tacky and environmentally wasteful, free us from some of this burden; we trash socks with holes and jettison broken toasters. But most of the baggage Americans drag around—those three tons of goods which the average family moves from one home to another—grew far heavier over the decades.[80]

In a similarly practical way, people may be compelled to shop by the collective logic of goods: the problem of not having something "everyone" else does. I am *not* referring here to any psychological impulse to emulate or to gain status points, but to practical concerns. When almost everyone has a telephone, anyone who wants to be connected to others must have a telephone or even a cell phone; when almost everyone drives a car, public transit fails and the job seeker or grocery shopper needs a car; and when almost everyone at the water cooler is talking about last night's hit television show, every worker who values collegiality feels compelled to have a television. Fully participating in society requires some version of the "standard package" of goods. (Recall that what Americans consider a basic income rises as average incomes rise. Recall also how welfare agencies extended their poverty-level budget to include hot water and telephones. Nowadays, computers and Internet connections are part of the standard package.) This may be the main way that possessions "possess" us, through their role in common practices. But, then, that is how all social norms possess us—like family obligations or Christmas gift giving. Having the normal set of goods is, as sociologist Lee Rainwater has argued, part of being a full member of a society. To be out of step is not only to risk practical losses, such as the chance to "network" professional colleagues on the Internet, but also to risk embarrassment or even shunning.* Thus, as a society becomes wealthier, individual members may be

---

* It is, of course, *possible* to resist. Some people, as I noted earlier, want to "live off the grid." But these few cases are notable precisely for being highly anomalous.

not only rich enough to buy more goods, but also compelled—not necessarily by emulation or uncontrollable desire, but by practicality—to buy
more goods.[81]

CONCLUSION

Average Americans now enjoy a volume and magnificence of goods that
would have dazzled even the wealthiest of Americans two centuries ago.
Many of these goods are surely superfluous. Just like the colonial cor-
respondent shocked by poor folks donning the hats of gentlemen and
the nineteenth-century traveler shocked by backwoods women buying
fancy soap, we are shocked by what seem like excesses in our day: athletic
shoes costing a half-week's wages, cell phones tossed aside to get the latest model, giveaway boxes with last year's fashions, and the like. Yet Tocqueville's claim that "the desire to acquire the good things of this world is
the dominant passion among the Americans" seemed about as true or as
false in the 2000s as in the 1830s. Americans' consuming urges seem no
more compelling and their materialism no more acute now, compared to
then. What mainly changed was the massive scaling up—the democratization of luxury. There were more goods and more Americans who could
desire and could acquire them.

As a consequence of greater affluence, the standards, expectations,
and even legal requirements for goods scaled up. Very few Americans today would be content to live in the dirt-floor cabins colonialists called
home and to share the straw mats that passed for beds; few would think
it proper for other Americans to live that way either. The sorts of people whom elites—and romantics like Thoreau—used to sneer at for their
cherished possessions could now without stigma aspire to many comforts
of life. Modern laws, including minimum wages, housing codes, workplace regulations, and welfare budgets, even codified Americans' right to
lives of comfort. Owning goods once thought luxuries became part of
living normal lives—and in many cases became socially necessary. It is
mostly in this social sense, rather than in terms of consumerist psychology, out-of-control envy, or unquenchable material desire, that modern
Americans "keep up with the Joneses."

The multiplication of goods, like growing security, helped expand the
culture of American voluntarism. More Americans could more fully participate as Americans, whether that meant affording readymade shirts in
the early nineteenth century or car-camping in the early twentieth century; and more could also express their identities in the language of goods,
as well, by the choice of fashion or of pastime. More Americans could
participate socially, whether that meant having chairs to seat visitors in

the eighteenth century or going tailgating at sports events with friends in the twenty-first century; and more could also use goods to compete for status in their social groups. More goods meant more possibilities, even if they meant, as well, a greater weight of possessions to shoulder—the three tons' worth in the moving van.

4 Groups

In 1905, Mrs. Alma A. Rogers of Portland, Oregon, proudly summed up the history of women's clubs in America: "Woman has at last made the fateful discovery that she is an individual, not an adjunct. Therefore, she thrills to the pulse of organization; and lo! The woman's club is born." In joyously declaring the simultaneous arrival of individualism and sisterhood, Mrs. Rogers expressed a strikingly American commitment to personal attainment through voluntary association, to *voluntarism*. As I sketched briefly in chapter 1, the American solution to the tension between the individual and the group is to assume that a person best reaches his or her personal ends with others in freely chosen fellowship.[1]

Centuries before Mrs. Rogers, the settlers of New England struggled with this tension. In 1630, John Winthrop addressed his Puritan followers as they sailed to New England and, in what would later become a classic American document, urged each one to submit to the group: "We must be knit together in this work as one man . . . [W]e must delight in each other, make others' conditions our own, rejoice together, mourn together, labor, and suffer together, always having before our eyes . . . our community as members of the same body." Winthrop had to exhort his shipmates to unite, because they were in fact *not* knit together, not organs of one body. They were members of separate families sailing on what was for most of them a commercial as much as a religious venture. Winthrop and his Puritans struggled against rank individualism and self-interest. About two centuries later, Ralph Waldo Emerson, descendant of New England ministers, endorsed the individualism that Winthrop warned against. In "Self-Reliance," Emerson wrote, "I appeal from your customs. I must be myself. I cannot break myself any longer for you, or you. . . . I will do strongly . . . whatever only rejoices me, and the heart appoints."

Emerson rejected any suggestion that the individual "make other's conditions our own" or submit to any group.[2]

The tension between knitting together and standing apart persists. In the 1970s, for example, the United States Supreme Court declared in Emersonian fashion that a married couple "is not an independent entity with a mind and heart of its own, but an association of two individuals each with a separate intellectual and emotional make-up." Yet the American public disagreed. In that same decade, over 70 percent of married respondents told a survey that they thought of their marriage as "a couple, it being very hard to describe one person without the other" rather than as "two separate people who make a life together." Americans managed the tension between their commitment to personal ends and their commitment to community through the evolving idea and practices of voluntarism, a covenant or contract between person and group.[3]

This chapter describes the evolution of Americans' relationships, in groups such as family, neighborhood, and church. Early settlement in the New World, despite Governor Winthrop's plea, occurred in conditions that promoted strong individualism. Then, during the colonial era, social groups congealed and curbed some of this individualism, gaining greater control over members. Beginning around the mid-eighteenth century and continuing for generations since, security, affluence, and new ideas expanded individuals' independence from and, thereby, their leverage in groups. More Americans, especially those who had been dependent— women, children, servants, the poor—joined in voluntaristic association, combining individual self-reliance and group belonging.

Some commentators sum up American social history as the "decline of community," arguing that Americans once lived in cohesive communities but then became isolated in the "lonely crowd." A more accurate description is the "unfolding of community." Early Americans tended to live in a few, nested groups: a household within a church within a village. Later Americans participated in several distinct groups, such as family, workplace, church, neighborhood, and club. This gave individuals more freedom within each group. They could, as Mrs. Rogers declared, simultaneously find their individuality and also "thrill to the pulse of organization."

In this chapter, I first elaborate the idea of American voluntarism that I introduced in chapter 1. The subsequent three sections discuss the colonial era, the nineteenth century, and the twentieth century. For each period, I review what we know about the relationships of individual Americans to their groups—to family, church, neighborhood, and other groups which emerge over time. The concluding section briefly considers the implications of more Americans engaging in more voluntarism.

VOLUNTARISM: A CONTRACT FOR INDEPENDENCE

Many Americans who devote time and effort to charitable work as aides in hospices or mentors in schools, for example, have an odd way of explaining why they do it. A minority tell researchers that they work to fulfill religious or moral obligations. Few speak of themselves as generous. Instead, these Good Samaritans tend to say that they find the work personally rewarding. Ironically, even as they are sacrificing themselves for others, they claim to be just satisfying themselves. They are not, of course, individualists even if they speak the language of individualism; they are American voluntarists.[4]

For centuries, observers, foreign and domestic, have described Americans as unusually individualistic, by which they have meant that Americans are, more than other people, loners, selfish, shrewd traders, self-expressive, defenders of liberty, rebels, or all of the above—and, most relevant to this chapter, that they are detached from family, neighborhood, and other social groups. One usually quotes Alexis de Tocqueville here, but Englishman Simon Ferrall, who toured America around the same time as the French aristocrat did, will serve:

> Perhaps there is nothing more remarkable in the character of the Americans than the indifference with which they leave their old habitations, friends, and relations. Each individual is taught to depend mainly on his own exertions, and therefore seldom expects or requires extraordinary assistance from any man. Attachments seldom exist here beyond that of ordinary acquaintances—these are easily found wherever one may go.[5]

Most human societies have treated individuals as components of a group, as "members [limbs] of the same body," in John Winthrop's terms. This "organic" understanding of persons seems strange to modern Americans. And it leads to behavior which also seems strange to modern Americans, such as marrying off young children, pursuing blood feuds, and conducting suicide missions. American culture is, by historical comparison, highly individualistic; it depicts society as comprised fundamentally of individuals, each unique, separate, and self-governing. Nonetheless, describing Americans as socially disconnected, the way Ferrall did, is a mistake. Americans are at least as socially engaged as are other Western peoples; they belong to as many or more groups and are as or more active in them. Americans also voice more loyalty to family, church, and nation than do other Westerners. In several ways, Americans are, by Western standards, relatively group oriented.[6]

What more accurately describes American culture than individualism is voluntarism. In the earlier and non-Western organic model, groups constitute people. Individuals are born into tribes, lineages, castes, age grades, religions, villages, and households; people are defined by those groups and forever committed to them. Kinship, tradition, insecurity, and sometimes law and physical force keep people in their inherited groups, creating very tight communities. Being a noble or a peasant or a member of this or that tribe pretty much determines who one is. The repressiveness of such strong communities can create ambivalence,* and members—despite or perhaps because they are so mutually interdependent—are often suspicious, cold, and imperious toward one another.[7]

In sharp contrast, Americans generally see "community" as an obvious and uncomplicated virtue; politicians, left and right, extol community. Americans are unconflicted in their affection for community, at least in part, because they typically *choose* their communities rather than inherit them. America's brand of individualism, as sociologist Ann Swidler suggests, may be thought of as the freedom to choose one's community. Americans have an unusually free choice of groups, churches, neighborhoods, clubs, and even families. (The great exception is one's racial group. America fixed slaves, Indians, and their descendants into a lower caste. Few Americans can as yet choose to be black or white.) In general, an American joins and participates in groups, but in principle cannot be drafted into or obliged to stay in them. What is most notable about America is not radical individualism, the principle of going it alone, but voluntarism, the principle that individuals choose with whom they go.[8]

To be sure, there is a strand of libertarian individualism in America, expressed for example by Emerson—"No law can be sacred to me but that of my nature" and "Why should we assume [responsibility for] the faults of our friend, or wife, or father, or child, because they sit around our hearth, or are said to have the same blood?"—and Thoreau, who, mocking the man who might care about helping widows and orphans, wrote that "It is not a man's duty . . . to devote himself to the eradication of any, even the most enormous wrong," but just to "wash his hands of it." But these are exceptional views.[9]

Mainstream American culture celebrates groups and community; they are the means to individual happiness. The evangelical Protestant congregation is the paradigm. Its theology presumes a unique, self-determining individual and insists that no priest, saint, or ancestor can intercede for that person with God. ("You've gotta walk that lonesome valley / You've gotta go there by yourself / Ain't nobody here can go there for you / You've

---

* To postwar Germans, for example, the term "community" (*gemeinschaft*) carries a whiff of Nazi *volk*-ish ideology. In South Asia, "communalism" brings to mind murderous rampages between Hindu and Muslim zealots.

gotta go there by yourself.") Crucially, however, the believer finds salvation not in a hermitage, a desert, or a lonesome valley, but in a church,
together with others of the faithful, testifying to his or her rebirth. This
theology and this form of church, as political scientist James Block well
argues, shaped American culture: the "new idiom of religion—combining
individualism with elective community—becomes the American character." A modern, mundane parallel is the gated community. Virtually anyone with the money can join or leave, but residents must accept strict
limitations on what color they paint their homes, where they park their
cars, and so forth in order to enjoy the benefits of the association. A third,
more complex example is contemporary marriage. Easier to enter and
easier to leave than it was generations ago, marriage remains to almost all
Americans central to personal fulfillment. As Emersonian as Americans
sometimes seem, they are committing themselves to churches, neighborhoods, and marriages—but only insofar as they choose those groups and
are not shackled to them. The individualism remains in the insistence on
free entry and exit.[10]

"Contractualism" or "covenantalism" is central to American voluntarism. Individuals make this implicit contract by joining the group: I am
free to stay or leave, but while belonging I owe fealty to the group. One
might also call this the "love it or leave it" rule. Modern American marriage has this character: Americans believe that a person should be free
to choose to marry or not and should be free to choose to leave an unhappy marriage or not, but so long as a marriage continues, the spouse
must be faithful. (Americans have little taste for discreet adultery à la
française.) Similarly, many Americans switch religions or denominations,
but those who do are at least as devoted to their newly chosen faiths as
are those who stay in their parents' churches. This is also how local activists in the San Diego area understood their commitments to their towns,
as explained by sociologist Richard Madsen:

> To be a member of a community means to fulfill the social dimensions
> of one's humanity through interaction with others. Belonging to a com-
> munity does not, though, entail the sacrifice of oneself for the good of
> the group. . . . [A]n individual must resist the twin temptations of sub-
> merging oneself in the group and of denying one's responsibilities to-
> ward the group.

Such activists do not feel obligated, for example, to stay forever—that
would be to sacrifice the self—but when they move, they feel obliged to
become activists in their new towns. This implicit contract helps explain
the conformism that many observers have historically charged to Americans: conformity is part of the deal. It also helps explain why Americans

are neither anarchists nor free lovers—positions one would expect of true libertarians—and why they more often defer to groups and group leaders than other Westerners do.[11]

With voluntarism comes equality. Historically, organic communities have been firmly hierarchical: patriarchs over households, lords over vassals, masters over apprentices, priests over laymen. Both the conditions of early America and the new ideas percolating there gave many subordinated colonists—women, children, servants, apprentices, small farmers, laymen—the longing, the license, and the leverage to demand greater equality. America's revolutionary generation made egalitarianism part of the call for independence. They challenged claims of divine or natural hierarchy. American democracy, in Tocqueville's words, "breaks the chain" of being from the king who rules by divine right to the lowest peasant "and frees each link." Too-strong assertions of equality unsettled many among the nation's founding elite. They rejected "unfair" inequalities based on birth or a king's favors, but they endorsed "fair" inequalities based on talent. The subordination of one man to another was wrong "*beside* that which arises from the difference of capacity, disposition, and virtue" (and, of course, race). They denounced radical "leveling." Equality in the American context is not equality of outcome, but equality of opportunity, treatment, and freedom. Nonetheless, this construction of equality still left average white men empowered to declare that they in fact were equal in "capacity, disposition, and virtue" and in rights. From early on, European visitors expressed shock at the presumptuous claims plain folk made for equal standing with their superiors; mere teamsters, for example, sat down at the dining table next to gentlemen and ladies; rough-hewn men even presumed to call one another gentlemen and to call gentlemen by their first names. Visitors saw equality as America's greatest "heresy."[12]

The heresy flourished on American soil. The vast expanse of available land and the shortage of laborers to work it gave average Americans the muscle to claim equality. The farmer who saw new land on the horizon could snort at the pretensions of the local gentry; the journeyman with several job options could challenge his master. Freedom to come and go gives individuals greater leverage to extract a better "contract," so that in the end groups serve members' interests rather than members serving groups' interests. Otherwise, people leave. Be it neighborhood, congregation, club, or, increasingly, marriage, if the group is "not working for you," you look for one that is.

I argue, following one school of historians, that cultural and material conditions in early America promoted voluntarism, this combination of individualism, group-orientation, contract, and egalitarianism. I also argue that this voluntarism spread and deepened over the centuries. More Americans gained more access to more social groups under more volun- taristic terms; many—especially women and youth—parlayed this into greater independence. Of course, no one is truly apart from the group; even the hermit is a product of society and even the yearning for freedom is learned from a group. But the terms of the relationship changed. That change, power shifting from the group as exercised by its leader, to aver- age members of groups, forms a central story line of this chapter.[13]

Voluntarism has its complexities, benefits, and costs. Sociologist Rob- ert Wuthnow, drawing from his 1990s study of small support groups like Bible study classes, expressed one sort of concern: "The social contract binding members together asserts only the weakest of obligations. Come if you have time. Talk if you feel like it. Respect everyone's opinion. Never criticize. Leave quietly if you become dissatisfied. Families would never operate by following these operating norms." Yet in the voluntaristic so- ciety, families *do* operate to some degree by these norms. Either spouse can leave a marriage that is "not working"; by the age of eighteen, chil- dren can move out. This independence, Wuthnow would point out, cuts both ways. Someone who can walk out can be walked out on—by friends, or coworkers, or a spouse. It can be an insecure social world. Moreover, as the individual's options expand, so does his or her burden to choose well and to re-choose each day (see chapter 6). No wonder, then, that some people seek to "escape from freedom" and to be in groups such as funda- mentalist sects that build a wall against the wider world, groups that try hard to remove the voluntarism from their voluntary associations.[14]

BORN LIBERAL? THE COLONIAL ERA

"Liberal" refers to the conviction, new to the modern world, that indi- viduals ought to be politically, economically, and socially independent of rulers, traditions, and communities. The question mark signals a debate among historians over whether early American society already followed liberal principles of personal independence or whether America became liberal only generations later. For many of the debaters, the answer osten- sibly has implications for twenty-first century politics. If America was al- ways liberal, then individualism would seem a fixed part of its culture and institutions. But if America became liberal only later, then the chances for establishing more collective institutions—more like those of north- western Europe—seem greater.

The affirmative side of the debate contends that the settlers brought with them ideas of individual liberty which were then germinating in Brit- ain. Combine that culture with several features of colonial America—

dissident Protestantism, the virtual absence of feudalism, the social diversity of the colonists, the demand and high pay for workers, the yeomanry made possible by seemingly inexhaustible land, the scattering of households across that land—and a voluntarist society quickly forms. (This would be truer of the North than the South). The negative side in this debate contends, instead, that the settlers brought with them communal values from the villages of Europe, often settled in tight-knit groups of subsistence farmers, and struggled together to survive on the frontier. They were *not* individualists; liberalism came only later, when commercial markets expanded. The evidence leans to the affirmative side of this debate.[15]

Classic organic communities, in the mold of old European villages, were rare even among the earliest North American settlements. (The Puritans may be an exception; I discuss them shortly.) The past held a weak grip on individuals. Friedrich Engels wrote in 1887 that America was "where no medieval ruins bar the way, where history begins with the elements of bourgeois society." And the present worked against strong communities. Most newcomers arrived as individuals; in the first generations, three-fourths of all white settlers between fifteen and sixty years of age came alone to America. Most came as indentured servants or deported criminals. They arrived free of the estates, lineages, villages, and churches into which they had been born and, several years later, the indentured became free of their New World masters, as well. Most of the other immigrants responded to publicity in Europe claiming that America offered white men the chance to become truly independent—rid of landlords with their game reserves and high rents, rid of nobles, creditors, bishops, and village elders. Once having paid off their debt for passage, settlers typically moved from place to place, usually to rural outposts so scattered that simply seeing other people was difficult. If they moved to towns, they usually settled among people of diverse nationalities, religions, and trades. Many lived in villages or towns with so much turnover, turmoil, and warfare that the communities could hardly have exercised the sort of social control found in the classic peasant village. Critically, they lived in far more equal conditions than Europeans did; by 1774, over 70 percent of white men owned land. As historian J. R. Pole has noted, "Much of the experience of life and work on the American continent operated to establish the primacy of the individual."[16]

On the other hand, much of that experience also dictated cooperation. Frontier life, historian Darren Rutman points out, necessarily entailed a "web of reciprocal obligations and responsibilities." Given limits of travel and communication, "how else was the world to be organized but on the basis of the small, direct, personal? . . . In cooperation lay the means for the subsistence of the individual." In rural New England, for example, farm wives bought, sold, traded, helped, nursed, and counseled one another. "Hallowell [Maine] women exchanged daughters the way they exchanged kettles and sleighs"; the girls went "from house to house, own, and kin's, and neighbors, doing what was needed—spinning or washing, etc.—when needed." When prominent New Hampshire farmer Matthew Patten logged his time, he found that he spent more of it on community business than working his land. In bartering, exchanging labor, managing commons, mounting a militia, providing emergency care, and satisfying other material demands, colonists needed their neighbors. Such cooperation, however, did not turn colonial neighborhoods into classic organic communities; mutual assistance entailed much more pragmatic and contractual arrangements. The Hallowell mothers, for example, kept careful accounts of their daughter exchanges. Hudson Valley farmers' records from around the start of the nineteenth century tracked exchanges of work:

> George Holcomb had threshed for William Douglas in March 1814, and noted that "Wm. Dixon with me for which Douglas indebted to me four days work and I am indebted to a days work to Dixon for his helping me today." Not quite a fortnight later Holcomb "chopped for Wm. Dixon in answer to his threshing for me at Wm. Douglasses a few days ago."

Cooperation rested on carefully counting favors; it was not or not simply a matter of social duty, moral obligation, or neighborly feeling.[17]

People often kept books inside the family as well. The harsh demands of survival unified wives, children, indentured servants, apprentices, and others under the rule of the household head; sentiment came second. In seventeenth-century Andover, Massachusetts, fathers and sons commonly wrote contracts stipulating that the father would deed land to the son in return for a specified annual payment after the elder's retirement. John Lovejoy bequeathed his home to his youngest son, Ebenezer, on the condition that Ebenezer provide his widowed mother "12 bushels of 'good and merchantable corne' consisting of 'six of Indian, 3 bushels of wheat & three of Rye,' 120 pounds of pork, 2 barrels of cider," and so forth.[18]

The ideologies as well as the conditions of the New World also worked against organic communities. Stressing self-reliance was common long before Tocqueville wrote in the 1830s that Americans "look after their own needs. [They] owe no man anything and hardly expect anything from anybody." Religious thought, basically Reformed Protestantism early on and evangelicalism later, emphasized God's direct relationship to the individual. Preachers during the eighteenth-century religious mobilizations told their audiences to seek God neither in an established church nor in theology, but in their own hearts (and in the ministers' new churches). Colonial political writers harped on self-reliance as the prerequisite for sustaining freedom and democracy. Slavery provided stark illustrations of what awaited those who lacked "competency," that is, independence. Most colonists, even as they collaborated to defend their settlements or cope with disease, were neither members of "one body" nor did they think of themselves as such. In both circumstances and consciousness, the new American society was considerably more "liberal," or voluntarist, than the Old World. This did not preclude it from becoming even more so.[19]

The Puritan Anomaly

But, what of those Puritan fellowships? The Puritans of seventeenth-century New England have gained, in the words of one historian, a "monopoly on publicity" about early America, such that even historians, in the words of another, "know more about the Puritans than any sane person should want to know." Although the Puritans still represent the colonial era in the popular imagination (Thanksgiving and all that) and their descendants shaped American letters (Emerson, Hawthorne, Longfellow, Adams, Dickinson, Frost, and so on), Puritan communities were atypical even within New England.[20]

Puritan leaders certainly tried to "knit" all individuals together into the same body, in Winthrop's language. In the mid-1600s, at the zenith of their culture, Puritan villagers held land in common, belonged to a single and strong church, resisted the intrusion of outsiders, and closely supervised one another's behavior. Leading minister Cotton Mather proclaimed, "If the neighbor of an elected saint [church member] sins, then the saint sins also" and so it is a duty to "admonish one another." And so they did, by fierce gossip, defamatory and often obscene billboards, and court suits. Local magistrates strictly enforced moral codes. One, for example, ordered the execution of Thomas Graunger in Plymouth in 1642 for bestiality. In Windsor, Connecticut, 20 percent of the adults in each decade found themselves charged with an offense, usually a morals violation. Magistrates also supported the church by compelling Sabbath attendance, paying ministers with tax money, and suppressing religious alternatives, to the point of executing and mutilating dissident Quakers. Mrs. Mary Dyer exasperated the Boston authorities by persistently returning from exile in Rhode Island to proclaim her religious dissents; they finally hanged her in the Commons in 1660.[21]

Authorities reinforced the power of the household patriarch, for example, by pressing feuding couples to stay married, sometimes at great cost to the wives. Even in relatively liberal Springfield, Massachusetts, the local court ordered a woman whipped for repeatedly calling her husband a fool. In the 1640s, New England legislatures passed laws prescribing a death sentence (never carried out) for grown children who rebelled against their parents. Historian Jack Greene explained the Puritans' social agenda in coming to America:

> The world puritans hoped to substitute for the one in which they lived used suspicion and mutual surveillance to achieve a tight social regimen and to suppress individual deviance and sin, exert tight control over the unruly forces of the market, diminish acquisitiveness and the covetousness or frivolous indulgence it engendered, locate every person in an appropriate calling, urge diligence and a careful use of time upon individuals, submerge the rampant assertion of self in a concern for the next world rather than this, and achieve a degree of communal unity virtually unknown in the fluctuating world of early modern England.

New England Puritanism was, wrote historian Michael Zuckerman, "a totalitarianism of true believers." Yet repeated efforts to suppress sin, hectoring by ministers, and frequent court suits point to the large gap between the total society the magistrates sought and the everyday reality of Puritan villages.[22]

Those villages could not really be communities the way European peasant villages were, much less the way the original Children of Israel were: organic, hierarchical groups into which generations of people were born and bound to one another. They were instead "intentional communities" formed by contracts among a self-selected elite. Also, much of Puritan theology, historian Perry Miller has explained, rested on the idea of covenants, one between God and man and one between man and society. Central to those covenants was free choice: "The individual voluntarily promised to obey civil and scriptural law, for the seventeenth-century Puritans believed that meaningful obedience could only grow out of voluntary consent, never out of coercion." In a sense, the effort of Winthrop and other Puritan leaders to form their followers into one body ran against the voluntarist grain of Puritanism itself. Even birth into the Puritan village did not guarantee full membership; choice did. In the early decades, churches required people to have and to describe a conversion experience before they could join. Townsfolk who rejected or were rejected by the church were not so much part of the community as they were subjects of it. In practice, Puritan magistrates, while they monitored much of social life, did not control, as premodern communities did, other behavior such as the crops people grew and the crafts they performed. Indeed, Puritan elders accepted the pursuit of individual wealth even if it meant growing inequalities. Finally, the Puritan model differed from peasant communities in persisting for only a few generations.[23]

Historian Kenneth Lockridge's classic study of Dedham, Massachusetts, *A New England Town*, illustrates the optimal Puritan case. The signatories of the 1636 Dedham Covenant designed, in Lockridge's phrase, a "Christian Utopian Closed Corporate Community." In its first half century, most of Dedham's several hundred residents belonged to the church and thereby exercised citizenship in the town. They were "almost hermetically sealed off from the rest of the world"; few people moved in or out. Citizens farmed relatively equal amounts of farmland and jointly held title to the yet undeveloped plots. They obeyed the church leaders and, unlike some neighboring towns, lived "entirely free of . . . prolonged disputes." In its second half century, however, Dedham experienced land shortages and subdivision, widening inequality, an influx of strangers, the growth of outlying hamlets, and repeated conflicts. The community became more democratic but also more geographically, economically, theologically, and politically fractured.[24]

Less secluded Puritan towns similarly grew more divided. Lawsuits and slander were commonplace, reaching one peak in the witchcraft accusations and executions of Salem in the 1690s. An eighteenth-century example is Concord, Massachusetts, home to the famed Minutemen. Factions there fought one another constantly before and through the Revolution. In 1776, to foster unity, sixty men of Concord's church came together for a day of "Fasting, Humiliation, and Prayer" and pledged to renounce all slandering, "Pride, Ostentation & Vanity." But a year later, factionalism returned. Within a century of their communities' founding, residents of many Puritan villages turned to trade and commercial farming, petitioned for divorce, watered down the standards for church membership, accepted more religious diversity, fought over a variety of issues, increasingly eluded community punishment for their sins, and left town. By the late 1700s, New England "congregations were on their way to becoming . . . centers of worship that could maintain a measure of peacefulness simply because the discontented could leave and join, or form, another group [church] whenever they pleased." As religious voluntarism emerged more clearly, so did doctrines of individual belief and salvation. Indeed, the Puritans' descendants, as Emerson best illustrates, emphasized religious voluntarism, personal expressiveness, and self-reliance. The roots of such thought can be traced back to the original theology and contractualism of the Puritans rather than to the authoritarian ways they actually ran their communities.[25]

Ultimately, the Puritans, as emblematic as they are, were an oddity. New England was the least commercialized, least mobile, most resistant to immigration, and most densely settled region among the colonies; it was most like rural England. Colonial government in seventeenth-century New England, acting on behalf of the church, controlled private life more and longer than elsewhere—perhaps more than even in England. Americans beyond New England lived on scattered homesteads rather than in compact villages, which meant that they were less involved with neighbors than the Puritans were; they more commonly grew export crops and were thus more attuned to the outside world; their towns were less isolated, more diverse, and more tolerant than the Puritan towns were; and American communities outside of New England included more slaves, indentured servants, and tenants and so were originally less egalitarian than those in New England. For such reasons, most scholars probably agree with historian John L. Brooke that "historians have long since abandoned any interpretation grounding the American nation in Puritanism." Puritan efforts to create organic communities cannot represent early America and cannot challenge the "born liberal" thesis. Nonetheless and ironically, the Puritans' *ideology of contractualism*, rather than their practices, influenced American culture and helped develop American voluntarism.[26]

Colonial Variations

If the story of the Puritan communities can be simplified as a "declension" from strict social control to greater voluntarism, the wider colonial story can be simplified as almost the opposite, the congealing of social control out of disorderly individualism—and then later a subsequent loosening into voluntarism. Only a few localities, say, Quaker and Mennonite settlements in Pennsylvania, were as tightly knit as the early Puritan villages. Salem, North Carolina, was one: a Moravian congregation owned the town, and church elders regulated residents' businesses. In many more places, however, the dispersion of homesteads weakened the community's sway over households; the shortage of women made family formation difficult; and most residents went unserved by any church. In the Chesapeake area, for example, the scarcity of women and the high mortality rate left many men unmarried and many children orphaned. In the South, informal liaisons often substituted for marriages. On the coasts of Georgia and the Carolinas, community commonly meant plantations of slaves with a few white supervisors. Even by 1724, only about one-third of white adults in coastal Virginia belonged to a church. And when Virginians did establish churches, their voluntaristic nature was evident: "Religion itself became more than ever a matter of choice. . . . [N]o longer did a particular faith simply 'come with the territory' as it had back in Europe." In sum, group life took time to form.[27]

Rural colonials—and 95 percent of Americans at this time were rural—nonetheless needed one another. The paucity of roads left many small localities on their own. (London was across an ocean and the colonial capitals often seemed so irrelevant that some villages did not even bother to send representatives to the legislature.) Where neighbors were nearby, they exchanged labor in barn raisings, harvests, and emergencies; traded produce; bartered for craft items; rented out their animals and sons to one another; banded together during wars and Indian raids, gave medical help; and relaxed together. Over time, local communities congealed in many regions. They built roads that connected farmsteads, and where roads crossed, up sprang hamlets and towns. More women arrived and settled the men down. Second and third generations matured, ministers started churches, and officials—some sent from London—instituted laws and courts. Groups formed and group influence over individuals intensified. Frontier isolation and strong individualism waned.[28]

In many an emerging colonial village or town, neighbors and town elders came to monitor residents' lifestyles, actions, and words; they were "morally intrusive and coercively communalistic." In isolated communities, one's local reputation mattered. Authorities devoted much effort to punishing residents who defamed their neighbors and, especially, who defamed the authorities themselves. Court records from throughout the colonies abound with complaints filed by the insulted against those who called them rogues or cuckolds or loose women or witches. Penalties could be severe. A Virginia man in 1624 who castigated the governor was sentenced to broken arms and having his tongue bored. In many places, local officials decided the prices merchants could charge and the wages laborers would earn. Sumptuary laws tried to regulate residents' clothing to stop ordinary folk from passing as gentlemen and ladies. Authorities tried to control drinking, sex, and family life, prosecuting and sometimes exiling wastrels and transients, overseeing husbands' exercise of authority, supervising unwed mothers, and binding out orphans to work in local households. In the South, legislatures tightened control over slaves, ending what had been loose mixing of the free and the bound. Social organization developed, authority ascended to power, and the individual's latitude narrowed.[29]

Churches were few and scattered; most colonials were "unchurched." Even in larger settlements, religious diversity and apathy left many people unconnected. In the late seventeenth century, for example, only about one in seven children born in Charles Parish, Virginia, was baptized. After 1680, established churches, notably the Anglicans in Virginia and the Congregationalists in New England, expanded and claimed more authority. New evangelical sects emerged, especially on the frontier. Congregations, where they could be sustained, became important, as there were few other places for social life. Religious participation started to rise, foretelling what would later be, in some places, a mid-eighteenth-century religious frenzy.[30]

Household authority tightened, too. By law and custom, authorities required every person to live in a household ruled by a free, adult male. Men's grip on their households varied, of course. Occasionally, a strong-willed woman might dominate a weak or alcoholic man, or neighbors might intervene to stop abuse of a wife. In New England, officials occasionally directed the patriarch to exercise more control over a rambunctious child or servant. On the other hand, Quaker families in the Delaware Valley were unusually egalitarian. For the most part, men governed firmly. Husbands controlled their wives' persons and property with only minor limitations, and fathers strictly ruled their children and stepchildren, working them at an early age or putting them out to labor on neighbors' farms. Control of land and dowries allowed fathers to constrict, if not determine, their sons' and daughters' marriage choices. (That was one reason colonial Americans tended to marry historically late, in their twenties.) Men could even direct their wives and children from the grave through detailed wills. Servants of various kinds—indentured immigrants, farmhands, maids, and apprentices, male and female, white and black, adult and child—shared a roof and broke bread with their masters; they were part of the household and ruled by the patriarch.[31]

The story of Rosina Schaeffer, a maid, although coming late in the eighteenth century, illustrates the power of the patriarchs. Jacob Hiltzheimer, the German immigrant whose diary I quoted in chapter 2, became an established figure in Philadelphia. He made these entries in 1786:

> May 22. Our servant maid, Rosina, was impertinent to her mistress.
> July 8. Had my servant maid, Rosina Schaeffer, taken to Lewis Weiss's, Esq., [a justice of the court of common pleas] on account of her insolent behavior to my wife and myself. Mr. Weiss ordered her to the Workhouse.
> August 9. Lewis Weiss, Esq., had my servant girl brought back from the Workhouse and asked her if she would go back to her master and behave as she ought to do. She answered, "No," upon which he ordered her back for another thirty days.
> August 24. Went with Mr. Franck to the Workhouse, who there spoke to my servant maid Rosina (being her countryman [probably Dutch]). She promised to behave better, upon which took her

> home, after paying £1 19s. 6d. for her lodging and board for forty-
> eight days.
>
> September 25. Sold my servant-maid, Rosina Schaeffer, to August Will
> for £20, and signed her over to him before Justice Farmer.

The feisty Rosina then seems to disappear from the scene.[32]

Colonial Americans, most living on scattered homesteads, the fringes of small towns, or on plantations, generally dealt with relatively few, mutually dependent, and interconnected neighbors. Puritans aside, the earliest generations experienced perhaps chaotic levels of individualism. Eventually, groups formed and solidified—households, churches, villages. Most people lacked "competency" and true self-reliance; they needed and deferred to those who had competency. "It was difficult for men and women of the premodern world to conceive of equality," wrote historian Laurel Thatcher Ulrich. "In the hierarchical structure which sustained the social order, one human being was of necessity almost always subject to another." The authorities in each group—community, church, household—reinforced one another's power. Even so, control of the individual was not nearly as complete or intense as that of the classical European community; America was still *comparatively* "liberal." Then an expanding liberalism, an evolving voluntarism, broke loose in the late eighteenth century.[33]

The Wider Revolution

As some of the colonial elite stirred rebellion against the British Empire, average Americans increasingly defied the authorities in their smaller communities. At one point, John Adams worried, "We have been told that our struggle has loosened the bonds of government everywhere; that children and apprentices were disobedient; that schools and colleges were grown turbulent; that Indians slighted their guardians, and Negroes grew insolent to their masters." This may be too grand a claim for the Revolution; reports of uppity behavior mounted for decades even before the battle at Concord. One observer complained, for example, that "the poorest day-laborer on the bank of the Delaware holds it his right to advance his opinion, in religious as well as political matters, with as much freedom as the gentleman." Some nongentlemen even asked to be called "Mister." How much American nationalism drove social unrest and how much social unrest drove nationalism is uncertain and debated by historians, but the parallels are evident. In the latter half of the eighteenth century, Americans increasingly demanded to renegotiate the implicit contracts between person and group.[34]

For instance, more wives resisted their husbands' rule. Suits for divorce, albeit few by modern standards, increased sharply. Because the Puritans treated marriage less as a sacrament and more as a civil contract (contractualism again!), New England magistrates had long been more lenient than the British in allowing an occasional divorce. But wives filed more divorce suits and in them often drew on political rhetoric. They charged men with domestic tyranny and claimed that women, too, had the right to pursue happiness, to expect love. Tom Paine, pamphleteer of the Revolution, supported their cause, arguing that people had the right to find their one God-given mate, if necessary by trying more than one marriage.[35]

Legal reforms following the Revolution granted women additional rights—for example, more control of the property they brought into a marriage—and better tools for claiming those rights. They also expanded the grounds for divorce to include verbal abuse, intemperance, and other poor treatment by husbands. Many more women, however, sought not to end marriages but to increase their leverage within them. They earned their own money churning butter or weaving, set up women's benevolent societies, and pulled their husbands into church. Revolutionary ideology supported greater female assertiveness by extolling the Republican wife and mother as the nurturer of citizens and the guardian of virtue; it placed the woman's contribution to the nation on almost the same plane as her husband's. Early trickles appeared of what would later be a flood of nineteenth-century feminist sentiments: ideas of romance, of marriage as mutual friendship, and of a more spiritual sexuality. The emerging standards, concludes historian Carl Degler, established that "women, like men, had interests and lives that were separate and different from those of other members of the family." Law and public opinion began shifting from viewing marriage as the absorption of one person by another (or even as a master-servant relationship) to viewing it as a love match between distinct and equal individuals. To be sure, only the glimmer of such change had appeared by 1800, and then mainly among the small, East Coast middle class, but it was on the horizon.[36]

Children of the urban affluent received—or wrested—greater respect, personal attention, and affection. Customary gestures of deference, such as bowing to parents or standing at attention while they ate meals, passed out of favor. Youths claimed more sexual freedom and greater choice in spouses. (A Philadelphia minister in the 1790s was bemused that one marrying couple found it "very odd" that he required their parents' permission.) To cite love as a reason for marrying, as young Americans increasingly did, observes Degler, "was the purest form of individualism; it subordinated all familial, social, or group considerations to personal preference." Some youths demanded even more. Calvin Heaton, of North

Haven, Connecticut, tried in 1788 to attach his father's farm for £1,000, claiming that it was owed him in return for farmwork he had done since he had come of age. (Eighteen years later, Calvin was the wealthiest man in North Haven.) College students, for whom the college served as "parent," grew rowdier, the unrest culminating in the murder of a professor at the University of Virginia. Some journeymen and apprentices left their masters' households to become "free laborers," living on their own and asking to be paid in cash on an hourly or piecework basis. (And we should not forget rebellious Rosina.) Increasingly, slaves on tobacco and rice plantations worked apart from their masters in teams supervised by overseers and black drivers, which, however bitter the life, increased their solidarity and their distance from owners. In these myriad ways, households slowly loosened their hold on their members.[37]

Religious Americans, disproportionately women, founded new congregations and divided older ones. Churches multiplied and democratized, especially during the First Great Awakening of the mid-1700s (and then again about a half-century later). Although most Americans still did not belong to a church, many joined one of a wildly diverse array of new evangelical movements, such as the Baptists and Methodists. Their lay leaders and circuit-riding preachers challenged the mainstream Anglican, Congregational, and Dutch Reformed denominations. The upstart sects appealed to folk spiritualism and growing democratic feelings in ways that ministers of the established churches could not. One of the latter reported, with great distaste, on a Baptist service he witnessed in the Carolina backwoods in the 1760s: "Extravagancies—One on his knees in a Posture of Prayer—Others singing—some howling—These ranting—Those crying—Others dancing, Skipping, Laughing and rejoycing. Here two or 3 Women falling on their Backs, kicking up their Heels, exposing their Nakedness to all Bystanders." "New-light" ministers preached that individuals should rely on "'self-examination' and their own private judgments, no matter that 'your Neighbors growl against you, and reproach you.'" They rejected the established churches' authority to interpret God and flattered their audiences by teaching that the humble were more attuned to God than were the elite. Evangelicals preached universal salvation rather than the election of the few and, above all, "the primacy of individual conscience." The springs of political dissent and religious dissent merged. By the time of the Revolution, the vocabularies of "the republican and evangelical traditions . . . became almost interchangeable."[38]

Hannah Heaton, a farmer's wife in North Haven, Connecticut, and mother of Calvin, mentioned above, got caught up. She had never been particularly religious until 1741 when, at age twenty, she heard famed revivalist George Whitefield preach. She sought deeper faith but with increasing frustration until one day she heard a voice and saw a vision; she had found "a new soul and a new body." For years, she recorded in her diary her struggles with satanic attacks on her faith, but also her feelings of God's reassurance. Despite her duties as wife and mother, Heaton immersed herself in private worship, dream interpretation, and religious readings. She refused to attend the required services at the official Congregational church in North Haven, because she felt the minister to be in error and in 1758 was fined for breaking the Sabbath. Heaton continued to resist conformity and in 1778 joined an evangelical church. Her intensity put off her religiously lax husband and estranged many people around her, but she nonetheless devoted her life to finding and expressing a personal faith. Similarly, Mrs. Lucy Mack Smith of New Hampshire decided, as others did, to follow her own reading of the Bible rather than the church's. She persuaded a minister to baptize her as, in effect, a Christian of her own personal denomination. Her son Joseph later founded the Mormon faith. The hold of the established churches—even in New England—was clearly weakening.[39]

Establishment ministers responded by relaxing their Calvinism. They tempered the notion that only the chosen few would gain eternal salvation and allowed instead that even the most degraded individuals— even criminals condemned to execution—could persuade God to save their immortal souls. Americans built more and more-diverse churches, sects, and spiritual groups as "voluntary societies for personal identification and salvation." New congregations formed of like-minded individuals, serving individual needs, enthusiasms, and salvation. We'll later see how this accelerated over the next few generations.[40]

Local communities' control also loosened—perhaps most dramatically around Massachusetts Bay, where that trend was viewed as a fall from grace. One sign of loosening was increasing crime and sexual license over the eighteenth century. On the eve of the Revolution, a third of the brides in some New England towns were already pregnant. Similarly, many New Englanders had surrendered to the practice of "bundling" (allowing courting couples to share a bed, albeit with a barrier between them). In the South and on the Western frontier, where local communities had been transient and loosely organized to start with, change was less stark. Yet whereas social groups had solidified and closed in the late seventeenth and early eighteenth centuries, they loosened and opened up in the late eighteenth century. Local politics involved increasingly more participation by common folk, more boisterous elections, and more crowd attacks on the authorities.[41]

Demographic and economic changes helped loosen the grip of household, church, and community on individuals. As populations grew, land became scarcer; younger sons moved away, some west to new land and some to the growing towns. The proportion who lacked property grew. At the same time, the swelling rhetoric of equality and freedom gave white men everywhere language with which to declare their independence against patriarch, minister, gentry, and magistrate. Then, the Revolution broke the dam. "In thousands of different ways," wrote historian Gordon Wood, "connections that had held people together for centuries were strained and severed, and people set loose in unprecedented numbers. The Revolution shattered traditional structures of authority and common people increasingly discovered that they no longer had to accept the old distinctions." General Washington himself confronted these challenges to old distinctions. A member of the Virginia gentry, he saw the "leveling spirit" of Northerners and backwoodsmen in his own army as threatening disorder, but any efforts to enforce hierarchy on the troops stirred up rumblings of insurrection. Even though colonial America was already, by Old World standards, a voluntaristic society, by the late eighteenth century it was more so. And there was more to come.[42]

SEARCHING FOR INDEPENDENCE AND INTIMACY:
THE NINETEENTH CENTURY

Population growth, urbanization, faster travel, restless moving, new kinds of work, and accumulating wealth provided more nineteenth-century Americans with more social groups to join and greater independence within each one; these changes widened and deepened voluntarism. And two relatively new sorts of groups emerged: workplaces and associations.[43]

Rebalancing the Family

"Few topics have gripped historians of early America," wrote one scholar in 2006, "as powerfully as the post-Revolutionary demise of patriarchal authority. . . . [S]cores of studies have shown how colonial America's rigidly structured social relationships softened. . . . The upshot of this decline in starchy paternalism was a widespread bourgeois embrace of affection and benevolence." Professionals, merchants, manufacturers, and even some well-to-do farmers tacitly renegotiated family life. For Americans on the cutting edge, family was no longer to be a matter of ruler and ruled, but a loving partnership. In this partnership, he earns income, she maintains a nurturing home, and the children concentrate on learning how to be adults who can replicate this world. One author of family advice wrote in 1833, "While . . . the father is engaged in the bustling affairs of active life, the mother, with almost irresistible sway, is forming the characters of the future." The emerging "nuclear" household of men of "competency" contained fewer people, often just parents and children and occasionally a widowed grandmother, spinster aunt, or a maid, but no longer farmhands, indentured servants, apprentices, boarders, neighbors' bound-out children, or orphaned relatives. The new family also had fewer children, but ones of higher "quality." Over the century, many in the middle class gradually adopted this model which scholars have variously labeled as bourgeois, domestic, separate-spheres, breadwinner, or Victorian. Most farmers, laborers, immigrants, and descendants of slaves—that is, most Americans—began emulating this model only generations later. (Typically, most had either been dependents in a large household or too poor to head anything but a small household.) Still, understanding the emergence of the middle-class, nuclear family in the nineteenth century is critical to understanding where American culture and character were headed.[44]

In 1870, a contributor to the *New York Times* described the new family pattern in a column entitled, "The Domestic Sphere":

> In certain respects woman *is* superior to man. . . . she is finer, softer, keener in perception, more delicate in sense, more scrupulous in almost every way. . . . Now, man, for the most part, takes—and properly takes—the lion's share of the toil, the cuffs, and the bruises of the world. . . . The just relation of the sexes is such that when the man's chief task for the day is done the woman's most important duty begins. It is the business of the woman to make a happy and sunny home. Hard as modern reformers may work to teach her to shirk it, this is her prime office.

Even women who seemed to challenge what was "her prime office" endorsed this ideal. Rhoda E. White, a daughter of Irish immigrants, rose to be the wife of a New York Superior Court justice, an influential activist, and eventually a close friend of Mary Todd Lincoln. In 1860, she wrote a letter to president-elect Lincoln in which she noted her political experience but insisted "I must not allow you to imagine me a *large virago-looking* woman politician, who belongs to a class (*I detest*) 'woman's rights.'" White went on to describe herself as the small and "not *awe*-inspiring" mother of eight children and detailed how she had personally educated them "while attending to my domestic duties." She clearly protested too much.[45]

The reaction of immigrants to the emerging family pattern illustrates its novelty. Pietist farmers from northern Europe who moved to the upper Midwest were shocked, historian Jon Gjerde reports, by the family life of Yankees. The immigrant patriarchs required everyone to sacrifice themselves in order to build up and pass on family estates. In their view, the native-born neighbors permitted their wives "sit home" all day rather than work, indulged their children by sending them to school and then letting them move away, and finally surrendered the family farm to retire in town.[46]

Finding one explanation for the emergence of the bourgeois family is difficult, given the intertwined economic, social, and ideological changes of the age; it is also unnecessary. Certainly, farming's decline changed many a man's role from the head of a small family business to a commuter bringing home a paycheck. (In 1820, 72 percent of American workers labored in agriculture; in 1900, only 37 percent did.) Rising income toward the end of the century freed many wives from weaving, selling home-churned butter, cooking for boarders, and similar homebound jobs. As I noted before, couples increasingly lived with fewer children, fewer relatives, and fewer nonrelatives, making for smaller and probably more intimate households. Advice books, novels, and ministers' sermons agreed that Americans—pointedly, men—should spend more time at home engaged in love, nurture, and religious practice. Architects designed houses to be shrines to Christian values and to serve as family redoubts; they recommended, for example, that children have their own rooms so as to draw them away from the streets. The bourgeois family was not "of the world," focused on the material; it existed instead, to summarize two scholars of family history, "for the sake of each [member's] emotional well-being and development."[47]

This new prescription for family life called for new sorts of men. Stern, sometimes even abusive men ran most American households. George C. Duffield recalled, "'the peace that passeth understanding' abode in our mother. Father, less filled with grace, enforced the rules of righteousness in the family, and to others outside, with stern exactness. . . . And my father's cabin was ruled as every other settler's." But in the new, emerging family, the father was to be not only a provider, sober and responsible, and a dispenser of strict justice, but also a loving husband and doting parent. Charles Cumming was such a man. The businessman moved his family to the Boston suburbs in 1877. He subsequently wrote many detailed notes about his children's development and managing the household in his wife's daybook. Although ahead of most men, Cummings foreshadowed the early-twentieth-century model of the middle-class husband who cared about and shared domestic duties, albeit under the supervision of the wife, who remained ruler of the home.[48]

The Victorian family, for all the castigation it received later, empowered women. Freed of outside work and often freed of household drudgery by a maid, the middle-class mother managed the home, directed the family's social life, took on what had been the father's role of moral tutoring, and presented the family to the world. (If the family experienced an economic setback, she typically contributed in ways that preserved her "natural" role, such as cooking for boarders, rather than going out to work.) To assume that these women felt oppressed is to read our sensibilities back into history. Compared to the chattel-like status of her grandmothers or great-grandmothers, being queen of the home was a great improvement. Increasingly, the bourgeois wife also had the luxury to step outside the home and press her values in the public arena through women's clubs and movements. Sophisticated European visitors—not just Norwegian farmers complaining about their Yankee neighbors—remarked on the elevated position of American wives.[49]

We can see women's increasing leverage in matters of sex and divorce. The Victorian model described women as too morally refined to have carnal thoughts, much less desires (reversing the previous century's image of women as lusty). This repression certainly constrained women. However, it also gave wives a way to control husbands' demands. With that and with crude but passable birth control methods, wives increasingly limited their pregnancies, thereby protecting their health and their time.[50]

A still small but growing number of wives took advantage of more liberal divorce laws. Early in the century, legal divorces were difficult to get; they typically required approval from a state legislature or a high judge. Women requested them when just walking out on their husbands would not suffice, when, for example, they wanted to keep property that they had brought into the marriage. In the 1840s, Abraham Lincoln's law office handled only about a half-dozen divorces a year, typically for women who charged their long-absent husbands with desertion, brutality, adultery, or drunkenness. State governments then made divorces easier and cheaper. They lengthened the list of complaints women could file, eventually including emotional distress and mental cruelty. The soaring and world-high American divorce rate that followed soon attained the status of a "social problem." Conservatives condemned divorce as a defiance of God, a threat to society, and an expression of rampant individualism. (Compounding the outrage, judges increasingly gave women custody of the children, which had originally been the father's alone.) Women's advocates preferred to describe divorce not as a cause of social disarray but as the solution to loveless marriages. At the end of the nineteenth century, husbands still legally ruled over their wives and their wives' property, but they had suffered substantial erosion of their power. Easier divorce and other legal changes, combined with increasingly active feminist movements, led Susan B. Anthony and Ida H. Harper to announce in 1900 "a complete legal revolution during the past half century" in married women's rights.[51]

One of those rights middle-class wives claimed was love. Women suing for divorce increasingly charged that their husbands were cold and inattentive (rather than just abusive), indicating new expectations for marriage. Wives nurtured higher expectations in part because their material needs were increasingly secure. The wave of nineteenth-century romanticism and sentimentality, dramatized in heartthrob novels of gallant love, could then work up their hopes. (See chapter 6 for a general discussion of Victorian-era sentimentality.) One cleric complained as early as 1809 about novels that stress "the omnipotence of *love* over all obligations." Middle-class weddings inflated from modest ceremonies conducted at home to all-out, white-gown, church rituals, with reception and honeymoon—the culmination of romance. We have no statistics of course, but it is highly likely that more spouses more often expressed their love to one another. Those same Midwestern Yankee farmers who were disdained by European immigrants for indulging their wives in turn criticized those immigrants for having loveless marriages.[52]

In the nineteenth century, most wives, of course, were yet to be mounted on a pedestal. Most rural, working-class, immigrant, and black women—that is, *most* women—did not even rule a separate sphere. They continued to work in the fields and in the mills, as servants, or as outworkers in their own homes. A rural woman wrote in 1874 of her "troubled life, unblest / 'From morn till night,' I said, in fretful tone / 'Tis endless toil, and thankless moil, alone." Poorer women's unions often lacked the stability of legal sanction and sacrament. Even some middle-class women worked for pay outside the home, teaching school for example, and many still shared chores with kin, servants, and neighbors. Nevertheless, the emerging Victorian model of the woman's small domestic sphere increasingly formed the ideal that most women sought, even if they were yet unable to live it. Historian Susan Glenn has described the feelings of women who immigrated from Jewish villages in eastern Europe to New York City near the end of the nineteenth century. They came from a culture in which the exemplary wife supported the family while the model husband immersed himself in religious study. But the young newcomers embraced instead the American breadwinner ideal: the husband should work in the world and the wife should fashion the home. For many, only their daughters or granddaughters achieved this ideal.[53]

Middle-class children of this era experienced the paradox of becoming both more enmeshed and more privileged in the family. Historically, fathers sent even young children out to work, or, more commonly, used them at home as laborers; parents treated children as miniature adults to be supervised rather than as fledglings to be nurtured. Historian Joyce Appleby describes how young men in the early 1800s often had to rebel against their fathers in order to go to school or to otherwise move up in the world. But circumstances changed for the children of the growing middle class: there were fewer children in each family; new ideologies described children as unformed clay to be shaped by love rather than as sinful creatures to be tamed by discipline; families increasingly lived in exclusively residential neighborhoods; and new sorts of jobs made schooling important. These developments brought each child more attention, more pampering, and more free time. They were, in the view of many outsiders, spoiled. One French visitor commented that "if the children irritated me, the parents maddened me. Their attitude can only be described as capitulation." A New England woman recalling her antebellum childhood wrote that "we were watched over and guarded day and night, indulged in everything which [mother] could possibly procure for us,—wept over, prayed over, but never controlled." Working-class children, on the other hand, continued to labor for their families, less frequently as farmhands but more often as factory hands, street hustlers, or casual laborers. Theirs was, in the words of historian Steven Mintz, a "useful childhood" rather than the "protected childhood" of middle-class children.[54]

At the same time, however, bourgeois parents tried to teach their sons self-reliance, for boys were to eventually strike out on their own and take the "cuffs and the bruises of the world." Mothers found help in this task from a growing number of advice books. One essayist gave parents this advice in 1816 on how to deal with their children's "follies and errors":

> by *moral* means; by example   by cogent and convincing appeals to understanding, and affectionate appeals to the heart:—and not so much, certainly not altogether, by corporeal punishment. . . . One of the most important objects of domestic government is so to train up children that they may have a due government of themselves when they shall come to be grown up men and women.

French visitor Michel Chevalier wrote, "as soon as they have their growth, the Yankees whose spirit now predominates in the Union quit their parents, never to return, as naturally and with as little emotion as young birds desert forever their native nests." Middle-class girls, too, were destined to leave for good, sometimes with a brief detour to decorous work, but relatively quickly to homes of their own. Guiding them required instilling the domestic virtues of sentiment, nurturance, and discipline.[55]

For such children, ultimately attaining the "competency" of a successful adult required, ironically, staying home longer, more parental supervision, and fewer escapades—a "protected childhood." Over the first half of the nineteenth century, the premarital pregnancy rate, a crude indicator of youth's independence, dropped considerably. One interpretation is that direct parental control increased as more teens and young adults stayed home longer, especially to attend school. Another interpretation is that parents actually supervised less, but that young people were learning "due government of themselves." At the same time, with immigration to the growing cities, undisciplined working-class children seemed to pose mounting and visible problems. Some American philanthropists responded with "child-saving" initiatives, such as Sunday schools, orphanages, YMCAs, settlement houses, and compulsory education, seeking to teach those children, too, self-government.[56]

Despite the growing empowerment of middle-class wives and children, the needs of the family, as determined by the head of the household, still trumped their interests. Both sexes, for example, expected women to defer their personal goals to care for others. Sarah Gillespie was a bright young woman from Iowa who in the 1880s repeatedly disrupted her teaching career to return home and nurse her often-ailing mother. In what was surely a common story, Sarah sacrificed much of her own life to her family duty. Also, women, although on an ever-higher pedestal and with more power than before, found that expectations for their performance also rose. Husbands, family, and community—and they themselves—expected them to make homes into "havens in a heartless world" and to lovingly mold children into superior adults. The emerging Victorian family model thus demanded intense emotional commitment from all.[57]

It required the greatest concessions from men. The general loosening of control over wives and children, together with the liberation of slaves and the flight of household servants, also meant, wrote historian Carole Shammas, the "disintegration in the powers of the household head." New laws loosened men's hold on wives and wives' property. And as farming gave way to wage work, fewer fathers could use a promised bequest of land as a leash on their sons. Reform campaigns subverted men yet more. Activists tried to shut down saloons, gambling dens, and brothels, and to restrain men's sexual demands on wives—essentially to *civilize* men. Many states passed laws requiring saloon keepers to heed any wife's demand that they cease serving liquor to her husband. And men faced rising expectations of them. They now owed their wives and children attention and affection as well as material support. It took years for male behavior to change noticeably, but by the 1870s, reformers were praising men who went home after work to spend time with their wives and children. These domesticating pressures irritated many men and spurred some backlash, including a spurt of violence against wives. Nonetheless, at the end of the century, American men—mainly middle-class but increasingly working-

class also—exercised notably less household authority than their grand-
fathers had. Men's "contract" with the family had, in contrast to wom-
en's and children's, deteriorated. Fewer homes were ruled with, in George
Duffield's words, a graceless father's "stern exactness."[58]

Opened Communities

Steamboats, canals, improved roads, better-designed wagons, and then
railroads comprised the transportation revolution that in the first half
of the nineteenth century opened up most of America's communities.
Faster, cheaper travel made communications and personal encounters
much easier, which, among other things, expanded marriage opportunities. Drawing on centuries of local marriage records, historian Daniel
Scott Smith documented how residents of Hingham, Massachusetts, a
small town fifteen miles south of Boston, found more of their spouses beyond the city limits as time passed. About 35 percent of marrying couples
in the 1700s involved a bride or groom not from Hingham; in 1950 about
75 percent did, with most of the change occurring in the nineteenth century. The transportation and communications revolutions connected
more American communities more tightly to the wider world. Chapter
2 recounted this story in terms of what market expansion meant for economic security; here my concern is with its implications for the cohesion
of local communities.[59]

For generations, most American farmers had at least dabbled in colonial and transatlantic markets, but in the early nineteenth century many
more grew more export crops for yet more distant customers. In addition, their wives took in work such as weaving and braiding palm-leaf
hats, their daughters spent a year or two before marriage tending machinery in factories, and everyone bought more goods shipped in from
many new sources. These developments focus our attention again on the
"Born Liberal" question discussed early in this chapter: were Americans
voluntarist from the start, or did they become so later? Many historians
point specifically to the antebellum era as the moment when Americans
fundamentally changed—and changed in two ways. One change, they argue, was psychological, that Americans became rational, calculating, self-
interested seekers of profits (I address this suggestion in chapter 6). The
other change, they argue, was social, that profit-seeking displaced local
fellowship and undermined the "moral economy." (Moral economy refers to a culture in which community values override individual material ambitions.) Many Americans of the antebellum era, particularly those
who felt injured by the new developments, described the changes around
them in just such terms, as moral collapse.[60]

In Salem, North Carolina, merchants and artisans in the 1830s and '40s faced growing competition from outside the community, but also growing opportunities. Both fear and ambition led them to challenge the church's restrictions on what they could make and sell and whom they could employ (including the church's injunction against using slaves). Eventually, church leaders conceded, loosened the constraints, and in 1856 finally dissolved their authority over businesses. Henry Leinbach, a local shoemaker, church elder, and loser in these struggles, commented during the 1830s debates: "Rough times, these. It appears there is little love among us any more . . . . Times are hard, and many people do not do as they wish others to do unto them." One of the winners in this transformation, on the other hand, spoke in a different, Emersonian language — "I relied on myself, I depended upon myself, I took care of myself" — the language of the ascending laissez-faire ideology.[61]

Many artisans found themselves outproduced and undersold by distant competitors. A resident of Salem in the 1830s noted that she preferred to order her shoes from Philadelphia because they "wear and fit better than any I have ever owned." She may have been one of those whom shoemaker Henry Leinbach had in mind when he referred to neighbors with "little love." Merchants had to compete with traveling salesmen and outside grain buyers. They made complex financial arrangements with out-of-town creditors. Farmers also encountered new challenges and opportunities. Eastern grain producers faced being undersold by Midwestern grain now arriving on canal boats. Other farmers found new markets in Europe for their crops, most notably for slave-produced cotton. The expansion and restructuring of the economy, including the removal of many legal restrictions on entrepreneurs, made new winners and losers. As I described in chapter 2, many Northern farmers sold out to their more successful neighbors and many farmers' sons had to either move west in search of new land or to become wage earners. In the cities, farm boys formed, together with immigrants, a growing laboring class toiling on wharves and in the warehouses. In the South, small-holding and tenant farmers fell further behind the plantation gentry. On the plantations themselves, mass production of cotton worsened conditions for the slaves. Inequality widened and that widening may explain the sag in Americans' physical well-being during this era.[62]

The economy often required and the new transportation now enabled more Americans to move farther more often. Millions moved west; millions moved east. Migrants from the countryside and immigrants from Europe multiplied the population of American cities sevenfold between 1830 and 1860, to over 3.5 million people — 12 percent of the population nationwide. Mobility marked the century. In 1861, Abraham Lincoln bid farewell to the people of Springfield, Illinois, as he left to take up the presidency in Washington. He addressed them, "my friends . . . whose kindness . . . I owe everything." Yet most Springfield residents had only recently arrived in town; very few had been there over a quarter-century earlier to extend any kindnesses to the young Lincoln. Other communities all over the country experienced similarly high levels of coming and going. An English woman visiting New York City wrote in 1842 of May 1, the day when customarily all rental leases expired, "From the peep of day till the twilight may be seen carts, which go at a rate of speed astonishingly rapid, laden with furniture of every kind, racing up and down the city, as if its inhabitants were fleeing from a pestilence." Foreign observers before and after this era described Americans as constantly on the move—"almost nomadic" in the words of Englishman James Bryce—but mobility was probably at its greatest in the middle decades of the nineteenth century.[63]

Migration brought diversity and disruption to America's towns and villages. Typically, an elite of merchants, lawyers, doctors, manufacturers, financiers, and, in the countryside, farmers with large holdings formed the leading circles in American communities. Such men, like Lincoln in Springfield, held both formal and informal positions of authority and they represented the town to the outside world. Their relatively settled lives, like their stately homes (many of which still stand), largely shape our images of the nineteenth century. But those images hide our view of most rural and small-town Americans, who were transient (their ramshackle dwellings crumpled long ago).[64]

In the cities, relatively new white-collar workers, such as bookkeepers, secretaries, tellers, and clerks of various sorts (almost all men in those days), formed into a lower middle class. Artisans made up the core of the stable manual class, but some of them began to employ others and became nascent industrialists. At the same time, the numbers of seamen, teamsters, day workers, factory employees, and other wage laborers grew greatly. Distinct city neighborhoods defined by residents' occupation, age, ethnicity, and income coalesced out of what had been streets of mixed uses and mixed residents. In upstate Kingston, New York, for example, Irishmen who came in the 1820s to work on the canals clustered near the waterfront, forming "New Dublin," a neighborhood that soon gained a fearsome reputation. In Detroit during the midcentury, "transient and unattached males—young lawyers, traveling businessmen, petty clerks, hotel waiters, and manual workers of all kinds—who concentrated in boarding houses and similar places downtown helped create

a 'bachelor subculture'" served by "saloons, billiard halls, and brothels."
New York's Bowery was the same writ larger. Repulsed by these urban
scenes, many affluent middle-class men removed their families from
downtowns, sometimes taking them as far as the new commuter suburbs, a ferry or long carriage ride away, thereby also reinforcing the domestic bourgeois family. As these residential enclaves developed, they demanded legal separation from the big city.[65]

The emergence of distinct neighborhoods combined with the growing
diversity, transiency, and inequality to undermine community consensus.
As early as the 1820s, according to one historian, "the traditional community, where every aspect of society—geographic, social, political, and
economic—overlapped, was dying out." The communities that still appeared to be tranquil and solidary were ones that growth passed by, such
as upcountry New England villages and Midwestern towns where the
trains never stopped. There, few newcomers arrived, many young people left, those who stayed intermarried, and one could imagine an *Our
Town* familiarity. Elsewhere, however, growth was common and fragmentation proceeded. In Underhill, Vermont, the rapid influx of newcomers and the arrival of evangelical ministries between 1800 and 1840 led
to repeated disputes over where in the sprawling township the Congregational and town meetinghouse should be located, disputes that drove
at least a couple of ministers first to distraction and then out of the community. Cultural diversity often led to intergroup tension. In rural Ohio,
immigrants from different regions of Germany escalated a dispute into
a church burning. In 1844, riots between Protestants and Irish Catholics
in Philadelphia left thirty or more dead in the streets—only one of several calamitous street battles among hundreds of less dramatic bloody
brawls in the antebellum era. Certainly, community conflict had a long
history, as we saw even in early Puritan towns. But the breadth and complexity of conflicts, and, more broadly, of estrangement from the local
society, grew.[66]

Expanding contacts with the outside, migration, growth, and diversity
rearranged neighboring relationships. As before, neighbors depended
on one another for practical everyday matters, for help in emergencies, and for some sort of social life; they exchanged labor at harvesting, responded to fires, helped nurse the ill, and attended church socials.
George C. Duffield described how an Iowa settler would, upon killing
a deer, bring neighbors around to share the venison. Such bonds may
or may not entail emotional commitment. A German immigrant to rural Illinois wrote in 1851 that "the Americans living around us are thor-
oughly good neighbors, ready and willing to be of help" but also that
when "doing business they have no conscience at all." Americans of this

era, as in the century before, saw a mixture of the practical and the social in relations with neighbors. The rare utopian settlement aside, Americans founded nineteenth-century communities as economic enterprises. Many were essentially real-estate speculations, bets on the caprice of weather and of railroad companies. As before, nineteenth-century neighbors tracked, calibrated, and enforced debts from their exchanges; failures to fully reciprocate led to acrimonious suits. In one critical development, however, Americans began untwining the strands that composed neighborhood ties. For example, common farmers started hiring outside help rather than neighbors to bring in harvests, and families started using professional undertakers rather than neighbors to prepare their dead for burial. We should not exaggerate the scale of these developments; farmers, for example, persisted in exchanging labor with their neighbors into the twentieth century. It would take generations for most Americans to see their neighbors as "only neighbors," as the people who just happen to live nearby but are neither practically nor socially critical. Yet the trend had begun.[67]

Given this unwinding and the growing connections to the outside world, local communities lost some hold over their residents. As in Salem, North Carolina, town and church elders in many places lost their authority to set prices and wages. In many towns, leaders lost control over voting. At one time, American elections typically proceeded by town meeting or voice vote; in some cases, official records listed who had voted for whom. This system obviously put pressure on electors to conform to the wishes of local elites. Later, having voters drop colored party "tickets" into a box still made their decisions public. Adoption of the secret "Australian ballot" late in the century ended local elites' ability to monitor people's votes (and electors' chances to sell their votes). Various external connections and opportunities provided residents with more independence from their neighbors. They could shop for nicer shoes, they could seek nicer spouses, they could plead their rights in state courts, and they could more easily pick up and leave—which Americans of the era did in great numbers.[68]

However, the loosening of local ties did not mean, as some read it, that Americans became isolated or without other forms of community. Historian Robert Wiebe has argued that the connecting of America's "island communities" to the wider world caused a loss of local control, a rise in alienation, and a backlash against modernity—a backlash, for example, of nativism. Perhaps, but Americans of the nineteenth century enthusiastically joined up with people in all sorts of groups: ethnic lodges, social clubs, lecture societies, fraternities, sisterhoods, and most especially, the prototype of the voluntary association, Protestant congregations.[69]

Salvation through Solidarity

In 1800, most Americans, whatever their beliefs, remained "unchurched." But the religious stirrings that had begun in the late eighteenth century swirled into a tornado by the 1830s, reaching many of the poorest and most far-flung Americans. Young, energetic, and plain-speaking preachers for new denominations like the Methodist Episcopalians, Disciples of Christ, and dissident Baptists drew enthusiastic audiences. Slaves found Christ, even though masters tried to hide him; free blacks established their own congregations. Revivals and camp meetings brought thousands of Americans together in prayer. Mystical sects built experimental communes. Americans founded new religions, and immigrants brought yet other ones. And religiously imbued social movements, notably abolitionism and temperance, mobilized millions.

Religious diversity and religious competition fed one another. When the states disestablished official churches in the early 1800s, they released yet more rivalry among faiths. It was, wrote historian of religion Martin Marty, "a textbook example of free enterprise in the marketplace of religion, a competition in which the fittest survived," one in which backwoods ministers found that their "first enemy was neither the devil nor the woman but the Baptist." The Catholic Church, a church by birth and for life in Europe, had in America to fend off challengers seeking to raid its flock. One priest dispatched to Maryland complained in 1821, "There are Swarms of false teachers [Methodist preachers] all through the Country, in every School house, in every private house—you hear nothing but night meetings, Class meetings, love feasts &c &c." Among Protestant churches, older Calvinist denominations suffered defections, particularly by those of modest means who rejected elitist doctrines of predestination. Churches proselytized through missions, camp revivals, and aid to the spiritually and often materially destitute. Evangelical ministers generally scorned what they considered to be overeducated, overfed, and overly boring reverends of old-line denominations, and those reverends scorned what they considered to be uneducated, unkempt, and undisciplined backwoods preachers. Later in the century, even atheists came together in formal association. This ferocious competition made church allegiances a matter determined not by people's birthplaces or family histories nor even by their own pasts, but by their choice renewed each day. More Americans joined organized religion, but still not most. One observer estimated that all the churches in Boston in 1867 could accommodate but one-fourth of the residents. Only by about 1900 did most Americans become effectively "churched."[70]

Ministers of the new religious movements typically preached an optimistic theology of individual conscience and democracy. Older ideas of
predestination implied that the hierarchy of this world carried into the
next, which in turn made average parishioners fear eternal damnation.
The evangelists brought a much happier gospel. Two of their hymns convey the new message:

> Can Christ our God a Moloch be,
> Pleas'd with his creatures' misery?
> Dooming nine-tenths of men that fell,
> To burning flames and endless hell? . . .
> Thy saving grace for all is free,
> And none are doom'd to misery.

And:

> Know then that every soul is free
> To choose his life and what he'll be
> For this eternal truth has giv'n
> That God will force no man to heav'n.

An old-line Massachusetts minister complained that the laity had begun
to "to think and act for themselves." Importantly, however, the evangelicals did not foster reclusive or solipsistic religion but instead the voluntary joining together of the faithful in revivals, camp meetings, and new
churches—not the personal church of Lucy Mack Smith but the strong
community of her son's Mormon church.[71]

The new congregations also provided sociability for millions of Americans whose predecessors had gone without. Especially in rural areas, people went to church to see, be seen, be entertained, meet the opposite sex,
hear the news, and deal with issues of common concern, as well as to exercise their faith. Much the same happened in the expanding immigrant
quarters of large cities. The Irish and Italians supported separate ethnic
parishes; Jews formed synagogues with coreligionists who had come from
the same regions of Europe. Black churches gave African Americans a
critically important space free of white surveillance, and regionally based
churches often comforted migrants—"Yankees" in Congregational and
Presbyterian churches, for example, and Southerners in Baptist and fundamental sects. Some churches even provided members with secular benefits, such as burial and life insurance.[72]

One gets a sense of the church's social role on the frontier from the diary of Kitturah Belknap. Born in Ohio in 1820, Belknap moved with her
husband to Iowa at age nineteen and then on to Oregon ten years later.

She worked a hard frontier woman's life, combining indoor tasks, such as spinning flax to make linen for sale, with occasional harvesting in the brutal sun. She bore nine children, five of whom were lost infancy or childhood. In June,1841, in Iowa, the then–twenty-one-year-old wrote in her diary about a forthcoming camp meeting and its social side:

> Now that the corn is layed by, George and I are going to take a vacation and go about ten miles away to a camp meeting. There are four young men and two girls going with us, but I made them promise there should be no sparking and they should all be in their proper places in time of service (for they were all members of the church). If they did not set a good example before the world and show which side they were on they could not go with me and they behaved to the letter.

British traveler Simon Ferrall's cynical description of an 1820s camp meeting may suggest why Kitturah Belknap was concerned:

> The girls, dressed in all colours of the rainbow, congregated to display their persons and costumes; the young men came to see the girls, and considered it a sort of "frolic" . . . . [T]he young married and unmarried women promenaded round the tents, and their smiling faces formed a striking contrast to the demure countenances of their more experienced sisters, who, according to their age or temperament, descanted on the folly, or condemned the sinfulness of such conduct.

In winter, Kitturah Belknap's family hosted traveling preachers and services, as in January 1844:

> The meeting is over and the house cleaned up. We had a good time and the house was packed every night. Good sleighing, and everybody seemed to be interested. . . . The meeting lasted for ten days. Had over twenty conversions, and I thought that was about the best time I ever had. I cooked by the fireplace and our one room served for the church, kitchen, dining-room, bedroom, and study for the preacher. Sometimes we had three or four as they came from adjoining circuits to help us thru the work.

In many communities, such informal meetings developed into physical, permanent churches.[73]

The founding of congregations, however, could also stir conflict. In the early 1800s, along the Vermont–New Hampshire border, an itinerant and untalented Freewill Baptist minister, William Smyth Babcock, repeatedly failed at starting a church. He finally established one after the woman he had newly married announced to the townsfolk that an angel had visited her with instructions for them. Shortly afterwards, other town women reported their own angelic visitors carrying contrary instructions. The witnesses' fevered competition led to Reverend Babcock's departure. In central Minnesota in the late 1800s, one observer claimed that the Lutherans "argued predestination in the saloons with their tongues . . . and settled [it] in the alley with their fists." Another recalled that "neighbor did not speak to neighbor. . . . Brothers and sisters were sundered from one another." In small or stagnant towns with only one or a few denominations, the church reinforced ties among local residents, but elsewhere, church involvement could draw residents' attention away from the community to sectarian loyalties. Protestant churches and their benevolent societies also mobilized members around national issues. Some denominations, for example, rallied against slavery, for the Union cause, and behind Lincoln's re-election in 1864.[74]

Congregations supervised members' morality as churches had done a century earlier, but less stringently. Church leaders exhorted congregants to self-discipline, insisted on standards, and on occasion investigated, tried, and excommunicated troublesome members. In upstate New York's Oneida County early in the century, Presbyterian, Methodist, and Baptist elders investigated congregants' family lives; they censured adulterers, wife beaters, and those whose domestic piety was deemed wanting. The antebellum First Presbyterian Church of Philadelphia suspended members found to play cards, swear, or drink. In the 1870s, a church in southern Illinois excommunicated a mill owner suspected of cheating his customers. Members who were moving away often bore letters of recommendation from their hometown ministers to churches in their new towns. Ministers and deacons continued to exercise authority over members of their own churches, but carried notably less authority in the wider community than they had in the eighteenth century.[75]

Ministers faced resistance when they tried to extend their writ beyond the church. One such effort in the 1820s involved trying to enforce the "Puritan Sunday" by banning commercial activities and, most heatedly debated, by ending Sunday mail delivery. Outside of New England, Americans had long conducted business or amused themselves after (or instead of) attending church services. Moreover, many immigrants brought along the "continental Sunday" devoted to pleasure, such as beer hall festivities. During periods of religious revival, the mainline Protestant ministers won Sunday prohibitions. In the 1840s, for example, some town fathers put chains across streets on Sundays to bar carriages. But the campaign to end Sunday mail, led by the Presbyterians, foundered on the resistance not only of businessmen but also of evangelical ministers and laymen who saw it as a power grab by a high-status church. Later in the century, Congress did suspend Sunday mail service, and state and

local "blue laws" closed down many businesses on Sunday. But those suc-
cesses depended on the churches combining forces with organized labor. In most places, Sunday in America ended up not being Puritan but
continental; it eventually included, scandalously, even baseball. Similarly,
church leaders encountered resistance to religious instruction in the public schools. Many wanted to transform the practice of using the Bible for
reading exercises into explicit teaching. The movement had some nomi-
nal success but eventually succumbed to public pressure that the schools
remain nonsectarian. By 1896, most American school districts did not require any Bible reading. More broadly, churches, even as they grew rapidly in number and size, increasingly confronted the ethos of religious democracy and voluntarism. They could welcome people in but could not
command them to come; they could count on the enthusiasm of members but could not cow the unchurched. Despite growing membership,
most nineteenth-century Americans remained outside churches. Abraham Lincoln was one. Skeptical as a young man, the Civil War led him to
believe in the hand of Providence and search for signs of God's will. Yet
even the later Lincoln of "firmness in the right as God gives us to see the
right" remained officially unchurched.[76]

Churchmen themselves recognized the contradiction they faced:
on the one hand, they represented absolute Authority, and on the
other hand, in an increasingly voluntarist society, they presided at the
whim of their congregants. Ministers who forgot who paid their wages
would soon be reminded. They tended flocks that increasingly led their
shepherds.[77]

Clubs

Grassroots Protestant congregations deviated from old-world, established, hierarchical churches; they were not unlike clubs. And social clubs
of all sorts multiplied over the nineteenth century: lyceums and debating societies, private libraries, choirs, reform movements, professional
guilds, sports teams, civic improvement leagues, Masons and other secret handshake brotherhoods and sisterhoods, temperance clubs, volunteer fire brigades, farmer cooperatives, political parties, art apprecia-
tion societies, self-education classes, abolitionist chapters, middle-class
women's civic improvement leagues, working girls' self-improvement
clubs, and black women's societies, the Grange, businessmen's confer-
ences, volunteer militias, immigrant societies, nativist societies—all
these and many other formal associations listed themselves in local city
directories and their meetings in the press. Many clubs belonged to state
and national federations, linking their members to compatriots around

the country. Many more Americans belonged instead or as well to local, often short-lived, informal associations, such as women's sewing circles, youth "gangs," and, in great number, groups of men meeting in pubs,
saloons, pool halls, and on baseball fields. Club life was noteworthy in
the colonial era—much of the American Revolution had been plotted
in merchants' taverns (see chapter 5)—but flourished much more in the
nineteenth century. Even in rural areas, middle-class people "flocked to
singing schools, dancing classes, and a wide variety of literary associations." By the later decades of the century, there were so many fraternal
and sororal orders such as the Red Men, Odd Fellows, and Pythian Sisters that "everyone seemed to be joining some temple, clan, castle, conclave, hive, or lodge."[78]

Young Henry Pierce provides a lively example. Pierce clerked for and
boarded with a Boston hat seller in the 1840s. He spent most of his evenings at one or another association—the Handel and Haydn Society, a
glee club, and less often, the Bachelor's Club or the Odd Fellows lodge.
At other times he entertained himself informally with fellow store clerks.
Unlike many up-and-coming white-collar workers, Pierce largely gave up
his memberships when he became a partner in the store and married.
Many others continued to be active long enough to become leaders of
major clubs and lodges. Blue-collar and laboring men often joined volunteer fire companies, clubs which typically devoted more time to carousing than to controlling fires. William Magear Tweed of New York City was
not himself of the working class; he helped out in his family's furniture
business and in off hours belonged to the Odd Fellows and Masons. But
Tweed also spent time with young men from the working class and the
underworld. He helped organize a nativist club and then a volunteer fire
company, both of which enlisted many of New York's notorious "Bowery
B'hoys." Tweed turned out to be a skillful leader and ferocious brawler; his
"Big 6" fire company, whose emblem was a tiger, promoted his climb to
power as Boss Tweed of the Tammany Hall political machine.[79]

Associations were easy to join and easy to leave. Yet while members
belonged, they submitted themselves to group control. It was in the clubs
as well as the churches of midcentury Jacksonville, Illinois, that many
newcomers planted themselves in the community, learned local norms,
found entertainment, paid dues for life and burial insurance, made professional contacts, obtained references, and occasionally faced censure
if they strayed morally. The Knights of Columbus, for example, banned
men who drank as part of their campaign to mold immigrant Catholics
into "middle-class respectability." Even unrespectable associations had
strong expectations of members. One Pennsylvanian recalled of the antebellum volunteer fire companies that fighting other companies at

whatever bodily risk "was no small part of the duties of firemen." These clubs were in a paradoxical relationship with their members similar to that of the churches: unable to coerce participation and relying on people's free choice to join and stay, they nevertheless made significant demands on those who belonged; loyalty was part of the deal.[80]

Tocqueville, like other observers, acclaimed America's associations. He argued that the lattice of voluntary groups joined citizens together so that they could do the work of the community—a theme picked up many generations later in the discussion of civil society (see chapter 5). But others worried that voluntary associations introduced factionalism. Washington and Madison, for example, decried clubs that might meddle in politics. Historians have picked up the debate. On the Tocquevillian side, Don Doyle has detailed the value of associations in nineteenth-century Jacksonville, Illinois: they united residents otherwise divided by religion, region, or politics; integrated young people and newcomers into the community; disciplined wayward members; provided sociability; sold insurance; and trained people in democracy by holding elections and providing forums for debate. They also "boosted" the town by beautifying it, handling public concerns like orphans and saloons, and recruiting new residents and businesses. In many ways, the associations *made* the local community. Skeptical scholars, however, argue that the voluntary associations instead widened community divisions. One club was for the Yankees, another for migrants from the South, one for Presbyterian women, one for businessmen, and so on. Historian Robert Hine wrote of Midwestern small towns: "A welter of voluntary associations bore off the individual's allegiance and . . . kept alive the spirit of the entire community only in superficial ways." One way that associations seemed divisive was that most tended to include members of the upper and middle classes and exclude the less–well-off members of the community. Also, associations often struggled against one another. For example, moral reform societies pushed temperance while German clubs defended their Sunday beer halls. Affiliations with national organizations, as in the case of churches, stirred cosmopolitan rather than local interest. Although the clubs brought some townsfolk together, particularly those of the middle class, and so were in that way integrating, on balance they reinforced the growing segmentation of most American localities.[81]

One particular kind of informal "group" is worth looking at more closely: *friendship*. Friendships, as we understand them today, probably proliferated only in the last couple of centuries (Jonathan and David, Damon and Pythias notwithstanding). In the nineteenth century in particular, middle-class Americans increasingly participated in emotionally intense same-sex friendships. In letters and diaries, urbane men and women revealed what were, by today's norms, highly romantic feelings and physical longings. Young Daniel Webster would address his closest friend as "dearest" and as "the only friend of my heart, the partner of my joys, griefs, and affections." Stimulated in part by a large reduction of postal rates around 1850 and in part by an expanding sentimental, even maudlin, culture (discussed in chapter 6), many Americans less precocious than Webster—and especially many women—used such expressions in their personal letters and journals. These writings testify to an expansion of freestanding friendships—freestanding in the sense that the relationships existed independently of groups like families or neighbors. Friendships are by nature idiosyncratic—consider the decades-long bond between antislavery firebrand Charles Sumner and romantic poet Henry Wadsworth Longfellow—and they were, by being independent, distinctively voluntary.[82]

The Workplace

Many Americans' social options also expanded, because they began working away from their homes. Most early Americans labored on farms, in artisan workshops, or at kitchen tables, alone or with their children, occasionally with apprentices, boarders, and once in a while with neighbors. A visitor to Lynn, Massachusetts, in 1780s described artisan quarters: alongside many houses in Lynn stood small, wooden buildings called "ten-footers." In the cramped space, a couple of journeymen shoemakers pounded away alongside their master in whose next-door home and under whose authority they lived. As I described in chapter 2, artisan masters built industrial "manufacturys," retail stores, and offices. They employed more workers and clerks, but employees by that time no longer lived in their employers' homes; they lived on their own. For masters, hiring and firing as business conditions demanded was more economical than remaining responsible for a worker's room and board. And workers themselves often preferred to take a higher wage at a new job rather than remain bound to a master and his household. Distinct places of work, separate from households or neighborhoods, emerged that provided a relatively new kind of social group: coworkers.[83]

Ties formed in workplaces typically extended beyond the job as men (much less often women) relaxed with coworkers in saloons and gambling spots. Some formed rowdy packs which toured the town in the evening. The most notorious were the New York Bowery's "Rude B'hoys," decked out in flashy clothes, mouthing off and ready for a round of fisticuffs. Young women in the textile mills often worked alongside their relatives but made new acquaintances and friends. Ties among coworkers fostered labor organization. Strikes and other labor actions, although waxing and waning as economic conditions changed, generally increased in tempo and vigor over the century. That so many gave up pay and even risked violence to express solidarity strongly testified to the importance of these worksite relationships.[84]

The work setting only began forming in the nineteenth century. In 1900, most Americans did not yet have a distinct workplace. The nearly one-third of men who were farmers did not, most women did not, and only some urban workers did. In 1880 in Philadelphia, for example, while almost all bookbinders worked a half-mile or more from their homes, most confectioners and cabinetmakers still worked inside their homes. Nonetheless, the workplace gradually emerged as an independent source of social membership.[85]

Quantity and Quality

Americans' social options multiplied. Growth, easier mobility, and new ideas opened up households and local communities, stimulated church foundings, fostered workplaces, and spurred associations. The diaries of upwardly mobile women in rural New England in the 1840s and '50s, writes historian Catherine Kelley, reveal "the ever-increasing pace of sociability." Accounts of dances, dinners, and other companionable events elbowed aside earlier descriptions of church Sundays and ministers' sermons. The *quality* of both the changed and the new relationships—their durability, reliability, intimacy—is harder to assess. More and more, these were voluntary relationships. Fathers could not be as patriarchal, neighbors as censorious, ministers as demanding, employers as arbitrary as in earlier eras. But individuals also had more decisions to make, juggling loyalties to multiple groups and figuring out who were their "real friends." (Falling in with bad friends motivated many a nineteenth-century cautionary novel.) Multiple group memberships may have generated—according to one *fin-de-siècle* theory—the emergence of true "individuality," because people had increasingly distinctive sets of social connections; they could, at least in theory, be different people in different settings. More social complexity also raised questions about the sincerity of acquaintances and the trustworthiness of strangers. If new social opportunities brought new "friend[s] of my heart," intensely personal relationships, they also brought new anxieties. Who would be and who would stay friends? In the nineteenth century, these changes and the issues they raised confronted mostly the growing middle class; in the twentieth century, they spread beyond.[86]

MORE GROUPS, MORE MEMBERS, MORE VOLUNTARISM: THE TWENTIETH CENTURY

In the middle of the twentieth century, American youth heard that they were a generation of conformists. David Riesman, whose *The Lonely Crowd* became the bestselling sociology book of the century and got him on the cover of *Time* magazine, argued that, whereas parents of the nineteenth century had installed in their children a moral "gyroscope" to sustain their independence, twentieth-century parents equipped their children instead with a social "radar" to track other people and better conform. Americans, Riesman and his coauthors famously said, had changed from "inner-" to "other-directed." Noted studies such as *Escape from Freedom* and *The Organization Man* made similar arguments, as did novels (Holden Caulfield's angst in *Catcher in the Rye*) and films (Uncle Murray's refusal to grow up in *A Thousand Clowns*). The president of Yale lamented the class of 1954's reputation as "the silent generation." Not long after such plaints about conformism, American youths' social radars apparently went haywire. A few spent the later '60s storming the barricades or "tuning in and dropping out"; many others cheered them on. And deeper changes were under way. Betty Friedan's *The Feminine Mystique* in 1963 heralded a transformation of gender roles. "I hear this over and over again," Mrs. Friedan said a year later. "Women are so delighted to know that there is nothing wrong with them for being bored with household drudgery and wanting to be a person in their own right, rather than an appendage to their children and husbands." When Reisman wrote a new preface to the twentieth-anniversary edition of *The Lonely Crowd*, he had second thoughts about whether young Americans were really marching in lockstep; he noted "a greater concern with autonomy and a rejection of adjustment as immoral compromise."[87]

In the twentieth century, most Americans came to experience the greater social options and the looser group constraints that middle-class Americans encountered in the nineteenth century. Women, in particular, stepped out energetically and in large numbers from under the shelter of home and husband. The wave of social changes crested in the late 1960s and early '70s, but the expansion of options started before and continued beyond those several years. Opportunities for belonging multiplied, and groups' hold on individuals loosened. By the end of the century, the wave of change subsided. In particular, time constraints on the middle class and financial constraints on the working class stalled the expansion of social opportunities, with the possible exception of Internet opportunities.

Beyond the Victorian Family

We can sometimes see social changes play out in the course of one person's life. "Alice Neal," born in 1928 to an Irish immigrant mother in Berkeley, California, became one of a cohort studied for life by researchers at the university. As a teen, Alice focused on friends and dating, with her only clear goal being marriage. "From 15 to 19 [1943–47] I was just crazy in the head. I pursued boys wildly, never had a moment when I wasn't chasing some boy, trying to get him to like me." At nineteen, she married, largely on the rebound, war veteran "George Neal." By 1959, over a decade later, Alice was a sociable, thirty-year-old homemaker raising three children in a comfortable marriage. In 1961, her life changed. Over George's objections, Alice took a part-time job in a store to help pay for their new house. She performed so well that in a few years the owner appointed her store manager. In 1971, forty-three-year-old Alice told university researchers that she was enjoying her job but having problems with her oldest daughter, who was living the turmoil of the era, including taking drugs and dropping out of college. Alice also reported that George was not earning much money and was acting immaturely. By 1982, at fifty-four, Alice provided stability for a sometimes chaotic, three-generation household coping with job disruptions and alcoholism. George, she said, was drinking more, had become dependent on her, and was not much of a romantic partner. Reflecting back on her life, the now middle-aged Alice described going out to work as its key moment and the job as her prime satisfaction. She had been a flighty girl dreaming of husband and children; she was now a businesswoman and the bedrock of her family. Every life story has its own particularities, but Alice Neal's illustrates some of what happened to women and families over the twentieth century.[88]

In 1892, suffragette Elizabeth Cady Stanton declared that, "in discussing the rights of woman, we are to consider, first, what belongs to her as an individual . . . [as] the arbiter of her own destiny." Women had come some way from Puritan John Winthrop's claim in 1645 that "a true wife accounts her subjection her honor and freedom." Stanton's statement was nonetheless still ahead of its time and brought controversy. In 1899, a sociologist, the Reverend Dr. S. G. Smith of Minnesota State University, asserted that "one of the greatest evils of modern civilization . . . is the woman wage-earner. Nature intends man to be the producer, woman the consumer." His comments in turn brought strong ripostes. One angry reader called him a "slap-dash sociologist" and wrote that "if a man cannot hold his own against the competition of women, he is poor stuff and entitled to no pity." Stanton's defenders emphasized women's need for income and intellectual stimulation. Yet even the early feminists were partly apologetic, admitting that a woman's primary role was indeed that of helpmate. It took much of the new century to make Elizabeth Cady Stanton's affirmation that women ought to be arbiters of their own destinies real in ways that she could have hardly forecast.[89]

With the exception of the baby boom (from the late 1940s to early 1960s — Betty Friedan's era of "household drudgery"), birth rates kept dropping until they leveled off at about 2 per woman around 1980. Although the average American woman at the start of the twentieth century spent most of her adulthood caring for children, the decline in births and the extension of lifetimes meant that, at the end of the century, the average woman spent most of her adulthood doing other, new things. One of those new things was getting advanced schooling; eventually more women than men went to college. And another new thing was going to work even when married and even while raising young children. Around 1900, poorer wives, notably black and immigrant ones, worked outside their homes, commonly as maids. Other wives either worked at home sewing collars, selling eggs, taking in laundry, and so on, or did not work for pay at all. Over the twentieth century, the proportion of wives officially counted in the labor force rose steadily — mounting even through the "Ozzie and Harriet" 1950s — from 5 percent in 1900 to 50 percent in 2000. Although hardly any married mothers with young children worked around 1900, about one in five did in 1960 and over three in five did in 2007.[90]

Economics — material needs and material dreams — drew most wives to outside jobs, but increasingly, new ideas about the nature of women also spurred, sustained, and justified working. As economic historian Claudia Goldin put it, it was a shift from wives who worked "because they and their families 'need[ed] the money' to those who are employed, at least in part, because occupation and employment define one's fundamental identity and societal worth." Americans who had once viewed work for women as an unfortunate necessity, as Elizabeth Cady Stanton's defenders did in 1899, came to see it as personal fulfillment. In the 1930s, three-fourths of Americans disapproved of a wife working if her husband could support her; and most school systems fired female teachers once they married. In the 1950s, wives at work were no longer an oddity, but still atypical. (It was new enough to lampoon; the famous "I Love Lucy" episode in which Lucy and Ethel try to work on a chocolate factory assembly line first aired in 1952.) By the 1980s, three-fourths of Americans *approved* of a wife working even if her husband could support her; and the government *defended* her right to work. Homemaking, in contrast, lost prestige. In 1977, the high school students of "Middletown," especially the girls, rated "being a good cook and housekeeper" not nearly as important a quality for a mother as had Middletown high school students fifty years earlier. As American women adopted more of the breadwinner role, American men adopted—slowly and in small steps, to be sure— some of the homemaker role.[91]

The two-job family became the norm for American women, although not the ideal for all of them. As late as the mid-2000s, about one-third of women agreed that "It is much better for everyone involved if the man is the achiever outside the home and the woman takes care of the home and family." (A generation earlier, two-thirds had agreed with this position). Half of women told interviewers that if they could they would stay home and raise children. The trend of wives working, in fact, leveled off around the turn of the millennium. College-educated women who came of age around 2000 were a bit likelier to stay home and have children earlier than were similar women about a decade before. The tidal wave of career women that emerged from the 1960s seemed to have quieted. Nonetheless, the long-term surge of wives taking on paid work and full careers is one of the major social changes of the twentieth century.[92]

Another major change was wives' increasing ability and willingness to leave marriages. Historically, marriages usually ended when the men walked out, but over the decades, more women initiated formal divorce proceedings. They filed about two-thirds of the cases in the twentieth century. And, often when men filed, it was in response to their wives' self-assertion. Court records allow researchers to snoop on marriages—on troubled marriages, at least. In the nineteenth century, divorcing couples complained about spouses who failed to meet the basic standards of the "separate spheres": husbands who did not bring home enough money, stay sober, or restrain their tempers, and wives who did not keep a nice house, provide enough sex, or safeguard their reputations. Continuing trends that had begun in the nineteenth century, twentieth-century couples increasingly complained about "cruelty," boredom (sexual and otherwise), and the absence of love. Wives increasingly charged that husbands denied them affection, companionship, and personal freedom. More Americans divorced, scholars conclude, not because more Americans lost faith in marriage, but in large part because more of them "load[ed] marriage with high expectations."[93]

Divorce rates rose exponentially from four per thousand married couples around 1900 to twenty-three per thousand marriages around 1980 and leveled off afterwards. Scholars attribute most of this rise to wives' growing self-reliance, which permitted them to leave marriages that failed to meet those rising expectations. Women gained greater independence through their greater earning power and through expanding legal rights. Divorcing kept getting easier, culminating in "no-fault" divorce in the 1970s. Unhappy spouses no longer needed to charge one another with grievous betrayals (before, many had to fake adultery in order to satisfy the law) or to move to an easy-divorce state. Now, couples could just agree that they were "incompatible." In 2005, the U.S. Supreme Court expressed the now no longer startling view—but one that would have made earlier jurists blanch—that a "state may not give to a man the kind of dominion over his wife that parents exercise over their children." (We'll see later about that dominion over children.) And the more women attained legal equality, the more the law assumed they had attained economic equality, leaving many divorced mothers with their children but also with little financial support.[94]

As divorce rates rose to unprecedented heights, marriage rates did *not* fall to unprecedented lows. Marriage rates rose greatly over the century and then they fell back. Between 1900 and 1960, the percentage of adult Americans who were married increased from under 60 to over 70 percent; it then declined by 2000 to about where it had begun a century earlier. (Marriage rates for African Americans, however, started dropping decades before 1960.*) In roughly the first half of the twentieth century, Americans married increasingly young, probably because economic opportunities for men generally improved. During the 1950s, half of American women married—as Alice Neal had—as teenagers. Then came the reversal: young Americans increasingly waited to marry, so that by the early 2000s women married at an average age of twenty-five.[95]

In the late twentieth century, middle-class Americans delayed marrying mainly to pursue college and postgraduate education; working-class Americans delayed marrying mainly to wait for jobs that could support a family. As they waited, more couples lived together without ceremony. In 2000, about half of all newlyweds had lived together before making their union official; many had lived with someone else before that relationship. Also, more women, often without stable relationships, had children while they waited to marry. In the 1990s, four in ten firstborn children arrived to unmarried women—compared to one in ten in the 1930s. Despite some celebrity cases, it was mainly less-educated women who became unwed mothers. Often, the babies' fathers walked away; in other instances, women preferred having a child as they waited for "Mr. Right" to show up with the right-sized paycheck. Two different trends thus developed for American women: college-educated women married, albeit

* Marriage rates among African Americans started dropping in the 1920s and '30s and continued falling, creating a large difference in marital status between black and other Americans by 2000. The massive migration of blacks from the rural South and then the collapse of manufacturing jobs in the North probably account for this divergence.

later than their mothers had, and raised children with a partner, while poorly educated women often had children early, remained unmarried, and raised their children alone. This divergence represented a stall or reversal in the long-term, growing inclusion of more Americans into the bourgeois way of life.[96]

Americans continued to value marriage, but they, especially women, increasingly insisted that marriages be financially sound, egalitarian, and serve personal needs. A leading student of the family concluded that "marriage has increasingly become less the pledge of permanent commitment than a conditional commitment to remain together as long as both parties are willing and able." Such marriages now also carried rising emotional and psychological expectations, a point to which I will return shortly.[97]

We can see how Americans continued to value marriage in yet another major development, the expansion of the "empty nest" stage. Because Americans lived longer and had fewer children, they spent more of their lives as childless couples. In 1900, about one in ten elderly Americans lived just with his or her spouse; in 2000, about five in ten did. More Americans spent many more years living with just a spouse, that same person across the table at breakfast each and every day. And research suggests that this is a generally happy stage of life—especially if the children remember to call.[98]

Women's greater independence drew charges from some quarters that they had become selfish, that the "new woman" sacrificed her marriage and children for personal interests. (We saw that similar charges had been made a century earlier.) Other observers worried that greater independence had been a snare for women, because it gave men easy access to sex and allowed them to shed their responsibilities, leaving the women to care for any incidental children. Women probably did feel ambivalent. In a 2007 survey, most female respondents said that American mothers were currently doing a worse job as parents than their mothers had a generation earlier. Only one in five employed mothers with children at home said that a full-time job was their ideal and an equal proportion said that staying home was their ideal. Most American women in the 2000s seemed to prefer a neotraditional arrangement: he works full-time, she works part-time. Yet, for all the uncertainty, greater equality seems to have improved how Americans, most clearly wives, felt about their marriages—and themselves. By the twenty-first century, American women, especially the educated and the employed, for the first time reported feeling as healthy as men did.[99]

Children, too, gained greater leverage within the family. Legal authorities in the twentieth century increasingly intervened on behalf of children against their parents. New laws, for example, banned child labor, required universal education and immunization, punished child abuse, and allowed officials to take away mistreated children. Public intrusion into family life seemed to reprise the control exercised by colonial New England magistrates—but now in reverse, to support the child rather than the parent. Inside the family, parents indulged children more; made fewer demands on them either to work or to do chores; forked over an allowance and padded it; and gave children more toys, clothes, and freedom. Surveys dating from the 1920s on asked Americans what values were most important to teach children. Early in the century, Americans stressed obedience and good manners; later, they stressed independence and thinking for oneself. Parents came to value autonomy in their children even if it meant encouraging rebelliousness. They, especially the middle class, parented more intensively, trying to "cultivate" their children into accomplished and self-confident adults by sowing more money and effort into their children's health, academic progress, and social life than parents a century earlier could or would.[100]

Increasing rates of divorce and unwed motherhood meant, of course, that more children after the 1950s lacked parenting of any kind from a father. That took a toll; children in fatherless homes face higher risks of school setbacks and emotional upsets. But white middle-class children spent relatively little time in such homes. It was a chronic issue for poorer children. (Here again we can see widening inequality in family life over the last few decades.) Most parents generally maintained and even increased the hours they spent with their children while still working and commuting more hours. They gave up leisure and other personal activities for one-on-one "quality time." Around 2000, to take a small illustration, most American children, even most adolescents, ate at least six dinners a week at home with one or more parents. Bourgeois parenting— generous, permissive, and yet intense—emerged among avant-garde middle-class parents in the nineteenth century and was typical by the end of the twentieth. Some children probably felt stifled by such close parenting; younger ones—those below driving age, especially—probably had less freedom to just roam about and get into adventures than their grandparents had. (A few older commentators have waxed nostalgic about their own unsupervised childhoods.) But the interests of children had risen in prominence and for many, perhaps most, American families become the focus of the household—a striking reversal of family life a century or two earlier.[101]

Children's empowerment, especially that of teens, also vexed parents. A *Newsweek* magazine cover declared, "Let's Face It, Our Teenagers Are Out of Control"—and that was in 1956. One concern of parents was, of course, sex. The twentieth century brought the practice of "dating," a new form of unsupervised courtship that allowed young people to explore a number of partners in search of true love. After World War II, practices changed. Couples paired off in high school—girls got "pinned" to signal the bond—and married early. Then, the cultural norms shifted back again to exploring the field. (In a 1960 Smokey Robinson hit, mother advises son: "Before you ask some girl for her hand now/Keep your freedom for as long as you can now/My mama told me/ 'You better shop around.'") Although the timing of the sexual revolution has been debated, it is clear that youth, particularly young women, experimented with sex at increasingly younger ages, starting most surely in the 1920s and accelerating thereafter. One study estimated that roughly a third of teenage girls had premarital sex in the 1950s, half did in the 1960s, and almost two-thirds did in the 1970s. Adult attitudes accommodated: Between the 1960s, when such survey questions were first asked, to the 1980s, Americans increasingly said that premarital sex was acceptable (although they increasingly disapproved of *extra*marital affairs). These liberalizing trends stalled in the 1980s, but American youth, especially in the middle class, claimed much more sexual independence at the end than at the beginning of the century (see, too, discussion of sex in chapter 6).[102]

Children also claimed independence by increasingly living on their own. In the nineteenth century, many adolescents left home, but it was to work in other households as spouses, servants, or apprentices. Those who wanted an education stayed with their parents. Over the twentieth century and especially after the 1950s, young middle-class Americans increasingly left home to live either on their own or with roommates. They could do so in part because families were wealthier and separate households more affordable. (In the economically strained 1970s and '80s, on the other hand, young adults stayed or returned home at slightly higher rates.) Leaving home, getting more schooling, and marrying later combined to create a new stage of life: not living with parents but not yet being fully, separately adult, for example, relying on parents' financial help. Yet another way young Americans showed their new autonomy was by pairing up with people their parents might not approve of. Bucking parents was not new—recall the novelty of love marriages in the late eighteenth century—but in the twentieth century young adults increasingly dated and married across ethnic, religious, and racial lines at rapidly rising rates; some even formed unions with partners of the same sex; and most spent at least some time just "living together." American parents largely accepted these changes; after all, they had themselves nurtured their children's self-direction and self-expression.[103]

While twentieth-century American culture advised husbands and wives *not* to sacrifice themselves to the marriage, it advised parents that they *should* sacrifice themselves for the children. This seeming paradox makes sense in a culture of voluntarism. Both adults freely enter marriage and must fulfill their obligations, yet ultimately each spouse retains the moral right to exit this voluntary association. In contrast, children arrive in families without choice. The parents, who are responsible, thus have in principle an unbreakable commitment; parents cannot legitimately exit parenthood. What the children reciprocally owe the parents, on the other hand, is a matter of their love, not a contract.[104]

All this unbinding of the family—later marriage or no marriage, increased premarital sex, more divorce, less childbearing, more women working, growing gender equality, cohabitation, child empowerment, and so on—brought what consequences? Some feared that these changes undermined the family's emotional and spiritual quality. Historian Christopher Lasch asserted in his 1977 lament for the Victorian family, *Haven in a Heartless World*, that "family life [has] become so painful, marriage so fragile, relations between parents and children so full of hostility." American survey respondents shared this bleak opinion of (other) Americans' families. Critically, however, Americans insisted that *their own* families were great and getting greater. Indeed, survey respondents reported high and sustained satisfaction with their own family lives through the tumultuous last decades of the century. This was so even in the face of still higher expectations. For example, marriage advisors increasingly told husbands and wives that they should aspire to be best friends and eternal, avid, and accomplished lovers. Similarly, elites raised the bar for how much parents had to attend to, nurture, and even befriend their children. Average Americans seemed to share these rising standards for families.[105]

At the same time, Americans endorsed rising standards for individual fulfillment, too, which pulled them in a different, if not opposite, direction. Those expectations could have led to avoiding marriage, but seem to have instead led to waiting longer, testing relationships in cohabitation, leaving the bad ones, and giving each member of the family "more space." In 1924, Robert and Helen Lynd described marriages in "Middletown" as dismal, but the Middletown researchers of 1977 concluded that "the quality of marriage seem[ed] to have improved substantially" in the intervening half-century. The survey data on Americans' evaluations of their marriages is mixed, but suggests that the quality seemed to be improve, at least for better-educated couples. Similarly, the emotional dimension of parent-child relationships—despite, or perhaps because of, intensive parenting—also seemed to improve over the century.

The remarkable consequence of the growing voluntarization of the family in the twentieth century is not that it engendered strains and dissolutions, which it surely did, but that it more often sustained or even expanded intimacy.[106]

The case of the missing grandmother illustrates this paradox of greater independence with greater affection. In the nineteenth century, the elderly, especially widows, lived with their adult children; by the twenty-first century, the elderly, even widows, commonly lived on their own. One explanation is that the aged—or their children or both—had always preferred living apart, but few could do so until the affluence, pensions, and Social Security of the twentieth century made separate households possible. Another explanation is that Americans' preferences changed, that they had come to care more about being independent than about being with family. The paradox I refer to is this: since the 1960s, young adults have increasingly told poll takers that grandparents living with their offspring was a *good* idea, while the elderly said that they generally *disliked* the idea. More adults seemed to express fondness, at least in theory, for living with their parents. The parents' reluctance probably reflected a desire for their own independence, but also a wish to not burden their children. (The elderly increasingly helped their children financially during this era.) That is, even as parents and adult children more often lived in separate homes, they expressed continuing, probably intensifying, concern for one another.[107]

The case of the missing grandmother also points to another important development in family life: the increasing ease of staying in touch. American women who left the farm for town in the early 1900s reported that they could check up on their aging mothers by ringing through the local telephone switchboard once a day. About a century later, people in the New York area made three hundred thousand calls to the Dominican Republic on a single day through only one out of hundreds of phone services; most of the calls were, we can assume, to kin. One caller told a reporter that he had given up writing letters home: "My mom expects a call at least once and really, a couple of times a week," he said. "She knows it's cheap and she knows it's easy, so if I don't call all the time, she cries." Similarly, a single dollar allows immigrants from Fujian Province in China to speak to family at home for nearly an hour. With cheap plane fare, many immigrants regularly visit family in India, Ghana, or Guatemala; they lead what sociologists call "transnational" lives. And Americans overseas do the same, most poignantly soldiers serving in Iraq who use phones, e-mail, and even web-camera connections to lead "virtual" family lives, talking screen to screen every day with their spouses and children.[108]

Most twentieth-century Americans absorbed the values of the nineteenth-century's avant-garde, bourgeois family; they increasingly sought companionship, gender equality, intensive parenting, and deeper feelings. For many, however, attaining such a family life remained a struggle. Economic conditions for the less educated, especially after the 1970s, forced more mothers into working more than they wanted and created other strains in relationships. For the poorest Americans, financial limitations, rising expectations, and growing independence, such as unwed mothers' expanding legal rights, led them to delay marrying until they could afford the bourgeois family they dreamed about.[109]

Around 2000, as most Americans struggled to sustain the bourgeois family, college-educated Americans formulated and adopted a yet newer model of the family. This model dissolved the old separation between the domestic and the worldly spheres; both husbands and wives entered careers and both nurtured children. Each member of the family could exercise greater independence, for example, pursuing separate interests and friends, but they still expected intense emotional bonding with family. (Alice Neal's aspirations may well have been for this kind of family.) The newest middle-class family was yet more voluntarist. More than ever, an American could leave the parental home or not, marry or not, divorce and remarry or not, parent or not. Still, when married or a parent, the new American spouse was expected to be fully committed to the marriage and any children. Ironically, then, middle-class Americans' emotional investments in family life were never greater.

Sociologist Andrew Cherlin has argued that this new family is less a vibrant institution and more a symbol of individual success. (Being married signals having "made it.") I suggest, instead, that when the new model works it enables both individual and joint success, both practical and emotional success. Although more Americans gained more options for personal achievement outside the family, for the great majority, having a fulfilling family life became even more central. (For most, being happily married *is* success rather than a token of success.) The transition to this model is complex, halting, and for some, still unattainable. Nonetheless, historian Stephanie Coontz seems about right: the "same personal freedoms that allow people to expect more from their married lives also allow them to get more out of staying single and give them more choice than ever before in history." "Marriage has steadily become more fair, more fulfilling, and more effective in fostering the well-being of both adults and children than ever. . . . It has also become more optional and more fragile and yet more important. The historical record suggests that these two seemingly contradictory trends are inextricably interwoven."[110]

The Dispersion of the Neighborhood

Sociologist Morris Janowitz once described Chicago neighborhoods in the mid-twentieth century as "communities of limited liability." Residents were involved but felt free to withdraw their "investments" if staying there no longer met their needs—another way of saying a voluntary community. Several kinds of American groups are of "limited liability," but the term applies particularly well to the twentieth-century locality. Americans settled into their neighborhoods for longer than ever before, but led less of their lives there than ever before.[111]

Increasingly, the American neighborhood was a suburban one. In 1900, about seven in ten Americans lived in rural towns or the countryside. By 2000, only two in ten did; half lived in suburbs. In 1993, the Bureau of the Census announced that it would no longer publish separate statistics for Americans who lived on farms, so few had they become. Within the cities, the most consequential development was the arrival of millions of poor African Americans from the rural South. In many places, the black population grew from negligible to a majority, which in turn stimulated white fear and resistance. Severe racial segregation developed and only started to subside after 1970; racial politics defined much of life in America's big cities. More than any other feature, even social class, the racial makeup of residents distinguished one urban neighborhood from another. Metropolitan areas polarized into black cores and white rings as middle- and working-class white Americans sought separation from blacks and sought—even more earnestly—the cheaper homes and greenery of suburbia.[112]

At the same time—and despite the myth of modern restlessness (see chapter 1)—Americans settled down. The nineteenth-century pattern of transient boarders and lodgers, floating "hobo" populations, and working-class families moving every year essentially ceased. In 1948, when the Census Bureau started to collect firm numbers, 20 percent of Americans had moved into their homes within the previous year. Except for a spike in the mid-1980s, that percentage steadily declined (through the baby boom and baby bust) to about 13 percent in the late 2000s. Americans settled down because employment became steadier; unemployment insurance provided income during layoffs; people could commute farther to work, which allowed families to stay put even when breadwinners changed jobs; and more families owned homes. The more-rooted Americans could invest themselves in their towns and neighborhoods, but it was a "limited liability" investment of limited scope. They remained free to move and freer than before to engage outside their neighborhoods.[113]

Isolation from the local community seemed to be a social problem at the beginning of the century–for *rural* Americans. Experts investigated what was called the "country life" problem—a problem most vividly illustrated by farm youth running off to "bright lights, big cities." Researchers concluded that farmers suffered from "excessive individualism," inability to cooperate, and disconnection from the wider society. Defenders of farm life have decried the reformers' disdain for country people, but many rural Americans did feel isolated. The nearly hundred thousand farm residents surveyed in 1908 by Theodore Roosevelt's Country Life Commission overwhelmingly reported themselves as dissatisfied with their inability to "get together for mutual improvement, entertainment, and social intercourse." A 1919 survey of ten thousand farm households found that "the farm woman [felt] her isolation from neighbors" and wanted more contact with other women. As late as 1940, anthropologists studying rural Landaff, New Hampshire, remarked on the solitude of women in the community; "visiting is extraordinarily infrequent," they noted. Rural women turned to new technologies, such as the radio and telephone, to overcome loneliness. (Phone calls, the anthropologists reported, were "frequent, detailed, and almost interminable.") The automobile and improved roads eventually brought many farm families closer to town, its entertainments, and its clubs. At the same time, however, cars and highways also drew families farther away from the rural neighborhood. When other anthropologists visited Landaff forty years later, in 1980, they also reported that its residents had relatively little social interaction with one another. They attributed isolation in 1980, however, not to physical distance, but to residents now finding their jobs and entertainment outside of Landaff.[114]

Changes in farming also helped dilute rural solidarity. Mechanization first encouraged cooperation as farmers borrowed and helped one another with the newly available harvesters, baling machines, and other technologies. But when the machines became cheaper, each farmer bought his own or purchased services from commercial providers. "We used to help each other," a Kansas farmer said in 1940. "Now it is every man for himself." Automobiles and trucks not only widened the range of social life, they made marketing and purchasing easier. Village merchants, doctors, and ministers saw customers, patients, and parishioners drive off to nearby towns or even beyond. The geographical range of rural Americans expanded.[115]

"Plainville," a village in the Ozark foothills, is a case in point. Even in 1940, when anthropologist Carl Withers studied its sixty-five families, residents already felt that their old isolation had broken and that neighbors were turning to the outside world. By 1955, when another anthropologist, Art Gallaher Jr. restudied Plainville, a recently completed interstate highway had brought new people to live in town and permitted residents to leave it more easily. The villagers and nearby farmers reported that there had been a decline in cooperation, visiting, and informal activities among immediate neighbors. Such reports must be treated with some skepticism—beware of nostalgia—but studies like those of Plainville confirm that rural Americans pushed their social lives farther and farther from the locality. As early as 1949, a sociologist concluded that "local [rural] communities today are proving inadequate for the needs of rural families. . . . Communities, through expanding human contacts, are forming new relationships that center around large and small cities." Expanding one's contacts did depend, of course, on being able to afford those new technologies of sociability. Most residents of a small town in Georgia told researchers in 1943 that the automobile, radio, and telephone had eased their feelings of isolation, but most of the nearby tenant farmers, largely African American, reported that the "world in which they move is pretty much restricted to their own community and the county." Connecting them to the wider world would take longer.[116]

Understanding what happened to the local community in cities is more difficult. Many observers early in the twentieth century expected that local social relations would wither under the power of modernity. Researchers in Chicago in the interwar years described its vibrant neighborhoods, especially those of immigrants, as doomed to melt into a bland mass society. Yet anthropologists and sociologists who continued to study city neighborhoods, especially those districts labeled as slums, typically declared them to be thriving. Residents engaged their neighbors, participated in distinctive local cultures, and defended their turf. William Whyte's *Street Corner Society* shows a classic example. Whyte described the "slum" of Boston's Italian North End on the eve of World War II as a tightly bound, if sometimes conflictual, community. North Enders knew one another well, shared local values, and formed a special society within American culture. What is difficult to judge from these reports is how typical places like the North End were and whether their intensity was indeed fading.[117]

Many developments that altered rural communities also changed urban ones. Faster transportation and communications enabled people to easily reach jobs, stores, and churches outside the neighborhood. In the early years of the twentieth century, for example, Slavic American workers in Detroit automobile factories and Chicago steel mills clustered in neighborhoods only a short walk from their jobs. Their sons followed them into those jobs but moved away from the plants to more comfortable homes in more pleasant neighborhoods. Because streetcars and highways made distance to jobs and family less critical, white workers could pick neighborhoods based on housing, local schools, and cost. Other social changes, such as having fewer children, wives taking jobs, television, and new housing styles (front stoops largely disappeared while backyards expanded) also sapped neighborhood involvement. On the other hand, countervailing developments, especially increasing home ownership, declining residential mobility, and growing neighborhood homogeneity, shored up local solidarity. Neighbors increasingly mobilized to deal with shared problems such as tax increases, the arrival of new ethnic groups, and development projects. Local activism culminated in the "community power" movements of the 1960s and the later "NIMBY" ("not in my back yard") campaigns to forestall incursions by businesses, low-income housing, or noxious city facilities. But such mobilizations were episodic. Overall, the balance of social changes worked against neighborhood solidarity.[118]

It makes sense, then, that by the end of the twentieth century Americans typically liked but did not mix much with their neighbors. City people told sociologists, as the residents of "Plainville" had told anthropologists, that there used to be more local camaraderie. In the 1920s, residents of both "Middletown" and central Los Angeles said that. Some harder evidence suggests that over the century Americans looked outside their neighborhoods more. One kind of evidence, which I presented earlier, is marriage records. They tend to show a modest widening in the geographical distances between urban brides and grooms over the century, implying that mixing with neighbors waned, although the pace of such change was greater in the nineteenth century.[119]

In sum, over the twentieth century, Americans became more rooted and vested in their local communities, but more thinly involved in them. Residents' interests, activities, and ties grew at a greater rate outside the locality than they did inside it. The major exceptions were poor, black Americans. Residential discrimination and segregation, which tightened until the last few decades of the twentieth century, confined them in narrow spaces, physically isolated them from good jobs, homes, and stores, and culturally estranged them from the wider society. Most Americans, however, found it increasingly easy to both invest in and withdraw from their local communities as their needs dictated. Given the great telescoping of space, that twentieth-century Americans sustained as much neighborhood involvement as they did, in homeowner associations, friendly relations, and occasional political mobilization, is noteworthy.[120]

The Social World of Work

The workplace supplanted the neighborhood as most adults' major setting for group life outside the family. With family farms disappearing,
most wives holding jobs, and longer commutes, more Americans spent
more time in the company of coworkers. (The often-heralded return to
working at home via the Internet had not yet arrived by the mid-2000s.)
In addition, fewer Americans worked alongside kin and neighbors as had
once been common. Coworkers increasingly formed an altogether distinct group.[121]

Americans made the workplace a site of social as well as economic life.
In the 1920s, Ora Pelletier, age sixteen, started working in the Amoskeag
plant in New Hampshire. Decades later, she recalled the sociable times
she and other teens extracted from the work day. "In the mill, people
stayed among themselves to talk about whatever they had to talk about.
Married people would be friendly, friendly enough to come and sit with us
sometimes during the noon hour. Other times they'd stay in their corner
and talk about their families and stuff like that. But we kids . . . [sat] in our
little corner and we'd have dinner together." In that same era, thousands
of young women went to work as department store sales clerks. Historian
Susan Porter Benson found that "solidarity [in each department] grew
out of the intense social interaction which co-workers shared; huddling,
or gathering together and talking, was the most universally remarked feature of saleswomen's work culture." Benson quotes an assistant buyer at
Filene's department store in Boston: "Call-downs [telling the salesgirls
to stop chatting] don't work here. They quiet down for a day, but it only
seems to give the jawbone a rest which improves its speed and stamina.
The next day they are at it, again."[122]

Sociability at work often led to social ties outside of work. Survey research in the last decades of the century found that roughly half of employed Americans drew at least one "close friend" from among their coworkers; about a fifth drew *most* of their close friends from among their
coworkers. The cultural diversity of work groups shows how distinctive
they are. Americans at the end of the twentieth century reported knowing and befriending more people of different races, genders, and even political convictions at work than in other settings. The workplace, to be
sure, was no multicultural Eden. Job discrimination, particularly against
African Americans, persisted throughout the century, and interracial and
interethnic fellowship did not often travel far from the office or assembly line. William Kornblum described steel workers in 1960s Chicago:
"White workers . . . may spend their entire occupational careers working with black men and still bar blacks from their neighborhood. Mexi-

cans . . . gain intimate knowledge about their Serbian workmates from the same neighborhood, but after work the two groups drink in different taverns." Nonetheless, the increasing diversity of coworkers illustrates how the work setting emerged as a major new source of personal bonds. The tension between work and home became a public issue near the end of the century as more women entered careers. This conflict was typically depicted as pitting individuals' economic interests against their personal ones, but work was not just about the money. Many people also felt the pull of work friends.[123]

Faith-Based Communities

In 1907, a delegation of ministers from the New York City Federation of Churches visited President Theodore Roosevelt to ask his assistance in halting an alarming decline in the churches' "hold on the people." Roosevelt promised his worried visitors "to aid the cause in every way possible." Ministers in the early twentieth century frequently raised such alarms. They blamed scientists who taught heresies such as evolution; they blamed congregants who spent Sunday mornings in their tin lizzies; and they blamed a popular culture for corrupting vulnerable minds. "The modern novel . . . is responsible for our empty pews. . . . [It] has taken the place of the pulpit," complained one priest—and that was before movies, radio, and television. The ministers could point to vacant, decaying church buildings all over rural America to illustrate their warnings. Historians too have concluded that the early decades of the twentieth century were years of a "religious depression." In the long run, however, the story of churches in the twentieth century turned out quite differently.[124]

Around 1900, perhaps half of American adults belonged to a church; by the 1950s, many more, about three-fourths, reported belonging. One reason for the surge was that midcentury Americans married earlier and had children earlier, both of which typically send people back to church, but religious enthusiasm also spurred them. Then membership slumped to about two-thirds of adults by 2000. One reason for the partial retreat was that Americans were now waiting much longer to marry and parent. Sociologist Robert Wuthnow recounted a pastor's comment: "It used to be that boys and girls got confirmed at 13, and you didn't see them again until they were 18 and came back to get married. . . . Nowadays, you don't see them again until they are 30 and come back to get married." Another reason for declining membership was disillusionment with organized religion, ministers, and, for some, the religious right. Many dropouts from the major denominations joined unaffiliated churches, new sects, or small "spiritual" groups.[125]

Attendance at religious services followed a similar trajectory of substantial increase up to about 1960 and modest decline later. Protestants and Jews, fragmentary surveys suggest, attended services quite *in*frequently in the early decades of the century; Catholics were much more regular. By midcentury, however, about five in ten Americans reported going to church at least weekly. In sharp to contrast to the ministers' complaints to Roosevelt in 1907, the Methodist Council of Bishops proclaimed in 1954: "Our people are attending public worship in larger numbers than we have ever known . . . . A new spirit has fallen upon our people." At the end of the century, about four in ten Americans told pollsters that they attended at least weekly.[126]

Catholics account for most, perhaps all, of the post-1950s sag in religious affiliation and attendance. According to one explanation, many Catholics turned away from the Church because they objected to the liberalization following Second Vatican Council in the early 1960s; according to another explanation, many turned away from the Church because they were disappointed by the timidity of the Vatican II liberalization. Catholicism was the only major faith whose members increasingly left the fold; about half of the dropouts became Protestants.[127]

Even as membership and attendance rose through most of the century, the public authority of the churches continued to recede. Ministers in 1957 — not to mention 2007 — could do even less than Roosevelt's visitors in 1907 to shape school curricula, political decisions, family law, or popular culture. And their control over their own members waned. Relatively few churches in twenty-first-century America could do as the First Presbyterian Church of Philadelphia did in the early nineteenth century — suspend members who drank or gambled.[128]

Voluntarism increasingly characterized Americans' connections to their churches. Religious options expanded as diversity increased; four-fifths of Americans claimed Protestantism in 1900, but only one-half did a century later. Tolerance of others' faiths grew. In 1924, almost all the high school students in Middletown agreed that "Christianity is the one true religion and all people should be converted to it"; by 1977, fewer than half of Middletown youth agreed. In many other ways as well — such as interfaith councils, union services, and declining anti-Catholicism and anti-Semitism — Americans came to accept religious diversity. Americans also accepted the growing tendency of people to marry across religious and denominational lines and then, in many cases, remain in their different faiths. About 40 percent of couples in 2007 lived that way, Baptist Bill Clinton and Methodist Hillary Rodham Clinton being a notable example. In 2006, survey respondents who had changed or left a religion overwhelmingly explained their moves as the result of disagreeing with the teachings of their original faith or finding a new religion "more fulfilling" or both, and few cited marrying. Even most churchgoers agreed that "one should arrive at his or her own religious beliefs independent of a church or synagogue." Most Americans, including most of those who called themselves "born again," said in a late-century poll that going to church was "something you do if you feel it meets your needs" rather than being a "duty or an obligation." In that spirit, American Catholics, by a ratio of over three to one, told pollsters in 2005 that "on difficult moral questions" they would more likely follow their own consciences than the teachings of Pope Benedict XVI. Such practices and statements indicate that Americans increasingly believed that people should invest themselves in a church, any church, but do so freely and only for so long as it satisfied a personal spiritual quest.[129]

If one church did not satisfy a person's needs or wishes, there was another church down the road. In 1998, about four in ten Americans reported that they had at least once "shopped around for a church or synagogue." In 2008, about half of survey respondents said they had switched faiths or denominations at least once in their adult lives. Also in 2008, a newspaper editor wrote that he and his three siblings were raised as mainline Protestants, but "these days my sister and my middle brother are born-again Christians, and my youngest brother is a Catholic. Me? I'm the Jew." The Jewish community had an apt phrase that captured these new developments. For decades, "Jew by Choice" referred to a convert; people born as Jews presumably had no choice in the matter. But what had been fate for millennia now became, in an increasingly voluntaristic society, a daily decision. All American Jews, the new saying went, were now Jews by choice.[130]

In the 1700s, when most Americans went unchurched, churches were, after taverns, one of the few, perhaps only, centers of sociability. In the early 2000s, when most Americans were churched, churches were only one of several centers of sociability. Still, about six in ten adults said they belonged to a church, about four in ten adults said they attended church services regularly, and three in ten said they were active in churches or affiliated groups. Perhaps one-fourth of adult Americans belonged to a church-based support or study group. The church provided many with a social life and most of their friendships. In 1979, Sociologist Nancy Ammerman studied a fundamentalist church in a New England suburb.

For many, almost every spare minute is spent on activities related to church. The church *is* their leisure activity. . . . For most members, their best friends are other members or at least others who attend a similar church. They share meals together, go on outings together, and do all the things that friends always do. . . . Throughout the week they are in touch by phone, go visiting prospects [for church membership] together, and eat in each others' homes. Their relationships are friendships in all the usual ways, but the focus of their lives together is the church.

Roughly one in seven twenty-first-century Americans rooted themselves in their churches this way.[131]

Voluntarism and religious tolerance did not undermine Americans' commitments to church. Whereas observers once thought that the freedom to choose vitiated religious commitment, sociologists now believe that it is "precisely this ability to choose that has kept religious organizations so remarkably healthy in this country." Americans who felt that they had picked their churches were more faithful to them; those who switched religions were typically at least as committed to their new faiths as those who had been born into them. Americans increasingly saw membership and attendance as an expression of free choice rather than a duty. Middletown residents in 1977 not only attended church more often than Middletowners had in 1924, but they more often reported positive reasons for attending, citing enjoyment and spirituality rather than mere habit. Given greater options to join and to leave, over the twentieth century more Americans embedded themselves in religious groups.[132]

Less Clubbing

Not all settings for social life expanded. As with neighborhoods, formal clubs became less important sources of belonging. Fraternal lodges, a great enthusiasm of the late nineteenth century, withered in the first half of the twentieth century. Up-and-coming young men found the Moose, the Red Men, and their kind déclassé, and instead joined service clubs like the Rotary and Kiwanis. But these too lost their vigor a few decades later. Women's organizations, many of which had been explicitly feminist during the suffrage movement in the years before World War I, shrank or turned their attention to homemaking after winning the vote. Many formal associations provided important services to members—health, life, and burial insurance, for example—but more such benefits at better terms became available from employers, insurance companies, and the government. The lodges, sisterhoods, and other societies had also provided entertainment, such as drinks and billiards for men and fashion shows and card games for women, but Americans increasingly found their entertainment at vaudeville theaters, movie palaces, dance halls, and eventually on television (see chapter 5). With marriages becoming more companionable, more men came home after work rather than go to the club (or the bar). By the last third of the twentieth century, the classic men's clubs were pale shadows of their vaunted reputations. The Masons, for example, lost about 40 percent of their members after 1960.[133]

The decline of the clubs led some observers to argue that contemporary Americans were no longer the "joiners" they were reputed to be and, furthermore, to suggest that this loss undercut American democracy. Other scholars contested this description; they argued that Americans actually joined more associations, not fewer, over the course of the century, but they joined new kinds of associations and many *informal* associations. Clubs with constitutions, officers, and dues—not to mention funny hats and ritual handshakes—comprised a shrinking segment of associational life. As far back as 1933, two sociologists reported that "one of the noticeable trends in rural social life [during the 1920s] . . . was the increase in informal recreation. In a number of places it was said that the tone of social life was set by informal groups rather than, as formerly, by organizations." Perhaps grandfather had belonged to the Elks, but grandson attended a weekly pick-up basketball game; perhaps grandmother had held office in the local art society, but granddaughter met friends to make pottery.[134]

Scholars furiously debated what happened to American club membership after about 1960. Some, like political scientist Robert Putnam in *Bowling Alone*, claimed that participation declined, that baby boomers and their children lacked civic-mindedness. His critics denied that club or club-like activities had really dropped. When the dust settled on this rhubarb, the conclusion seemed to be that Americans in the latter half of the twentieth century joined roughly the same number of formal associations as Americans had before but participated less actively in them. In the middle of the century, towns had many formal clubs for people from the highest social class (country clubs and civic associations, for example) to almost the lowest class (the lodges and ethnic social clubs). Many men went after work to a men's club, a union hall, or the "poor man's club," the bar. Many middle-class homemakers devoted parts of their days to women's clubs or civic organizations like the Parent-Teacher Associations. That kind of social life waned after the 1950s. As a sixty-eight-year-old member of the Los Angeles Knights of Columbus told a reporter in 1996, "There's just so much more to do now. . . . When my dad was alive, the Knights and Elks were a major part of a man's social life because there wasn't much else." Watching television and, later, surfing the Internet provided a lot of that "so much to do"; so did the housework and child care that husbands undertook to partly make up for the hours their wives now spent working and commuting. Despite the distractions, many Americans nonetheless created new kinds of formal and informal associations, from book clubs, choirs, hiking groups, and mutual support circles to activist organizations, such as Habitat for Humanity. Many made time, in smaller chunks and less regularly, to participate. In the end, they could not match the hours that their parents gave to older sorts of organizations. Club life has been waning since midcentury and certainly since the late nineteenth century when "everyone seemed to be joining some temple, clan, castle, conclave, hive, or lodge."[135]

As the competition for their time increased, Americans changed their involvement in a familiar direction, toward more voluntarism. The classic lodge or club held their members through dues, elected offices, insurance programs, rules about attending meetings, and public censure for misbehavior. Mutual support groups, Bible study classes, Saturday morning soccer games, and unscheduled get-togethers have little of that hold on individuals. Maybe the participants in these less structured and less demanding groups are more emotionally invested in them than their parents were in the Kiwanis and PTAs; many such groups focus on spirituality and personal concerns. In any case, the new types of groups were clearly more voluntaristic. They were, in the terms of sociologist Robert Wuthnow, "loose connections"—or, in other terms, associations of especially limited liability.[136]

Just Friends

"Loose connections" can also describe the kinds of friendships that emerged most distinctively among the middle class in the nineteenth century and then proliferated in the twentieth: intimate ties outside of any particular group. Schoolmates, army buddies, or coworkers who stay close long after school, military service, or changing jobs, or people who become pals after being introduced by mutual friends or simply chancing upon one another—these pairs might be called "just friends." They see one another when they want to and only because they like one another. We can reasonably assume, although there are no studies that test the proposition, that more Americans had more such friends over the twentieth century. At the end of the century, roughly one-fifth of Americans' personal relationships were "just friends." As the increasing availability of mail made it easier for nineteenth-century friends to stay friends even at a distance, so too have telephones, automobiles, airplanes, and now the Internet made it easier for twentieth- and twenty-first century friendships to persist. Around the end of the twentieth century, however, it appears that Americans saw friends of all sorts less often than they did at midcentury. The evidence is murky, but longer hours of work for married couples, longer commutes, and more time at home in the evenings (watching television in particular; see chapter 5) probably reduced the time Americans spent in the physical company of friends—be they "just friends" or any friends.[137]

Dispersed Voluntarism

Twentieth-century social life, for all its seemingly sharp swerves—particularly the apparent lurch from 1950s *The Lonely Crowd* conformity to 1960s rebelliousness—evolved in a general direction. Cultural and material developments enabled more Americans to participate in more voluntaristic groups. Sociologist Barry Wellman has used the terms "personal communities" and "networked individualism" to describe social connections that "supply support, sociability, information and a sense of belonging separately to each individual. It is the individual, not the household or the group, that is the primary unit of connectivity." Most Americans did not yet participate heavily in such idiosyncratic social networks, but that has been the overall direction of change.[138]

In the twenty-first century, the so-called online community exemplified a person's ability to form a social group around his or her individual interests. The Internet explosion loosed an avalanche of studies on such communities (in part, I suspect, because researchers could conduct much of their "field work" from the comfort of their office chairs). One study, for instance, described online and offline social life among fans of the television show "Buffy the Vampire Slayer" (1997–2003). As one-dimensional as such groups may appear, participants often bring friends into them and friendships can emerge from them. Moreover, the general research on the social consequences of the Internet suggests (as of this writing) that Internet use more often generated and sustained group life than undermined it. What could be more voluntaristic than a "community" one joins by typing in an e-mail address and exits by sending an "unsubscribe" message?[139]

Population growth, urbanization, technology, and affluence multiplied individuals' social options in the twentieth century. More Americans, notably women, could choose among more jobs, neighborhoods, schools, churches, and other settings, each of which opened up opportunities for belonging in voluntary communities. Greater security allowed more Americans to explore and extend their search for social ties beyond the family and locality; the widow joining a retirement community is but one illustration.

While this summary may capture most of the century, the last few decades seem to tell a more complex story. Growing economic strains appear to have produced greater joint work hours for middle-class couples and even greater difficulties for the poor and less educated. We saw that family difficulties since about 1960 have been concentrated among the less educated, and there are other indications that those who were relatively marginal to mainstream American society became yet more marginalized in this era.[140]

Cultural changes in the twentieth century also expanded voluntarism for most Americans. Congress and the courts, under pressure from social movements and public opinion, extended—some say invented—rights, like the right to privacy. Individuals could leverage laws against all sorts of groups, from their families to the nation, and could use law to restrain authorities, such as employers, police, and even democratic majorities. In the twentieth century, American law, which had once backstopped the authority of groups and their leaders—husbands over wives, bosses over workers, and so forth—increasingly empowered individuals against the group. Liberation ideologies—for women, children, ethnic and sexual minorities, the disabled, and so on—spread claims of autonomy throughout society. These long-term trends gave more Americans greater latitude to form social connections with whom they wished under better terms. Twenty-first century voluntarism was not just for property-holding white men, as it was when Emerson pronounced the virtue of doing "whatever only rejoices me," but for most Americans.

Many observers, however, viewed the developments of the twentieth century not with Emersonian celebration but with trepidation. The "culture wars" of the 1990s, as exaggerated as they were by politicians and the press, raised serious questions about the scope and consequences of voluntarism. In 2005, Pope Benedict XVI voiced these concerns when, just before being elected to the papacy, he denounced "a dictatorship of relativism which does not recognize anything as definitive and has as its highest value one's own ego and one's own desires." The critique of egoism may, in the American context at least, need qualification: it was not rampant individualism, but spreading voluntarism. Americans continued to join groups—to marry, remarry, and parent; to join churches or smaller spiritual circles; to invest in their neighborhoods, hang out with coworkers, and stay in touch with old friends—and to be devoted to them. But Americans also increasingly insisted on contracting membership and relationships on favorable terms and retaining the option of exit. Qualifying the egoism charge, however, does not dismiss the concerns of cultural conservatives. At what point does having more options for more people to exit more groups create a society in which too little is certain, too little can be counted on, and people are too often left behind—sometimes by just an "unsubscribe" e-mail?[141]

CONCLUSION

So, Mrs. Alma A. Rogers, celebrator of women's clubs in 1905, was not as inconsistent as she may have seemed when she said that women discovered their individuality as they discovered their clubs. A culture of voluntarism encouraged Americans to define and refine their individuality in covenants of fellowship. That culture widened and deepened over time, most especially changing the experience of women. More Americans gained more options for belonging to more groups, and they translated those options into better terms in the "contracts" with their groups. This trajectory was not apparent in the first century or so in many parts of the colonies, places where society was still emerging out of frontier settlements. But by the Revolution, the direction was set. In particular, middle-class women steadily developed independence and influence within the family, first in the Victorian model, which gave them reign at home; then in the early twentieth-century companionate model, which demanded that husbands keep courting their wives; and most recently in the twenty-first-century model, which presumes equal rights to personal happiness. Women gained leverage because they were increasingly empowered—by rising security and affluence, by new law, and by new ideologies—to avoid or leave unsuitable matches. Overwhelmingly, women used that leverage to improve rather than to leave family life. Working-class women were a generation or two behind this trend, but for the most part, they followed. The same is true for youth. Eighteenth-century children served their parents or other adults to whom their parents assigned them; twentieth-century children were doted on by their parents. Others, such as servants and apprentices, who once lived in households under the thumb of a patriarch, gained independent families. In their churches, neighborhoods, workplaces, and clubs, Americans found more alternatives, more "communities of limited liability," more independence, and thus more power to meet their personal needs.

Space does not permit me to explore in depth why voluntarism spread and strengthened, but the reasons must include the momentum of early-American ideals about individual rights, the recent willingness to enforce in law those individual rights against group interests (recall the Supreme Court's declaration that a marriage was an association of independent individuals), the growing security and affluence that permits such ideals to become real, and the proliferation of social circles—kin, neighborhoods, workplaces, churches, clubs, and free-floating friendships—in an industrialized, urban society.

This story of American belonging is not one more account of how American character was corrupted by rising individualism, egoism, or selfishness. Americans did not turn into free lovers, free thinkers, ramblers, rebels, or anarchists; they remained by Western standards remarkably committed to family, church, community, job, and nation—quite bourgeois. Americans handled the tension between individual liberty and society through an implicit covenant between member and group, which allowed free exit to whomever felt unserved but required commitment to the group by whomever stayed. Over three centuries, more Americans emerged from exclusion (recall the rural women who wrote to Country Life Commission investigators about their isolation) or dependent inclusion (recall the bound apprentices) to claim voluntary inclusion. Voluntarism explains how Americans could simultaneously combine independence and attachment—for example, residential mobility with neighborhood activism, religious switching with religious enthusiasm, easy dissolution of family ties with strong "family values." Recall that in 1976, with divorce rates peaking, 70 percent of married Americans preferred to describe their marriages as a "couple who cannot be separated" rather than as "two separate people" (see p. 96). Americans still insisted on the ideal of marital melding—so long as the marriage "works" for each partner. In the last few decades of this history, however, this growing social inclusion seemed to have stalled. Social opportunities constricted for average Americans and marginalized Americans became more marginalized. History is not a steady progression, so this stall may be a passing era. Or not.[142]

Finally, while voluntarism is central to American culture, its expansion could have—may have had—problematic consequences. If families, congregations, neighborhoods, associations, and friendships increasingly depend on meeting each individual's whims—if group entryways are revolving doors—then groups may not operate reliably. How well, for example, can a family nurture both adults and children if it seems provisional, a matter of "until inconvenience do us part" rather than "until death do us part"? How well can a church provide fellowship and existential meaning if its theology, rules, and authority are always up for debate? Journalist Alan Ehrenhalt addressed the issue in 2000 when he asserted that "if it is true to say of 1950s America that it was a world of limited choices, it is also fair to call it a world of lasting relationships." The 1950s of which he wrote was already long past the era of truly limited choices. In the 2000s, it was not clear—indeed, it was hotly debated—whether American voluntarism had passed its optimal point.[143]

5 *Public Spaces*

Under overcast skies, at 6 PM, Saturday, May 18, 1895, A. M. Rothschild & Co. opened the doors of its new department store at State and Van Buren streets in Chicago for only two hours—not to sell any goods, but to permit the public to view what the *Chicago Tribune* called a new "establishment of stupendous proportions." Rothschild & Co. also was giving away 31,000 souvenirs to visitors. Within minutes, crowds had fully jammed the store and taken over blocks of State Street. About 150 police officers responded and ordered the emporium closed. The crowd, largely of women, stayed on until a rain shower came up and dispersed the sightseers. A reporter noted that, while a few women had items crushed in the throng—a hat, and a carton of eggs—no one was seriously hurt. A couple of years later, a 6 AM opening in Boston of a different sort also drew a vast crowd: the trolley line's first subway section. Thousands, mostly men, gathered around, hoping to ride one of the lead cars underground. As the first trolley approached the subway opening, "the entrance to the great tunnel was marked by a canal of humanity. The passengers aboard the car had packed themselves in like sardines, and the black mass yelling like a jungle of wild animals, dipped down the incline for the underground run to Park st." Passengers joked about elbows poking backs and feet stomping toes. Spilling out into yet more hordes at Park Street, the passengers hurrahed in good spirits "and a crowd of swarthy Italians yelled: 'Bravo, bravo, bravissimo!'"[1]

These sorts of experiences, increasingly common in nineteenth-century cities, contrasted dramatically with the everyday life that most Americans a few generations earlier had led on isolated farms and in small towns. More Americans were now encountering more people more often in public spaces. Critically, they encountered "strange" people whom they did not know and who were distinctively, culturally different, such as the "swarthy Italians." These encounters did not always go well, as nineteenth-century episodes of urban disorder and mob violence dramatized. But remarkably, most contact among strangers, often full-body contact in trolley cars or ballparks, increasingly went well, as demonstrated by the thriving street life and public entertainments of the early twentieth century. Contact and coordination among strangers is a distinguishing feature of urban, particularly of modern urban, life. Similarly, dealing with strangers is a feature of political, particularly modern political, life. This chapter describes how Americans learned to handle life in public spaces, both literal public spaces and the metaphoric public spaces of politics. Another important aspect of this history, however, is its later phase, when Americans retreated partway from public spaces into their private and parochial spaces. By the end of the twentieth century, Americans had left some of the buzzing confusion of the streets for the voluntaristic circles of family, friends, coworkers, and cocongregants.[2]

We often contrast being in public to being in private, but people generally move in three kinds of spaces. The space inside the home is *private*, inhabited by people who are either intimates or invited in by intimates. In sharp contrast, places such as main streets, plazas, and commons are, at least in large communities, clearly *public* sites where strangers typically encounter one another. The vague but nonetheless important space in between the private and the public is *parochial* space. Nominally public and open to strangers, parochial spaces operate as if reserved for acquaintances and friends. The neighborhood bar is a classic example, a space where "everyone knows your name" and where people whose names are not known and who do not at least look like they fit in are unwelcome.* A park bench favored by group of elderly men, a small church, a pick-up basketball court, a suburban cul-de-sac, and women's clubs like Mrs. Rogers's (see chapter 4, p. 95) are parochial spaces. In the smallest of communities, all the space that is not private may be parochial; locals stare at strangers even on Main Street. People in larger communities more easily distinguish parochial from public spaces.[3]

The boundaries of private, parochial, and public can be vague and shifting but are still consequential. Many constitutional struggles, say over the Fourth Amendment, concern precisely where to draw the line that bounds private space. Neighbors sometimes fight over whether a few square yards of sidewalk or driveway are private, parochial, or public. The previous chapter in effect addressed the history of private and parochial

---

* "Virtual space" also divides in three. An e-mail is presumably private; a comment in a by-invitation discussion group is parochial; posts to an open Web site are fully public.

spheres, such as home and club; this chapter is about the history of Americans' engagement in public spaces.

This history also informs a debate about Americans' civic participation. At question is whether modern Americans participate less in the deliberations of their democracy than earlier generations did. Some scholars argue that Americans, starting in the late nineteenth century, surrendered to mass society—to big business, big government, big media—by not voting, not organizing, not paying attention to politics. Other scholars argue that Americans withdrew from the public arena much more recently, as a sort of collective depression following the 1960s. Yet others deny that modern Americans withdrew from civic participation at all; instead people changed *how* they participated—voting less often, perhaps, but lobbying and marching more often. Ironically, sages in earlier eras often worried about *too much* civic engagement by the wrong people or in the wrong ways—for example, immigrants voting or temperance mobs burning down beer halls. Participation in the political public space is the topic of this chapter's second part. It tells of an historical arc in popular political involvement. The first part of the chapter covers the history of Americans' participation in physical public spaces such as State Street in front of A. M. Rothschild & Co. or Boston's MBTA. It, too, describes an arc.[4]

ENTRIES AND EXITS: AMERICANS IN PUBLIC

Paris and Tokyo, it has been said, have long enjoyed vibrant public spaces because their living quarters are so cramped. To meet someone or just to relax, people must go out to cafés or restaurants. By this logic, we would expect Americans, who have long enjoyed big-sky elbow room and who increasingly have lived in spacious suburban houses, to have become private, homebound people. There is some truth in that expectation. But the story, of course, is more complex; it entails the rise of cities, technological inventions, literature, economic growth, group tensions, and much more. Public spaces became more alluring and drew millions, but Americans' homes became better appointed, too, allowing more Americans to ask, "Why don't we just stay in?"[5]

Secluded: Early Americans

Seventeenth- and eighteenth-century Americans rarely entered public spaces, that is, places with strangers. More than nine in ten lived outside of cities until well into the nineteenth century, and while the countryside and villages had many social moments, these happened in parochial spaces. Starting in 1785, Mary Ballard, whose New England diary I drew from in the last chapter, kept track of her frequent visits with neighbors. As a midwife, she knew many people, but they were locals; she rarely encountered strangers. American communities were too sparsely settled, even more so outside New England, to sustain really public spaces. Churches, where they existed, welcomed all who sought fellowship in prayer, but in practice they grew from and served small, parochial groups. Most men of the era glimpsed the public world only occasionally, perhaps at open markets, more often at the local tavern or "pub"—a term derived from "public house," a place open to all. The history of taverns shows us how limited the public realm of early America was.[6]

Colonial-era taverns existed, as the subtitle of one study put it, "For the Entertainment of Friends and Strangers." Rural inns on local turnpikes or at trail intersections attracted both travelers and locals. Typically, authorities licensed the taverns to provide wayfarers with food, a bed (usually shared with other guests), boarding for horses if any, and, often, legal alcohol. In many communities, the tavern was the only gathering place, so judges used them to hold trials, officials to hold town meetings, and merchants to negotiate deals. But taverns provided much more, especially to local men. In back-country North Carolina, for example, "Patrons certainly drank, but they also ate, slept, sang, danced, smoked, made love, played various games (on which they often bet), fought, conducted club meetings, watched traveling exhibitions, sent and received mail, held political discussions and celebrations, and did business with their neighbors, with peddlers, and with itinerant craftsmen." Public houses could be found everywhere and they outnumbered churches; they were "Americans' most important centers of male sociability." Respectable women, for the most part, stayed away. In larger towns, taverns served distinct clienteles—this one sailors, that one clerks. Politics and pubs stimulated one another. Men heard the latest news at the tavern, argued over it, and organized in reaction to it. (John Adams complained about having to cultivate the "crowd in the tavern.") Taverns often had their individual political affiliations, and tavern keepers stepped up to become officeholders in colonial and state legislatures. In these myriad ways, the American tavern from the mid-1600s into the 1800s was first and primarily a *parochial* space in that it relied on its local regulars, but it also served as a portal to the public arena and visitors from that arena. Local men encountered strangers there. Alexander Hamilton once reported that he had "dined at a tavern with a very mixed company of different nations and religions. There were Scots, English, Dutch, Germans, and Irish; there were Roman Catholicks, Church men, Presbyterians, Quakers, Newlightmen, Methodists, Seventh day men, Moravians, and one Jew." And in these encounters, locals joined in conversations about the outside world.[7]

The Salem Village witchcraft trials in the late 1690s provide us a sense of the tavern's role as a gateway. The key split in the village, as described by historians Paul Boyer and Stephen Nissenbaum, pitted families who largely engaged in subsistence agriculture and lived far from the growing *town* of Salem against families who had commercial interests and lived closer to the town. Four taverns of Salem Village stood on the road to Salem Town. Conservative folks had long seen the mixing of locals with strangers at the taverns as a threat to social stability. A generation earlier, village selectman had approved one tavern license specifically on the condition that the keep sell liquor only to passing strangers, that the inn be a "rendezvous point for outsiders—and *only* for outsiders." In 1692, two of the four tavern keepers were hanged as Salem "witches," emphasizing the taverns' continuing and suspect connection to the public world.[8]

The classic early-American tavern declined in the antebellum era as rail travel, postal service, and other modern improvements provided competing services. Its descendants, the bars and saloons of the mid-nineteenth century, often became yet more parochial spaces. Some continued to connect their clients, especially migrants and immigrants, to the wider world, serving, for example, as mail drops, but they rarely served as public meeting grounds for strangers. Indeed, encounters between strangers, especially those of different backgrounds, often led to barroom violence.[9]

However rarely American men of the eighteenth and early nineteenth centuries encountered strangers, American women lived yet more circumscribed lives. European visitors, such as Tocqueville and English novelist Frances Trollope, noted the absence of middle- or upper-class women in public places. In the antebellum era, such women started leaving their homes more often, but it was typically to *parochial* spaces, such as meetings of church sisterhoods or lecture societies, rather than the streets or plazas. Most women who regularly ventured into public were the urban poor who used city streets to hawk goods or get to their jobs, perhaps as washerwomen. There they passed loiterers, hucksters, and gangs, men who assumed that unaccompanied women were available for the taking. In a notorious 1793 case, a seventeen-year-old working-class girl in New York City charged that she had been lured off the street into a whorehouse and raped by the scion of a wealthy family. The defendant's attorney argued that the sex had been consensual and that the alleged victim was clearly a strumpet, proven by the well-known fact that no innocent woman would walk the streets unescorted. (The jury's almost instant acquittal of the defendant led to three days of rioting.) When circumstances required "respectable" women to enter public spaces, authorities made strenuous efforts to shield them from strangers. Post offices, for example, attracted pickpockets and other idlers, so postmasters of large offices set up separate windows and lines for those women who needed to personally deposit and collect their letters. Concerns about women in public helped spur the postal system to provide mail drop boxes in residential neighborhoods and free home delivery in 1863. By the 1880s, women in five hundred cities no longer needed to visit the town post office, but in effect could communicate to kin and friends from their private and parochial spaces.[10]

Religious revivals provided a special opportunity for women and children, in town and country, to mingle with crowds of strangers. Celebrity evangelists roused the emotions of hundreds in jammed city halls, but the rural camp meetings drew Americans who were largely inexperienced with public spaces. A revival week after the harvest provided an exceptional chance for neighbor and stranger alike to pray, sing, witness, and party together. (Recall how Kitturah Belknap organized a post-harvest vacation at a camp meeting in 1841, as discussed in chapter 4.) People would travel from miles around and plant a temporary "city" of thousands of believers who had come to witness their faith. The less religious attendees, largely men, lurked on the outskirts, seeking fun and making fun, campaigning for office, or selling food and sin. Rural Americans viewed camp meetings as special in great measure because they were unusually public events for people who typically lived secluded lives.[11]

Americans increasingly entered the public realm "virtually," especially through newspapers and novels. New technologies and new policies vastly expanded the volume of communications. In place of hearing twice-told tales from travelers or reading fragmentary accounts in occasional letters, more people, mainly men, read the papers. In 1800, the new nation had 92 newspapers; in 1860, 3,725—a direct result of the federal government's subsidy of postal delivery for newspapers and its aggressive distribution of post offices. In 1800, 903 post offices served the nation; in 1860, over 28,000 did. European visitors were astonished at the "newspaper reading animal[s]" Americans had become. Old woodcuts show men at a post office, pub, or store crowded together as one of them reads aloud the news. In some communities, the post office was the only place other than church open on Sundays, and men would rush there as soon as the mail had arrived, staying on to drink and play cards with neighbors (at least, until Sunday blue laws stopped Sabbath deliveries; see chapter 4, p. 129). Mail and newspapers alerted even remote settlers to matters publicly debated in the big cities and in Europe—and did so with increasing speed. In 1799, it took about twelve days for people in Boston to learn of George Washington's death in Alexandria, Virginia, but in 1830, it took them less than two days to learn of Andrew Jackson's State of the Union address. Middle-class women focused, especially after 1830, on advice books, sermons, women's magazines, and especially sentimental novels, which provided a window to a world full of morality tales lightened with frissons of romance. One young New York woman reported in the 1800s that all she knew of the news were small items in the newspaper pointed out to her by her husband, but a novel, she reported, "sent me to rest with my eyes drowned in tears."[12]

In the nineteenth century, women of the growing middle class re-treated with their novels further into the privacy of the home. As de-scribed in the previous chapter, these women, unlike their mothers and grandmothers, no longer needed to sell eggs or butter; they gave up what-ever temporary jobs they may have had in the mills or in country schools; and they moved with their families away from the hurly-burly and in-sults of city centers onto the quieter streets uptown or even into more secluded suburbs. At the same time, American houses became more in-viting places in which to retreat. Affluent families in the antebellum era added comforts such as heavy furniture, utensils, decorations, and occa-sionally, new rooms. Managing the home engaged wives' energies and tes-tified to their skills; maids helped them deal with the public world. The emerging ideology of the "domestic sphere" (discussed in chapter 4) de-scribed middle-class antebellum homes as private refuges from a cruel public sphere. For increasingly many women, being home was more than fleeing public spaces; it was a positive virtue.[13]

Other women still could not avoid public spaces. Some of the farm-ers' daughters who left home to work in factories remained in town, of-ten in transient jobs; some found work in the trades—in 1845, for exam-ple, women comprised almost half of Charleston's bookbinders. Many more worked as maids or washerwomen. Most women who worked for pay—by weaving, making hats, or parts of shoes—worked at home, but even they had to confront the public world of city streets to shop, visit kin, or conduct chores. There they often encountered insult and injury. Antebellum etiquette books made clear that women in public should an-ticipate stares, comments, and badgering, if not worse. Urban working-class men, of course, were very much creatures of the streets. There they plied trades, bought and sold, and sought entertainment.[14]

In the earliest generations, then, the great majority of Americans—ru-ral men, and women almost everywhere—either had little opportunity to participate in public spaces or good reasons to avoid them. By necessity, many city men and poorer city women tramped the streets to conduct or find work or to escape dim interiors, but America was still an overwhelm-ingly rural nation. Proportionately few Americans positively enjoyed the public life: tavern regulars, street corner loiterers, apprentices out on the town, or the rare urban aesthete—say, Walt Whitman. In his ode, "Crossing Brooklyn Ferry" (1856), Whitman describes his reactions: "Crowds of men and women attired in the usual costumes, how curious you are to me! / On the ferry-boats the hundreds and hundreds that cross, returning home, are more curious to me than you suppose." Few average Americans saw these scenes, and many who could avoided them.

Into the Buzzing Confusion: The Postbellum Years

The Civil War dragged millions of young men out of their neighborhoods and into the wider world. Farm boys from rural New England and frontier Minnesota found themselves not only facing battlefields of terror but sharing campgrounds with strangers, such as Irish draftees from New York, German immigrants, and even black soldiers. Some recruits literally fell homesick and others' survival depended in part on staying close to comrades from their hometowns. Yet many soldiers, perhaps most, once having seen the outside world, the public spaces, reacted the way many liberated slaves did: they couldn't go—or stay—home again.[15]

In the late decades of the nineteenth and early decades of the twentieth centuries, vastly more Americans than before—and most notably, more middle-class women—participated in public life. The booming growth of large cities, new technologies such as the streetcar, new enterprises such as popular theater, and a churning economy ensured that. Between 1860 and 1920, the proportion of Americans living in cities of over fifty thousand people tripled from about one in ten to about three in ten. Increasing productivity gave American workers more time off and more money to explore recreational outlets. Railroads, trolleys, and eventually automobiles carried rural and suburban residents into the cities and ferried city residents around town. Businessmen developed new public venues for shopping and recreation, such as department stores, baseball stadiums, museums, dance halls, vaudeville houses, and amusement parks. City fathers provided other public spaces, particularly large nature parks—New York's Central Park being the most famous. So well attended were many of the public attractions that promoters began specializing them by style and class, differentiating "highbrow" from "lowbrow" theaters, concerts, and exhibitions. The surge of attendance led to frequent crushes, like the jam of window shoppers who charged Chicago's Rothschild & Co. in 1895, and occasional clashes over how to use these spaces. For example, immigrants held boisterous picnics and played sports in the new urban parks, while the native-born middle class campaigned to preserve the parks for quiet contemplation; immigrants staffed and shopped at peddler markets, while the middle-class complained about the congestion, dirt, and incivility of those markets.[16]

Men still dominated public spaces. Starting as a gentlemen's recreation and popularized during the Civil War, baseball became nationally organized, professional, and commercial in the 1860s and '70s. Mark Twain described the sport as "the very symbol . . . of the drive and push and rush and struggle of the raging, tearing, booming nineteenth century"; its immense popularity spurred the building of ever larger ballparks. One built in 1896 in Philadelphia accommodated an unprecedented sixteen thousand spectators seated with room for another five thousand to stand (in many parks, fans could stand along the foul lines); only thirteen years later, thirty-five thousand crowded into the new Shibe Park. Occasional Ladies' Day promotions notwithstanding, ballparks, like horse-racing tracks, boxing rings, and similar places, were masculine to the point of disrepute. Ball club owners tried strenuously to elevate the sport, but gambling, drinking, cursing, and fisticuffs nonetheless accompanied the early game.[17]

Men also had saloons, billiard halls, brothels, and early burlesque houses. Especially for immigrants and laborers, saloons provided parochial spaces for hearty conversation, gambling, news of homelands, rooms for organizational meetings, loans of money, "free lunches," and sexual entertainment. Some saloons still retained the public character of old-time taverns. Many keeps, for example, set up shop where tram lines intersected so they could attract commuters transferring between lines. Saloons stimulated the greatest cultural battles of the late century. Middle-class Protestant reformers pointed to the drunkenness, violence, and neglected families that the saloons seemed to spawn and tried to shut them down or strictly regulate them. Immigrants and the working class, and, of course, the alcohol interests fought back. It took a few decades, but the anti-saloon forces eventually triumphed.[18]

For all the testosterone in the air, women increasingly stepped out onto city streets, in part because those streets became less dangerous and in part because women asserted claims to them. Historian Mary Ryan has described "the provision of public space for women [as] a major civic project during the latter half of the nineteenth century." Women dominated that grand new public space described in chapter 3 and at the top of this chapter: the department store. Dazzling emporia, such as Macy's, opened in the 1880s and provided women with places to meet friends for shopping and lunch, but also places to join hundreds of strangers scanning items on the sales counters or listening to the store pianist. The doors were open to all who had the time to enter, even factory girls, whether to buy or just to look. Filene's in Boston opened its famous "Automatic

Bargain Basement" in 1909; it was so successful that it sustained the company through the Depression. An Italian visitor, recounting his exertions trying to navigate through crowds of women heading for the stores on Boston's Washington Street, wrote that "the Public here is a common noun of the feminine gender." In 1866, an etiquette guide had cautioned women against lingering in front of shop windows for fear of molestation; but an 1891 guide encouraged women to enjoy window shopping without noting any danger. About a generation later, middle-class women stepped out in the late hours, joining men in tasting the naughty pleasures of cabarets, dance halls, and the other venues of nightlife.[19]

Toward the end of the nineteenth century, entire families enjoyed yet other public places. The new "museums" tended to be more like P. T. Barnum's freak shows than the staid institutions we know today, but both kinds drew visitors. Burlesque houses turned into partly sanitized vaudeville shows. City fathers provided family-appropriate playgrounds and parks (where in the 1890s young women even dared to peddle about on bicycles in their "bloomers"). Many trolley and ferry entrepreneurs built outdoor amusement centers at the end of their transport lines to promote weekend business. A streetcar ride west out of downtown San Francisco to the ocean brought fun-seekers to an enormous public pool for all ages and genders, beachside rides, shooting galleries, and concessions. In New York City, on Saturday half-holidays in the summer, working-class families took the 25-cent round trip to Brighton Beach to dip in the water, look at carnival sights, taste the new "hot dog," bounce around on a train-like device that rolled and coasted, and marvel at the electrically lit walkways as night fell. Each summer after the turn of the century, Coney Island amusement parks attracted millions of people in almost all their varieties: families and singles; workers, clerks, and businessmen; Italians, Jews, and Yankees. African Americans, however, it is important to note, found themselves either barred from amusement parks and entertainment places or channeled into segregated sections. Those Americans who were allowed into the parks shared in a festive "timeout" from Victorian constraints, wearing informal clothing, taking thrill rides, spending uninhibitedly, and toying with controlled sexual titillation.[20]

In rural areas, improved rail service and then, after the turn of the century, cheap automobiles allowed many more families to visit towns, attend county fairs, and even tour the country. Train companies organized outings to the seashore or mountains for the holidays. By transferring from city streetcar lines to inter-urban trolleys, city folk took a day in the country and country folk took a day in town. In 1899, a farm family living near Rockport, Illinois, could take a special excursion train to Sauerkraut

Day at Forreston or to a revival with Billy Sunday at Flagg Center. One of the early members of the Country Church movement who was both a minister and sociologist worried in 1912:

> In those states in which the trolley system has been extended in the country . . . Sunday becomes for country people a day of visiting the town and in great numbers they gather at the inter-urban stations. The city and town on Sunday is filled with careless, hurrying groups of visitors, sight-seers and callers, who have no such fixed interest as that to be expressed in churchgoing or in substantial social processes.

Henry Ford's Model T really brought rural Americans into public spaces in the 1910s and '20s. Farmers went to town much more often and now brought their wives and children along, turning what had been grueling marketing trips into days and nights of entertainment. Rural women in particular eagerly took to driving and praised the automobile for letting them escape the house. Celebrity home economist Christine Fredrick declared in 1912 that "the car has wrought my emancipation, my freedom. I am no longer a country-bound farmer's wife. . . . The auto . . . brings me into frequent touch with the entertainment and life of my neighboring small towns—with joys of bargains, library, and soda-water." Rural Americans joined in the national craze for auto-camping, driving to see the natural wonders of the West and fabled Hollywood. Automobile campgrounds attracted, as public spaces commonly do, diverse sorts of people and "undesirables" like hoboes. The motor hotel business, pioneered by Howard Johnson, sprung up to ease travelers' discomforts with snug, secure, and not-too-public lodging.[21]

Movies greatly expanded Americans engagement in public spaces. Families in working-class neighborhoods flocked to converted stores to see new feature films, some of which even had plots. One-fourth of all New Yorkers, by one estimate, saw a movie in a single week in 1910. The nickel movies gained a reputation as safe spaces for women, who comprised perhaps 40 percent of the typical audience, but the ones in working-class neighborhoods still seemed a bit rough; audiences, for example, cat-called actors on the screen. Entrepreneurs built more sedate and controlled settings, even some "movie palaces," for middle-class families. By 1918, about three-quarters of urban white families went to the movies; they more than doubled their weekly visits by 1930. In rural areas, small-town cinemas attracted farm families, first weekly by horse wagon and later more often by car. Films were so popular that movie attendance dwarfed that of virtually all the competitors—theaters, vaudeville, museums, and the rest—combined; even saloons lost customers.[22]

Most other venues, like department stores, continued to expand. Americans in the 1920s enthusiastically crowded into dance halls, bistros, and sports stadiums. Attendance at major league baseball games jumped more between the 1910s and '20s than in any other decade in the century. Stirred by ragtime in the 1910s, young people in the '20s joined the dancing craze in clubs and on campuses. The nightlife was by then attracting not just the dandies and hustlers but the middle class, too. The center of nightclub swing was Harlem in its Renaissance, featuring famous performance spaces like the Cotton Club. In bitter irony, many of these popular entertainments relied on African American traditions and performers, and yet at the same time, like the amusement parks, these clubs segregated African American customers or barred them altogether.[23]

In these ways, late-nineteenth- and early-twentieth-century Americans—men to start with, but increasingly women and children, too—went out in public more than ever before. They not only out went of the house but also out of the neighborhood. Americans mixed with people like themselves and, more importantly, with people unlike themselves—which sometimes created problems along with excitement. City governments developed policing and regulations—for example, rules against picnicking in parks—to handle nuisances, petty crimes, and intergroup tensions in public spaces. They did not always succeed. In 1919, a race riot broke out in Chicago when black youngsters swam across an unmarked line dividing the white and "colored" sections of the beachfront. Life in public mixed adventure with anxiety for more city—and increasingly, country—people.[24]

Early-twentieth-century American cities pulsated with public life in part because, if the Paris-Tokyo theory of urbanity (p. 163 above) is true, crowded city apartments squeezed people into the streets. Between the Civil War and World War I, millions of immigrant families from abroad and single migrants from rural America landed in the big cities. The better-off boarded with widows or struggling couples. The poorer jammed into small apartments, sometimes sharing rooms with other families and occasionally sleeping in shifts on cots or table tops. In these circumstances, the outdoors—the stoops and streets and parks—provided some room to stretch.[25]

However, a countertrend could be detected. As urban working-class Americans went more often to more diverse sorts of public spaces, more middle-class Americans moved into homes that provided respite from public spaces. Housing construction costs dropped, mortgages became available, and trolley lines rolled out toward the countryside, allowing even families of middling income—those headed by clerks, skilled artisans, teachers, and such—to buy homes buffered by distance from the downtown tumult. The new houses provided more rooms, running water, better lighting, and increasingly, indoor toilets and central heating. Inexpensive, mass-produced furniture, rugs, wallpaper, and prints made possible that cushioned, contentedly stuffed Victorian look. By their location and architectural design, the new houses provided more privacy from outsiders. Middle-class and even lower-middle-class Americans could thus have both: excursions into the public world a streetcar ride away and havens in the private world. The experience probably helped accentuate the contrast between public and private spaces—and the appropriate behavior and moral tone for each one—more than ever before.[26]

An 1884 book of moral instruction entitled *Right and Wrong, Contrasted* paired images of a city and a suburban street. The first picture displays dilapidated housing, a mother with several children running about, one man clubbing another, and a distraught girl tugging on her drunken father's sleeve. The second picture shows stately houses, decorative front yards, tall trees, a horse and carriage, and a well-dressed couple strolling on the sidewalk. Accompanying the images is the message:

> The [city] neighborhood here shown is a representation and true type of hundreds of localities. . . . The scene tells its own story—a tale of brutal passion, poverty, base desires and crime. [In the suburb,] How great the difference! Intelligence, refined taste and prosperity. . . . [W]hatever morality, good sense and culture can do to make people better and happiness is to be sought in such homes.

As noted in the previous chapter, good Victorian husbands returned to these suburban homes after work, and good Victorian wives did not work at all. Bourgeois and aspiring families cultivated domestic rituals which later generations took to be immemorial and sacrosanct, like the family dinner hour and the family-based Christmas. What middle-class Americans may have let slip over the course of the twentieth century as they elaborated both their public and their private activities was their participation in *parochial* spaces. Men spent less time in bars and fraternal lodges, women less time in social clubs, and families less time with neighbors (see chapter 4). Increasingly, middle-class families conducted funerals privately and commemorated the Fourth of July with kin and friends rather than as open, neighborhood events. In the same era, poor and blue-collar city residents, of course, continued to live in cramped flats and to endure the noise, jostling, and the dangers of the public streets. They sought to imitate the private lifestyles of the middle class, but they succeeded in doing so only decades later.[27]

Coming Home

In 1962, saxophonist Cannonball Adderley lamented the decline of the jazz club scene in America—a consequence, he said, of so many top musicians taking better-paying television work and leaving only "second-raters doing road jobs." That was but one way that television undercut public venues; it mainly did so by enticing entertainment seekers to stay home. The trek home started, however, long before 1962. Even as Americans in the early twentieth century enjoyed going out, many in the 1920s started staying in. The fashionable crowd had discovered the new pastimes of hosting card games and of listening to the brand-new entertainment, radio. (Twenty-first century Americans need to remember that radios used to be large pieces of furniture, highly unportable.) An Albany, New York, newspaper editor reported in 1928:

> One night last week we . . . enjoy[ed] a relaxed evening with friends. For three hours hardly a word was spoken and all ears were strained to catch every word and note coming from the radio loud-speaker. We've heard tell that the motion picture industry is getting panicky because people are staying home with their ears tuned to earphones and loud-speakers instead of going to the movies. I might be sticking my neck out, but I think this new entertainment medium is great and will be around for a long time.

In 1920, virtually no American homes had radios; fifteen years later, about two-thirds did. Rural Americans in particular kept buying radios right through the Depression. They followed shows programmed directly to them, such as the "Grand Ole Opry," and ones targeted to city people, such as "Amos 'n' Andy." A Wisconsin mother told interviewers that her daughter "would rip into her chores and she'd come in and flop down on the floor and listen to 'Amanda of Honeymoon Hills.'" Another farm woman praised radio in 1925 for keeping her children happy and at home. Radio brought the sounds of public spaces, such as band performances in New York nightspots, into the quiet, cloistered houses of Americans across the great heartland.[28]

The Great Depression kept yet more Americans at home, because it deprived many of the money and perhaps also of any enthusiasm for stepping out. Moviegoing began its long decline in the 1930s, despite the era's spate of "happy time" films; baseball attendance sagged; and nightclubs closed. Americans spent much of their remaining income on automobiles for work, commuting, and occasional travel, but largely turned homeward. Robert and Helen Lynd, who had studied "Middletown" in the mid-1920s, came back several years later to see how residents had adjusted to the Depression. They found that some new public activities drew people out. New Deal work projects, for example, provided recreational facilities, such as a swimming pool. But people in Middletown had largely retreated home; they were even reading more library books than before. Several government initiatives to re-energize the economy also made home life more appealing. Financing policies (and after World War II, the G.I. Bill) lowered the cost of buying; home ownership in turn led more people to stay put and stay in. So too did rural electrification and telephone service and the agricultural extension agents who encouraged people to buy household goods (see chapter 3, p. 68). Then, the arrival of war in late 1941 further curtailed going out.[29]

On VE and VJ days, Americans celebrated the war's end with public merrymaking commemorated in iconic images such as that of a sailor kissing a passing woman in New York's Times Square. But 1945's street parties did not signal the revival of public life—just the opposite. As economic conditions improved, even working-class Americans could afford more spacious and comfortable homes. In 1910, the average American house or apartment had more people than rooms; by 1970, the average home had about two rooms for each person. In 1920, about one-third of American homes had electric service and one-fifth had toilets; by 1970, virtually all homes had both. Air conditioning, another mundane item that, like window screens, had major social consequences, had become commonplace by the end of the century. Not only did artificial cooling open up the Sunbelt to great migration, it allowed more Americans to stay indoors. In the 1950s, one woman told *House Beautiful* magazine that "television and air-conditioning are bringing families together again." Average Americans could now enjoy the bourgeois home and its domestic lifestyle.[30]

The postwar baby boom further rooted people to their homes. Americans who married at twenty rather than twenty-five and had three children instead of two had less time, money, and interest in public activities. Family duties encouraged many, especially mothers, to involve themselves in their children's schools and in church activities, but discouraged other public outings. When the baby boom eventually receded, the domesticity boom did not. To be sure, 1960s and '70s young adults—the baby boomers themselves—delayed marrying and parenting and could provide the "demographic," as marketers put it, for public activities. They traveled, attended concerts, and ate out. Other trends, however, outweighed the demographics and discouraged public life.[31]

One was mass suburbanization, the postwar move of millions to the suburbs and exurbs. Americans had been moving out from the city centers for generations, but the numbers doing so multiplied after World War II. The Levitts and other developers used factory-style production techniques to build "instant" towns on what had once been farmland. Although the projects sometimes supplied essential neighborhood facilities like schools, they typically presumed that residents would drive miles for most services and entertainment. Eventually, suburban shopping malls satisfied some of the demand for shopping, recreation, and public mingling, but they were small imitations of city stores, venues, and streets. Culture critics charged suburbia with producing a variety of ills. They said it weakened family life or perhaps overheated it, isolated individuals or perhaps forced sociability on them. These fears were overblown, but low-density housing did have consequences. It attracted people who preferred a home-centered life and encouraged others to develop those interests, working on their houses and gardens, for example. The longer job commute, especially as more wives went to work, took time away from public—and parochial—activities. In 1985, historian Kenneth Jackson summed up the change from city spaces to suburban developments: "Residential neighborhoods have become a mass of small, private islands; with the back yard functioning as a wholesome, family-oriented, and reclusive place."[32]

Americans moved to the suburbs largely for detached, single-family homes at affordable prices; they did because they could increasingly afford to and because the government paved the way with new highways and suburban growth policies. Americans also moved out to the suburbs in part to flee racial change, racial tension, and crime. Millions of poor African Americans in search of jobs had moved to the major Northern cities. The proportion of blacks in New York and Chicago, for example, rose from under 10 percent before World War II to 40 percent by 1980. Whites fled from black neighbors even faster than the native-born had fled the Irish in the nineteenth century. The resulting concentration of poor people in the inner cities, combined with the loss of urban manufacturing jobs, led to an upsurge in street crime and periodic racial disorders in the 1960s—and to vivid television images of both. Even more whites then left the cities; others simply avoided them. Disorders and departures fed one another. Deserted streets and vacant stores encouraged yet others to leave, further undermining cities' public spaces. Even bars, long the vexation of middle-class reformers, succumbed as Americans increasingly preferred to drink at home. Chicago, for example, lost 60 percent of its taverns in the second half of the century. Neighborhood drugstore soda fountains also dwindled away. Public venues, such as downtown baseball stadiums, lost customers.[33]

The vicious cycle stopped and even reversed in select American cities around 1990. Crime receded, investment dollars flowed in, housing renovation and construction surged, and affluent people—particularly those who were young, unmarried, and childless—came to play and even to live in downtowns. New Yorkers were startled to see new homes spring up in the once–"bombed-out" South Bronx, and Southern Californians were surprised to find that downtown Los Angeles, for years a bleak night-time landscape of vacated office buildings, had become a chic neighborhood. An urban historian described the revival of downtown Denver as "returning to its roots as a noisy, sometimes raucous, people-filled urban village." Some urban scholars found the turnaround so startling that they described it as a "touristification" of cities. Yet this renaissance touched only some metropolitan areas—those that were better connected to the global information economy and those that were most culturally interesting, such as New York, San Francisco, and Boston, but not cities like St. Louis, Detroit, and Buffalo. Even in the fortunate metropolitan areas, the revitalization of some inner-city neighborhoods only underlined the still larger trend of suburban sprawl—and the homebound lifestyle it encouraged.[34]

The greatest subversion of public life—and the reason for Cannonball Adderley's blues—coincided with the start of mass suburbanization: television. Although radio had already kept some people home some of the time, television was revolutionary. In 1950, only one in ten American households owned a television, and few Americans watched. Nonetheless, newspapers already reported major erosions in public activities, at least in the larger cities. In April, San Francisco's minor league baseball team, the Seals, complained that fans were staying home to watch their games on television. In July, a University of Southern California sociologist announced a study showing that television was holding families at home. He conducted a survey that matched ninety-four television-owning households with ninety-four television-less neighbors. Most of the television-owning respondents said that they were going out less (few of the nonowners said that). "Turn it on at 3 PM and watch until 10 PM. We never go anywhere," complained one. The set owners did, however, report *hosting* more visitors than before. "Sometimes I get tired of the house being used as a semiprivate theater," said one interviewee. "I have almost turned off the set when some people visit us." And not surprisingly, three-fourths of television-owning respondents said they were going to movies less often. Professor Edward McDonagh noted what he saw as a positive byproduct: "the family is home together, rather than at the theater with strangers." Later in the decade, transportation officials in New York City and in Lima, Ohio, reported major losses of evening ridership because, they assumed, people were staying home to watch television. In 1958, a study conducted at the University of California, Los Angeles, concluded that the movie industry was in substantial and permanent decline. The studios could anticipate some short-term improvement, the author concluded, mainly from a forthcoming demographic surge in teenage baby boomers, but "the huge theater audience is gone," largely because of television. Why not? Watching television was easier and cheaper.[35]

By 1960, nearly nine in ten households had a television set and almost everyone watched every day. By 1990, the average household owned more than two sets and Americans spent more time watching television than doing anything else besides working and sleeping. Depending on how one counts, around 2000, Americans averaged from two-and-a-half to four-and-half hours a day watching television. Over the years, the Gallup poll occasionally asked people to list their favorite ways to spend an evening. In 1938, television was not an option. In 1960, 28 percent named television as their favorite, more than any other evening activity; by 1974, 46 percent picked television. Many Americans—from a third to a half—confessed to interviewers that they watched too much television.[36]

Watching television probably reduced Americans' literacy, increased their weight, distorted their views of the world, reduced their volunteering, encouraged their children's aggression, and may have been addictive—although these research findings are contested. In any case, watching so much television certainly led Americans to curtail public engagement. They spent less time on other at-home activities, such as sleeping and reading, but also less time on outside activities, such as attending movies, playing sports, going to meetings, or otherwise being in public spaces. Movie attendance, as the 1958 UCLA report predicted, dropped by about 80 percent and never recovered; horse race attendance grew into the early 1970s and then plummeted; major league baseball kept its attendance up by roughly doubling the number of teams, while minor league baseball collapsed. Television helped keep America home.[37]

Since 1980, another at-home technology has drawn Americans' attention: computers. By 2003, three in five American homes had a computer, and most had Internet access—as we would expect, homes of the highly educated much more often than those of the less educated. In 2009, about a third of Americans told pollsters that an Internet connection was a necessity of life to them. Yet unlike television, computer use did *not* revolutionize how Americans spent their time. Americans cut back on television and perhaps sleep in order to write e-mails and surf the Net, but they did not further cut back significantly on public activities. Moreover, while electronic communications connected Americans to the outside— to news, videos, and chats (and a lot of shopping and pornography) from literally around the world—Americans overwhelmingly used the technology to communicate with family and friends rather than enter the world of strangers. The Web was as much a parochial as a public space.[38]

The broadcast technologies of the twentieth century—radio, television, Internet—pose a fascinating paradox and a series of questions. The media bring the great outside inside. Millions of Americans "virtually" attended Lindbergh's landing in France, Bobby Thomson's pennant-winning home run in New York's Polo Grounds, Jack Ruby's murder of Lee Harvey Oswald in Dallas, the landings on the moon, and the destruction of Manhattan's World Trade Center towers. For decades, observers have speculated about the consequences of virtual participation at a distance. Would space be obliterated and location no longer matter now that people could "be" anywhere at anytime or all the time? The answer seems to be no; distance still matters. Would the new media draw people into the wider world and press them to be more engaged in the public realm? The answer, by the start of the twenty-first century, was a mixed one. People around the nation wore the same clothes, listened to the same songs, recognized the same celebrities, and laughed at the same jokes in large measure because of radio, television, and the Internet. But Americans, with minor exceptions such as calling in to talk radio or posting a comment to a Web site, watched rather than participated in or exposed themselves to this virtual "world of strangers." In fact, concerns about meeting strangers in virtual space spread about as fast as Internet connectivity itself. A California assemblyman, for example, posted warnings to parents in 2008: "There are many hidden dangers for our kids lurking on the Internet. . . . The old adage 'Don't talk to strangers' also applies while online."[39]

In simple, physical terms, Americans of the early twenty-first century were out in public more than ever before, thanks to growth of urban areas, factory and office jobs, college education, and women commuting to work. Much of that physical exposure, however, had qualities of the virtual. In 2005, about nine in ten American workers drove to work, about eight, alone in their cars. (Here is one way that New York City is really different: most New Yorkers used public transit.) They entered typically parochial workplaces with few strangers. Even when they went shopping at the mall, retailers tried to provide them with an environment of people who at least *looked* parochial. For example, in 1992, one mall reported training its security staff to help foster that "warm, safe feeling." Increasingly, as well, Americans bought homes in semiprivate, gated neighborhoods to keep the public world at bay. Whatever the increasing incidental exposure Americans had to public space, they turned in their discretionary time to parochial and especially private space. The march out of private homes into public spaces in the decades before 1900 to shows, department stores, zoos, movies, and ballparks turned around in the decades before 2000 to the comfort, warmth, safety, electronic entertainment, and mail-order deliveries of home. In 1987, trend-spotter Faith Popcorn declared that "cocooning"—staying home rather than going out for leisure time—was "in." One headline writer defined it as a "Desire for a Cozy, Perfect Environment Far From the Influences of a Madding World." Fifteen years later, forecasters declared, as forecasters do, a reversal: "The End of Nesting." Nonetheless, the turn-of-the-century movement was, as it had been for several preceding decades, homeward.[40]

Not of the Crowd

Over the centuries, Americans entered public spaces and learned to cope with the crowds of strangers there. From the occasional days when isolated farmers heard about the outside world in travelers' stories at the local tavern (his wife at home awaiting his retelling) to the many evenings when couples watched movies at the local cineplex seated among hundreds of strangers, Americans' experiences in the public realm multiplied enormously. The cultural and psychological implications of this transformation of everyday life are not well understood. Commentators during the period of its greatest expansion speculated that the public experience created everything from constant anxiety to a sense of universal fellowship. (The research literature suggests that any consequences were far less dramatic.) Edgar Allan Poe told a story in 1840 that he placed in London but could have happened in New York, which illustrates the wonderment. Sitting at the window of a coffeehouse, the narrator observes the passing multitudes, identifying one category of humans after another by their clothes, posture, and facial expressions—the junior clerks and the upper clerks, the gentry, the gamblers, and so on. One face in particular draws his attention. The narrator lurches out of the coffee shop and spends hours following this man who, he discovers, becomes agitated and distressed when alone; the man needs to mix with the masses to find any tranquility. He is a new sort of person, "the man *of* the crowd." Americans' immersion in crowds, however, did not expand indefinitely. Over the twentieth century, for more and more Americans, the attractions of private spaces—the comforts and conveniences of home, the ability to import what one wanted from the outside world electronically and by doorstep delivery, the power to distance oneself from what one did not want—and the attractions of parochial spaces—sheltered neighborhoods, private health clubs, a selection of churches—eventually outpaced the new excitements and enticements of the public spaces. If cramped quarters had pushed Parisians, Tokyoites, and New Yorkers of the nineteenth century into the streets, spacious quarters brought many twentieth-century Americans back indoors. Increasingly, Americans turned back home, away from the public arenas.[41]

The history cannot, of course, be rewound. In the twenty-first century, even the most rural or suburban of Americans regularly encounters the public world of strangers not only in virtual spaces through electronic media but also in real spaces, such as large outlet stores, national parks, and stadiums. Still, Americans' preference for the private and the parochial, for the small voluntary community, has become easier for more Americans to attain.

THE POLITICAL PUBLIC

Americans at the end of the twentieth century seemed to also turn away from the political arena. Assessing whether and why this was so preoccupied many political scientists who worried about the "vanishing voter" and "the strange disappearance of civic America." Bipartisan commissions investigated Americans' apparent political apathy. Political operatives deflected blame from themselves. "The consultants," a reporter noted at a professional conference in 1990, "were particularly annoyed at the theory that their negative commercials turn voters off. 'We've had a decline in participation ever since John Kennedy's election,' said Tom Edmonds, a Republican consultant. 'People just don't care.'" Americans' seeming political disengagement since 1960 contrasted sharply with the upswell of political enthusiasm that marked the eighteenth and nineteenth centuries.[42]

Deferential Politics

Although Americans increasingly built their lives across local boundaries (see chapter 4), localism remains a striking distinction of American politics. Virtually every administrative district of more than a few thousand residents has its own elected officials, police, school system, taxes, and laws governing construction, land use, traffic, and much more. Almost all American factions extol grassroots democracy and local control; we might even call it *parochial* politics. This localism has its origins in America's earliest years. Many of the first settlers emigrated from England in part because they resented the new British dynasty's efforts to tighten its control of village life. Much of the Revolution's energy came from Americans' resistance to the king's deputies who ruled colonial governments. And many of the difficulties George Washington had in conducting the

War of Independence came from trying to get these same locally oriented Americans to join together against the British. Before the Revolution, the colonists understood that Britain, thousands of miles and several months away, ultimately determined Americans' legal status, economic conditions, and risk of war. Day to day, however, Americans commonly ignored the authorities in London and in the colonial capitals. Town and village authorities, as I noted in the previous chapter, particularly those in the North, regulated much of the market, such as the prices of some foods and wages; assisted the needy (so long as they were worthy locals); and tried to regulate residents' private lives. "Most Americans were proud that they lived in such [isolated] communities and that their communal standards were often parochial and idiosyncratic," wrote one historian. "Often their central corporate aspiration was to be left alone in their secluded villages to shape their lives as they collectively saw fit."[43]

In the seventeenth and early eighteenth centuries, the collective view of what was fit was usually the view of a very small group in each locality. Of course, only white, property-owning (and typically Protestant) men could vote, but few of them bothered. Election turnouts were well below half of those eligible. Where town meetings decided matters, the attendees typically deferred to the local elite. Early American culture was far more egalitarian than Europe's, but it still gave the duty of governing to a handful of presumably virtuous, dispassionate, disciplined "stewards" of the community. In moments of crisis, constituents might storm out to vote or demonstrate their fury in other ways, perhaps by running off the tax collector or locking an official in the smokehouse. Typically, however, early Americans deferred to "gentlemen." In return, gentlemen promised good order, disinterested civic virtue, and periodic treats. Young George Washington, for example, lost his first run for the Virginia House of Burgesses in 1755. He made sure in the next election to enlist some of the local gentry to support his candidacy, line up early, and publically announce their vote for him. Washington also "spent 239.6s. out of his own pocket" for a variety of drinks, totaling "160 gallons of liquor to be served to the 391 voters of the district."[44]

Events in the decades running up to the Revolution, however, shook this deferential system. Colonial elites in conflict with the crown and with one another increasingly enlisted voters (and vigilantes) in their struggles, however distasteful that was to them. Gentlemen accused one another of stirring up the "passions" of the masses. In Philadelphia in 1764, the stirring up included distributing German-language pamphlets and bringing German immigrants to the polls, to the dismay of many leaders of English stock, including Benjamin Franklin. Once released, populist passions could be neither dammed nor channeled; they merged with the general upwelling of social egalitarianism described in the previous chapter. Ideologies of deference gave way to the ideology that all white men, not only "natural" leaders, had voice in the political arena. Tom Paine's "Common Sense" asserted as much and drew fire from John Adams for its "absurd democratical notions."[45]

Democratic notions spurred the Revolution, and the Revolution, like many revolutions, further stimulated democratic demands. The rambunctious egalitarianism that European visitors remarked upon only expanded with the Revolution and into the Jacksonian era's "passion for equality" described by Tocqueville. Grassroots groups declared their independence against central authorities to the point of violence, as in Shay's Rebellion. The right to vote, already widespread by English standards, expanded as state legislatures eliminated religious tests and repealed wealth requirements (or allowed inflation to render them moot). Local governments established more frequent elections for more offices. The transportation revolution spread political news widely and cheaply; it also made both campaigning and voting easier. The principle that the people should defer to stewards of high prestige drowned under the wave of populist democracy and factional competition. New sorts of men not of the gentry stood for election. Politicians had to abandon classical oratory for a "middling" rhetoric—not too elevated, not too vulgar—to appeal to the increasingly empowered middle classes.[46]

American men of the new Republic discussed public affairs and entered electoral politics. Organized parties mobilized to support candidates, complain to government, and debate policy issues. The well-off still controlled many decisions behind closed doors, but they now had to present, defend, and compromise their decisions in meeting halls jammed with demanding citizens. Similarly, Americans learned to petition and pressure Congress, notably around the Sunday mail dispute (mentioned in chapter 4). Abolitionists picked up these lobbying techniques. Elections became more contested, more cantankerous, and more vicious than those of the colonial era. The editor of a major Whig paper, for example, charged that "General [Andrew] Jackson's mother was a COMMON PROSTITUTE, brought to this country by British soldiers! She afterward married a MULATTO MAN," for whom she bore the future president. Indeed, to American elites, Jackson personified the intrusion of the mob and its passions into politics. Philadelphia lawyer Sydney George Fisher marked the succession of Martin Van Buren to the presidency in his diary on March 4, 1837: the transition ended "an administration [Jackson's] distinguished by ignorance, folly, passion, and corruption . . . [and] a career sufficient refutation of the absurd idea . . . that people are competent to self-government." Election days in the antebellum era confirmed such contempt, because balloting often occurred amidst riotous carnivals, surpassing even George Washington's 1755 kegger. One 1830 account reported that an "election in Kentucky lasts three days, and during that period whiskey and apple toddy flow through our cities and villages like the Euphrates through ancient Babylon." In 1842, German immigrant farmer Jacob Schramm wrote home about elections in Indiana: "I do not go to elections. The whole business repels me because I see nothing but the filthy, self-serving ways of the money-hungry and unworthy who vie for official positions." The numbers suggest, however, that he was in the minority; in the 1840s, about 80 percent of eligible Indiana voters turned out for the presidential elections.[47]

Voting statistics for the earliest years of the American Republic are sketchy, but they generally show that typically many fewer than half of those eligible took part. Then, starting roughly around 1820, perhaps sparked by the Panic of 1819, voting turnout rates climbed sharply, eventually peaking around 1890. They rose in part because of legal changes, notably states' reduction of property requirements for voting and addition of polling places, and in part because of political changes, particularly the emergence of two-party competition. Perhaps as well, American men got more interested in electoral campaigns.[48]

Contemporary observers like Fisher described average Americans of the antebellum years as politically enthused, punch-drunk with the prospect of grasping power. But how deeply people were politically engaged is uncertain. In one obvious respect, most Americans stood outside politics: women could not vote; slaves and even free blacks could not vote; and in some places propertyless men, Catholics, and Jews still could either not vote or not hold office. Nonetheless, many white men (and occasionally their wives) plunged zealously into partisan politics, with its noisy rallies, torchlight parades, and beer taps. Historians Glenn Altschuler and Stuart Blumin have argued that this democratic enthusiasm was episodic and thin, largely limited to election day. On other days, including those devoted to selecting party nominees, antebellum politics remained a private game of courthouse lawyers and seekers of government contracts. Most respectable folk, like Jacob Schramm, kept their distance most of the time. Other scholars, however, argue that genuine political interest did run deep. They point out that newspapers of the era were heavily partisan and that towns held several election days a year. However much antebellum Americans were politically energized, we can question how much of it was a matter of responsible citizenship, of civic-mindedness. In the nineteenth century, entertainment, spirited team competition, partying, and simple bribery, as well as special economic and ethnic interests, drew American men into the political arena.[49]

Popular Politics Peaks

Nothing mobilized Americans politically like the intensifying struggle over extending slavery. It divided families and friends the way politics hadn't since the Revolution. Partisan energies stoked violence in celebrated instances such as John Brown's raid on Harper's Ferry and the now-forgotten street brawls between abolitionists and Southern sympathizers. During the war, the antidraft riots in New York City took the lives of dozens of black men and scores of largely Irish-American rioters. The war profoundly touched every distant hamlet. Local governments had to raise companies and then cope with the absence of so many young men and the creation of so many young widows. At the same time, Lincoln's activist administration enacted income taxes, homestead grants, a transcontinental railroad, and other nation-building initiatives, all of which also pulled Americans into national politics.[50]

After Appomattox, state and especially local government spending outpaced the federal budget. Cities handled rapid population growth by investing in police departments, street paving, water treatment, and other infrastructure. Town residents argued and voted on these issues and struggled as well over hot-button topics like alcohol policies and compulsory schooling. Postbellum federal politics increasingly mattered, too, especially as regional economies knitted together into a national one (excepting the South). Issues like hard money versus soft, high tariffs versus low, and labor versus capital bubbled in the political pot. Voting rates soared, driven by these controversies, political machines shepherding new immigrants to the polls, and the familiar enticements of revelry, liquor, jobs, and money. In the 1880s and '90s, over three-fourths of eligible voters outside the South voted in congressional, off-year elections. (The South was politically another country, one that suppressed not only black votes, but poor white votes, too.) One scholar wrote that "everyone who was eligible [and physically able] to vote . . . went to the polls. And they did so in nearly every election." Some historians consider the closing decades of the nineteenth century to be the heyday of popular democracy (outside the South); others are skeptical.[51]

To what extent do the high turnouts and the election hoopla of the late nineteenth century show that Americans were civically minded? An answer to that question would help answer another big question about this era: why did the turnouts and hoopla plummet after the turn of the century? Voting rates for congressional elections outside the South dropped from over 75 to about 50 percent in the 1920s and leveled out, with modest undulations, at a little above 50 percent into the twenty-first century. Some historians suggest that Americans' high involvement in the 1880s and '90s followed from simple self-interest. Parties had the organization, patronage, and money to bring men to the polls on election day by cajoling, entertaining, treating, and paying them to vote (perhaps more than once). In an oft-cited 1892 report, Trinity College Professor J. J. McCook "reached the startling conclusion that 16 per cent of the voters of Connecticut were up for sale, at prices ranging from two to twenty dollars. What is more, he found that three-fifths of . . . [these voters] were not shiftless lodgers or ignorant immigrants, but the descendants of virtuous Yankee yeomen." Even when men's election-day enthusiasm was genuine, the skeptics argue, it did not spring from disinterested citizenship but instead from a desire to get their, their relatives', and their ethnic groups' cut of the jobs, contracts, and status that politics offered.[52]

Starting in the late 1890s, public enthusiasm for politics, including voting, plummeted. Four sorts of changes may have contributed to that loss of energy: more complex electoral procedures, fewer inducements, party realignment, and perhaps deeper social trends. First, new rules discouraged the poor and minorities from voting. In the South, formal discrimination through poll taxes and rigged literacy tests largely replaced the violent suppression of votes. In one generation, African American voting rates went from over half of adult men to nearly zero; white rates dropped by a third. Outside the South, good-government reformers — largely educated and affluent progressives who worried about the baneful influence of uneducated and poor voters — enacted stricter conditions for being able to vote, such as longer residency requirements, more complex ballots, and English-only procedures. Other Progressive moves, including at-large city council elections and professionalizing city administrations, distanced local government from average voters. Many reforms made it harder for the less sophisticated to vote and to understand their options. Most states banned ballot symbols, such as donkeys and elephants, which could assist the illiterate, and many cities required that all candidates be listed without party identification.[53]

Second, as to incentives, the secret ballot itself, which became common around 1890, undercut vote selling.* Parties stopped directly buying votes and some voters stopped voting. Civil service reform undercut indirect incentives to vote by taking thousands of government jobs out of party leaders' hands. That in turn reduced the kickbacks that holders of patronage jobs paid the parties, which, further on, meant that the

---

* In 2008, a Minnesota college student tried to work around this problem. He offered his vote up for sale on the Internet and pledged to provide photographic proof from the voting booth that he had kept the deal. The county attorney charged the student with a felony, violating an 1893 law against vote buying or selling.

parties had less money for parades, beer kegs, and hoopla. (A twenty-first-century experiment showed that even today a block party can bring out voters.) Reformers also suppressed the boisterousness of election-eering—and the deadly violence that often accompanied it. For many American men, these sorts of changes helped transform elections from exciting, fun, and sometimes profitable outings into straight-laced, bor-ing exercises of civic virtue.[54]

Third, political realignment began with the severe 1893 depression that started under a Democratic administration. The Republicans com-bined their base of socially conservative evangelicals with new voters at-tracted by the message of restoring prosperity. They were able to domi-nate many Northern states and left the South to virtual one-party rule by the Democrats. For much of the early twentieth century, then, competi-tion between the parties in most states faded and parties had less need, as well as fewer tools, to draw voters to polls.[55]

Fourth, broader social changes may have also depressed early-twentieth-century voting and electioneering. New, exciting public en-tertainments—baseball, vaudeville, movies, and so on—drew younger people away from old-fashioned political speeches and parades. The bit-ter ethnic divisions that had energized many Americans to vote, notably disputes over alcohol and schooling between foreign-born Catholics and native Protestants, faded as immigrants assimilated. Some scholars also argue that the rise of large-scale, national organizations—government, media, manufacturing, and commerce—undermined average Ameri-cans' sense that they could control events in their local communities. To many Americans, things seem to be decided by powers far away; national tides swamped what Robert Wiebe called "island communities." Voting declined, it is argued, because Americans began feeling disempowered. These propositions are contestable, but there are more than enough ex-planations, from changes in procedures to changes in Zeitgeist, to ac-count for the growing abstention of so many Americans from the politi-cal arena.[56]

Political Retreat

That abstention drew attention and concern. In an August 2, 1924, edito-rial, the *Los Angeles Times* bemoaned the low rates of voting:

> With what heart would Washington and his brave men have endured
> that awful winter at Valley Forge had they known... that 50 per cent
> of the sixth or seventh generation of Americans whom they were free-
> ing from... political bondage voluntarily would re-enter it?... [But

America] will emerge, rise and shine. Her people will take heart. And no better time for heart-taking can be found than the fourth day of next November [election day] and no better inspiration than the necessity for retention in office of that able chieftain, Calvin Coolidge.

Coolidge was retained, but turnout remained low. Fredrick J. Haskin, journalist and author of an often-reprinted text on American government, reported that the early returns, turnouts of under one-half of eligible voters, shocked the leaders of the League of Women Voters and American Legion. They had mounted a national campaign to get out the vote and now "are at a loss to understand why so many citizens are slackers with respect to the fundamental duty of citizenship." A year and half later, Haskin reported on the renewal of the national campaign to get out the vote, a campaign driven by the concern that the government was "largely in the hands of selfish minorities and organized cliques because the busy mass of the population is willing to let some one else attend to its politics." In the end, one-third of the eligible voted in 1926. Although it was largely the absence of working-class, immigrant, and black voters that accounts for the great drop-off from the 1880s (and, in part, also some women's hesitancy to exercise their newly granted suffrage), the get-out-the-vote campaigners focused their concern on the smaller drop-off among white middle-class voters. Their abstention from politics, reformers feared, yielded power to unenlightened and corrupt voters—echoing, of course, a chronic worry about American politics.[57]

The residents of Middletown also noticed the drop in political activity around them. In the 1920s, wrote Robert and Helen Lynd, "elections are no longer the lively centers of public interest they were in the nineties. . . . Today torchlight processions and horns no longer blast out the voters or usher in newly elected officials." They went on to quote a local businessman who decided to listen to the radio rather than attend a political speech, a speech he could read about in the next day's paper. The Lynds also explain Middletowners' political passivity by their cynicism toward corrupt politicians—although there is little reason to think that contempt for politicians was new and made the difference.[58]

After the doldrums of the 1920s, political participation resurged, although not among those whom the good-government activists would have preferred. Distress from the Great Depression and inspiration from the New Deal impelled workers and immigrants and their children to become voters. World War II and the postwar boom then solidified much of a generation's commitment to the party of Franklin Roosevelt. ("Mr. Roosevelt," one worker famously said, "is the only man we ever had in the White House who would understand that my boss is a son of a bitch.")

Turnout never regained the levels it reached in the nineteenth century, but from the 1930s to 1970, over half of eligible voters outside the South voted, even in nonpresidential elections. The New Deal administration also mobilized voters by funneling much of its aid and jobs through local Democratic political machines and, later, by engaging veterans through the G.I. Bill. On the larger public stage, millions of workers joined unions and manned strike lines; deadly violence flared between union members and employers' security forces.[59]

The generation that grew up in the Depression, fought in World War II, and subsequently enjoyed an unprecedented economic boom—later labeled the Greatest Generation—largely sustained its political involvement through middle age. In the mid-1960s, the noted political scientist Robert E. Lane hailed an emerging "politics of consensus in an age of affluence." Growing wealth, equality, and stability allowed the nation to replace divisive, ideological politics with government by agreement and expertise. Then things fell apart. A generation later, Lane published a far more pessimistic essay in which he worried about a "rising malaise" of American democracy. After the 1960s, the numerous baby boomers and the boomers' children did not participate in politics nearly as much as their parents had. They showed less interest, knew less, campaigned less, and voted less. Voting rates among those eligible to vote dropped by about ten points from the early 1960s to the early 1970s and stayed relatively low afterwards.* Trying to understand this second, twentieth-century era of dropping involvement has kept political scientists busy for decades.[60]

Unlike reforms of the early twentieth century, post-1960s rule changes, such as simpler registration, absentee balloting, and multilingual instructions, should have raised voting rates, but they increased turnouts little. Awarding eighteen-to-twenty-year-olds the right to vote in 1971 *reduced* turnout rates, because relatively few of them voted, but that cannot explain the scale of the post-1960s decline. Something else was going on.[61]

Interest, too, seemed to wane. Between 1966 and 2000, the percentage of college freshmen who agreed that it was very important or essential to keep "up to date with political affairs" dropped by over half to about 25 percent. (Interest in politics, however, appeared to rise around 2000.) At the end of the twentieth century, Americans, especially younger ones, knew less about public affairs than Americans used to know, or they knew no more than earlier generations did in spite of having gotten more schooling. For example, teenagers surveyed in 2000 were much less likely than teenagers surveyed in 1977 to know that Churchill was English.[62]

---

* From 2000 to 2008, voting rates in presidential elections rose back to near-1960 levels, but that re-engagement had not yet shown up in off-year elections.

The old inducements to participate and to vote, such as bribes, alcohol, and jobs, were long gone, and other inducements—entertainment, for one—may have also had less draw. Politics, like everything else, could not compete with the home screen; the spread of television seemed to undermine political interest and turnout. Americans engaged less in elections also, some argue, because they increasingly used other tactics to influence government: "politics by other means." Demonstrations, boycotts, writing checks, organized lobbying, and most especially lawsuits seemed to promise clearer, faster results than voting in election after election. (Consider *Brown v. Board of Education* on ending segregation, *Roe v. Wade* on allowing abortion, and more recent court rulings curbing affirmative action.) Increasingly, some Americans also preferred to do their civic duty in small parochial groups, like church social action committees. As several scholars have pointed out, intense involvement in such groups may not only draw people away from the public arena, it may even build barriers between groups.[63]

And yet young Americans' greater abstention from politics after the mid-1960s—the drop-off was largely among young adults—may need little more explanation than the political history of those years. Civil disorder in the cities, the assassinations of Martin Luther King Jr. and Robert Kennedy, more civil disorder in the cities, a costly and futile war, street demonstrations against that war, rising crime rates, and then the scandal of a president entangled in illegal acts and forced to resign—all that happened between 1965 and 1974. Add in economic stagnation after 1970 and polarization of the political parties and one might ask, Why wouldn't Americans give up on politics? On the other hand, one could also ask why frustration did not mobilize Americans to "throw the bums out"? The thesis that America's political traumas suffice to explain political abstention runs into a puzzle, however: similar declines in voting occurred in other Western nations. A different thesis is that the political parties, especially the Democrats, "demobilized" voters by focusing on television advertising and cultivating rich donors rather than on grassroots organizing. The success the religious right had in the early 2000s and the Obama campaign had in 2008 through door-to-door work provides anecdotal support for this explanation.[64]

Finally and most broadly, perhaps Americans' withdrawal from elections was a symptom of a deeper political alienation after the mid-1960s. Perhaps the can-do, lets-get-organized spirit that observers since Tocqueville's time had ascribed to Americans had dissipated. During roughly the same period, Americans were much more negative when answering survey questions such as, "How much of the time do you think you can trust government in Washington to do what is right?" Before the mid-

1960s, nearly three in four Americans answered "just about always" or "most of the time"; in the 1980s and '90s, about *one* in four did; the proportion rebounded in the 2000s to nearly two in four. One exhibit of Americans' skepticism is their view of John F. Kennedy's assassination. In 1966, about half told pollsters that it had been a conspiracy; from 1976 on, about three-fourths did. Researchers have attributed declining trust in government to concrete political events, such as the Vietnam War; increasing economic inequality and ethnic diversity; a growing disdain for established institutions throughout Western societies; and even rising popular expectations for what government *should* do.[65]

What Americans mean by these distrusting answers is puzzling, especially when we find out that Americans' trust of *local* government did not drop; that their trust of the national government soared after one its worst failures, the attacks of 9/11; and that people who express distrust are no less likely than the trusting to participate politically. Perhaps the question captures nothing more than Americans' emotions about the national scene—how much respect, disgust, or patriotism they feel at the moment.[66]

Summing up, starting around 1970, at least several events and trends led young Americans to withdraw from politics. Given that some seemed to return, in some ways, to politics in the 1990s and 2000s, the best account may be this: the combination, on the one hand, of unusually favorable conditions for political engagement before the mid-1960s—the New Deal's political mobilization, a relatively popular war, family-building, and strong economic growth—with, on the other hand, unusually unfavorable conditions immediately after the mid-1960s—political traumas, an unpopular war, economic stagnation, and television—produced a downward lurch in Americans' political engagement. By the 2000s, however, Americans had returned to their "normal," early-twentieth-century level of involvement, one that was still notably below that of the late nineteenth century and that of people in other Western nations.

For all the modern concern and debate about political involvement, we should not lose sight of the larger picture: only by the late twentieth century, with women's suffrage and civil rights laws, could most adult Americans even claim full participation in politics. Participating or not became largely a matter of choice and personal enthusiasm, not of forced exclusion. The arc of Americans' enthusiasm for politics roughly approximates that of their general engagement in public spaces: peaking sometime in the nineteenth century. Many details are specific to politics, such as the way revisions of election rules around 1900 fettered poorer voters and the way fluctuations in party competition determined turnouts. And the timing of the two are not quite the same. Still, we can see some rough parallels: over the nineteenth century, an expanding public arena—more travel, communications, events, and attractions, as well as more democratic politics—drew more Americans out of their earlier seclusion. Then in the twentieth century, for various reasons, some specific and some common (like television), Americans stepped back from both buzzing public spaces and bewildering politics to their more comfortable, less threatening, private and parochial spaces.

WHOM DO YOU TRUST?

A seemingly new trope spread in popular film and television after 1960: the secret conspiracy controlled by people in authority, even by the president himself (for example, *Chinatown*, the *Bourne* trilogy, works by director Oliver Stone, and *The X-Files*, with its catchphrase, "Trust No One"). Whether as spur or symptom, the media participated in the surge of distrust Americans expressed for the national government. It also participated in what seems like a post-1960s surge of distrust of other Americans. The press printed and broadcast stories that carried implicit and sometimes explicit messages that people could not be trusted—stories about both serious and petty crime and about derelictions of duty, such as the Catholic priest sexual abuse scandal. On Christmas Eve 2001, to take a stark instance, a young mother allowed a woman at a Chicago bus terminal to hold her baby for a moment while she struggled with her bags and an older child. The supposed Good Samaritan fled with the baby (who was found a few days later in West Virginia). "I probably should have said no," said the mother, "because I know you can't trust everyone."[67]

Researchers since the mid-twentieth century have systematically studied people's trust and distrust of other people. In particular, many surveys asked respondents around the world this question: "Generally speaking, would you say that most people can be trusted, or that you can't be too careful in dealing with people?" Clinical psychologists have used variations of this question to identify misanthropic personalities, but social scientists used it to assess people's worldviews. The proportion of Americans who answered (to a short version of this question) that most people can be trusted rose from about two-thirds in the 1940s and '50s to about three-fourths around 1960. But then the proportion sank. In later surveys (using the full version of the question), the percentage of respondents who expressed trust fell from over 50 percent in the 1960s to about 40 percent by the 1990s, perhaps rising a bit in the early 2000s. Fewer Americans expressed trust *not* because particular individuals had lost faith in "most people," but because each decade, fewer young Americans coming of age said most people can be trusted than did those born before them. And people tend to stick with their youthful worldview for the rest of their lives. This generational change in the United States is distinctive among major Western nations.[68]

What does replacement of older, trusting Americans with younger, distrusting ones tell us? That Americans' character changed? That the people Americans encountered became less trustworthy? Or that American culture became more cynical? The survey item works, as intended, as a crude personality test. Although logically one can agree with both parts of the question—that most people can be trusted *and* that you can't be too careful—the question forces one to choose. Respondents who choose the trusting answer tend to be more positive, upbeat, generous, and honest than those who give the "can't be too careful" answer. Still, it is unlikely, and against other evidence, that trusting personalities died out so quickly and were replaced so quickly by cynical personalities. More likely, young Americans answered the question in a way that reflected how the world looked to them around the time that they entered adulthood.[69]

Perhaps there were more people one had to "careful" about. Robert Putnam suggests that Americans became less honest and trust*worthy*, for example, running stop signs more often. Others argue that Americans became more materialistic and their greed made them increasingly suspicious. Or perhaps specific social and political events disillusioned young Americans. In place of their parents' and grandparents' euphoria from a "good war" won and economic success, young people whose introduction to adulthood was the Vietnam War, a crime wave, Watergate, racial tension, and growing inequality learned caution. Or in the end, perhaps academics have made too much out of a roughly fourteen-point drop in positive answers to one question.[70]

If Americans coming of age after the 1960s seemed increasingly suspicious, it would be hardly a new trend in American history; it may be a throwback. Many generations worried that strangers they met were frauds or assailants and that crowds of strangers could become mobs. Nativist reactions against immigrants of all sorts, including the Irish, Italians, Chinese, and others, broke out often in the nineteenth century. In the next chapter I describe how bourgeois Americans of the eighteenth and nineteenth centuries suspected that strangers whom they met were not whom they purported to be. Someone of low standing could be trying to pass as a gentleman; he might even be a confidence man. For example, readers of the *New York Daily Times* in 1852 learned of a Señor De Castro, alias Valencia, who charmed "fashionable circles in the South" and New York with fanciful tales of his military adventures. He swept women off their feet—when necessary, affecting a tubercular cough to gain their sympathy—and lived the high life on credit from his new friends, all despite having spent a term in the city's Tombs prison. The question, whom can you trust these days? must have been muttered by many *Daily Times* readers. Perhaps the distrust is as much a reflection of withdrawal from public spaces as a cause of it.[71]

CONCLUSION

How might one evaluate the parabola that this chapter has described? From the colonial era to the turn of the twentieth century, Americans rushed into public spaces; then they increasingly stepped back into their private and parochial spaces. Almost all commentators decry the civic disengagement of the twentieth century; few publically agree with Philadelphian Sidney George Fisher when in 1837 he dismissed the "idea . . . that people are competent to self-government," and few would agree with the Progressives around 1910 who claimed that only the well-informed should have voice. Post-1960s disengagement from electoral politics—be it from frustration, distrust, complacency, or disgust—is by these lights a social problem. Most commentators also see a social problem in contemporary Americans' avoidance of public spaces, believing that a viable democracy and a vibrant culture require intermingling and interchange among diverse people. Political scientist Robert Lane argues that, although intimate social ties are important for social order, "democracy must include strangers and the unfamiliar and the dissimilar." Privatism and parochialism, many fear, breed suspicion and intolerance which, in turn, corrode liberal democracy and impair problem-solving. From that perspective, the fact that large homes and fast cars enabled suburban Americans to turn increasingly homeward, away from their fellow citizens, may be, as historian Kenneth Jackson argues, a problem. Ironically, though, the peak years of American street life were also the years of street battles among Americans of different backgrounds and the twentieth-century withdrawal from the streets coincides with greater intergroup tolerance, integration, intermarriage, and multiculturalism.[72]

Certainly, twenty-first-century Americans spend much more of their lives in the public "world of strangers" than their occasional tavern-going and revival-attending eighteenth-century ancestors could imagine. The recent retreat from public spaces, however, does fit the American preference for groups of like-minded people freely chosen and easily exited, for the small voluntaristic communities of family and friends.

6 *Mentality*

Sometime in the 1850s, Abraham Lincoln gave his wife a copy of a popular advice book he had closely studied, Mary G. Chandler's *The Elements of Character*. Early in the book, Mary Todd Lincoln would have read, "Weak and helpless as we may be in the affairs of this life, there is, however, one thing over which we have entire control . . . one thing left which misfortune cannot touch, which God is ever seeking to aid us in building up, and over which He permits us to hold absolute control; and this is Character. For this, and for this alone, we are entirely responsible." Building character, constructing a better self for which one is "entirely responsible," has for centuries been an American project. Later generations used the term character less and psychological jargon more, but the construction project was much the same. In 2007, for example, entrepreneurs of "positive psychology" offered to teach people to "understand how our thoughts drive our feelings and our actions . . . [to] utilize a concrete set of skills to think more accurately . . . [and] apply these skills . . . to become more resilient, productive, and successful." Mary G. Chandler would have approved.[1]

Over the generations, more Americans participated in more such self-conscious self-improvement. Slowly shedding an old-world fatalism, they saw greater possibilities to control the world and themselves. With new knowledge, new technologies, and more options, planning and calculation could be increasingly effective. Critically, self-construction involved examining and molding one's emotions. Middle-class Americans learned and taught their children to check feelings of aggression and to nurture feelings of sympathy and affection. Greater self-control, self-determination, and self-absorption—and the "entire responsibility" for one's character—may have carried psychic costs in worry and regret. The Lincolns certainly were tortured souls.

This chapter addresses historical changes in Americans' mentality. The first part recounts how more Americans engaged in deeper self-inspection and character improvement. The second considers whether and how modern Americans thought differently than their forbears. Specifically, did Americans become more skeptical, rational, intelligent? The third part considers how Americans' emotional experiences developed, addressing in particular the affective consequences of their psychological history. Did Americans, for example, suffer more psychological disorders? Did they become more or less happy? Across these diverse topics, we see the extension of American voluntarism, both in the elaboration of personal independence and the cultivation of sympathy. Before turning to the history, consider the proposition that there *could even be* historical changes in mentality.

HISTORY AND MENTALITY

The frequency and skill with which modern Americans dissect their and others' psychologies is a fascinating historical development. People draw on a young science of the mind which offers novel ways of imagining the self. Around 1900, for example, Sigmund Freud first defined "sublimation" (diverting a sordid impulse into an acceptable channel), a concept that educated Americans today apply to each other's behavior and that historians apply to people who lived long before Freud. One can wonder, however, whether sublimation existed before 1900; was it discovered or invented? Some psychological conditions, or at least discussion of them, have come and gone over time. In the nineteenth century, doctors commonly diagnosed troubled middle-class women with "neurasthenia"; in the twentieth century, similar women were said to suffer from "nervous breakdowns." Both syndromes had their periods of attention and then seemed to fade away, at least in the United States. Similarly, the "melancholic" personality arrived in antebellum America and then seemed to leave a few decades later. Americans learned psychology in school—millions took college psychology courses in the 1990s alone—and from the mass media—programs such as "Dr. Joyce Brothers" and "Dr. Phil." No surprise, then, that Americans were alert to clinical traits in themselves and others. (A Woody Allen character complains to his girlfriend, "Why do you always reduce my animal urges to psychoanalytic categories?") This profusion of psychological ideas and discussions, among both professionals and lay people, means that there certainly is a history of *talk* about mentality.[2]

Popular theories of mentality changed over American history. Puritans described human nature as innately willful and corrupt, romantics as inherently good, and social reformers as a blank slate. Thinking of people as hydraulic systems, as Freud taught in the early twentieth century, leads to talk about releasing anger and sublimating lust. Thinking of people as learning machines, as B. F. Skinner taught a few decades later, leads to discussing patterns of punishment and reward. And thinking of people as genetically prewired leads to conversations about evolution and protein inhibitors. Our task here, however, is to get past the talk about mentality, if possible, and find out whether and how actual mentality changed.[3]

We can assume that mentality changed historically. Psychologists and anthropologists assure us that the human psyche is malleable, that people in different cultures tend to think and feel and even perceive the world differently. Anthropologist Clifford Geertz has argued, for example, that the "Western conception of the person as a bounded, unique, more or less integrated motivational and cognitive universe, a dynamic center of awareness, emotion and judgment and action organized into a distinctive whole" is "a rather peculiar idea within the context of the world's cultures." Scholars claim psychic variation across history, too. British sociologist Anthony Giddens is one of many who describes the late twentieth century on both sides of the Atlantic as a new era of pervasive unease and anxiety. Others wonder whether rationality or neuroticism emerged recently in American history. These are the sorts of issues at stake.[4]

Definitive evidence about the minds of people long ago eludes us. We can turn to surveys and other social psychological studies to describe the thoughts and feelings of Americans since the middle of the twentieth century, but we have nothing comparable for earlier generations. Letters, diaries, and memoirs provide glimpses of some people's thinking, but usually only of literate and self-conscious people, and even then we must often read between the lines to make out the authors' states of mind. Literary fiction vividly illustrates how a few Americans—usually the authors and the authors' circle—thought and felt, but only vaguely portrays what ordinary people were thinking and feeling.* Many historians turn to old advice books, with their explicit directions about how people ought to think and feel (and behave) to understand people of earlier eras. I do, too. Yet what authors of advice books recommended often differed from what people practiced; and even the practices they described were not necessarily typical. One famous book, *Lord Chesterfield's Letters*, was for decades the model for other advice books. The instructions from an otherwise little-noticed nobleman to his illegitimate son are famous for their

---

* Even fiction for mass audiences may only tell us about the fantasies of their readers. Few nineteenth-century men, for example, experienced the violent capers of dime-novel heroes, and few nineteenth-century women experienced dramatic romances.

cynicism and sycophancy. In 1779, writer Mercy Otis Warren addressed Chesterfield's advice concerning women: "He was never noted to be successful in any of his gallantries, but that which brought Mr. Stanhope [the son] into this world." Such limitations and complications have led some scholars to lower their aspirations; they settle for telling the history of psychological *standards* as sketched in prescriptive books, sermons, and other media. If, however, we want to understand the history of people's characters rather than the history of the debates about their characters, we must make the best of what evidence is in hand. And in the end, even historians who disavow studying actual mentalities do in fact end up at least implicitly claiming to know how psyches changed—as well they should, since that is the gripping question.[5]

MAKING ONE'S "SELF" ONESELF

In 1978, M. Scott Peck, a Connecticut psychiatrist, published *The Road Less Traveled: A New Psychology of Love, Traditional Values and Spiritual Growth*. Ten million copies of this advice book sold in the next three decades, and it appeared on the *New York Times* bestseller list for eight years. Peck's prescription combined psychotherapy, New Age spiritualism ("our unconscious is God"), and a strong dose of self-discipline. In 2002, Rick Warren, the minister of an independent evangelical church in Orange County, California, published *The Purpose Driven Life: What on Earth Am I Here For?* Warren's advice book would sell twenty-five million copies in only three years, dominate the *New York Times* list, and spawn a Web site with its own set of services, materials, and activities (http://www.purpose drivenlife.com). Warren went on to conduct the invocation at the inauguration of President Obama in 2009. Rejecting Peck's therapeutic approach, Warren stressed instead submission and service to God as the path to a fulfilling life. "It's not about you," the book begins, "pleasing God is the first purpose of your life." However different Warren's religious and Peck's secular guides—Peck was even attacked by fundamentalists—both books told readers to work hard on improving their characters. Peck wrote that attaining growth meant "a life of continuous and never-ending stringent self-examination"; Warren directed readers to keep journals, make lists, and draft mission statements in order to plan and track their progress in attaining "God's ultimate goal for your life . . . character development."[6]

Peck's and Warren's counsels follow a long tradition in Western culture. Perhaps the most famous American self-improver was Benjamin Franklin. Franklin descended from a line of Puritan self-inspection enthusiasts who dissected their behavior, as well as that of their children and neighbors, for signs of salvation or damnation. Franklin famously described in his autobiography how he "conceiv'd the bold and arduous project of arriving at moral perfection," developed a list of thirteen virtues, and checked off his progress in a ledger. (The virtue of chastity, which he defined as engaging in sexual intercourse only "for health and offspring," proved a major challenge.) Through publications such as *Poor Richard's Almanack*, Franklin proselytized for self-analysis and self-betterment. I borrow Franklin's term and describe in this section Americans' efforts at "self-perfection," a task that involves explicitly holding up one's "self," one's character or personality, to the light as an object to be honed. This mission assumes, as does Western culture and especially American voluntarism, that at the core of each person is a one-of-a-kind self. It also assumes that each person has enough control of his or her mind and circumstances to improve that self. Even in early America, many people engaged—if not at Franklin's virtuoso level—in self-perfection. Over the generations, more Americans participated in more self-conscious self-perfection.[7]

Working on Sincerity

Few were as compulsive as Franklin, but many colonial Americans studied their characters. Keeping a diary helped them monitor their progress—and also provided later historians with some insights into their minds. While most diarists simply chronicled weather endured, tasks accomplished, and debts owed, increasingly many recorded their wishes for transformation. The teenage George Washington copied maxims from an advice manual into an exercise book later entitled *Rules of Civility*, precepts ranging from "Drink not nor talk with your mouth full" to "A Man ought not to value himself of his Achievements, or rare Qualities of wit; much less of his riches Virtue or Kindred." Eliza Lucas Pinckney was a successful plantation manager before she married at age twenty-two. A year later, in 1745, she wrote, "I am resolved . . . to govern my passions, to endeavor constantly to subdue every vice and improve in every virtue and in order to [do] this I will not give way to any the least notions of pride, haughtiness, ambition, ostentation, or contempt of others . . . but to endeavour after all the contrary Virtues, humility, charity, etc, etc." Evangelical movements often required converts to write or dictate testimonials of their rebirth—being reborn being one route to self-perfection—and in these testimonies average Americans recounted their struggles to remake themselves.[8]

In the generations following the Revolution, more Americans worked more explicitly and more deeply on their personalities (and on the personalities of their children). Self-perfecters like Eliza Pinckney charted the war in themselves between good and evil passions. Mary Chandler, in the book bought by Lincoln, told readers that "to build a Character requires a plan, no less than to build a house." Kenyon College student and future president Rutherford B. Hayes, like other young, middle-class Americans, kept the requisite diary and wrote in 1841 that "by keeping a diary . . . I expect to promote a stability of character." Many turned to books adapted from English aristocratic models (Lord Chesterfield's in particular), but American guides gave a more democratic spin to their counsel. For example, they told readers not to defer excessively to their betters nor to patronize their lessers—albeit thereby recognizing that there were indeed betters and lessers. Manuals instructed readers on how to present themselves to advantage in good company. Don't fawn, slouch, get angry, grimace, laugh out loud, scratch, or pick your nose; do seem "easy and affable," effortless. And certainly control your passions. Other antebellum books stressed character more than manners, trying to instill adherence to those Franklinesque virtues such as honesty, sobriety, piety, and self-discipline. One 1838 book encouraged the reader: "*you may be whatever you will resolve to be.*" Yet other advice books, premised on the increasingly popular notion that experience shaped character from infancy, taught parents how to form the "moral habits" in their children that would effectively determine their adult natures. Well-known author Lydia Child instructed mothers in 1831 to rely not on rules and punishments but on "inspiring sentiments" in the child. "If you inspire in him the right feelings, they will govern his actions." That is, shape the children's minds so that they will want to do right or at least feel guilty if they do not do right.[9]

These same self-conscious Americans, particularly urban young men seeking their way in business, engaged in all sorts of self-improvement activities—lectures, libraries, debating societies, art courses, musical performances, and the like—and then reviewed their improvement in diaries and letters. Evangelical movements, particularly during the Second Great Awakening, roughly 1790 to 1840, provided much different uplift to much wider audiences. Preachers explained that "works" and personal regeneration—temperance, restraint, faith, charity, attention to domestic duties—would bring not only salvation in the world to come, but also a better life in the world at hand. Superficial conformity, however, would not suffice; a full rebirth of the self was required. Many, disproportionately young women, heeded the preachers' calls. As mothers, they increasingly shouldered the burden of morally improving their children. In Brattleboro, Vermont, for example, women's societies emerged from the churches focused not on missionary work but on becoming better molders of Christian children. Self-examination and self-reform, as well as child examination and child reform, occupied the attention of the rising bourgeoisie and aspiring bourgeoisie.[10]

In the antebellum years, advisors to the middle class valued a personality that was genial, sensitive, informed, and religious, but especially self-disciplined—a personality that seemed to suit the emerging commercial economy. A man who was irritable, ignorant, and regularly drunk could still succeed as a farmer but was doomed as a clerk or tradesman. Traits like congeniality, advice books stressed, were important for economic success. A book I quoted in chapter 4 urged parents "to train up children that they may have a due government of themselves." Character improvement also helped the native middle class defend their status. While others—the increasingly visible immigrants, the poor, the black, and also the idle rich—were unmannered, impulsive, and decadent, "we" behaved better. Some advice books explicitly drew such comparisons. Bourgeois character traits eventually became virtues independent of any practical advantage they provided. Middle-class Americans came to feel that someone who was loud, profane, and reckless was, by the very fact, offensive and immoral—just as in a later era someone who was dirty and smelly was plainly offensive and immoral.[11]

These standards for personal character democratized by the 1820s; the advice books multiplied and reached wider audiences. In the 1830s, Boston's William Ellery Channing, a founder of Unitarianism, argued that "self-culture" was open to even the meanest laborer. He called on the masses to realize that all have the power of "acting on, determining, and forming ourselves." He continued, "you were not created . . . like the inferior animals. If you will, you can rise. . . . Awake! Resolve earnestly on Self-culture." Even many immigrants and working-class natives joined in self-perfecting, whether willingly or under duress. Reformers founded organizations to strengthen character, such as Sunday schools, YMCAs, settlement houses, and the Boy and Girl Scouts. Public schools, designed in part to round up loose children from the streets, sought to ingrain in them the discipline to sit still and pay attention, obedience to proper authority, self-reliance, and values fit for a modern, Christian nation. This values agenda stirred cultural conflict, particularly between Protestant authorities and Catholic parents, but the "Americanization" project pressed on.[12]

As more Americans created—or at least presented—a better self, they increasingly wondered about the sincerity of other people's self-presentations. Because manners books were now common, because Jacksonian America's democratic culture encouraged social climbing, and because growing cities meant encountering more strangers, middle-class Americans worried more about being fooled by bad characters. Lord

Chesterfield's well-known advice to polish one's surface appearance underlined the threat of pretense. Scandals, notably involving men of the
cloth, provided stark examples of people who were not whom they appeared to be. (Recall also the 1852 case of the gallant poseur, Señor De
Castro, on p. 193.) Underlining the concern, moralists and advice givers stressed the importance of projecting sincerity by one's clothes, conversation, and correspondence. And people tried. Teenager Sarah Connell, writing in her diary in the early 1800s, rejected the Chesterfield-like
advice found in many manners books. She condemned the person who
"act[ed] foreign to his nature" and prayed, "May I ever view my heart
cloth'd in sincerity." In love letters of the era, sweethearts wrote at length
about shucking false fronts and revealing to one another only their honest, heartfelt emotions. Thus, many in the middle class were busy projecting sincerity and worrying that others were only projecting sincerity.[13]

Practicing to be sincere sounds, of course, like hypocrisy. Mocking
our nineteenth-century ancestors for their hypocrisy, for their suspect-
ing other people's self-presentations while working on their own, is easy.
But bourgeois Americans of that era tried to improve their characters
and sought moral rectitude, seriousness of purpose and of demeanor, piety, and proper formality in public, while at the same time, as I will describe later, they worked on feeling and expressing warmer sentiments in
private. Living with contradictions was hardly particular to the Victorians, although they seemed to worry about it a lot.

Finding (or Making) the Real Me

However self-absorbed the Victorians may have been, introspection only
expanded in the twentieth century. The spread of new ideas—notably,
Freud's notions that the mind is complex and that governing it is hard
work, the expansion of higher education with all those Intro to Psych
classes, and the rising tide of how-to-be-better books and, later, how-I-
was-so-bad talk shows prodded and equipped many Americans to perfect
themselves. In midcentury, essayist Alfred Kazin observed of Freudian-
ism that "no other system of thought in modern times, except the great
religions, has been adopted by so many people as a systematic interpretation of individual behavior." Americans gained psychological sophisti-
cation; they learnt analyst-speak about instincts, drives, complexes, and
syndromes. A 1988 survey found that as many as half of adult Americans
had once bought a self-help book. And the professionals were there to
help, too. In 2007, there were 180,000 psychologists, psychiatrists, psychiatric aides, and psychiatric technicians in the United States. Indeed,
Americans in the mid- to late-century, various scholars have argued, wal-

lowed in a therapeutic hot tub. Certainly, a lot of quasi-therapy happened in corporate headquarters, factories, schools, churches, clubs, and self-help groups, as well as on psychiatrists' couches. For middle-class Americans and increasingly for others, too, one's life tasks included perfecting one's self.[14]

Some people went in search of their *real* selves, a twist on creating a new self. Advice books and personal diaries describe a growing quest for, in Daniel Bell's terms, the self's "unique, irreducible character free of the contrivances and conventions, the masks and hypocrisies, the distortions [created] by society," increasing efforts to unshroud that true self, to give it full expression. Magazine writers and college students alike were more likely toward the end of the twentieth century to describe themselves in terms of a deep and lasting character rather than in terms of their social positions—for example, more likely to say "I am a caring person" than "I am a member of the Jaycees."[15]

Consistent with the theme of authenticity, late-twentieth-century moral authorities soft-pedaled propriety and restraint while urging openness and gregariousness. Experts increasingly diagnosed shyness, not as an expression of virtuous modesty, but as a problem that people needed to fix. People, of course, learn both kinds of styles, both how to be "natural" and "authentic" as well as how to be artful and polished. And people monitor how well they conform in each case. Indeed, trying to be appropriately "open" and "natural" probably requires more intensive self-management than does just following rules. For example, as women increasingly joined men in schools and at jobs on equal footing, each person became more responsible for controlling any sexual implications of his or her behavior, words, and body language. This emphasis on informal authenticity did not dry up the river of etiquette books and advice columns. Instead, professional guidance gushed out in yet wider streams—and sometimes on startling topics, such as how to have better sex. Even child-care expert Benjamin Spock, who was commonly caricatured as overly permissive, proposed techniques to instill self-management in children. Even the authentic, supposedly natural self required cultivation.[16]

The authentic self presents, in principle, one consistent, honest personality to the world. Much earlier, Lord Chesterfield had no problem advising his son to don whatever personality suited an occasion, hypocrisy notwithstanding. The young George Washington duly copied down advice such as "if you have reason to be [angry] . . . Shew it not put on a Chearfull Countenance." But, as young Sarah Connell expressed it, true authenticity seemed to require consistency, not acting "foreign" to one's nature. Some theorists argue that modern life fractures such consistency. Individuals play diverse roles, each with different audiences, and therefore each costumed with a different persona—perhaps shy at work, high-spirited with friends, authoritarian at home.* Presumably, the premodern individual projected the same personality to the same small group of intimates all day long. Some argue, moreover, that the modern juggler of personalities suffers psychological disorientation and stress as a result of all this costume-changing. (A few scholars claim, in contrast, that role-switching creates mental and social dexterity.) Intriguing as the theory of multiple personas is, little evidence suggests that Americans suffered psychologically from the proliferation of social groups. Nonetheless, whether pressed by multiple roles or not, modern Americans came to value authenticity. Not being "two-faced" was increasingly one goal of self-perfection.[17]

The very work of self-perfecting may exact psychological costs; it could cause strain and lure one into self-obsession. Sociologist Richard Sennett once wrote, "Each person's self has become his principal burden . . . this concern has proven to be a trap rather than a liberation," and that trap includes narcissism. There is the noted case of "Sheila," a woman interviewed in the 1985 study *Habits of the Heart*, who professed a religion of "Sheila-ism." Such cathedral-sized hubris, however, seems rare; most Americans engaged in far more modest self-perfecting.[18]

Over the course of American history, more Americans engaged in more self-fashioning in more sorts of ways. After the 1960s, the extension of young adulthood—more years between leaving parents and settling into career and family—provided more Americans yet more time for self-exploration and self-work. Mass college education, with its "to thine own self be true" ideology, contributed to the project. Self-fashioning became, like so much else, democratized—and also professionalized, analyzed, and medicalized. Many took up the intense disciplines of yoga, long-distance running, or psychoanalysis to learn how to relax, be spontaneous, or genuine—never mind the irony. These endeavors, along with simpler efforts at self-improvement such as dieting and spiritual ones such as seeking the "purpose driven life," were part of more self-perfecting by more Americans. The American mentality this chapter explores became increasingly the product of self-consciousness and purposeful change. Benjamin Franklin would have been proud.[19]

* In 2009, the *New York Times* reported that Facebook, the social networking Internet site, "enabled users to create many 'friend lists'—one for college buddies, another for work friends, another for family—and control the information they share with each. This makes it possible to distribute party photos with only our best friends, and family reunion photos with just your family" and thereby avoid the potential embarrassment of revealing the "wrong" self to the wrong group.

THINKING

People in different cultures think somewhat differently. For example, when Americans explain why people do what they do, they tend to say it was because of the person's character or preferences; when Saudi Arabians explain, they more often point to the circumstances that the person faced. When Americans encounter logical contradictions, they typically try to determine which option is true; Asians more often try to reconcile the alternatives. One can suppose, then, that people in different historical eras may also have thought differently. In this section, I explore whether and how Americans' ways of thinking may have changed over the centuries.[20]

Rational Thinking

European scholars of the late nineteenth and early twentieth centuries commonly contrasted the minds of "premodern" people—meaning both tribal people in distant lands *and* peasants in their own societies—to the minds of modern, educated Westerners like themselves. Premoderns, they said, thought simply, guided by tradition and superstition; moderns thought complexly, critically, and strategically. (This image of "primitive" people is wrong. Indigenous peoples were and are much more pragmatic, innovative, and clever than Westerners imagined.) Some scholars have translated this comparison to America, even though this nation never had a significant peasantry. They describe the evolution of a new American culture "emphasizing rationality, specialization, efficiency, cosmopolitanism, and an interest in the future." Americans, the argument goes, came to anticipate, plan ahead, and weigh options; they came to think like scientists, demanding logic and evidence.[21]

Where might we see—or not—the rise of rationality? One period historians have closely studied is the antebellum era of "market revolution" discussed in a couple of previous chapters. Some claim that the expansion of commerce transformed Americans, notably farmers but also the rising bourgeoisie, into what a traveling Englishman called a "guessing, reckoning, expecting, and calculating people"—into little capitalists. Other historians are skeptical that Americans' psychology changed so radically, positing instead that behavior changed but not mentality; the opening of markets permitted Americans, who were already a reckoning people, to trade and profit more.[22]

In this debate, historians have, for the most part, had to infer psychology from behavior. Before the 1820s or so, American farmers left much of their land untilled, much of their produce unsold, and much of their

day for leisure—all habits that can be read as signs of economic "irrationality." When many started later to sell more produce on the open market, they appeared to have become more rational, more calculating. But
these farming practices are ambiguous evidence: did earlier farmers in
the eighteenth century neglect commercial opportunities because they
lacked "calculating egotism" or because they simply lacked commercial
opportunities? Researchers have looked, therefore, for other evidence
of rationality. They have examined farmers' account books. Yankee farmers kept detailed ledgers of income and outgo even before the expansion
of commercial agriculture; they seemed to be capitalists-in-waiting. Yet
here, too, some ambiguity remains. Eighteenth-century farmers' and merchants' ledgers display evidence of hardheaded business practices, such as
keeping track of tiny debts and demanding repayment from heirs. During
the War of Independence, Philadelphia-area farmers haggled with Continental officers over the rent of wagons and horses and risked their lives
in order to sell their products to the British troops for better prices and
harder currency. And yet farmers' and merchants' ledgers also display evidence of seeming irrationality, such as carrying debts for years without
charging interest.[23]

One study compared the 1799 and 1820 ledgers of merchants in Kingston, New York, a small town on the Hudson River. In 1799, most farmers
bartered their produce for finished goods at the local store, trading "in a
business-like manner that emphasized rational calculation" and the quick
settling of accounts. In 1820, owners of large farms instead sold much of
their produce to outside buyers for cash, but small-scale farmers, many
forced by grain competition from the Midwest to shift into dairying and
wood harvesting, still sold to the local merchants. The Kingston story,
in the end, tells of new connections to larger markets and their exploitation by those who had the means; it does *not* tell, it seems, the story of
farmers and merchants turning into calculating profit seekers. Another
study of the same region in the early nineteenth century points out that
local merchants, who should have been the shrewdest reckoners in the
community, kept ledger books that looked much like those of farmers:
casual, sloppy, and ignorant of sound accounting procedures. Similarly,
both merchants and farmers often surrendered their best business judgments for social ends, such as employing feckless relatives. Neither the
comparison of farmers before and after the early 1800s nor the comparison of farmers to merchants suggests that the market revolution brought
a rationality revolution. From the beginning, English settlers, North and
South, came with the idea of farming both for themselves *and* for market cash. The problem was making farming pay off while adhering to the
principle of "safety first," as historian Gary Edwards put it: setting aside

enough land for subsistence foods and easily tradable crops while gambling on volatile commercial crops only with extra land. At first, they muddled along, as the ledgers reveal. Later, new tools provided all Americans, especially those in commerce but also farmers, with better ways to do their accounting. The tools ranged from simple arithmetic instruction books to, eventually, farm management computer software. Historians will continue to debate the mindsets of early American farmers, but the evidence suggests that the expansion of markets did not spur a revolution in rational calculation; it provided more reason to calculate and more tools to calculate with.[24]

Another front in the rationality debate addresses the issue of whether faith succumbed to rationality. Skeptics have regularly assailed Americans' religious beliefs as irrational, be it journalist H. L. Mencken mocking evangelical politician William Jennings Bryan in the 1920s or scientists fulminating against Christian fundamentalism in the 2000s. Critics have often predicted the "end of faith"—futilely. Conventional wisdom assumes that over the generations Americans became doubting, empirical, reasoning children of the Enlightenment; they no longer needed to, or could, believe in a spiritual realm and in a God who manages the world. Thomas Jefferson, a poster child for the Enlightenment in America, produced a version of the New Testament from which he had literally snipped out all things supernatural—virgin birth, the resurrection, and all the miracles in between. In the end, however, Americans did *not* abandon faith. (Speaking of presidents, it is worth considering that America's first presidents were at best deists or Unitarians, while a few of America's latest presidents were evangelical Christians.) Piety was neither as common in early America nor as rare in modern America as most people assume.[25]

I noted in chapter 4 how "unchurched" early Americans were. Even many of the churchgoers were, as many churchgoers are today, more social than pious participants. On Sundays in seventeenth-century Virginia, for example, whites came from miles around to the local Anglican church, but only a few, mainly the elderly, took communion. Many, if not most, early Americans mixed versions of Christian tenets with heretical superstitions and occult practices. At times, surges—"awakenings"—of Christian enthusiasm breached the indifference. As described before, such moments of enthusiasm became more common as the eighteenth century turned into the nineteenth. Diary writers of the antebellum era filled pages with religious intensity. Harriet Newell, a missionary who died overseas in 1812 at age nineteen, wrote, "I should be willing to have every thing for God; willing to be called by any name . . . and to undergo any sufferings, if it would but make me humble, and be for his glory." A quite different woman, Sarah Grimke, a Southern abolitionist and feminist, wrote of "never [experiencing] any feeling so terrific as the despair of salvation . . . I felt as if my doom was irrevocably fixed, and I was destined to that fire which is never quenched." Less literary Americans of the nineteenth century thronged to catch the fever of evangelical preachers. Christian faith, like church membership, rose, albeit with swells and ebbs, over the generations following the Revolution.[26]

By the twentieth century, secular intellectuals expressed astonishment that their countrymen had not abandoned belief. In 1922, Mencken defined faith "as an illogical belief in the occurrence of the improbable." Yet at the start of the twenty-first century, 80 to 90 percent of Americans told pollsters they believed in and prayed to God; almost as great a proportion said they never doubted the existence of God (while most doubted evolution); most agreed that God continues to perform miracles; and four in five agreed that He would grade them on Judgment Day. Skeptics, but also people of faith, pointed out that modern Americans had a shallow understanding of Christianity. Probably so—but probably no shallower than that of earlier generations. For example, both in 1950 and in 1990, only about half of American adults could name of one of the four gospels. In one notable religious development, Americans over the twentieth century became less theologically dogmatic; many fewer insisted that their denomination had the only path to salvation. In a 2008 survey, two-thirds agreed that "many religions can lead to eternal life"; most even granted the possibility of immortality to those of no faith. Nonetheless, Americans kept professing their own creeds (and remained suspicious of those who professed atheism). About as many Americans reported praying daily in 1999 as did fifty years earlier; more Americans said they believed in life after death; about half of Americans surveyed in 2004 reported that they had had a life-changing spiritual experience; and one-third specifically reported a "born-again" experience. Sales of religious and religiously themed books, such as Rick Warren's and, even more dramatically, Tim LaHaye's (his *Left Behind* series of novels concerning the End Times had sold sixty-five million copies as of 2008), remained robust. One editor of such books recalled that "in the '60s, everyone was saying that religion was fading away. I remember sitting in a sociology class and the professor calmly explaining that religion would continue to play less and less of a role in people's lives. That was wrong."[27]

Philosophers of the modern condition have long explored the existential crisis of the Enlightenment's rational man, like Jefferson, facing a universe with neither eternal salvation nor present meaning. But most Americans, it seems, do not sense that crisis or do not sense it any more than their ancestors did. Most by far continue to avow their faith in life everlasting or some vaguely spiritual version of the same and, since more believe in heaven than in hell, about one in eight is perfectly sanguine.[28]

Perhaps the better historical comparison for tracking (ir)rationality is not the level of Americans' Christian faith, but their belief in the non-Christian supernatural. In the early colonial era, occult practices challenged the church. Almanacs, coveted in large part because of their astrological information, outsold Bibles; and many people, not just the accused witches of Salem, suffered accusations of and punishment for making black magic. In the eighteenth century, interest in the occult apparently declined under the assault of school teachers and evangelical Christianity. But such magical thinking persisted in various forms, in utopian sects for example, into the nineteenth and twentieth centuries. Around 2000, 30 to 40 percent of Americans said that they believed in ghosts, about 20 percent said that they believed in witches, and most (including M. Scott Peck) said they believed in some kind of paranormal phenomena, such as extrasensory perception or astrology. Strikingly, the proportion of Americans professing occult beliefs seemed on the rise, especially among younger people.[29]

The persistence of Abrahamic faith for most Americans and some sort of New Age spiritualism for others challenges the assumption that modern life made people "rational" in the sense that science is rational. This persistence is especially striking—and for many scientists disheartening—given that for generations schools have taught more Americans to think more scientifically. Or perhaps this persistence challenges the assumption, expressed by Mencken, that rational thinking and faith are incompatible. In any case, while the church as an institution has changed, ceding social power and even claims on individuals' time to other institutions (recall the ministers' complaints in the early 1900s about parishioners skipping out on Sunday services, p. 151), modern Americans are remarkably close to their ancestors in having faith.[30]

I've discussed rationality in terms of business practices and faith. Yet another angle is to ask whether Americans became more "logical" in the IQ sense. At first look, that certainly seems to be the case. So-called intelligence tests, particularly those that measure how well subjects handle abstract and nonverbal problems, show "massive gains" in test-takers' scores over the twentieth century. An average score for an American in 2000 would have qualified him or her as a genius a few generations earlier. Does this mean that modern Americans are that much smarter than their great-grandparents? Probably not. Rather, more Americans have been more extensively trained on the particular cognitive skills these tests measure, such as reading and decoding visual abstractions. Consider how contemporary children learn in art class to draw perspective, something that was a mystery to painters centuries ago, how they manipulate numbers at a complexity beyond the educated of earlier generations, how they encounter far more writing—from schoolbooks to billboards—than their ancestors did, and how they can decipher many more visual patterns, such as traffic signals, product logos, and board games. Even television, notwithstanding its pernicious effects, trains children, through fast cuts in a scene, to understand multiple angles of vision.[31]

Given the plasticity of the human brain, the improvement in diet, the multiplication of symbols in the environment, and the extension of literacy, modern Americans should handle abstractions better and score higher on IQ tests than their forebears. Those skills, however, do not necessarily translate into a greater ability to solve real-life problems, such as how to handle a troubled relationship, or to successfully match means to ends, such as how to wrangle a promotion at work. Rather than becoming smarter or more rational, Americans gained new tools with which to make better-informed, more systematic decisions. The most important source of such tools has been the school. Most children before the twentieth century went to school episodically and briefly, but by 2000, almost all fourteen- to seventeen-year-olds attended school and had attended school, excepting summers, for many years. Formal schooling provides skills, such as reading, writing, and arithmetic, that earlier generations of children, working as farmhands, servants, or laborers, could rarely obtain. Moreover, schools instill subtle bourgeois talents, such as punctuality, self-discipline, planning, team play, and articulateness (from those awkward recitations and oral presentations). Even if only some of the youngsters dragooned into classrooms acquired only some of these abilities, the cognitive "skill set" of the nation improved. Americans generally did not become more self-interested, sharp-eyed, or strategic than their ancestors had been, but, like the antebellum farmers and merchants who eventually learned modern bookkeeping, they became better equipped to cope. These skills in turn promoted a sense of control.[32]

In Control

In 2002–3, the Pew Research Center interviewed representative samples of people in forty-four nations, asking, among other things, questions to tap their basic views on life. At a ratio of two to one, Americans were the most likely (closely followed by Canadians, but far ahead of Europeans) to *reject* the proposition that "success in life is pretty much determined by forces outside our control." Americans believe more than others that, at least in principle, a person is responsible for his or her fate. To some extent, believing it can make it so. People who think they control their lives typically act accordingly and then tend to do better as a consequence, confirming their self-confidence. For example, ill people who think they can speed up their recovery tend to pursue treatment more aggressively and improve their chances over those of people who are fatalistic. Even people who are deluded that they are in control act in goal-oriented and often successful ways. This can-do conviction probably distinguished early Americans from Europeans; it fits voluntarism well. Historically, people's sense of control appears to have expanded as the means for actually being in control spread—means outside the person, such as wealth, expert services, newspapers, and calculators, and also means inside the person, such as literacy, numeracy, time-consciousness, and self-discipline.[33]

Colonial yeoman farmers probably felt empowered when they understood the contrast between their situation and those both of European peasants and slaves in America. Many certainly took umbrage at being treated as dependents by Mother England. Adherence to this notion of individual responsibility grew. In the eighteenth century, Americans increasingly viewed others' poverty as self-inflicted, rather than as a consequence of fate or God's will (see chapter 2). Religious developments in early America catered to and further stimulated the idea that ordinary people could decide both their earthly and their eternal lives. Growing evangelical sects challenged the orthodox doctrine that a person's everlasting destiny was predetermined or waited on God's unknowable grace. Everyone, they said, could secure their salvation by faith, reborn faith, or expressions of faith such as good works. (For the established Protestant churches, doctrines that granted believers a hand in their salvation implied the heresy that ordinary people could change the mind of God; for new denominations, that heresy was a great sales pitch.) The religiously based temperance movement similarly stressed self-determination. Reverend Lyman Beecher sermonized in 1826 that "unless you intend soon to resign your liberty forever, and come under a despotism of the most cruel and inexorable character, you must abandon the morning bitters, the noontide stimulant, and the evening bowl." In tune with such messages, authors of autobiographies in the nineteenth century increasingly explained their moral accomplishments as the product, not of God's grace, but of their own hard work.[34]

Growing security and wealth were, of course, the bases for an expanding sense of control. Without predictability, the ideology that success in life is in one's own hands sounds hollow. With greater predictability, more Americans took initiatives. In one major example, they took control of their childbearing, and birth rates plunged in the nineteenth century. Economic explanations for that drop—that children became less valuable as farmhands—while valid, are incomplete; they do not account for much of the drop's timing and geography. Americans, mainly women, began thinking that the arrival of children was not merely God's will or Nature's course, but their decision. Thus, births declined most in those parts of the country where education expanded, liberal denominations predominated, cities grew, and the native-born concentrated. The birth control publications women read and the comments they wrote in their diaries also suggest that they increasingly sensed that they could and should exercise birth control. A woman in the elite Shippen family of Pennsylvania wrote a sister in the late 1700s: "It gives me great pleasure to hear of your prudent resolution of not increasing your family. . . . I have determined upon the same plan; and when our Sisters have had five or six, we will likewise recommend it to them." The Shippen sisters were part of the avant-garde; many more women followed. A somber corollary of feeling in greater control of birth was feeling in greater control of death. Middle-class Americans came to think that infant and child deaths were neither random nor due to God's inscrutable will; parental diligence could prevent such tragedies (see chapter 2, pp. 28–29). Bearing fewer but longer-lived children both revealed and reinforced the growing sense, first among the bourgeoisie and later among other Americans, that life in general was controllable. "Will it and it is thine," counseled an 1856 advice book. "No longer grovel as though the hand of fate were upon thee."[35]

Over the long course, more Americans could anticipate and manage other life transitions, too. As I noted in chapter 2, school-entering and -leaving, first job, marriage, retirement, and death, as well as parenting, became more standardized, predictable, and common. Random shocks, like the early death of a parent or the failure of a farm, became rarer, allowing Americans to make and carry out plans. Historian John Modell wrote that young people gained more control over their lives and came "increasingly to value the expression of personal choice." It is ironic, but sociologically understandable, that as individuals wrested greater control of their lives from arbitrary events, they chose increasingly similar paths through life. After around 1970, Americans' life transitions became again somewhat irregular, in large part because of economic difficulties that delayed careers and marriages (and in part because of cultural shifts like the acceptance of cohabitation). The reduction in the predictability of the life course, if my argument is right, would have slowed Americans' growing sense of control.[36]

Mass schooling also helped fuel a sense of control. To be sure, the children whom officials forced into early-twentieth-century classrooms hardly felt in control. Critics claimed then and still do that schools did little more than instill deference. But in the long run, those who get more schooling gain a stronger sense of efficacy, which they then display by taking charge in various arenas from planning their families to engaging in politics.[37]

At home, parents increasingly pressed their children to be autonomous. The theme shows up in children's literature, among other places. Children's books of the early nineteenth century stressed the virtues of duty and fulfilling family roles. Later, the lead characters became more independent (*Huckleberry Finn* may have been a harbinger), so that by the late twentieth century, storybook heroes were typically competent children operating beyond parental oversight. Similarly, over the twentieth century, fewer Americans told survey interviewers that children ought to be taught obedience and decorum, and more Americans listed independence and personal responsibility as the critical virtues to be taught.[38]

Thanks to the development of psychological testing, we have estimates from the late 1950s onward of how much Americans thought they controlled their lives or thought that such control was generally possible. Many studies asked Americans questions like, "When you . . . make plans ahead, do you usually get to carry out things the way you expected, or do things usually come up to make you change your plans?" and "Do you agree or disagree: becoming a success is a matter of hard work; luck has little or nothing to do with it?" The surveys suggest that Americans' sense of personal efficacy rose to a peak around 1960, then dropped some, and then stabilized. Americans' sense specifically of *political* efficacy, that they had some say in politics, definitely dropped in the 1960s and 1970s. Those were years, of course, of assassinations, urban disorder, the Vietnam War, and other traumas, so one can understand why Americans' sense of political power also suffered (see chapter 5). The coincidence of the two trends, political and personal efficacy, suggests that the social turmoil of those years may have also weakened Americans' sense of personal control, of how much command they had of their own lives.[39]

Over several generations, more Americans seemed to have gained a greater sense of control. They made increasingly many decisions that bespoke such confidence, such as having fewer children (because each would live and thrive), borrowing money and investing it in education and homes, and planning for retirement. Some observers believe that such self-assurance was an illusion, because twentieth-century Americans actually lost control of their lives to the leviathans of government, business, and media. It is difficult to weigh how much individuals became empowered—in expanded rights, greater wealth, and more education, for example—against how much they may have become disempowered—

by more bureaucracy and broader surveillance, perhaps—but the first probably outweighed the second. The trend to a greater sense of can-do probably required both greater real security and the spread of new ideas from the bourgeoisie. As with other trends, a growing sense of efficacy was not irreversible; in the 1960s and '70s, it seemed to stall.[40]

The Price of Choice?

Modern Americans gained far more options than any people before them. Women in antebellum Boston and Charleston, for example, had few choices, Jane and William Pease tell us in *Ladies, Women, and Wenches*. Almost all were either married, roomers in relatives' homes, or disreputable. Modern women can choose among significantly more life options. But the question arises: can modern American women—and men—handle the greater number of options before them and make optimal choices, or do they instead suffer from a surfeit of options, from a "tyranny of choice" that their ancestors were spared? Indeed, some scholars suggest that more options produce less rational choosing.[41]

Americans gained more choices as their security, wealth, and social groups multiplied. Many of the new options were mundane, such as consumer goods, travel, entertainment, and food. Between 1976 and 2005 alone, the average supermarket more than quadrupled the number of distinct products it carried to forty thousand items. But many of the new options were more profound, such as places to live, churches, careers, spouses, and even what sort of self to cultivate. "Being 'modern' means being *able to choose*," according to one analyst; it means being *forced* to choose according to another. Most Americans see choice as freedom, and thus all to the good. So do most economists, who assert that economics is about "how people choose" to "improve their well-being." Indeed, economists are distinctive, said a famous economist, because they embrace the principle that the "good is an aggregation of many individuals' assessments of their own well-being" so that "the highest morality is respecting [individual] choices."[42]

But along came psychologists (and some economists, too), as I discussed in chapter 3, to question how well people actually choose and how satisfying their choices really are. New research undermines the assumption that expanding choices necessarily brought greater good for the greatest number. Nobel Prize winner Daniel Kahneman, his collaborator Amos Tversky, and others showed that people often choose in what seem to be illogical ways. People, for example, often choose based on how a choice is couched. (Is a stock purchase described as an "investment" or as a "gamble"? What about a lottery ticket?) When they choose, people often follow some incidental cue, use rules of thumb, fall back on habits, and "satisfice" instead of optimize. Choosing successfully seems bounded by limits of time, resources, skill, knowledge, and the peculiarities of the mind. Indeed, individuals may not know what really is good for them, so respecting their choices may *not* be the highest morality. (How moral is it to let children choose their own meals? Or poorly educated workers their own retirement plans?) Some psychologists have taken the critique of rational choice a step further and reversed economists' fundamental premises by contending that simply *having* more options actually *reduces* people's ultimate satisfaction.[43]

Experimenters find that giving subjects more options raises the odds that they make poor choices, choices they later regret, or no choice at all, whether it's buying jam or saving for retirement. Just having to choose can wear people out. People in option-rich situations seem to retreat from the complexities of decision-making and to obsess about the options not taken. (Recognition of this behavior led benefits experts to recommend "opt-out" systems, which assign health and retirement plans to employees, in place of "opt-in" ones, which require employees' active decision-making.) Skeptics of the choice-is-debilitating thesis point out its reliance on studies that investigate either trivial decisions, such as buying jam, or esoteric decisions, such as picking retirement plans. When people face serious choices for which they have information—say, where to buy a home, whom to marry—having more alternatives may well produce better and more satisfying choices. Perhaps. In another study, college seniors who maximized their job searches by looking more and gathering more information did indeed end up with better-paying jobs, but they also were more disappointed with their jobs than the seniors who just "satisficed." Some scholars have concluded from such research that modern Americans suffer from having too many options. Psychologist Barry Schwartz wrote that "when self-determination is carried to extremes, it leads not to *freedom* of choice but to *tyranny* of choice."[44]

Schwartz and others thus repeat a point made by theorists a generation or two earlier who warned that people could not handle the glut of options offered by modernity, especially when authorities do not guide their choices. Psychologist Kenneth Keniston wrote in 1965, "Many Americans have come to experience this freedom [the increase in choice] as at best a mixed blessing and at worst as an acute problem; the demand that one choose and make commitments in the face of an enormous variety of socially available options is increasingly felt as a heavy demand." And so people seek to escape from freedom, as psychoanalytic philosopher Erich Fromm put it in a book by the same name. Even earlier, classical sociologist Emile Durkheim argued that modernity released constraints on people's aspirations and those aspirations, left to soar unfettered, carried people to a state of anomie—endless desire and ultimate frustration. Choice-less premoderns, in contrast, were presumably content in their innocence. Greater choice, then, may have left modern Americans not more satisfied, but more uncertain, anguished, and regretful.[45]

To support this inference, Schwartz and others point to survey evidence suggesting that Americans felt more miserable as the end of the twentieth century approached, evidence we shall explore in depth in the next section on emotions. And yet individuals who have more options—the educated and the affluent—and citizens of nations that provide more options—richer countries—report themselves as feeling *better*, not worse, than people with fewer options. These facts raise an intriguing possibility: perhaps we should distinguish between the immediate psychology of making choices and the psychology of living in a choice-rich society. When someone faces a plethora of options—even in buying a car or picking a house—having many options can be taxing and lead to second-guessing, especially if the chooser insists (irrationally!) on seeking the single best option. But living in a world of many options—having many ways of traveling, many neighborhoods to live in, and so on—probably leads *in the long run* to a set of more satisfying outcomes.[46]

Rethinking

Modern Americans probably think not all that differently from earlier generations; they are probably no more or less self-interested, clever, or rational. But modern Americans gained access to a wider range of mental tools (such as literacy and methods for self-control) and technical tools (such as bookkeeping and media) that, together with a cornucopia of options, made it easier to attain their ends. One consequence of such changes should have been that more Americans came to think of themselves as more personally empowered. That in turn may have led them to demand more choices. Certainly, modern Americans did demand choices their ancestors might not have imagined—women to work any job, religious minorities to express their beliefs, people with scorned sexual identities to be "out," youth for more liberties—all amounting to what legal scholar Lawrence Friedman called the "republic of choice."

All this thinking and choosing still operated within the limits of the human mind, within "bounded rationality," with mistakes and misunderstandings. But with greater knowledge, cognitive training, increasing wealth, and technological aids, the boundaries of that rationality widened. The long-run expansion of choices and of individuals' cognitive skills to choose probably also gave Americans a greater sense of responsibility for themselves. Americans, we saw, are especially likely to believe that people are captains of their own fates. That sense of responsibility, some speculate, may have made Americans that much more anxious—which brings us to the topic of emotions.

FEELING

In 1782, Alexander Hamilton wrote a friend about his seven-month-old son: "It is agreed on all hands that he is handsome; his features are good. . . . His attitude in sitting, is, by connoisseurs, esteemed grace-ful. . . . If he has any fault in manners, he laughs too much." Whether or not Hamilton meant to be droll, his closing remark fit in an era when people of standing might see infants as being *too* happy and might press children to restrain their laughter—much in contrast to our own when it seems there can never be a child who laughs too much.[47]

All humans recognize a common set of physiological and visual signs associated with emotions; for example, the "smiley face"—☺—means happiness. But people vary from culture to culture in when, whether, and how they express feelings. They experience differently tinged emotions in somewhat different contexts and at different rates. To take simple examples, most Americans would feel embarrassed to share common public baths as the Japanese do, while most Japanese probably would feel embarrassed by an American's friendly bear hug. It makes sense, therefore, that there would also be comparable historical variations. For instance, in an era when the death of a child is understood as the will of an inscrutable God, it would engender sadness and resignation; in another era when the death is interpreted as resulting from poor parenting, it would engender sorrow and guilt; and in a third era when it is considered the product of others' decisions (say, polluted tap water), it would engender grief and anger. Here is another example of the plasticity of emotions: public campaigns in the late nineteenth century to develop habits of cleanliness, such as daily washing, succeeded when Americans came to viscerally abhor filth, to feel disgust at the sight of a dirty face. Emotions—which ones, how often they occur, and how they are expressed—have a history.[48]

Telling the history of emotions, like telling the history of thinking, requires the researcher to infer what is inside people from outward signs, what they say and do. Some scholars renounce any effort to track people's actual feelings and claim that they can only write the history of emotion *rules*, such as the injunction not to get angry at a child; they commonly find those rules in the same advice books that counseled Americans on manners and self-presentation. We want to use those guides, but also to see through them to Americans' actual emotions. It appears that Americans increasingly felt affection and tenderness, decreasingly expressed aggression, and generally learned to modulate their negative emotions. Monitoring and molding emotions are key aspects of perfecting the self.[49]

Eighteenth- and nineteenth-century elites carefully attended to their emotions. Recall George Washington's *Rules of Civility*, which included admonitions such as "Shew not yourself glad at the Misfortune of another" and "Make no Shew of taking great Delight in your Victuals." Washington was trying to regulate how he expressed his emotions. (According to one historian, "Washington was a man of strong passions, which he struggled to keep in check. For him the worst slavery was to be in bondage to unbridled passion and not in 'full possession of himself.'") Increasingly, people of high status also tried to regulate the feelings themselves. Middle-class Philadelphians of the eighteenth century saw emotionality as a lower-class habit—one to avoid lest one lose social standing—and a habit that could also produce physical or mental illness. "An overriding feature of 18th-century middle-class life was an interest in health preservation through self-restraint, with an emphasis on emotional self-control. . . . What was desirable was to eliminate feelings of anger, to moderate the emotions of fear and grief." Advice books cautioned against too-vivid displays, warning, for example, against laughing loudly in genteel company. Young girls in particular had to practice restraint. Late-eighteenth- and early-nineteenth-century emotional culture began redefining women, at least middle-class women, as "passionless." Unlike the bawdy women of an earlier England or those sensual black and immigrant women, middle-class American women were to be modest and lacking in "carnal motivation." By the end of the nineteenth century—just before the Freudian revolution—experts advised that "perfect inhibition is the sign of perfect mental health."[50]

Learning to inhibit some feelings and emotional displays—such as "great Delight in your Victuals" or wails of grief—were not, however, the only kind of "emotion work" that nineteenth-century Americans performed. They also cultivated the experience and expression of desirable feelings.

Sympathy and Sentimentality

Beginning in the late eighteenth century and accelerating through the nineteenth century, middle-class Americans increasingly subscribed to sentimental "feeling rules." Proper persons (especially women), had "sensibility"; they felt others' emotions, especially their pain, and then expressed—demurely—sympathetic emotional resonance. A young woman's letter to her fiancé illustrates this tuning-fork responsiveness: "I feel *intensely* . . . more than words can express every thrill of joy which bursts from your heart—and every sigh of sadness which is breathed from your bosom." Leading spokesmen for the Revolution and the new Republic played similar emotional chords when they castigated England for its *unfeeling* cruelty toward the colonists and praised Patriots' egalitarian *sympathies* for the oppressed.[51]

Romance, of course, provided many opportunities for sentimental expression, and many middle-class women of the nineteenth century immersed themselves in the romantic sentimentality of novels. (Recall from chapter 4 the minister who in 1809 complained about novels that stress "the omnipotence of love," and from chapter 5, the woman whose novels sent her to bed "drowned in tears.") Increasingly, love was not reserved for star-crossed couples, nor was it something to hope would develop during marriage; it became a prerequisite for marriage. Indeed, being capable of loving—a person or a value—became a prerequisite for true character. Lincoln marked this passage in Mary Chandler's *Elements of Character*: "The motive power in man is Affection. What he loves he wills, and what he wills he performs. Our Character is the complex of all that we love." Conduct guides urged sustained tenderness between spouses; couples' letters and diaries increasingly expressed passion; and, as I reported in chapter 4, charges in divorce cases included more complaints about the withholding of love. Ellen Coile Graves of Philadelphia provided a telling variation on such complaints in 1844. Mrs. Graves wrote to the court in response to her husband's divorce petition that, although he had imagined that the two would eventually grow to love one another, she could not wait and live without love: "I am not one of those lukewarm Creatures who can bestow their affection upon all alike. . . . I *cannot compel* myself to love. . . . I did wrong very wrong in marrying you without feeling sincere attachment but believed that you was capable of attaching me to you by kind and affectionate treatment." Alas, his kindness did not spark her passion.[52]

Parents' feelings toward their children also intensified; they found in them innocence and wonder (as did Hamilton relatively early), which made their loss all the more crushing. Whereas mothers had once written fatalistic, matter-of-fact reports of their children's deaths, mothers in the antebellum era more often wrote anguished, detailed accounts of the experience (chapter 2, p. 23). Henry Wadsworth Longfellow's wife, traumatized and obsessed by the death of her infant daughter, was "haunted by thoughts of what might have been avoided, the most pitiless of all." Easing the torment a bit, nineteenth-century clerics no longer depicted deceased infants' souls as doomed because they had not had a chance to repent of original sin, but instead described them as angelic messengers called back to God's throne. The Civil War inflamed the emotional cords linking parents to the young sons they saw off to battle. Soldier boys reported intense longings, to the point of illness, for home. And parents whose sons had died eagerly welcomed descriptions of their deaths, which would reassure them that their sons had died a "good death" with peace of mind and reconciliation to their Savior.[53]

Antebellum sentimentality focused a great deal on death. Middle-class Americans solemnized death with intense expressions of grief (for example, elaborate mourners' clothing) and with romantic melancholy. Even the deaths of urchin newsboys in the big cities occasioned elaborate funerals and maudlin press coverage. A new form of internment developed. The forested cemetery enabled mourners to plumb depths of feeling seemingly unreachable in simple churchyard plots or cold mausoleums. In these parks, nature, which the emerging urban culture romanticized, could be captured and cultivated to promote the experience of the sublime. Transcendentalist poet William Ellery Channing made the connection at the dedication of Sleepy Hollow Cemetery in Concord, Massachusetts, in 1855:

> No abbey's gloom, nor dark cathedral stoops
> No winding torches paint the midnight air
> Here the green pines delight, the aspen droops
> Along the modest pathways, and those fair
> Pale asters of the season spread their plumes
> Around this field, fit garden for our tombs.

Later, wooded, gothic cemeteries gave way to park-like cemeteries.[54]

More generally, the contemplation of death inspired melancholy, a poignant emotion many Victorians reached for, turned over and around, and cherished. In the early 1800s, the teenage daughter of a Massachusetts businessmen described in her diary how, as she sat by her window at twilight, "a sweet melancholy diffused itself over my heart. Memory recalled a thousand tender scenes; the silent tear fell, from an emotion, which it was impossible to control." Such melancholic sentimentality provided fodder for Mark Twain's parodies, as in his character Emmeline Grangerford. Huckleberry Finn discovers the recently deceased teenager's doleful art and poetry. Emmeline's drawings of tear-streaked mourners carried titles like "And Art Thou Gone Yes Thou Art Gone Alas," her scrapbook contained notices of deaths and suffering, and her treacly poetry delivered lines about anything "just so it was sadful." In the end,

Huck concludes, "I reckoned that with her disposition she was having a better time in the graveyard." Literary experts have noted that there were plenty enough models in the real world to inspire the character of Emmeline. However pretentious the Emmelines of antebellum America were, they reflected the emerging bourgeois attachment to strong sentimentality.[55]

Bourgeois Americans imbued the world beyond the family with sentimentality, too. In chapter 4, I noted how the circle of intimacy widened to include friendships. Victorians expressed their feelings about same-sex friends with such intense terms of affection and longing that they sound, to modern ears, homoerotic. Daniel Webster referred to his "partner of my joys, griefs, and affections," and young Virginia attorney William Wirt passed on greetings from two of his friends to a third as "send[ing] their love piping hot." Middle-class women were even likelier to write down such endearments, to report that the thought of meeting a friend "makes me feel hot and feverish," and that they longed to snuggle in bed. Only later, historians of sexuality report, did American culture draw a clear line between feelings of fondness and feelings of erotic attraction. However sincere these intense expressions, and we can assume that private diaries and letters were usually sincere, they were also conventional for the times. Correspondents could turn to letter manuals for boilerplate emotional phrases; some of these manuals even included prepared texts that swear to the sincerity of the author's sentiments.[56]

Sentimentality spread into public life. The great reform movements of the nineteenth century, such as abolitionism, temperance, child protection, and first-wave feminism, mobilized middle-class Northerners' responses to others' pain and suffering. Parents used household pets to cultivate children's feelings of compassion, which in turn spurred the movement against cruelty to animals. Displays of physical torment, most famously in stage performances of *Uncle Tom's Cabin*, aroused pathos. Words and pictures depicted the oppressed—slaves, children, captives of war—"bound or chained, stripped to the waist, and whipped until the blood poured down and pieces of flesh flew, and the victims writhed with pain." One historian refers to a "pornography of pain," which displayed obscene yet transfixing suffering. Anguish at such displays showed the observer to be a delicate and sensitive soul, another sign that he or she was superior to the brutish, unfeeling masses. Still, more Americans were genuinely repelled by what historically had been common, unremarkable cruelties. They experienced what German sociologist Norbert Elias called the "civilizing process," learning to feel revulsed by what had once been ordinary, be it piggish eating, public urinating, or sadistic fighting.[57]

The process was slow in evolving and spreading; casual acceptance of bear-baiting, lynching, eye-gouging, and wife beating persisted in nineteenth-century rural and working-class communities. Barroom culture celebrated—and juries excused—outbursts of righteous anger and murderous violence (see chapter 2). Despite the efforts of reformers and governments, emotional recoil from such scenes came later, after the turn of the century, in these working-class social worlds.[58]

Young, educated, twentieth-century Americans may have found the florid sentimentality of their grandparents' era a bit much, even laughable at times. Still, the underlying code of sympathy and sensibility spread. Tugging at heartstrings—in, say, Norman Rockwell paintings* or human interest features on television news—worked. Sentimentality spread in part because more Americans joined the middle class and also because middle-class culture prescribed sentimentality in more contexts. Evolving standards dictated that modern parents should adore their children ever more, that they should guide children by seduction and camaraderie rather than intimidation, and that fathers should nurture, not just discipline. Benjamin Spock, the great midcentury advisor of parents, wrote that "a man can be a warm father and a real man at the same time." Many men no doubt had difficulty meeting these new standards, but they still had to deal with others' rising emotional expectations. Teens in 1977 "Middletown" were much likelier to want their parents to respect their opinions and spend time with them than were Middletown teens in 1924. Marriage ideology similarly raised the expectations for couples beyond simple affection and partnership to higher standards: companionship, esteem, and never-flagging love. The expansion of gift-giving, stretched to include friends and coworkers as well as family (and encouraged, of course, by merchants), also widened the sphere of sentimentality. In the public arena, social movements of the twentieth century extended the targets of sympathy beyond orphans and abandoned pets to include virtually every piteous victim, from hungry children half a globe away to polar bears and coral reefs. Modern sentimentality may have lost its Victorian flounces, but it still grew. Note that this sentimental code remained consistent with a code of expressive restraint. A good middle-class American felt the pain of, say, abandoned pets, but did not howl or rant about it; he or she instead sympathized deeply and engaged in measured reform. Those who raged, who acted out their sentiments, who lost control even in a good cause, garnered little sympathy.[59]

* Rockwell's sentimentalism appeared not only in his iconic *Saturday Evening Post* odes to small-town Americana, but also in his later, more political art. *The Problem We All Live With* critiques racism through the figure of a victimized but plucky little black girl.

Stay Cool and Warm

More Americans absorbed the bourgeois emotional culture, some willingly as they joined the middle class and others unwillingly, pressed by
teachers, bosses, and police. First-generation immigrant memoirs and
novels commonly describe parent-child battles over what was more
shameful, the new-world decorum or the old-world fervor. A Sicilian
American youth, for example, dreaded family picnics in the park; he felt
embarrassed because his people ate their spaghetti "with pagan abandon"
while "American families munch[ed] neatly cut sandwiches." In the long
run, the children and Americanization won that struggle. Another park
example is the Fourth of July. Many immigrants celebrated their patriotism with commotion, alcohol, and gunfire, but authorities ultimately
managed to repress their enthusiasm as they established the "safe and
sane" Fourth. Similarly, the children of Jewish immigrants from eastern
Europe modified their fathers' noisy and disorderly prayer services to imitate the reverence and quiet awe of Protestant high churches. Despite
some resistance, the bourgeois culture of sentimentality without histri-
onics gained wider adherence.[60]

The twentieth century, especially after World War I, brought some re-
laxation of emotional restraints, some greater latitude for individual expression. Etiquette expert Emily Post, for example, loosened up during
the 1920s, partly in response to readers' complaints. Middle-class Americans had perhaps become sufficiently secure in their social positions to
allow playful displays of working-class or even of black cultural styles—
think, for example, of young swells dancing the Charleston in the 1920s.
Nonetheless, emotional self-discipline remained part of the modern
self.[61]

Peter Stearns, the leading historian of emotions, has labeled the twentieth century (at least up to the 1960s) as the era of "American cool." He argues that the emerging emotion rules dictated less intense expressions of
feelings and perhaps even less intense *experience* of feelings than in the Victorian era. Stearns finds evidence for this claim in the twentieth-century
advice literature. Counselors told parents to dampen upsetting emotions,
such as fear, jealousy, and anger, in their children and also in themselves
when around their children. Workplace experts advised employers on
how to tamp down anger among employees. Doctors recommended control of bodily impulses, especially gluttony. Stearns argues that experts
also warned against allowing positive emotions to get too intense, telling
mothers in particular not to smother their children with love.[62]

Moral authorities surely pressed Americans to curtail their anger and
their children's outbursts—"Use your words!" parents learned to insist.

Physical aggression declined; Americans brawled less often. It is not clear, however, that advice givers pressed Americans to stifle positive emotions, such as love, pride, and sympathy—to think the laughing child, as Hamilton perhaps did, too crude. Indeed, some authorities encouraged more emotion. They urged fathers to buddy up with their children, counseled young couples to be intimate friends and passionate lovers, developed team-building exercises for employees, promoted children's self-esteem, and evangelized for a "soft Jesus." Twentieth-century Americans increasingly endorsed teaching children values such as tolerance, sympathy, and helping. For example, only one-fifth of survey respondents born before 1920 but one-third of those born in the 1940s and 1950s chose being "considerate of others" as one of the top three values they held for children. Most Americans came to embrace religious, racial, and moral diversity, at least in principle, even to the point of mock-worthy political correctness. One study described middle-class Americans at the end of the century as "tolerant to a fault"; almost the only people who garnered criticism were those who criticized other people. Tolerance is, of course, a "cooler" sort of emotion than either hate or love, but it usually presumes feelings of sympathy or even empathy, the willingness to see the world from another's vantage point. Tolerance education and diversity celebration are squarely in the American tradition of sentimentality. To be sure, overexpressiveness even of a positive emotion—say, a group hug at an office party—can make some Americans uncomfortable and would usually be discouraged, but that is because nice, empathetic people do not make other people uncomfortable. The "American cool" of the twentieth century seemed to be about suppressing hostile or disturbing emotions, but also about cultivating warm ones, especially sympathy and sensibility, in low-key ways.[63]

Both Stearns's thesis of the "cool" twentieth century and my variant of it face at least one potentially huge objection: that Americans became increasingly impulsive, vulgar, and self-indulgent, especially when it came to sex. In 1976, Daniel Bell wrote that American culture was "at war" with bourgeois convention; it now promoted intemperance and hedonism. (And "nothing epitomized the hedonism of the United States better," Bell wrote from Cambridge, Massachusetts, "than the State of California.") Stearns resolves this seeming contradiction by arguing that blatant sex, violence, and coarseness are largely confined to the media. On television sitcoms, for example, coworkers constantly insult one another although real coworkers rarely do. The emotionality of the media, Stearns suggests, allows Americans to vicariously "compensate" for the emotional repression of their real lives. This is unpersuasive. Yes, the volume of sex, violence, and verbal abuse in the media is orders of magnitude greater than in American reality. In the 1990s, for example, an average child "witnessed" thousands of murders on television. But claiming that a libertine popular culture simply relieves the tension of inhibited lives underestimates the social changes of the twentieth century. Consider sex.[64]

The Sex Case

Americans at the start of the twenty-first century surely encountered more open sexual expression more often than earlier generations had. (Could any of our ancestors have imagined confronting magazines, displayed child-height at market check-out counters, with covers promising to reveal the secret of greater orgasms? Never mind movies, television, and Internet pornography.) Earlier generations were hardly innocents, however. Even middle-class Americans of previous eras encountered public displays of lust. Some colonial towns prosecuted fornicators and other towns openly tolerated bawdyhouses. Early novels revolved around the threat of seduction and abandonment; popular almanacs printed ribald jokes and doggerel. Journalists of the new Republic competed in recounting (or inventing) politicians' sexual escapades and in reporting details of sensational trials that revolved around sex and violence; printers in the nineteenth century turned out volumes of pornography and thinly cloaked pornography in cheap magazines. Prostitution was legal and common. Red-light districts flourished in the big cities, and respectable folks would cross paths with prostitutes on the streets or in the theaters. Even in their own homes, with few rooms and few beds, it was hard for American adults to hide sexual activity from children and boarders. There seems never to have been an age of innocence. Nonetheless, American public and private sexuality did change.[65]

The Puritans often confronted cases and discussions of bastardy, impotence, adultery, and bestiality. Further south and west in the colonies, bawdiness was commonplace; bonded servants and slaves often suffered as reluctant sexual partners. William Byrd II, a member of Virginia's political and intellectual elite in the early 1700s, recorded escapades in his "secret diary," which suggest that he and his friends "rogered," or tried to, virtually every woman they encountered. The cultural imagery of the pre-Revolutionary era depicted women as just as libidinous, if not more so, than men. Data on premarital pregnancies imply that premarital intercourse rose sharply in the colonies. By the late 1700s, roughly one-third of all firstborn children had been conceived before marriage—although typically such conceptions were a prelude to marriage (though not always: Abraham Lincoln's mother, Nancy Hanks, was probably the illegitimate issue of a Virginia planter and Lucy Hanks). Open expressions of sexuality increased, perhaps a reflection of the general loosening of group controls, in the Revolutionary era. In Philadelphia, for example, respected men acknowledged their illegitimate children, and streetwalkers plied their trade with little interference.[66]

Premarital, extramarital, and public sex became more constrained in the nineteenth century, although not as constrained as the "proper Victorians" stereotype would imply. Among the bourgeoisie, public manners often covered more intensely sexual private lives; the romantic sensibility of the age encouraged sex along with intimacy, love, and marriage. At the same time, widespread prostitution openly testified to the double standard that permitted or even encouraged men to at least start their sexual lives outside of marriage. (An 1859 travel guide reviewed New York City's brothels: Miss Thompson's place at 75 Mercer Street, for example, "accommodates a number of handsome lady boarders, who are agreeable and accomplished.") Among the working classes, enough "loose" behavior persisted to provide middle-class readers with cautionary—and titillating—tales. Frontier camp revivals, I have pointed out before, had a sexual underground. All this granted, there was something Victorian about the Victorians. Premarital pregnancy rates dropped substantially in this era. Young, middle-class women indulged premarital passion up to, but not including, intercourse; that was reserved for marriage. Doctors and feminists counseled married women against having sex too frequently. Restraints—both external, such as chaperonage, and internal, such as religious guilt—seemingly increased over the course of the nineteenth century.[67]

Franker sexuality re-emerged, particularly for middle-class women, as the nineteenth century turned into the twentieth. New marital advice books emphasized understanding and enjoying sex. One warned: "Don't let anyone tell you that 'sex will take care of itself.' The sex act is not so simple or instinctive." By the 1920s, married couples were probably having sex more frequently and more equitably than ever. Unmarried Americans, notably middle-class "new women" going to college or doing office work, participated in the emerging culture of public "dating" and sexual experimentation. Young working-class women, also working outside the home and allowed to enjoy public entertainments, participated in the dating culture, too, although their relative poverty led many to more explicitly trade sexual favors for being "treated" to dinners, shows, and amusements. Explicit discussion of sex, often presented as "sex hygiene," appeared in books, plays, and films, and in the public schools. Around midcentury, the famous Kinsey studies of sexuality appeared, stimulating shock, titillation, and widespread conversation about sex. Purveyors of sex talk justified their work in part by citing the Freudian idea that sex was "an insistent force demanding expression" and claiming that its proper expression needed expert guidance. Meanwhile, authorities suppressed prostitution as a threat to health, morals, and the intimacy of the family. There was more sex—good sex and bad sex.[68]

By the second half of the twentieth century, the increase in premarital sex was clear. About 30 percent of women born around 1940 had premarital intercourse before they turned twenty; about 60 percent of women born around 1960 did. Recall that roughly a third of teenage girls in the 1950s had premarital sex, but almost two-thirds in the 1970s did (see chapter 4). Premarital pregnancies are still, as they were in colonial New England, a pretty clear marker of premarital sex. One in two first-time mothers in the 1990s had conceived her child before marriage, compared to only one in seven in the 1940s. Unlike colonial-era premarital pregnancies, however, modern ones did *not* usually lead to marriage, but instead to single mothering. Cohabiting, a public revelation of what had once been illicit, became common. By 2000, young couples typically lived together before getting married—to each other or to someone else. As sexual behavior changed, so did public attitudes: Americans' acceptance of premarital sex increased rapidly in the 1960s and 1970s. In 1968, The Supremes had a hit recording, "Love Child," which included the lyrics, "My father left, he never even married mom / I shared the guilt my mama knew / So afraid that others knew I had no name." Only seven years later, First Lady Betty Ford described the possibility of her daughter having a premarital affair as "perfectly normal." The post-1960s surge in premarital sex leveled off in the 1980s, and teenage sexual intercourse actually declined in the 1990s and 2000s. Similarly, the liberal trend in public opinion toward approving premarital sex leveled off. Neither opinions nor practices, however, had returned by the mid-2000s to anywhere near pre-1960s inhibition.[69]

Public displays of sexuality did not level off, but kept proliferating: men's picture magazines, adult cable television, blue comedy, four-letter-word hit songs, semi-nudes in advertisements, pornographic Web sites, and the like. It is unclear whether homosexual behavior increased, but the public visibility (and public acceptance) of homosexuals certainly continued to grow into the 2000s.[70]

Return to the puzzle that motivated this pocket history of sex in America: if Americans increasingly restrained their emotions, became "cool," how do we understand the sexual openness of the later twentieth century? One answer could be that the public vulgarity really was just as great in earlier periods (see the penny press, theater balconies, public prostitution, and so forth). But let us assume that sexual openness did grow. Stearns says that a hedonistic popular culture was an escape

valve for Americans' repressed impulses. The history of sexuality, however, makes it unlikely that modern Americans sought vicarious outlets
for a repressed sexuality, because they actually expressed their sexuality
more. Post-1960s Americans, especially women, recognized, analyzed,
managed, and probably had more sex with more partners than their forebears had going back at least to the early eighteenth century.[71]

Nor was twentieth-century sexuality a story of primal urges unloos-
ened, teeth-gnashing critics notwithstanding. Americans still disapproved of sex among minors and, from the 1970s through the mid-2000s,
increasingly deplored extramarital sex. They legislated against sexual ha-
rassment, tried to equalize the sexual freedom of men and women, expanded sex education in the schools, and in other ways constructed a
self-conscious, nuanced, and—dare I say—"sentimental" sexuality. In her
history of middle-class youth in the Roaring Twenties, historian Paula
Fass concludes that peer groups directed individuals' sexual experimentation and dictated that intercourse be predicated on love, because "the
young were true romantics."* In sum, both trends—increasing efforts to
accentuate positive emotions and eliminate negative ones, *and* increasing sexuality, both private and public—were not contradictory trends.
Instead, cultivating an explicit, managed, and sympathetic sexuality was
part of constructing a sensitive and sentimental self.[72]

As to the torrent of sexual coarseness in the popular culture: like much
else in the vastly expanded marketplace of the twentieth century (say, fried
food and loud music), more marketers sold more sex to more and younger
people. The volume was greater in the twentieth century, but it is unlikely
that Americans' crudity and sensation-seeking were greater than when
Virginia planters "rogered" slaves, serving wenches, and widows alike, or
when street broadsheets reported salacious details of scandalous trials almost hour-by-hour, or when women could be grabbed on city streets by
gangs of ruffians. Sexuality, like sentimentality and anger, became part of
increasing emotion management, of self-conscious self-perfecting, rather
than the unbridled release of id (—even in California).[73]

Accounting

Americans of the twentieth century less often felt—or at least less often expressed—the more virulent, hostile emotions common to everyday life in earlier centuries. Of course, aggression remained abundant,

---

* Sentimentality colors even relatively casual sex: The student newspaper at Berkeley, like many others, publishes explicit sexual advice columns. The authors usually
provide, along with mechanical directions, a moral etiquette admonishing patience,
self-control, and sensitivity to one's partner.

whether expressed verbally in television dialogue or physically in child battering. The surge of homicidal violence in the 1970s and '80s in part reflected what can happen when young, unattached men who cannot settle financial disputes or control their sense of injured honor carry guns — much as did barroom violence of the nineteenth century. But, overall, negative emotions slowly subsided. At the same time, twentieth-century Americans embraced a sentimentality and a sympathy toward others that became almost taken for granted and, in many ways, institutionalized, from charitable campaigns and environmentalism to laughing babies in advertising.[74]

What might have produced such historical changes in emotional standards and experiences? Most explanations point to economics. A crude version argues that nineteenth- and twentieth-century capitalists generated, stifled, or channeled human emotions to produce Americans who were, on the one hand, driven, repressed workers and, on the other hand, hedonistic, expressive consumers. To find succor from the harsh economic world, the middle class built "havens" of feminine love in the home. Other analysts suggest that the emergence of modern jobs, particularly service and professional jobs that require teamwork and pleasing customers, led aspirants to the middle class to cultivate in themselves and in their children the "soft skills," such as emotional self-control and sympathy, which are needed to succeed in such an economy. Research does show a connection between jobs and mentality. Working-class parents, for example, tend to instill in their children the deference useful in laboring and service jobs; middle-class parents push their children to be self-assertive and take initiative. So it is plausible that, in some form, as Americans' work lives changed over time, their child rearing may have followed, and then the American personality as well. Historian Thomas Haskell has made another sort of economic argument. Success in commerce, he suggests, required interpersonal deftness, moderation, trustworthiness, a sense of responsibility, and the ability to estimate far-off consequences. These psychological habits in turn fostered a wider sense of humanitarian sympathy and obligation. A different, simpler, economic explanation is that growing wealth and security allowed Americans to turn their attention and effort toward "luxuries," such as romance and benevolence. In a world that was less short, nasty, and brutish, more Americans could aspire to new purposes, including—like those girls yearning for "a thousand tender scenes"—perfecting a better, more sensitive self.[75]

Norbert Elias's "civilizing process," referred to earlier, presents a different, noneconomic explanation. Insistence on manners and self-restraint emerged from the European royal courts. Rulers of the Middle Ages needed to tame courtiers' explosive and violent temperaments. The effort took centuries and spread to the wider society. Americans experienced the last stages of that Western cultural evolution. For Elias, the driving force is emerging nation-states' need to guarantee stability and the security of its citizens. I cannot and need not adjudicate among these explanations here; I only point out that some historical evidence suggests that cultural changes, the ways people thought and felt, preceded the economic ones.[76]

From the possible causes, we turn to the possible consequences of modern emotionality. On the surface, at least, stronger emotion management produced a more civil and sentimental society. But some would argue that it only displaced dark drives and impulses into other channels. Or perhaps emotional self-control produced stress. One source argues, for example, that the anger Victorian women repressed then emerged in the form of psychosomatic illnesses. Emotion management might cause mental illness, which brings us to the issue of disorders.[77]

Feeling Disorders

Abraham Lincoln was famously a melancholy man; one can read the weariness and worry on the skeletal face of his memorial statue. Lincoln's sadness issued not only from the war and the loss of his sons, however; even as a young man, Lincoln frightened his friends with spells of depression—describing himself as "the most miserable man living"—and intimations of suicide. Distress was all around him. Lincoln's father had episodes of the "blues"; the violent madness of a nineteen-year-old neighbor impelled Lincoln to write a poem about the "howling, crazy man"; and the widowed Mary Todd Lincoln attempted suicide. Lincoln's story illustrates historian Page Smith's thesis that "anxiety and despair, as much as confidence and optimism, have characterized our history from the beginning." The question is how commonly Americans in different eras experienced what psychologists call "mood disorders."[78]

Many commentators claim that Americans became more vulnerable to a variety of syndromes, such as anxiety, narcissism, and neuroses.* Erich

---

* A methodological caution: the frequency of explicit disorders like the madness of Lincoln's neighbor can increase or decrease even if there is little change in average people's mental health. This can happen if variation in health widens. At one time, people may be all middling in their levels of stress. Over the years, more people may feel great and more people may also feel terrible, so terrible that disorders appear. Then, observers would see no change or perhaps an improvement on average and yet also see more episodes of mental disorder. For such reasons, changes in psychiatric hospitalizations, addictions, or suicides may or may not tell us about what is happening to people in general.

Fromm wrote in *The Sane Society* that people in the modern world are deeply alienated and therefore highly vulnerable to mental illness. Mass consumer culture narcotizes the pain, he said, but it is insufficient. Some people fall into extreme pathological behavior, while most people just endure anxiety, guilt, and unhappiness. Support for such claims, however, is almost always inferential, drawing on theory, personal experience, popular literature, declarations by contemporary observers, or just the authors' impressions—not solid evidence.[79]

One might try to find evidence in rates of admissions to mental institutions, for example. But changes in those rates do not reflect changing rates of mental illness; they more closely reflect changing policies toward mental illness. Between 1903 and 1940, the number of Americans in state mental hospitals roughly tripled, mainly because officials began using such institutions to house the elderly poor or other bothersome people. Later, fewer of the elderly were poor, and even they found housing. In the 1960s, state governments emptied out the mental hospitals as part of a yet newer reform, encouraged by both civil libertarians and tax cutters, to free the ill from forced confinement. Mental illness did not decline substantially; many of the disturbed simply ended up on the streets. In similar ways, changes in how doctors diagnose and treat people shape counts of the mentally ill. I mentioned at the top of this chapter the nineteenth-century rise and fall of "neurasthenia." In the 1810s, Philadelphia doctors replaced many diagnoses of insanity with "delirium tremens" as a label more suitable for middle-class men. In the 1970s, the American Psychiatric Association decided that homosexuality was no longer to be classified as a disorder; instantly, millions were "cured." More recently, diagnoses of bipolar disorder increased 4,000 percent in one decade. The immense difficulty of finding out who and how many people actually suffered psychological disorders in the past may explain why historians of mental illness typically study the development of psychological institutions, theories, standards, and professions rather than incidences of illness itself. I try, nonetheless, to extract from what evidence there is a history of the disorders themselves, with a focus on depression, the most common mood disorder and the one scholars most often attribute to modernity. I draw on fragmentary reports to describe the earlier eras and on statistical indicators, such as suicide rates, alcoholism, and surveys to detect trends in the twentieth century.[80]

Mental illness was well-known in colonial and nineteenth-century America. Page Smith points to the "cosmic loneliness" of life in the wilderness, to anxieties about salvation, to common reports of upset stomachs, and to high rates of alcoholism among early Americans. The chronic pain so many suffered (see chapter 2, p. 20) caused depression and perhaps suicide. Official documents record the names of many people who were "distempered" or "distracted" or had "fits," because local governments had to care for some of the ill and manage their property. Often, the disturbed were simply tolerated: a Watertown, Massachusetts, schoolmaster in the 1740s occasionally strode about town naked and sometimes had to be dragged out of meetings for creating a disturbance; an upcountry Carolina man who had fled Georgia around 1800 for killing one his slaves lived in a hollow log, ranted about witches, and pulled out fourteen of his teeth because he thought his kin were hiding inside them. To get officially noticed as insane, as these men did, people had to act bizarrely or repeatedly endanger lives. In such cases, relatives and neighbors testified that the person was delusional, violent, and, perhaps most critically, unable to manage his or her normal affairs. For example, many Connecticut women in the 1840s who suffered postpartum depression and could therefore no longer do their wifely chores ended up in Hartford's Retreat for the Insane; that failure to perform qualified them for admission.[81]

Remaining unlisted in the records — and therefore uncountable — were the many more Americans whose functioning was not so impaired (they may have been "blue" like Lincoln's father or even suicidal as Lincoln may have been) or those who, even if quite ill, found care among relatives. Some families were solicitous and humored the insane; others just coped with them. The family of John Wells, a South Carolina farmer, kept him chained and handcuffed for ten years before sending him to an asylum. Such stories, of course, do not give us any clear sense of how frequent disorders were. Still, biographies, passing accounts, and literary references suggest that serious mental illness was probably more common in the eighteenth and nineteenth centuries than in the twentieth. Of more substance than such anecdotes are reports that farm women, particularly in the sparsely settled West, suffered greatly from mental distress; their depression became one of the key Country Life problems investigated during the Theodore Roosevelt administration.[82]

At the same time, in the bursting cities of the nineteenth century, native migrants and foreign immigrants contributed substantially to the national tally of mental illness. We see their contribution in the rising rates of suicide. Social scientists have long used suicide rates as markers of depression rates, among other things. Official suicide rates fluctuate in response to many circumstances besides depression, such as religious doctrines, access to weapons, availability of life saving procedures, and bureaucratic rules for classifying deaths. Yet they do reflect, albeit crudely, variations in actual depression. European scholars of the late nineteenth century interpreted a contemporary increase in suicide rates as a sign that modernization was creating psychological trauma. Recorded rates of suicide in the

United States also rose toward the end of the nineteenth century, in large measure because of suicides by immigrants from Central Europe.[83]

Many of those immigrants found "taking the gas" to be a relatively easy means of ending their pain. While some newcomers struck gold in the New World, many others struck out. Arriving in New York in 1890, Charles Fischer, a well-educated clerk from Stuttgart, Germany, failed in real estate, the saloon business, and finally china plate decorating. During his travails, his wife betrayed him; after their divorce, he lost touch with his only child. At 10:00 PM on a Saturday evening in 1896, he entered his small rented room on East Third Street, sealed up every crack, wrote a few letters, and turned on the gas. In his letter to his mother, he wrote, "I cannot stand this much longer. If I don't get work within two weeks I will have to go out on the street and work as a laborer." Mrs. Ida Blohm, a forty-year-old dressmaker, was also an immigrant from Germany. She was widowed and had left her young son behind in the Old Country. In late 1895, she started a new job as a cook at the Cooper Union Hotel, but left it after a dispute with another employee. She took a room on the top floor of a boarding house and soon after connected one end of a rubber hose to the burner of a gas chandelier and placed the other end in her mouth. Her body was found several weeks later.[84]

Over the twentieth century, suicide statistics became more complete, accurate, and trustworthy. They show essentially *no net change* over a hundred years; the rate was about ten or eleven suicides per hundred thousand Americans in 1900, in 1950, and in 2005. Official suicide rates should have gone up simply for technical reasons, because other causes of death declined and because increasingly professional recordkeeping classified more deaths as suicides. Both considerations imply that Americans' underlying propensity to commit suicide probably went down; their underlying propensity to *attempt* suicide is much harder to estimate. This overall constancy, however, hides two major changes. First, from the middle to the end of the twentieth century, suicides by the elderly declined. Second, in about the same period, suicides by *young males*, especially teenage boys, rose—although they dropped after the early 1990s. (These two trends are evident in other Western nations, too.) The approximate halving of suicide rates among the elderly is perhaps easy to understand. The lives of the elderly clearly improved over those years; they became healthier, wealthier, and more independent, and their spouses lived longer. Since the mid-1980s, antidepressant drugs may have further reduced suicides. However, explaining the approximate tripling of suicide rates among boys and young men from 1950 to 1994 is more difficult. It may be, some research suggests, that boys suffered psychologically from rising rates of divorce and single parenting, or it may be that the baby boom

strained families, schools, and employment so much by the 1960s and
'70s that it generated despair among some young men. The decline after 1994 may indicate in part an abating of such stresses and in part the
effectiveness of some drug treatments. Pooled together, overall suicide
rates in American cities increased in the nineteenth century (we know
much less about rural America) and then nationally changed little over
the twentieth century.[85]

Substance abuse, especially heavy drinking, can also indicate emotional distress. Rates of alcohol consumption reflect many other things
as well as despair: styles of sociability, fluctuations in price, ease of access, and even water quality (often, beer was healthier for children to
drink than the local water). In the eighteenth and early nineteenth centuries, employers often paid laborers in alcohol, farmers honored barn-
raising neighbors with drinks, doctors prescribed alcohol to anesthetize
pain, and party leaders rewarded voters with free libations. The lifestyle
of working-class men commonly included binges. Nonetheless, alcoholism is connected, at least in modern populations, to anxiety and depression; some people drink heavily as a form of self-medication. Alcoholism,
crude records suggest, declined from the nineteenth into the twentieth
century. Death rates for cirrhosis of the liver generally declined, excepting a spurt in the 1960s and '70s, and reached their lowest point in mid-
2000s. Rates of overall alcohol consumption followed about the same
path. As in the case of young men and suicide, the 1960s seem distinctive; the burst in addiction during those years was an exception during a
long decline in alcoholism.[86]

People, of course, abuse other substances as well, including many items
in the growing pharmacopeia of drugs that Americans take for physical or
psychological relief—or just for fun. Over the nineteenth century, many
Americans, notably middle-class women, began using and becoming dependent on morphine, opium, laudanum, and cocaine; use of these drugs
peaked in the 1890s. Many, if not most, nineteenth-century addicts probably got hooked after their doctors prescribed one of these drugs to treat
any of a vast array of physical and psychological symptoms. Wounded
Civil War soldiers often became addicted to morphine; laborers in brutal jobs, such as dock work and mining, found cocaine a useful stimulant;
other Americans medicated themselves for emotional reasons. As early as
1830, a doctor in Knoxville, Tennessee, wrote poetry about the wonders
of opium: "It clears the cloudy font of wrinkled care / And soothes the bosom of despair!" An opium dealer remarked in 1877 that "since the close
of the [Civil] War, [Southern] men once wealthy, but impoverished by the
rebellion, have taken to eating and drinking opium to drown their sor-
rows." And an 1897 Sears Roebuck ad read, "If you . . . have to undergo an

unusual amount of hardship, always keep a bottle of our Peruvian Wine of Cocoa near you" (at $10 per dozen bottles). Some women used opium and morphine as feminine "substitutes for alcohol." Medical practice changed, new laws curtailed some drugs, and eventually drug addiction in the twentieth century, at least among the middle class, declined. Drugs became more of a problem for lower-class youths, and the drugs of choice changed from opium and morphine to heroin and cocaine.[87]

Because many people use drugs for recreation rather than for emotional numbing, drug use does not necessarily indicate mental distress. The twentieth-century trends are nonetheless interesting. Illicit drug use took a major and fateful lurch in the 1960s and 1970s when the baby boomers grew up. More teens and young adults tried drugs, especially marijuana, and tried them earlier in their lives than previous generations had and more than subsequent generations would. By one estimate, only 2 percent of Americans who were teenagers before 1960 had ever tried marijuana, but about half of teenagers in the 1970s and early '80s eventually tried it. Use of other drugs also rose during that period, albeit less dramatically. The proportion of Americans who experimented with and the proportion who regularly took drugs seemed to peak around 1980 and then declined. Baby boomers largely gave up drugs, and fewer children of boomers used drugs than their parents had. A telling national survey conducted in 1997 asked *parents* of teenagers, most of whom had been teenagers themselves in the 1960s and early '70s, whether they had ever tried marijuana; 55 percent said yes, they had tried it. When asked whether they had ever "had a problem with marijuana or any other illegal drug," about 20 percent said yes. But, when asked whether they "smoked [marijuana] from time to time nowadays," only 5 percent said yes. A relative few of the '60s and '70s drug experimenters never stopped, but illicit drug use decreased as the century closed.[88]

A more direct way to estimate rates of mood disorders is to diagnose people in person. Impractical as it is to get nationally representative samples of Americans onto a psychiatrist's couch, researchers have deployed mass surveys that include short questions to assess symptoms. They ask respondents such questions as "Have you ever had 2 weeks or more when nearly every night you had trouble falling asleep?" and "Have you ever had 2 weeks or longer when you lost the ability to enjoy having good things happen to you, like winning something or being praised or complimented?" Certain patterns of answers, researchers assume, indicate that the interviewee has a mental disorder. Results from one survey suggested that about half of adult Americans living in 2002 would experience a diagnosable disorder sometime in their lives, one-sixth of them suffering a major depressive disorder, and most of those enduring at least one such episode before they turned twenty. Unfortunately, such surveys began only in the late 1950s. To try to look further back in time, some researchers compared the reports of older respondents to those of younger ones and concluded from that comparison that there must have been a major increase in symptoms during the twentieth century. There must have been, they suggested, an "epidemic of depression." However, more recent scholarship shows that this well-publicized claim is, because of technical problems, highly dubious. Moreover, comparing surveys conducted in the middle of the century to those conducted later does *not* reveal an increase in depression-revealing answers. There was no such epidemic.[89]

The next question may be why Americans did not become *less* depressed since the 1950s. Generally and despite some economic slippage, Americans gained much after 1950; they became healthier, longer-lived, better-educated, and so on. Perhaps changes of other sorts—especially during and after the 1960s—offset those material gains. Economic insecurities, declining rates of marriage, strains as wives went to work, cultural turmoil (remember the story of "Alice Neal" from chapter 4), more television-watching, or even more introspection may have cancelled out the improvements. Each claim has its adherents and some evidence. Take, for example, the issue of sleep. With women's growing employment, round-the-clock commerce, longer commutes, and new entertainment opportunities at night—especially television—Americans at the end of the century slept fewer hours than their parents or grandparents did. The trend fits with increasing complaints by Americans in the later decades that they felt pressed for time. Sleeplessness tends to generate psychological disorders. All things considered, the best estimate is that depression rates stayed roughly the same over the century.[90]

Together, these various strands of evidence suggest that Americans around 2000 were less often insane or seriously disturbed than Americans were around 1800. Vulnerability to milder disorders, like Thomas Lincoln's "blues," probably rose and fell, perhaps in step with economic cycles. Psychological distress seemed to increase in the later decades of the nineteenth century as immigration surged and industrialization accelerated, and it then stabilized or probably declined for much of the twentieth century. The noteworthy exception to this conclusion is that young people, particularly young men, apparently experienced a swelling of distress during the 1960s and '70s. (Their younger siblings and children were less psychologically vulnerable.) Many Americans recall "the sixties" as the era "that had robbed them of hope"; they point to crime, the undermining of authority, family disruptions, duplicitous government, and the like. Indeed, major social changes tested Americans during those years—from the civil rights and feminist movements to the rapid expansion of college and increasing delay of marriage. Perhaps the sixties were special because several social trends crested at once. Or perhaps, as some social scientists suggest, the trends themselves emerged from a deeper demographic current, the 1950s baby boom and its long-unfolding consequences.[91]

Happiness

The bottom line for all these emotional trends is arguably happiness: have Americans become more or less happy? At the start of the twenty-first century, many scholars turned to this question; even economists got happiness-happy. Although classical thinkers had pondered happiness and survey researchers had studied it for decades, modern economists had rarely addressed it—perhaps because studying happiness seemed mawkish, best left to mushy-headed sociologists and psychologists who could with a straight face ask interviewees, "Taken all together, how would you say things are these days—would you say that you are very happy, pretty happy, or not too happy?" Then economists discovered that the methods they used to figure out people's "utilities" were deeply flawed. Their assumption that people had a ranked set of preferences, examined the choices available to them, and then picked the one with highest payoff increasingly seemed naive. People too often made illogical, self-punishing, or quickly regretted decisions (see section above on choice). Economists could no longer take a buyer's choice as a "revealed preference."* Many economists turned to happiness as the ultimate utility and to the happiness question as its best measure, arguing that respondents' answers were valid reflections of how much they took pleasure from, say, their jobs, reputations, or children.[92]

Many new happiness scholars focused in particular on an apparent paradox first presented by economist Richard Easterlin: America became wealthier over the last few decades of the twentieth century, but average American happiness, as reported in surveys using the happiness question, stayed flat. Why did growing national wealth not bring more national happiness? The puzzle is relevant to this book's larger purpose, because expanding wealth is a central force in American history; how wealth affects people's feelings bears on how we understand Americans' emotional history. Two different kinds of answers to the seeming paradox emerged.

* Noted psychologist Daniel Kahneman and noted economist Alan Krueger wrote in 2006 that "people often make choices that bear a mixed relationship to their own happiness.... [T]heir choices do not necessarily reflect their 'true' preferences, and an exclusive reliance on choices to infer what people desire loses some of its appeal."

One kind points to the psychology of happiness. Beyond a basic level, many scholars said, more money does not make people happier, because people adapt to having the money (so the thrill is gone), or because wealth just whets the desire for more, or because being happy depends on making more than the guy next door, or because people have a biological "set point" of happiness. The second kind of answer points to countervailing forces. Wealth brought happiness, but other historical trends in the late twentieth century, such as rising divorce rates, time pressures, and social turmoil, negated the joys of affluence. For all this debate, there is probably *no paradox at all*: in the last few decades of the century, unlike generations before, average Americans did not really get much wealthier. National wealth grew, but the gains largely went to a top few. So why would we expect average Americans to get much happier? Conclusion: on average (notorious celebrities aside), the more wealth people have, the happier they tend to be. The research around the supposed Easterlin Paradox has expanded our understanding of happiness, but leaves us still with the question, did Americans become more or less happy over the course of our history?[93]

However murky mass surveys may be as measurements of national happiness, descriptions of Americans' happiness before the 1950s rest on even thinner evidence. As with other emotions, historians can more easily track *expectations* than actual experiences of happiness. Those expectations of happiness probably increased over the course of American history. They received a boost, for example, when Thomas Jefferson, drafting the Declaration of Independence, took the conventional list of inalienable rights that had been circulating among activists in the colonies, "life, liberty, and property," and replaced the last entry with "the pursuit of happiness." Over the nineteenth century, women filing for divorce increasingly asserted their rights to personal happiness, charging husbands with shirking their duty to provide that happiness. And the expanding commercial culture promised more pleasure in more goods.[94]

Alexis de Tocqueville, among others, claimed that such pursuit of happiness generated a characteristic American *un*happiness. He wrote in the 1830s that American equality, with its promise of universal success, bred sadness. "In America I saw the freest and most enlightened men placed in the happiest circumstances that the world affords, it seemed to me as if a cloud habitually hung upon their brow, and I thought them serious and almost sad, even in their pleasures." Poor people in hierarchical societies hoped for little and were content with even less, but the egalitarian Americans "are forever brooding over advantages they do not possess. . . . Besides the good things that [the American] possesses, he every instant fancies a thousand others that death will prevent him from trying if he does

not try them soon. This thought fills him with anxiety, fear, and regret."
About a decade later, New York minister Henry Bellows made a similar
observation: "All strangers who come among us remark the excessive anxiety written in the American countenance." Bellows explained the American anxiety, in a preview of French sociologist Emile Durkheim's concept
of anomie, this way: "There are no bounds among us to the restless desire to be better off; and this is the ambition of all classes of society. . . .
In other lands, if children can maintain the station and enjoy the means,
however moderate, of their father, they are happy. Not so with us." The
implication, then, is that the egalitarian, high-expectations, can-do culture of America bred a never-satisfied ambition, which could only mean
chronic unhappiness.[95]

The historical fragments are too sparse to confidently reconstruct a
history of American happiness. But contemporary differences among nations may by analogy suggest what happened. Worldwide studies show
that people are likelier to say they are happy—setting aside differences
of individual temperament—if they are economically secure, healthy and
active, religious, busy with friends and groups, and married (having children at home, however, is a bit of a downer). People are also likelier to
report being happy if they live in a country that is affluent; has a democratic, effective, and economically active government; has a culture that
is individualistic; and has citizens who feel free and who trust one another.* On most of these counts, social change in America from the early
nineteenth through the middle of the twentieth centuries should have
raised Americans' national happiness. Because of the social psychology of
emotions—people accustom themselves to improvements, evaluate their
circumstances by comparing themselves to others, and so on—the increase in happiness would not have been proportional to the scale of the
social changes, but still noticeable. Towards the end of the twentieth century, some of these presumably uplifting trends stalled or reversed. Most
Americans experienced income stagnation, they married later, and the
American welfare state retrenched. The flattening out of Americans' reported happiness after 1970 seems understandable.[96]

Of course, this analogy—treating historical differences like cross-
national differences—is a crude estimate at best. Fragmentary survey
data starting in the late 1940s allow us to track happiness reports over
sixty years. Upbeat reports increased from the end of World War II to
about 1960 and then slumped a bit during the 1970s and '80s, roughly leveling out afterwards. Some research suggests that we do better comparing

* Comparatively, Americans ranked in the middle in reported happiness among
Western nations around 2000.

generations rather than decades. From that point of view, it appears that baby boomers, roughly those who were teenagers between 1960 and 1980, were and remain distinctively downbeat. Overall, the best summary is that average Americans' happiness probably rose significantly—albeit with ups and downs—through most of the nation's history, slumped among baby boomers, and has been roughly steady since about 1970.[97]

Yet the reader may well ask, is happiness really the bottom line, the ultimate "utility"? Would we judge a bovine happiness—some sort of bellyful-, chemical-, or television-induced contentment—superior to a richer but more strained life? Would we discount tragedies because people typically recover their spirits? Would we dismiss the historical reductions in child mortality, physical debilitation, discrimination, and the like because they yield only moderate returns in happiness? Most readers would answer no, I suspect. Such answers imply that there is some yet more profound bookkeeping we would want to do.

REFLECTING

Bookkeeping is, in some sense, what this chapter has been about: listing, lining up, tabulating the changes in the American psyche. And bookkeeping also describes much of what Americans learned to do with their psyches. Benjamin Franklin's checklist of virtues may have been a cartoon symbol of it, but the project of systematic self-examination and self-perfection became increasingly widespread and normal. Psychological recordkeeping, as well as the conventional versions of accounting, expanded Americans' powers of calculation. The growing voluntaristic culture both raised their sense of empowerment and encouraged a set of emotional habits suited to group life, such as self-discipline, sympathy, and sentimentality. All this working on the self, insisted on by cultural leaders from Mary Chandler in 1854 to Oprah Winfrey in 2004—the introspection, the emotion management, the conviction that one is whoever one wants to be—both liberated and burdened Americans. Similarly, the expansion of choices, from the mundane like foods to the profound like spouses, both enriched and taxed modern Americans. The question then arises whether Americans paid a psychic or emotional price for all this freedom and opportunity and for being "entirely responsible" for their Characters (in Mary Chandler's terms). The evidence suggests, most generally, no. There were generations, notably that of the baby boomers, when it seems that the turmoil of social change took some toll. Over the long run, however, were it not for the anxieties that accompany the freedom to be whoever one wants to be, the bookkeepers of happiness would have detected growing joy.[98]

7 Closing

Much of the controversy swirling around U.S. Supreme Court decisions in recent decades concerns the principle of "originalism." Should the Court read the Constitution for the explicit meaning the words had to its authors in 1789 and apply those denotations in modern times? Or should the Court read the Constitution for its implicit principles and, as exponents of the "living Constitution" would have it, adapt the document to fit modern life? The death penalty is one of the issues at stake. The Constitution explicitly assumes its use, and death sentences were commonly applied at the time the Founding Fathers composed the nation's charter. Voices on the modern Court have charged, however, that America's evolving culture requires accommodations. In 1972, Justice Brennan wrote, "*Today* death is a uniquely and unusually severe punishment. . . . [It] stands condemned as fatally offensive to human dignity"—as a violation, in other words, of Elias's "civilizing process." Significantly, both sides of this debate see sufficient continuity in American culture and character to argue about how best to apply today either the explicit words or the implicit principles of men now two centuries dead.[1]

This continuity is a striking feature of American culture. To be sure, there have been important changes, spikes, sideways moves, and reversals, but what seemed socially distinctive about America in the eighteenth century still seems distinctive in the twenty-first. The major change has been the broadening and deepening of that distinctive culture and the incorporation into it of more Americans who had been—because of gender, race, age, servitude, poverty, and isolation—less than full participants.

More Americans engaged more fully in American voluntarism. That voluntarism presumes an independent, self-governing, and self-reliant individual. Over the generations, more people gained the "competency" that colonial Americans thought necessary to be such a person. Greater security, more wealth, and the proliferation of groups made autonomy more possible for more Americans. More also gained the cognitive tools to practice competency, especially the sense that they controlled their fates and even could mold their own characters. Personal empowerment permitted even more independence from the authority of other people. But critically, American individualism was and is coupled with intense, freely given fellowship—group belonging by voluntary contract or covenant. More Americans developed the personal skills, including the self-discipline and emotional reactions, such as sympathy, needed to fully and freely participate in marriages, churches, neighborhoods, workplaces, clubs, and free-floating friendships. Americans' social evolution, then, involved a balancing act between, on the one hand, maintaining independence, the freedom to exit groups, and, on the other hand, committing to groups enough to make them benefit all. (A prime example of this is couples "working" on their marriages.) For increasingly many, voluntarism became imaginable, desirable, and possible.

In other ways besides voluntarism, we see striking continuities in American culture and character. Americans, for example, continued to be avid accumulators of goods, the major historical change being not more desire, but the deluge of goods that could be desired and the greater means with which to scoop them up. Americans over the generations also remained believers, perhaps even more theologically sophisticated believers. And working on the self, trying to perfect one's character, continued a discipline practiced over the centuries by a few, but now by masses.

How could there be so much continuity of culture and character over centuries of enormous social change? Between 1800 and 2000, industrialization overturned an agricultural society, tens of millions of people from disparate cultures moved in, rural residents became urbanites and then suburbanites, children learned new skills, modern technologies altered the mechanics of human contact, and people who had little came to have so much. Many wise observers have argued that radical changes in American culture and character must have followed—that, for example, a people who had once been "producer oriented" became "consumer oriented," the once-ascetic became hedonistic, the once–inner-directed became other-directed, the once–community-oriented became individualistic, the individualistic conformist, the simple-minded sophisticated, believers became skeptics, the social became lonely, the giving became selfish, and so on. These assertions largely remain only that, unproven. Far less really changed. Perhaps such continuity testifies to the resilience of national cultures, the way people can craft new circumstances to sustain old practices. (The Japanese, too, modernized while staying

distinctively Japanese.) In the case of immigration, to take one challeng-ing circumstance, America has been able to incorporate, remold, and ac-culturate—to Americanize—people from vastly different backgrounds.*
Americans commandeered growing wealth, technology, and education,
for example, to energize existing patterns, like voluntarism, and pursue
existing goals, like luxury goods.[2]

For all the continuities, American character did change in some ways.
The vast expansion of physical and economic security, greater stability
and predictability, and the abundance of food, goods, and services en-dowed more individuals with more freedom and confidence to plan their
own futures, to demand autonomy, and to expand equality. Abundance, as
historian David Potter emphasized, made liberty and equality—and de-mocracy—possible for the masses. "In other societies, liberty—the prin-ciple that allows the individual to be different from others—might seem
inconsistent with equality—the principle that requires the individual to
be similar to others; but in America 'liberty,' meaning 'freedom to grasp
opportunity,' and 'equality,' also meaning 'freedom to grasp opportunity,'
have become almost synonymous. . . . [It is a] politics of abundance rather
than a politics of individualism." In the eighteenth century, apprentices
chafed at masters' rules; in the twentieth century, African Americans de-manded political voice. Growth, industrialization, and modern commu-nications weakened the hold of groups and groups' rulers—household
patriarchs, church elders, local elites—on individuals. Psychologically,
Americans became no "smarter," but more of them picked up various
skills and tools that made them more effective and feel more effective.
Americans' emotional skills also seemed to increase as they learned to
better examine their emotions, master the ones that could damage rela-tionships, and nurture those that sustain relationships. And more Ameri-cans managed to do more of this while largely maintaining, even improv-ing, their equanimity and good cheer.[3]

RECENT PAST AND NEAR FUTURE

I have made sweeping summaries covering broad expanses of time. It is
worth narrowing our gaze to the recent past, both because of its rele-vance and because of its fascinating reversals. The 1950s were an era of
exceptional—perhaps peak—domesticity, calm, safety, and satisfaction.
We cannot ignore the underside of '50s, such as the racial caste system
in the South, the stifling of many women's ambitions, and the pockets of

---

* As I noted in chapter 1, for all the celebration of multiculturalism, it is striking how
rapidly immigrants' children and grandchildren become culturally American.

intense poverty. But "middle Americans" felt, quite reasonably, that it was a good time. Then came the extended 1960s, roughly 1963 to 1973. They were years of continuing prosperity, but also of dislocation, especially for the young, the baby boomers. Some significant developments during those years particularly affected, lastingly, the generation of Americans then in their teens and early adulthood: delays in marrying, more divorces, a drop in voting, backsliding in church adherence, a spurt in drug taking and drinking, a rise in young male suicides, earlier sexual experiences, liberalization of social attitudes, and an ebb in reported happiness. Some of what happened in the mid-1970s and the '80s can be seen as fallout from, reaction to, or recovery from the extended '60s. Why the '60s were really so disruptive—it was not just in popular imagination—has been answered in various ways. Demographers emphasize the numbers: baby boomers went through years of competition, with their siblings for parents' attention, classmates in crowded schools, and coworkers on the first rungs of career ladders; the competition took a toll. Culture critics stress that baby boomers were the first generation to grow up immersed in, perhaps reared by, television. Political analysts point to the traumatic events of the era, especially the Vietnam War and its draft. The cultural collision of the hyper-disruptive '60s into the hyper-domestic '50s reverberated for decades. Baby boomers remain a distinctive cohort of Americans—for example, less happy and more suicide-prone than their parents or children.[4]

The case of the boomers reminds us that, although I have sought in this book to summarize, to simplify, the broad sweep of Americans' experience from the colonial era to the new millennium, that history involves many tos and fros, ups and downs. We saw the rise, fall, and rise of Americans' heights, fluctuations in church involvement, the flow and ebb of public life in American cities, surges and declines in criminal violence over the centuries, and so forth.

The years after 1973 were yet another ebb. After a period of strong economic growth, average Americans' economic fortunes stagnated and then plunged in the late 2000s. Historically, Americans had done materially better than Western Europeans, but by the twenty-first century, average Americans' economic security was no better and in some respects worse than that of average Western Europeans. (Wealthy Americans remained at the top.) Economic inequality had widened considerably. Many have written in detail about the causes and consequences of this growing economic inequality. Here, I note only that widening inequality, in educational attainment as well as in wealth, stalled or even reversed the inclusion of Americans within the mainstream culture. The gaps in security, fortune, and lifestyle between the middle class—roughly now defined as people with college degrees—and the marginal have widened. The gaps manifest themselves in many ways, for example, in family life. Since 1960, children of college-graduate women have commonly lived with two parents, but children of poorly educated women increasingly lived only with one. The prospect that the history of growing inclusion will reverse is significant.[5]

Predicting where these recent trends will take Americans is unwise and potentially embarrassing. (Just ask the reporter who wrote a story in 1985 entitled "Home Computers: Why the Craze is Fizzling Out.") Demographers can foretell, barring catastrophes, how many seventy-year-olds there will be in fifty years based on how many twenty-year-olds there are today. But foreseeing changes in the kinds of cultural and psychological topics discussed in this book is another matter. Savants of the 1950s totally missed what became "the sixties"; and writers in "the sixties" hardly expected the culture of the Reagan '80s. In the thirty-five years after 1815, the cost of shipping goods around the United States dropped by at least 95 percent. In the thirty-five years after 2015, energy costs could also drop sharply—or they could rise sharply—and the economic circumstances of American society would change drastically. It is unlikely that such changes would alter the bedrock culture and character of this society, but they would certainly affect the numbers who could fully participate.[6]

There is no guarantee that the centuries-old direction of social change in America—more security, goods, social life, control, voluntarism—will continue. Any major historical break in Americans' good fortune—such as catastrophes from global warming, global war, or global competition—could reverse trends: more Americans impoverished or marginalized, people's rights curtailed, individuals circling the wagons or falling back on kin, the shriveling of voluntarism. It is the spirit of American voluntarism to believe, however, that much of that future is in our control.

CODA

Finally, there is a question that always lurks around books like this: have the changes been for the better or the worse? It is not easy to answer and Americans themselves are ambivalent. For example, in 1939 a national survey asked respondents whether they thought that "Americans were happier and more content . . . during the horse-and-buggy days instead of now," and 62 percent said yes. However, asked whether they "would rather have lived during the horse-and-buggy days," 69 percent said no.

It is hard to argue, although perhaps Henry David Thoreau would have, that attaining longer, healthier, less pain-filled, more comfortable lives is anything but good. And almost all Americans today would agree, although John Adams might not have, that making American society more inclusive, empowering more people, and extending equality was good. The widespread applause for Barack Obama's ascension to the presidency, even by many who had not voted for him, was in part Americans applauding themselves for expanding the circle.[7]

The cultural and characterological aspects of modernity can still be debated, nonetheless. It is difficult to evaluate the ultimate implications of moving from a society of small, hierarchical circles, where competency was held by the few and the others understood their place; where life and death and one's role during the few years inbetween was a given; and where most people fatalistically accepted how they lived and who they were, to a society of vastly more choices, where individuals are much more empowered and are expected to build their own social bonds, to control their lives, and to constantly improve themselves. Whether these developments are good or bad depends on who judges. In terms of sheer privilege and power, white men of property lost a lot over the last three centuries; Americans who were not white men of property gained a lot. But the judgment also depends on what one values. Many white men of property, for example, learned to value companionate marriages, independent children, and political equality. From whoever's perspective, the changes certainly posed burdens along with options—the freedom that Erich Fromm argued people tried to escape—and judging that trade-off is an individual matter in our voluntaristic society.

Notes

Chapter One

1. Duffield, "An Iowa Settler's Homestead" ("thousand," para. 7) and "Frontier Church Going." Duffield makes no mention of his mother's social or emotional role. Ripken and Bryan, *The Only Way I Know*, 17–18, and Ripken, *My Story*, 7–8 ("set shot," 7).

2. Popular debunking: K. Davis, *Don't Know Much About History* (Plymouth, 21); Loewen, *Lies My Teacher Told Me*. Family meals: historian John Gillis writes: "In the early nineteenth century, bourgeois households everywhere still ate on the run and only rarely in family groups. There was neither a time nor a place for the family dinner: the dining room as we know it had not yet been invented, and the big meal was still located closer to noon" ("Making Time for Family," 8); see also J. Gillis, *A World of Their Own Making*: "Everything that we now call 'quality times,' namely those highly ritualized times-out-of-time whose origins we trace back to the Victorian era . . . have actually increased over the last century and a half" (5). Christmas: J. Gillis, *A World of Their Own Making*, 100ff; Nissenbaum, *The Battle for Christmas*; L. Schmidt, *Consumer Rites*.

3. "The Changing American Family," *New York Times* (hereafter, *NYT*), May 18, 2001; Patricia Cohen, "Midlife Suicide Rises, Puzzling Researchers," *NYT*, Feb. 19, 2008. In the 2000s, about 14 percent of Americans changed homes each year; in the early 1950s, about 20 percent did (http://www.census.gov/population/socdemo/migration/tab-a-1.xls). See also Cohn and Morin, "American Mobility." More: C. Fischer, "Ever-More Rooted Americans"; see also chapter 4.

4. Parts of chapters 4 and 6 address religion. Overviews: Finke and Stark, *The Churching of America*, and Fischer and Hout, *Century of Difference*, ch. 8.

5. Fear: a 1996 survey asked respondents to pick one of eighteen areas in which America had declined the most. Nineteen percent picked "crime and safety," 14 percent "family life," and 12 percent "moral and ethical standards" (Hunter and Bowman, "The State of Disunion," vol. 2, table 5). For rates of violence, see chapter 2, below.

6. Braverman, *Labor and Monopoly Capital*, is the key source on "deskilling." Zakim, *Ready-Made Democracy*, ch. 3, describes the case of antebellum tailors who lost

their independence when new technologies and specialization allowed manufacturers to make cheaper clothes. Overall, however, Americans did *not* suffer deskilling (e.g., Spenner, "Temporal Change"; Oestreicher, "The Counted and the Uncounted"; Lebergott, *The Americans*, 371–72; Prude, "Capitalism, Industrialization, and the Factory," 93; Attewell, "The Clerk Deskilled," and Fischer and Hout, *Century of Difference*, ch. 5). Much depends on how one characterizes nineteenth-century farming. Farmers were nominally independent, but most were so vulnerable to weather, debt, and price cycles that they felt dependent and fled the farms.

7. See chapter 2 for an extended discussion.

8. Romanticizing: Eibach et al., "When Change in the Self"; Hagerty, "Was Life Better?"; Rosenzweig and Thelen, *The Presence of the Past*. Crowe, "Good Fences" and "Community Size," describes how Austrian villagers exaggerated the sociability of their parents' lives and the loneliness of their own. Coontz remarked in "The Challenge," that public audiences refuse to "hear" findings about the 1950s that clash with their memories. Historian Eugen Weber, in *Peasants into Frenchman*, noted that, while many of the French elite circa 1914 "grieved over the death of yesterday," "few who grieved were peasants . . . . [Their] past was a time of misery and barbarism" (478). *Gemeinschaft* and scholars: Lears, *Fables of Abundance*, 103. See also B. Turner, "A Note on Nostalgia"; C. Fischer, "Finding the 'Lost' Community."

9. Toulmin and Goodfield, *The Discovery of Time*, 233. P. Stearns, "The Idea of Postindustrial Society," also points out tendencies to exaggerate differences. Dickens: "It was the best of times, it was the worst of times . . . in short, the period was . . . like the present period."

10. Zambia: Ault, "Making 'Modern' Marriage"; Maori: J. N. Wilford, "Anthropology Seen as Father of Maori Lore," *NYT*, Feb. 20, 1990. Birthdays: Chudacoff, *How Old Are You?* Faux customs: Bodnar, *The Transplanted*, 46–48. There is by now a large literature on *The Invention of Tradition* (a book edited by Hobsbawm and Ranger).

11. "Collective memory": Hobsbawm and Ranger, *The Invention of Tradition*; Kammen, *Mystic Chords of Memory*; and J. Gillis, *Commemorations*. New England woods: Bowden, "The Invention."

12. Mexican Americans, like whites, saw the past as mostly about either their families or the whole nation, but, like blacks, they saw progress (Rosenzweig and Thelen, *The Presence of the Past*).

13. Narratives: "Explanation resides in an achieved sense of dramatic inevitability . . . [so that] the plot as a whole viewed in retrospect rings true"(P. Abrams, "History, Sociology," 10. See H. White, "The Value of Narrativity," *Content of the Form*, and *Metahistory*; see also Berkhoffer, *Beyond the Great Story*; McCloskey, *If You're So Smart*, ch. 2; and Hexter, *Doing History*. Lincoln: Wills, *Lincoln at Gettysburg*. Tides in historians' thinking: e.g., Kessler-Harris, "Social History"; Novick, *That Noble Dream*, part IV; Wiener, "Radical Historians" (with subsequent comments in the same issue); Hughes, "Contemporary Historiography"; and J. Block, *A Nation of Agents*, ch. 1. National standards: e.g., Wiener, "History Lesson"; McDougall, "Whose History?" (quotation about cynicism); and special issue, "Social History and the American Political Climate," of the *Journal of Social History* (vol. 29, 1995).

14. Progress: Manuel and Manuel, *Utopian Thought*; Nisbet, *History of the Idea of Progress*; Iggers, "The Idea of Progress"; P. Wagner, "Modernity." Iggers argues that "the idea of progress has run its course in social thought and historiography, but not quite" (64). Marty, "The Idea of Progress," describes a recent shift toward pessimism in theology. As noted earlier, most respondents to a mid-1990s survey expressed a sense of decline (Rosenzweig and Thelen, *The Presence of the Past*, 132–37). See Best, "Social Progress," on sociologists' gloominess.

15. A vast literature covers modernization theory. Nolte, "Modernization and Modernity," is a good short overview; see also Adelman, "Modernization Theory and Its Critics"; Appleby, "Modernization Theory"; Grew, "More on Modernization"; P. Stearns, "Modernization and Social History"; P. Wagner, "Modernity"; and Haferkamp and Smelser, *Social Change and Modernity*. Major historians using modernization theory include R. Brown, *Modernization*; and Wiebe, *The Search for Order*. Canonical nineteenth- and twentieth-century authors include Karl Marx, Ferdinand Tönnies, Emile Durkheim, Max Weber, and Talcott Parsons. Raymond Williams's *The City and the Country* and Leo Marx's *The Machine in the Garden* explore the cultural roots of these ideas.

Variants: (1) In the economic version, new technologies, systems of production, means of distribution, or combinations thereof compelled—albeit with some "cultural lag" (Ogburn, "How Technology Causes Social Change")—new social arrangements, such as smaller families, and new forms of consciousness, such as consumerism. Mainstream economics stresses technological innovations like steam power (e.g., N. Rosenberg, *How the West Grew Rich*; Boorstin, *The Americans*). Classical Marxism stresses capitalists' gathering of wage laborers into new systems of manufacturing. Some neo-Marxists argue that the expansion of markets changed work and consumption (e.g., Sellers, *The Market Revolution*; see also discussions in chapters 3 and 4 of this book).

(2) A more sociological variant contends that an increase in scale created a "mass society." The consolidation of nation-states, for example, expanded communications and commerce. Vast and continental institutions invaded what were formerly "island communities," in the phrase of historian Robert Wiebe (*The Search for Order*), transforming Americans' experiences from the small, local, and informal to the large, national, and formal. People became estranged members of the "lonely crowd." (On historians' "organizational synthesis": e.g., Brinkley, "Prosperity, Depression, and War"; Galambos, "Technology, Political Economy, and Professionalization"; and Adelman, "Modernization Theory and Its Critics.") In the last century, mass society theory was represented by thinkers such as Eric Fromm, C. Wright Mills, Robert Nisbet, and David Reisman (of *Lonely Crowd* fame). More recent exponents include Giddens, *The Consequences of Modernity*; and C. Calhoun, "The Infrastructure of Modernity." Among the many criticisms of mass society theory, see Coser, *In Defense of Modernity*; and Bender, *Community and Social Change in America*. Another close variant focuses on "structural differentiation." Growth leads to specialization in work but also in other spheres. Where the family once produced goods, taught the young, cared for the ill, and so forth, now businesses, schools, and hospitals serve those ends. People face a

fragmented and confusing social world; many fall between the cracks. (Durkheim's *Division of Labor in Society* and *Suicide* are classic statements. See also the work of mid-twentieth-century structural functionalists led by Talcott Parsons.) Although often attacked, the structural differentiation thesis remains—at least, implicitly— influential. (See Tilly, *Big Structures, Large Processes, and Huge Comparisons*; Tiryakian, "Dialectics of Modernity.")

(3) The cultural variant of modernization theory reverses the causal order: Changes in culture and consciousness precede material changes. Max Weber's thesis that the "Protestant ethic" produced capitalism is well-known, but his argument that "rationalization" characterizes the modern world is also important. Others have pointed to declines in religious faith or in fatalism, or to increases in individualism or scientific thinking, or to other changes in mentality as the transformation that launched modernity. (See Zuckerman, "Dreams"; Henretta, "Social History"; R. Brown, *Modernization*, esp. ch. 1 [and the review by Henretta, "'Modernization'"]; R. Wells, "Family History"; D. Bell, "The Return of the Sacred"; Tiryakian, "Dialectics of Modernity"; and Swidler, "The Concept of Rationality.") Some, like Inkeles and Smith, in *Becoming Modern*, were more explicitly psychological, suggesting that certain cognitive skills made modernization possible. Post-1960s European scholars stressed changes in "discourse," i.e., modes of apprehending the world (P. Wagner, *A Sociology of Modernity*, ch. 1, for an example and overview). Nolte, "Modernization and Modernity," points out that disdain for optimistic modernization theories led many analysts to prefer the word "modernity" or even "post-modernity" when really pursuing the same argument.

16. Modernization theories draw on teleological nineteenth-century notions about evolution which modern biology has moved beyond (Bock, *Human Nature and History*; R. Collins, "Upheavals"). Problems assuming organic coherence: e.g., M. S. Archer, "The Myth of Cultural Integration." The complexity and disorderliness of "traditional" societies: Tilly, *Big Structures, Large Processes, and Huge Comparisons*; Bendix, "Tradition and Modernity Reconsidered"; Boudon, "Why Theories of Social Change Fail"; D. Smith, "'Modernization'"; Appleby, "Values and Society"; Tipps, "Modernization Theory," esp. 213; Gusfield, "Tradition and Modernity"; and Nolte, "Modernization and Modernity." Others criticize modernization theory for being ethnocentric, or conservative, or deterministic. Judt, "A Clown in Regal Purple," claims that the theory serves "a multitude of ideological [largely anti-Marxist] purposes" (69). Fox-Genovese and Genovese, "The Political Crisis," wrote that social history "as a whole is sinking into a neoantiquarian swamp presided over by liberal ideologues, the burden of whose political argument—notwithstanding the pretense of not having a political argument—rests on an evasion of class confrontation" (214). Adelman, "Modernization Theory and Its Critics" reviews such critiques. They have led some theorists to talk instead about "modernity." Modernization theory's (non)applicability to the United States: Nugent, *Structures of American Social History*, ch. 1; P. Wagner, "The Resistance"; and K. Wilkinson, "Rural Community Change." Inglehart and Wenzel, *Modernization, Cultural Change, and Democracy*, conclude that "industrializing societies in general are not becoming like the United States, as a pop-

ular version of modernization theory assumed" (47) Pervasiveness: e.g., Zunz, "The Synthesis of Social Change." Defenders of modernization ideas include P. Stearns, "Modernization and Social History"; Grew, "More on Modernization"; and Adelman, "Modernization Theory and Its Critics."

Alternatives: Marxists demand the insertion of class conflict, but as I noted earlier, the Marxist theory of history is a version of modernization theory. The cultural or critical studies school lambasts the standard model but actually just flips the story from romance to tragedy, charging, for example, that economic growth enslaves people. Some repudiate telling any grand narrative at all, preferring to recount small stories, "microhistory" (Magnússon, "The Singularization of History"). Yet even the little stories are "plot-ful" and imbedded with theory; telling usually conveys explanation (e.g., Berkhoffer, *Beyond the Great Story*, 37). The small stories' typical moral is about local resistance to the grand sweep of modernization. The "cultural turn": Bonnell and Hunt, *Beyond the Cultural Turn*. Clifford Geertz explicitly eschewed explanation, but even his "interpretations" were embedded with causal explanation (Swidler, "Geertz's Ambiguous Legacy"; Sewell, "Whatever Happened"). For general discussion of these topics, see Appleby et al., *Telling the Truth about History*.

17. Avalanche: Appleby, "Recovering America's Historic Diversity." Greene and Pole, "Reconstructing," have a different metaphor: "a severe case of intellectual indigestion" (7). Larger framework: Hays, "On the Meaning." Peter Stearns, editor of the *Journal of Social History*, wrote, "To some observers, social history is not so much a field or an approach as a collection of separate subjects, tied together only by their novelty" ("The New Social History," 14). See also Henretta, "Social History"; Zunz, "The Synthesis of Social Change"; Bender, "Wholes and Parts"; Kessler-Harris, "Social History"; Berkhoffer, *Beyond the Great Story*; and P. Stearns, "The Old Social History and the New." On the other hand, Anderson and Cayton, "The Problem of Fragmentation," are not worried: "If social historians choose to stress multivalence, specificity, and texture, what point is there in asking whether their findings can be synthesized into larger wholes? . . . Should we tell stories at all, if doing so requires us to reduce . . . [such complexities] to linear chronological form?" (300). As I suggested earlier, this is no answer at all. Tipps, "Modernization Theory," is one critic despondent because there seems to be no alternative to modernization theory.

18. Hays, "On the Meaning"; Bender, "Wholes and Parts"; and P. Stearns, "The Old Social History and the New," review a few takes on the central issues for American social history. See, as examples of alternative foci, Nugent, *Structures of American Social History*; Berthoff, *An Unsettled People*; and R. Brown, *Modernization*.

19. Competency: Vickers, "Competency and Competition"; Bushman, "Markets and Composite Farms." Virtue: "A family farm offered the key to a life of 'virtue'— a word then used to mean wholesome, productive, public-spirited independence" (D. Howe, *What Hath God Wrought*, 44).

20. A key source on voluntarism is D. Fischer, *Albion's Seed*. See also C. Fischer, "Paradoxes of American Individualism" and the extended discussion in chapter 4 of this book.

21. Humpty Dumpty: R. M. Collins, "In Retrospect," 328. Overview of national

character studies: R. Wilkinson, "On American Social Character." Assimilation swamps multiculturalism in America: e.g., Lieberson et al., "The Course of Mother-Tongue Diversity"; E. Morawska, "In Defense of the Assimilation Model"; Alba, "Assimilation's Quite Tide"; Kazal, "Revisiting Assimilation"; Portes and Hao, "Bilingualism and Language Loss"; and Fischer and Hout, *Century of Difference*, 41–56.

22. Homicide: United States Bureau of the Census, *Statistical Abstract*, 2008, table 301; international "Murders," http://www.nationmaster.com/graph/cri_mur_percap-crime-murders-per-capita (accessed Apr. 28, 2008). D. Fischer's *Albion's Seed* strongly asserts lasting regional diversity (linked to British regional diversity). Recent histories of "Atlantic" societies argue for commonalities across borders. Cross-cultural psychology, however, emphasizes national distinctions (Triandis, "Cross-Cultural Studies"; McCrae and Terracciano, "National Character"; Inglehart and Welzell, *Modernization, Cultural Change, and Democracy*).

23. Outsiders repeatedly described America as exceptional: Tocqueville, *Democracy in America*; Woodward, *The Old World's New World*; Lawson-Peebles, "America as Interpreted." Critics of exceptionalism include Fredrickson, "From Exceptionalism to Variability" ("ill repute," 588); Rodgers, "Exceptionalism"; Tyrell, "American Exceptionalism"; Appleby, "Values and Society"; and most scornfully, Zuckerman, "The Dodo." Overviews: Kammen, "The Problem of American Exceptionalism"; Woodward, "The Comparability of American History"; D. Bell, "'American Exceptionalism' Revisited"; D. Ross, "The New and Newer Histories"; R. Wilkinson, *The Pursuit of American Character*; the collections edited by Shafer, *Is America Different?*; and Curry and Goodheart, *American Chameleon*.

Sociologists have argued that some feature of the United States — individualism, affluence, early democratization, ethnic diversity, etc. — rendered American workers apolitical and conservative (e.g., Lipset, *American Exceptionalism*; Lipset and Marks, *It Didn't Happen Here*). Critics reply that American workers were not so passive, pointing, for example, to labor violence in the late nineteenth century. Instead, employer coercion and state repression explain the weakness of organized labor in America (e.g., Voss, *The Making of American Exceptionalism*). Gerber, "Shifting Perspectives," is a recent overview. Criticisms claiming that exceptionalists postulate that the United States is immune to general social laws (e.g., to Marxist theory) or that they assert American superiority are incorrect readings. On inequality: T. Smith, "Social Inequality"; Shapiro and Young, "Public Opinion." Religiosity: Greeley, "American Exceptionalism." Patriotism: Rose, "National Pride." Voluntarism: C. Fischer, "Just How Is It."

24. Quantum: Rosenthal, *The Era of Choice*.

25. I am clearly inspired here by the *Annales* school. Marc Bloch's *The Historian's Craft*, remains an excellent guide.

26. Even the valuable *Encyclopedia of American Social History*, by Cayton et al., is inevitably limited (C. Fischer, "In Search of the Plot").

27. This assertion can spark an immediate dissent: Was not the late twentieth century marked precisely by cultural disruptions, by postmodernism, multiculturalism, "hybridity," etc.? Not really. Cultural diversity within the United States can be ex-

plained as minor variations within a larger, shared culture. Asian college students, for example, may insist on their ethnic identities, but they are not clamoring for arranged marriages or foot binding.

28. "Contestants": Fowler, *The Dance with Community*, 121. (For more on community, see C. Fischer, "Finding the 'Lost' Community"; comments on Wiener, "Radical Historians.") Some dismiss a "value-free" social science as impossible, if not undesirable. The difficulty of suspending values does not, however, justify abandoning the effort, any more than occasional contamination in medical experiments leads doctors to throw away their gloves. Earlier work: C. Fischer et al., *Inequality by Design*, document growing income inequality and persisting racial chasms in America.

Chapter Two

1. As late as 1900, 62 percent of families had a child under sixteen die; by 1976, it was down to 4 percent (Uhlenberg, "Death and the Family"). Ann Rutledge: Gannett, "'Overwhelming Evidence.'"

2. Annan: "'Humanity is Indivisible,'" *NYT*, Dec. 11, 2001. The 9/11 attacks had surprisingly transient psychological effects. Various polls in the fall of 2001 reported an increase in feelings of worry. In October 2001, 27 percent of survey respondents said that they changing their personal lives to reduce the chances of being a terrorist victim (Saad, "Americans' Mood"). Yet soon after, Americans largely returned to pre-9/11 private habits and concerns. For example, employment in Manhattan dipped in 2002, but resumed its steady upward climb by the next year ("County Business Patterns [1998–2005]: Number of Employees," http://censtats.census.gov/cgi-bin/cb-pnaic/cbpsect.pl). See below on post-1970s economic insecurity. Johnson-Hanks's studies in Africa (e.g., "When the Future Decides") show how great uncertainty leads people to forego planning and engage instead in "judicious opportunism," day-by-day grasping of whatever may come up. Finally, some readers may think of the literature on the "risk society"; I address that in note 93 of this chapter.

3. In 1900, a black baby boy had a life expectancy sixteen years shorter than that of a white boy; in 2000, the deficit was down to six years. 1850: Preston and Haines, *Fatal Years*, table 2.2. Twentieth-century statistics: United States Bureau of the Census, *Historical Statistics*, 56. Recent statistics: idem, *Statistical Abstract*, 2000, tables 116–20. Childbearing: R. Wells, *Revolutions in Americans' Lives*, 222. Men at twenty: Modell, "Changing Risks." See also Vinovskis, "Death"; Klein, *A Population History of the United States*. Average woman: Watkins et al., "Demographic Foundations." Diaries and letters: Dye and Smith, "Mother Love," 329–30. After World War I: H. Green, *The Light of the Home*, 166. Robustness: Height is a good proxy for health, and average height increased over the long term—although not without reversals (see discussion of antebellum era later in this chapter)—Komlos, *The Biological Standard of Living in Europe and America*; Costa and Steckel, "Long-Term Trends"; and Steckel, "Heights and Health." Europeans surpassing Americans: Steckel, "Stature and the Standard of Living"; Komlos and Lauderdale, "Underperformance in Affluence."

4. See Steckel, "Nutritional Status"; Costa, "Height, Wealth, and Diseases"; Fogel,

"Nutrition and the Decline in Mortality" (meat, 466); S. McMahon, "A Comfortable Subsistence"; R. Wells, *Revolutions in Americans' Lives*; Nugent, *Structures of American Social History*; Klein, *A Population History of the United States*; and health citations in previous note. New England and the South: Vinovskis, "Death." Puritan descendants: Fogel, *The Fourth Great Awakening & The Future of Egalitarianism*, 19. Views of Americans: Lawson-Peebles, "America as Interpreted"; J. Evans, *America*; Woodward, *The Old World's New World*.

5. Indians: S. Cook, "The Significance of Disease" (quotation, 497); Snow and Lanphear, "European Contact" (children, 26–27); S. Cook, "Interracial Warfare." Slaves: Berlin, *Many Thousands Gone* (death rate, 122); Butler, *Becoming America* (5 years, ch. 1). Indentured servants: R. Lane, *Murder in America*, 42.

6. Evacuation: e.g., S. Wolf, *Urban Village*. Teeth: Darnton, "The Pursuit of Happiness." Pain: Crane, "'I Have Suffer'd'" (Franklin, 375). Hog fat: Ekrich, *At Day's Close*, 289. Alcohol for pain a century later: Larkin, *Reshaping Everyday Life*, 91–92. Psychological consequences: modern people in chronic pain suffer high levels of psychological problems, commonly including depression. Psychological difficulties can increase feelings of pain, but the causal direction largely runs from pain to depression, especially for the pain common in earlier eras, such as untreated injuries. See, for example, Gatchel, "Comorbidity of Chronic Pain."

7. Diary: Dye and Smith, "Mother Love," 334–35. See also R. Wells, *Facing the "King of Terrors."* Hiltzheimer, *Extracts from the Diary of Jacob Hiltzheimer of Philadelphia*. "Emotion work": "trying to change in degree or quality an emotion or feeling. . . . 'to manage' an emotion or to do 'deep acting'" (Hochschild, "Emotion Work," 561).

8. Smith and Hacker, "Cultural Demography," argue that New Englanders overestimated mortality risks (Mather, 379). Epitaphs: Vovelle, "A Century and One-Half," esp. 540. See also R. Wells, *Facing the "King of Terrors."* See chapter 6 of this volume on sentimentality around mourning.

9. Costa and Steckel, "Long-Term Trends." See also Fogel, *The Fourth Great Awakening & The Future of Egalitarianism*, 58–59; idem, "Nutrition and the Decline in Mortality"; Steckel, "Heights and Health"; idem, "Stature and the Standard of Living"; idem, "Heights and Human Welfare"; Steckel and Floud, conclusions to *Health and Welfare During Industruialization*; Komlos, *The Biological Standard of Living in Europe and America*; idem, "The Height and Weight"; idem, "Shrinking."; Haines et al., "The Short and the Dead"; Maloney and Carson, "Living Standards"; and Chanda et al., "Convergence." The finding of antebellum regression has been challenged (e.g., Soltow, "Inequalities," 149), but seems to be the generally accepted as real.

10. Steckel and colleagues stress disease (Costa and Seckel, "Long-Term Trends"; Steckel, "Heights and Health"). Komlos argues for diet theory (Komlos, *The Biological Standard of Living in Europe and America*; idem, "The Height and Weight"; idem, "Shrinking"; and Sunder, "The Height of Tennessee Convicts"). Chanda et al., "Convergence," indict coal production. Haines et al., "The Short and the Dead," indict mainly disease transmission. Shammas, *The Pre-Industrial Consumer*, 146ff, points to the shift away from milk and cheese.

11. Schenectady: Wells, *Facing the "King of Terrors,"* 41–44. New York: Burrows and

Wallace, *Gotham*, 589–91. Quotation from *New York Evening Post*: John Noble Wilford, "How Epidemics Helped Shape the Modern Metropolis," *NYT*, Apr. 15, 2008. Frontier: Faragher, *Sugar Creek*, 88–89.

12. Class and height: Komlos, *The Biological Standard of Living in Europe and America*, 103; Fogel, "Nutrition and the Decline in Mortality." Class and child mortality: Davin, "The Era"; Costa and Steckel, "Long-Term Trends." Lincoln: 1868 memoir by Elizabeth Keckley, *Behind the Scenes*, http://digilib.nypl.org/dynaweb/digs/wwm9713/@Generic__BookTextView/877 (accessed Jan. 1, 2002).

13. Death sentiment: e.g., Wells, *Facing the "King of Terrors"*; Douglas, "Heaven Our Home"; S. Scott, "'Earth Has No Sorrow'"; Dye and Smith, "Mother Love" (Child Mary, 337); and Hoffert, "'A Very Peculiar Sorrow.'" Ayer: Blauvelt, "The Work," 583. Chapter 6 in this volume discusses the rise of sentimentality in general and the garden cemetery movement in particular.

14. Malaria: Faragher, *Sugar Creek,* 90–91. Lincoln: Donald, *Lincoln*, 26. Industrial hazards: e.g., Wallace, *Rockdale*, 148–50; Knights, *Yankee Destinies*, ch. 4; Kleinberg, *The Shadow of the Mills*, 27. City accidents: R. Lane, *Violent Death in the City*. Streetcar conductor: Anonymous, "Experience," 17. Farming: Even in 2005, the death rate in "agriculture, forestry, fishing, and hunting" was above average and the fatality rate far higher than in any other industry (National Center for Health Statistics, *Health, United States, 2007*, tables 49 and 50).

15. Public health: e.g., Meeker, "The Improving Health"; Tarr, "Water and Wastes"; Ferrie and Troesken, "Water"; Cutler and Miller, "The Role of Public Health Improvements"; Dowling, *Fighting Infection*, ch. 2; Preston and Haines, *Fatal Years*, ch. 1; R. Wells, "The Mortality Transition"; and Klein, *A Population History of the United States*, ch. 3, as well as general urban histories, such as Chudacoff and Smith, *The Evolution of American Urban Society*. Working-class water: Kleinberg, *The Shadow of the Mills*, 90–99. New York and Boston: Teaford, *The Unheralded Triumph*, 247–50.

16. Hoy, *Chasing Dirt* (Beecher, 22); R. Wells, *Revolutions in Americans' Lives*, 129ff; Cowan et al., "Clean Homes"; Cowan, *More Work for Mother*; Wilkie, "Submerged Sensuality."

17. New York: Burrows and Wallace, *Gotham*, 1197. Schenectady: Wells, *Facing the "King of Terrors,"* 186–88. Reduced death rates: see previous note. Inequality and health: D. Smith, "Differential Mortality"; Costa and Steckel, "Long-Term Trends."

18. Most notably, infant mortality dropped from over 10 percent to under 1 percent. See United States Bureau of the Census, *Historical Statistics*, 56–57; and idem, *Statistical Abstract*, 2007, tables 98 and 106; Klein, *A Population History of the United States*, ch. 4–6. Diseases: Dowling, *Fighting Infection*, esp. ch. 13; C. Rosenberg, "What It Was Like"; and R. Wells, *Revolutions in Americans' Lives*. Tuberculosis: United States Bureau of the Census, *Historical Statistics*, 58; idem, *Statistical Abstract*, 2000, table 126. AIDS: idem, *Statistical Abstract*, 2000, table 215. AIDS vs. TB: Cohen and Elder, "Major Cities." Accidents: Holinger, *Violent Deaths in the United States*; Zopf, *Mortality Patterns and Trends in the United States*, 191; Lebergott, *The Americans*, 519; and Tarr and Tebeau, "Managing Danger." Maturity: Between 1850 and 1990, the onset of menstruation and the age of boys' puberty dropped by about three years (Mintz, "Life

Stages," 2012). Disabilities among the elderly: Costa, "Understanding the Twentieth-Century Decline."

19. R. Wells, "The Mortality Transition"; Tarr and Konvitz, "Patterns "; Tarr, "Infrastructure"; H. Green, *The Uncertainty of Everyday Life*, 177–81; Isaacs and Schroeder, "Where the Public Good Prevailed." Cutler and Miller, "The Role of Public Health Improvements," estimate that clean water systems alone cut overall big-city mortality by half. Schenectady: R. Wells, *Facing the "King of Terrors,"* 181. Personal hygiene: Hoy, *Chasing Dirt*; Cowan et al., "Clean Homes"; Cowan, *More Work for Mother*; H. Green, *The Uncertainty of Everyday Life*, 181–86; and P. Stearns, *Battleground of Desire*, ch. 8.

20. Levenstein, *Revolution at the Table*; P. Williams, "Foodways"; Lebergott, *The American Economy*; Fogel, *The Escape from Hunger and Premature Death*, who credits nutritional changes for most of the health improvements. Food spending: Cox and Alm, "Time Well Spent"; Jacobs and Shipp, "How Family Spending"; C. Brown, *American Standards of Living*; and Fischer and Hout, *Century of Difference*, ch. 6. Craig et al., "The Effect of Mechanical Refrigeration," estimate that refrigeration alone contributed upwards of 5 percent to the growth in American heights. Depression: Levenstein, *Revolution at the Table*, ch. 17; Wu, "How Severe"; World War II: C. Brown, *American Standards of Living*, 195. However, Komlos and Lauderdale, "Underperformance in Affluence," find that white men born in the Depression and the War grew a bit shorter than earlier and later cohorts.

21. Increasing importance of medical technology: Cutler and Meara, "Changes in the Age Distribution." Funerals vs. medicine: Lebergott, *Pursuing Happiness*, 123.

22. Fogel, *The Fourth Great Awakening & The Future of Egalitarianism*, 143. Extension of health and longevity: Costa, "Unequal at Birth"; Daniel Scott Smith, "Differential Mortality"; Davin, "The Era"; Costa and Steckel, "Long-Term Trends"; Komlos, *The Biological Standard of Living in Europe and America*, 103ff; Fogel, *The Escape from Hunger and Premature Death*, ch. 2; Fischer and Hout, *Century of Difference*, ch. 4; Soltow, "Wealth"; Keppel et al., "Trends in Racial and Ethnic-Specific Rates." Some research suggests that after about 1980, the well-off improved their health more rapidly than the poorly off (Krieger et al., "The Fall and Rise"; Ezzati et al., "The Reversal"; and Warren and Hernandez, "Did Socioeconomic Inequalities").

23. Height: Komlos and Lauderdale, "Underperformance in Affluence." Longevity: Kinsella, "Changes in Life Expectancy," table 1. As late as 1960, Americans' life expectancy at birth was about a year longer than the average for Organisation for Economic Co-Operation and Development nations; in 2003, it was a half-year below that average, and about one to three or more years shorter than those of comparable large nations like France and Sweden (*OECD Fact Book 2007*, http://lysander.sourceoecd.org/vl=4845173/cl=26/nw=1/rpsv/factbook/11-01-01.htm). The dire situation of American blacks cannot explain the difference, since native-born American whites fell behind Europeans of all racial origins.

24. North Dakota: Dickson, "Prosperity Rides." Death rates: United States Bureau of the Census, *Historical Statistics*, 58, and table 16. Obesity: Between ca. 1978 and ca. 1991, the percentage of Americans who were obese, as *measured* on a scale,

increased from 14 to 22 percent (Flegal et al., "Overweight") and between 1991 and 1998, the percentage whose *self-reported* weights and heights classed them as obese increased from 12 to 18 percent (Mokdad et al., "The Spread"). Strauss and Pollack, "Epidemic Increase," show major increases after 1986, especially for blacks and Hispanics. Cutler et al., "Why Have Americans," point to the drop in the real cost of calories (see also Bill Marsh, "The Overflowing American Dinner Plate," *NYT*, Aug. 3, 2008). Polls: Panagopoulus, "The Polls—Obesity." Disability: Lakdawalla et al., "Are the Young?" Some scholars strongly dissent to the "obesity epidemic" (e.g., Campos et al., "The Epidemiology"), but there seems to be scientific consensus on its reality (e.g., commentary that accompanies this article in the *International Journal of Epidemiology*).

25. The 65-plus: Carter et al., *Historical Statistics of the United States*, table Aa185; United States Bureau of the Census, *Statistical Abstract*, 2008, tables 7 and 10. See Fischer and Hout, *Century of Difference*, ch. 4; Katz and Stern, *One Nation Divisible*, ch. 3; Hareven, "Historical Changes in the Life Course"; and Watkins et al., "Demographic Foundations." Financial support: Schoeni and Ross, "Material Assistance."

26. Dye and Smith, "Mother Love." See also J. Burnham, "Why Did Infants"; T. Kelly and Kelly, "Our Lady"; and R. Wells, *Facing the "King of Terrors."* Milk: "It is Mothers' Problem," *NYT*, Nov. 11, 1910. Birth rate: see chapter 4, p. 117; R. Wells, *Revolution in Americans' Lives*; Smith and Hacker, "Cultural Demography." Other factors must have also been important, however, because the birth rate dropped before and faster than the death rate.

27. The secularization argument: e.g., Norris and Inglehart, *Sacred and Secular*; and Inglehart, "Globalization and Postmodern Values." See discussion regarding the "soft" Jesus and similar changes in chapter 6.

28. Costa and Kahn, "The Rising Price," estimate from wage data that Americans' monetary valuation of a life grew about thirtyfold over the twentieth century. See also Zelizer, *Pricing the Priceless Child* and *Morals and Markets*.

29. Normality: Newman, "Dead Bodies," 55.

30. Lawyering: Donald, *Lincoln*, 150. Lincoln, "Address Before the Young Men's Lyceum," http://quod.lib.umich.edu/l/lincoln/ (accessed May 11, 2008). The editors added the note about the Alton lynching. Fear: In 2007, nearly 40 percent of respondents said that there was some area near their homes that they were afraid to walk to at night (Gallup, "Crime Issues"). Greatest decline: Hunter and Bowman, "The State of Disunion," vol. 2, table 5.

31. Gurr, "Historical Trends"; Eisner, "Long-Term"; Österberg, "Criminality"; Feldberg "Urbanization"; A. Gillis, "Crime and State Surveillance"; Parrella, "Industrialization and Murder"; R. Lane, "On the Social Meaning of Homicide"; idem, *Murder in America*; Monkkonen, *Murder in New York City*; idem, "Homicide"; Eckberg, "Estimates"; Zahn, "Homicide"; and Spierenburg, "Violence and Culture." On the fear of night attacks in the early modern period: Ekrich, *At Day's Close*. Anthropologist Elizabeth Colson (*Tradition and Contract*) has pointed out that even in small, traditional, non-Western societies, conflict and violence were endemic. Modern cross-national comparisons: Gartner, "Victims"; Shelly, "The Development"; Gallup poll, "A World-

wide Look at Crime," *San Francisco Chronicle*, Nov. 15, 1984, 6. Rates: Bureau of Justice Statistics, "Homicide Trends," http://www.ojp.usdoj.gov/bjs/homicide/ (accessed May 13, 2008); Barclay and Tavares, "International Comparisons." Although some explain the differences in terms of race, even among whites alone the American rates are exceedingly high. American violence is concentrated in particular groups (see Grandin and Lupri, "Intimate Violence"; Ouimet, "Crime in Canada") and some indict a "culture of honor" explanation for that pattern, particularly in the South (e.g., Cohen and Nisbett, "Field Experiments"; Dixon and Lizotte, "Gun Ownership," and subsequent comments in the *American Journal of Sociology*, Jul. 1989; Ellison, "An Eye for an Eye?"), which also may explain American-European differences.

32. Drake: Appleby, *Recollections of the Early Republic*, 44–45. Wars: Butler, *Becoming America*, 118–19. General violence: see, in addition to citations in the previous note, R. Lane, *Murder in America*, ch. 2; Friedman, *Crime and Punishment*, ch. 1, 2; S. Wolf, *As Various as Their Land*, 252–54; S. Block, "Bringing Rapes to Court"; and Roth, "Child Murder."

33. Frontier: Wade, *The Urban Frontier* (St. Louis, 289); Gorn, "'Gouge and Bite'"; idem, "'Good-Bye Boys'"; see also Way, "Evil Humors." Gangs: Wade, *Urban Frontier*; Laurie, *Working People of Philadelphia*. Liquor: Lender and Martin, *Drinking in America*; Kaplan, "New York City Taverns." Like dogs: Faragher, *Sugar Creek*, 153. Women's risks: Moore, "'Justifiable Homicide'"; Pease and Pease, *Ladies, Women, & Wenches*, ch. 7; and M. Smith, *Breaking the Bonds*. Infanticide: Roth, "Child Murder." Infanticide increased perhaps because transportation and urban growth made it easier to hide the victims or perhaps because children were becoming less economically valuable. "Daily fabric": Larkin, *Everyday Shaping*, 287.

34. Unpunished violence: Steinberg, "The Spirit of Litigation"; Monkkonen, "The American State"; and R. Lane, *Murder in America*, ch. 4. Chesterfield case: Moore, "Justifiable Provocation."

35. Gangs: e.g., Laurie, *Working People*; Gilfoyle, "Strumpets and Misogynists"; Schneider, *Detroit and the Problem of Order*; Way, "Evil Humors"; and Ryan, *Civic Wars*. Indians: "The Indians—A War of Extermination," *New York Daily Times*, Dec. 26, 1855. On the South, slavery, and violence, see esp., R. Lane, *Murder in America* (Jefferson, 88). Southern rates of homicide continually lead those of the nation (see note 31 above).

36. Freidman, *Crime and Punishment*, 69ff; Monkkonen, *America Becomes Urban*, 229ff. Urban-rural: e.g., Monkkonen, *Murder*, ch. 1; Eckberg, "Stalking"; C. Fischer, *The Urban Experience*, ch. 8.

37. Visnovskis, "Death"; J. D. Hacker, "The Human Cost." Conscription: Stewart, "Civil War," 132. Kemp, "Community and War," discusses the effects on local communities.

38. Louisiana: Vandal, *Rethinking Southern Violence*, 84. Tucson: Hand, *Whiskey, Six-Guns*, 153, 224, 189ff. Dunn-Elliott: "The Week," *The Nation*, May 17, 1883, 415, and "The Week," *The Nation*, May 24, 1883, 436. J. Adler, "It Is His First," discusses the persistence of jury indifference to homicide into early twentieth-century Chicago. The era's violence: R. Lane, *Violent Death in the City* and *Murder in America*, ch. 5;

Gurr, "Historical Trends"; Monkkonen, *Murder in New York City*; and several contributions to Graham and Gurr,*Violence in America*. Post-bellum saloon violence: e.g., E. Parsons, "Risky Business"; J. Adler, "'My Mother-in-Law.'"

39. See studies by R. Lane, Gurr, and Monkkonen, cited in previous note, who emphasize the "civilizing" effects. See also Rugh, "Civilizing the Countryside"; Marsh, "Suburban Men."

40. Even homicide statistics are problematic for the first few decades. For example, in the early years, deaths by motor vehicle were listed as murders and many states did not report their figures. Eckberg, "Estimates," provides corrections (see also Eckberg, "Stalking"; Zahn, "Homicide"). Rates rose a bit from 1900 to 1920 for various reasons, including better recording of infanticides and the great waves immigration (see J. Adler, "'Halting the Slaughter'"). Homicide rates rose again during Prohibition but dropped rapidly afterwards to a nadir just before 1960 (Fox and Zawitz, "Homicide Trends" and updates from the *Vital Statistics* Web site, http://www.cdc.gov/nchs/products/vsus.htm). Nonfatal violence: The increasing use of firearms probably meant that assaults that would not have become murders in earlier years became fatalities in later ones.

41. R. Lane, *Murder in America*; Monkkonen, *Murder in New York*; Gurr, "Historical Trends"; P. Stearns, *Battleground of Desire*, ch. 6; Kasson, *Rudeness and Civility*. Male living patterns: Fischer and Hout, *Century of Difference*, ch. 4. The shrinking of a male-only culture also shows up in the falling number of saloons, pool halls, and flophouses (Duis, "The Saloon"; Rosenzweig, *Eight Hours for What We Will*, ch. 7, 8; and Schneider, "Skid Row").

42. Fear: Saad, "Fear"; Hood, "Changing Perceptions." Police reports, as collected annually by the *FBI Uniform Reports*, http:// www.fbi.gov/ucr/ucr.htm, show escalating violent and property crime rates through the 1970s. Annual victimization surveys, however, show *declining* reported rates for both violent and, especially property crime from the mid-1970s on (Bureau of Justice Statistics, "National Crime Victimization Survey," http://www.ojp.usdoj.gov/bjs/cvict.htm; accessed Nov. 25, 2008).

43. A sample of the vast literature includes Cohen and Land, "Age Structure"; O'Brien et al., "The Enduring Effects"; Gartner and Parker, "Cross-National Evidence"; Steffensmeier et al., "Relative Cohort Size"; Miethe et al., "Social Change"; and Baumer, "Poverty." Television: e.g., Centerwall, "Television" vs. Jensen, "The Invention of Television."

44. Blumstein and Wallman, *The Crime Drop in America*; Rosenfeld, "The Crime Drop"; Jencks, "Is Violent Crime Increasing?"; and Fox and Zawitz, "Homicide Trends." Zimring, *The Great American Crime Decline*, finds many of the explanations weak and stresses the Canadian comparison. He and Rosenfeld suggest hard-to-calculate cultural shifts. Victimization surveys: Bureau of Justice Statistics, "National Crime Victimization Survey," http://www.ojp.usdoj.gov/bjs/cvict.htm. (Surgeon General David Satcher's "Youth Violence: A Report " of 2000 shows continuing high levels of self-reported violence among youngsters.) Black life expectancy: Beltrán-Sánchez et al., "An Integrated Approach," 8.

45. "The Decline of New York," *Time*, Sept. 17, 1990, 36. Gallup: "Poll Topics and

Trends: Crime," http://www.gallup.com/poll/topics/crime.asp (accessed Jul. 4, 2007), except for a 1965 poll on whether crime in the community was increasing, retrieved from Lexis-Nexis, and the data on children's safety, from "Children and Violence," http://www.gallup.com/poll/topics/child_violence.asp (accessed Aug. 13, 2002). Unfortunately, survey data are not available that would allow us to gauge public fears before the run-up in crime in the 1960s.

46. Risk and sexual assaults: Kilpatrick et al., "Criminal Victimization"; Resnick et al., "Prevalence of Civilian Trauma." On differential rates, see Bureau of Justice Statistics, "Victim Characteristics," http://www.ojp.usdoj.gov/bjs/cvict_v.htm (accessed Aug. 11, 2002). Explanations: See notes 38 and 39, and also Zimring, *The Great American Crime Decline*. Several scholars, such as Roger Lane, invoke Norbert Elias's theory (*The Civilizing Process*) that the transition from feudal to modern Europe entailed increasing self-control of bodily functions and of anger and growing revulsion to violence.

47. The research is complicated, but generally the more their exposure to news coverage of crime, especially on local television, the more some Americans see danger and fear it (Heath and Gilbert, "Mass Media"; Chiricos et al., "Fear, TV News"; Weitzer and Kubrin, "Breaking News"; and Liska and Baccaglini, "Feeling Safe"). Whether Americans' exposure to crime reports increased historically is harder to establish; recall the "yellow journalism" and scandal broadsides of earlier centuries. But it is plausible that television multiplied the presentation of crime. Ethnic diversity generates fear: Covington and Taylor, "Fear of Crime"; Quillian and Pager, "Black Neighbors"; and Sampson and Raudenbush, "Seeing Disorder." Whether Americans encountered increasing diversity in their neighborhoods over the decades is hard to establish, in part because of what "diversity" meant. But it is likely that neighborhood ethnic diversity generally increased, especially after 1870 and then after 1950 (e.g., Fischer and Hout, *Century of Difference*, ch. 7).

48. Herndon, *Unwelcome Americans*, 162–64. Herndon, "'Who Died,'" gives more details of colonial Rhode Island's poor relief programs.

49. Bruchey, *Enterprise*; Lebergott, *The Americans*; Henretta, "Wealth and Social Structure"; Temin, "Free Land"; D. Smith, "Female Householding"; Larkin, "Rural Life"; and Main and Main, "The Red Queen." Hessians: D. Fischer, *Washington's Crossing*, 63. General descriptions: Hawke, *Everyday Life*; S. Wolf, *As Various as Their Land*. Soil depletion: Gross, *Minutemen*, 87. Southern homes: Charles Ball, in Appleby, *Recollections of the Early Republic*, 114.

50. Virginia: Rutman and Rutman, *A Place in Time*. Five years: Butler, *Becoming America*, ch.1. Food and rice: S. Wolf, *As Various as Their Land*, 166, 168. Indentured: Bailyn, *Voyagers to the West*, 166–89; Fogleman, "From Slaves"; and Grubb, "Babes in Bondage?" Slaves vs. servants: Danbom, *Born in the Country*, 48–49. Overviews: Berlin, *Many Thousands Gone*; Earle, "Rural Life."

51. Wars: Butler, *Becoming America*, 118–19. New England depletion and mobility: Greven, *Four Generations*; Gross, *Minutemen*; Lockridge, *A New England Town*; Henretta, "Families and Farms," 9; and Main and Main, "The Red Queen?" See also

Lemon, *The Best Poor Man's Country*; Rutman and Rutman, *A Place in Time*; and Danbom, *Born in the Country*, ch. 2 and 3. Lincoln: Donald, *Lincoln*, 21.

52. Historians disagree on the timing of widening inequality, some locating it during the antebellum "market revolution" (e.g., Henretta, "Wealth and Social Structure"). The evidence for pre-Revolutionary widening seems stronger: Butler, *Becoming America*, ch. 2; Danbom, *Born in the Country*, ch. 3; Rutman, "Assessing"; Shammas, "A New Look"; Greven, *Four Generations*; Innes, *Labor in A New Land*; S. Wolf, *Urban Village*; S. Warner, *Private City*; Nash, "Poverty and Politics"; idem, *The Urban Crucible*; Oestreicher, "The Counted and the Uncounted"; Main and Main, "The Red Queen?" and Sarson, "Yeoman Farmers."

53. See previous note and Herndon, *Unwelcome Americans* (blind man, 8); Murray, "Bound by Charity" (the orphanage); Jones, "The Strolling Poor"; B. G. Smith, "The Material Lives"; Trattner, *From Poor Law to Welfare Law*: ch. 2; S. Wolf, *As Various as Their Land*, 166ff; Haber and Gratton, *Old Age and the Search for Security* (Charleston 1770, 214n8); Gross, *Minutemen*, 90–91; J. Alexander, "Poverty" (Philadelphia, 16); and Burrows and Wallace, *Gotham*, 146–47, 192–93. On changes, see also Nash, "The Social Evolution"; Rutman, *Winthrop's Boston*. Ideology: Olivas, "'God Helps Those.'" Conflict: a classic story is Boyer and Nissenbaum's *Salem Possessed*; see also Nash, *Urban Crucible*.

54. Growth: e.g., Gallman and Wallace, introduction to *American Economic Growth*; Costa and Steckel, "Long-Term Trends"; Bruchey, *Enterprise*; Taylor, *The Transportation Revolution*; and D. Howe, *What Hath God Wrought*. Lincoln: http://gi.grolier.com/presidents/ea/bios/16plinc.html (accessed Feb. 25, 2002). Peters and Illinois: Faragher, *Sugar Creek*, 55, 59.

55. See Danbom, *Born in the Country* (cotton statistics, 74–75); J. Larson, "Business Culture"; and particular studies, such as Nobles, "Breaking into the Backcountry"; Faragher, *Sugar Creek*; and Wermuth, "New York Farmers." Transportation: G. Taylor, *The Transportation Revolution*; Sellers, *The Market Revolution*; and D. Howe, *What Hath God Wrought*.

56. D. Howe, *What Hath God Wrought* (panic, 42–47); Sellers, *The Market Revolution*; Rothenberg, *From Market-Places to Market Economy*; Bruchey, *Enterprise* (slave owner percent, 238); Larkin, "Rural Life"; and Earle, "Rural Life." New York: Wermuth, "New York Farmers." Sangamon: Faragher, *Sugar Creek*, 144–45. Plantation owners vs. small landholders: Edwards, "Men of Subsistence." Mobility: see also Winkle, *The Politics of Community*: ch. 5; and Johnson, *Shopkeepers' Millennium*, ch. 2. According to Wallace, *Rockdale*, a "working family had about a 10 percent chance of remaining in the Rockdale district for more than ten years" (64).

57. Dawley, *Class and Community*; Dublin, *Transforming Women's Work* (Fowlers, 85–88); and Wallace, *Rockdale*.

58. Licht, *Industrializing America*; Bruchey, *Enterprise*; Gallman and Wallace, *American Economic Growth*; Gilje, *Wages of Independence*; Wilentz, *Chants Democratic*; and P. Johnson, *Shopkeepers' Millennium*. Bragg: Appleby, *Inheriting the Revolution*, 77–78. Pratt: Dawley, *Class and Community*, 27–28.

59. Blumin, *The Emergence of the Middle Class*; Ryan, *The Cradle of the Middle Class*; P. Johnson, *Shopkeepers' Millennium*; K. Jackson, *Crabgrass Frontier*; Bushman, *The Refinement of America*; Gilekson, *Middle-Class Providence, 1820–1940*; Sellers, *The Market Revolution*; Carnes, "The Rise"; and C. Kelly, "'Well Bred Country People.'" Lincoln: e.g., Guelzo, *Abraham Lincoln*, 56–63.

60. Rural artisans: Stott, "Artisans" (County Tailor, 104). Workers' mobilization: e.g., Wilentz, *Chants Democratic*; Laurie, *Working People of Philadelphia, 1800–1850*, ch. 4; Oestreicher, "Urban Working-Class Political Behavior"; idem, "Labor"; Foner, *The Story of American Freedom*, ch. 3; Sellers, *The Market Revolution*; and Huston, *Securing the Fruits of Labor*. The militants were relatively few and "de-skilling" (as elaborated by Braverman, *Labor and Monopoly Capital*) was proportionally uncommon. See, e.g., Stott, "Artisans"; Lebergott, *The Americans*, 371–72; Attewell, "The Clerk Deskilled"; Spenner, "Temporal Change"; P. Adler, "Marx"; and Prude, "Capitalism, Industrialization, and the Factory," 93.

61. Laurie, *Working People of Philadelphia*; Sellers, *Market Revolution*; Wilentz, *Chants Democratic*; P. Johnson, *Shopkeepers' Millennium*; Nash, "Social Evolution"; Bushman, "Family Security"; and Oestreicher, "Labor." Urban mobility: Blumin, "Residential Mobility"(Philadelphia); P. Johnson, *Shopkeepers*, ch. 2; Doyle, *The Social Order of a Frontier Community*, 92; Wallace, *Rockdale*, 64; Alcorn, "Leadership and Stability"; and Parkerson, "How Mobile." Inequality: although Soltow, "Inequalities," dissents, most historians describe the nineteenth century as one of widening inequality, especially in the cities. See Steckel and Moehling, "Wealth Inequality"; Lindert, "Three Centuries"; Costa and Steckel, "Long-Term Trends"; Shammas, "A New Look"; Margo, "History of Wage Inequality"; and J. Main, "Note."

62. Lebergott, "Changes in Unemployment"; Trattner, *From Poor Law to Welfare State*; Kiesling and Margo, "Explaining"; and Hannon, "The Generosity"; for examples, see Faragher, *Sugar Creek*, 138–39; Winkle, *The Politics of Community*, ch. 3; and Lyons, *Sex Among the Rabble*, ch. 8 (with respect to single mothers). Watkinson, "'Fit Objects,'" describes a community with more generous attitudes (the Percifull case is presented there). Jerome: Appleby, *Recollections of the Early Republic*, 162.

63. Kolchin, *American Slavery*, ch. 4; Blassingame, *The Slave Community*. Slave memories: Mellon, *Bullwhip Days*, 116, 118, 122, 180 (I have converted Mellon's transcriptions of dialect into standard English).

64. Jerome and Cook in Appleby, *Recollections of the Early Republic* (Cooke, 234). M. Archer, "Small Capitalism," found that half of Detroit entrepreneurs in the late nineteenth century substantial enough to get themselves recorded in official records failed within four years.

65. Foner, *Reconstruction*, 125ff; Goldin, "War"; Fredrickson, "Nineteenth-Century American History"; and Bruchey, *Enterprise*, 254–59.

66. Foner, *Reconstruction* (planter, 104); Kolchin, *American Slavery*, ch.7 (one-fifth, 218). Maddox and Moses: Mellon, *Bullwhip Days*, 126, 181, 182 (dialect standardized). Property estimate calculated from Goldin, "War," 952.

67. Licht, *Industrializing America*; Bruchey, *Enterprise*; and Danbom, *Born in the*

Country. Ratios calculated from United States Bureau of the Census, *Historical Statistics*, 139.

68. Danbom, *Born in the Country*; Barron, *Those Left Behind*. Kansas: E. Bell, "Culture of a Contemporary Rural Community." Two-thirds: Hurt, "Rural Life," 1238. Meyerowitz, "Women and Migration," describes rural women's migration to Chicago.

69. Licht, *Getting Work*. San Francisco: Kleppner, *Continuity and Change*, 97. Pittsburgh: Kleinberg, *The Shadow of the Mills*, 20–21. Massachusetts: Keyssar, *Out of Work*, ch. 2. Asmokeag: Hareven, *Family Time and Industrial Time*. 3.5 million: Sautter, *Three Cheers*, 36. Shoe industry and floaters: Dawley, *Class and Community*, 139–42. Tramps: Monkkonen, *Tramping*, 5; see also Schneider, "Homeless Men"; Altschuler and Saltzgaber, "The Limits"; and DePastino, *Citizen Hobo*. Carter and Savoca, "Labor Mobility," contest the standard description of high job turnover; still, by their estimates, workers in the nineteenth century averaged between eight and thirteen years on a job, compared to the late-twentieth-century norm of eighteen years.

70. Keyssar, *Out of Work*, 166.

71. R. Robinson, "Economic Necessity"; Folbre, "Women's Informal"; Goldin, "Household"; S. Glenn, *Daughters of the Shtetl*; Peel, "On the Margins"; Chudacoff, "Success and Security"; and Modell and Hareven, "Urbanization and the Malleable Household." For a personal story of making it through the recession of 1870, see Shumsky, "Frank Roney." Servants: Katzman, *Seven Days a Week* (mother, 12; statistics, 284). Pittsburgh: Kleinberg, *The Shadow of the Mills*, 81–82. Houses: e.g., Luria, "Wealth."

72. Relatives: e.g., Hareven and Lagenbach, *Amoskeag*; Hareven, *Family Time and Industrial Time*. Ethnic associations: Conzen, *Immigrant Milwaukee;* J. Smith, *Family Connections*; Bodnar et al., *Lives of Their Own*; and Barton, *Peasants and Strangers*. New York: Osterud, *Bonds of Community*, 61ff. Orphans: Adams, *The Transformation of Rural Life*, 103–4. Residential mobility: Hall and Ruggles, "'Restless'"; Monkkonen, *Walking to Work*; and Kleinberg, *The Shadow of the Mills*, 121. Thernstrom's 1973 summary (*The Other Bostonians*, table 9.1) shows only a small increase in residential stability by the twentieth century, but he notes that those who moved changed from blue- to white-collar and thus presumably from forced to voluntary migration, including many to the suburbs (see also C. Fischer, "Ever-More Rooted Americans"). Lebergott, *The Americans*, estimates that 56 percent of husband-wife families were poor in 1900 (508); Keyssar, "Poverty," reports an estimate of 40 to 45 percent of Americans that year. Overviews: M. Katz, *In the Shadow of the Poorhouse*; Trattner, *From Poor Law to Welfare State*; and Levine, *Poverty and Society*. Local studies: Altschuler and Saltzgaber, "The Limits"; Osterud, *Bonds of Community*, 61ff. Private efforts to redeem the poor: Boyer, *Urban Masses and Moral Order*. Although Civil War veterans' and widows' pensions amounted to over 40 percent of the federal budget in 1893, they covered only about 10 percent of all widows (Holmes, "'Such is the Price'"). Poem: Haber and Gratton, *Old Age*, 129. Holtzman: Bruce Weber, "Jerome Holtzman, 82, 'Dean' of Sportswriters, Dies," *NYT*, Jul. 22, 2008. Bell: "Daniel Bell," *Encyclopedia of World Biography*, http://www.encyclopedia.com/doc/1G2-3404700545.html.

73. Even the wages of the unskilled increased, although with a sharp drop in the 1870s (David and Solar, "A Bicentenary Contribution," table B1). Occupations: Carter et al., *Historical Statistics of the United States,* "Occupations," Series Ba1033–4213. See also Lebergott, *The Americans*; Licht, *Industrializing America*, ch. 5. Middle-class sub-urbs: Jackson, *Crabgrass Frontier*; Warner, *Streetcar Suburbs*; and Binford, *The First Sub-urbs*.

74. By one estimate, over half of those coming to America circa 1900 went back home (Gould, "European," 70, 86).

75. Between 1900 and 2000, the proportion of Americans aged sixty and over who were in the labor force grew from about 50 to about 67 percent, despite the fact that older men increasingly retired and young adults increasingly extended their educa-tion. Obviously, more official jobs per capita must have been created (United States Bureau of the Census, *Historical Statistics*, 131–32). Wages: In 1999, the average full-time employee earned about $32,000 a year (median salary, not including fringes; United States Bureau of the Census, *Statistical Abstract*, 2001, tables 620, 621); in 1900, he or she earned $418 (mean salary; idem, *Historical Statistics*, 164). The 1900 earnings were worth about $10,000 in 2008 dollars (calculated from *Historical Statis-tics*, 164, and *Statistical Abstract*, 2000, table 692). Bread: 1900 work time for manu-facturing employees, *Historical Statistics*, 170, 210, and 213; 1999 estimate based on av-erage wages of $32,000, 40 hours per 52 weeks of work, and bread at $1.36 a pound (*Statistical Abstract*, 2001, table 706). Poverty 1900: Lebergott, *The Americans,* 508. Poverty 2000: 4.7 percent of married couple families were at poverty level (among all families, 9 percent were), http://www.census.gov/hhes/poverty/histpov/hstpov4 .html (accessed Mar. 28, 2002). The rising standard for poverty: G. Fisher, "Is There?" An important indicator of increasing security is that Americans spent less of their money on the basics—food—and more on extras—recreation (Costa, "American Living Standards"; Fischer and Hout, *Century of Difference*, ch. 6; see further discus-sion in chapter 3 of this book). Middle-class jobs: Fronczek and Johnson, "Occupa-tions: 2000," and Fischer and Hout, *Century of Difference*, ch. 5. Levittown: See per-sonal testimonies in Stewart Bird (Director), *Building the American Dream: Levittown, NY* (New York: Cinema Guild, 1994); Gans, *The Levittowners*.

76. On the narrowing of economic differences, see Fischer and Hout, *Century of Difference,* ch. 6. Goldin, "Labor Markets," credits changes in market conditions over changes in government policy for improving labor's position. For example, men started retiring earlier a few decades before Social Security, although the old-age pensions accelerated the process (see also Gratton and Rotondo, "Industrializa-tion"; S. Carter and Sutch, "Myth"). Boarding: Lebergott, *The American Economy*, 93–94; Peel, "On the Margins"; and Harris, "The Flexible House."

77. Overviews: Danbom, *Born in the Country*; Adams, *The Transformation of Rural Life*; Baron, *Mixed Harvest*. The "country problem": United States Senate, *Report of the Country Life Commission*; Ward, "The Farm Woman's Problem." Forest: Larkin, "Rural Life." Dust Bowl: Egan, *The Worst Hard Time* (Chicago, 150–51). Dakotans: *Main Street in Crisis*, ch. 1. Iowa: Ossian, "Bandits."

78. Regarding farm families earning only a fraction of their income from the land,

see previous note and Lobao and Meyer, "The Great Agricultural Transition." Although increased productivity is the short story, the full story includes other factors, including the politics of the New Deal—see Fligstein, "The Transformation."

79. Overview: D. Kennedy, *Freedom from Fear*. See also Bruchey, *Enterprise* (Ford, 452); H. Green, *The Uncertainty of Everyday Life*, 73ff. Suicide rates for white males: Pierce, "The Economic Cycle," table 2. Oklahoma City: Egan, *The Worst Hard Time*, 128. Sons and mothers: Bolin, "The Economics." Failing: Chambers, *Seedtime of Reform*, 191ff.

80. Republicans: Lebergott, *The Americans,* 472–73; Bruchey, *Enterprise*. Security theme: D. Kennedy, *Freedom from Fear*, 247.

81. Cycles: Romer, "Changes." Although Romer de-emphasizes pre–World War I economic volatility, she shows that recessions were distinctly less frequent and less severe after 1945 than before 1920. The interwar years were the most volatile. Unemployment: United States Bureau of the Census, *Historical Statistics*, 135, with corrections for 1890–1930 from Romer, "Spurious Volatility," table 9; Bureau of Labor Statistics Web site: "Employment status," ftp://ftp.bls.gov/pub/special.requests/lf/aat1 .txt (accessed Mar. 31, 2002). Goldin, "Labor Markets," concludes that while the frequency of unemployment declined, those unemployed stayed jobless longer. The unemployed, however, had more financial help and, indeed, may have delayed their return to work because of those supports. Job stability: Jacoby and Sharma, "Employment Duration"; Carter, "The Changing Importance"; Carter and Savoca, "Labor Mobility." Work less: Moore and Hedges, "Trends"; Whaples, "Hours"; Owen, *Working Lives*; Costa, "The Wage and Length." I calculated the 30 percent estimate for fewer hours based on a work week of roughly 50–60 hours×52 weeks in 1900 versus one of 40 hours×50 weeks in 1970 (United States Bureau of the Census, *Historical Statistics*, 168–69).

82. United States Bureau of the Census, *Historical Statistics*, 178, 139; United States Department of Labor, Bureau of Labor Statistics, http://stats.bls.gov/news.release/ union2.t01.htm (accessed Apr. 1, 2002). See Keyssar, *Out of Work*, ch. 7; R. Jensen, "The Causes and Cures"; and many standard sources on labor history. See Goldin, "Labor Markets," on whether unionization was a secondary factor.

83. United States Bureau of the Census, *Historical Statistics*, 344, 1056; idem, *Statistical Abstract*, 2000, tables 851, 177. Insurance: Zelizer, *Morals and Markets*; Kaufman, *For the Common Good*; Beito, *From Mutual Aid to the Welfare State*. See also spending on insurance in C. Brown, *American Standards of Living*.

84. Overview of the government's role: Moss, *When All Else Fails*; Sautter, *Three Cheers for the Unemployed*; Keyssar, *Out of Work*; Brock, *Welfare, Democracy, and the New Deal*; and M. Katz, *In the Shadow of the Poorhouse*. Pensions: McClintock, "Civil War Pensions." Hopkins: D. Kennedy, *Freedom from Fear*, 173. Administrating issues: Richards, *Closing the Door to Destitution*; Quadagno, *The Color of Welfare*; Lieberman, "Race, Institutions"; and Kirby, *Rural World Lost*, ch. 2 (Talmadge quote, 59). Onethird: Danbom, *Born in the Country*, 212. Rural suspicion: Moe and Taylor, "Culture"; Wynne, "Culture." Adams, *The Transformation of Rural Life*, reports that even in the 1960s, residents of southern Illinois farmlands still drew over a third of their income

from government, only 5 percent from the land itself (213), and also quotes a local author criticizing the poor for demanding help "as a civil right" (148).

85. Social Security's consequences: Haber and Gratton, *Old Age and the Search for Security*; Aichenbaum, *Old Age in the New Land*; and Duncan and Smith, "The Rising Affluence." On the details of elderly needs, see also Gratton, "The Poverty"; Carter and Sutch, "Myth." On living alone, McGarry and Schoeni, "Social Security" (ratios from table 1), update earlier studies, such as Kramarow, "The Elderly"; Costa, "A House of Her Own"; and Hareven and Uhlenberg, "Transition to Widowhood," which also demonstrate the role of Social Security. (See also Jason Fields and Casper, "America's Families," table 6.) Retirement: Owen, *Working Lives*, ch. 4; United States Bureau of the Census, *Historical Statistics*, 132; idem, *Statistical Abstract, 2000*, table 644. Men and pensions: Costa, "Displacing the Family."

86. Changes through the mid-1990s are discussed in Fischer et al., *Inequality by Design*. Wages surged in the latter half of the 1990s, but the stagnation resumed after 2000 (David Cay Johnston, "Average Incomes Fell for Most in 2000–5," *NYT*, Aug. 21, 2007) and then came the recession of 2007–9. See Levy, *The New Dollars and Dreams*; Danziger and Gottschalk, *America Unequal*; Jacob Hacker, *The Great Risk Shift*; Piketty and Saez, "The Evolution"; Browne, "The Baby Boom"; and Sawhill and Morton, "Is the American Dream?" Workers reported more hours on the job and a greater fear of losing their jobs in 1997 than in 1977 (Families and Work Institute, *The 1997 National Study of the Changing Workforce*; Hout and Hanley, "Working Hours"). The best estimate is that between the mid-1970s and the mid-1990s, involuntary job turnover increased and worries about job security increased, especially for those below the top rungs (Fligstein and Shin, "The Shareholder"). The numbers would look worse were over two million Americans not in prison in 2005 (Solomon Moore, "Justice Dept. Numbers Show Prison Trends," *NYT*, Dec. 6, 2007; Western and Beckett, "How Unregulated?"). Some data suggest that year-to-year variability in household incomes increased after the 1970s, although these results are murky (A. Stevens, "Changes"; Gottshalk and Moffitt, "Changes"; Valetta, "Recent Research"; Jacob Hacker, *Great Risk Shift*; and Yellin, "Economic Inequality"; cf. Congressional Budget Office, "Trends" vs. Dynan et al., "The Evolution" and Jacob Hacker, "Trends"). The percentage of Americans under sixty-five without health insurance rose from 14.5 percent to 16.4 percent between 1984 and 2007, and even more sharply for those near the poverty level (National Center for Health Statistics, *Health, United States, 2006*, table 133; for 2006: idem, "Health Insurance Coverage," http://www.cdc.gov/nchs/fastats/hinsure.htm. Unemployment insurance: Greenstein and Stone., "Addressing"; Moira Herbst, "Layoffs Flood a Weakened Unemployment System," *Business-Week*, Dec. 7, 2008; McMurrer and Chasanov, "Trends." Debt: see Sullivan et al., *The Fragile Middle Class*, and discussion in the next chapter. Private pension plans shifted away from defined benefit plans to defined contribution plans with more employee pay-in. In 1975, active participants in defined benefit plans outnumbered those in defined contribution plans by over two to one; by 1997, the ratio had reversed (Edward Wyatt, "Pension Change Puts the Burden on the Worker," *NYT*, Apr. 5, 2002; Jacob Hacker, *Great Risk Shift*, ch. 5.)

87. Family incomes did rise after 1970, but only because couples worked more hours. Some experts argued that technological advances increased living standards, but they were mesmerized by electronics. The key, big-ticket elements of the American middle-class lifestyle—housing, health care, and college–did not keep pace with costs (Fischer et al., *Inequality by Design*, 115, 257n28; Weller, "The Middle Class"; and Tamar Lewin, "College May Become Unaffordable," *NYT*, Dec. 4, 2008). Survey data show growing anxiety, at least among the nonaffluent. In 1988, 26 percent of American respondents described America as the "haves" and "have-nots," but in 2007, 48 percent did; in 1988, 17 percent labeled themselves "have-nots," but in 2007, 34 percent did (Allen and Dimock, "A Nation"). Middle-class identification: the rise and then stall, even decline, is especially evident after controlling for education—analysis by the present author of the American National Election Survey and the GSS and analysis by Michael Hout of the GSS; see also Hout, "How Class Works," table 1A.2. Job insecurity: Fullerton and Wallace, "Traversing"; Kalleberg, "Precarious Work." In 1964, "yes" answers to, "Are you better off now than you were 5 years ago?" outnumbered "no" answers 49 to 16; in 1996, it was 57 to 16, but in 2008, it was 41 to 31 (P. Taylor et al., "Inside," 7; Hout, "Money and Morale"; Families and Work Institute, *The 1997 National Study of the Changing Workforce*; Jacob Hacker, *The Great Risk Shift*, passim). Falling behind Europeans: see earlier notes 3 and 23 about heights and longevity; on hours, Huberman and Minns, "The Times," esp. table 3; and on mobility, Sawhill and Morton, "Is the American Dream?" Deciding whether Americans or Europeans have a higher standard of living partly depends on how one values private income and goods compared to other private "utilities," such as vacation time and assured health care, and compared to public goods, such as low rates of violence and accessible mass transit. Boarders: John Leland, "Homes at Risk, More Owners Consider Taking in Boarders," *NYT*, Jul. 16, 2008.

88. Those with poor job preparation or those facing social or personal barriers were often left behind; the 1990s expansion was accompanied by more work instability, health crises, and homelessness for the less–well-off (Valletta, "Recent Research"). Better than parents: P. Taylor et al., "Inside the Middle Class," 11. Proportion of gross national product: Plotnick et al., "The Twentieth-Century Record," 279–80. Government: Moss, *When All Else Fails*.

89. Psychological effects: e.g., Liker and Elder, "Economic Hardship"; Elder et al., "Families"; Conger et al., "Couple Resilience"; and Hobfoll et al., "Resource Loss." Note that people vary; those with more social and psychological resources cope better with the same economic shocks. Child employment: Licht, *Getting Work*, ch. 2; Mintz, "Life Stages," 2018; Goldin, "Labor Markets"; Waters and Briggs, "The Family Economy"; and Moehling, "State." Mobility: C. Fischer, "Ever-More Rooted Americans"; Long, *Migration and Residential Mobility*.

90. S. Schmidt, "Long-Run Trends," shows more worry about job security in the 1980s and 1990s than 1970s (at comparable points in the business cycle). General Social Survey (GSS) data show that, except for college graduates, Americans aged twenty-five to sixty-two were likelier in the early 2000s than in the 1970s to be pessimistic about their families' finances (my analysis; see also Hout, "Money and Morale").

91. Confidence, see R. Wells, *Revolutions in Americans' Lives* and *Uncle Sam's Family*; Modell, "Changing Risks"; idem, *Into One's Own*; and Smith and Hacker, "Cultural Demography." Standardization: Modell citations immediately above; Uhlenberg, "Changing Configurations"; Chudacoff, *How Old Are You?*"; Hareven, "Historical Changes in the Life Course"; D. Stevens, "New Evidence"; Stanger-Ross et al., "Falling Far"; and Fischer and Hout, *Century of Difference*, 86–87. "Postmaterialism": Inglehart, "Globalization and Postmodern Values"; idem, *Modernization and Postmodernization*; and Inglehart and Welzel, *Modernization, Cultural Change, and Democracy*. The idea has roots in Abraham Maslow's notion of a hierarchy of needs and is consistent with Daniel Bell's claim, in *The Cultural Contradictions of Capitalism,* that nineteenth-century pursuits of material gain came to be replaced by twentieth-century pursuits of pleasure.

92. Americans' demand for a risk-free society: e.g., Friedman, *Total Justice*; Burnham, "Why Did Infants?" "Colossal lure": David Frum quoted by George F. Will, "Up From Geniality," *Newsweek*, Sept. 5, 1994, 75–76. The literature on government support "crowding out" civic society support suggests real but modest effects far from cancelling out the benefits (e.g., Gruber and Hungerman, "Faith-Based").

93. Schlesinger: Sam Tanenhaus, "History, Written in the Present Tense," *NYT*, Mar. 4, 2007. In 2005, there was Judith Warner's *Motherhood in the Age of Anxiety*. Textbooks: Carl Degler, *Affluence and Anxiety, 1945 to the Present*; Gary Donaldson, *Abundance and Anxiety, America 1945–1960*; Ernest May, *Anxiety and Affluence, 1945–60*. And then there is Horowitz's 2004 *The Anxieties of Affluence*. (Interestingly, Harvey Green characterized the years *before* this period as the epoch of "uncertainty" in *The Uncertainty of Everyday Life, 1915–1945*.) To be sure, the twentieth century brought new, real threats. From the 1950s through the 1980s, one-third to one-half of Americans told pollsters that they expected or worried seriously about a nuclear war (T. Smith, "A Report: Nuclear Anxiety"). But the broader claim is that the gains in security brought feelings of insecurity. Peter Stearns (Stearns and Haggerty, "The Role of Fear"; P. Stearns, "Fear and Contemporary History") argues that modern Americans became fearful of fear itself, trying to avoid or suppress it for their children rather than confront it. Media scares: Glassner, *The Culture of Fear*; Best, *Damned Lies and Statistics*. Advertising: Marchand, *Advertising the American Dream*; Hoy, *Chasing Dirt*; and Strasser, *Satisfaction Guaranteed*. Among the critiques of such claims is J. Martin, "The Myth"; see also chapter 3 of this book. "Risk society" theorists claim that anxiety has become pervasive because there are new dangers that can be so catastrophic, about which average people obsess but for which tradition provides no guide (Beck, "From Industrial Society"; Giddens, *Modernity and Self-Identity*, ch. 5). My dips into this literature leave me unconvinced. It is hard to credit the image of a premodern people unconsumed by the risks they faced, be it disease, enemies, or the natural catastrophe ("Yea, though I walk through the valley of the shadow of death.").

94. Commager, *The American Mind*, 407; see also Norris and Inglehart, *Sacred and Secular*. Terror management theory in social psychology emphasizes the role of faith in soothing existential dread. See the discussion in ch. 6 of secularization theory. Life after death: my analysis of the GSS item "postlife" (English-language interviews only for comparison). In 1998, the GSS asked a slightly different question ("afterlife"),

and 59 percent said that they "definitely" believed in life after death. See Greeley and Hout, "Americans' Increasing Belief."

95. House prices: Downes and Zabel, "The Impact"; Figlio and Lucas, "What's in a Grade?" College savings: "529 Plan Data," College Savings Plan Network, http://www.collegesavings.org/529PlanData.aspx (accessed May 20, 2008). Planning: Sánchez-Jankowski, *Cracks in the Pavement*, identifies two general strategies the very poor typically have toward money: hoarding or spree-ing. See also Johnson-Hanks, "When the Future Decides."

96. Dakotans: Stock, *Main Street in Crisis*, 40; Adams, *The Transformation of Rural Life*, on attitudes toward government. Poll: Gallup, http://www.gallup.com/poll/27286/Government.aspx (accessed May 20, 2008). Americans in 2000 said by more than 2 to 1 that charitable organizations can do a better job of helping people in need than can the government (Kaiser Family Foundation, "Attitudes toward Government," questions 27, 34, 44a, 45). See also idem, "Why Don't Americans?"; and Frieden, "Public Needs").

Chapter Three

1. "Shopping: Super Deals," *Money Magazine* Jul. 27, 1998, 88–90; Bernice Kanner, "Mall Madness: Big, Bigger, Biggest," *New York Magazine*, Mar. 29, 1993, 18–19. Filene's: Benson, *Counter Cultures*, 83; Leach, *Land of Desire*. Store openings: "Crowds at Macy's Fall Opening," *NYT*, Sept. 18, 1894 ("crowning"). Virginia: Martin, "Common People." Three tons: Mayflower, "America on the Move," http://www.mayflower.com/moving/mayflower-newsroom/press-releases/2008/interesting-moving-facts-2008.htm (accessed Dec. 16, 2008).

2. See, e.g., Lasch, "The Culture of Consumption," on "a whole culture pervaded by the ideal of consumption" (1381). "Worshiping": Solomon et al., "Lethal Consumption," 129.

3. Thoreau: *Walden*, 7, 17. For generations, "commentators have worried about threats that profligacy, extravagance, materialism, and affluence pose to American society" (Horowitz, *The Morality of Spending*, xviii; idem, *The Anxieties of Affluence*). Survey: Wuthnow, *Poor Richard's Almanac*, 249. In a 2002 poll, about half of Americans picked the option "Consumerism and commercialism are a threat to our culture" over the option "not a threat"—a proportion, however, lower than that of other Western peoples (Mead, "The Community's Pulse"). See also Shi, *The Simple Life*; Woodward, *The Old World's New World*; Wuthnow, *Poor Richard's Almanac*; Schudson, *Advertising*, ch. 5; and idem, "Delectable Materialism." Academic critiques of consumption include Fox and Lears, *The Culture of Consumption*; Collier, *The Rise of Selfishness in America*; Gottdiener, "Approaches to Consumption"; Schor, *The Overspent American*; Richter, *Enchanting a Disenchanted World*; and Borgmann, *Technology and the Character of Contemporary Life*. For overviews of scholars' opinions, see Steigerwald, "All Hail," and subsequent comments in the same issue; Zukin and Maguire, "Consumers and Consumption"; Zelizer, "Culture and Consumption"; and Fourcade and Healy, "Moral Views."

4. Anthropologist: D. Miller, "The Poverty," 226.

5. Zelizer, "Culture and Consumption"; idem, *The Purchase of Intimacy*; and idem, *The Social Meaning of Money*. See also Douglas and Isherwood, *A World of Goods*; Csikszentmihalyi and Rochberg-Halton, *The Meaning of Things*.

6. Carson et al., *Of Consuming Interest*; Greene and Pole, *Colonial British America*; Shammas, *The Pre-Industrial Consumer*; Breen, "The Meaning"; idem, "'Baubles'"; Main, "The Standard of Living"; Carr and Walsh, "The Standard of Living"; Perkins, "The Consumer Frontier"; and Rothenberg, *From Market-Places to a Market Economy*. York: Carr and Walsh, "The Standard of Living," tables 11 and 4. Acquisition of what had been luxury goods: S. Wolf, *As Various as Their Land*, 50. Domesticity that the goods permitted: Shammas, "The Domestic Environment." Comfort: Crowley, "The Sensibility"; idem, *Invention of Comfort*; and Bushman, *Refinement of America*, 267ff.

7. Perkins, "The Consumer Frontier"; Breen, "'Baubles'"; Jaffee, "Peddlers"; Bruegel, "'Time'"; Innes, "Fulfilling"; Ulrich, *Good Wives*, ch. 1; Walsh, "Urban Amenities"; S. Wolf, *As Various as Their Land*, 189ff; and Sellers, *The Market Revolution*, 155–57.

8. Advertising and "shopping experience": Bushman, "Shopping and Advertising" (China Ware, 249). Virginia: A. Martin, "Common People," 47, 46. Philadelphia: Doerflinger, "Farmers." Gender: Perkins, "The Consumer Frontier," 496; Dierks, "Letter Writing," 474. See also Breen and Jaffee in previous note.

9. Mather: Staloff, "Where Religion," 8. "Orgy": S. Wolf, *As Various as Their Land*, 189, who also notes that increasingly "frequent, bitter references to female extravagance as the cause of everything from domestic discomfort to financial ruin and the corruption" (79). Tea: Shammas, "The Domestic Environment," 14. Elite complaints and sumptuary laws: Shammas, *The Pre-Industrial Consumer*, 218–19; Calvert, "The Function"; and Thompson, *Rum Punch & Revolution* (Philadelphia: 117–18).

10. Revolutionary criticisms: Huston, *Securing the Fruits,* 55; Breen, "Narrative"; idem, "'Baubles'" (Harvard and Yale); Zakim, "Sartorial Ideologies." Appleby, "Consumption in Early Modern Thought," dissents by suggesting that consumption was not of major concern in this era.

11. B. G. Smith, "The Material Lives," 202. Housing: e.g., Crowley, *Invention of Comfort*, ch. 3. Extravagance: Paul Dudley quoted in Greene, *The Intellectual Construction of America*, 105. Beds: M. Smith, *Breaking the Bonds*.

12. Overviews: Larkin, *The Reshaping of Everyday Life,* ch. 3 (clothing, 187–89); D. Howe, *What Hath God Wrought*; and Blumin, *The Emergence of the Middle Class*, ch. 5. Production and distribution: Taylor, *The Transportation Revolution;* Dawley, *Class and Community*, 90ff; Zakim, "Sartorial Ideologies"; idem., *Ready-Made Democracy* (inch-ruler; clothing); Scranton, "Manufacturing Diversity." The cost of shipping by land dropped 95 percent between 1815 and 1850, and the carrying capacities of riverborne vessels went up a hundred times (Gienapp, "The Antebellum Era," 106). See also Perkins, "The Consumer Frontier"; Rainer, "The Sharper Image"; Jaffee, "Peddlers of Progress"; Walsh, "Consumer Behavior"; Clemens, "The Consumer Culture" (mirrors, stoves, and clocks); and Garvan, "Effects of Technology." Work time for chair: United States Bureau of the Census, *Historical Statistics*, table D716.

13. Quackenbush and Sylvester, "Letter of Jacob Schramm." Bok, "The Americanization," 78.

14. Washington: Walsh, "Consumer Behavior," 227. Donald, *Lincoln*, 27–28. Duffield, "Frontier Church Going." Howe, *What Hath God Wrought*, 32, notes that ordinary country people went barefoot most of the time and lacked outdoor privies.

15. Marketing: Tedlow, *New and Improved*; Strasser, *Satisfaction Guaranteed*; Schlereth, *Victorian America*, ch. 4; Scranton, "Manufacturing Diversity"; Boorstin, *The Americans*, 89ff; and Moskowitz, *Standard of Living* (flatware, bathtubs). Department stores: Leach, "Transformations"; idem, *Land of Desire*; Benson, *Counter Cultures*; and D. Cook, "The Mother as Consumer." Glennie, "Consumption," dissents, arguing that the department store was not really a major departure in marketing. Rural America: Schlereth, "Country Stores"; Baron, *Mixed Harvest*, ch. 5; Ownby, *American Dreams in Mississippi*; Fuller, *The American Mail*; idem, *RFD*; Blanke, *Sowing the Americans Dream*, esp. 214–15; Dickson, "Prosperity Rides"; Kolb and Polson, "Trends"; Bureau of Business Research, "The Automobile"; and Atwood, "Routes."

16. Marchand, *Advertising and the American Dream*; Schudson, *Advertising*; and Pope, *The Making of Modern Advertising*. Ewen, *Captains of Consciousness*, most strongly makes the claim about creating needs. Schudson is most skeptical of such claims. Toothbrushes: Larkin, *Reshaping*, 92. See also Olney, *Buy Now, Pay Later*, ch. 5. Further discussion of the issue is picked up later, in note 44. Studies of ads' messages include Pollay, "The Subsiding Sizzle"; Belk and Pollay, "Images."

17. Credit: Calder, *Financing the American Dream*. Entertainments: e.g., Barth, *City People*; Cullen, *The Art of Democracy*; and Nasaw, *Going Out*. Victorian styles: Green, *The Light of the Home*; Garvan, "Effects of Technology." Goods life: Schlereth, *Victorian America*, 141.

18. C. Brown, *American Standards of Living*; Lebergott, *The Americans*; idem, *Pursuing Happiness*. Immigrants: Barton, *Peasants and Strangers*; Bodnar et al., *Lives of Their Own*; Heinze, *Adapting to Abundance*; and Glenn, *Daughters of the Shtetl*. Social workers and budgets: Horowitz, *The Morality of Spending*, 124–25; Rainwater, *What Money Buys*, 44–49; and C. Brown, *American Standards of Living*, 79–82.

19. Cathedrals: Charles DeKay, "Surface Impressions of New York," *NYT*, Jan. 13, 1897. Shoplifting: Leach, *Land of Desire*; Abelson, *When Ladies Go A-Thieving*.

20. Spending: Shammas, *The Pre-Industrial Consumer*, 132; C. Brown, *American Standards of Living*; Horowitz, *The Morality of Spending*, appendix A; Lebergott, *Consumer Expenditures*; Jacobs and Shipp, "How Family Spending"; and recent Bureau of Labor Statistics reports on consumer expenditures at http://www.bls.gov/cex/. Work time: Cox and Alm, "Time Well Spent," 5. Changing diets: Levenstein, *Revolution at the Table*; P. Williams, "Foodways"; and Lebergott, *The American Economy*, 104–5.

21. In 1918, laborers spent 71 percent of their budgets on food, clothing and shelter, while managers and professionals spent 66 percent on those items, a five-point difference. In 1988, laborers spent only 38 percent on these basics, while managers and professionals spent only 33 percent, still a five-point difference. C. Brown, *American Standards of Living*, presents these class analyses. See previous note for other studies of spending.

22. 1918: Estimated from United States Department of Labor, Bureau of Labor Statistics, "The Cost of Living," 455. Automobile spending represented over two-

thirds of new major durables expenditures: Olney, *Buy Now, Pay Later*, 9–22. Middletown: Lynd and Lynd, *Middletown*, 255; and Jensen, "The Lynds Revisited," for corrected spending on automobiles. 2005: United States Department of Labor, Bureau of Labor Statistics, Consumer expenditure survey. Berkeley: Peixotto, *Getting and Spending*, 196. The automobile: e.g., Flink, *The Automobile Age*; Rae, *The American Automobile*; Fischer and Carroll, "Telephone and Automobile Diffusion"; and C. Fischer, *America Calling*, appendix D.

23. Housing tenure: United States Bureau of the Census, *Historical Statistics*, table N243; idem, *Statistical Abstract*, 2007, table 956. (Home ownership escalated between 1995 and 2005 in part because of the easing of credit limits, which then turned into the 2007–9 sub-prime mortgage crisis.) Spending trends: see sources cited above in notes 20 and 21. History of home ownership: Myers and Shammas, "Housing Standards"; Chevan, "The Growth"; Luria, "Wealth"; Harris, "Working-Class"; idem, "The Flexible House"; Tobey et al., "Moving Out"; Peel, "On the Margins"; and Land, "Be a Patriot." Tastes: e.g., Marsh, "From Separation to Togetherness."

24. Olney, *Buy Now, Pay Later*, focuses on automobile purchases; see also Olney, "Avoiding Default," on proportions and terms; Calder, *Financing the American Dream*; Leach, *Land of Desire*; and Mandell, *The Credit Card Industry*. Installment figures: United States Bureau of the Census, *Historical Statistics*, series X552, using the CPI adjustment.

25. Statistician quoted in *Literary Digest*, "Fallacies as to the High Cost of Living," Feb. 24, 1912, 400. Strauss: Leach, *Land of Desire*, 266. See also Lynd, "The People as Consumers." See Horowitz, introduction to *The Anxieties of Affluence*, for overview of critiques.

26. Kline, *Consumers in the Country*; Tobey, *Technology as Freedom*; L. Cohen, *A Consumer's Republic*; M. Jacobs, "'Democracy's Third Estate'" (Croly, 28); Olney, "Avoiding Default"; and R. M. Collins, "In Retrospect." FDR and Sears: Potter, *People of Plenty*, 60.

27. Long-term equalization and post-1973 reversal: C. Brown, *American Standards of Living*; Soltow, "Wealth"; Fischer and Hout, *Century of Difference*, ch. 6; Slesnick, *Consumption and Social Welfare*; and Cutler and Katz, "Rising Inequality?" Cheap imports: Zukin, *Point of Purchase*, ch. 3; Basker, "Selling." Around Christmas 2005, for example, most *low-income* Americans had DVD players and cable television (Carroll, "Americans Inventory"). Designer aesthetics: Nickles, "More is Better."

28. Inequality, of course, involves not just consumer goods like televisions but also "goods" like medical care, which have remained or became more unequal. Class distinction by goods is a familiar topic of study since at least Veblen (Bourdieu, *Distinctions*; McCracken, *Culture and Consumption*; Lunt, "Psychological Approaches"; Felson, "Invidious Distinctions") and is picked up later in this chapter.

29. Chinese: N. Park, "Cultural Strains," 153; Israeli: Bartov, "Measures," 299. Domestic critics include Riesman, *The Lonely Crowd*; Whyte, *Organization Man*; and Boorstin: *The Americans*, 427. See review of critiques in Donaldson, *The Suburban Myth*.

30. In 1970, only 6 percent of sixth-graders had television sets in their bedrooms

(Rideout et al., *Kids & Media @ the New Millennium*, 21; see also Tara Parker-Pope, "A One-Eyed Invader in the Bedroom," *NYT*, Mar. 4, 2008). Various periodizing: P. Stearns, *Consumerism in World History*, p. x, suggests 1700; Seller, *The Market Revolution*, 155–57, picks the 1820s; Zukin, *Point of Purchase*, 257ff, and Leach, *Land of Desire*, choose the 1870s; Baritz, *The Good Life*, Lynd, "Consumers," Sussman, "Culture and Civilization," and McGovern, "Consumption" and "Consumption and Citizenship," pick the 1920s; and Schor, *The Over-Spent American* and *Do Americans Shop Too Much?* and Strasser, *Satisfaction Guaranteed,* pick the late twentieth century. One historian: David Levine, cited by Shammas, "Explaining Past Changes," 62. Clunas, "Modernity," pushes the transition back even to ancient Greece. See also Glennie, "Consumption"; McCracken, *Culture and Consumption*, ch. 1; A. Martin, "Makers"; Cross, *An All-Consuming Century*; Ritzer, *Enchanting a Disenchanted World*; Brewer and Porter, *Consumption and the World of Goods*; and Miller, *Acknowledging Consumption*.

31. Consumerist culture is defined variously. Don Slater defines a consumer culture as synonymous with a market culture and modernity (*Consumer Culture and Modernity*, ch. 1), but that is too broad; markets have been with us for millennia and consumerism is a more specific, more psychological issue. Quotations: Leach, *Land of Desire*, xiii; Dreiser, *Sister Carrie*, 19; Ritzer, *Enchanting a Disenchanted World*, 28.

32. "Do not need": P. Stearns, *Consumerism in World History*, p. ix, who also discusses various models of consumerism. See Zelizer, "Culture and Consumption"; Agnew, "Coming Up for Air"; A. Martin, "Makers, Buyers, and Users"; McCracken, *Culture and Consumption*; D. Miller, *Material Culture and Mass Consumption*; and Belk, "The Human Consequences." The subfield of consumer psychology is reviewed in Cohen and Chakravarti, "Consumer Psychology." Sharon Zukin has pointed out that one could alternatively define a consumer society by some more objective criteria, such as the spending on marketing or the proportion of time spent buying (pers. comm., May 26, 2004). But such a formulation avoids the question of whether a consumer society alters character—a question that Zukin herself has significantly explored: "The cumulative effect [of the *intensifications* of shopping] . . . is that they . . . persuade us to see the entire world as a shopping experience. Ultimately, a new culture depends not just on the production of consumer goods but on the production of consumers"(*Point of Purchase*, 257).

33. "Keeping up with Joneses" was the name of a comic strip began in 1913 about a family jealous of its neighbors (http://www.wordorigins.org/index.php/site/comments/joneses_keep_up_with_the/; accessed Jul. 18, 2007; Matt, *Keeping Up with the Joneses*, 42). Boston: Breen, "The Meaning of Things," 255. Immigrant: Glenn, *Daughters of the Shtetl*, 160–61; see also Heinz, *Adapting to Abundance*; L. Cohen, "Embellishing a Life of Labor." Hummer: Schulz, "Vehicle of the Self," pp. 77–78. Children: Pugh, *Longing and Belonging*, describes how low-income parents feel pressed to accommodate the pleas their children make. Consumption as status marking is central to analyses such as Bourdieu's *Distinctions*. Scholars invoke emulation when they say that, at some key moment, Americans shifted from judging one another by how they earned their money (a "producer ethic") to judging one another by how they spent their money (a "consumer ethic"). See, e.g., Fox and Lears, introduction to *The*

Culture of Consumption (see Lears, "Beyond Veblen," for second thoughts); Bauman, "The Self." Reisman, *The Lonely Crowd*, ch. 3, suggests that the drive to consume shifted from a nineteenth-century wish to stand out to a twentieth-century desire to conform. The literature on advertising's appeals to status is vast, including Ewen, *Captains of Consciousness*, and Fox, *The Mirror Makers*.

34. Shoplifters: Abelson, *When Ladies Go A-Thieving* (1895 quote, 55). "Wanting and desiring . . . lie at the very heart of . . . modern consumerism" (Campbell, "I Shop Therefore," 28). Addictive habits: Csikszentmihalyi and Rochberg-Halton, *The Meaning of Things*, 229. See also Bauman, "Consuming Life," 25; R. Frank, *Luxury Fever*, ch. 12. Zombie: Ritzer, *Enchanting a Disenchanted World*, 89. Explicit claims of hedonism: Collier, *The Rise of Selfishness*; D. Bell, *The Cultural Contradictions of Capitalism*; and Sussman, "Culture and Civilization." Students of advertising have adopted the concept of "hedonic consumption," "which designates those facets of consumer behavior that relate to the multi-sensory, fantasy and emotive aspects of one's experience with products" (Hirschman and Holbrook, "Hedonic Consumption"). From means to ends: "What sets the members of consumer society apart from their ancestors is the emancipation of consumption from its past instrumentality that used to draw its limits. . . . [C]onsumption is its own purpose and so is self-propelling" (Bauman, "Consuming Life," 12–13).

35. P. Stearns, *Consumerism in World History*, most explicitly forwards this thesis. See also Zukin, *Point of Purchase*: "We shop because we long for value . . . that we no longer get from religion, work, or politics" (8). Gottdiener, "Approaches"; Cross, *The All-Consuming Century*; Lears, "From Salvation to Self-Realization"; Lasch, "Culture of Consumption"; Lynd, "The People as Consumers"; and Dumenil, *The Modern Temper*, ch. 2. Entertainment: Somers, "The Leisure Revolution" ("steam," 138); Barth, *City People*. Advertising: see esp. Marchand, *Advertising and the American Dream*. For a critique of compensation as an explanation, see C. Fischer, "Comment on 'Anxiety.'" For a rare demonstration of compensatory inclination to spend, see Rucker and Galinsky, "Desire to Acquire."

36. Rejecting earlier theories: Agnew, "Coming Up for Air," writes, "[W]e now stand corrected. . . . [H]istorians have . . . rejected the Weberian dichotomies between Puritanism and Romanticism and, correspondingly, between saving and spending, and in some instances, they have also abandoned the classic Marxist distinction between use-value and symbolic value. Finally, they have revalued the political and moral dimensions of fantasy, fetishism, dream, and wish. . . . As a result, the productionist, supply-side, and hegemonic interpretation of consumer culture has been shaken, if not overthrown" (5–6). Lears in 1989 rejected the "notion of a shift from a Protestant 'producer culture' to a secular 'commercial culture'" ("Beyond Veblen," 77n8; see also his *Fables of Abundance*).

Self-expression: Sociologists will recognize the influence of Bourdieu's *Distinction*. Belk's essay, "Possessions," has been influential in consumption studies. See Arnould and Thompson, "Consumer Culture Theory," with its emphasis on "consumer identity projects." Key works on goods as symbols start with Douglas and Isherwood, *A World of Goods*. See also Baudrillard, "Consumer Society" ("system of meaning," 48);

Featherstone, *Consumer Culture and Postmodernism*; D. Miller, *Acknowledging Consumption*; McCracken, *Culture and Consumption*; Applbaum, "The Sweetness of Salvation"; and Schudson, "Delectable Materialism." "Self-creation" through goods: Holt, "Postmodern Markets," in Schorr, *Do Americans Shop Too Much?*, 67. Strasser, "Making Consumption Conspicuous," regrets this revisionism, as does Steigerwald, "All Hail."

Hummers: Schulz, "Vehicle of the Self." African Americans: Lamont and Molnár, "How Blacks Use Consumption"; K. Charles et al., "Conspicuous Consumption."

37. De Vries, "Review of *Consumerism in World History*." A database search shows that "consumerism" rarely appeared in the economics literature over the last fifteen years of the twentieth century—just when historians and sociologists rediscovered the topic—and almost never in the sense used here. Similarly, Schor's *Overspent American*, a major statement of the consumerist thesis, was ignored by mainstream economists. To be sure, a few economists believe that buying can be irrational. Keynes, for example, described consumers as motivated by "enjoyment, short-sightedness, generosity, miscalculation, ostentation and extravagance" (Lebergott, *Consumer Expenditures*, 45).

38. McCloskey, "The Economics of Choice," 150. "Gratification": Campbell, "I Shop Therefore," 34. Most economists assume that there are personal, a priori preferences and that external forces like marketing cannot change them (see Rhoads, *The Economist's View of the World*, ch. 9). In John Kenneth Galbraith's words, the economists' slogan is: "The consumer wants more. [Ours] is not to reason why, but to satisfy" (quoted by Rhoades, *The Economist's View of the World*, 62). Premoderns: American Indians eagerly adopted Western goods (C. Miller and Hamell, "A New Perspective"; Butler, *Becoming America*, 142). The "cargo cults" of Pacific Islanders provide another case. Necessities in 2006: Morin and Taylor, "Luxury or Necessity?" The Roper Poll asked people about what they "don't know how they could get along without" (P. Liberatore, "Home Computers—Why the Craze is Fizzling Out," *San Francisco Chronicle*, Jul. 5, 1985).

39. Subsistence budgets: Rainwater, *What Money Buys*; Horowitz, *The Morality of Spending*; and G. Fisher, "Is There?" Smith and Marx: Schudson, *Advertising*, ch. 4. "Relative deprivation," the tendency for people to make evaluate themselves based on their "reference groups": Runciman, *Relative Deprivation and Social Justice*; Merton, *Social Structure and Social Theory*, ch. 10, 11 (more on this later, in chapter 6).

40. The 2006 poll asked "What, if anything, do you think that you or your spouse spend too much money on?" Only 21 percent said nothing (Gallup survey, the iPOLL Databank, http://www.ropercenter.uconn.edu/ipoll.html; accessed Aug. 1, 2007). For similar results in 1978, see report in Rhoades, *The Economist's View*, 165; and in 1997, see survey conducted by EDK Associates (Center for a New American Dream, pers. comm., Nov. 13, 1997). Earmarking: Zelizer, *Social Meaning of Money*. Twelve-step programs: Debtors Anonymous (http://www.debtorsanonymous.org/)—the symptoms—and Spenders Anonymous (http://www.spenders.org/home.html)—the first step. Entertainment: Zukin, *Point of Purchase*. "Get along": Rainwater, *What Money Buys*; G. Fisher, "Is There?"

41. A sample of works on this topic includes these (others are cited in the discussion

of choice in chapter 6): Cohen and Chakravarti, "Consumer Psychology"; McFadden, "Economic Choices"; idem, "Free Markets"; Henrich et al., "In Search"; Bargh, "Losing Consciousness"; Vohs and Faber, "Spent Resources"; Lowenstein et al., "Projection Bias"; and Kahneman and Thaler, "Anomalies."

42. The literature on advertising history is large. See Ewen, *Captains of Consciousness*; S. Fox, *The Mirror Makers*; Laird, *Advertising Progress*; Lears, *Fables of Abundance*; idem, "From Salvation to Self-Realization"; Marchand, *Advertising the American Dream*; Packard, *The Hidden Persuaders*; Pope, *The Making of Modern Advertising*; and Schudson, *Advertising*. On admen's psychological models, see esp. Curti, "The Changing Concept"; Marchand, *Advertising the American Dream*; and Laird, *Advertising Progress*. On other aspects of marketing, see Leach, *Land of Desire*; Strasser, *Satisfaction Guaranteed*; Tedlow, *New and Improved*; and Zukin, *Point of Purchase*. Farm daughters: Barron, *Mixed Harvest*, ch. 6. Research on ads: Belk and Pollay, "Images of Ourselves"; idem., "Materialism and Magazine Advertising"—although their evidence is only suggestive and apparently has not been replicated.

43. "Suckers": used by early admen (Curti, "The Changing Concept," 340–41).

44. Some authors try to sidestep the effectiveness issue by stating that they only study the marketers (e.g., Leach, *Land of Desire*, xiv; R. Fox and Lears, introduction to *The Culture of Compensation*, x). Typically, they go on to draw conclusions about the consumers anyway. Boasts of admen (such as selling soup and toothpaste [Strasser, *Satisfaction Guaranteed*, 95]) are informative, but not necessarily because they are to be believed. Admen are certain that ads make people want things they would not otherwise want (which is different than telling consumers about new products), but many scholars are skeptical (e.g., Schudson, *Advertising*; Olney, *Buy Now, Pay Later*, ch. 5; and Stewart, "Speculations"). Laird argues that "commercial messages . . . better represent the creators than their audiences" (*Advertising Progress*, 93). I concluded, in *America Calling* (ch. 3), that telephone salesmen and admen were often poor receivers, broadcasters, or creators of the public's concerns. Pollnay's "The Subsiding Sizzle" depicts cycles in advertising over the twentieth century and implies that changes follow fashions in the ad industry more than responses of consumers. Skeptics also point to examples of failed campaigns. For instance, Howard, "A 'Real Man's Ring,'" describes how efforts to market a man's engagement ring in the 1920s failed; years later, American men bought such bands as a byproduct of World War II patriotism. Lasch's response is that advertising matters not in promoting particular products but in promoting "images of the good life in which happiness depends on consumption" ("The Culture of Consumption," 1387). Children: Wilcox et al., "A Report."

45. Employment in retail trade: United States Bureau of the Census, *Historical Statistics*, 840; idem, *Statistical Abstract*, 2007, table 606. Trade as proportion of national income, from 11 percent in 1929 to 8 percent in the 2000s: idem., *Historical Statistics*, 839, 224; idem., *Statistical Abstract*, 2007, tables 649, 654. The dollars spent on advertising ranged around $150 to $300 per capita (in 2008 dollars) until the postwar years and then escalated rapidly afterwards. As a percentage of the gross domestic product, however, advertising spending ranged from 2.1 to 3.4 percent before World War II (the high point was 1910) and 2.0 to 2.5 percent afterward (2.2 in 2005) (*Historical*

Statistics, 855; *Statistical Abstract*, 2007, table 1261). For 1980, the Television Bureau of Advertising, http://www.tvb.org/rcentral/mediatrendstrack/tvbasics/basics17.html (accessed Jan. 22, 2003). Thus, advertising's share of the nation's economy shrank just during the historical era in which consumerism presumably took over. Increasing distrust and inefficacy of advertising: Banwari, "Public Assessment," 35; Zanot, "Public Attitudes."

46. R. Frank, *Luxury Fever*. 1815 Taxation: Carson, "The Consumer Revolution." Luxuries and necessities: Morin and Taylor, "Luxury or Necessity?" (Had the question offered an option such as "useful, but not necessary," many fewer respondents probably would have answered "necessity.") In a 1997 national survey, the median American estimated that he or she did not "really need" about 15 percent of purchases (EDK Associates, reported by the Center for a New American Dream, pers. comm., Nov. 13, 1997).

47. See discussion on p. 73 on "need," as well as sources such as Shammas, *The Pre-Industrial Consumer*, 132; and C. Brown, *American Standards of Living*.

48. The concern over spending comes out most sharply in Lynd and Lynd, *Middletown*. Pianos: Shammas, "The Domestic Environment"; Calder, *Financing the American Dream*, ch. 4. Immigrants: Heinze, *Adapting to Abundance*; E. Morawska, *For Bread with Butter*, ch. 6; and Joselit, *The Wonders of America*. Farmers: United States Senate, *Report of the Country Life Commission*; Ward, "The Farm Woman's Problem." Young women: Peiss, *Cheap Amusements*; Meyerowitz, "Women and Migration"; and idem, *Women Adrift*. Stockings: Matt, "Frocks." Women's clubs: Breckinridge, *Women in the Twentieth Century*; Wilson, *American Women in Transition*. Divorce: E. May, "The Pressure." In *Great Expectations*, Elaine May describes women's rising expectations for intimacy as well. Men: Swiencicki, "Consuming Brotherhood"; Duis, "The Saloon"; Kingsdale, "The 'Poor Man's Club'"; and Rosenzweig, *Eight Hours for What We Will*. Alcohol: In 1905, wage earners in New York City spent over 2 percent of their expenditures on alcohol (More, *Wage-Earners' Budgets*, 96, 102); in 1909, Chicagoans spent 4.4 percent (Kennedy, *Wages and Family Budgets*, 72)—both probably underestimates, because they did not really include saloon drinking or families with alcoholic husbands. In 2000, about 1 percent of middle-income Americans' spending and 3 percent of poor Americans' spending went to alcohol (calculated from the 2000 Consumer Expenditure Survey, http://data.bls.gov). See also Swiencicki, "Consuming Brotherhood."

49. Pride: Carson, "Consumer Revolution," 660. Child: M. Barton, "The Victorian Jeremiad," 61. Virginia: Greene, "Society, Ideology, and Politics," 69–75. Bellows, "The Influence of the Trading Spirit," 111–12.

50. Overviews of consumption in the eighteenth and early nineteenth centuries: Glennie, "Consumption"; P. Stearns, "Stages of Consumerism"; A. Martin, "Makers, Buyers, and Users"; and De Vries, "Between Purchasing Power." Debates about luxury: Crowley, "The Sensibility." Breen's "Narrative," "The Meaning of Things," and "'Baubles of Britain'" (soap reference, 451) are important studies. Colonial elites: Lockridge, "Colonial Self-Fashioning," 282. Adams: Carson, "The Consumer Revolution," 521. Kentucky: Perkins, "The Consumer Frontier," 508. Virginia: A. Martin,

"Common People"; also S. Wolf, *As Various as Their Land*, 64–66. Specific kinds of spending: Shammas, "Changes in English and Anglo-American Consumption"; idem, *The Pre-Industrial Consumer*; idem, "The Domestic Environment" (42 percent tea services, 13); Bruegel, "Time"; Jaffee, "Peddlers"; Calvert, "The Function of Fashion"; Carson, "The Consumer Revolution" ("pissing," 505); Chappell, "Housing a Nation"; Walsh, "Urban Amenities"; Main, "The Standard of Living"; and Perkins, "The Consumer Frontier." On tax: Carson, "The Consumer Revolution," 661–62. The $200 can be translated into 2008 dollars via the consumer price index, yielding $2,900, but that reflects nearly two centuries of dropping food and manufacturing costs. Using the number hours of unskilled work it would take to buy these goods in 1815 and 2008 is a better translation, a more-accurate updated price is $37,000. Either way, there was a lot of "luxury" in 1815. (Conversion estimates: http://measuringworth.com/uscompare; accessed May 28, 2008.)

51. Overviews: Nissenbaum, *The Battle for Christmas*, ch. 6 (Stowe, 134); L. Schmidt, *Consumer Rites*; and idem, "The Commercialization of the Calendar." Ryan, *Women in Public*, notes that antebellum newspapers in December blared "TOYS, TOYS, TOYS" and "DOLLS, DOLLS, DOLLS" (39). On modern American attitudes, see M. Gillespie, "Merry Christmas." In a 2000 Gallup poll, 84 percent of respondents said there was "too much . . . emphasis on gifts and presents at Christmas these days" and in a 2006 poll, 85 percent said that Christmas was "too commercialized" (Roper Center for Public Opinion Research, http://www.ropercenter.uconn.edu/ipoll.html; accessed Jul. 31, 2007). On gifting and social ties: Caplow, "Rule Enforcement"; idem, "Christmas Gifts"; and Zelizer, *The Social Meaning of Money*, ch. 3. Thanksgiving: Pleck, "The Making." Independence Day: Applebaum, *The Glorious Fourth*; Kamen, *Mystic Chords*. Heinze, *Adapting to Abundance*, describes how Jewish immigrants adapted Chanukah to mimic Christmas gift-giving (72–78; *Tribune* quote, 73). Broadening of gift-giving: e.g., Owen, *American Dreams in Mississippi*, 93–94. My claim that much purchasing is for gifts is extrapolated from a British survey (Schudson, *Advertising*, 142). Schor, *The Overspent American*, 88–89, reports that 25 percent of sales occur during the Christmas season. The 3 percent of consumer dollars is based on the Consumer Expenditure Surveys of 1990 and 2000 (http://www.bls.gov/cex/csxstnd .htm). Household budget surveys show a rise of gift spending from about 2–3 percent in the early part of the century to about 7 percent of all spending near the end (C. Brown, *American Standards of Living*, table 1.3). Different definitions of "gift" explain the different percentages; Brown includes charity but explains that it is mostly personal gifts and that the noncash component also increased. Economists have been puzzled by the seeming irrationality of gifts, especially noncash gifts, because they violate the principle that individuals know their own utilities best (Waldfogel, "Gifts"; List and Shrogen, "The Deadweight Loss," plus replies following the article).

52. D. Bell, *The Cultural Contradictions of Capitalism*, 21. Calder, *Financing the American Dream*, 23, 26. Black ink: e.g., Jackson Lears, "The American Way of Debt," *NYT Sunday Magazine*, Jun. 11: "There never was a golden age of thrift. Debt has always played an important role in Americans' lives" (13).

53. Indentured: Fogleman, "From Slaves," table 1, 44; Klein, *A Population History*

of the United States, 47; in Middlesex, Virginia, 1688, almost half the population were bound laborers (Rudman and Rudman, *A Place in Time*). Farmers: Kulikoff, *From British Peasants to Colonial American Farmers*, 217ff. Farmers keeping track: e.g., Osterud, *Bonds of Community*, 216–22, and Pruitt, "Self-Sufficiency." Jefferson left his "heirs with crushing debts that required the dismantlement of Monticello and selling off of all his remaining slaves" (Ellis, "Money," 588). Mann, *Republic of Debtors,* ch. 3, on bolting planters and Morris. See also Perkins, "The Consumer Frontier" (storekeepers' ads, ledgers); S. Wolf, *As Various as Their Land*, 192–93; Shammas, *The Pre-Industrial Consumer*, ch. 9; Ownby, *American Dreams in Mississippi*, 9, 19; Calder, *Financing the American Dream* ($880, 40; wages from United States Bureau of the Census, *Historical Statistics*, table D475). Pawnbrokers: Woloson, "In Hock."

54. Calder, *Financing the American Dream*; Olney, *Buy Now, Pay Later*; Mandell, *The Credit Card Industry*; Tobey, *Technology as Freedom*. Debt numbers calculated from United States Bureau of the Census, *Historical Statistics*, tables D405–6 and A351; and Board of Governors, "Flow of Funds," table D.3, divided by number of households.

55. Overviews ca. 2000 include Weller and Douglas, "One Nation"; Kish, "Perspectives"; and Lansing, "Spendthrift Nation." 1890 Estimates: Calder, *Financing the American Dream*, 40. In 2007, the mean household income was about $67,600 and all debts amounted to about $118,600 per household. (Medians would be more appropriate, but Calder reported means for 1890. See Board of Governors, "Flow of Funds," table D.3 for 2007 debt data and Bureau of Census, "HINC-01," for 2007 income data.) Increasing home ownership and larger homes: Chevan, "The Growth"; C. Brown, *American Standards of Living*; Cox and Alm, "Time Well Spent"; and *Statistical Abstract, 2000* and *Statistical Abstract, 2002*, table 922. Increasing use of borrowed money: Tobey et al., "Moving Out." In the 1940s, homeowners' remaining debt represented about 15 percent of the value of residential real estate; by the 2000s, that percentage was over 50 percent (Board of Governors, "Flow of Funds," table B.100; Louise Story, "Home Equity Frenzy Was a Bank Ad Come True," *NYT*, Aug. 15, 2008; Maki, "The Growth of Consumer Credit"; and analysis reported above). Mortgage debt will reasonably go up when interest rates drop, as they did toward the end of the century and into the 2000s.

Contemporary consumer debt is usually overestimated because Americans began using credit cards for items such as groceries and as sources of temporary small loans ("floats"). On the other hand, some home mortgage debt is home equity loans used to purchase consumer goods (see Garner, "Can Measures?"; Kennickell et al., "Family Finances"; and Virginia Postrel, "The Case for Debt," *Atlantic Online*, Nov. 2008, http://www.theatlantic.com/doc/print/200811/debt).

Bankruptcies probably increased because of legal and cultural changes, including the extension of easier credit to the economically marginal, rather than any dramatic escalation in debt (Garner, "Can Measures?"; Sullivan et al., *The Fragile Middle Class*; Garrett, "The Rise"; and American Bankers Association, "Consumer Credit Delinquency Historical Fact Sheet," http://www.aba.com/default.htm; accessed May 28, 2008)—at least until the mortgage crisis of 2008–9.

56. The personal savings rate is defined as the difference between national after-

tax income and national spending. Twentieth century: Carter et al., *Historical Statistics of the United States*, table Ce1–126; Bureau of Economic Analysis, National Income and Product Accounts tables, 2003, http://www.bea.doc.gov/bea; Lansing, "Spendthrift Nation," 1. On whether savings rates (inversely) indicate overbuying, J. Martin, "The Myth," found that savings rates did not fall in the first part of the century even as mass consumption expanded. From 1947 to 1982, another consumer boom period, the national savings rate actually rose, from 5 to 11 percent of income. Direct surveys of individual consumers' budgets show a drop in saving from 1973 to 1988, but the 1988 rate was still higher than in 1950 or 1935 (C. Brown, *American Standards of Living*, 13–15). On the spending-investment conflation, see M. Rogers, "Measuring"; Vurley and Villani, "The Personal Savings Rate"; Olney, *Buy Now, Pay Later*. Most sources identify changes in Americans' spending strategies after the 1970s as being due to the "wealth effect" (esp. Maki and Palumbo, "Disentangling"), earnings stagnation and inequality (e.g., Krueger and Perri, "Does Income Inequality?"), and greater credit availability. (For a skeptical note, see Christopher Flavelle, "Debunking the 'Wealth Effect,'" *Slate Magazine*, http://www.slate.com/id/2193287/; accessed Jun. 10, 2008.) Lower savings may, however, also reflect psychological change, greater "discounting" of future income among people raised in a boom economy (Parker, "Spendthrift in America?"). Americans, however, got the message (Morin, "Feeling Guilty"). On the 2008–9 drop in spending: Catherine Rampell, "Shift From Spending to Saving May Be Slump's Lasting Impact," *NYT*, May 10, 2009.

57. New Deal programs: Tobey, *Technology as Freedom*. Calder, *Financing the American Dream*, is an excellent overview.

58. One complication is that a higher wage makes the "opportunity cost" of a leisure hour higher and another is that some consumer goods require leisure time, e.g., to enjoy RV travel (Paul DiMaggio, pers. comm., Nov. 13, 2008).

59. Americans work more hours: Steven Greenhouse, "Americans' International Lead in Hours Worked Grew in 90's, Report Shows," *NYT*, Sept. 1, 2001. On the historical trends, see, e.g., Whaples, "Hours of Work"; Moore and Hedges, "Trends in Labor"; Costa, "The Wage and the Length" (note on class differences, table 5); Fischer and Hout, *Century of Difference*, ch. 5; and Fogel, *The Escape from Hunger and Premature Death*, ch. 4.

60. McGovern, "Consumption"; Cross, *Time and Money*; Schor, *Overworked American*; and P. Stearns, *Consumerism in World History*. Lindsey, *Age of Affluence*, quotes Daniel Bell writing of the postwar "Treaty of Detroit" that General Motors "may have paid a billion for [labor] peace. It got a bargain," because the deal ended class conflict (69).

61. Hochschild, *The Time Bind*; Schor, *Overworked American;* Peter T. Kilborn, "Tales from the Digital Treadmill," *NYT*, Jun. 3, 1990; Hamilton, "Work and Leisure"; Kacapyr, "Are We Having Fun Yet?"; and Robinson and Godbey, "Busyness as Usual." Data and analysis: United States Bureau of the Census, *Statistical Abstract*, 2007, table 587; Jerry Jacobs, "Measuring Time at Work"; Jacobs and Gerson, "Who Are the Overworked Americans?"; idem, "Overworked Individuals"; Aguiar and Hurst, "Measuring Trends"; and Hout and Hanley, "The Overworked."

62. Matthaei, *An Economic History of Women in America*, ch. 10; Leach, "Transformations"; and Gordon and MacArthur, "American Women." This argument would imply that the consumer impulse struck only women, because men cut back their weekly hours and retired earlier, and children largely stopped working. There is also a timing problem: the argument typically places the time of transition in the 1920s, but if we count farmers' and shopkeepers' wives as "really" working for pay, then women's participation rates did not take off until the 1940s (Fischer and Hout, *Century of Difference*, 101–5). Among the factors drawing wives into the paid labor force were the availability of higher wages; new kinds of jobs, particularly clerical ones; fewer children to care for; easing housework demands; growing cultural acceptability and legal rights for workingwomen; and after the 1970s, efforts to supplement falling husbands' incomes. See Goldin, "The Quiet Revolution"; idem, "Labor Markets"; Chafe, *The American Woman*; Degler, *At Odds*; and Leibowitz and Clurman, "Explaining Changes." A different gender story is that shopping became the main duty of modern middle-class wives and more shopping required more income from both spouses. Anecdotes about nineteenth-century housewives in department stores fit, but there is little evidence in support.

63. Shammas, "Changes in English and Anglo-American Consumption," 197. See also Shammas, "Explaining Past Changes"; Martin, "The Myth." Martha Olney, *Buy Now, Pay Later*, found changes in Americans' spending on major consumer durables during the 1920s. Most of that new spending was for cars, which in that decade became available on easier credit terms and became a practical technology for average urban Americans (rather than a leisure good of the rich)—an investment as well as a consumer expenditure—despite the tut-tutting of experts (p. 67).

64. Russell Belk's paper-and-pencil test of materialism includes measures of possessiveness, (non)generosity, and envy (Belk, "Materialism" [definition, 265]; idem, "The Human Consequences"; Ger and Belk, "Cross-Cultural Differences"). See also Kassner and Kanner, *Psychology and Consumer Culture*. Tocqueville: *Democracy in America*, 534, 536. Qutb, "Fundamentalism." On views of Americans, see also Woodward, *The Old World's New World*; Lipset, *First New Nation*, 114. Poll: Wuthnow, *Poor Richard's Almanac*, 246. Reagan: Wuthnow, "A Good Life," 15.

65. Scholarly claims of rising materialism: Sussman, "Culture and Civilization"; P. Stearns, *American Cool*, ch. 7; Leach, *Land of Desire*; and Carson, "The Consumer Revolution"; as well as (implicitly, at least) most critiques of consumer society. Postmaterialism: see citations in chapter 2, p. 268n91. Some psychologists have turned the postmaterialism thesis on its head by suggesting that material security undermined faith in the afterlife which, in turn, increased existential anxiety, which, in turn, led people to seek solace in materialism (e.g., Solomon et al., "Lethal Consumption").

66. More messages: between 1900 and 2000 alone the number of new book titles per capita grew sixfold (United States Bureau of the Census, *Historical Statistics*, 808; idem, *Statistical Abstract*, 2001). Add the newer electronic media and obviously information and images multiplied (even if newspapers declined). The "simplicity" theme in American culture: Shi, *The Simple Life*. Barton, "The Victorian Jeremiad," reviews the critiques of the Gilded Age. Contemporary instances: e.g., Ralph Blumenthal

and Rachel Mosteller, "Chasing Utopia, Family Imagines No Possessions," *NYT*, May 17, 2008 (one carton); and Web sites to assist in simpler living, such as http://www.simpleliving.org/ and http://www.newdream.org.

67. Schama, "Perishable Commodities." American portraits: Jaffee, "The Ebenezers Devotion"; Lovell, "Copley"; and Smithsonian Portrait Gallery, "Eye Contact: Modern American Portraits," http://www.npg.si.edu/cexh/eye/index.html (accessed Feb. 6, 2004). Craven, "The Development," 259–61. I conducted a mini-study of modern portrait photography. Using the Google search engine, I took one top-listed photographer from ten different metropolitan areas and examined the portfolios each displayed on his or her Web site. Occasionally, a family posed in front of a marble staircase or on a yacht, but overwhelmingly the subjects posed in nature scenes or in front of studio backdrops. They dressed casually and were shown smiling or laughing. The message was: we are a loving and fun-loving family. Halle, "The Family Photograph," draws similar conclusions.

68. Howells: Bronner, "Reading Consumption," 14–15. Money in literature: W. Griswold, "American Character," 756.

69. E.g., Bushman, *The Refinement of America*; Clifford, *The American Family Home*; Handlin, *The American Home*; Volz, "The Modern Look"; and Grier, "The Decline." Merish: "'The Hand'" ("civilizing," 489); idem, "Sentimental Consumption." Immigrant aspirants' furnishings: Heinze, *Adapting to Abundance*, ch. 6.

70. D. Cohen, "The Murder of Maria Bickford," says that murder stories before this period rarely discussed possessions. In the same era, a domestic murder case revolved around the relative virtues of the husband and the deceased wife. One witness impugned the husband by testifying that his wife "had two chemises and one dress. I would not give 50 cents for all her clothing" (S. Moore, "'Justifiable Homicide'").

71. Colonial-era advice, which I discuss in chapter 6, more commonly pushed readers to appear more elite than they were. Women authors: M. Kelley, "The Sentimentalists"; although see Merish, "Sentimental Consumption." Anti-consumption: Shi, *The Simple Life*. Middle-class movements: L. Cohen, *A Consumer's Republic*; McGovern, "Consumption and Citizenship." Kline, *Consumers in the Country*, however, describes government encouragement to buy appliances. Consumers Union, *CU Buying Guide 1937*, 24.

72. Children: P. Stearns, "Consumerism and Childhood"; idem, *American Cool*, ch. 7; idem, *Anxious Parents*; Matt, "Children's Envy"; Cross, *Kids' Stuff*, ch. 8; and Pugh, *Longing and Belonging*. Cross, *The Cute and the Cool* writes that "ads told adults what they wanted to hear—that if children with their 'natural' needs wanted something, then adults had the right to indulge them" (80). Children want too much: 90 percent agreed (Wuthnow, "A Good Life," 5; Mellissa Walker, "Narrative Themes"). Not necessarily their own: 60 percent of parents of children aged ten or older in 2002 said that their child never "spends too much money shopping" (the iPOLL Databank, The Roper Center for Public Opinion Research, http://www.ropercenter.uconn.edu/ipoll.html; accessed Aug. 1, 2007).

73. Rehn and Sköld, "'I Love The Dough'"; S. Lee, "Prosperity Theology."

74. Sermons: Boyer and Nissenbaum, *Salem Possessed*, read the minister's sermons

denouncing money in the second way, as revealing worries about his salary. Puritan village conflicts: see chapter 4.

75. Robert Wuthnow sees the materialism complaint about others as a language for saying that something has gone wrong in America. "It symbolizes impending corruption in our values . . . thinking about our self-interest too much" (*Poor Richard's Almanac*, 275). Studying materialism as a psychological construct: Mannion and Brannick, "Materialism"; Ger and Belk, "Cross-Cultural Differences"; Richins, "The Material Values Scale"; and Kasser and Kanner, *Psychology and Consumer Culture*. One poll asked, from 1975 through 1990, "What comes closest to expressing your personal idea of success?" In 1990, 13 percent said "being wealthy" (up from 6 percent in 1975) while about 40 percent gave answers such as being a good husband or father, being true to God, and being true to yourself (Ladd and Bauman, *Attitudes Toward Economic Inequality*, 51; a 2008 survey: Morin, "Who Wants to Be Rich?"). A 1990s poll asked people to rate things that "would make them more satisfied with their lives." Half or more rated items such as "spend more time with my family and friends" and "do more to make difference in my community" highly, while about one-fifth or fewer picked items such as "nicer car, bigger house, or more nice things" ("Thinking about Values," *The Public Perspective*, Feb.–Mar. 1997, 13).

76. Seniors: Ovadia, "Suggestions"; Rahn and Transude, "Social Trust"; and Easterlin and Crimmins, "Changes." Trzesniewski and Donnellan, "Rethinking 'Generation Me,'" see a weaker, more ambivalent trend. (Note that seniors also gave increasing emphasis to living near their families and being leaders in their communities.) The college freshman studies are from UCLA's Higher Education Research Institute, specifically Hurtado and Pryor, "Looking at the Past." In the early 1970s, 37 percent rated being financially well-off highly; from the early 1990s though 2006, about 73 percent did. In 1971, 50 percent said they were attending college "to be able to make more money"; 75 percent did in 1991; and 69 percent did in 2006 (Astin, "The Changing"; Hurtado and Prior, "Looking at the Past"; and Dey et al., *The American Freshman*). Undergraduate business majors rose from under 15 percent in the 1960s to almost 25 percent in 1990, and settled at 22 percent in 2005. (1960 data: Charlene Hoffman, National Center for Educational Statistics, Jul. 15, 1998; 1970: National Center for Educational Statistics, "The Condition of Education 2000–2002," table 36–2, http://nces.ed.gov, accessed Jul. 17, 2003; 1980–2005: idem, Digest of Education Statistics, 2007, table 28–1, http://nces.ed.gov/, accessed Jul. 30, 2007.) Paul DiMaggio suggests that the increase in business majors may have been an artifact, the result of enrollment shifts to public and community colleges in that era (pers. comm., Nov. 13, 2008). Good life surveys: Roper Reports 03–1, courtesy of courtesy of Paul Abbate and Jon Stiles, Sept. 13, 2004. See also the trend on "What comes closest to expressing your personal idea of success?" cited in the previous note.

77. Economic insecurity: on most indicators, the high point of financial answers was around the early 1990s. Levy, *Dollars and Dreams*, documents the economic struggle of reaching adulthood in those years. See also Easterlin and Crimmins, "American Youth," and subsequent comments from and rejoinders to Ronald Inglehart. Rahn and Transude, "Social Trust," disagree with this interpretation. (See also Conrad,

"Where Have All") An economic insecurity explanation cannot easily account for the increase in the percentage of Americans who rated vacation homes and swimming pools as part of the "good life." The special '60s: The college freshman data suggest a slight decline in financial success answers during the 1960s and majoring in the liberal arts rose during the 1960s. See also the study showing that Dartmouth and University of Michigan students placed less emphasis on careers and more on leisure and religion from the 1950s into the 1960s (Hoge and Hoge, "The Return of the Fifties?" table 1).

78. Zelizer, "Culture and Consumption," 349.

79. Wuthnow, *Poor Richard's Almanac*. The political ascendance of market ideology starting in 1980 is part of this story. The influential "Law and Economics" movement, the work of Gary Becker on marriage, and the best-selling book *Freakonomics*, coauthored by economist Steven Levitt, illustrate how analysts turned economics' lenses on many topics originally outside the field's domain, to topics such as family life, crime, and friendship. One manifestation may be the possibility that teaching students economics makes them more self-interested (see debate on this in the 1996 *Journal of Economic Perspectives*, vol. 1).

80. Economists' notions of "loss aversion" and the "endowment effect" suggest that people may overestimate the value of what they have (compared to what they could have). Three tons: see note 1.

81. Rainwater, *What Money Buys*.

Chapter Four

1. Rogers, "The Women's Club Movement," 348.

2. Winthrop, *A Modell of Christian Charity*, 47–48 (spelling modernized); Emerson, "Self-Reliance," 31. See also Cayton, *Emerson's Emergence*, ch. 9.

3. Court: Glendon, *Rights Talk*, 163. Survey: Veroff et al., *Inner American* (results, 169, question, 566).

4. Wolfe, *One Nation, After All*, ch. 7; Wuthnow, *American Mythos*; and Madsen, "Contentless Consensus." Bellah et al., *Habits of the Heart*, is a classic treatment of how Americans explain themselves to themselves.

5. Ferrall, *A Ramble of Six Thousand Miles*, ch. 4.

6. Individualism: in 2004, the Library of Congress listed over 850 English-language books with the keyword "individualism." About 4,000 sociology and political science articles since 1960 deal with "individualism" (according to a search on J-Stor; http://www.jstor.org). Anthropological studies have generally agreed that there is a "distinctively American individualism" like that I describe (Moffatt, "Ethnographic Writing," 215; see also Spindler and Spindler, "Anthropologists View"). Psychologists' cross-cultural studies point—albeit with many complexities and qualifications— to the same conclusion (Oyserman et al., "Rethinking Individualism"; Shweder and Bourne, "Does the Concept?"). A sample of works that explore American individualism: Abercrombie et al., *Sovereign Individuals of Capitalism;* Arieli, *Individualism and Nationalism in American Ideology*; Bellah et al., *Habits of the Heart*; Bellah, "Is

There a Common?"; J. Block, *A Nation of Agents*; Curry and Goodheart, "Individualism"; Gans, *Middle-Class Individualism*; Hoover, *American Individualism*; Lukes, "The Meanings"; Pole, *American Individualism and the Promise of Progress*; Shalhope, "Individualism"; Swart, "'Individualism'"; Swidler, "Cultural Constructions"; Thomson, *In Conflict No Longer*; Tocqueville, *Democracy in America*; and Wolfson, "Individualism." On the other hand, the various dimensions of individualism do not necessarily cohere as a package—see Halman, "Individualism?" and C. Fischer, "Just How Is It?" My approach is outlined in C. Fischer, "Paradoxes of American Individualism."

Americans' engagement: e.g., Curtis et al., "Voluntary Association Membership"; idem, "Affiliating." Hollinger and Haller, "Kinship," report Americans to be somewhat less involved with kin but somewhat more involved with friends than Europeans (cf. Bruckner and Knaup, "Networks"; Farkas and Hogan, "The Demography"). Loyalty: surveys such as the World Values Survey and the International Social Survey Programme show that Americans are as or more likely to endorse family duties (e.g., rejecting divorce), religious commitments (e.g., attending church), loyalty to an employer, and patriotism than other Westerners (C. Fischer, "Paradoxes of American Individualism"; idem, "Just How Is It?").

7. See Blum, "The European Village"; M. Bloch, *French Rural History*; Heberle, "The Normative Element"; M. Walker, *German Home Towns*; Fleming, *Villagers and Strangers*; and S. Freeman, *Neighbors*. On suspiciousness, see also Wylie, *Village in the Vaucluse*; Foster, "Interpersonal Relations"; O. Lewis, "Further Observations"; and Banfield, *Moral Basis of a Backward Society*. Organic or "corporate" community vs. communal relations: Fischer et al., *Networks and Places*, 7–12. Germans: Joas, "Communitarianism." Southeast Asia: The Coalition Against [Indian] Communalism, http://cac.ektaonline.org/ (accessed Jan. 5, 2005).

8. Swidler, "Cultural Constructions." D. H. Fischer describes the "principle of voluntary action" as the distinctive feature of American culture and subsumes within it individualism, democracy, pluralism, capitalism, and libertarianism (*Albion's Seed*, 3). See also Breen, "Persistent Localism"; Varenne, *Americans Together*; D. Howe, *Making the American Self*; and Perry, "The American Cast." Oyserman et al., "Rethinking Individualism," summarize from the psychological literature: "Americans do feel obligated to family, often as strongly as others do, though they view these obligations as voluntary. . . . Empirical literature . . . found that Americans interacted with more groups, felt they could choose their groups more freely, and were more at ease with strangers than others"; and "Americans are individualists as defined by their responses to [psychological measures] . . . but it is equally clear that Americans are relational and feel close to group members, seeking their advice" (40, 45).

9. Emerson, "Self-Reliance." Thoreau, "Civil Disobedience," part 1, paragraph 13.

10. Protestantism: Max Weber was also struck by the connection to Protestant sects (Kalberg, "Max Weber's Analysis"). Traditional song, "Lonesome Valley." J. Block, *A Nation of Agents*, 277. Private neighborhoods: Blakely and Snyder, *Fortress America*; Barton and Silverman, *Common Interest Communities*. Marriage: ca. 2000, 93 percent of teenagers said they wanted to marry and 91 percent of those said they would like to have children (Gallup poll, Lyons, "Kids and Divorce"). Marriage

"work": see rise of "companionate" marriages in Mintz and Kellogg, *Domestic Revolutions*, and interviews in Swidler, *Talk of Love*. My general argument is indebted, in part, to Swidler, "Cultural Constructions"; Zuckerman, "The Fabrication of Identity"; J. Block's *A Nation of Agents*.

11. Anthropologist Hervé Varenne, in "Is Dedham American?" also invokes the "love it or leave it" principle (235). Marriage attitudes: Thornton, "Changing Attitudes"; C. Fischer, "Just How Is It?"; and Swidler, *Talk of Love*. Religious switching: Roof and McKinney, *American Mainline Religion*, 177–81; Hoge et al., "Types." Local activists: Madsen, "Contentless Consensus," 450–51. Conformity: Lipset, *First New Nation*, 107ff, states that many nineteenth- and twentieth-century foreign commentators on the United States described Americans as very concerned about "opinion." The conformity, Lipset argues, is part of American egalitarianism. Themes of covenant and contract wind through much of American history: The dissident sects, like Winthrop's Puritans, formed voluntary compacts among themselves and a covenant with God. Many other European settlers came as contractually bound servants. Rebellious colonists organized as committees and declared compacts. Sociologist Robert Bellah, in particular, has noted in *The Broken Covenant*, ch. 1, the uneasy tension between the American covenant as one based on "civic virtue" (the common good) versus one based on utilitarian values (the greatest individual returns for the greatest number). What is more striking than the ideological tensions is how conditions necessitated compacts—practical contracts and, in some cases, more elevated covenants.

12. Tocqueville, *Democracy in America*, 508. Heresy: Woodward, *The Old World's New World*, 107. Cmiel, *Democratic Eloquence*, 56–57, 69, traces how American language, including terms of address, was democratized. Huston, *Securing the Fruits of Labor*, locates both individualism and egalitarianism in work and the popular labor theory of value. But egalitarian ideology applies to much more—to religious and political standing, and to "respect." G. Wood, *The Creation of the American Republic*, explores the tension between equality of opportunity and of outcome, quoting Thomas Shippen, an acquaintance of Jefferson, on "capacity, disposition" (emphasis added, 72; see also 70–75). See also Pole, "Equality"; Hemphill, "The Middle Class Rising"; Swart, "'Individualism'"; G. Wood, *The American Revolution*, 50ff; and Foner, *The Story of Freedom*.

13. Thomson, *In Conflict No Longer*, has argued that from the 1920s through the 1950s, American writers described individuals' struggles to defend their unique selves *against* society and after the 1950s described individuals developing their uniqueness *through* communities. Thomson might consider this chapter as reflective of the second trend, but this voluntarism is deeply, historically rooted.

14. Wuthnow, *Sharing the Journey*, 6. "Escape": The phrase is Erich Fromm's, *Escape from Freedom*. New groups: Davidman, *Tradition in a Rootless World*; Kaufman, *Rachel's Daughters*; and Ault, *Spirit and Flesh*. Some more extreme groups, often labeled "cults," try to sever all outside connections of and possible exits for members.

15. Overviews of the debate: Appleby, "The Vexed Story of Capitalism"; G. Wood, "The Enemy is Us"; Feller, "The Market Revolution"; and in the popular press,

G. Wood, "Inventing American Capitalism"; and Jill Lepore, "Vast Designs," *New Yorker*, Oct. 29, 2007, 88–92. An important sample of the debate: Henretta, "Families and Farms"; idem, "Reply"; Lemon, "Comment." Surely oversimplifying, these works frame the debate: Claiming early liberalism: Innes, *Labor in a New Land*; Greene, *Pursuits of Happiness*; idem, *The Intellectual Construction of America*; Rothenberg, *From Market-Places to Market Economy*; D. Fischer, *Albion's Seed*; Lemon, "Spatial Order"; idem, *The Best Poor Man's Country*; S. Wolf, *Urban Village*; idem, *As Various as Their Land*; Blumin, *The Urban Threshold*; Bushman, "Markets and Composite Farms"; and Greenstone, "Political Culture." Claiming later liberalism: Sellers, *The Market Revolution*; Shain, *The Myth of American Individualism*; Henretta, "The Slow Triumph"; idem, *The Origins of American Capitalism*; Wilentz, "Society, Politics"; Lockridge, *A New England Town* (cf. the afterword in the 1985 edition); Wall, *Fierce Communion*; Bushman, *From Puritan to Yankee*; Shalhope, "Individualism"; and Countryman, "American Liberalism."

16. Engels: P. Wagner, "The Resistance," 38. On who came: Fogleman, "From Slaves," 44, table 1; Bailyn, *Voyagers to the West*, 166–89, table 5.6; Kulikoff, *From British Peasants to Colonial American Farmers*, 194ff (70 percent, 127). Greene, *The Intellectual Construction of America*, discusses the enticements to immigrate. Turnover: J. Potter, "Demographic Development." Studies showing early American settlements as *not* being tight, corporate communities include Zuckerman, *Friends and Neighbors*; S. Wolf, *Urban Village*; idem, *As Various as Their Land*; Innes, *Labor in a New Land*; Hine, *Community on the American Frontier*; Lemon, *The Best Poor Man's Country*; Rutman and Rutman, *A Place in Time*; Blumin, *The Urban Threshold*; and L. Becker, "Diversity."

17. Rutman, "Community," 294, 301. New England: Ulrich, *A Midwife's Tale*, 81, 87; see also Ulrich, *Good Wives*, esp. ch. 2–3. New Hampshire: Thompson, "The Life Course." Hudson Valley: Bruegel, "The Social Relations" (Holcombe, 543). See also Lamoreaux, "Rethinking the Transition" and citations in previous note. To see what "duty" looks like even in a post-feudal society, see Collier, *From Duty to Desire*.

18. Andover: Greven, *Four Generations*, 91ff (Lovejoy quotation, 95). Note, too, the common practice of "binding out" one's children as servants.

19. Tocqueville, *Democracy in America*, 506–8; see also Pole, *American Individualism*, 9. This capsule summary blends over 150 years of tumultuous history. Still the literature indicates that, while a liberal culture became more explicit from the seventeenth to the late eighteenth century, it was present early on: Foner, "The Meaning of Freedom" and *The Story of American Freedom*; Wiebe, *Self-Rule*; Furstenberg, "Beyond Freedom"; Huston, *Securing the Fruits of Labor*; Arieli, *Individualism and Nationalism in American Ideology*; Curry and Valois, "The Emergence of an Individualistic Ethos"; Shalhope, "Individualism"; Henretta, "The Slow Triumph"; and R. Welter, *The Mind of America*. On Protestantism's connection to individualism, see esp. J. Block, *A Nation of Agents*. See also Bellah, "The Protestant Structure"; Seligman, *Modernity's Wager*, ch. 4; Witten, *All is Forgiven*; Marty, *Pilgrims in Their Own Land*; and MacCulloch, *The Reformation*. Political thought: Greene, *Pursuits of Happiness*, ch. 8; idem, *The Intellectual Construction of America*, ch. 3; Foner, *Story of American Freedom*,

ch. 2; Furstenberg, "Beyond Freedom"; Kulikoff, *From British Peasants to Colonial American Farmers*, 125–27; and D. Fischer, *Albion's Seed*, 410–18.

Shain, *The Myth of Individualism*, argues the other side, that "Americans were able to realize traditional European communal ideals in their locally autonomous, consensual, and unusually democratic peasantlike villages" (63), but is ultimately unpersuasive, especially in applying the term, "peasantlike." Rural sociologist Kenneth Wilkinson, "Rural Community Change," seems more accurate: "Save among isolated . . . enclaves, . . . the European tradition of *gemeinschaft* has never fitted American communities. The time since settlement has been too short and the structural conditions were there too briefly to support . . . the development of sacred bases of solidarity apparently necessary for *gemeinschaft*" (118–19).

20. "Monopoly": Bowden, "The Invention" (also Lears, "Intellectuals," 2452). "Sane": Edmund Morgan, cited in Butler, *Awash in a Sea of Faith*, 317. On atypicality: Greene, *Pursuits of Happiness*; Zuckerman, *Friends and Neighbors*; and Kammen, *Mystic Chords of Memory*. A sample of studies on colonial New England towns: Bissel, "Family, Friends, and Neighbors"; Boyer and Nissenbaum, *Salem Possessed*; Bushman, *From Puritan to Yankee*; Demos, *A Little Commonwealth*; Greven, *Four Generations*; Gross, *The Minutemen and Their World*; Innes, *Labor in a New Land*; Lockridge, *A New England Town*; Melvoin, "Communalism"; Rutman, *Winthrop's Boston*; and Zuckerman, *Peaceable Kingdoms*.

21. Mather: R. Thompson, "'Holy Watchfulness,'" 521. State support: e.g., Holifield, "Peace"; Melvoin, "Communalism." Windsor: Bissel, "Family," ch. 7. Execution: Marty, *Pilgrims in Their Own Land*, 61, 86. Social control: Kamensky, *Governing the Tongue*; Ulrich, *Good Wives*, ch. 3 (on gossip); D. Fischer, *Albion's Seed*, 199–205 (on "ordered liberty"). Colonial authorities in later years forced more religious tolerance onto Massachusetts (Breen and Foster, "The Puritans' Greatest Achievement").

22. Marriages: e.g., Wall, *Fierce Communion*. Fool: Innes, *Labor in a New Land*, 123. Children: Kamensky, *Governing the Tongue*, 102ff; also Demos, *Little Commonwealth*. Agenda: Greene, *Pursuits of Happiness*, 37. "Totalitarian": Zuckerman, *Peaceable Kingdoms*, 6. Godbeer, *Sexual Revolution in Early America*, reviews some of the gaps between principle and practice. More positive interpretations of Puritan communities include Shain, *The Myth of American Individualism*, and R. Brown, *Modernization*.

23. Puritan vs. peasant communities: Lemon, "Spatial Order," 95, and Bender, *Community and Social Change in America*, who states that the former were "socially constructed and not the precipitate of tradition . . . the product of decision rather than peasant inertia" (64). Cases that more closely fit the peasant model were Southern plantations and the Hudson Valley estates with tenant farmers (Bruegel, "Unrest"). Theology: P. Miller, *The New England Mind*, ch. 13, 14, explains that New England Puritans escaped one Calvinist conundrum—that predestination leaves people with no reason to be good—by postulating that God agreed to "yoke Himself" in a covenant with Man and there is thus a quid pro quo for salvation. The corresponding social philosophy is a social contract between ruled and ruler. Miller notes that this contractualism contradicted Winthrop's call for organic wholeness; the two themes coexisted in tension. Free will: Breen and Foster, "The Puritans' Greatest Achieve-

ment," note: "The Massachusetts Puritans organized churches, towns, indeed, the entire commonwealth upon the contractual model" (12). On Puritan economic inequality, see, e.g., Staloff, "'Where Religion and Profit.'"

Lockridge defended the "peasant" label in *A New England Town*, his study of Dedham, Massachusetts (further discussed on p. 106). See also Shain, *The Myth of American Individualism*, for application of the peasant analogy. By the simplest definition of peasantry—"small agricultural producers who labor mostly for their own consumption" (S. Frank, "Peasantry," 555)—Dedham and other places qualify, but so would independent yeoman farmers in isolated homesteads on the American plains. A more distinctive definition of peasantry, including "their domination by powerful outsiders . . . [as] exploited subordinates" (ibid.), would *not* cover Dedham and its sister towns. Cultural features usually attributed to typical peasantry, such as being tradition-bound and serving as vassals, are hard to apply to the Puritans. The "peasant" label seems more a metaphor than a scientific classification. In the afterword to the 1985 edition of his book, Lockridge makes no reference to peasantry, writing instead about "localism."

24. Lockridge, *A New England Town* (quotations, 64, 15).

25. Slander and lawsuits: e.g., R. Thompson, "'Holy Watchfulness.'" Boyer and Nissenbaum, *Salem Possessed*, describe lines of division between the circle of accusers and that of the accused which roughly matched those between adherents to early subsistence economy and those engaged in commerce—between the old Puritans and the new liberals (see also Latner, "The Long and Short"; and special July 2008 issue of *William and Mary Quarterly* on *Salem Possessed* introduced by Kamensky, "Salem Obsessed"). Concord: Gross, *Minutemen*. The story of increasing division is generally labeled the "declension" of New England Puritanism and recounted by Lockridge, *A New England Town* (although Lockridge later denied that his is a story of declension); Greven, *Four Generations;* Bushman, *From Puritan to Yankee;* Zuckerman, *Peaceable Kingdoms;* Conroy, *In Public Houses;* and Drink and Lacey, "Gender." See also Breen and Foster, "The Puritans'"; D. Smith, "Parental Power"; idem, "All in Some Degree"; Cott, "Divorce"; Innes, *Labor in a New Land;* Pruitt, "Self-Sufficiency"; debate in *William and Mary Quarterly*, Oct. 1985, 553–63. Standards for membership: because younger generations were not having conversion experiences, the Massachusetts churches agreed in 1662 to the "halfway covenant," awarding partial memberships to youth who had been baptized. Tolerance: Kamensky, *Governing the Tongue*, 184ff. "Congregations were on their way": Holifield, "Peace," 569. New Englanders as individualists: e.g., Lemon, "Spatial Order"; Innes, *Labor in a New Land*. Indeed, other Americans tended to view Yankees as shrewd self-aggrandizers (Pedersen, *Between Memory and Reality*, ch. 2; Sellers, *Market Revolution*, ch. 12).

26. Atypicality: D. Fischer, *Albion's Seed*, 184–86. Historians have described New England as also economically backward, but that is challenged by G. Main and Main, "The Red Queen?"; Brooke, Review of *Innerworldly Individualism*, 556. Michael Zuckerman, *Friends and Neighbors*, notes that New England provides "our preeminent—almost our only—account of Western modernization. . . . [But] of all the colonial regions, only New England began with a measure of medieval community from which

departures could be calculated" (7). Greene and Pole, "Reconstructing," state that "it has become powerfully obvious that [the decline of community model] fundamentally distorts the experiences of all colonies outside New England" (11). See also, e.g., Innes, *Labor in a New Land*, esp. the epilogue; Conzen, "Community Studies," 128; S. Wolf, *Urban Village*, 155–59; idem, *As Various as Their Land*, ch. 7; Hawke, *Everyday Life*, 20ff; Nash, "Social Development"; P. Williams, "New England"; and the exchange between James Lemon and Betty Pruitt in "Communications," *William and Mary Quarterly*, 3rd Ser., 42 (Oct., 1985), 553–63. Lockridge, in the afterword to *A New England Town*, later noted that covenanted communities were not common even in New England. Also, dispersed settlements were more common than concentrated Puritan villages even in New England (J. Wood, "Village and Community").

27. Views south of New England include Greene, *Pursuits of Happiness* (who explicitly contrasts ascent to order there with the Puritan descent); Rutman and Rutman, *A Place in Time* (Virginia church estimate, 125); Lemon, *The Best Poor Man's Country*; idem, "Spatial Order"; Nash, "Social Development"; S. Wolf, *Urban Village*; idem, *As Various as Their Land*; Zuckerman, *Friends and Neighbors*; D. Fischer, *Albion's Seed*; and Greene and Pole, *Colonial British America*. Moravian: Shirley, "The Market." Southern marriage: Godbeer, *Sexual Revolution*, ch. 4; Carr and Walsh, "The Planter's Wife." "More than ever": Marty, *Pilgrims in Their Own Land*, 108.

28. Isolated: Noble, "Backcountry"; Melvoin, "Communalism"; and Breen, "Persistent Localism." Congealed: Greene, *Pursuits of Happiness*; Rutman and Rutman, *A Place in Time*; Lemon, "Spatial Order"; Nash, "Social Development"; and Shammas, *A History of Household Governance*.

29. "Morally intrusive:" Shain, *Myth of Individualism*, 73. Virginia: Hawke, *Everyday Life*, 99. On talk, see also Kamensky, *Governing the Tongue*; Wall, *Fierce Communion*. Sumptuary: e.g., Shammas, *The Pre-Industrial Consumer*, 218–19. Example of exiling: Herndon, "Women." Slavery: Berlin, *Many Thousands Gone*; Fredrickson, *White Supremacy*.

30. Churches outside New England: see Jon Butler's work: *Awash in a Sea of Faith*; "Magic"; *Becoming American*, ch. 5; and "Religion" (one in seven baptized, 66). See also Marty, *Pilgrims in Their Own Land*; C. Cohen, "The Post-Puritan Paradigm"; Lemon, *The Best Poor Man's Country*; and Rutman and Rutman, *A Place in Time*. About half of the households in Germantown, Pennsylvania were nonattendees as late as 1770–1800 (S. Wolf, *Urban Village*, 215–16).

31. Shammas, *A History of Household Governance*; Kulikoff, *From British Peasants*, 231ff; Mintz, *Huck's Raft*, ch. 1–2; Wall, *Fierce Communion*, ch. 3; D. Fischer, *Albion's Seed*, 677–80; G. Main, *Peoples of Spacious Land*, 74–94. Greven, *Four Generations*, ch. 4 (age at marriage, 37). Quakers: Levy, "The Birth"; D. Fischer, *Albion's Seed*, 481–85. Child rearing: Hessinger, "Problems"; Lystad, *At Home in America*; and Lewis, "Mother Love." Leasing out children: e.g., Demos, *Little Commonwealth*, 113.

32. Hiltzheimer, *Extracts from the Diary of Jacob Hiltzheimer of Philadelphia*, 88–99. (Parsons, Hiltzheimer's nineteenth-century descendant and editor, fails to include Rosina in the diary's index, although he does include "Roger, prize ox.")

33. Ulrich, *A Midwife's Tale*, 8.

34. Adams: Foner, *The Story of American Freedom*, 16. Delaware: Zuckerman, "Tocqueville, Turner, and Turds" (see also comments following that article in June, 1998 issue of the *Journal of American History*). Mister: G. Wood, *The American Revolution*, 120. See also McDonnell, "Popular Mobilization"; Appleby, *Inheriting the Revolution*, ch. 5; Shalhope, "Individualism"; and Hemphill, "The Middle Class Rising."

35. Norton, "The Evolution"; Cott, "Divorce"; Riley, *Divorce*; Basch, *Framing American Divorce* (Paine, ch. 1); M. Smith, *Breaking the Bonds*; Rothman, "Sex and Self-Control"; Sievens, "'The Wicked Agency'"; Mintz and Kellogg, *Domestic Revolutions*, ch. 3; and S. Wolf, *As Various as Their Land*.

36. See previous note and Degler, *At Odds* (quote, 189); R. Bloch, "Changing Conceptions" ("spiritualization," 44); Klepp, "Revolutionary Bodies"; Eustace, *Passion is the Gale*; and Lewis, "The Republican Wife." Shammas, *A History of Household Governance*, ch. 3, dissents and doubts that any serious change in family life occurred this early.

37. Decline in deference: Mintz, *Huck's Raft*, ch. 3 (bowing, 59). Sex and marriage: e.g., D'Emilio and Freedman, *Intimate Matters*; D. Smith, "Parental Power"; Smith and Hindus, "Premarital Pregnancy"; Rothman, "Sex"; Godbeer, *Sexual Revolution*, ch. 7, 9; S. Wolf, *As Various as Their Land* (Philadelphia, 74); Degler, *At Odds* (love, 14); Lantz et al., "Pre-Industrial Patterns"; Demos, *Past, Present, and Personal* (murder, 102); Graff, *Conflicting Paths*; Greven, *Four Generations*; Wall, *Fierce Communion*; Zuckerman, "Tocqueville, Turner, and Turds" (and the comments that follow); Alexander, "Adolescence"; Salinger, "Labor"; and Nash, "Social Evolution." Heaton: Lacey, "The World of Hannah Heaton," 298. Shammas, *A History of Household Governance*, ch. 3, dissents, arguing that colonial fathers never had much control over marriages, for example. Slavery: Rutman and Rutman, *A Place In Time*; Kolchin, *American Slavery*.

38. "Extravagancies": Nobles, "Breaking," 653. "Self-examination": G. Wood, "Religion," 182. "Primacy": Hatch, *Democratization*, 35. Interchangeable: Noll, "The American Revolution," 631. J. Block, *A Nation of Agents*, argues persuasively that the Great Awakening of the midcentury was "the pivotal event in the emergence of a distinctive American culture" (184). On religion in this era, see Butler, "Religion in Colonial America," and other works by Butler cited above in note 30. See also Marty, *Pilgrims in Their Own Land*; Stark and Finke, "American Religion"; Finke, "Religious Deregulation"; Bonomi and Eisenstadt, "Church Adherence"; and case studies such as P. Moore, "Family Dynamics"; S. Wolf, *Urban Village*; Gross, *Minutemen*; Rutman, *Winthrop's Boston*; Rutman and Rutman, *A Place in Time*; and Kling, *A Field of Divine Wonders*. See also earlier citations regarding religion in New England, note 25.

39. Lacey, "The World." Smith: Hatch, *Democratization*, 43.

40. Condemned: D. Cohen, *Pillars of Salt, Monuments of Grace*. "Voluntary societies": Lemon, *The Best Poor Man's Country*, 113. J. Block, *A Nation of Agents*, 192: "The whole society was quickly awash in personal religious choice." See general sources on religion in earlier notes, such as Butler, *Awash in a Sea of Faith*; and Marty, *Pilgrims in Their Own Land*.

41. New England's "declension" is discussed in note 25 above. See also Greene, *Pursuits of Happiness*; Wall's afterword in *Fierce Communion*; and Godbeer, *Sexual Revolu-*

tion (pregnancies and bundling, ch. 7). Crime: S. Wolf, *As Various as Their Land*, 253. Politics: Nash, "The Transformation"; Beeman, "Deference, Republicanism"; B. C. Smith, "Beyond the Vote"; P. Thompson, *Rum, Punch & Revolution*; and discussion in the next chapter.

42. G. Wood, *The American Revolution*, 131. Washington: D. Fischer, *Washington's Crossing*, 20–24.

43. Social contexts and social networks: C. Fischer, *To Dwell among Friends*; Feld, "The Focused Organization."

44. "Few topics": McWilliams, "Marketing," 162. Overviews of the changes: Mintz and Kellogg, *Domestic Revolutions*; Coontz, *The Social Origins of Private Life*; and Degler, *At Odds*. Advice giver: J. Lewis, "Mother's Love," 14. Prescott, "'Why She Didn't Marry Him,'" illustrates the model's eventual spread westward. Demographic changes: the average size of (nonslave) households in 1790 was 5.8 and was 4.8 in 1900; broader declines came later (Kobrin, "The Fall"; R. Wells, *Revolutions in Americans' Lives*; idem, *Uncle Sam's Family*; Seward, *The American Family*; and Nugent, *Structures of American Social History*). Between 1850 and 1900, the number of non-relatives in American households dropped by about a quarter, of siblings by about a third, of distant relatives by about 40 percent, and of children by nearly one-fifth—from an average of 2.8 to about 2.2 (calculated using Carter et al., *Historical Statistics of the United States*, table Ae320–480). In contrast, households with a grandparent actually increased, because age at marriage dropped, the elderly lived longer, and middle-class families could better afford to take them in (Ruggles, *Prolonged Connections*; idem, "Multigenerational Families"). "Quality": Parkerson and Parkerson "'Fewer Children'"; D. Smith, "'The Number and Quality of Children.'"

45. "The Domestic Sphere," *NYT*, Jun. 12, 1870. White: Letter of Rhoda E. White, Dec. 15, 1860, Abraham Lincoln Papers, Library of Congress, http://memory.loc.gov/ammem/alhtml/malhome.html (accessed Dec. 24, 2008; original emphasis).

46. Gjerede, *The Minds of the Midwest*.

47. The "separate spheres" description of nineteenth-century family life is controversial. B. Welter, "The Cult of True Womanhood," is a key text, while M. Kelley, "Beyond the Boundaries," illustrates the criticisms. Buhle, "Feminist Approaches," gives a good overview. See also Kerber, "Separate Spheres"; Ryan, *The Cradle of the Middle-Class*; J. Lewis, "The Republican Wife"; and idem, "Mother's Love." In the end, the thesis that a special and increasingly "naturalized" domestic role for women grew over the century is roughly accurate. Employment: United States Bureau of the Census, *Historical Statistics*, table D-152. Demographic changes: e.g., R. Wells, *Revolution in Americans' Lives*; Nugent, *Structures of American Social History*; D. Smith, "'Early' Fertility Decline"; Watkins et al., "Demographic Foundations"; Ruggles, "Multigenerational Families"; and sources cited in note 44 above. Work-home separation: Blumin, *The Emergence of the Middle Class*; Matthaei, *An Economic History of Women in America*, ch. 5; Jackson, *Crabgrass Frontier*; and Binford, *The First Suburbs*. Housing and private space: C. Clark, *The American Family Home*; Marsh, "From Separation"; Wall, *Fierce Communion*, 144ff; Coontz, *The Social Origins of Private Life*; and J. Gillis, *A World of Their Own Making* (although he focuses on the postbellum era). "For the sake": Mintz and Kellogg, *Domestic Revolutions*, 45.

48. Duffield, "An Iowa Settler's Homestead." Cummings: Marsh, "Suburban Men," 173–74. See also, e.g., Prescott, "'Why She Didn't Marry Him.'"

49. H. Green, *Light of the Home*, gives details; see also Matthews, *"Just a Housewife."* Ryan's *Cradle of the Middle Class* describes the child-forming duties; J. Lewis, "Mother's Love," and Dye and Smith, "Mother Love," outline the emotional tasks. Women's activism: A. Scott, "On Seeing"; Varon, "Tippecanoe"; Baker, *The Moral Frameworks of Public Life*, ch. 3; and Ryan, *Cradle of the Middle Class*, ch. 3. Shammas, *A History of Household Governance*, and Demos, "The Changing Faces," among many others, review the decline of men's authority. D. Howe, *What Hath God Wrought*, summarizes the antebellum household: "The man was 'head of the house' by both law and custom, and he could exploit the labor of the other family members, as his predecessors had done for centuries. Yet in practice, the other members of the household enjoyed increasing autonomy in white America" (36). Visitors: Woodward, *The Old World's New World*.

50. Cott, "Passionlessness," argues that the angelic image of women empowered them. See also M. Smith, *Breaking the Bonds*, 83ff. Births: the emerging consensus is that the nineteenth-century drop in fertility was not simply a response to economic modernization, but preceded it, and that shifts in cultural attitudes, including a greater voice for wives, best accounts for it. See R. Wells, *Revolution in American Lives*; contributions in Vinovskis, *Studies in Historical Demography;* Klepp, "Revolutionary Bodies"; D. Smith, "'The Number and Quality of Children'"; Parkerson and Parkerson, "'Fewer Children'"; Haines and Guest, "Fertility in New York State"; and overviews by Hirschman, "Why Fertility Changes," and Juster and Vinovskis, "Changing Perspectives."

51. Lincoln: McDermott, "Love and Justice." General histories: Cott, *Family Vows*; Shammas, *A History of Household Governance*; Griswold, "Law, Sex"; Riley, *Divorce*; Basch, *Framing American Divorce*; Hartog, *Man and Wife in America*; Friedman, *Law in America*, ch. 4; and Degler, *At Odds*, 166ff (Anthony and Harper, 332). Emotional grounds for divorce: J. Gillis, *A World of Their Own Making*, ch. 7; Mintz and Kellogg, *Domestic Revolutions*, ch. 3; and Stearns and Stearns, *Anger*.

52. Histories of marriage and the family generally describe the elevation of love: Degler, *At Odds*; Cott, *Public Vows*, ch. 6; J. Gillis, *A World of Their Own Making*, ch. 4 (on weddings, ch. 7); and Coontz, *Marriage: A History*. Divorce complaints: R. Griswold, "Law, Sex"; Basch, *Framing American Divorce*; Riley, *Divorce*; Prescott, "'Why She Didn't Marry Him.'" Nineteenth century marital love: Lystra, *Searching the Heart*; Rothman, "Sex"; and D'Emilio and Freedman, *Intimate Matters*. Cleric's complaint: Appleby, *Inheriting the Revolution*, 178 (ch. 6 more generally). Loveless: Gjerde, *The Minds of the West*, ch. 6.

53. Women without a "separate sphere": Osterund, *Bonds of Community*; Hansen, *A Very Social Time*; Gjerde, *The Minds of the West*; Boydston, "The Woman"; and Schwartzberg, "'Lots of Them Did That.'" See also notes 51 and 52 on marriage and divorce. Poem from McMurry, *Families and Farmhouses*, 91. Immigrants: S. Glenn, *Daughters of the Shtetl;* Heinze, *Adapting to Abundance*.

54. Overviews: Mintz, *Huck's Raft*, ch. 4–8; Mintz and Kellogg, *Domestic Revolutions*, ch. 3; Degler, *At Odds*, ch. 5; Kett, "The Stages of Life"; and Vinovskis, "Ameri-

can Families." Specific studies: Ryan, *The Cradle of the Middle Class*; Lystad, *At Home in America*; Rodgers, "Socializing Middle-Class Children"; Bruegel, "The Social Relations"; Nissenbaum, *The Battle for Christmas*, ch. 4. Appleby, *Inheriting the Revolution*, 170–73. Visitor: Woodward, *The Old World's New World*, 128. New England woman: Graff, *Conflicting Paths*, 125.

55. Cuffs and bruises: "The Domestic Sphere," *NYT*, Jun. 12, 1870. Advice books: Hemphill, *Bowing to Necessities*, 66ff. 1816 Advice: "The Brief Remarks," from the *Connecticut Courant*, reprinted in the *Newport Herald*, Feb. 3, 1816, via Early American Newspapers, http://infobank.newsbank.com (original emphasis). Chevalier quoted in F. Furstenberg, "Industrialization," 333. Ryan's *Cradle of the Middle Class* is an essential source.

56. See general sources in note 54. Rothman, "Sex," is one who argues that pregnancy rates responded to inculcated self-control rather than supervision. Child-saving: e.g., Boyer, *Urban Masses and Moral Order*; Mintz, *Huck's Raft*, ch. 4. Pregnancy and marriage: The classic study is Smith and Hindus, "Premarital Pregnancy."

57. Gillespie: Abel, *Hearts of Wisdom*. Havens: See Lasch, *Haven in a Heartless World*. Women's child-centeredness: Hessinger, "Problems." The discussion of psychological attachments is further developed in chapter 6.

58. Disintegration: Shammas, *A History of Household Governance*, xiii. Inheritance and control: e.g., Ruggles, "The Decline." Saloons: Duis, *The Saloon*; Kingsdale, "The 'Poor Man's Club'"; P. Johnson, *A Shopkeeper's Millennium*, ch. 4; Kaplan, "New York City Tavern"; and E. Parsons, "Risky Business" (the saloon-keeper laws). Sex: Degler, *At Odds*, ch. 12; D'Emilio and Freedman, *Intimate Matters*. New family man: Marsh, "Suburban Men"; K. White, "The New Man." Backlash: J. Adler, "'My Mother-in-Law'"; S. Moore, "Justifiable Homicide." Duffield, "An Iowa Settler's Homestead."

59. Transportation: e.g., the price of shipping freight from the American interior to New York City dropped by 95 percent in the first part of the century (G. Taylor, *The Transportation Revolution*; Larson, "Transportation and Mobility"). Communications: R. Brown, *Knowledge is Power*; Pred, *Urban Growth*; John, "Communications"; and D. Howe, *What Hath God Wrought*, ch. 6. Hingham: D. Smith, "Parental Power," 426 (ca. 1850, the rate was 48 percent and ca. 1900 it was 32 percent). Other colonial-era estimates are comparable (Bissel, "Family," table 30; Rutman and Rutman, *A Place in Time*, 12).

60. Market integration: Sellers, *The Market Revolution* (cf. commentary in Stokes and Conway, *The Market Revolution in America*; Ellis et al., "A Symposium on Charles Sellers"); P. Johnson, "The Market Revolution"; Rothenberg, *From Market-Places to a Market Economy*; Dublin, *Transforming Women's Work*; idem, "Rural Putting-Out Work"; and Wallace, *Rockdale*. Bushman, "Markets and Composite Farms," summarizes the literature ca. 1998 and concludes that American farmers were market actors long before this era, albeit they usually reserved some land for basic subsistence.

61. Salem: Shirley, "The Market" (quotations, 245, 244). Similar stories are in Watson, "'The Common Rights'"; Kulik, "Dams."

62. For overviews, see, in addition to the studies cited in note 60, Wilentz, "Society"; Gilje, *Wages of Independence*; Rothenberg, *From Market-Places to a Market Econ-*

omy; Nash, "The Social Evolution"; and Danbom, *Born in the Country*, ch. 4. Case studies: Shirley, "The Market" (shoes, 232); Blumin, *The Urban Threshold*; P. Johnson, *Shopkeepers' Millennium*; Faragher, *Sugar Creek*; Wilentz, *Chants Democratic*; Tangires, *Public Markets and Civic Culture*; Wermuth, "New York Farmers"; and Friend, "Merchants and Markethouses." Changing laws: Horowitz, *The Transformation of American Law*; Bruchey, *Enterprise*; Henretta, "The Slow Triumph"; and Wright, "The First Phase."

63. Migration from crowded and depleted lands: Gross, *Minutemen*; Greven, *Four Generations*. Migration more generally: Larkin, *Reshaping*, 207–8; Friedeburg, "Social and Geographical Mobility"; Hudson, *Plains Country Towns*; D. May, *Three Frontiers*; and Gjerde, *The Mind of the West*. Cities: United States Bureau of the Census, *Historical Statistics*, 12; Nash, *The Urban Crucible*; idem, "The Social Evolution"; and Knights, *Yankee Destinies*. High population turnover is "one of the central findings and now one of the central themes of nineteenth-century social history" (Darroch, "Migrants," 217). Visitors: Woodward, *The Old World's New World*, 71–75. Moving day: Scherzer, *The Unbounded Community*, 20, 234n20. Springfield: Winkle, "The Voters" (only 1 percent of the men who voted in the 1850s voted in every year from 1850 to 1860). Other examples of high turnover: fewer than one in ten men who voted in the election of 1850 in Clinton, Ohio, also voted there in 1860 (Winkle, *The Politics of Community*, ch. 5); only one-third of Jewish immigrants and 8 percent of Italian immigrants in Manhattan in 1880 were there ten years later (Kessner, *The Golden Door*, 142). See also Wallace, *Rockdale*; Gregson, "Population Dynamics"; Doyle, *The Social Order*; D. May, *Three Frontiers*; Thernstrom, *The Other Bostonians*, 225–27; Simmons, "Changing Residence"; Knights, *Plain People of Boston*; Alan Burstein, "Immigrants"; Allen, "Changes." *Long-distance* migration rates may have increased after the nineteenth century as national employment markets grew (Rosenbloom and Sundstrom, "The Decline"), but overall turnover probably declined. Parkenson, "How Mobile?" and Davenport, "Duration," dissent, but recent research sustains the general opinion that mobility declined after the nineteenth century (e.g., Hall and Ruggles, "'Restless'"; Ferrie, "The End?" 212) and clearly during the twentieth century (C. Fischer, "Ever-More Rooted Americans").

64. How minorities of persisters formed the "core communities": Alcorn, "Leadership"; Winkle, *Politics of Community*; and Faragher, *Sugar Creek*.

65. Class diversity: Nash, "The Social Evolution"; Blumin, *The Emergence of the Middle Class*; idem, *The Urban Threshold*; P. Johnson, *A Shopkeeper's Millennium*; S. Warner, *The Private City*; Gilekson, *Middle-Class Providence*; Reid, "The Seeds"; Wilentz, *Chants Democratic*; Story, "Social Class." Kingston: Blumin, *The Urban Threshold*. Detroit: Schneider, *Detroit and the Problem of Order* (quotation, 40). On urban differentiation, see also Nash, *The Urban Crucible*; Chudacoff, *The Age of the Bachelor*, ch. 1; Binford, *The First Suburbs*; Frisch, *Town into City*; Jackson, *Crabgrass Frontier*; Scherzer, *The Unbounded Community*; S. Warner, *Streetcar Suburbs*. For much of the nineteenth century, new suburban towns sought to join cities in order to benefit from infrastructure investments, but they later insisted on staying apart (e.g., Brookline, Massachusetts, see Karr, "Brookline").

66. "Traditional community": R. Brown, *Modernization*, 120. Descriptions of cohesive communities come largely from towns that peaked in the nineteenth century (Barron, *Those Who Stayed Behind*; Pedersen, *Between Memory and Reality*; and Osterud, *Bonds of Community*). On community fragmentation and conflict: C. Wagner, "Town Growth" (Vermont); Gjerde, *The Minds of the West*, ch. 4 (church burning, 111); Reid, "The Seeds"; Boyer, *Urban Masses and Moral Order* (Philadelphia, 69); Ryan, *Civic Wars*; Baker, *Moral Frameworks of Public Life*; Scherzer, *The Unbounded Community*; and Sellers, *The Market Revolution*.

67. Hine, *Community on the American Frontier*; Lingeman, *Small Town America*. A case study of towns as economic speculations: Hudson, *Plains Country Towns*. Hansen, *A Very Social Time*, describes changing customs of shared work in antebellum New England. Venison: Duffield, "Frontier Church Going." German: Danbom, *Born in the Country*, 81. Persistence of farm exchanges: Adams, *The Transformation of Rural Life*; Pederson, *Between Memory and Reality*; and Harper, "Changing Works." Burial: R. Wells, *Facing the "King of Terrors."* On the calculations of exchanges, see note 17 above. On the sociology of neighboring: Keller, *The Urban Neighborhood*; C. Fischer, *The Urban Experience*, ch. 5.

68. Voting: Winkle, *The Politics of Community*; Fredman, "The Introduction"; Bourke and DeBats, "Identifiable Voting"; and Farragher, *Sugar Creek*, 141.

69. Wiebe, *The Search for Order*: "[The] society that had been premised upon the community's effective sovereignty, upon its capacity to manage affairs within its boundaries, no longer functioned.... [C]itizens in towns and cities across the land sensed that something fundamental was happening to their lives, something they had not willed and did not want, and they responded by striking out at whatever enemies their view of the world allowed them to see" (44). See also Wiebe, *Self-Rule*.

70. Marty, *Pilgrims in Their Own Land*, 169, 173. See also D. Howe, *What Hath God Wrought*, ch. 5; Finke and Stark, *The Churching of America* and "Turning Pews into People"; Stark and Finke, "American Religion"; Hatch, *The Democratization of Christianity* (priest's complaint, 141); Butler, *Awash in a Sea of Faith*; R. Brown, "The Emergence of Urban Society" (who reports about a sevenfold increase in Massachusetts church foundings from before to after the Revolution); Holifield, "Toward a History"; R. Moore, *Selling God*; Bodnar, *The Transplanted*, ch. 5; J. Turner, *Without God, Without Creed*; Johnson, "Supply-Side?"; Conzen et al., "Forum"; and Dolan, "The Search." Although some argue that involvement was already high (e.g., M. Carroll, "Upstart Theories"), most historians are skeptical about early affiliation. Waxhaws, South Carolina, for example, was "churched" before 1800, but well under 50 percent of adult whites were members (P. Moore, "Family Dynamics," 43–44). Evangelical efforts notably included the mobilization of women auxiliaries (Ryan, *Cradle*; Blackwell, "Surrogate Ministers") and youths (P. Moore, "Family Dynamics"). Boyer, *Urban Masses and Moral Order*, provides an overview of reform movements. Boston's pews: McCrossen, *Holy Day, Holiday*, 60. Hansen, *A Very Social Time*, 140, reports that about half the New England diarists she studied attended church regularly around the Second Great Awakening. Baker, *Moral Frameworks*, 187n1, estimates that as late as the 1890s, under 20 percent of residents in an upstate New York region were church members, although more than that attended (9ff).

71. Moloch: Solomon Wiatt, "Against the Calvanian Doctrine," in Hatch, *The Democratization of Christianity* (233, and "think for themselves," 125). Know then: "The Freedom," in J. Block, *A Nation of Agents*, 395.

72. E.g., Hansen, *A Very Social Time*, ch. 6; Pederson, *Between Memory and Reality*, ch. 5. Ethnicity and region: Bodnar, *The Transplanted*, ch. 5; Wirth, *The Ghetto*; Gjerde, *Minds of the West*; and Barron, *Those Who Stayed Behind*. Welfare: Kaufman, "The Political Economy."

73. Belknap, "Commentaries," 199, 207–08; Ferrall, *A Ramble of Six Thousand Miles*, ch. 3. Duffield, "Frontier Church Going," gives a more sympathetic description of a camp meeting.

74. Babcock: Juster and Hartigan-O'Conner, "The 'Angel Delusion.'" Lutherans: Gjerde, "Conflict and Community," points out that regional origins and class divisions fueled tensions, but the theological issues were real. Churches and politics: Carwardine, *Lincoln*, 274ff; and more generally, Newman, "One Nation under God."

75. Control: Ryan, *Cradle of the Middle Class*, ch. 1 (Oneida); Doyle, *The Social Order of a Frontier Community* (letters of reference, 165–67); Laurie, *Working People*, ch. 2 (Presbyterians, 45–46); Adams, *The Transformation of Rural Life*, 58ff (mill owner); Baron, *Those Left Behind*; P. Johnson, *A Shopkeeper's Millennium*.

76. Sunday: John, "Taking Sabbatarianism"; McCrossen, *Holy Day, Holiday*; Mirola, "Shorter Hours"; and Laband and Heinbuch, *Blue Laws*. Schools: R. Moore, "Bible Reading." Most outside churches: Marty, *Pilgrims in Their Own Land*, 208–12; he also notes Lincoln's nonmembership, 220. Guelzo, *Abraham Lincoln*; Carwardine, *Lincoln*. Lipset, *First New Nation*, 82ff, reports several instances of political resistance to churches in the antebellum era.

77. Ministers' tensions: e.g., Gjerde, *The Minds of the West*, 66–73, 115–31. Competition with organizations and activities: Kaufman, "The Political Economy"; R. Moore, *Selling God*.

78. Nash, "The Social Evolution," describes the early stages of associational growth in the late eighteenth century. The rise of associations in town and country during the early nineteenth century: R. Brown, "The Emergence of Urban Society"; Blumin, *The Emergence of the Middle Class*; idem, *The Urban Threshold*; Appleby, *Inheriting the Revolution*; Von Hoffman, *Local Attachments*; and C. Kelly, "'Well Bred'" (singing schools, 458). Scherzer, *The Unbounded Community*, describes their role in mid-century New York City; Conzen, *Immigrant Milwaukee*, describes their role among immigrants. Gamm and Putnam, "The Growth," provide some numbers. Skocpol makes the case that national federations provided the bulk of *formal* associations (Skocpol, "How Americans" and "United States"; Skocpol et al., "A Nation"; Skocpol and Oser, "Organization"). Clawson, "Fraternal Organizations," 1659, estimates that, by 1900, 20 percent or more of men belonged to a fraternal order. Kaufman, *For the Common Good?* 41, estimates that between 20 percent and 50 percent of white men belonged, but the upper range seems high; see also Beito, *From Mutual Aid*. Further studies include A. Scott, "On Seeing"; idem, "Most Invisible"; Gilekson, *Middle-Class Providence*; Doyle, "The Social Functions"; Beito, "To Advance"; Reitano, "Working Girls"; and Singleton, "Protestant Voluntary Organizations." On informal groups, see Duis, *The Saloon*; idem, "Whose City?"; Rosenzweig, *Eight Hours for What We Will*;

Barth, *City People*; and Peiss, *Cheap Amusements*. "Everyone seemed": Schlereth, *Victorian America*, 213.

79. Pierce: Blumin, *The Emergence of the Middle Class*, 214–15. Tweed: Anbinder, "'Boss' Tweed"; Burrows and Wallace, *Gotham*, 823. Fire companies: e.g., Laurie, *Working People of Philadelphia*, ch. 3.

80. Doyle, *The Social Order of a Frontier Community*; idem, "The Social Functions." Knights: Koehlinger, "'Let Us Live.'" Fire companies: S. Martin, *Killing Time*, 134. Functioning of associations, e.g., Hine, *Community on the American Frontier*; Barron, *Those Who Stayed Behind*, ch. 6; and previous citations on associations in note 78.

81. See Doyle, "Social Theory," on the debate. Doyle, "The Social Functions" and *The Social Order of a Frontier Community*, makes the integrative argument for associations. See also Gilekson, *Middle-Class Providence*; Barron, *Those Who Stayed Behind* (who argues that associations ameliorated divisions by facilitating compromises, 121–22). Fears of factionalism: readers have noted that Tocqueville is not as sanguine about voluntary associations in the second volume of *Democracy in America* (e.g., Schudson, *Good Citizen*, 101). See Gross, *The Minutemen*, about Concord in the 1790s: "The voluntary associations served to set off neighbors from one another, to nurture attachments separate from the whole community . . . the community had lost a certain moral unity" (175). See also Schudson, *The Good Citizen*, 54ff; Hine, *Community on the American Frontier* (welter, 137–38); Atherton, *Main Street on the Middle Border*; and Martin, *Killing Time*, 64. Divisions among immigrants: Conzen, *Immigrant Milwaukee*, ch. 6; Bodnar, *The Transplanted*, ch. 4; and Wirth, *The Ghetto*. Class: Skocpol (see note 78) states that national federations tended to be cross-class associations, but local studies suggest class stratification. Kaufman and Weinberg, "Social-Capital Formation," report some class mixing in the lodges of Buffalo's 1894 Knights of Pythias, but divisions by ethnicity (as well as race). In general, Kaufman, *For the Common Good*, argues that associational life promoted division. See also Ryan, *Cradle of the Middle Class*, ch. 3; Singleton, "Protestant Voluntary Organizations"; and Schneider, *Detroit and the Problem of Order*. The balance of unity and segmentation no doubt varied among communities. On the translocal nature of the associations, see Skocpol et al., "A Nation of Organizers"; R. Brown, "The Emergence of Urban Society."

82. Silver, "Friendship" and "'Two Different Sorts,'" makes the historical argument about the founding of friendship. Beginning with Smith-Rosenberg's "The Female World," studies of intimacy in nineteenth-century letters have become a major industry. Rotundo, "Romantic Friendship," extended the work to friendships between high-status young men (Webster, 3). Hansen, "'Our Eyes,'" claims that such ties existed among the working-class men, but reports only one (49). Henken, *The Postal Age*, discusses the burst of letter writing and its sentimental conventions; see also John, "Communications," 2357. Sumner-Longfellow: Blue, "The Poet." See also Yacovone, "'Surpassing the Love'"; Hansen, *A Very Social Time*; and Jabour, "Male Friendship."

83. Lynn: Dawley, *Class and Community*, 17. Emergence of shops: Wilentz, *Chants Democratic*, ch. 1–3; D. Gordon et al., *Segmented Work*; P. Johnson, *Shopkeeper's Millennium*, ch. 2; and Stott, "Artisans." Factories: Dublin, *Transforming Women's Work*; Wal-

lace, *Rockdale*; Licht, *Industrializing America*; Hareven and Langenbach, *Amoskeag*; and Kleinberg, *The Shadow of the Mills*.

84. Wilentz, *Chants Democratic*; Laurie, *Working People*; S. Glenn, *Daughters of the Shtetl*; Rosenzweig, *Eight Hours for What We Will*; Duis, "The Saloon"; Kingsdale, "The 'Poor Man's Club'"; Meyerowitz, *Women Adrift*; Hareven and Langenbach, *Amoskeag*; Voss, *The Making of American Exceptionalism*; and Ostreicher, "Labor." The Bowery Boys and their like: Burrows and Wallace, *Gotham*, 754ff; Chudacoff, *The Age of the Bachelor*, ch. 1.

85. Distances: Hershberg et al., "Journey to Work," table 2.

86. C. Kelly, "'Well Bred,'" 465. Theories of individuality: e.g., Simmel, *Individuality and Social Form*; Coser, *In Defense of Modernity*. Sincerity: Halttunen, *Confidence Men and Painted Women*, and the discussion in chapter 6 of this book.

87. Riesman, *The Lonely Crowd* (1969 comment, xxv); cover of *Time*: "Freedom—New Style," Sept. 27, 1954 (cover portrait by Ernest Hamlin Baker). "Yale Head Holds Liberty Menaced," *NYT*, Aug. 28, 1954. Friedan: Joan Cook, "'Mystique' View Backed by Many, Author Finds," *NYT*, Mar. 12, 1964. An overview of these trends is Thomson, *In Conflict No Longer*.

88. Clausen, *American Lives*, ch. 11. For some similar accounts, see Gerson, *Hard Choices*.

89. Winthrop and Stanton: Kerber, "Can a Woman?" 152, 153. The 1899 sociologist: "A Slap-Dash Sociologist," *NYT*, Dec. 4, 1899 ("poor stuff"); "Position of Women as Wage-Earners," *NYT*, Dec. 24, 1899. "Women in Business," *Los Angeles Times* (hereafter, *LAT*), Jun. 23, 2001, also displays a defense of women working.

90. Birth rates, longevity, and related changes: Fischer and Hout, *Century of Difference*, ch. 4; Klein, *A Population History of the United States*; and Ruggles, "The Transformation." White women's "total fertility rate" dropped from about 4 percent in 1900 to a low of 1.8 percent in 1980 and rose to 2.05 percent in 2000 (Haines, "Fertility and Mortality"; the late rise: Vere, "'Having it All'"). Time: An average woman in 1900 would have a first birth at twenty-five, see a fourth child leave home when she was fifty-two, and die at sixty-four, having spent twenty-eight (57 percent) of her forty-four adult years with a child at home. An average woman in 2000 is projected to have a first birth at twenty-five, see her second and last child leave home when she is forty-eight, and live to eighty-one, spending twenty-three (38 percent) of her sixty-one adult years with a child at home. Watkins et al., "Demographic Foundations," present more sophisticated calculations up to 1980 with the same import. College: e.g., Buchmann and DiPrete, "The Growing Female Advantage." Married mothers' employment: United States Bureau of the Census, http://www.census.gov/compendia/statab/tables/09s0578.xls. See also Folbre, "Women's Informal"; Degler, *At Odds*, ch. 15; Chafe, *The American Woman;* Owen, *Working Lives*; Cookingham, "Working after Childbearing"; Goldin, "Lifecycle"; and Leibowitz and Klerman, "Explaining Changes."

91. Cultural issues around women entering the labor force: Goldin, "The Quiet Revolution" (quotation, 1); Meyerowitz, "Beyond the Feminine Mystique"; and Matthews, *"Just a Housewife."* "I Love Lucy" "Job Switching" episode, "I Love Lucy,"

dir. William Asher, originally aired Sept. 15, 1952. Attitudes: R. Simon and Landes, "Women and Men's Attitudes"; Farley, *The New American Reality*, 43–48; Caplow, *Middletown Families* (survey, 377); and Molly O'Neill, "Drop the Mop, Bless the Mess: The Decline of Housekeeping," *NYT*, Apr. 11, 1993. Survey on whether wives should work: Gallup polls analyzed in Fischer and Hout, *Century of Difference*, ch. 9; see also Thornton, "Changing Attitudes." Men doing homemaking: Hochschild, *The Second Shift*; Bianchi et al., *Changing Rhythms of American Family Life*, ch. 5; and Tamar Lewin, "Men Assuming Bigger Share at Home," *NYT*, Apr. 15, 1998, which reports a study by the Family and Work Institute.

92. "Achiever": Analysis of the General Social Survey item "fefam," which asks whether it is better for the wife to stay home, shows a shift from 37 percent disagreement in 1977 to 64 percent disagreement in 2000–6; 22 percent of women born before 1921 disagreed and 76 percent born after 1960 disagreed. Wishing to stay home: Saad, "Women Slightly More Likely." Return of college-educated women: Vere, "'Having it All.'" (The trend does not apply to less-educated young women, presumably because they are more constrained.) Percheski, "Opting Out?" finds a leveling-off rather than a decline in working among professional women born 1966–75.

93. Friedman and Percival, "Who Sues?"; Brinig and Allen, "'These Boots,'" 126–27; E. May, *Great Expectations*; Riley, *Divorce*; and R. Griswold, "Law, Sex." "Load[ed] marriage": R. Griswold, "Divorce," 288. Lynd and Lynd, *Middletown*, report that the grounds for divorce had shifted from adultery and abandonment toward "cruelty" between 1890 and 1920 (122–23). They quote advice columnist Dorothy Dix with approval: "The reason there are more divorces is that people are demanding more of life than they used to" (128).

94. Rates: Stevenson and Wolfers, "Marriage and Divorce," figure 1; Haines, "Marriage and Divorce Rates." (Informal separation rates were high early on; see Schwartzberg, "'Lots of Them.'") Also, divorce rates briefly spiked right after World War II.) Goldstein, "The Leveling," concludes that a post-1980s downturn was real, but Schoen and Canudas-Romo, "Timing Effects," conclude that rates only leveled off after 1980. Complicating matters, divorce rates continued to climb for less-educated women but dropped substantially for more educated ones (Martin, "Trends"). See also Schlereth, *Victorian America*, 280–81; F. Furstenberg, "Divorce"; Cherlin, *Marriage, Divorce, Remarriage*; idem, *The Marriage-Go-Round*; Riley, *Divorce*; Cott, *Public Vows*; and Hartog, *Man and Wife in America*. Most scholars emphasize women's work as the prime mover in rising divorce rates rather than cultural changes: Espenshade, "Marriage"; Cherlin, *Marriage, Divorce, Remarriage*; Riley, *Divorce*, 145ff; Ruggles, "The Rise of Divorce" (and the commentary following it); Ono, "Historical Time"; economic analyses in Becker et al., "An Economic Analysis"; Fuchs, *How We Live*; and Stevenson and Wolfers, "Marriage and Divorce." Supreme Court: Bob Egelko, "Alito's Record has Feminists Ready for Battle," *San Francisco Chronicle*, Nov. 20, 2005.

95. "Adults" who married refers to those aged eighteen to eighty-five with spouse present: calculated from IPUMS data, http://www.ipums.umn.edu (accessed Nov. 2, 2007). Racial contrast: numbers from Carter et al., *Historical Statistics of the United*

States, table Af148–175. Although the racial difference existed in the nineteenth century, it widened greatly after the 1940s (Fischer and Hout, *Century of Difference*, ch. 4). Analysts disagree whether this racial difference arose from cultural patterns, economic circumstances, migration to from the rural South, or from yet broader social trends that simply affected whites later. Certainly, the shift from a farm to an industrial population is a major part of the story. See, e.g., Bennett et al., "The Divergence"; Cherlin, *Marriage, Divorce, Remarriage*; Pagnini and Morgan, "Racial Differences"; and Fitch and Ruggles, "Historical Trends." Age at marriage: Fischer and Hout, *Century of Difference*, figure 4.5; Fitch and Ruggles, "Historical Trends"; and Haines, "Long-Term Marriage Patterns." Early 2000s: Johnson and Dye, "Indicators of Marriage and Fertility"

96. Marriage rates: see previous note and Goldstein and Kenny, "Marriage Delayed?" Later marriage: Fischer and Hout, *Century of Difference*, ch. 4; Cherlin, *Marriage, Divorce, Remarriage*; idem, *The Marriage-Go-Round*; F. Furstenberg et al., "Growing Up"; and Danziger and Rouse, "The Price of Independence." Working-class delay: Lichter et al., "Race and the Retreat"; Sweeney, "Two Decades"; Edin and Kefalas, "Unmarried"; Reed, "Not Crossing"; and Ellwood and Jencks, "The Growing Differences." Cohabitation: Smock, "Cohabitation"; Cherlin, "Towards a New Home." In 2002, 37 percent of married Americans (and 51 percent of those under fifty) told the Gallup poll they lived together before marriage (Jones, "Public Divided"). See also Raley, "Recent Trends"; Graefe et al., "Life Course Transitions." Premarital pregnancies: Bachu, "Trends in Marital Status"; Parnell et al., "Nonmarital Pregnancies"; and Akerlof and Yellin, "New Mothers."

97. Nineteenth century: in antebellum Boston and Charleston, about one-third of adult white women never married, which is a much higher rate of spinsterhood than existed in 2000 America (Pease and Pease, *Ladies, Women, & Wenches*, 10–11). For pro-family attitudes, see sources cited in the previous note. "Willing and able": F. Furstenberg, "Family Change," 152; Cherlin, "The Deinstitutionalization."

98. Empty nest: Hareven, "Aging," 446; Fischer and Hout, *Century of Difference*, ch. 4; L. and White and Edwards, "Emptying the Nest."

99. On the redefinition of marriage, see Hartog, *Man and Wife in America*; Cott, *Public Vows*; and Riley, *Divorce*. The arguments about "selfishness" appeared in many places. One arena was in the abortion debate (Luker, *Abortion and the Politics of Motherhood*). Survey: Pew Research Center, "Motherhood Today"; idem, "Fewer Mothers." Increasingly egalitarian views: see survey research cited in note 91. Positive consequences of equality (at least for women): Amato et al., *Alone Together* (a rare longitudinal study); Schnittker, "Working More." Wilcox and Nock, "What's Love?" find negative consequences in an early 1990s survey (but see critique by Springer, "Research or Rhetoric?"). Reports of happiness, however, slumped a bit for women from 1973 to 2008 — although not for married women (my analysis of GSS item "happy"). We can assume that the gender role transition has had its complications and frictions.

100. Zelizer, *Pricing the Priceless Child*, is a classic study. State intervention: e.g., Kellogg and Mintz, *Domestic Revolutions*, ch. 6. Fewer chores: Goldscheider and Waite, *New Families, No Families?*, ch. 9; P. Stearns, *Anxious Parents*, ch. 5. Allowances: Zelizer,

The Social Meaning of Money, ch. 2. Work vs. school: an average child in the 1880s worked about 7 years while living at home, compared to about 2.5 years for a child in the 1970s (Modell et al., "Social Change")—and the latter probably kept all or most of the money. Parental devotion: P. Stearns, *Anxious Parents*; F. Furstenberg, "Family Change"; Russell, "What's Wrong?"; and Bahr, "Changes in Family Life." Child rearing values: Alwin, "From Obedience"; idem, "Changes"; idem, "Childrearing"; idem, "From Child-Bearing"; Lystad, *At Home in America*; and Staples and Smith, "Attitudes." The GSS asked respondents what is "important for a child to learn to prepare him or her for life?" From 1973 through 2004, even controlling for education, later cohorts increasingly emphasized responsibility, consideration, interestedness, thinking for oneself, working hard, and helping others, and decreasingly pointed to cleanliness, fulfilling gender roles, obedience, studiousness, and popularity. "Cultivating" parenting typifies twentieth-century middle-class parents rather than "natural" parenting, which allows children to develop on their own—a more typically working-class style (Lareau, *Unequal Childhoods*, esp. 246; Gans, *The Urban Villagers*, 54ff).

101. The fate of children of single parents has been very controversial, but they do run a greater risk of academic and social difficulties (McLanahan and Sandefur, *Growing Up with a Single Parent*; McLanahan, "Life Without Father"). Overall, the proportion of children in one-parent households declined from 10 percent to 7 percent between 1900 and 1960. Then the rate for black children in a one-parent household grew from 16 percent to 38 percent by 2000 and for white children from 6 percent to 18 percent. For white children of college-educated parents, the rate grew from 2 percent to 10 percent (Fischer and Hout, "The Family in Trouble"). See also McLanahan, "Diverging Destinies."

Parents' time with children: fragments of data suggest that parents spent *more* time with their children between the 1920s and 1970s and beyond (Bryant and Zick, "Are We Investing Less?"; Bahr, "Changes"; and Caplow et al., *The First Measured Century*, 88–89). Since the 1970s, parents have generally squeezed out yet more time, even just one-on-one time, despite mothers' work and fathers' household chores expanding (Bianchi et al., *Changing Rhythms of American Family Life*). These data accord with Americans' recollections. In a 1997 survey, 58 percent of respondents (68 percent of fathers, 50 percent of mothers) said they spent more time with their children than their parents had spent with them; 19 percent said less (10 percent of fathers, 25 percent of mothers; http://institution.gallup.com, question qn22; accessed Nov. 5, 2007). Estimating how much total adult attention children received is harder (Folbre et al., "By What Measure?"). We have to take into account who children lived with in each era. Children ca. 1900 were likelier to live in an extended household with other adults. Black children clearly experienced substantial declines in the chances that they lived with even two adults. At least since 1960, increasingly more white children (of non–college-educated parents) also experienced this change (Fischer and Hout, *Century of Difference*, ch. 4). All this implies a drop in contact time. However, declining birth rates work the other way, allowing each child a greater share of parents' attention, even aside from the more "intensive" parenting. Further evidence, although mixed, suggests that individual American children, on average, got as much or more personal time with parents as the century progressed, even into the later decades of two-job couples and economic strain. (Showing more time: Sandberg and Hofferth, "Changes"; idem, "Changes . . . A Correction"; and Sayer et al., "Are Parents?" table 3. Bahr et al., "Trends," find a decline in kids' time with parents between 1977 and 1999 in Muncie. See also Putnam, *Bowling Alone*, 100–1; Pew Research Center, "Motherhood Today.") Increasing parental time is much likelier to be true for white children of better-educated parents and not for the disadvantaged.

Meals: in a 2003 census survey, over 70 percent of children under eleven and 58 percent of twelve-to-seventeen-year-olds ate dinner seven nights a week with at least one parent (J. Dye and Johnson, "A Child's Day," table 4). From 1997 to 2005, parents reported in Gallup polls that their family ate dinner together at home a median of five or six times a week (Gallup Brain, questions 35, 41, 18, and 20). Putnam, *Bowling Alone*, 100–1, however, reports data suggesting a decline since the 1970s.

Critiques of doting on children: Steven A. Holmes, "Children Study Longer and Play Less, a Report Says," *NYT*, Nov. 11, 1998; Cross, "The Cute."

102. *Newsweek*: Mintz, *Huck's Raft*, 291. Common accounts of dating describe an increase, at least among middle-class girls, of sexual experimentation in the early 1900s and 1910s, and another increase, this time of premarital intercourse, starting in the 1960s. Overviews on dating and sexuality: Modell, "Dating"; Rothman, *Hands and Hearts*; Bailey, *From Front Porch to Back Seat*; D. Smith, "The Dating of the American Sexual Revolution"; D'Emilio and Freedman, *Intimate Matters*; Seidman and Rieder, "A Review"; and Mintz and Kellogg, *Domestic Revolutions*. Other studies (e.g., Petigny, "Illegitimacy,"; Bachu, "Trends") suggest that there was more continuous than discontinuous change over the last sixty-plus years of the century. Laumann et al., *The Social Organization of Sexuality*, 322–33, show that the greatest declines in age at first intercourse were in the 1960s and '70s. See also Farley, *The New American Reality*, 61–63; Seidman and Rieder, "A Review," 333; Pennington, "It's Not A Revolution"; Modell, *Into One's Own*; and Peiss, *Cheap Amusements*. Attitudes: Harding and Jencks, "Changing Attitudes"; T. Smith, "The Sexual Revolution"; and Thornton, "Changing Attitudes."

103. Leaving home: see Goldscheider and Goldscheider, "Leaving"; idem, "Moving Out"; D. Stevens, "New Evidence"; Gutmann et al., "Three Eras"; Stanger-Ross et al., "Falling Far"; Kobrin, "The Fall"; Ruggles, "The Demography"; and Michael et al., "Changes." On extended semi-independence: F. Furstenberg et al., "Growing Up"; C. Smith, "Getting a Life"; and Schoeni and Ross, "Material Assistance." Intermarriage: Rosenfeld and Kim, "The Independence"; Lieberson and Waters, *From Many Strands*, ch. 6, 7; Kalmijn, "Intermarriage"; Qian and Lichter, "Social Boundaries"; Fischer and Hout, *Century of Difference*, 45, 202; and Pagnini and Morgan, "Intermarriage."

104. In 1999 and 2000, the World Values Survey (http://www.worldvaluessurvey.org) asked respondents to choose between (a) "parents' duty is to do their best for their children even at the expense of their own well-being," or (b) "parents have a life of their own and should not be asked to sacrifice their own well-being for the sake of their children." Most Americans, 85 percent, chose answer (a), by far highest among fifteen Western nations (my analysis).

105. Lasch, *Haven in a Heartless World*, xvi. Rating marriage: e.g., in 1992, Gallup asked respondents whether they were satisfied with "the state of the American family"; only 32 percent said yes. However, in 1995, they asked how satisfied respondents were with "your family life" and 64 percent said "very satisfied" (Gallup Brain, questions 6e and 4q, http://institution.gallup.com/; accessed Jun. 10, 2008). Similarly, almost all Middletown interviewees in 1977 rated their marriages as happier than those of their friends (Caplow et al., *Middletown Families*, 128). From 1972 to 1994, the GSS asked respondents to rate their satisfaction with their family lives; the percentage picking "a great deal" or a "very great deal" varied around the 75 to 80 percent range throughout; the only movement was a slight upward trend for the married and college educated (my analysis).

Expectations: Many family histories (Degler, *At Odds*; J. Gillis, *A World of Their Own Making*, ch. 7; Cott, *Public Vows*; Mintz and Kellogg, *Domestic Revolutions*, ch. 6; P. Stearns, *Anxious Parents;* Laslett, "The Family"; and Cherlin, *The Marriage-Go-Round*) have stressed the intensifying emotional (rather than material) focus of the family. Romantic expectations: Shumway, "Something Old"; Swidler, *Talk of Love*; and idem, "Saving the Self." Parenting: Middletown III replications of high school student surveys show that students' standards for good parents shifted toward matters like mutual respect and time and away from having parents of high status (Bahr, "Changes"; Bahr et al., "Trends").

106. Consistent with the growing emphasis on individual fulfillment, Americans became more tolerant of new family patterns—divorce, spinsterhood, cohabitation, and even single motherhood—as legitimate, if not desirable, alternatives to marriage (Thornton, "Changing Attitudes"; Veroff et al., *The Inner American*, ch. 4; Lyons, "Kids and Divorce"). Marriage quality: Caplow et al., *Middletown Families*, ch. 6, 135. Veroff et al., *The Inner American*, esp. 162, report on matched surveys conducted in 1957 and 1976; notably, more 1976 respondents claimed to have happy marriages and emphasized companionship and love. More also reported marital problems, but the researchers interpreted that as evidence that American couples were more frankly trying to deal with higher marital expectations. Amato et al., *Alone Together*, analyzed matching 1980 and 2000 surveys of under-fifty-year-olds. They found that couples less often did various things together, suggesting more independence, but also found general improvements in the marriages themselves, notably a drop in marital conflict. (A Canadian study found a decline in time from 1986 to 2005 respondents spent with family, due mainly more work hours; Turcotte, "Time Spent"). The GSS has asked, "Taking all things together, how would you describe your marriage?" (item labeled "hapmar").Between the 1970s and 2000s, those saying "very happy" dropped from 67 percent to 62 percent, most of that early on—but it was essentially unchanged for college graduates (my analysis). On the economic strains less-educated couples faced, see Amato et al., *Alone Together*; Gerson and Jacobs, "The Work-Home Crunch"; and the discussion in chapter 2 of this book. Children: we have little solid evidence on the quality of parent-child ties (see note 101 on time spent together). The Middletown replications suggest somewhat more emotional connection later in the century (Bahr, "Changes"; Bahr et al., "Trends."). The 1957

and 1976 surveys conducted by Veroff et al., *The Inner American*, ch. 5, reveal more of a focus on the emotional side of the parent-child bond in 1976.

107. Studies try to isolate how much of the decline in three-generation households is due to changing demographics (the elderly living longer and having had fewer children), changing economics (the elderly getting wealthier), or changing preferences. See Ruggles, "The Decline"; McGarry and Schoeni, "Social Security"; Schoeni, "Reassessing"; Goldscheider and Lawton, "Family Experiences"; Costa, "A House of Her Own"; idem, "Displacing the Family"; Hareven and Uhlenberg, "Transition to Widowhood "; and Kramarow, "The Elderly." More generally, see Cherlin and Furstenberg, *The New American Grandparent*. Attitudes: Fischer and Hout, *Century of Difference*, ch. 4, esp. 92–93. (The skeptic could argue that parents and children were both disingenuous in answering the survey question. Perhaps, but absent other evidence, we should take people's word.) Umberson et al., "As Good as It Gets," find that older people feel better about their marriages if they do not live with adult children. Elderly giving: By one estimate, ca. 1990, the average middle-class American in his or her young thirties received a couple of thousand dollars and a couple of hundred hours of help a year from parents (third- and fourth-quartile families in tables 12.4 and 12.5 in Schoeni and Ross, "Material Assistance").

108. Telephone: C. Fischer, *America Calling*. New York phone cards: Susan Sachs, "Immigrants See Path to Riches in Phone Cards," *NYT*, Aug. 11, 2002. Transnationalism: e.g., Levitt, "Salsa and Ketchup." Iraq: Lizette Alvarez, "An Internet Lifeline for Troops in Iraq," *NYT*, Jul. 8, 2006.

109. Amato et al., *Alone Together*, note the negative effects on marriage of economic strains and also of wives working who would rather not. Delay: Edin and Kefalas, "Unmarried." In a 2001 poll of twenty-year-olds, four-fifths agreed that "it is extremely important . . . to be economically set before you get married" (Cherlin, "The Deinstitutionalization," 856).

110. Cherlin, "The Deinstitutionalization" and *The Marriage-Go-Round*, argues that marital norms have become less binding. I would argue that they have changed; new expectations matter, e.g., that a good husband listens to his wife. Coontz, *Marriage, A History*, 310, 301.

111. Janowitz, *The Community Press*, 210ff. The phrase "communities of limited liability" has been used by numerous urban sociologists since. E.g., Greer, *The Urban View*, 82, contrasts such neighborhoods with the indigenous community based on constraint.

112. Fischer and Hout, *Century of Difference*, ch. 7. Farmers: "Few Farmers Left to Count," *NYT*, Oct. 10, 1993. Rural decline: Brunner and Kolb, *Rural Social Trends*; Adams, *The Transformation of Rural Life*; Gallaher, *Plainville Fifteen Years Later*; and Lobao and Meyer, "The Great Agricultural Transition." Suburbanization: Jackson, *Crabgrass Frontier*; Clifford Clark, *The American Family Home, 1800–1960*; M. Foster, *From Streetcar to Superhighway*; and C. Fischer, *The Urban Experience*, ch. 9. Segregation: Massey and Denton, *American Apartheid*, is the standard; Drake and Cayton, *Black Metropolis*, describe the history in Chicago. Segregation after 1970: Logan et al., "Segregation"; Fischer et al., "Distinguishing the Levels and Dimensions."

113. Mobility: C. Fischer, "Ever-More Rooted Americans." Numbers: United States Bureau of the Census, "Geographical Mobility/Migration." Nineteenth-century rates: see note 63 above. Home ownership: Chevan, 'The Growth"; Clifford Clark, *The American Family Home, 1800–1960*; and Handlin, *The American Home*. Tobey et al., "Moving Out," argue that the New Deal pressed home ownership explicitly to encourage residential stability.

114. Country Life: United States Senate, *Report of the Country Life Commission*; Baker, "The Farmer"; and Ellsworth, "Theodore Roosevelt's." Barron, *Those Who Stayed Behind*, 41–50, is one critic of the Country Life reformers. The 1908 survey: Larson and Jones, "The Unpublished Data." The 1919 survey: Ward, "The Farm Woman's Problem"; Bailey and Snyder, "A Survey." Landaff: MacLeish and Young, "Landaff" (quotations, 61–62); F. Schmidt et al. "Community Change." See also Brunner and Kolb, *Rural Social Trends*; Kolb and Polson, "Trends"; Pederson, *Between Memory and Reality*; Adams, *The Transformation of Rural Life*; Koerselman, "The Quest"; Neth, "Leisure"; Bell, "Culture of a Contemporary Rural Community;" Bloomquist et al., "Sublette"; Moe and Taylor, "Irwin"; and Clough and Quimby, "Peacham." Technology in rural America: e.g., Flink, *The Automobile Age*; Berger, *The Devil Wagon*; Interrante, "'You Can't'"; Fuller, *RFD*; and C. Fischer, *America Calling*.

115. "Every man:" E. Bell, "Culture of a Contemporary Rural Community," 73. Pederson, *Between Memory and Reality*, 230, quotes a local minister saying that once families were able to work on their own, they chose to do so. See also Adams, *The Transformation of Rural Life*; Koerselman, "The Quest." The automobile's effect on villages: see citations in previous note; Moline, *Mobility and the Small Town*; Bruner and Kolb, *Rural Social Trends*; Bureau of Business Research, "The Automobile"; and Johansen and Fuguitt, "Changing Retail Activity."

116. West [Withers], *Plainville*; Gallagher, *Plainville Fifteen Years Later*. See also Luloff and Krannich, *Persistence and Change in Rural Communities*. Sociologist in 1949: Ensminger, "Rural Neighborhoods," 60. Georgia: Wynne, "Culture," 56.

117. Chicago sociologists: the main statements include Park, "The City," and Wirth, "Urbanism." Illustrative studies include Wirth, *The Ghetto*, and Zorbaugh, *The Gold Coast and the Slum*. Later inner-city neighborhood studies: Whyte, *Street Corner Society*; Gans, *The Urban Villagers*; Suttles, *The Social Organization of the Slum*; Hannerz, *Soulside*; Jankowski, *Islands in the Street*; E. Anderson, *Streetwise*; and Kefala, *Working-Class Heroes*. A couple of the later studies, like Anderson's, raise doubts about the solidarity in late-twentieth-century, inner-city, largely black neighborhoods.

118. Workers: Kornblum, *Blue-Collar Community*; Zunz, *The Changing Face of Inequality*. See also Alba et al., "White Ethnic Neighborhoods"; idem, "Immigrant Groups"; Lieberson, *Ethnic Patterns in American Cities*; Hawley and Zimmer, *The Metropolitan Community*; Zimmer, "The Metropolitan Community"; and my earlier discussion of journey to work on p. 215. Architecture: e.g., Clark, *The American Family Home*, 193ff. Mobilization: historical studies of neighborhood activism include Miller, "The Role"; Arnold, "The Neighborhood"; Scherzer, *The Unbounded Community*; Nicolaides, "The Neighborhood"; Karr, "Brookline"; Jackson, *Crabgrass Frontier*, ch. 8; and Weiss, "Planning Subdivisions." More recently, residential commu-

nity associations and gated communities have helped defend American middle-class suburbs and neighborhoods (e.g., Blakely and Snyder, *Fortress America*; Arnold, "The Neighborhood"). The political power of American localities: Logan and Molotch, *Urban Fortunes*, ch. 5; Monkkonen, *America Becomes Urban*; and Tropea, "Rational Capitalism."

119. Liking neighbors: In surveys, Americans tend to rate their local communities relatively highly. In a 2004 Harris Poll, 84 percent said they "felt good" about "the city, town, or county" in which they lived vs. 55 percent for the "state of the nation"; 77 percent felt good about the "morals and values of people in your community" vs. 55 percent about "morals and values of Americans in general" (Harris Interactive, Oct. 2004, iPOLL Databank, The Roper Center for Public Opinion Research, http://www.ropercenter.uconn.edu/ipoll.html; accessed Dec. 28, 2008). Recollections: Lynd and Lynd, *Middletown*; McClenahan, *The Changing Urban Neighborhood* (Los Angeles). Studies trying to measure change in neighboring objectively are mixed: among those indicating a decline early in the twentieth century are B. Lee et al., "Testing," and C. Fischer, *America Calling*, ch. 7. For more recent decades, several have relied on surveys about how often respondents got together with neighbors. They tend to show modest declines since the 1960s (e.g., Guest and Wierzbicki, "Social Ties"; Putnam, *Bowling Alone*, 106–7, 460n36). Those suggesting little change include K. Campbell, "Networks Past," and A. Hunter, "The Loss of Community" (before the 1960s); while DeStefano ("Pressures") found a small *in*crease between 1978 and 1990 in the percentage of Americans who reported that most of their closest friends lived in the community. Marital distances: some studies report modest but real increases. D. Smith ("Parental Power," 426) estimated that in Hingham the in-town marriage rate dropped from 32 percent in 1900 to 26 percent by the 1950s. See also R. Abrams, "Residential Propinquity" (Philadelphia); Dinitz et al., "Mate Selection," 350 (Columbus, Ohio, 1939 to 1949); C. Fischer, *America Calling*, 206–9 (California towns before World War II). Reporting no change were Moline, *Mobility and the Small Town*, 120, in a small Illinois town before 1930, and Scherzer, *Unbounded Community*, 179–86 (and pers. comm., Sept. 26, 1997), for Manhattan in the nineteenth century. See Scherzer, *Unbounded Community*, 179–86, and Shannon and Nystuen, "Marriage, Migration" on methodological problems which may underestimate the change.

120. See note 112 above on segregation trends. W. Wilson, *The Truly Disadvantaged*; E. Anderson, *Streetwise*; Cutler and Glaeser, "Are Ghettos"; and Jargowsky, *Poverty and Place*, among many others, document the isolating effects of racial segregation.

121. Work at home declined from 7.2 percent of all workers in 1960 to 2.3 percent in 1990 and rose back to 3.6 percent in 2005. Excluding the self-employed, only about 1 percent of workers in 2000 worked at home (United States Bureau of the Census, "Working at Home: 2000," http://www.census.gov/population/www/cen2000/phc-t35.html, accessed Nov. 18, 2007; idem, "Most of Us Still Drive to Work—Alone," press release CB07-CN.06, Jun. 13, 2007, http://www.census.gov/Press-Release/www/releases/archives/american_community_survey_acs/010230.html, accessed Nov. 15, 2007). Self-employment rates dropped substantially from the nineteenth century,

from over 40 percent to under 10 percent around 1970 and then leveled off (Stein-metz, and Wright, "The Fall," table 3). Even among nonagricultural workers alone, self-employment declined after World War II (Hipple, "Self-Employment," tables 1 and 2). Kin and neighbors: in the nineteenth century, employers often hired whole families to work together in factories. In the twenty-first century, remnants of this trend continued but declined, especially as jobs changed (see, e.g., Hareven, *Family Time and Industrial Time*; Kornblum, *Blue-Collar Community*; and on immigrant hir-ing, Waldinger, *Still the Promised City*). Similarly, nineteenth- and twentieth-century factories often drew workers from the immediate neighborhood or provided worker housing (Wallace, *Rockdale*; Dublin, *Transforming Women's Work*; Hareven and Lagen-bach, *Asmokeag*; and Kleinberg, *The Shadow of the Mills*) and that, too, diminished.

122. Pelletier: Hareven and Lagenbach, *Amoskeag*, 185. Saleswomen: Benson, *Coun-ter Cultures*, 245. See also S. Glenn, *Daughters of the Shtetl*; Halle, *America's Working Man*; Kornblum, *Blue Collar Community*; and numerous other studies of the work-place.

123. Hodson, "Work Life," summarizes about 150 ethnographic studies of work-places. In the vast majority of studies "friendships extend[ed] beyond the workplace" (appendix, 239). Friends from work: Marks, "Intimacy." In a 1965–66 survey, white men in the Detroit area reported that they had met about one-fourth of their clos-est male friends at work (Fischer et al., *Networks and Places*, 51). In the 1985 GSS, over one-third of the people with whom employed respondents "discuss[ed] important matters" were coworkers (my analysis). Heterogeneous coworkers: in 1990, 38 per-cent of white workers said they worked in an all-white workplace; in 2006, 28 percent did (GSS item labeled "racwork," my analysis). See also Estlund, "Working Together"; Tomaskovic-Devey et al., "Documenting Desegregation"; Mutz and Monday, "The Workplace"; and Briggs, "'Some of My Best Friends.'" In a 1985 survey of New York-ers, half of whites reported working where "most people are of your own race," while seven in ten reported living in neighborhoods that were mostly of their own race (differences for blacks were similar; Maureen Dowd, "Divisions Between Races Per-sist in New York City, Poll Indicates," *NYT*, May 14, 1985). Persisting (albeit declin-ing) job discrimination is very well documented. Herring, "Is Job Discrimination Dead?" provides one overview. Kornblum, *Blue Collar Community*, 37. A large litera-ture emerged in the 1990s on home and work, e.g., Gerson and Jacobs, "The Work-Home Crunch"; Hochschild, *The Time Bind*.

124. Overviews of the church in the twentieth century: Fischer and Hout, *Century of Difference*, ch. 8; Marty, *Pilgrims in Their Own Land*; Roof and MacKinney, *American Mainline Religion*; and Finke and Stark, *The Churching of America*. Roosevelt: "Non-Church Going," *NYT*, Apr. 21, 1907. Novels: "Priest Denounces Realistic Novels," *NYT*, Jan. 27, 1903. Complaints about Sunday baseball were legion. The rural church crisis: Madison, "Reformers"; United States Senate, *Report of the Country Life Com-mission*; Barron, *Those Left Behind*; Brunner and Kolb, "Rural Social Trends"; and Ma-cLeish and Young, "Culture." Depression: Handy, "The American Religious Depres-sion"; see also Lynd and Lynd, *Middletown*; Caplow et al., *All Faithful People*, 284ff.

125. Early membership data: Finke and Stark, "Turning Pews into People"; Caplow

et al., *A Faithful People*, 29; and Herberg, *Protestant Catholic Jew*, 47–48. Recent data: the Gallup poll's affirmations of membership ran from about 72 percent of their respondents between 1936 and 1946, peaked at 80 percent in 1956, then declined to about 70 percent in the 1980s, 68 percent in the 1990s, and 63 percent in the mid-2000s (my analysis of Gallup Brain data, http://institution.gallup.com/; accessed Dec. 29, 2008). The percentage who "dropped out" of a faith increased noticeably among GSS respondents who came of age in the 1960s (Hout and Fischer, "Explaining the Rise"). See Winesman, "Religion in America?" for Gallup data. See also debate between Dougherty et al., "Recovering the Lost" and Smith and Kim, "Counting Religious Nones" and Kosmin and Keysar, "American Religious Identification Survey" for 2008 data. Some survey respondents report "no religion" but nonetheless belong to churches; many others among these report religious belief. Family formation leads to church membership: e.g., C. Smith, "Getting a Life"; Wuthnow, "Myths" (pastor, 5). On switching to new forms of churches and spiritual groups, see, Wuthnow, *The Restructuring of American Religion*, ch. 6; Dougherty et al., "Recovering the Lost"; Pew Forum, "Faith in Flux."

126. Attendance rates are controversial, because people exaggerate their attendance and we don't know if the degree of exaggeration has changed (see Hadaway et al., "What the Polls," and *ASR,* "A Symposium."). Estimates for early twentieth century: see summary in Fischer and Hout, *Century of Difference*, 203, 343n53; Butler, "Protestant Success"; Sarna, *American Judaism,* 224–5, 404n38, 404 n41, for both Jewish and Christian rates. The Lynds counted Sunday church attendance in *Middletown* in the 1920s and found that only about one-fifth of the town's adults were typically there (358); Caplow et al., *A Faithful People*, found increased attendance in Middletown fifty years later. Ethnographers in rural America in the 1940s reported low rates (e.g., Moe and Taylor, "Irwin, Iowa"; E. Bell, "Culture of a Contemporary Rural Community"); follow-up studies found similar or higher rates (Luloff and Krannich, *Persistence and Change*). Later twentieth century: Methodist council quoted by Herberg, *Protestant Catholic Jew*, 51. For overviews, see Finke and Stark, *The Churching of America*; Fischer and Hout, *Century of Difference*, ch. 8; and Chaves and Anderson, "Continuity and Change." Survey reports of attendance suggest a rise to ca. 1960 (American National Election Survey, tables 1B.5a and b, http://www.electionstudies.org/nesguide/gd-index.htm#5; accessed Jun. 12, 2008) and then a modest decline afterwards (Presser and Stinson, "Data Collection"; Firebaugh and Harley, "Trends"; Sasaki and Suzuki, "Changes"; Hout and Greeley, "The Center Doesn't Hold"; Putnam, *Bowling Alone*, ch. 4; Gallup and Lindsay, *Surveying the Religious Landscape*; Gallup, "Catholics Trail"; and, for high school seniors, Hurtado and Prior, "The American Freshman"). Contributions to churches probably followed a similar trajectory (Caplow et al., *A Faithful People*, 85; Lebergott, *Pursuing Happiness*, 143; Ronsvalle and Ronsvalle, "An End?" and Amerson and Stephenson, "Decline or Transformation").

127. Fischer and Hout, *Century of Difference*, ch. 8. Finke and Stark, *The Churching of America*, argue that liberalization alienated traditional Catholics. Greeley, *Religious Change in America*, and Hout and Greeley, "The Center Doesn't Hold," argue that the Vatican's conservatism alienated young Catholics. See also N. Glenn, "The

Trend"; idem, "Review of Greeley"; and Astin, "The Changing." Switching: according to a 2007 survey, 28 percent of American adults have changed religions since childhood (including to no religion—44 percent if we include denominational change), but about one-third of raised Catholics said they had left the faith (Pew Forum on Religion & Public Life, "U.S. Religious Landscape," 26; idem, "Faith in Flux"). Catholics account for attendance decline: e.g., Saad, "Church-Going among U.S. Catholics." Wuthnow, *The Restructuring of American Religion*, 88–91, largely relies on an early Gallup poll to claim a dramatic increase in switching since the 1960s, but GSS data suggest that only Catholics (and perhaps Jews) increasingly switched out (Fischer and Hout, *Century of Difference*, ch. 8). Studies that discount any increase in switching include Sherkat, "Tracking "; Hout et al., "The Decline"; Sullins, "Switching"; T. Smith, "Are Conservative Churches Growing?"; and Stump, "The Effects."

128. C. Smith, introduction to *The Secular Revolution*; Chaves, "Secularization." Presbyterian: Laurie, *Working People*, 45–46.

129. Middletown: Caplow et al., *All Faithful People*, 94; idem, "The Middletown Replications." Also on tolerance: Pew Forum on Religion & Public Life, "Many Americans Say." Waning of denominational tension: e.g., Wuthnow, *The Restructuring of American Religion*, ch. 5. Intermarriage: e.g., Pagnini and Morgan, "Intermarriage"; Kalmijn, "Shifting Boundaries." For a case study: Fishman, *Double or Nothing*. The 40 percent: Pew Forum on Religion & Public Life, "U.S. Religious Landscape," 8. Reasons for switch: Gallup poll, http://www.gallup.com/poll/1690/Religion.aspx; Pew Forum on Religion & Public Life, "Faith in Flux." On increasing diversity and tolerance, see Fischer and Hout, *Century of Difference*, ch. 8. On increasing voluntarism, see esp. Roof and McKinney, *American Mainline Religion*, ch. 2 ("arrive at own beliefs," 57, based on a 1978 Gallup survey; a 1988 replication showed similar results); Warner, "Work in Progress"; Madsen, "The Archipelago of Faith." "Meets your needs": Roof, *Spiritual Marketplace*, 86 (the text erroneously describes the results in reverse—Wade Clark Roof, pers. comm., Mar. 28, 2005). Pope: Jeffrey Jones, "U.S. Catholics' Reactions."

130. Shopped: GSS question "shoprel" asks respondents if they had ever "shopped around for a church"; see also Wuthnow, *The Restructuring of American Religion*, ch. 5. The 2008 switchers: Pew Forum on Religion & Public Life, "Faith in Flux." Three siblings: Dana Jennings, "Religion Is Less a Birthright than a Good Fit," *NYT Week in Review*, Mar. 2, 2008, 7. "Jews by Choice": e.g., Cohen and Eisen, *The Jew Within*: "They [moderately affiliated Jews] want to be Jewish because of what it means to them personally. . . . It is voluntarist in the extreme: assuming the rightful freedom of each individual to make his or her Jewish decisions" (35–36). A similar comment about Catholics: Dolan, "The Search."

131. Attendance: my analysis of GSS questions labeled "churhmem," "attend," "memchurh" and "actchurh," which ask about membership and attendance. Small groups: Wuthnow, *Sharing the Journey* (see also Wuthnow, *Restructuring of American Religion*, ch. 6, and *Loose Connections*). Ammerman: *Bible Believers*, 106–7; see also Ault, *Spirit and Flesh*. Estimate of one-seventh: In the 1972–2006 GSS, 13 percent of respondents were in a fundamentalist denomination and reported attending church

"nearly every week" or more; 28 percent were in any kind of church and reported attending every week or more; and 7 percent were in any kind of church but attended more than once a week (my analysis). One-seventh seems a fair guess of the percentage who were heavily involved.

132. Choice: Ammerman, "Organized Religion" (quotation, 203). Switching as spiritual seeking: Sherkat and Wilson, "Preferences." (In the 1987 GSS, most switchers explained their move as a matter of marriage, family, or friends, but about one-third cited a religious reason. In the 2008 Pew Forum on Religion & Public Life, "Faith in Flux" survey, the most common explanations were about spiritual disappointment or searching.) Switchers' commitments: Roof and McKinney, *American Mainline Religion*, 177–81; Hoge et al., "Types"; Jacques, "Changing Marital," 393. Middletown: Caplow et al., *All Faithful People*, ch. 3.

133. Membership trends are uncertain, given the variety of associations, but, discounting the Depression, probably rose and fell. Early twentieth century: Household budget surveys (C. Brown, *American Standards of Living*) show that the percentage of families paying associational membership fees dropped from 1918 to 1935 and then rose strongly to 1973. Putnam's estimates (*Bowling Alone*, figure 8) show sharp increases in membership from 1900 to 1930, a sag, and then rapidly climbing rates that peaked in 1960. Caplow et al., *Middletown Families*, 84, report rates of membership exceeding 80 percent in 1977, surely an increase. See also Steiner, "Recreation"; Brunner and Kolb, *Rural Social Trends*; Hudson, *Plains Country Towns*; Lynd and Lynd, *Middletown*, ch. 19; L. Warner, in *Democracy in Jonesville*, ch. 8; McBee, "He Likes Women"; Gamm and Putnam, "Association-Building"; Skocpol, "The Tocqueville Problem"; Breckinridge, *Women in the Twentieth Century*; and W. G. Wilson, *The American Woman in Transition*. Kaufman, *For the Common Good?* and Beito, *From Mutual Aid to the Welfare State*, stress the welfare aspects of associations' rise and fall. Skocpol, "Voice," adds additional explanations.

134. "Noticeable trends": Brunner and Kolb, *Rural Social Trends*, 266. See also general sources in the previous note.

135. Putnam, "Bowling Alone" and "Tuning In," initially claimed, based on GSS data, that membership had declined between 1974 and 1994. Later analyses suggested, however, that the decline was negligible (Lipset, "Malaise and Resiliency"; Nie et al., *Education and Democratic Citizenship in America*; Greeley, "The Other Civic America"; Wuthnow, "Bridging?" 89ff; T. Smith, "Trends in Voluntary Group Membership"; Costa and Kahn, "Understanding the American Decline in Social Capital"; Paxton, "Is Social Capital?"; Rotolo, "Trends"; and Rotolo and Wilson, "What Happened?"). New kinds of groups: see Wuthnow, *Sharing the Journey*; Schudson, *The Good Citizen*, 298. In *Bowling Alone* (ch. 9), Putnam questioned the numbers and "civic-ness" of the kinds of groups Wuthnow stresses. He also supplemented the GSS with surveys showing less active participation in groups. From another research direction, Bianchi et al., *Changing Rhythms of Family Life* (ch. 5), found that parents' time budgets reveal a decline in time spent in organizations from 1965 through 2000s. A case study of decline: Fost, "Farewell." Nationally, the total number of formal, nonprofit associations more than doubled between 1968 and 2000 (Caplow et al., *Recent Social Trends,*

75–76; United States Bureau of the Census, *Statistical Abstract*, 1998, table 1295; idem, *Statistical Abstract*, 2002, table 1261; Putnam, *Bowling Alone*, figure 7; and Skocpol, "Associations"), but trends in rates of membership are harder to pin down. For descriptions of associational life in small-city America in the midcentury, see Warner and Lunt, *Yankee City* (Newburyport, MA) and Warner, *Democracy in Jonesville* (Morris, IL). Knights member: Peter Y. Hong, "Bowling Alley Tour Refutes Theory of Social Decline," *LAT*, Mar. 18, 1996. Effects of television: Putnam, *Bowling Alone*, ch. 13, is more persuasive than television's defenders, such as Ray, "Technological Change"; Uslaner, "Social'"; and Norris, "Does Television?" See more discussion of television in chapter 5. Housework and childcare: Bianchi et al., *Changing Rhythms of Family Life*. "Everyone seemed": Schlereth, *Victorian America*, 213.

136. Wuthnow, *Loose Connections*.

137. I first used the term "just friends" in this sense about 1980 (Fischer et al., *Networks and Places*, 50; C. Fischer, *To Dwell among Friends*, 40–42, 114–17). See also Wellman, "The Community Question"; Giddens, *Modernity and Self-Identity*, ch. 3 (who writes of the "pure relationship"); Spencer and Pahl, *Rethinking Friendship*; Oliker, "The Modernisation." One-fifth estimate: From the 1965–66 Detroit-area study of white men, 26 percent (Fischer et al., *Networks and Places*, 50); the 1977 northern California survey, 23 percent (C. Fischer, *To Dwell among Friends*, 41), and the 1985 GSS, about 20 percent (my analysis). Technology and friendships: C. Fischer, "Gender and the Residential Telephone"; idem, *America Calling*, ch. 8; and Scharff, *Taking the Wheel*. The Internet: Wellman, "Connecting Communities"; Boase and Barry Wellman, "Personal Relationships"; Bargh and McKenna, "The Internet"; DiMaggio et al., "Social Implications," 314–19; Katz et al., "The Internet"; and Ito et al., "Living and Learning" vs. Hampton and Wellman, "Long Distance Community"; Quell et al., "Isolation."

Less frequent contact since ca. 1960: Veroff et al., *The Inner American*, 479–80 (although they report an increase in turning to friends when in distress, 481–83); Putnam, *Bowling Alone* (ch. 6 and esp. 458n15); Costa and Kahn, "Understanding the American Decline in Social Capital" (who find less decline than Putnam and attribute much of it to women's work and economic inequality); Bianchi et al., *Changing Rhythms of American Family Life*, ch. 5 (time-budget data); J. Robinson and Godbey, "Busyness" (on much the same data); and Turcotte, "Time Spent" (Canadian data). The GSS data are mixed—slightly more frequent reports of seeing friends outside the neighborhood and fewer of getting together with neighbors (my analysis); Guest and Wierzbicki, "Social Ties"; Monti, "Private Lives." One complication is whether the researcher simply describes changes in contact or seeks to estimate what those changes would have been had other coincident trends—most notably, the rise in educational attainment and later age of marriage—not occurred? Putnam's findings (in *Bowling Alone*) are strong because he controls for education. Finally, a well-publicized study reported that respondents to the 2004 GSS had substantially fewer people with whom they "discuss[ed] important matters" than did respondents to the 1985 GSS (McPherson et al., "Social Isolation"). But that finding is almost certainly an artifact (C. Fischer, "The 2004 GSS Finding").

138. Wellman, "Physical Place," 238.

139. *Buffy*: Gatson and Zweerink, "Ethnography Online." Many observers expressed concerns about the thinness of Internet "communities"; see, e.g., C. Calhoun, "Community without Propinquity." Research at the Annenberg School finds that members of on-line communities put great store in those relationships ("Online World As Important to Internet Users as Real World?" 2007, http://digitalcenter.org; accessed Jan. 29, 2008). A fraction of the ballooning Internet research literature is listed in note 137 above.

140. Inequality: see earlier discussion on family and esp. Martin, "Trends"; also Wuthnow, "Bridging?"; Fischer and Hout, *Century of Difference*, passim. A few studies suggest that economic, ethnic, and racial heterogeneity in American communities has modestly led to social withdrawal (e.g., Costa and Kahn, "Civic Engagement"; Putnam, "E Pluribus Unum.") Given the vast rise in immigration and in economic inequality since about 1970, we might therefore expect a modest reduction in social ties and the ones who probably would suffer most would be those most disadvantaged to start with.

141. Culture wars: R. Williams, *Cultural Wars in American Politics*; Fiorina, *Culture War?*; and Fischer and Mattson, "Is America Fragmenting?" Pope Benedict XVI: Tom Heneghan, "Ratzinger Sounds Doctrinal Alarm Before Conclave," Reuters News Service, http://today.reuters.co.uk (accessed Apr. 19, 2005).

142. Survey: see note 3.

143. Ehrenhalt, "The Lost City," 244.

Chapter Five

1. "Big Show in Itself," *Chicago Tribune*, May 19, 1895. J. N. Taylor, "First Car Off the Earth," *Boston Globe*, Sept. 1, 1897.

2. Classic statements about modern life—notably Simmel's "The Stranger"—focus on encounters among strangers, especially rural newcomers, to the city.

3. Private and public: Seligman, "Between Public and Private"; Weintraub, "The Theory and Politics"; Laslett, "The Family"; Hareven, "The History of the Family"; Coontz, *The Social Origins of Private Life*; Bender, *Community and Social Change in America*, 128–36; and Hansen, *A Very Social Time*. For some writers, such as Seligman, the emergence of a *private* sphere entails modernity, but that conflates privatism with individualism. Parochial space: A. Hunter, "Private, Parochial and Public"; Lofland, *The Public Realm*; idem, *A World of Strangers*; idem, "Social Life"; and Hansen, *A Very Social Time*.

4. Democracy debate: Wiebe, *Self-Rule*; Valelly, "Vanishing Voters"; Putnam, "Tuning In"; idem, *Bowling Alone*; Skocpol, "The Tocqueville Problem"; Schudson, *The Good Citizen*; Ladd, *The Ladd Report*; Skocpol and Fiorina, *Civic Engagement in American Democracy*; and C. Zukin et al., *A New Engagement?*

5. The comment about Paris I heard from historian Oscar Handlin, Harvard University, 1969; about Tokyo from Abraham Fischer, personal conversation, 2007. American homes ca. 2000 had notably more rooms than European homes (United

Nations, *Compendium on Human Settlements Statistics*, table 16) and surely more square footage. Crowding in American homes dropped greatly over the centuries, while house sizes have grown (Lebergott, *The American Economy*, 3–5; Doucet and Weaver, "Material Culture").

6. See S. Wolf, *As Various As Their Land*, ch. 7, for an overview of public—really parochial—life. Ballard: Ulrich, *A Midwife's Tale*, esp. 99ff. (also Ulrich, *Good Wives*, ch. 3).

7. Rice, *Early American Taverns*; Thompson, *Rum Punch & Revolution*; Conroy, *In Public Houses* (Adams, 225); Clemen, "Shall I Not"; Thorp, "Taverns" ("Patrons certainly," 674); Criblez, "Tavernocracy"; Larkin, *The Reshaping of Everyday Life* ("sociability," 281); S. Wolf, *As Various as Their Land*, esp. 221–3; and Gilfoyle, "The Urban Geography," on related urban institutions. Hamilton: quoted by Alan Taylor, "Worlds within Words," *The New Republic*, Jul. 29, 2002, 35.

8. Boyer and Nissenbaum, *Salem Possessed*, 96–7, 101–2. (See chapter 4, note 25, for more on this study.)

9. Tavern decline, see note 7. Bars: Kaplan, "New York City Tavern Violence"; Gorn, "'Good-Bye Boys'"; and Kingsdale, "The 'Poor Man's Club.'"

10. Trollope: "In America, with the exception of dancing, which is almost wholly confined to the unmarried of both sexes, all the enjoyments of men are found in the absence of women. They dine, they play cards, they have musical meetings, they have suppers, all in large parties but all without women" (quoted in Simmons, *Star-Spangled Eden*, 40); Tocqueville: "American women never manage the outward concerns of the family" (ibid., 41). See also Ryan, *Women in Public*, ch. 2. Rape: Burrows and Wallace, *Gotham*, 407–8. Bourgeois: e.g., Hemphill, *Bowing to Necessities*, ch. 6. Post offices: Henkin, *The Postal Age*, ch. 3.

11. Revivals: Johnson, *A Shopkeepers' Millennium*, ch. 5; Bruce, *And They All Sang Hallelujah*; Kling, *A Field of Divine Wonders*; Larkin, *Reshaping of Everyday Life*, 278–81; Butler, *Awash in a Sea of Faith*; and Finke and Stark, *The Churching of America*. Belknap, "Commentaries," 199.

12. John, "Communications"; idem, "Taking Sabbatarianism Seriously" (Sunday post office, 547); Schudson, "Journalism" ("animals," 1897); R. Brown, *Knowledge is Power* ("tears," 170); Pred, *Urban Growth*, ch. 1 (spread of news); Henkin, *The Postal Age*; Degler, *At Odds*, 377–79; and Bushman, *The Refinement of America*, ch. 9.

13. Less work: Dublin, *Women at Work*; idem, *Transforming Women's Work*; Boydston, "The Woman"; Gabin, "Women and Work"; and Matthews, "Just a Housewife." Leaving downtown: Blumin, *The Emergence of the Middle Class*; Jackson, *Crabgrass Frontier*. Homes: Chappell, "Housing"; Clifford, *The American Family Home, 1800–1960*; Handlin, *The American Home*; Bushman, *The Refinement of America*, ch. 8; Larkin, *The Reshaping of Everyday Life*, ch. 3; Garvan, "Effects of Technology"; and Matthews, *"Just a Housewife,"* ch. 1.

14. Charleston: Pease and Pease, *Ladies, Women, & Wenches*, ch. 3. Danger of the streets: ibid., ch. 7; Kaplan, "New York City Tavern Violence," 610–13; Moore, "'Justifiable Provocation'"; S. Block, "Bringing Rapes to Court"; Godbeer, *Sexual Revolution in Early America*, 294 (who notes the frequency of rape during the Revolutionary War); and Kasson, *Rudeness & Civility*, 128–30.

15. Kemp, "Community"; Clarke, "So Lonesome." Hometown comrades: Costa and Kahn, *Heroes and Cowards*.

16. Overview: Barth, *City People*. Leisure time: Costa, "The Wage and the Length"; Whaples, "Hours." On the "brows": DiMaggio, "Cultural Entrepreneurship"; L. Levine, *Highbrow, Lowbrow*. Conflict: Rosenzweig, *Eight Hours for What We Will*; Couvares, "The Triumph of Commerce"; and Bluestone, "'The Pushcart Evil.'"

17. Barth, *City People*, ch. 5 (Twain, 182; Philadelphia, 184, 189); Rader, *Baseball*; Nasaw, *Going Out*, ch. 8; Peiss, *Cheap Amusements*; Kasson, *Amusing the Million;* Rosenzweig, *Eight Hours for What We Will*; and Schlereth, *Victorian America*, ch. 6.

18. Overview: Duis, *The Saloon*. See also Kingsdale, "The 'Poor Man's Club'"; Rosenzweig, *Eight Hours for What We Will*; Chudacoff, *The Age of the Bachelor*, ch. 4; Couvares, "The Triumph"; Swiencicki, "Consuming Brotherhood"; and Schlereth, *Victorian America*, 225–29.

19. Ryan, *Women in Public*, 78, also wrote: "By the 1870s . . . [legal and police] controls combined with urbanites' mental maps and the proliferation of semipublic institutions to create some semblance of order amid the confusion of public spaces. . . . [P]laces for [the woman's] amusement were the centerpiece of the new network of semipublic institutions" (62–64). Street etiquette: Peiss, *Cheap Amusements*; Kasson, *Rudeness & Civility*, 131. Security: see the discussion in chapter 2, p. 31 above; Schneider, *Detroit and the Problem of Order*; and Boyer, *Urban Masses and Moral Order*. Assertiveness: see chapter 4. Department stores: e.g., Leach, *Land of Desire*; Barth, *City People* (Italian, 121). Clubs: Benson, *Counter Cultures*, 84ff. Filene's: *Encyclopedia Britannica*, http://search.eb.com/eb/article-9034257. Nightlife: Erenberg, *Steppin' Out*, ch. 1–3; Nasaw, *Going Out*.

20. Nasaw, *Going Out*; Barth, *City People*; Kasson, *Amusing the Million*; Peiss, *Cheap Amusements*, 115ff (also on Coney Island); Rosenzweig, *Eight Hours for What We Will*; Cranz, "Changing Roles"; Schmitt, *Back to Nature*; Mintz, *Huck's Raft*, ch. 8; and Couvares, "The Triumph." San Francisco: "Amusing America," San Francisco Public Library, http://sfpl.org/news/onlineexhibits/amusing/ (accessed Jan. 15, 2008). New York: Burrows and Wallace, *Gotham*, ch. 64.

21. Excursions: Moline, *Mobility and the Small Town* (Rockport, 35); C. Fischer, *America Calling*, 213. Minister: W. H. Wilson, *The Evolution of the Country Community*, 128. Automobiles: Murphy, "How the Automobile"; Moline, *Mobility*; Wik, *Henry Ford and Grass-Roots America*; Berger, *The Devil Wagon in God's Country*; and C. Larson, "A History." Women: Scharf, *Taking the Wheel*; Interrante, "'You Can't Go to Town.'" Fredrick: Scharf, "Reinventing the Wheel," 7. Rural travelers: Belasco, *Americans on the Road*; Brunner and Kolb, *Rural Social Trends*; West, *Plainville, U.S.A*; Moe and Taylor, "Culture" (and other volumes in the USDA's "Rural Life Studies" of the 1940s); Adams, *The Transformation of Rural Life*; and Pedersen, *Between Memory and Reality*.

22. Gabler, *An Empire of Their Own*; Nasaw, *Going Out*; Peiss, *Cheap Amusements* (140, 148 for statistics); Dulles, *America Learns to Play* (exceeding other venues, 295); Rosenszweig, *Eight Hours for What We Will*; and Duis, *Saloon* (292–93 on decline). Rural moviegoing: e.g., Moline, *Mobility and the Small Town*; Neth, "Leisure and Generational Change." Attendance in 1918: C. Brown, *American Standards of Living*, 74.

Weekly attendance grew from forty million to ninety million between 1922 and 1930 (United States Bureau of the Census, *Historical Statistics*, 399–40).

23. Cullen, *The Art of Democracy*; Nasaw, *Going Out*, ch. 9; Peiss, *Cheap Amusements*; Rothman, *Hands and Hearts*, 292–93; Erenberg, *Steppin' Out*; and Light, "The Ethnic Vice Industry." Race: Nasaw, *Going Out*; Erenberg, *Steppin' Out*. Baseball attendance grew about 60 percent between the 1910s and 1920s (United States Bureau of the Census, *Historical Statistics*, 399–40).

24. Many histories attend to the problems of public disorder. See chapter 2; also Schneider, *Detroit and the Problem of Order*; Boyer, *Urban Masses and Moral Order*; R. Lane, *Murder in America*; and Gurr, *Violence in America*. Lofland, *A World of Strangers*, discusses the sociological issues. 1919: Drake and Cayton, *Black Metropolis*, ch. 4.

25. The percentage of Americans living in cities with populations of over 500,000 peaked at 18 percent in 1950 (United States Bureau of the Census, *Historical Statistics*, 11; Fischer and Hout, *Century of Difference*, ch. 7). Boarding houses: Peel, "On the Margins"; Meyerowitz, *Women Adrift*; S. Glenn, *Daughters of the Shtetl*; Knights, *Yankee Destinies*; Chudacoff, *The Age of the Bachelor*; and Gamber, "Away." Immigrants: J. Barton, *Peasants and Strangers*; Bodnar, *The Transplanted*; Bodnar et al., *Lives of Their Own*; and Rischin, *The Promised City*.

26. Wright, *Building the American Dream*, ch. 6; Marsh, "'From Separation'"; Doucet and Weaver, "Material Culture"; Clifford, *The American Family Home*; Handlin, *The American Home*; Warner, *Streetcar Suburbs*; and Jackson, *Crabgrass Frontier*. House facilities: Garvan, "Effects of Technology"; Lebergott, *The American Economy*, 93ff; H. Green, *The Light of the Home*; McMurry, *Families and Farmhouses*, ch. 4; and Tarr, "The Evolution." Accentuating the public-private contrast: Coontz, *The Social Origins of Private Life*; Laslett, "The Family."

27. Morality: Wright, *Building the Dream*, 98. Between roughly 1880 and 1920, native-born, white, middle-class married women *reduced* their work outside the home: Goldin, "Labor Markets" and "The Quiet Revolution"; Folbre, "Women's Informal"; and Fischer and Hout, *Century of Difference*, ch. 4. Elaborating family life: J. Gillis, *A World of Their Own Making*; Lasch, *Haven in a Heartless World*; and Coontz, *The Social Origins of Private Life*. Funerals: Wells, *Facing the "King of Terrors,"* ch. 8. July Fourth: Ryan, *Civic Wars*, 235ff; Rosenzweig, *Eight Hours for What We Will*, ch. 3; and C. Fischer, *America Calling*, 213. Immigrant aspirations: S. Glenn, *Daughters of the Shtetl*; Pederson, *Between Memory and Reality*, ch. 9; Gjerde, *The Minds of the West*; and Heinze, *Adapting to Abundance*.

28. Adderley: "Laments That Studio, TV Jobs Lure Good Musicians From Road," *Chicago Daily Defender*, Sept. 27, 1962. Leisure changes in the 1920s: Steiner, "Recreation and Leisure." Albany editor: Walter Ames, "Radio Moving In On Movies— Twenty-Five Years Ago," *LAT*, Aug. 10, 1953. Radio: United States Bureau of the Census, *Historical Statistics*, 796; Lundberg et al., *Leisure*, 186; Dulles, *America Learns to Play*, 329; Brunner and Kolb, *Recent Social Trends*, 265; S. Craig, "'The More They Listen'"; Willey and Rice, *Communication Agencies and Social Life*; Barron, *Mixed Harvest*, 215–25; Kline, *Consumers in the Country* (1925 woman, 123); and Neth, "Leisure."

29. Baseball attendance: United States Bureau of the Census, *Historical Statistics*,

399. Movies peaked at ninety million weekly admissions in 1930, lost ground but rose again to ninety million in the late '40s, and dropped to forty million in 1960 (ibid., 340). Middletown: Lynd and Lynd, *Middletown in Transition*, ch. 7. Home ownership: rates from the late nineteenth century into the 1920s were about 40 percent, spiked at 46 percent in 1930, dropped, and then rose largely due to government. See United States Bureau of the Census, *Historical Statistics*, 646. See also Tobey et al., "Moving Out"; Tobey, *Technology as Freedom*; and Chevan, "The Growth." Homeowners tend to stay put and be more locally involved (e.g., Guest et al., "Neighborhood Context"; Kasarda and Janowitz, "Community Attachment") and to be more often homebodies (Michelson, *Environmental Choice*; Gans, *The Levittowners*).

30. "V-J Day in Times Square," photograph by Alfred Eisenstaedt, 1945. Ownership: see previous note. The typical home had fewer residents as households included only the nuclear family and child-bearing dropped (e.g., Laslett, "The Family"; Harris, "The Flexible House"; and Fischer and Hout, *Century of Difference*, ch. 4). See also C. Clark, *The American Family Home*; C. Brown, *American Standards of Living*. Air conditioning: Between 1970 and 2006, the percentage of newly built, single-family homes with *central* air-conditioning rose from 34 to 89 percent (United States Bureau of the Census, *Statistical Abstract*, 1999, table 1201; and idem, *Statistical Abstract*, 2008, table 936). *House Beautiful*: quoted in Shove, *Comfort, Cleanliness and Convenience*, 45. Jackson, *Crabgrass Frontier*, credits much of Americans' withdrawal to home life to such comfort technologies.

31. Munch, "Cooperative Motherhood," describes a prototypical parochial involvement of the sort celebrated in Putnam's *Bowling Alone* (ch. 3) description of the 1950s and '60s associational activity. Demographics: In the 1960, under 20 percent of Americans were aged fifteen to twenty-nine, the lowest percentage in generations; in 1980, 27 percent were, the highest percentage since 1910 (Carter et al., *Historical Statistics of the United States*, table Aa185–286). On later marriage and child rearing, see Fischer and Hout, *Century of Difference,* ch. 4.

32. Perhaps the single best overview in the vast literature on suburbia is Jackson, *Crabgrass Frontier* (quotation, 280); see also Muller, *Contemporary Suburban America*. A key sociological study is Gans, *The Levittowners*. Culture critics: Donaldson, *The Suburban Myth*. For what scholars knew about the effects of suburbia (to 1984): C. Fischer, *The Urban Experience*, ch. 9; B. Schwartz, *The Changing Face of the Suburbs*. A more recent study is Oliver, "Mental Life." Longer commutes, along with television, are explanations that Putnam, *Bowling Alone*, gives for declining public participation.

33. Percentages: Gibson and Jung, "Historical Census." Crime: see chapter 2; rates rose first and fastest in the largest cities (C. Fischer, "The Spread of Crime"). "White Flight": Massey and Denton, *American Apartheid*; Farley et al., "Stereotypes and Segregation"; Zubrinsky and Bobo, "Prismatic Metropolis"; Cutler et al., "The Rise and Decline"; and Fischer and Massey, "The Ecology of Racial Discrimination." The fall of urban public life: Jackson, *Crabgrass Frontier*; Nasaw, *Going Out*; Jane Jacobs, *The Death and Life of Great American Cities*. Taverns and soda fountains: Oldenburg, *The Great Good Place*, 9, 78.

34. Crime decline, see chapter 2, pp. 000–000; it was particularly steep in the large cities and especially New York City. Urban revival: Birch, "Who Lives Downtown"; Kennedy and Leonard, "Dealing"; Jargowsky, "Stunning"; Florida, "Cities"; Domina, "Brain Drain." New York: "Left to Die, the South Bronx Rises From Decades of Decay," *NYT,* Nov. 13, 1994. Los Angeles: "Living Gets Loftier in Downtown L.A.," *LAT,* Nov. 22, 2005. Denver: Brooke, "Denver Stands Out in Trend Toward Living in Downtown," *NYT,* Dec. 29, 1998. "Touristification": e.g., Hannigan, *Trend Report on the Postmodern City.*

35. Survey: McDonagh, "Television and the Family." News stories: "Seal Bosses Fret as Fans Stay Home in Droves (TV)," *LAT,* Apr. 14, 1950; "SC Study: TV Owners Staying Home, Poll Reveals," *LAT,* Jul. 12, 1950; "Bus Line to Quit; Video Blamed [Lima, OH]," *NYT,* Jul. 3, 1951; "TV Found Factor in Transit Traffic Drop," *NYT,* Oct. 22, 1953; Thomas M. Pryors, "Movies' Decline Held Permanent," *NYT,* Apr. 7, 1958.

36. Television ownership: Carter et al., *Historical Statistics of the United States,* table Dg129; United States Bureau of the Census, *Statistical Abstract,* 2000, table 910. Television watching: In a 1950 Gallup poll (#460, question 20c), 75 percent said they had *not* watched in the prior three days; in a 1955 poll (#545, q. 13b), 55 percent said they *had* watched the day before; in a 1965 poll (#722, q. 1c) over 90 percent reported watching some television on a typical day (all items from "Gallup Brain," at http://institution.gallup.com/). Hours: Various estimates from the GSS ("tvhours" item, original numbers logged); United States Department of Labor, Bureau of Labor Statistics, "American Time Use," table 1; Nielsen, "Nielsen Media Research Reports; United States Bureau of the Census, *Statistical Abstract,* 2008, table 1098. The variability is partly a function of method, but also of what it means to "watch" television. Does it count if we are doing something else at the same time? Television as a favorite evening activity in Gallup surveys: Compare the top seven choices for 1938 and 1974 as reported in J. Robinson, "'Massification'" and J. Robinson and Godbey, "The Great American." After 1974, fewer Gallup respondents cited television as their favorite, but more answered "staying home with my family" or "relaxing," both of which surely included some television watching. From 1960 to 2005, the percentage of respondents citing those two activities or television as their favorite rose from about 50 percent to about 65 percent (my estimates from Saad, "There's No Place"; J. Carroll, "Family Time"). Whether television watching declined after the 1970s is unclear (compare the GSS "tvhours" item vs. J. Robinson and Godbey, "Busyness," table 1; Bianchi et al., *Changing Rhythms of American Family Life,* table 5.8). Too much television: Gallup poll reports for 1977 (#990, q. 5a), 1990 (August, q. 25; December, q. 22), and 2003 (December, q. 32, from "Gallup Brain," http://institution.gallup.com/). In each case, twice as many said too much as said too little.

37. Some summaries of the enormous literature on television: Comstock et al., *Television and Human Behavior,* ch. 4, 8; Cordelian, "Television"; Wartella and Mazzarella, "A Historical Comparison"; T. Williams, *The Impact of Television;* Kubey and Csikszentmihalyi, *Television and the Quality of Life;* and Putnam, *Bowling Alone,* ch. 13. Literacy: N. Glenn, "Television Watching"; Gaddy, "Television's Impact." Obesity: Ching et al., "Activity Level." Volunteering: Borgonovi, "Divided We Stand." Ag-

gression: Hoghen, "Factors Moderating"; Comstock and Paik, "The Effects"; and Centerwall, "Television." Distortions: e.g., O'Guinn and Shrum, "The Role of Television"; Shrum et al., "The Effects of Television"; Roemer et al., "The Treatment"; and Gilens, "Race and Poverty." Where the time for television comes from: J. Robinson and Converse, "Social Change," 40–44; J. Robinson and Godbey, "The Great American." Most studies have problems disentangling television's effects from selection effects. However, the few longitudinal studies—most notably, T. Williams, *The Impact of Television*—present results that are consistent with the claims I make. Movies: per capita attendance was over thirty movies a year before 1950 and about five from 1970 on—Carter et al., *Historical Statistics of the United States*, tables Dh388–89. Horse races: ibid., table Dh337. Baseball: ibid., table Dh328, 337. Bellamy and Walker ("Did Televised Baseball?") blame *radio* broadcasts of major league teams more than television. Attendance at cultural events declined or stagnated when one would have expected an increase, given incomes and education (e.g., DiMaggio and Mukhtar, "Arts Participation"). Americans' use of the outdoors peaked in the 1970s and then slowly declined (Pergams and Zaradic, "Evidence").

38. Computer availability: Day et al.," Computer." Necessity: Morin and Taylor, "Luxury or Necessity?," 2. The evidence on time shifts is muddled: DiMaggio et al., "Social Implications"; Wellman, "Connecting Communities"; Gershuny, "Web Use"; Veenhof, "The Internet"; Robinson and Martin, "IT and Activity"; and Robinson and De Haan, "Information Technology." Parochial use: see also notes 137 and 139 in chapter 4.

39. Speculations include the works of Marshall McLuhan and Meyrowitz, *No Sense of Place* (cf. C. Fischer, *America Calling*, ch. 1). Castells, *The Rise of Network Society*, ch. 6, discusses the persistence of place. Television and shared symbols: Beniger, "Does Television Enhance?"; Cerulo, "Television." Passive activity on the Internet: see Schradie, "The Digital Divide," for analysis of Pew surveys. California: Roger Niello, "Keep Your Kids Safe," http://republican.assembly.ca.gov/member/5/?p=article&sid=144&id=208349 (accessed Jan. 29, 2008).

40. Out of the home: survey response rates have declined since the 1970s partly because more people are away (Tom Smith, National Opinion Research Center, pers. comm., Jan. 30, 2008). Commuting: United States Bureau of the Census, "Most of Us Still Drive to Work—Alone," http://www.census.gov/Press-release/www/releases/archives/american_community_survey_acs/010230.html. Malls: Just how private or public malls are is matter of legal debate—L. Cohen, *A Consumer's Republic*, ch. 6; see also, "Court Ruling on Protests Curbs Malls in California," *NYT*, Dec. 25, 2007; "The Mall as Cocoon," *NYT*, Apr. 21, 1992 ("warm" quotation). Gated neighborhood numbers: Sanchez et al., "Security"; El Nasser, "Gated Communities More Popular," *USA Today*, Dec. 12, 2006; Palen, *The Urban World*, 129–30. Gated communities generally: Blakey and Snyder, *Fortress America*; Romig, "The Upper Sonoran Lifestyle." Americans' home-clinging: In 2003, over 80 percent of Americans polled ranked at-home activities as among their top three choices for spare time, compared to 66 percent of Western Europeans (Mary Kissel, "Leisure Pursuits Differ by Country," *Wall Street Journal*, Jul. 22, 2003). Cocooning: "Life Style in the '90s, According to Popcorn,"

LAT, Jan. 16, 1987; "The Essence of Cocooning," *LAT*, Aug. 7, 1987 ("cozy"); "Currents: Victorian Parlors Re-enacted," *NYT*, Sept. 8, 1988; "The End of Nesting," *Wall Street Journal*, May 16, 2003.

41. The research literature on life in crowds falls within the social psychology of city life. Classical statements include Simmel, "The Stranger"; R. Park, "The City"; Wirth, "Urbanism"; Gans, "Urbanism." For a literature review, see C. Fischer, *The Urban Experience*.

42. Valelly, "Vanishing Voters"; Putnam, "The Strange Disappearance"; "Study Says TV's Blare Obscures Community," *LAT*, Jun. 25, 1998; Robin Toner, "Consultants Ponder Coming Elections," *NYT*, Jul. 10, 1990.

43. American localism: Logan and Molotch, *Urban Fortunes*, ch. 5; Monkkonen, *America Becomes Urban*. Market regulation: Sheridan, "The Domestic Economy"; Rothenberg, *From Market-Places to a Market Economy*; and Nash, *The Urban Crucible*. Welfare: Trattner, *From Poor Law to Welfare State*, ch. 2; D. Jones, "The Strolling Poor." Personal regulation: See chapter 4 of this book. "Most Americans": Shain, *The Myth of American Individualism*, 50. On early localism: Breen, "Persistent Localism"; Nobles, "Breaking." In surveys, Americans generally rate and prefer state and especially local governments over the federal government (e.g., Kaiser Family Foundation, "Attitudes toward Government").

44. Low participation: Butler, *Becoming America*, ch. 3; Schudson, *The Good Citizen*; and Greene, "Social and Cultural Capital." Case studies: Lockridge, *A New England Town*; Gross, *The Minutemen*; and Innes, *Labor in a New Land*. Political deference: see also Greene, "Society, Ideology, and Politics"; Robertson, "Voting Rites." Estimates for average legislative elections in the mid-eighteenth century are well below 50 percent, occasionally spurting into the 60 percent range (Butler, *Becoming America*, 97–98; Kolp, "The Dynamics"; Nash, "The Transformation"; and Beeman, "Deference" [also the Washington story, 417–18]). Turnouts for a comparably privileged population in 1996–2004 presidential elections—male, white, twenty-five-plus years old, homeowner—were about 70 percent or more (my analysis of the GSS, discounting some for exaggeration). A popular account of voting history: Jill Lepore, "Rock, Paper, Scissors: How We Used to Vote," *The New Yorker*, Oct. 13, 2008 .Crowd action: B. C. Smith, "Beyond the Vote" (smokehouse), as well as Nash, "The Transformation"; and Beeman, "Deference."

45. See previous note and: Nash, *The Urban Crucible*; McDonnell, "Popular Mobilization"; Morris, "Social Change"; Zuckerman, "Tocqueville, Turner, and Turds"; Conroy, *In Public Houses*; J. Block, *A Nation of Agents*, ch. 7 (Adams, 269); Appleby, *Inheriting the Revolution*, ch. 5; Shalhope, "Individualism"; and Hemphill, "The Middle Class Rising."

46. Democratic stirrings: see chapter 4, pp. 110–111; Zuckerman, "Tocqueville, Turner, and Turds"; Pasley, " The Cheese"; Robertson, "Voting Rites"; Schudson, *Good Citizen*, 91ff; Wiebe, *Self-Rule*; Ryan, *Civic Wars*; Foner, *Story of American Freedom*, ch. 1; Ellis, "The Market Revolution"; Morris, "Social Change"; Newman, "One Nation"; and Varon, "Tippecanoe." Ideology: compare Wood, "Republicanism," to Wilentz, "Jacksonian Democracy." Rhetoric: Cmiel, *Democratic Eloquence*. D. Howe,

What Hath God Wrought, ch. 6, stresses transportation and communications; see also R. Brown, *Knowledge is Power*; Henkin, *The Postal Age*; and Sellers, *The Market Revolution*.

47. See sources in previous note, such as Foner, Schudson, and Wiebe. Public meetings: Ryan, *Civic Wars*, ch. 3. Sunday mail: John, "Taking Sabbatarianism." Jackson and Kentucky: Simmons, *Star-Spangled Eden*, 40, 10. Fisher, *A Philadelphia Perspective*, 24–25. Quackenbush and Sylvester, "Letter of Jacob Schramm," 279. Indiana: Carter et al., *Historical Statistics of the United States*, table Eb77.

48. Statistics: Carter et al., *Historical Statistics of the United States*, tables Eb114–122. Formisano, "Deferential-Participant Politics"; Ratcliffe, "Voter Turnout."

49. Altschuler and Blumin challenge the common image of a highly politicized "party era" in "Where Is the Real America?"; "Limits"; and *Rude Republic*. For critiques, see commentary after "Limits" (pp. 886–909 of the *Journal of American History* 84, Dec. 1997); Becker, "Involved Disengagements"; Neely, *The Boundaries of American Political Culture in the Civil War Era*. See also Schudson, *The Good Citizen*, on self-interest. For more on nineteenth-century electoral blandishments, see p. 186 below.

50. See Altschuler and Blumin, *Rude Republic*, ch. 5; Ryan, *Civic Wars*; Skocpol, "How Americans Became Civic"; Kemp, "Community"; and Althschuler and Saltzgaber, "The Limits of Responsibility." Keegan, *A History of Warfare*, notes that the Civil War's mobilization represented "about the maximum a society can tolerate while continuing to function at normal levels of efficiency" (355); also, casualties were at unprecedented levels.

51. Spending: Holcombe and Lacombe, "The Growth"; Heer, "Taxation"; and L. White, "Public Administration." Urban projects: e.g., Monkkonen, *America Becomes Urban*. Conflicts over the role of government: Ravitch, *The Great School Wars*; Gjerde, *The Minds of the West*, ch. 10; Rosenzweig, *Eight Hours for What We Will*; Brown and Warner, "Immigrants"; Oestreicher, "Urban Working-Class Political Behavior"; and McCormick, "The Party Period." Voting: Carter et al., *Historical Statistics of the United States*, tables Eb114–122. Congressional elections refer to both presidential and off-year elections. "Everyone": Kornbluth, *Why America Stopped Voting*, xii.

52. Arguing for the meaningfulness of nineteenth-century voting: Wiebe, *Self-Rule*; Ryan, *Civic Wars*; Kornbluth, *Why America Stopped Voting*; Burnham, "Triumphs"; and Beckert, "Involved Disengagement?" Skepticism: Altschuler and Blumin, *Rude Republic*; Schudson, *The Good Citizen*; McCormick, "The Party Period"; Fredman, "The Introduction" (McCook, 206); and Argersinger, "New Perspectives." Kleppner, in *Who Voted?* and *Continuity and Change in Electoral Politics*, is one researcher who saw electoral enthusiasm as genuine, but as a sort of "political confessionalism" tied to ethnicity and religion (*Who Voted?* 47).

53. See general sources in previous note such as Kleppner and Kornbluth and Von Hoffman, *Local Attachments*, ch. 7.

54. Heckelman, "The Effect"; idem, "Revisiting"; Mayfield, "Voting Fraud"; Argersinger, "New Perspectives." Experiment: Addonizio et al., "Putting the Party Back." Vote seller: Christina Capecchi, "College Student's Offer of a Vote for Sale Draws Unwanted Attention," *NYT*, Jul. 5, 2008.

55. McCormick, "Life"; Formasino, "The Party Period" (with comment by Holt, "The Primacy"); Jenkins et al., "Constituency Cleavages."

56. Wiebe, *The Search for Order* and *Self-Rule* ("island communities"); McCormick, "Public Life"; Brinkley, "Prosperity, Depression, and War"; Sussman, *Culture as History*; and Galambos, "Technology, Political Economy, and Professionalization."

57. Turnouts for off-year elections outside the South probably indicate political interest best. During 1878–1894, they averaged 71 percent, 1900–1914, 62 percent, and 1918–30, 43 percent (Carter et al., *Historical Statistics of the United States*, tables Eb114–122). *Los Angeles Times* stories: "Our Apathetic Voters," Aug. 2, 1924; Fredric J. Haskin, "Minority Rules United States," Dec. 10, 1924; and "Drive Begun to Get Out Vote," Jul. 2, 1926. Gidlow, "Delegitimizing Democracy," describes the 1920s get-out-the-vote campaign and ideology in detail. See also studies on voting decline cited in note 52.

58. Lynd and Lynd, *Middletown*, ch. 24 (quotation, 416).

59. Excepting 1942 and 1946, the non-South off-year turnouts from 1934 to 1970 exceeded 50 percent for the first time in twenty years; they didn't come close from 1974 through at least 2006. For a general description, see D. Kennedy, *Freedom from Fear*. Voting: Kleppner, *Who Voted*, ch. 5 ("son of bitch," 83); Oestreicher, "Urban Working-Class Political Behavior"; Gamm, *The Making of New Deal Democrats*. Machines: Stave, "The New Deal." GI Bill: Mettler, "Bringing."

60. Putnam, *Bowling Alone*; M. Franklin et al., "Generational Basis"; W. Lyons and Alexander, "A Tale." R. E. Lane, "The Politics of Consensus"; idem, "The Decline of Politics"; cf. R. E. Lane, *The Loss of Happiness in Market Democracies*, ch. 11. Voting data: McDonald and Popkin, "The Myth"; Michael P. McDonald, "United States Election Project," http://elections.gmu.edu/voter_turnout.htm (accessed Jan. 1, 2009).

61. Kleppner, *Who Votes*, ch. 6; Putnam, *Bowling Alone*; Brady et al., "Who Bowls"; Schudson, *The Good Citizen*; Dalton, *Citizen Politics in Western Democracies*; Gray and Caul, "Declining Voter"; Caren, "Big City?"; Fitzgerald, "Greater Convenience"; Gronke et al., "Convenience Voting"; and Blais, "What Affects Voter Turnout?" (eighteen-to-twenty-year-olds voting). Elimination of Southern states' rank discriminatory tactics like literacy tests and poll taxes certainly boosted voting there. By 1960, non-Southern voting rates had recovered from their lows in the 1920s. A couple of the post-1960s off-year elections have official non-Southern turnout rates just under 40 percent (Carter et al., *Historical Statistics of the United States*, tables Eb-114–22), but those are biased by the inclusion of ineligible voters (mainly noncitizens and felons) in the denominator. A proper estimate puts the post-1970 off-year-election rates in the low-to-middling 40 percent range (McDonald and Popkin, "The Myth").

62. Verba et al., *Voice and Equality*, table 3.6, suggest that nonvoting political activity like lobbying *increased* between 1967 and 1987, but later data suggest a small decline through the mid-1990s (Putnam, *Bowling Alone*, ch. 2). National Election Survey (NES) data show that activity such as lobbying people to vote and using bumper stickers sagged during the mid-1970s but recovered by the 2000s (http://www.electionstudies.org/nesguide/gd-index.htm; accessed Mar. 6, 2008). Declining response rates to the NES raise questions about whether the resurgence is real (Bur-

den, "Voter Turnout"), but this pattern holds for off-year elections alone, which seem less sensitive. Interest: NES data indicate that interest may have revived in the 1990s and 2000s (http://www.electionstudies.org/nesguide/gd-index.htm; accessed Mar. 6, 2008); see also Higher Education Research Institute, "Most of the Nation's"; idem, "The American Freshman"; Dalton, *Citizen Politics*, 22–24; Putnam, *Bowling Alone*, 35–36; and Zukin et al., *A New Engagement?*, 82ff. Knowledge: N. Glenn, "Television Watching"; Delli Carpini and Keeter, "Stability and Change"; Jennings, "Political Knowledge"; and T. Smith, "Changes in the Generation Gap." Churchill: J. Carroll, "Teens' Knowledge." Education: Rising school attainment should have boosted turnout, but Tenn, "An Alternative Measure," finds that it is *relative* education that matters.

63. Gentzkow, "Television." Other means: Zukin et al., *A New Engagement?*; Crenson and Ginsberg, *Downsizing Democracy*; Schudson, *The Good Citizen*; Wuthnow, *Acts of Compassion*; and idem, *Loose Connections*. Putnam, *Bowling Alone*, especially regarding "bonding" vs. "bridging" social ties. Teixeira, *The Disappearing American Voter*, ch. 2, finds that declining church attendance accounts for part of the drop in voting.

64. Historical explanations: Mansbridge, "Social"; Weaver et al., "The Polls"; Gilens, *Why Americans Hate Welfare*; Kleppner, *Who Votes*; King, "The Polarization"; Teixeira, *The Disappearing American Voter*, ch. 2. Overseas: Gray and Caul, "Declining Voter Turnout." Demobilization: Rosenstone and Hansen, *Mobilization, Participation, and Democracy in America*; Crenson and Ginsberg, *Downsizing Democracy*; and Valelly, "Vanishing Voters."

65. The trust numbers are calculated from the NES, http://sda.berkeley.edu/ (see also http://www.electionstudies.org/nesguide/gd-index.htm#5). Gallup's trust responses are lower but parallel to the NES's through 2004 and then drop ("Gallup Brain," http://institution.gallup.com/). Assassination: Gallup, *The Gallup Poll: Public Opinion 2001*, 95, and after 2001, "Gallup Brain." Overviews of the literature on distrusting government include Nye et al., *Why People Don't Trust Government* (see also the conclusion, by Nye and Zelikow); Levi and Stoker, "Political Trust"; Wills, *A Necessary Evil*; and Lipset and Schneider, *The Confidence Gap*. Specific studies: Dalton, "The Social Transformation"; Inglehart, "Postmaterialist Values"; Cantril and Cantril, *Reading Mixed Signals*; Pew Research Center, "Deconstructing Distrust"; Kaiser Family Foundation, " Why Don't Americans Trust?"; Lipset, "Malaise and Resiliency"; Putnam, *Bowling Alone*, ch. 2; King, "The Polarization"; Hetherington, "The Effect of Political Trust"; Weakliem and Borch, "Alienation"; Karp, "Explaining Public Support"; Brooks and Cheng, "Declining"; Rosenzweig and Thelen, *The Presence of the Past*, esp. 132–3; and Cook and Gronke, "The Skeptical American." More recent studies suggest that heterogeneity undermines such trust (Costa and Kahn, "Civic Engagement"; Putnam, "E Pluribus Unum").

66. Local government: Gallup, *The Gallup Poll: Public Opinion 2003*, 354-5; idem, "Trust in Government," http://www.gallup.com/poll/5392/Trust-Government.aspx; accessed Mar. 5, 2008 (also, trusting the federal government in international and domestic affairs did not drop much); Pew Research Center, "Federal Government's"; and Jennings, "Political Trust." 9/11: See Gallup poll, "Trust in Government." Not

correlated: Hetherington, "The Political Relevance"; Zukin et al., *A New Engagement?* 106. In one study, more respondents explained their distrust in terms of politicians' dishonesty and the federal government's inefficiency that in any other ways (Kaiser Family Foundation, "Attitudes toward Government," q. 46).

67. Baby: Jodi Wilgoren, "Toddler Reported Abducted in Bus Terminal," *NYT,* Dec. 27, 2001; John W. Fountain, "Girl Abducted at Bus Station Is Found in West Virginia," *NYT,* Dec. 28, 2001.

68. Overviews: T. Smith, "Factors Relating to Misanthropy"; Uslaner, *The Moral Foundations of Trust*; Putnam, *Bowling Alone*, ch. 8; Nannestad, "What Have We Learned?"; Jennings and Stoker, "Social Trust"; Hardin, "Solving the Problem"; and Stolle and Hooghe, "Review Article." Truncated versions of the question appear as far back as 1942, but the first major uses include M. Rosenberg, "Misanthropy"; Rotter, "A New Scale"; and idem, "Generalized Expectancies." The earliest surveys asked only the first half, "Do you think," yes or no (Erskine, "The Polls"; T. Smith, "Factors Relating to Misanthropy"). "Yes" answers *increased* from 1940s to ca. 1960. The longest series are from the NES (1964 on) and the GSS (1972 on), both available on-line (e.g., http://sda.berkeley.edu/), and both reported in many sources. The post-1960s numbers are from the NES. (N.b., NES results show an upswing to 47 percent in 2000–4, but some of that rise was due to occasional telephone interviews [Arthur Lupia, Institute for Social Research, pers. comm., Mar. 18, 2008]. Method-constant, 45 percent is a better estimate.) The GSS trend is more uniformly declining: about 43 percent trusting answers in the 1970s, 36 percent in the 1990s, and 33 percent in 2006–8 (English interviews only for comparability). The decline is largely a cohort rather than a period effect (R. Robinson and Jackson, "Is Trust?"; my analysis). Annual surveys of high school seniors also show a steady decline (T. Smith, "Factors Relating to Misanthropy"; Rahn and Transue, "Social Trust"). The percentage of American respondents born after 1950 who gave trusting answers to surveys taken between 1982 and 1999 was fourteen points lower than for respondents of the same age who were born in the 1930s. In no other nation is the difference that great and in many, particularly in northern Europe, later generations were *more* trusting (my analysis of eleven major countries in the World Values Survey, http://www.worldvaluessurvey. org, accessed Mar. 19, 2008; see also Nannestad, "What Have We Learned?," 421–22; Stolle and Hooghe, "Review Article," 158).

69. In one study that allowed it, over three-fifths of respondents agreed with each position (Wuthnow, "Trust," 163; see also 1983 GSS experiment reported in T. Smith, "Factors Relating to Misanthropy"). Another found that American students were both more trusting *and* more cautious than students in Japan, which researchers interpreted as a reflection of Americans' concerns about crime (A. Miller and Mitamura, "Are Surveys?"). Another found UCLA students to be more cautious than Brigham Young undergraduates (Dekker, "Generalised"). People who answer in a trusting manner do not necessarily trust others more in action, but seem themselves more worthy of trust (Rotter, "Generalized Expectancies"; idem, "Interpersonal Trust"; and Glaeser et al., "Measuring Trust"). The question may really test how respondents prefer to present themselves. On the rapidity (or not) of personality change, see chapter 6.

70. Less honest: Putnam, *Bowling Alone*, ch. 8; Rahn and Transue, "Social Trust." Uslaner, *Moral Foundations*, ch. 6, contends that rising inequality explains most of the decline in trust responses (see also Uslaner and Brown, "Inequality, Trust"). Increasing crime: The NES trust series correlates –.64 with the homicide rate lagged four years (my analysis; see also C. Fischer, "The Public and Private Worlds"). Increasing diversity: Costa and Kahn, "Civic Engagement"; idem, "Understanding the American Decline"; Putnam, "E Pluribus Unum"; Alesina and La Ferrara, "Who Trusts Others?; and Stolle et al., "When Does Diversity?." Uslaner, "Does Diversity?," dissents. Changing meanings: responses to the trust question are sensitive to preceding questions (T. Smith, "Factors Relating to Misanthropy"), and survey researchers know that the meanings of words drift over time. Too much: political scientist and trust expert Russell Hardin concluded that scholars have learned virtually nothing from all this research (quoted by Nannestad, "What Have We Learned?," 431).

71. "Adventure of a Confidence Man," *New York Daily Times*, Oct. 21, 1852. On the speculation that personal distrust reflects withdrawal from public spaces: The highly trusting American survey respondents of the 1950s and '60s were adolescents between 1910 and 1930, years of much public activity; the least trusting respondents of the 1990s were adolescents roughly in the 1950s, years of less public life.

72. R. E. Lane, *The Loss of Happiness*, 250. Expressions of concern about withdrawal from public spaces include Jane Jacobs, *The Death and Life of Great American Cities*; Putnam, *Bowling Alone* (see his distinction between "bonding" and "bridging" ties); Wuthnow, *Loose Connections*; and Jackson *Crabgrass Frontier*, 280–82. Street battles: see chapter 2; Ryan, *Civic Wars*. Tolerance: Many sociological studies demonstrate increases in verbal tolerance and also in behavior (see reviews in Fischer and Hout, *Century of Difference*, ch. 3, 8).

Chapter Six

1. Chandler, *The Elements of Character*, 8; gift noted in Fleischner, *Mrs. Lincoln and Mrs. Keckly*, 173; Guelzo, *Abraham Lincoln*, 105. Training program: Adaptive Learning Systems, http://www.adaptivlearning.com/main_windows.htm (accessed Feb. 2, 2007. Positive Psychology: http://www.ppc.sas.upenn.edu/index.html (accessed Feb. 2, 2007).

2. See collection edited by Pfister and Schnog, *Inventing the Psychological*; Reddy, "Against Constructionism"; Gergen, "History and Psychology"; Stearns and Stearns, "Emotionology"; Morawski, "Educating the Emotions"; Zuckerman, "The Fabrication of Identity"; and Veroff et al., *The Inner American*. Neurasthenia may have come back as chronic fatigue syndrome—Abbey and Garfinkel, "Neurasthenia"; Schäfer, "On the History"; see also Barke et al., "Nervous Breakdown." Courses: Over four hundred thousand students enrolled in undergraduate psychology classes in 1995–96, for example (American Psychological Association, http://research/apa.org/gen6.html; accessed Mar. 22, 2000); and in the mid-2000s, over eighty thousand earned bachelor's degrees in psychology each year (National Center for Education Statistics, table 261, http://nces.ed.gov/programs/digest/d07/tables/dt07_261

.asp?referrer=report). Psychologist Joyce Brothers had a syndicated advice show on network television in the 1950s and 1960s; psychologist Phil McGraw has had his own television program since 2002. Woody Allen: *Annie Hall* (dir. Woody Allen, dist. MGM, May 30, 2000).

3. Curti, *Human Nature in American Thought*; Pfister, "On Conceptualizing." See also collections such as Stearns and Lewis, *An Emotional History of the United States*; Pfister and Schnog, *Inventing the Psychological*.

4. Cross-cultural psychology: Markus and Kitayama, "Culture and the Self"; idem, "Culture, Self,"; Shweder and Bourne, "Does the Concept?"; Iyengar and Lepper, "Choice"; Mezulis et al., "Is There a Universal?" and Geertz, *Local Knowledge*, 59. Anxiety: Giddens, *Modernity and Self-Identity*.

5. Ordinary folks: Hansen, *A Very Social Time*, has employed a collection of "middling" Americans' diaries to good use. Sobel, *Teach Me Dreams*, draws on the life stories that converts to nineteenth-century sects were asked to write upon their "new birth." Bjorklund, *Interpreting the Self*, draws on a wide range of autobiographies. Oral histories conducted by Works Progress Administration interviewers during the Depression are available online (http://lcweb2.loc.gov/wpaintro/wpahome.html). Lord Chesterfield: e.g., Hemphill, "Class, Gender." Warren: Hayes, "Mercy Otis Warren," 620. Standards: in 1985, Peter and Carol Stearns, "Emotionology," called for studying the cultural standards for emotions, rather than chase after experienced emotions. Gergen, "History and Psychology," argues that all historians *can* study is the "discourse" of emotions.

6. Peck: *The Road Less Traveled* (unconscious, 281; self-examination, 51). Sales: obituary of Scott Peck by Adam Bernstein, *San Francisco Chronicle*, Nov. 28, 2005. Fundamentalist attacks: Charles Leerhsen, "Peck's Path to Inner Peace," *Newsweek*, Nov. 18, 1985, 79. Warren: Warren, *The Purpose Driven Life* ("not about,"17; pleasing God, 69; "God's ultimate," 173). Sales: Ann Rodgers, "'Purpose-Driven' Life Author to Speak Here Friday," *Pittsburgh Post-Gazette*, Nov. 9, 2005. Journalist Malcolm Gladwell also noted the conjunction between these two books, adding that the "self-help genre . . . is fundamentally inward-focused" ("The Cellular Church," *The New Yorker*, Sept. 12, 2005, http://www.newyorker.com/archive/2005/09/12/050912fa_fact_gladwell; accessed Jan. 2, 2009). See also McGee, *Self-Help, Inc.*

7. Foucault et al., *Technologies of the Self*, reviews famous cases of self-perfecting; see also Elias, *The Civilizing Process*. P. Wagner, "Self," summarizes social science approaches to the self. Colonial and antebellum Americans: D. Howe, *Making the American Self;* Hoffman et al., *Through a Glass Darkly*. B. Franklin, *Autobiography,* 82, 84. Scholars typically use "self-fashioning"—attributed to literary scholar Stephen Greenblatt—to describe efforts people make to conform (e.g., Lockridge's "Colonial Self-Fashioning" is about Virginia gentry trying to fit in with London culture). I mean to cover a wider range of self-work, including developing countercultural dispositions. Many historians adopt Warren Sussman's distinction between character and personality (in "'Personality'"). I am not persuaded of the distinction's historical reality (see Eustace, *Passion is the Gale*, 67) and use the terms interchangeably.

8. Washington: "George Washington's Rules of Civility," Colonial Williamsburg,

http://www.history.org/Almanack/life/manners/rules2.cfm (accessed Jun. 23, 2005); "Washington's School Exercises," Papers of George Washington, http://gwpapers .virginia.edu/documents/civility/ (accessed Jun. 23, 2005). Diaries and early self-perfecting:, Sobel, *Teach Me Dreams* (Pinckney, 17–18; church essays, ch. 1); idem, "The Revolution"; C. Kelly, "Well Bred"; Augst, *The Clerk's Tale*, ch. 1; Lockridge, "Colonial Self-Fashioning"; and Isaac, "Stories." R. Brown, *Knowledge is Power*, 6, points out that perhaps only one in a hundred diaries in the archives provide more than cursory entries.

9. Chandler, *The Elements of Character*, 13. Augst, *The Clerk's Tale*, ch. 1, describes antebellum diary writing. Hayes: M. Wood and Zurcher, *The Development of a Postmodern Self*, 72. Advice books: Hemphill, *Bowing to Necessities*; idem, "The Middle Class"; idem, "Class, Gender"; Schlesinger, *Learning How to Behave*; Kasson, *Rudeness and Civility*; Bushman, *The Refinement of America*; and Augst, *The Clerk's Tale* ("*whatever you will resolve*," 57). Haltunnen, *Confidence Men*, 28, attributes the quote to education reformer William A. Alcott. Child rearing advice: Hessinger, "Problems"; Rodgers, "Socializing Middle-Class Children"; Ryan, *Cradle of the Middle Class*; Mintz and Kellogg, *Domestic Revolutions*, ch. 3; Mintz, *Huck's Raft*, ch. 4; Stearns and Stearns, *Anger*; and J. Lewis, "Mother Love" ("moral habits," from *Mother's Magazine*, 212). Nineteenth-century ideology of character improvement: D. Howe, *Making the American Self*. Lydia Child: from *The Mother's Book*, in D. Davis, *Antebellum American Culture*, 23–24.

10. Self-improvement: Blumin, *The Emergence of the Middle Class*; R. Brown, *Knowledge is Power*; Bushman, *The Refinement of America*; and C. Kelly, "'Well-Bred Country People.'" Augst, *The Clerk's Tale*, ch. 2, stresses that the culture called for personal reports in letters and diaries. The evangelical role: Hatch, *The Democratization of American Christianity;* Ryan, *The Cradle of the Middle Class*; Johnson, *Shopkeepers' Millennium*; Sobel, *Teach Me Dreams*; D. Howe, "Protestantism, Voluntarism, and Personal Identity"; Appleby, *Inheriting the Revolution*, ch. 6; Noll, "The American Revolution"; Finke and Stark, *The Churching of America;* Lindman, "Wise Virgins"; and Blackwell, "Surrogate Ministers" (Brattleboro).

11. Ryan, *Cradle of the Middle Class*, and P. Johnson, *Shopkeepers' Millennium*, stress the economic payoff. D. Howe, *Making the American Self*, and Haskell, "Capitalism" illustrate other approaches. Dawley, *Class & Community*, 32ff, describes businessman Benjamin Franklin (!) Newhall, who exhibited the classic personality of the up-and-coming entrepreneur. "Train up": see chapter 4, note 55 re 1816 advice.

12. Advice books: Hemphill, *Bowing to Necessities*, 131ff; Bushman, *The Refinement of America* (on the upwardly striving and on reformers' aspirations, 420ff). Channing, *Self-Culture*. New institutions: e.g., Boyer, *Urban Masses and Moral Order*. Schools: Ravitch, *The Great School Wars*; Bodnar, *The Transplanted*, ch. 7; Mintz, *Huck's Raft*, ch. 4; and Lassonde, "Learning."

13. The central work on the antebellum sincerity is Halttunen's *Confidence Men*; see also Wood, "Conspiracy," 412ff. Chesterfield's popularity: R. Brown, *Knowledge is Power*, 348n7; Haltunnen, *Confidence Men*, 94ff. Chesterfield wrote, for example: "Mankind . . . are more governed by appearances than by realities . . . . Few people

have penetration enough . . . to examine beyond the exterior; they take their notions from the surface, and go no deeper" (Chesterfield, *Letters to His Son*, letter CXLI). Scandals: a clergyman's crimes is told in Pilarczyk, "The Terrible Haystack Murder"; the most famous case is the adultery scandal of Rev. Henry Ward Beecher in the 1870s. Connell: Blauvelt, "The Work," 578. Letters: Lystra, *Searching the Heart*.

14. P. Stearns, *The Battleground of Desire*, ch. 6 (and Stearns's work generally); Dumneil, *Modern Temper*, 146–47; Wouters, "Etiquette Books," part one; idem, "Etiquette Books," part two; Heinze, "Schizophrenia Americana"; Curti, "The Changing Concept'"; Sussman, *Culture as History*; J. Morawska, "Educating the Emotions"; and Pfister and Schnog, *Inventing the Psychological*; McGee, *Self-Help, Inc*. (1988 survey). Alfred Kazin, "The Freudian Revolution Analyzed," *NYT Sunday Magazine*, May 6, 1956, 22. Psychiatrists, etc: United States Department of Labor, Bureau of Labor Statistics, Occupational employment, http://www.bls.gov/oes/current/oes_alph.htm (accessed Jun. 30, 2008). Americans increasingly interpreted problems psychologically: Veroff et al., *The Inner American,* ch. 3; Pescosolido et al., "Americans' Views"; Phelan et al., "Public Conceptions." Therapeutic ethos: Lears, "From Salvation"; Weiss, *American Myth of Success*, ch. 7; and Wuthnow, *Sharing the Journey*.

15. Turner, "The Real Self"; Bjorklund, *Interpreting the Self*; M. Wood and Zurcher, *The Development of a Postmodern Self*; Thomson, *In Conflict No Longer*; Lears, "From Salvation"; Benton "Self and Society"; and Arditi, "Etiquette Books." D. Bell, *The Cultural Contradictions of Capitalism*, 19. See also Wouters, "Etiquette Books," part one; Lears, *No Place of Grace*; Benton, "Self and Society"; Babbitt and Burbach, "A Comparison"; Thomson, "The Transformation"; and Veroff et al., *The Inner American*, ch. 3.

16. P. Stearns, "Girls, Boys, and Emotions," reports a brief decline in advice literature early in the twentieth century and then a resurgence. McGee, *Self-Help, Inc*, 11, reports a doubling of self-help books between 1972 and 2000. Shyness: McDaniel, *Shrinking Violets and Caspar Milquetoasts*. Sex manuals long predated the twentieth century but were directed at married couples and were less frank. Spock: Graebner, "The Unstable World," notes, for example, that Spock insisted that "discipline must be internalized. A properly led child, argues Spock, will want to go to bed on time" (623). An excellent study of modern middle-class child rearing is Lareau's *Unequal Childhoods*.

17. Theories of the multiple self: James, *The Principles of Psychology*, 293ff; Simmel, *Conflict and the Web of Group Affiliations*; Coser, *In Defense of Modernity*; Giddens, *Modernity and Self-Identity*; Gergen, *The Saturated Self*; Bjorlund, *Interpreting the Self*, ch. 6; Smith-Lovin, "The Strength of Weak Identities." Psychological studies on whether people (almost always undergraduates) who report themselves as being different in different situations also appear to be psychologically troubled seem to conclude that there is no connection. Baird et al., "On the Nature," seems definitive as of late 2006; see also Donhaue et al., "The Divided Self"; Sheldon et al., "Trait Self"; Menagahan, "Role Changes"; and Bigler et al., "The Divided Self." Facebook: Riva Richmond, "On Networking Sites, Learning How Not to Share," *NYT*, Jan. 29, 2009.

18. Sennett, *The Fall of Public Man*, 5, 8. The narcissism hypothesis: Battan, "The 'New Narcissism'"; Giddens, *Modernity and Self-Identity*, ch. 5; Thomson, *In Conflict*

No Longer, ch. 2; and Crocker and Park, "The Costly Pursuit." Twenge et al., "Egos Inflating," claims that college women's narcissism increased after the 1970s, but see Trzesniewski et al., "Is 'Generation Me'?" People who "ruminate" about their shortcomings do seem to suffer some depression and anxiety (Mor and Winquist, "Self-Focused"). Sheila-ism: Bellah et al., *Habits of the Heart*, 221.

19. Extended adulthood: Furstenberg et al., "Growing Up"; Settersten et al., *On the Frontier*; and Arnett, "Learning." Danziger and Rouse, "The Price," find that the delay of marriage is not really explainable economically and suggest a cultural dimension.

20. Culture and thinking: Lehman et al., "Psychology and Culture," 695–700; Nisbett et al., "Culture and Systems of Thought"; and Al-Zahrani and Kaplowitz, "Attributional Biases" (Saudis). See also Nisbett, *The Geography of Thought*.

21. Tönnies, *Community and Society*, exemplifies the classic argument, that "rational will" was replacing "natural will" (37; collective, timeworn, unreflective action). Add Weber, Simmel, and Durkheim, as well. "Rationality" can be defined in several ways; mine is close to what Swidler, "The Concept of Rationality," calls "rationalism," efficiently matching means to ends. Native peoples: e.g., Root, *Fountain of Privilege*, 61–77. On applications to America: e.g., R. Brown, "Modernization" (quotation, 533) and *Modernization*. Other examples include Giddens's focus, in *The Consequences of Modernity*, on "reflexivity" and Coser's argument, in *In Defense of Modernity*, that modernity produces sophisticated thought; and the general works of Talcott Parsons.

22. Sellers, *The Market Revolution*, is the key text (Englishman, 153); also Henretta, "Families and Farms"; idem, "The 'Market'"; Christopher Clark, "The Consequences"; Kulikoff, "The Transition"; Merrill, "Putting 'Capitalism'"; and Shain, *The Myth of American Individualism*. Skeptics include Bender, *Community and Social Change in America*, who wrote that early Americans "did not lack rationality, a concern for efficiency, or a willingness to work hard on behalf of their self-interest. What they lacked . . . was an autonomous economic institution legitimizing and facilitating the pursuit of economic goals" (113). See also Appleby, "The Vexed Story of Capitalism"; Rothenberg, *From Market-Places to a Market Economy*; G. Wood, "The Enemy"; Nobles, "Breaking"; Innes, "Fulfilling"; Greene, *Pursuits of Happiness*; and Feller, "The Market Revolution." See Lamoreaux, "Rethinking," for an excellent overview.

23. "Calculating egotism": Sellers, *The Market Revolution*, 202. Farmers' practices, see the previous note. Selling to soldiers: Doerflinger, "Farmers," 193–94. Account books, see also Breugel, "The Social Relations"; Mann, "Rationality"; and Perkins, "The Consumer Frontier."

24. Wermuth, "New York Farmers" ("rational calculation," 182). See also Perkins, "The Consumer Frontier." Lamoreaux, "Rethinking," presents the farmer-merchant comparison. Market-oriented from the start: Bushman, "Markets and Composite Farms," esp. 356ff; Edwards, "Men of Subsistence" (safety first, 310–11). Accounting: P. Cohen, *A Calculating People*. Computers: Peter Lewis, "The Executive Computer: A New Crop of Services Take Root," *NYT*, Apr. 9, 1989.

25. Early-twentieth-century attacks on religion: C. Smith, *The Secular Revolution*. Early-twenty-first-century attacks: George Johnson, "A Free-for-All on Science and

Religion," *NYT*, Nov. 21, 2006. The literature on "secularization theory," which posits that moderns have abandoned faith, is enormous. Secularization itself can mean several different things, including removing religious content and authority from institutions, such as colleges or government, declining church participation (see discussion in chapter 4), or declining faith (see Somerville, "Secular Society"). These edited collections provide overviews: Bruce, *Religion and Modernization*; Stout and Hart, *New Directions in American Religious History*; and C. Smith, *The Secular Revolution*. See also Swatos and Christiano, "Secularization Theory"; Chaves, "Secularization"; Warner, "Work in Progress"; and Finke and Stark, *The Churching of America*. In the 1990s, about half of religion scholars believed that secularization remained the "dominant" trend in the West (Stout and Taylor, "Studies of Religion"). Jefferson: *The Jefferson Bible: The Life and Morals of Jesus of Nazareth*. Jill Lepore, "The Founders' Attitude Toward Religion," *New Yorker*, Apr. 14, 2008, 71–74, covers some of the founders' deism; Grasso, "Deist Monster," some of the controversy around deism.

26. Butler, *Awash in a Sea of Faith*; Marty, *Pilgrims in Their Own Land*; Hatch, *Democratization of American Christianity*; and Finke and Stark, *The Churching of America*. Virginia: Isaac, "Evangelical Revolt," 353. Religion and superstition: Butler, "Magic"; Godbeer, *The Devil's Dominion*. Diaries: Appleby, *Inheriting the Revolution*, ch. 6 (Newell and Grimke, 187); Gillespie, "'The Clear Leadings'"; and Bjorklund, *Interpreting the Self*, ch. 3.

27. Overviews of thinking and research on Americans' faith: Sherkat and Ellison, "Recent Developments"; Swatos and Christiano, "Secularization Theory"; and S. Bruce, *Religion and Modernization*. Surveys show remarkable stability in answers about faith. I drew the poll results from various sources, including Pew Research Center for the People and the Press surveys on religion (such as "Evenly Divided," 65, re: Judgment Day); Gallup and Castelli, *The People's Religion*; regular surveys by the Gallup Organization, particularly the "Religion" page, http://www.gallup.com/tag/Religion.aspx (accessed Jan. 26, 2006); Kosmin and Keysar, "American Religious Identification Survey"; and data from the NES, http://www.electionstudies.org (accessed Jun. 11, 2008). For studies, see: Fischer and Hout, *A Century of Difference*, ch. 8; Greeley, *Religious Change in America*; Greeley and Hout, "Americans' Increasing Belief"; Duncan, "Facile Reporting"; Chaves and Anderson, "Continuity and Change"; and Caplow et al., *Middletown Families*. Bishop, "Americans' Belief," is critical, arguing that belief in a personal God has declined. Some data show a shift from certainty to questioning in the 1960s, e.g., in 1964, 77 percent claimed to have no doubts about God and in 1981, 63 percent did, but that trend flattened afterwards (61 percent of English-language interviewees said they had no doubts in the 2006–8 GSS panels). Close reading suggest that there may have been a modest uptick in skepticism in the 1960s, perhaps after a modest uptick in faith in the 1950s.

Mencken: quoted at http://www.positiveatheism.org/hist/quotes/mencken.htm (accessed Jun. 11, 2006). Evolution: Americans may have grown even more skeptical of evolution recently (Miller et al., "Public Acceptance"; Plutzer and Berkman, "Trends"). Suspicion of nonbelievers: Edgell et al., "Atheists As 'Other.'" Life-changing event: T. Smith, "The National Spiritual Transformation Study." Shallow understanding: George Gallup Jr., "Americans Celebrate Easter," wrote of Americans' "glaring lack of knowledge about the Bible, basic doctrines, and the traditions of [their] own church[es]." Gospels: In 1950, 47 percent could name one of the four; in 1990, 50 percent could (retrieved from Lexis-Nexis Academic Search, accession numbers 0150256 and 0159719; accessed Jun. 5, 2006). See also Gallup, *Religion in America*. Tolerance: e.g., Pew Forum on Religion & Public Life, "Many Americans Say." Book sales: Linz, "A Religious Country"; Hart, "Changing Social Attitudes." Editor: John Wilson, quoted in Ron Charles, "Religious Book Sales Show a Miraculous Rise," *NYT*, Apr. 9, 2004. Left Behind: "Left Behind (series)," Wikipedia, http://en.wikipedia.org/wiki/Left_Behind_(series) (accessed Jun. 24, 2008)

28. In the 1990s, 86 percent of respondents to the GSS said they definitely or probably believed in heaven (65 percent definitely) and 73 percent definitely or probably believed in hell (52 percent definitely; GSS items "heaven" and "hell"). Histories of American religion generally describe a muting of the hellfire-and-damnation theme in favor the loving-arms-of-God theme.

29. Early occultism: Butler, "Magic"; Godbeer, *The Devil's Dominion*. Contemporary belief: Newport, "Seven Out of Ten"; D. Moore, "Three of Four"; Baylor Institute, *American Piety in the 21st Century*, tables 19, 21; various poll questions on related topics at the Roper Center Public Opinion Archives, http://www.ropercenter.uconn.edu/; and Lexis-Nexus "Academic Universe," http://web.lexis-nexis.com/universe.

30. Faith and reason: there is essentially no connection between whether an American believes in heaven and his or her attitude about the promise of science (calculated from the 1981 to 2000 World Values Surveys, http://www.worldvaluessurvey.org/services/index.html; accessed Nov. 15, 2006). See also Norris and Inglehart, *Sacred and Secular*, 67–68.

31. Overviews: Flynn, *What is Intelligence?*; Neisser et al., "Intelligence"; Neisser, *The Rising Curve*; and Fischer et al., *Inequality by Design*. Specifically on the increase in Americans' IQ scores: Flynn, "The Mean IQ," and "Massive IQ Gains"; Storpfer, *Intelligence and Giftedness*; and Greenfield, "The Cultural Evolution." There is some debate about what happened the late twentieth century to Americans' knowledge, reading, and verbal ability. See: e.g., Wilson and Gove, "The Intercohort Decline," and critiques in the Apr., 1999 issue of the *American Sociological Review*; Caleb Crain, "Twilight of Books," *The New Yorker*, Dec. 24 and 31, 2007, http://www.newyorker.com/arts/critics/atlarge/2007/12/24/071224crat_atlarge_crain; and Yang and Land, "A Mixed Models Approach." The last identified the 1940–50 birth cohort as the one with the highest vocabulary score in the GSS, but that cohort was roughly the same one that formulated the vocabulary test.

32. Plasticity: e.g., M. Wolf, *Proust and the Squid*; Donald McNeil, "In Raising the World's I.Q., the Secret's in the Salt," *NYT*, Dec. 16, 2006; Crain, "Twilight of Books" (see previous note). Education: United States Bureau of the Census, *Statistical Abstract*, 1999, tables 1425 and 1426; Fischer and Hout, *Century of Difference*, ch. 2; and Fischer et al., *Inequality by Design*.

33. Surveys: Pew Research Center, "Views of a Changing World," 107–8. Americans score at or near the top on this topic in many international surveys. Overviews on the

sense of control: Gecas, "The Social Psychology"; Ross and Mirowsky, "Social Structure." This tendency—also called "internal (versus external) locus of control" or ob-
versely as "powerlessness" or "helplessness"—has proven to be one of the more enduring and consequential psychologists have defined (Lefcourt, "Durability").

34. Insisting on independence: e.g., Foner, *The Story of American Freedom*; F. Furstenberg, "Beyond Freedom." See also G. Wood, "Religion"; Marty, *Pilgrims in Their
Own Land*, esp. ch. 10; D. Howe, "Protestantism, Voluntarism, and Personal Identity"; and Laurie, *Working People of Philadelphia*, ch. 2. Beecher: D. Davis, *Antebellum American Culture*, 397. Autobiographies: Bjorklund, *Interpreting the Self*, ch. 4;
R. Weiss, *The American Myth of Success*.

35. Johnson-Hanks, "When the Future Decides," (and following discussion in
June 2005 issue of *Current Anthropology*) demonstrates how unpredictable circumstances generate fatalism. Birth rates: R. Wells, *Revolutions in Americans' Lives*; idem,
Uncle Sam's Family; Vinovskis, "American Families"; idem, *Studies in Historical Demography*; Hirschman, "Why Fertility Changes"; Juster and Vinovskis, "Changing Perspectives"; D. Smith, "'Early' Fertility Decline"; and J. D. Hacker, "Economic, Demographic" (marriage). Studies stressing the sense of control and related issues: Klepp,
"Revolutionary Bodies"; Guest and Tolnay, "Children's Roles"; Parkerson and Parker-
son, "'Fewer Children'"; D. Smith, "'The Number and Quality of Children'"; Gjerde,
Minds of the West; Watkins, "From Local to National Communities"; G. Main, "Rock-
ing the Cradle"; Haines and Guest, "Fertility in New York State"; and T. Kelly and J.
Kelly, "Our Lady." Shippen sisters: Klepp, "Lost, Hidden," 100. Death: e.g., Dye and
Smith, "Mother Love "; Smith and Hacker, "Cultural Demography"; and P. Stearns,
Revolutions in Sorrow, 38–39. "Will it": Bjorklund, *Interpreting the Self*, 66.

36. Modell, *Into One's Own*, 330–31; idem, "Changing Risks." See also Uhlenberg,
"Changing Configurations"; Chudacoff, *How Old Are You?*; Stevens, "New Evidence";
Hareven "Historical Changes in the Life Course"; Stanger-Ross et al., "Falling Far
From the Tree"; F. Furstenberg, "Family Change"; F. Furstenberg et al., "Growing
Up is Harder to Do"; Danziger and Rouse, "The Price of Independence"; Shanahan,
"Pathways to Adulthood"; and Fischer and Hout, *Century of Difference*, 86–87.

37. More education, other things being equal, predicts a greater sense of control
or mastery (e.g., Ross and Mirowsky, "Age and the Gender Gap," and "Life Course
Trajectories," suggest that the education payoff has increased historically; see also
Schieman and Plickert, "How Knowledge"). Critics charge that schooling inculcates
passivity (e.g., Graff, *The Legacies of Literacy*). While schools surely taught (and teach)
deference and *sitzfleisch* (sitting patiently), they also provided children with tools for
efficacy, such as reading and, indeed, time-consciousness. Even bureaucratic skills,
such as complaining through channels, are in the long run more effective than alternatives, such as punching one's supervisor.

38. Children's literature: Lystad, *At Home in America*. Survey: See work of Duane
Alwin: "From Obedience," "Changes in Qualities," "Religion," and "From Child-
Bearing." See also Staples and Smith, "Attitudes."

39. Personal efficacy: I compiled a list of personal efficacy questions that were repeated at least once in national surveys. Inspection suggests a modest increase into

the early 1960s, then a drop, followed by little change from about 1980 on. (Sources: Lexis-Nexis Academic Search, References, Polls, accession numbers 0272319, 0042586, 0127782, 0257475, 0192134, 0328496; Veroff et al., *The Inner American*, 117; NES questions V626, V628, V627, V629, accessed through Survey Data & Analysis Web site, http://csa.berkeley.edu:7502/; GSS "getahead" question, accessed through same site, accessed Jun. 9, 2006.) Mirowsky and Ross, "Life Course Trajectories," find increases in sense of control over recent cohorts, as do Trzesniewski and Donnellan, "Rethinking 'Generation Me.'" Twenge et al., "It's Beyond," find a decline in internal locus of control scores for student samples between 1960 and the 1980s and little change later.

Political efficacy: Lipset and Schneider, *The Confidence Gap*; Nye et al., *Why People Don't Trust Government*; and Dalton, *Citizen Politics in Western Democracies*. The key data are questions asked by the NES from 1952 through 2004, such as "People like me don't have any say about what the government does." They generally show a modest increase in reported efficacy from 1952 to 1960, then a deep and prolonged drop, bottoming out around 1990, with a modest rebound in the 2000s. See http://www .electionstudies.org/nesguide/gd-index.htm#5 (accessed Jun. 19, 2006).

40. Disempowerment: See mass society theorists such as Mills, *The Power Elite*; Nisbet, *Quest for Community*; Riesman, *The Lonely Crowd*; Wiebe, *The Search for Order* and *Self-Rule*; Brinkley, "Prosperity, Depression, and War"; and Lasch, *Haven in a Heartless World*. For example, Jackson Lears, "From Salvation to Self-Realization," argued that the "decline of autonomous selfhood lay at the heart of the modern sense of unreality" (9). Yet closer empirical work casts doubt on such claims. For example, bureaucratic work does not reduce and may even increase the sense of efficacy (Kohn, *Class and Conformity*; Kohn and Schooler, "Occupational Experience"). Historians make more empirically persuasive arguments that Americans became more empowered—perhaps even too much so; see Foner, *The Story of American Freedom*; Friedman, *The Republic of Choice*; and Potter, *People of Plenty*.

41. Pease and Pease, *Ladies, Women, & Wenches*. Tyranny: B. Schwartz, "Self-Determination."

42. Supermarkets: Vohs et al., "Making Choices," 883. More places: as the commuting radius increased, residential options increased geometrically well into the late twentieth century (e.g., Levinson and Kumar, "The Rational Locator"). More churches: see discussion of religious switching in chapter 4. More careers: over the twentieth century, the number of distinct jobs roughly doubled (Fischer and Hout, *Century of Difference*, ch. 5). Spouses: with urbanization, increased schooling, and declining ethno-religious barriers, spouse options grew (Kalmijn, "Shifting Boundaries"; C. Schwartz and Mare, "Trends"; and Fischer and Hout, *Century of Difference*, ch. 3). More selves: D. Howe, *Making the American Self*, notes that the "capacity to choose is at the heart of political freedom as Americans have conceived of it, and the capacity to choose or revise one's own identity is perhaps the ultimate exercise of that capacity" (257). Friedman, *Republic of Choice*, adds the consumer rights movement as a force for expanding choice. "Able to choose": Rosenthal, *The Era of Choice*, ix (original emphasis). Giddens, *Modernity and Self-Identity*: "We have no choice but to choose"

(84). In 1981, 73 percent of polled Americans said that they had more choice than their parents did (Thomson, *In Conflict No Longer*, 123). Most Americans: Westerners, particularly Americans—and particularly well-educated ones—are more invested in having choice than are Asians (Markus and Kitayama, "Culture, Self"; Snibbe and Markus, "You Can't Always Get"; and Iyengar and Lepper, "Choice"). "How people choose": the American Economic Association's answer to the question, "What is Economics?" http://www.vanderbilt.edu/AEA/students/WhatIsEconomics.htm (accessed Jun. 27, 2006). "Good is an aggregation": Laurence Summers, "Morning Prayers Address," Harvard University, Sept. 15, 2003, http://www.president.harvard.edu/speeches/2003/prayer.html (accessed Jun. 27, 2006).

43. There is by now a vast literature in behavioral economics and irrational decision-making: e.g., Kahneman, "A Perspective"; Loewenstein, "The Creative Destruction." Wolfe, "Hedonic Man," is an accessible overview. "Bounded": H. Simon, *Models of Man*. Not knowing what is good: Kahneman and Thaler, "Anomalies." Loewenstein, "The Creative Destruction," concluded that "we should . . . move away from the idea that the key to enhancing people's happiness is to give them more of what they want" (503). However, psychological research suggesting that more options are worse than fewer ones seemed not to have gotten any attention from economists, at least as of mid-2000s.

44. Studies: Iyengar and Lepper, "When Choice" (choosing gourmet jams); Iyengar and Jiang, "The Psychological Costs"(retirement plans); B. Schwartz et al., "Maximizing Versus Satisficing." B. Schwartz, "Self-Determination" and *The Paradox of Choice*, reviews the literature; see also McFadden, "Free Markets." Choosing is tiring: Vohs et al., "Making Choices." Opt-out: "Investing: How to Make Employees Take Their 401(k) Medicine," *NYT*, Nov. 13, 2005. Skeptics: Chernev, "Product Assortment," shows that when people have formulated preferences before facing choices, the number of choices does not pose a problem. Kahneman and Tversky's analysis suggests that people operate on two different systems, one intuitive and the other deliberative (Kahneman, "A Perspective on Judgment"). Similarly, scholars have pointed out that using norms or "meta-rules" (e.g., I'll choose the first flavor that is not chocolate, or I'll give this decision just fifteen minutes) may be irrational in any particular case, but sensible as a long-term strategy (see Kelley and Thibaut, *Interpersonal Relations*, on norms). Job study: Iyengar et al., "Doing Better." Tyranny: B. Schwartz, "Self-Determination," 81 (original emphasis); idem, *The Paradox of Choice*. See also Loewenstein, "The Creative Destruction."

45. Keniston, *The Uncommitted*, 261. Daniel Bell in 1976: "The sociological problem of . . . our time . . . arises because individuals . . . are constantly faced with the problem of choice . . . and no longer find authoritative standards or critics to guide them" (*The Cultural Contradictions of Capitalism*, 90). More recent comments along these lines include Giddens, *Modernity and Self-Identity*; Ehrenhalt, "The Lost City." Durkheim: *Division of Labor in Society*, and esp., *Suicide*.

46. B. Schwartz, *The Paradox of Choice*. I review some of the research on wealth and well-being in the later section on happiness. See Inglehart et al., "Development, Freedom, and Rising Happiness," on cross-country comparisons. Abraham Fischer

suggested the point that more options in the long run will yield more optimal outcomes. One can assume that, in general, people who have more choices will, on average and in the long run, however they choose, do better than those with fewer options, and also assume that those who do better will in the long run feel better.

47. Chernow, *Alexander Hamilton*, 167; see also Letter to Colonel Richard K. Meade, "The Works of Alexander Hamilton," http://oll.libertyfund.org/Home3/HTML.php?recordID=0249.09 (accessed Jul. 2, 2006). See also Kotchemidova, "From Good Cheer."

48. Cultural variations in emotions: Mesquita et al., "Culture and Emotion"; Scherer and Wallbott, "Evidence"; and Kitayama and Markus, *Emotion and Culture*. Noted psychologist Jerome Kagan discusses historical changes in *What is Emotion?*, ch. 5. Infant deaths: Dye and Smith, "Mother Love." Sociology of emotions: S. Gordon, "The Sociology"; Hochschild, "Emotion Work"; and idem, *The Managed Heart*. Sociologists tend to argue that emotions themselves can be invented; others argue that there are universal emotions which are only managed culturally; see Reddy, "Against Constructionism." Cleanliness: Hoy, *Chasing Dirt*; Cowan, *More Work for Mother*; Strasser, *Never Done*; Wilkie, "Submerged Sensuality"; and P. Stearns, *Battleground of Desire*, ch. 8.

49. History of emotions: Stearns and Stearns, "Emotionology," and the large corpus of work by Peter Stearns, including, *Anger, American Cool,* and *Battleground of Desire*. See also Kasson, *Rudeness and Civility*; Stearns and Lewis, *An Emotional History of the United States*. Rosenwein, "Worrying about Emotions," 824, critiques the focus on rules: "Its emphasis, then, is not on how people felt or represented their feelings but on what people thought about such matters as crying in public, getting angry, or showing anger physically. It assumes that what people think about feelings they will eventually actually feel."

50. "Washington's School Exercises," Papers of George Washington, http://gwpapers.virginia.edu/documents/civility/ (accessed Jun. 23, 2005). Strong passions: D. Fischer, *Washington's Crossing*, 14. See Halttunen, *Confidence Men*, ch. 4, on the cultivation of feelings themselves. Philadelphia: Jacqueline Miller, "An 'Uncommon Tranquility,'" 129, 139; Eustace, *Passion in the Gale*. Victorian girls: P. Stearns, *Anxious Parents*, ch. 4. Passionless: Cott, "Passionlessness" ("carnal," 233); R. Bloch, "Changing Conceptions"; Godbeer, *Sexual Revolution*, ch. 8; Pease and Pease, *Ladies, Women, & Wenches*. "Perfect inhibition:" Sicherman, "The Paradox of Prudence," 894. See also other works by P. Stearns cited in previous note; Hemphill, "The Middle Class Rising"; idem, *Bowing to Necessities*; Kasson, *Rudeness and Civility*; D. Howe, "Protestantism, Voluntarism, and Personal Identity"; idem, *Making the American Self*; and Rodgers, "Socializing Middle-Class Children."

51. "Feel intensely": Lystra, *Searching the Heart*, 45. Political appeals: Andrew Burstein, "The Political Character of Sympathy." On the emergence of sympathy: Eustace, *Passion is the Gale*, ch. 6.

52. Sentimentality and young romance: Lystra, *Searching the Heart*; Rothman, *Hands and Hearts*; and R. Bloch, "Changing Conceptions." Novels: R. Brown, *Knowledge is Power*, ch. 7 ("tears," 170); Appleby, *Inheriting the Revolution*, 178ff ("omnipo-

tence," 178); W. Griswold, "American Character"; M. Kelley, "The Sentimentalists." Demands for love in marriage: Prescott, "'Why She Didn't Marry Him'"; F. Furstenberg, "Industrialization"; D'Emilio and Freedman, *Intimate Matters*; R. Griswold, "Law, Sex"; M. Smith, *Breaking the Bonds*, ch. 2 (Graves complaint, 70); Basch, *Framing American Divorce*; Riley, *Divorce*. Lincoln: "Mr. Lincoln and Friends," http://www .mrlincolnandfriends.org (accessed Feb. 9, 2007).

53. Sentiment in family life: J. Lewis, "Mother's Love"; Cross, *The Cute and the Cool*, ch. 1; Lystad, *At Home in America*; Degler, *At Odds*; J. Gillis, *A World of Their Own Making*, ch. 8; Mintz and Kellogg, *Domestic Revolutions*, ch. 3; and M. Anderson, *Approaches to the History of the Western Family, 1500–1914*. Quaker families seemed to embody this emotionality earlier than others (B. Levy, "The Birth"), while rural and working-class parents did later (Hansen, *A Very Social Time*, 105). Infant deaths: Dye and Smith, "Mother Love" (Longfellow, 343); Hoffert, "'A Very Peculiar Sorrow'"; see also chapter 2 of this volume. Soldiers: Clarke, "'So Lonesome'"; Matt, "You Can't"; Faust, "The Civil War Soldier"; and S. Scott, "'Earth Has No Sorrow'."

54. Douglas, "Heaven Our Home"; R. Wells, *Facing the "King of Terrors"*; P. Stearns, *Revolutions in Sorrow*, ch. 3; H. Green, *The Light of the Home*; Halttunen, *Confidence Men*, ch. 5, 6; Sloane, *The Last Great Necessity*; Wills, *Lincoln at Gettysburg*, ch. 2; and Schmitt, "Grave Matters." Newsboys: DiGirolamo, "Newsboy Funerals." Channing: "Sleepy Hollow," poem reprinted with Emerson's dedication, http://www.rwe .org/?option=com_content&task=view&id=91&Itemid=42 (accessed Jul. 4, 2006).

55. Teenager: Blauvelt, "The Work of the Heart," 579. Emmeline: *Huckleberry Finn*, ch. 17. One oft-cited model is Julia Moore, "The Sweet Singer of Michigan" (Rachels, "Julia A. Moore").

56. Friendships: Smith-Rosenberg, "The Female World"; D'Emilio and Freedman, *Intimate Matters*, 125–30 ("feverish": Emily Dickinson, 126); Oliker, "The Modernisation of Friendship"; Rotundo, "Romantic Friendship" (Webster, 1); Jabour, "Male Friendship" ("piping hot," 95); Yacovone, "'Surpassing'"; and Hansen, "'Our Eyes Behold.'" Yocavone and Hansen contend that romantic friendship existed among working-class men, too, but confess that there is little evidence to show that. Manuals: Halttunen, *Confidence Men*, 119–22. Henkin, *The Postal Age*, ch. 4, discounts the letter manuals, saying that Americans learned florid styles from one another.

57. Pets: Grier, *Pets in America*, ch. 3. Movements: E. Clark, "'The Sacred Rights'"; Haskell, "Capitalism," parts 1 and 2; Halttunen, "Humanitarianism and the Pornography of Pain" ("bound or chained," 320); Rozario, "Delicious Horrors"; Boyer, *Urban Masses and Moral Order*; and Mintz, *Huck's Raft*, ch. 8. Civilizing: Elias, *The Civilizing Process*; De Swaan, "Widening Circles."

58. Adler, "'My Mother-in-Law'"; idem, "'Halting the Slaughter'"; idem, "'We've Got a Right'"; Gorn, "'Gouge and Bite,'"; idem, "'Good-Bye Boys'"; Kaplan, "New York City Tavern Violence"; R. Lane, *Murder in America*; Monkkonen, *Murder in New York City*; idem, "Homicide in Los Angeles"; Larkin, *The Reshaping of Everyday Life*, 293ff; E. Parsons, "Risky Business"; and Way, "Evil Humors ."

59. Children: Zelizer, *Pricing the Priceless Child*; Rodgers, "Socializing Middle-Class Children"; the work of Peter Stearns, such as *Anxious Parents* and *American Cool*;

Stearns and Haggerty, "The Role of Fear"; and Stearns and Stearns, *Anger*. Fathers: Marsh, "Suburban Men"; J. Weiss, *To Have and to Hold*, ch. 3 (Spock, 89); Parke and Stearns, "Fathers"; and Families and Work Institute, *The 1997 National Study of the Changing Workforce*. Middletown: Caplow et al., *Middletown Families*, 377; Bahr, "Changes in Family Life." Survey data in the 1990s and 2000s show that parents report spending more time with their children than in earlier generations (Russell, "What's Wrong?"; Bianchi et al., *Changing Rhythms of American Family Life*). Couples: Mintz and Kellogg, *Domestic Revolutions*, ch. 6; Coontz, *Marriage*, esp. ch. 9–12; J. Weiss, *To Have and to Hold*; and E. May, *Great Expectations*. The working class trailed in meeting the new marriage model (Komarovsky, *Blue-Collar Marriage*; also Shumway, "Something Old"; P. Stearns, *Battleground of Desire*, ch. 7). Gift giving: e.g., Zelizer, *The Social Meaning of Money*; see also discussion in chapter 3, p. 80. Humanitarianism: Rozario, "Delicious Horrors."

60. Immigrants: Berrol, *Growing Up American*, ch. 4 ("pagan," 85); I. Howe, *World of Our Fathers*, 271ff. Fourth: Rosenzweig, *Eight Hours for What We Will*, ch. 3; Appelbaum, *The Glorious Fourth*. Jews: Sarna, *American Judaism*, ch. 4.

61. Emily Post: Schlesinger, *Learning How to Behave*, 52–58. P. Stearns, *Battleground of Desire*, sees informalization as part of greater self-discipline: "Manners became more informal while demands for systematic emotional control became more stringent" (154). Status security: Wouters, "Etiquette Books," part one.

62. P. Stearns, *American Cool*, "Girls, Boys, and Emotions," and other works; see also Kasson, *Rudeness and Civility*. Lears, *Fables of Abundance*, suggests that such "cool" became part of twentieth-century advertising, overturning the more "carnivalistic" style of the nineteenth. Fear: Stearns and Haggerty, "The Role of Fear"; P. Stearns, "Suppressing Unpleasant Emotions." Anger: Stearns and Stearns, *Anger*. Mother love: Shields and Koster, "Emotional Stereotyping."

63. Less aggression: see discussion in chapter 2, pp. 34–36; see also P. Stearns, *Battleground of Desire*, ch. 6. Encouraging positive emotions: P. Stearns, *Anxious Parents*, includes many examples, although he interprets them as coddling children. Couples: E. May, *Great Expectations*; J. Weiss, *To Have and to Hold*; D'Emilio and Freedman, *Intimate Matters*; Mintz and Kellogg, *Domestic Revolutions*, ch. 6; and Coontz, *Marriage*, ch. 12. "Soft Jesus" refers to the growing emphasis in Protestantism on a forgiving rather than a judgmental Jesus, to loving rather than damning the sinner. See Witten, *All is Forgiven*; Wuthnow, *Sharing the Journey*; Finke and Stark, *The Churching of America*; Mike Anton and William Lobdell, "Hell Losing Its Fire in American Sermons," *San Francisco Chronicle*, Jul. 6, 2002; and in reaction, David Murrow, "Why Men Hate Going to Church," http://www.pastors.com/article.asp?ArtID=7978 (accessed Jul. 11, 2006): "Pastors often focus on Jesus' tenderness and empathy. This is a good thing, but presenting soft Jesus week after week runs the risk of turning men off. What man wants to follow Mr. Rogers?" Child rearing values: the studies described chapter 4, p. 141, which show a shift to independence, also show a move toward considerateness. See Alwin, "Childrearing Goals," "From Obedience," and "Changes in Qualities." I analyzed the GSS and found a similar increase across generations in preference for attributes like consideration and helping others versus traits

such as mannered, obedient, clean, and popular. The consideration findings are from that work. (GSS items ask about which "qualities may be desirable for a child to have" [1973–83] and which are "most important for a child to learn to prepare him or her for life" [1984–].) Tolerance of different races: Schuman et al., *Racial Attitudes in America*; Wilson, "Cohort." Tolerance of religions: Caplow et al., *All Faithful People*, ch. 4. Tolerance of family patterns: Thornton, "Changing Attitudes." Tolerance of political opinions: J. Davis, "Patterns"; Blendon et al., "The 60s and the 90s." "Tolerant to a fault": Wolfe, *One Nation After All*, 278. Politically correct: the Wikipedia entry for "political correctness" is consistent with my recollection of its history: http://en.wikipedia.org/wiki/Politically_correct (accessed Jul. 12, 2006).

64. D. Bell, *The Cultural Contradictions of Capitalism* (California, 70). Similar charges: Burnham, *Bad Habits*; James Collier, *The Rise of Selfishness*; Bellah et al., *Habits of the Heart*; and Janowitz, *Social Control of the Welfare State*. Sociologist Ralph Turner, "The Real Self," described a shift from the "institutional self"—people defined themselves by the roles they played—to the "impulsive self"—people defined themselves by their inward traits, especially those that seemed natural. While there is evidence that Westerners decreasingly defined their identities by roles and increasingly by personalities, this is not "impulsive." Defining and presenting a self requires considerable introspection and systematic effort. Perhaps what Turner saw is better described as a shift from the institutional to the psychological self. (See Thomson, "Individualism"; idem, "The Transformation"; Benton, "Self and Society"; Buchmann and Eisner, "Images of the Self.") Historian Warren Sussman characterized the great change (in 1905, he specified) as a shift from a culture of internalized, moralized, self-disciplined "character" to one of "personality," flashy self-presentation in pursuit of approval. The best evidence for Sussman is found in advertising and the media's fascination with celebrities, but as a description of how people actually behaved or felt, it does not match the evidence well. (See Sussman's "Personality'" and other essays in his *Culture as History*. Lowenthal, "Biographies," and Riesman, *The Lonely Crowd*, make similar claims.) Stearns on escapism: *Battleground of Desire*, passim. The argument assumes, thanks to Freud, that emotions are "hydraulic" forces, which most modern psychologists would discount, and a "compensation" model of human behavior, which also has little support (see Hunt, "Anxiety"; C. Fischer, "Comment on 'Anxiety'"). Television murders: Scott Stossel, "The Man Who Counts the Killings," *Atlantic Monthly*, May, 1997, 86–104.

65. Overviews: D'Emilio and Freedman, *Intimate Matters*; Degler, *At Odds*; Godbeer, *Sexual Revolution in Early America*; Lyons, *Sex Among the Rabble*; and Odem, "Sexual Behavior." Journalism: e.g., D. Cohen, "The Murder of Maria Bickford." Prostitutes: Gilfoyle, "The Urban Geography"; Claudia Johnson, "That Guilty Third Tier."

66. Godbeer, *Sexual Revolution in Early America;* D. Fischer, *Albion's Seed* (passages on "sex ways"; Byrd, 300–3); Kulikoff, *From British Peasants*, 227ff; and T. Foster, "Deficient Husbands" (on impotence). Smith and Hindus, "Premarital Pregnancy." The usual estimated rate of premarital pregnancies is 30 percent, but that is based on births to parents settled and respectable enough to get recorded in local documents,

so the true rate was surely higher. Donald, *Lincoln*, 20, discusses Hanks. Philadelphia: Lyons, *Sex Among the Rabble*; see also M. Smith, *Breaking the Bonds*, on adultery charges.

67. D'Emilio and Freedman, *Intimate Matters*, ch. 4, 5 (Miss Thompson, figure 15); Rothman, "Sex and Self-Control"; idem, *Hands and Hearts*; Lyons, *Sex Among the Rabble*, ch. 6–8; Lystra, *Searching the Heart;* Pease and Pease, *Ladies, Women, & Wenches*, ch. 7; P. Stearns, *Battleground of Desire*, ch. 3; K. White, "The New Man"; and Smith and Hindus, "Premarital Pregnancy." Restraints: Cott, "Passionlessness"; C. Rosenberg, "Sexuality, Class, and Role"; and Degler, *At Odds*, ch. 11.

68. More sex in marriage: Coontz, *Marriage*, ch. 12; P. Stearns, *Battleground of Desire* ("Don't let anyone," 206); E. May, *Great Expectations*, ch. 6; Landale and Guest, "Ideology and Sexuality"; H. Green, *Light of the Home*, ch. 5; and David and Anderson, "Rudimentary Contraceptive Methods." Premarital experimentation: D. Smith, "The Dating of the American Sexual Revolution"; Rothman, *Hands and Hearts*; Bailey, *From Front Porch to Back Seat*; Modell, "Dating"; idem, *Into One's Own*; Clement, *Love for Sale*; Mintz, *Huck's Raft*, ch. 11; Fass, *The Damned and the Beautiful*, ch. 6; Meyerowitz, *Women Adrift*; Glenn, *Daughter of the Shtetl*; Peiss, *Cheap Amusements*; and Spurlock and Magistro, *New and Improved*. Public discussion: Burnham, "The Progressive Era Revolution"; J. Martin, "Structuring"; and D'Emilio and Freedman, *Intimate Matters*, ch. 10 ("needing expression," 223). Kinsey: Igo, *The Averaged American*, 236ff.

69. On how much of a revolution the post-1960 "sexual revolution" actually was: Seidman and Rieder, "A Review"; T. Smith, "American Sexual Behavior"; Petigny, "Illegitimacy"; Wells and Twenge, "Changes in Young People's Sexual Behavior and Attitudes"; Pennington, "It's Not A Revolution"; Goldin and Katz, "The Power of the Pill"; and Lindberg et al., *Teen Risk-Taking*. Intercourse by age nineteen: Hofferth et al., "Premarital," table 3; Advocates for Youth, "Adolescent Sexual Behavior." See also Laumann et al., *The Social Organization of Sexuality*, 197–99, 213–14, 322–33, who found a big change between the 1933–42 and the 1943–52 birth cohorts. First births: Bachu, "Trends." Declining rates of teen sex: Federal Interagency Forum on Child and Family Statistics, "Sexual Activity," http://www.childstats.gov/americaschildren/beh4.asp (accessed Jun. 27, 2008); Nicholas Bkalar, "Teenagers Changing Sexual Behavior," *NYT*, Aug. 25, 2008. Cohabitation: Smock, "Cohabitation"; Fitch et al., "The Rise"; Jeffrey Jones, "Public Divided." (In 2002, 51 percent of married respondents under fifty said they had lived together before marriage). Fear of AIDS does not seem to explain the recent decline (Tremblay and Ling, "AIDS Education"). Attitudes: Thornton, "Changing Attitudes"; Harding and Jencks, "Changing Attitudes"; and T. Smith, "The Sexual Revolution." The percentage of respondents to the GSS who said that premarital sex was "not wrong at all" rose from 27 percent in 1972 to 44 percent in 1991 and rose a bit in the later 2000s (44 percent through 2006, 55 percent in 2008—"premarsx" item; my analysis). The annual survey of college freshmen found that the 1990s cohorts had become relatively conservative on casual sex (Higher Education Research Institute, "Most of the Nation's"). Betty Ford: J. Weiss, *To Have and to Hold*, 170.

70. Sex in twentieth-century culture and media: D'Emilio and Freedman, *Intimate*

Matters, ch. 12; P. Stearns, *Battleground of Desire*. Homosexuality: D'Emilio and Freedman, *Intimate Matters*; T. Smith, "American Sexual Behavior"; C. Turner et al., "Same-Gender Sex." Attitudes: The percentage of GSS respondents who said that "sexual relations between two adults of the same sex" (item "homosex") was always wrong dropped from about 75 percent in the 1970s to about 50 percent in 2008 (English-language interviews for comparability); see also A. Yang, "The Polls."

71. The data are sparse but suggest an increase in lifetime sexual frequency (D'Emilio and Freedman, *Intimate Matters*, esp. 336–38). So do most concomitant changes, such as the earlier puberty and onset of sexual initiation, more partners, longer lives, better health, fewer years widowed, ease of birth control, and greater privacy. On the other hand, the rise in divorce and in women's employment might have suppressed frequency of sex.

72. The percentage of GSS respondents who said that sex among fourteen-to-sixteen-year-olds was "always wrong" ("teensex") increased a bit, from 67 percent in 1986 to about 72 percent in the late 2000s. The percentage who said that "a married person having sexual relations with someone other than the marriage partner" ("xmarsex") was "always wrong" increased much more, from 70 percent in 1973 to about 83 percent in 2006–8 (English interviews for comparability). In regressions, the cohort effect on the extramarital question, younger generations more conservative, was robust. Actual extramarital affairs: an increase has been reported (Tara Parker-Pope, "Love, Sex and the Changing Landscape of Infidelity," *NYT*, Oct. 28, 2008), but the data are unclear. In the GSS, it appears that admissions of affairs peaked among baby boomers, although later marriages may not have been sufficiently "at risk" and earlier respondents may have repressed or forgotten. In any case, the gross rate of survey respondents admitting infidelity stayed essentially unchanged from 1991–93 (15 percent) to 2006–8 (17 percent) (my analysis of GSS "evstray" item, English interviews for comparability). Fass, *The Damned and the Beautiful*, ch. 6, 273.

73. Planters: D. Fischer, *Albion's Seed*, 298–306. Media: D. Cohen, "The Murder of Maria Bickford"; idem, *Pillars of Salt, Monuments of Grace*. Women grabbed: see chapter 5 of this book.

74. On violence, see discussion in chapter 2.

75. Capitalist manipulation: e.g. Sellers, *The Market Revolution* ("Human energy was capped and channeled to market production at its deepest springs in gender and libido," 258). Some of the consumerism literature makes similar claims (see ch. 3 of this book). D. Bell argues that the cultural contradictions of capitalism lie precisely in promoting ascetic industriousness in workers and hedonistic indulgence in consumers (*The Cultural Contradictions of Capitalism*). Haven: e.g., Lasch, *Haven in a Heartless World*. Occupational fit: Ryan, *Cradle of the Middle Class*; P. Stearns, *Battleground of Desire*; Riesman, *The Lonely Crowd*; Kohn, *Class and Conformity*; Kohn and Schooler, "Class"; and Lareau, "Invisible Inequality." Lareau and Kohn show the connection between class and psyche. See also Haskell, "Capitalism," parts 1 and 2. Affluence: The central argument draws from Abraham Maslow's notions of a hierarchy of needs. See, e.g., D. Potter, *People of Plenty*; Inglehart, *Culture Shift in Advanced Industrial Society*; and Lindsey, *The Age of Abundance*.

76. Elias, *The Civilizing Process*. See also De Swaan, "Widening Circles"; L. Stone, *Family, Sex, and Marriage in England, 1500–1800*. Foucault would probably fit here, although his interpretation hardly treats the changes as positive. For an Elias-like analysis of Swedish social history, see Frykman and Lofgren, *Culture Builders*.

77. Illness: Stearns and Stearns, *Anger*. Rosenwein, "Worrying," critiques "hydraulic" models of emotions.

78. R. Miller, "What Is Hell?"; Hirschhorn, "Mary Lincoln's"; Donald, *Lincoln*, esp. 87–88; Kushner, *Self-Destruction*, 132–44. E. Wilson, *Patriotic Gore*, 122–23, notes the poem (the text of "My Childhood Home" is available on-line). P. Smith, "Anxiety and Despair," 417; see also Tocqueville, *Democracy in America*, vol. 2, ch. 13.

79. Fromm, *The Sane Society*, esp. ch. 5. Battan, "The 'New Narcissism,'" and Alan Hunt, "Anxiety," discuss problems in historians' claims about psychological changes.

80. Mental institutions: Sutton, "The Political Economy"; Scull, "Psychiatry"; R. Fox, "The Intolerable"; and Luchins, "Social Control." Tripling: Grob, *Mental Illness and American Society, 1875–1940*, ch. 3. "Delirium tremens": Osborn, "A Detestable Shrine." Bipolar: Benedict Carey, "Bipolar Illness Soars as a Diagnosis for the Young," *NYT*, Sept. 4, 2007. McCandless, *Moonlight, Magnolias, & Madness*, 8, notes that histories of insanity are typically histories of institutions.

81. P. Smith, "Anxiety and Despair." Pain and depression: Crain, "'I Have Suffer'd,'" 385. See also Eldridge, "'Crazy Brained'"; Jimenez, "Madness" (Watertown schoolmaster); McCandless, *Moonlight, Magnolias, & Madness* (Carolina, 17); Moran, "The Signal"; and Goodheart, "The Concept" (Hartford mothers). Grob, *Mental Illness, 1875–1940*, writes: "Individuals who ended up in asylums [in the nineteenth century] usually manifested some form of extreme behavior . . . rather than marginal behavioral symptoms" (9).

82. Wells: McCandless, *Moonlight, Magnolias, & Madness*, 147. The distress of farm women was a commonplace observation at the turn of the twentieth century, although some observers questioned it (C. Taylor, "The Rise," 31; Kline, *Consumers in the Country*, 88ff). The widespread nature of the observation, however, including by rural Americans themselves, convinces me. See United States Senate, *Report of the Country Life Commission*; Ward, "The Farm Women's Problems." Immigrants: Kushner, "Immigrant Suicide."

83. The classic study is, of course, Durkheim's *Suicide*, but there were similar claims before and after; see Kushner, "Suicide, Gender" and *Self-Destruction in the Promised Land*. The depression-suicide link: Kessler et al., "Trends"; Cutler et al., "Explaining the Rise"; Maimon and Kuhl, "Social Control." Nineteenth-century American rates: There was not much of a trend in New York City before the Civil War (Kushner, *Self-Destruction*, table 2); and there was an increase in turn-of-the-century San Diego (ibid, figure 4.1) and in Philadelphia from about five per hundred thousand residents in midcentury to about twelve by its end (R. Lane, *Violent Death in the City*, ch. 2). On measurement issues, see Pescosolido and Mendelsohn, "Social Causation."

84. Fischer, "Poverty Drove Him to Suicide," *NYT*, Apr. 20, 1896. Blohm, "Dead in a Room Five Weeks," *NYT*, Jan. 10, 1895.

85. Crude suicide rates peaked at about eighteen per hundred thousand Americans in 1908 and again in 1932, but there was no overall trend. Age-adjusted rates, starting in 1950, show little change for men and a 50 percent decline for women, from six in 1950 to four in 2005. For males aged fifteen to twenty-four, rates more than tripled from six in 1950 to twenty-two in 1990 and went down to sixteen in 2005; for males sixty-five and older, rates dropped sharply from fifty-three to thirty. (Sources: 1900–1940: National Office of Vital Statistics, *Vital Statistics*; 1950–2005: National Center for Health Statistics, *Health, United States, 2007*. See also Holinger, *Violent Deaths in the United States*.) Noteworthy is that rates went up substantially from 1999 to 2005 only for baby boomers (NCHS, "Deaths: Final Data for 2005," http://www.cdc.gov/nchs/nvsr/nvsr56/nvsr56_10.pdf, table 9; accessed Jan. 7, 2009). Efforts to statistically explain the trends, particularly among young men: Pampel, "Cohort Size"; McCall and Land, "Trends"; Stockard and O'Brien, "Cohort Variations"; idem, "Cohort Effects"; O'Brien and Stockard, "A Common Explanation"; Eckersley and Dear, "Cultural Correlates"; and Cutler et al., "Explaining the Rise." Holinger et al., *Suicide and Homicide among Adolescents*, review earlier studies. The significance of antidepressants is under debate. While they do reduce rates of suicide, perhaps substantially, the historical connection is uncertain. For example, rates for women declined steeply before and through the mass introduction of antidepressants ca. 1990. See Grunebaum et al., "Antidepressants," and Gibbons et al., "Early Evidence" vs. Safera and Zito, "Do Antidepressants?"

Data on *attempts* at or *thoughts* of suicide probably would better measure depression than statistics on completed suicides. Such data are slim and recent. The National Comorbidity Surveys found no change in suicidal thoughts or tries among eighteen–to–fifty-four-year-olds between ca. 1991 and ca. 2002, but estimated that there was more lifetime interest in suicide among younger cohorts (Kessler et al., "Trends in Suicide"; idem, "Prevalence of and Risk"). However, these surveys excluded the groups with the fastest-dropping suicide rates, the elderly, and lifetime estimates are prone to recollection bias (discussed below, see note 89).

86. History of alcohol: Lender and Martin, *Drinking in America*; Rorabaugh, *The Alcoholic Republic*. Sociability: Duis, *The Saloon*; Rosenzweig, *Eight Hours for What We Will*; and Kingsdale, "The 'Poor Man's Club.'" Anesthesize: e.g., Osborn, "A Detestable Shrine," 124–25. Alcoholism as indicator of psychological distress: e.g., Swendsen et al., "The Comorbidity." Deaths rates for cirrhosis of the liver: 22.1 per 100,000 in 1920, 11.2 in 1950, 17.8 in 1970, and 9.2 in 2004–5 (National Institute of Alcohol Abuse and Alcoholism, "Age-Adjusted Death Rates of Liver Cirrhosis," http://www.niaaa.nih.gov/Resources/GraphicsGallery/cirrtext.htm). Annual alcohol consumption: about 2.2 gallons per person in 1900, a low of 1.5 during the Depression, a peak of 2.8 in 1980, and about 2.2 in the mid-2000s (idem, "Apparent Per Capita Ethanol Consumption," http://www.niaaa.nih.gov/Resources/DatabaseResources/QuickFacts/AlcoholSales/consum01.htm; accessed Jun. 29, 2008). Responses to Gallup poll question, "Do you have occasion to use alcoholic beverages such as liquor, wine, or beer or are you a total abstainer?" show little variation in the postwar era, ranging between 60 percent and 70 percent "yes" (idem, "Percent Who Drink Beverage Alco-

hol," http://www.niaaa.nih.gov/Resources/DatabaseResources/QuickFacts/Alcohol Consumption/PercentAlcoholGender.htm, accessed Jun. 29, 2008; supplemented by the "Gallup Brain," http://institution.gallup.com, accessed Jun. 29, 2008). The annual survey of high school seniors shows a decline in reported drinking from 1975 to 2005 (Johnston et al., "Demographic Subgroup Trends").

87. Courtwright, *Dark Paradise* ("substitute," 59); idem, "The Hidden Epidemic" (opium dealer, 66); Jones, "Selected Aspects" (Knoxville doctor, 2; Sears, 12); Hickman, "'Mania Americana'"; and Spillane, *Cocaine*, esp. 92ff.

88. Trying drugs by generation: R. Johnson and Gerstein, "Initiation"; see also Kessler et al., "Lifetime Prevalence." Although such estimates depend on retrospective reports, which are skewed (see note 89 below), the cohort effects are large enough to show real change. Teenagers' parents: my analysis of a 1997 ABC/Washington Post survey (Study 2175, Inter-University Consortium for Political and Social Research [distributor], http://dx.doi.org/10.3886/ICPSR02175). Polls asking "Have you, yourself, ever happened to try marijuana?" show a substantial rise in "yes" answers from 1969 (4 percent) to the mid-1980s (about 35 percent), a pattern consistent with a surge and then a drop in experimentation (Pew Research and Gallup poll results available from the Roper Center for Public Opinion Research iPoll Databank, http://www.ropercenter.uconn.edu/data_access/ipoll/ipoll.html). National surveys of Americans twelve and older show steady declines in drug use from 1979 to 1998 (Carter et al., *Historical Statistics of the United States*, tables Ec951–974 [by Douglas Eckberg]), with use in the previous month dropping from 14 to 6 percent. More recent surveys used new procedures which probably raised the rate, so there was likely no real change between 1998 and 2004 (Office of Applied Studies, "Results from the 2004 National Survey," ch. 9.) Surveys of high school seniors, 1975 to 2005, show a peak of about 50 percent using any illicit drug in the past *year* in 1979, a decline, and a small rebound, finishing at about 40 percent in 2005 (Johnston et al., "Demographic"). Methodological issues make parsing small fluctuations in such surveys unwise. We can probably assume that underreporting became less common as drug use, at least of marijuana, became less stigmatized. (Support for legalization of marijuana tripled between 1969 and 2005: J. Carroll, "Who Supports Marijuana Legalization?"). So the best conclusion is of a general downward trend in use since ca. 1980 (see also Menard and Huizinga, "Age, Period.") Never stopped: some discussions of suicide trends (note 85 above) speculate that an increase after 2000 in suicide among middle-aged Americans may reflect drug use (e.g., Patricia Cohen, "Midlife Suicide Rises, Puzzling Researchers," *NYT*, Feb. 19, 2008).

89. Sample questions: "Baseline NCS Interview Schedule," http://www.hcp.med .harvard.edu/ncs/Baseline_NCS.php (accessed Aug. 31, 2006). Disorder rates: Kessler et al., "Lifetime Prevalence."

The claim of a depression "epidemic" rests on the finding that younger and older people were about *equally likely* to report episodes of distress some time during their lives. Because the younger had been "at risk" for far fewer years, their underlying lifetime propensity for depression must be *much higher* than that of older people. Ergo, depression increased over the century. Using this method, Weissman et al.,

"The Changing Rate," concluded that Americans of every birth cohort from 1935 on had more episodes of major depression and experienced them earlier in life than had members of the previous cohort. E.g., fewer than 1 percent of Americans who were thirty-five years old in the 1940s reported ever experiencing a major depression, but 10 percent of Americans who were thirty-five in the 1980s reported one. Kessler et al., "Lifetime Prevalence," estimate that Americans born around the late 1970s had three times the chances of ever having a major depressive disorder than those born around the early 1950s (see also Klerman et al., "Birth-Cohort Trends").

Despite the attention the "epidemic of depression" got (e.g., Daniel Goleman, "A Rising Cost of Modernity: Depression." *NYT*, Dec. 8, 1992), strong reservations arose. (1) The validity of such survey questions for assessing depression has been questioned (A. Horwitz and Wakefield, "The Age of Depression" and *Loss of Sadness*). (2) Differences by age in recalling an episode do not reliably indicate historical change. One problem is the way recollection works. The older people are, the more they forget upsetting experiences, and, when people remember traumas, they tend to misplace the episodes closer to the present. In one study, most of the people who had been hospitalized for major depression could not, twenty-five years later, recall it well enough to be categorized as ever having had a case of depression (Andrews, "Recall"; also G. Simon and VonKorff, "Recall"; G. Simon, "Is the Lifetime Risk?"—with a response and a rejoinder in *Journal of Clinical Epidemiology*, vol. 49, 1996, 1077–8; Paten, "Recall Bias"; Costello et al., "10-Year Research"). Recall problems probably explain why Weismann et al., "The Changing Rate," concluded, oddly, that young adults in France, Italy, and Germany were less depressed during World War II than comparable young adults were during the 1950s and '60s. Even scholars who have used the recall method admit that it may be an artifact of memory (e.g., Kessler et al., "Lifetime Prevalence," 600; see also Frombonne, "Increased Rates"). Another artifact is differential mortality: people with major depression tend to die at a high rate, which means that they never show up in later surveys as older depressed people (e.g., Paten, "Recall Bias"). (3) To the extent that more Americans became more psychologically wise, self-aware, and forthcoming in the late twentieth century (reasonable assumptions, see, e.g., Veroff et al., *The Inner American*) the likelier they were to look for, identify, and report melancholy feelings (see Phelan et al., "Public Conceptions"; Klerman et al., "Birth-cohort Trends," 692). On the other hand, perhaps introspection produces real melancholy; people who ruminate about themselves also tend toward depression (Ingram, "Self-Focused"; Mor and Winquist, "Self-Focused").

The sorts of studies that can avoid most such biases (although not the last one) compare similar samples of people answering the same questions in different eras. There are few of these and they cover only the last half-century at best. In general, they suggest *no net change* in rates of depression. Veroff. et al., *The Inner American*, contrasted a 1976 survey with one conducted in 1957 and concluded, "American [mental] well-being generally has remained constant" (57). They credit increasing psychological awareness and frankness for the 1957–76 differences they did find. (Note, also, that the unemployment, inflation, and homicide rates in 1976 were double those of 1957; it had been a stressful two decades.) Other studies that suggest constant or declining psychological difficulties: Srole, "The Midtown Manhattan"; Amato et al., *Alone Together*, 57–60; Roberts et al., "Changes"; Kasen et al., "Depression"; Costello et al., "10-Year Research"; Kessler et al., "Prevalence and Treatment"; and Y. Yang, "Is Old Age Depressing?" More complex results: Swindle et al., "Responses," found that 26 percent of GSS respondents in 1996 reported feeling an oncoming nervous breakdown, compared to about 20 percent in the 1957 and 1976 Veroff studies. That small change may be substantive, may reflect different survey methods, or may reflect more openness about psychological issues. The GSS item "life," which asks people whether they find life exciting, routine, or dull, showed a slight increase in "exciting" responses from the 1970s to 2000s (my analysis). Twenge, "The Age of Anxiety," reports that measures of anxiety among youth increased from 1950 to around the late 1980s, but Twenge and Nolen-Hoeksema, "Age, Gender," report that depression symptoms *de*creased among children from 1980 to 1998. (In addition, the Twenge methodology has been questioned; see note 18 above.) Summing all this up, the fairest conclusion is that any substantive change in depression or related conditions since roughly 1960 has not been demonstrated.

90. Late-twentieth-century changes that might have increased depression: changes in family, including mothers working and the delay in getting married; strains in living up to rising economic expectations amid economic stagnation (Frank, *Luxury Fever*; Schor, *The Overworked American*); television (Kubey and Csikszentmihalyi, *Television and the Quality of Life*; Comstock et al., *Television and Human Behavior*; and by implication, Putnam, *Bowling Alone*); and increased self-absorption. Sleep: in 1942, 36 percent of Gallup poll respondents reported getting less than eight hours of sleep; in 2001, 71 percent did (Saad, "Americans' Mood"). Between 1982 and 2005, the percentage of GSS respondents who said they "always" felt rushed rose a bit, from 25 percent to 31 percent. J. Robinson and Godbey, "The Great American Slowdown," found that complaints about time pressure rose from the 1960s to the mid-1990s (and then leveled off), although, by their measures, actual time pressures had relaxed. See also Jacobs and Gerson, "Who Are the Overworked Americans?"; Presser, "The Economy."

91. Economic cycles: e.g., Osborn, "A Detestable Shrine." Several studies cited above point to the distinctiveness of the 1960s and 1970s: the surges in youth suicide, alcoholism, and drug use, for example; the happiness studies cited below are consistent. "Robbed of hope": Rosenzweig and Thelen, *The Presence of the Past*, 133. Fischer and Hout, *Century of Difference*, ch. 9, discuss the "extended 1960s" as a period of unusually sharp cultural divisions. The baby boom argument derives from Richard Easterlin and is pursued in many studies, such as Pampel, "Cohort Size"; McCall and Land, "Trends"; and R. Johnson and Gerstein, "Initiation of Use."

92. From 1987 to 1999, fewer than four economics articles per year treated "happiness"; from 2000 to mid-2006, over twenty-six per year did (tabulated from the "EconLit" database, http://www.econlit.org). Easterlin, "Does Money Buy Happiness," laid the foundation for an economics of happiness in the early 1970s, but few built upon it until much later. Classical: D. McMahon, "From the Happiness." The rise of behavioral economics and the discovery of choice paradoxes undercut the

"revealed preference" assumptions. See Kahneman and Krueger, "Developments" ("people often make," 3); Loewenstein, "The Creative Destruction"; Gilbert, *Stumbling on Happiness*; Frey and Stutzer, "Happiness Research"; idem, *Happiness and Economics*; Di Tella and MacCulloch, "Some Uses"; Layard, *Happiness*; Koszegi and Rabin, "Choices"; and the symposium "Life Satisfaction and Welfare Economics" in the *Journal of Socio-Economics*, Apr. 2006. A clearinghouse of happiness research is Rutt Veenhoven's World Database of Happiness (http://www1.eur.nl/fsw/happiness/; accessed Oct. 20, 2006) and the *Journal of Happiness Studies*. Validity issues: see sources above and T. Smith, "Happiness"; Blanchflower and Oswald, "Well-Being"; Deiner et al., "Subjective Well-Being"; Veenhoven, "Developments"; Biswas-Diener et al., "The Psychology"; and a more recent caution: Kahneman et al., "Would You Be Happier?"

93. Easterlin, "Does Money Buy Happiness?" (The "paradox" seemingly appears in some other countries, too.) Posing the paradox: see sources in the previous note such as Easterlin and Layard, as well as Easterlin, *Growth Triumphant*; idem, "Income"; R. E. Lane, *The Loss of Happiness*; Ott, "Did the Market?"; Franks, *Luxury Fever*; and Binswanger, "Why Does?" On the (un)reality of the paradox: Hagerty and Veenhoven, "Wealth and Happiness Revisited," Easterlin's reply, "Feeding the Illusion," and a rejoinder, Veenhoven and Hagerty, "Rising Happiness"; see also Veenhoven, "Is Life Getting Better?"; Di Tella and MacCulloch, "Gross National Happiness"; Deaton, "Income, Health"; Inglehart et al., "Development, Freedom, and Rising Happiness"; and C. Fischer, "What Wealth-Happiness Paradox?" (GDP per capita grew greatly after 1970, but average Americans' earnings were flat). Stevenson and Wolfers, "Economic Growth," analyzed a massive amount of data and concluded both that income increased happiness "across countries, within countries, and over time" and that happiness was flat in America because average Americans' wealth was flat (2). See also Hout, "Money and Morale." On the general correlates of happiness, including the effects of national-level conditions, see also Di Tella et al., "The Macroeconomics"; Di Tella and MacCulloch, "Partisan Social Happiness"; Radcliff, "Politics, Markets"; Pacek and Radcliff, "Assessing"; Diener and Suh, "National Differences"; and Hagerty, "Social Comparisons." The large literature on happiness that preceded economists' entry includes: Cantril, *The Pattern of Human Concerns*; Bradburn, *The Structure of Psychological Well-Being*; and Diener and Suh, *Culture and Subjective Well-Being*.

94. "Pursuit": Maier, *American Scripture*; Darnton, "The Pursuit of Happiness." Divorces: Riley, *Divorce*; R. Griswold, "Law, Sex"; and E. May, *Great Expectations*. On goods: Leach, *Land of Desire*, and ch. 3.

95. Tocqueville: *Democracy in America*, 536. Bellows, "The Influence of the Trading Spirit," 111. Treadmill: see sources cited in note 93 above.

96. Argyle, "The Causes," provides a literature review. I also extracted the list of personal and national traits that correlate with happiness from various cross-national survey analyses, including Diener and Suh, "National Differences"; Helliwell, "How's Life?"; Frey and Stutter, *Happiness and Economics*; Inglehart et al, "Development, Freedom, and Rising Happiness"; Di Tella and MacCulloch, "Gross National Happiness"; Di Tella et al., "The Macroeconomics of Happiness"; Radcliff, "Politics, Markets"; Pacek and Radcliff, "Assessing"; Lucas and Clark, "Do People?" (vs. Zim-

mermann and Easterlin, "Happily?"); Lucas, "Time Does Not"; and Lucas et al., "Unemployment." (See also citations in note 92.) I subsume under economic well-being income, unemployment, hours of work, and inflation. I focus on what seemed the strongest predictors. For a catalog of the correlates of happiness, see Veenhoven, "World Database." In 1995–2005, the United States ranked *seventeenth* in average happiness, at about the same level as Belgium, the Netherlands and Germany, above the French and British, and notably below the Danish and Swiss (Veenhoven, "Average Happiness").

97. Crude estimate: differences among nations cannot prove historical change in a single nation. Also, people of different cultures answer such questions differently. For example, Eastern Europeans tend to be morose in the international comparisons and Asians place less weight on individual happiness (e.g., Sastry and Ross, "Asian Ethnicity").

Trends: The Gallup happiness question, asked from 1946 through late 2008 shows, after smoothing, a low point of about 40 percent "very happy" in the immediate postwar years, a peak just above 50 percent around 1957, a trough around 45 percent in the mid-1980s, and another rise to above 50 percent around 2005—then sliding to 45 percent in late 2008 (my analysis of the "Gallup Brain" data, http://institution.gallup.com; accessed Jun. 30, 2008). Season-to-season and year-to-year fluctuations in this series suggests that there is a lot of noise. See also Erskine, "The Polls" and Bradbuurn, *The Structure of Psychological Well-Being*, 41, for early estimates. "Very happy" answers to the GSS item (starting in 1973; 1972 had a technical fluke) are at 36 percent in the mid-1970s, decline marginally to about 34 percent in the late 1980s, and then level off to about 33 percent in the 2000s (my analysis). The Pew surveys, using a "ladder" ranking question, show a rise from 1987 to the end of the 1990s, a flattening, and then a sharp drop in 2008 (Taylor, "Inside the Middle Class," 81). The short gloss is that between World War II and 2008 happiness ratings rose notably, then slumped a bit, flattened out, and finally took a fall during the 2007–9 recession.

Among recent studies of these trends are Stevenson and Wolfers, "Economic Growth"; Inglehart et al., "Development, Freedom, and Rising Happiness"; Hout, "Money and Morale"; Yang, "Social Inequalities"; C. Fischer, "What Wealth-Happiness Paradox?"; and Schnittker, "Diagnosing." Generations: Yang, "Social Inequalities"; Cohn, "Baby Boomers."

98. Oprah Winfrey: "Want to Get in Touch with Your Soul? Oprah sits down with leading spiritual thinkers and authors to talk about matters of the soul," such as "Elizabeth Lesser, author of *The Seeker's Guide: Making Life a Spiritual Adventure*" (http://www2.oprah.com/spiritself/oss/ss_oss_main.jhtml; accessed Jul. 1, 2008). Baby boomers: We saw distinctive rates of distress, unhappiness, and perhaps even extramarital affairs (note 72 above).

Chapter Seven

1. Brennan, Concurring Opinion, *408 U.S. 238 Furman v. Georgia*, sec. IV, Jun. 29, 1972, http://www.law.cornell.edu/supct/html/historics/USSC_CR_0408_0238_ZC1.html (accessed Jul. 8, 2008; emphasis added).

2. Adapting new technology: see C. Fischer, *America Calling*, esp. ch. 1. Assimilation: see chapter 1, note 21.

3. D. Potter, *People of Plenty*, 92, 126.

4. These claims are drawn from the previous chapters. See also J. Davis's "Did Growing Up?"; Fischer and Hout, *Century of Difference*, passim. Boomers' problems: see discussion in the previous chapter.

5. Versus Europeans: the United States ranks average or below-average among advanced nations in life expectancy and related health issues (such as height, e.g., Komlos and Lauderdale, "Underperformance in Affluence"), employment, leisure, educational skills, and even ownership of computers. We are often misled by some measures, notably the per capita Gross National Product, which rank the United States near the top. They mislead because, given America's much greater inequality, the well-being of the very top masks difficulties of the rest. (See: e.g., OECD data, http://stats.oecd.org, accessed Jul. 13, 2008; United States Bureau of the Census, "Children's Well-Being"; Fischer et al., *Inequality by Design*, ch. 5.) How do Americans rank in happiness? It depends on the measure and method: near the top (Inglehart et al., "Development, Freedom, and Rising Happiness") or middling (Veenhoven, "Average Happiness"). Much of Fischer and Hout, *Century of Difference,* addresses the education gap.

6. Computers: P. Liberatore, "Home Computers—Why the Craze is Fizzling Out," *San Francisco Chronicle*, Jul. 5, 1985. Shipping: Gienapp, "The Antebellum Era," 106.

7. 1939: Erskine, "The Polls."

Abbreviations

AER	American Economic Review
AHR	American Historical Review
AJS	American Journal of Sociology
ARS	Annual Review of Sociology
AQ	American Quarterly
ASR	American Sociological Review
DEM	Demography
JAH	Journal of American History
JCR	Journal of Consumer Research
JEH	Journal of Economic History
JEP	Journal of Economic Perspectives
JER	Journal of the Early Republic
JIH	Journal of Interdisciplinary History
JPSP	Journal of Personality and Social Psychology
JSH	Journal of Social History
JUH	Journal of Urban History
NBER	National Bureau for Economic Research
POQ	Public Opinion Quarterly
SF	Social Forces
SSH	Social Science History
WMQ	William and Mary Quarterly

Works Cited

Abbey, Susan E., and Paul E. Garfinkel. 1991. "Neurasthenia and Chronic Fatigue Syndrome: the Role of Culture in the Making of a Diagnosis." *American Journal of Psychiatry* 148:1638–46.

Abel, Emily K. 2000. *Hearts of Wisdom: American Women Caring for Kin, 1850–1940*. Cambridge, MA: Harvard University Press.

Abelson, Elaine S. 1989. *When Ladies Go A-Thieving: Middle-Class Shoplifters in the Victorian Store*. New York: Oxford University Press.

Abercrombie, Nicolas, Stephen Hill, and Bryan S. Turner. 1986. *Sovereign Individuals of Capitalism*. London: Allen & Unwin.

Abrams, Philip. 1980. "History, Sociology, Historical Sociology." *Past and Present* 87 (May): 3–16.

Abrams, Ray H. 1943. "Residential Propinquity as a Factor in Marriage Selection: Fifty Year Trends in Philadelphia." *ASR* 8 (June): 288–94.

Abramson, Paul R., and Ronald Inglehart. 1995. *Value Change in Global Perspective*. Ann Arbor: University of Michigan Press.

Adams, Jane. 1994. *The Transformation of Rural Life: Southern Illinois, 1890–1990*. Chapel Hill: University of North Carolina Press.

Addonizio, Elizabeth M., Donald P. Green, and James M. Glaser. 2007. "Putting the Party Back into Politics: An Experiment Testing Whether Election Day Festivals Increase Voter Turnout." *PS: Political Science & Politics* 40: 21–27.

Adelman, Melvin. 1993. "Modernization Theory and Its Critics." In Cayton, Gorn, and Williams 1993, 347–58.

Adler, Jeffery S. 1997. "'My Mother-in-Law Is to Blame, But I'll Walk on Her Neck Yet': Homicide in Late-Nineteenth-Century Chicago." *JSH* 31 (Winter): 253–76.

———. 2001. "'Halting the Slaughter of the Innocents': The Civilizing Process and the Surge of Violence in Turn-of-the-Century Chicago." *SSH* 25 (Spring): 29–51.

———. 2003. "'On the Border of Snakeland': Evolutionary Psychology and Plebian Violence in Industrial Chicago, 1875–1920." *JSH* 36 (Spring): 541–60.

———. 2003. "'We've Got a Right to Fight; We're Married': Domestic Homicide in Chicago, 1875–1920." *JIH* 34:27–48.

———.2006. "'It Is His First Offense. We Might As Well Let Him Go': Homicide and Criminal Justice in Chicago, 1875–1920." *JSH* 40 (Fall): 5–24.

Adler, Paul S.1990. "Marx, Machines, and Skill." *Technology and Culture* 31 (October): 780–812.

Adrian, Lynne M., and Joan E. Crowley. 1991. "Hoboes and Homeboys: The Demography of Misdemeanor Convictions in the Allegheny County Jail, 1892–1923." *JSH* 25 (Winter): 345–71.

Advocates for Youth. 1997. "Adolescent Sexual Behavior: I. Demographics." Fact sheet. Washington DC: Advocates for Youth.

Agnew, Jean-Christophe. 1990. "Coming Up for Air: Consumer Culture in Historical Perspective." *Intellectual History Newsletter* 12:3–21.

Aguiar, Mark, and Erik Hurst. 2006. "Measuring Trends in Leisure: The Allocation of Time over Five Decades." Working paper 12082. Cambridge, MA: NBER.

Aichenbaum, W. Andrew. 1978. *Old Age in the New Land.* Baltimore: Johns Hopkins University Press.

Akerlof, George A., and Janet L. Yellin. 1996. "New Mothers, Not Married." *Brookings Review* 14 (Fall): 18–22.

Al-Zahrani, Saad Said A., and Stan A. Kaplowitz. 1993. "Attributional Biases in Individualistic and Collectivistic Cultures: A Comparison of Americans with Saudis." *Social Psychology Quarterly* 56 (September): 223–33.

Alba, Richard D. 1995. "Assimilation's Quiet Tide." *Public Interest* 119: 3–18.

Alba, Richard D., John R. Logan, and Kyle Crowder. 1997. "White Ethnic Neighborhoods and the Assimilation Process: The Greater New York Region, 1980–1990." *SF* 75 (March): 883–909.

Alba, Richard D., John R. Logan, Brian J. Stults, Gilbert Marzan, and Wenquan Zhang. 1999. "Immigrant Groups in the Suburbs: A Reexamination of Suburbanization and Spatial Assimilation." *ASR* 64 (June): 446–60.

Alba, Richard D., Ruben G. Rumbaut, and Karen Marotz. 2005. "A Distorted Nation: Perceptions of Racial/Ethnic Group Sizes and Attitudes toward Immigrants and Other Minorities." *SF* 84 (December): 901–19.

Alcorn, Richard S. 1974. "Leadership and Stability in Mid-Nineteenth-Century America: A Case Study of an Illinois Town." *JAH* 61 (December): 685–702.

Alesina, Alberto, and Eliana La Ferrara. 2002. "Who Trusts Others?" *Journal of Public Economics* 85:207–34.

Alexander, John K. 1973. "Poverty, Fear, and Continuity: An Analysis of the Poor in Late Eighteenth-Century Philadelphia." In Davis and Haller 1973, 13–36.

Alexander, Ruth M. 1993. "Adolescence." In Cayton, Gorn, and Williams 1993, 2037–50.

Allen, James P. 1977. "Changes in the American Propensity to Migrate." *Annals of the Association of American Geographers* 67 (December): 577–87.

Allen, Jodie T., and Michael Dimock. 2007. "A Nation of 'Haves' and 'Have-Nots'?: Far More Americans Now See Their Country as Sharply Divided Along Economic Lines." *Pew Research Center for the People & the Press*, September 13. http://pewresearch.org/pubs/593/haves-have-nots.

Almond, Gabriel A., Marvin Chodorow, and Roy Harvey Pearce. 1982. *Progress and Its Discontents*. Berkeley: University of California Press.

Altschuler, Glenn C., and Stuart M. Blumin. 1997. "Limits of Political Engagement in Antebellum America: A New Look at the Golden Age of Participatory Democracy." *JAH* 84 (December): 855–85.

———. 1997. "Where Is the Real America: Politics and Popular Consciousness in the Antebellum Era." *AQ* 49(2): 225–67.

———. 2000. *Rude Republic: Americans and Their Politics in the Nineteenth Century*. Princeton, NJ: Princeton University Press.

Altschuler, Glenn C., and Jan M. Saltzgaber. 1988. "The Limits of Responsibility: Social Welfare and Local Government in Seneca County, New York 1860–1875." *JSH* 22 (Spring): 515–38.

Alwin, Duane F. 1986. "Religion and Parental Child-Rearing Orientations: Evidence of Catholic-Protestant Convergence." *AJS* 92 (September): 412–40.

———. 1987. "Childrearing Goals." *ISR Newsletter* (Spring/Summer): 3–4.

———. 1988. "From Obedience to Authority: Changes in Traits Desired in Children, 1924–1978." *POQ* 52 (1988): 33–52.

———. 1989. "Changes in Qualities Valued in Children in the United States, 1964 to 1984." *Social Science Research* 18:195–236.

———. 1996. "From Child-Bearing to Child-Rearing: The Link Between Declines in Fertility and Changes in the Socialization of Children." *Population and Development Review* 22 (Supplement): 176–96.

———. 1996. "Coresidence Beliefs in American Society, 1973 to 1991." *Journal of Marriage and the Family* 58 (May): 393–403.

Amato, Paul R., Alan Booth, David R. Johnson, and Stacy J. Rogers. 2007. *Alone Together: How Marriage is America is Changing*. Cambridge, MA: Harvard University Press.

American Sociological Review. 1998. "A Symposium on Church Attendance in the United States." 63 (February): 111–45.

Amerson, Philip, and Edward J. Stephenson. 1997. "Decline or Transformation? Another View of Mainline Finances." *Christian Century* 114 (February 5): 144–51.

Ammerman, Nancy Tatom. 1987. *Bible Believers: Fundamentalists in the Modern World*. New Brunswick, NJ: Rutgers University Press.

———. 1997. "Organized Religion in a Voluntaristic Society." *Sociology of Religion* 58 (Fall): 203–16.

Anbinder, Tyler. 1995. "'Boss' Tweed: Nativist." *JER* 15 (Spring): 109–16.

Anderson, Elijah. 1990. *Streetwise: Race, Class, and Change in an Urban Community*. Chicago: University of Chicago Press.

Anderson, Fred, and Andrew R. L. Cayton. 1993. "The Problem of Fragmentation and the Prospects for Synthesis in Early American Social History." *WMQ* 3rd Ser., 50 (April): 299–310.

Anderson, Michael. 1995. *Approaches to the History of the Western Family, 1500–1914*. 2nd ed. Cambridge: Cambridge University Press.

Andrews, Gavin, K. Anstey, H. Brodaty, C. Issakidis, and G. Luscombe. 1999.

"Recall of Depressive Episode 25 Years Previously." *Psychological Medicine* 29 (July): 787–91.

Anonymous. 1903. "Experience of a Street Car Conductor." Repr. in *Plain Folk: The Life Stories of Undistinguished Americans*, ed. David M. Katzman and William M. Tuttle, 14–21. Urbana: University of Illinois Press, 1982.

Appelbaum, Diana Karter. 1989. *The Glorious Fourth: An American Holiday, an American History*. New York: Facts on File.

Applbaum, Kalman. 1998. "The Sweetness of Salvation: Consumer Marketing and the Liberal-Bourgeois Theory of Needs." *Current Anthropology* 39 (June): 323–50.

Appleby, Joyce. 1978. "Modernization Theory and the Formation of Modern Social Theories in England and America." *Comparative Studies in Society and History* 20 (April): 259–85.

———. 1984. "Values and Society." In Greene and Pole 1984, 290–316.

———. 1992. "Recovering America's Historic Diversity." *AHR* 79:419–31.

———. 1993. "Consumption in Early Modern Thought." In Brewer and Porter 1993, 162–73.

———, ed. 1997. *Recollections of the Early Republic: Selected Autobiographies*. Boston: Northeastern University Press.

———. 2000. *Inheriting the Revolution: The First Generation of Americans*. Cambridge, MA: Harvard University Press.

———. 2001. "The Vexed Story of Capitalism Told by American Historians." *JER* 21 (Spring): 1–19.

Appleby, Joyce, Lynn Hunt, and Margaret Jacobs. 1994. *Telling the Truth about History*. New York: W. W. Norton.

Archer, Margaret S. 1985. "The Myth of Cultural Integration." *British Journal of Sociology* 36 (September): 333–53.

Archer, Melanie. 1995. "Small Capitalism and Middle-Class Formation in Industrializing Detroit, 1880–1900." *JUH* 21 (January): 218–55.

Arditi, Jorge. 1999. "Etiquette Books, Discourse and the Deployment of an Order of Things." *Theory, Culture, and Society* 16 (4): 25–48.

Argersinger, Peter H. 1985–86. "New Perspectives on Election Fraud in the Gilded Age." *Political Science Quarterly* 100 (Winter): 669–87.

Argyle, Michael. 1999. "Causes and Correlates of Happiness." In Kahneman, Diener, and Schwartz 1999, 353–73.

Arieli, Yehoshua. 1964. *Individualism and Nationalism in American Ideology*. Cambridge, MA: Harvard University Press.

Arnett, Jeffrey Jensen. 1998. "Learning to Stand Alone: The Contemporary American Transition to Adulthood in Cultural and Historical Context." *Human Development* 41:295–315.

Arnold, Joseph L. 1979. "The Neighborhood and City Hall: The Origin of Neighborhood Associations in Baltimore, 1880–1911." *JUH* 6 (November): 3–30.

Arnould, Eric J., and Craig J. Thompson. 2005. "Consumer Culture Theory (CCT): Twenty Years of Research." *JCR* 31 (March): 868–82.

Astin, Alexander W. 1998. "The Changing American College Student: Thirty-Year Trends, 1966–1996." *Review of Higher Education* 21 (Winter): 115–35.

Atherton, Lewis. 1954. *Main Street on the Middle Border*. Bloomington: Indiana University Press.

Attewell, Paul. 1989. "The Clerk Deskilled: A Study in False Nostalgia." *Journal of Historical Sociology* 2 (December): 357–88.

Atwood, Roy Alden. 1987. "Routes of Rural Discontent." *Annals of Iowa* 48:264–73.

Augst, Thomas. 2003. *The Clerk's Tale: Young Men and Moral Life in Nineteenth-Century America*. Chicago: University of Chicago Press.

Ault, James M. Jr. 1983, "Making 'Modern' Marriage 'Traditional:' State Power and the Regulation of Marriage in Colonial Zambia." *Theory and Society* 12 (December): 181–210.

———. 2004. *Spirit and Flesh: Life in a Fundamentalist Baptist Church*. New York: Knopf.

Babbitt, Charles E., and Harold J. Burbach. 1990. "A Comparison of Self-Orientation Among College Students Across the 1960s, 1970s, and 1980s." *Youth & Society* 21 (June): 472–82.

Bachu, Amara. 1999. "Trends in Marital Status of U.S. Women at First Birth: 1930 to 1994." *Current Population Reports, Special Studies*, P23–197. Washington DC: U.S. Bureau of the Census.

Bahr, Howard M. 1980. "Changes in Family Life in Middletown, 1924–77." *POQ* 44 (Spring): 35–52.

Bahr, Howard M., Colter Mitchell, Xiaomin Li, Alison Walker, and Kristen Sucher. 2004. "Trends in Family Space/Time, Conflict, and Solidarity: Middletown 1924–1999." *City & Community* 3 (September): 263–91.

Bailey, Beth L. 1988. *From Front Porch to Back Seat*. Baltimore: Johns Hopkins University Press, 1988.

Bailey, I. M., and M. F. Snyder. 1921. "A Survey of Farm Homes." *Journal of Home Economics* 13 (August): 346–56.

Bailyn, Bernard. 1986. *Voyagers to the West*. New York: Vintage.

Baird, Brendan M., Kimdy Le, and Richard E. Lucas. 2006. "On the Nature of Intraindividual Personality Variability: Reliability, Validity, and Associations With Well-Being." *JPSP* 90 (3): 512–27.

Baker, Paula. 1984. "The Culture of Politics in the Late Nineteenth Century: Community and Political Behavior in Rural New York." *JSH* 18 (Winter): 167–94.

———. 1985. "The Farmer as a Social Problem." Paper presented to the Organization of Americans Historians, Minneapolis.

———. 1991. *The Moral Frameworks of Public Life: Gender, Politics, and the State in Rural New York, 1870–1930*. New York: Oxford University Press.

Banfield, Edward C. 1958. *The Moral Basis of a Backward Society*. New York: Free Press.

Bargh, John A. 2002. "Losing Consciousness: Automatic Influences on Consumer Judgment, Behavior, and Motivation." *JCR* 29 (September): 280–85.

Bargh, John H., and Katelyn Y. A. McKenna. 2004. "The Internet and Social Life." *Annual Review of Psychology* 55: 573–90.

Baritz, Loren. 1982. *The Good Life: The Meaning of Success for the American Middle Class*. New York: Harper & Row.

Barke, Megan, Rebecca Fribush, and Peter N. Stearns. 2000. "Nervous Breakdown in 20th-Century American Culture." *JSH* 33 (Spring): 565–84.

Barnes, Andrew E., and Peter N. Stearns, eds. 1989. *Social History and Issues in Human Consciousness*. New York: New York University Press.

Barron, Hal S. 1984. *Those Who Stayed Behind: Rural Society in Nineteenth-Century New England*. New York: Cambridge University Press.

———. 1997. *Mixed Harvest: The Second Great Transformation in the Rural North, 1870–1930*. Chapel Hill: University of North Carolina Press.

Barth, Gunther. 1980. *The Rise of Modern City Culture in Nineteenth-Century America*. New York: Oxford University Press.

Barton, John J. 1975. *Peasant and Strangers: Italians, Rumanians, and Slovaks in an American City, 1890–1950*. Cambridge, MA: Harvard University Press.

Barton, Michael. 1989. "The Victorian Jeremiad: Critics of Accumulation and Display." In Bronner 1989, 55–71.

Barton, Stephen E., and Carol J. Silverman, eds. 1994. *Common Interest Communities: Private Governments and the Public Interest*. Berkeley: University of California, Institute of Governmental Studies Press.

Bartov, Hannoch. 1963. "Measures of Affluence." Repr. in Handlin and Handlin 1997, 292–317.

Basch, Norma. 1999. *Framing American Divorce: From the Revolutionary Generation to the Victorians*. Berkeley: University of California Press.

Basker, Emek. 2005. "Selling a Cheaper Mousetrap: Wal-Mart's Effect on Retail Prices." *Journal of Urban Economics* 58:203–29.

Battan, Jesse F. 1983. "The 'New Narcissism' in 20th-Century America: The Shadow and Substance of Social Change." *JSH* 17: 2 (Winter): 199–220.

Baudrillard, Jean. 1988. "Consumer Society." In *Jean Baudrillard: Collected Writings*, ed. M. Poster, 29–56. Oxford: Polity Press.

Bauman, Zygmaut. 1998. "The Self in a Consumer Society." *Echoes,* Post-Modernity Project, University of Virginia (Winter): 27–30.

———. 2001. "Consuming Life." *Journal of Consumer Culture* 1 (1): 9–29.

Baumer, Eric. 1994. "Poverty, Crack, and Crime." *Journal of Research in Crime and Delinquency* 31 (August): 311–27.

Baumgartner, Frank R., and Jack L. Walker. 1988. "Survey Research and Membership in Voluntary Associations." *American Journal of Political Science* 32 (November): 908–28.

Baylor Institute for Studies of Religion. 2006. *American Piety in the Twenty-First Century: New Insights to the Depth and Complexity of Religion in the US.* Waco, TX: Baylor University.

Becker, Gary S., Elisabeth M. Landes, Robert T. Michael. 1977. "An Economic Analysis of Marital Instability." *Journal of Political Economy* 85 (December): 1141–88.

Becker, Laura L. 1982. "Diversity and Its Significance in an Eighteenth-Century Pennsylvania Town." In Zuckerman 1982, 196–221.

Beckert, Sven. 2000. "Involved Disengagement? Reconsidering the Golden Age of Participatory Democracy." *Reviews in American History* 28.4 (2000): 560–56.

Beeman, Richard R. 1992. "Deference, Republicanism, and the Emergence of Popular Politics in Eighteenth-Century America." *WMQ* 3rd Ser., 49 (July): 401–30.

Beito, David T. 1999. "To Advance the 'Practice of Thrift and Economy': Fraternal Societies and Social Capital." *JIH* 29 (Spring): 585–613.

———. 2000. *From Mutual Aid to the Welfare State: Fraternal Societies and Social Services, 1890–1967.* Chapel Hill: University of North Carolina Press.

Belasco, Warren. 1979. *Americans on the Road: From Autocamp to Motel, 1910–1945.* Cambridge, MA: Harvard University Press.

Belk, Russell W. 1985. "Materialism: Trait Aspects of Living in the Material World." *JCR* 12 (December): 265–80.

———. 1988. "Possessions and the Extended Self." *JCR* 15 (September): 139–68.

———. 1999. "I Shop, Therefore I am." *American Anthropologist* 10 (March): 182–85.

———. 2004. "The Human Consequences of Consumer Culture." In Ekstrom and Brembeck 2004, 67–85.

Belk, Russell W., and Richard W. Pollay. 1985. "Images of Ourselves: The Good Life in Twentieth Century Advertising." *JCR* 11 (March): 887–97.

Belknap, Kitturah Penton. 1849. "The Commentaries of Kitturah Penton Belknap." Repr. in *Covered Wagon Women: Diaries & Letters from the Western Trails.* Vol. 1. *1840–1849,* ed. Kenneth L. Holmes, 189–230. Lincoln: University of Nebraska Press, 1995.

Bell, Daniel. 1982. "The Return of the Sacred: The Argument about the Future of Religion." In Almond, Chodorow, and Pearce 1982, 501–23.

———. 1989. "'American Exceptionalism' Revisited: The Role of Civil Society." *Public Interest* 95 (Spring): 38–56.

———. 1996. *The Cultural Contradictions of Capitalism.* Twentieth anniversary edition. New York: Basic Books.

Bell, Earl H. 1942. "Culture of a Contemporary Rural Community: Haskell, Kansas." *Rural Life Studies* 2. Washington DC: USDA: Bureau of Agricultural Economics.

Bell, Joyce M., and Douglas Hartman. 2007. "Diversity in Everyday Discourse: The Cultural Ambiguities and Consequences of 'Happy Talk.'" *ASR* 72 (December): 895–914.

Bellah, Robert N. 1975. *The Broken Covenant: American Civil Religion in a Time of Trial.* New York: Seabury.

———. 1998. "Is There a Common American Culture?" *Journal of the American Academy of Religion* 66 (3): 613–25.

———. 2002. "The Protestant Structure of American Culture: Multiculture or Monoculture?" *Hedgehog Review* 4 (Spring): 7–34.

Bellah, Robert N., Richard Madsen, William M. Sullivan, Ann Swidler, and Steven M. Tipton. 1985. *Habits of the Heart: Individualism and Commitment in American Life.* Berkeley: University of California Press.

Bellamy, Robert V. Jr., and James R. Walker. 2004. "Did Televised Baseball Kill the 'Golden Age' of the Minor Leagues? A Reassessment." *Nine* 13 (1): 59–73.

Bellows, Henry W. 1845. "The Influence of the Trading Spirit Upon the Social and Moral Life of America." Repr. in Davis 1979, 111–12.

Beltrán-Sánchez, Hiram, Samuel H. Preston, and Vladimir Canudas-Romo. 2008.
    "An Integrated Approach to Cause-of-Death Analysis." Unpublished paper, Pop-
    ulation Studies Center, University of Pennsylvania.

Bender, Thomas. 1978. *Community and Social Change in America*. New Brunswick,
    NJ: Rutgers University Press.

———. 1986. "Wholes and Parts: The Need for Synthesis in American History"
    JAH 73 (June, 1986): 120–36.

Bendix, Reinhard. 1967. "Tradition and Modernity Reconsidered." *Comparative
    Studies in Society and History* 9:292–346.

Bengston, Vern L. 1975. "Generation and Family Effects in Values Socialization."
    ASR 40 (June): 358–71.

Beniger, James R. 1983. "Does Television Enhance the Shared Symbolic Environ-
    ment? Trends in Labeling of Editorial Cartoons, 1948–1980." *ASR* 48 (February):
    103–11.

Bennett, Neil G., David E. Bloom, and Patricia H. Craig. 1989. "The Divergence of
    Black and White Marriage Patterns." *AJS* 95 (November): 629–722.

Benson, Susan Porter. 1986. *Counter Cultures: Saleswomen, Managers, and Customers in
    American Department Stores 1890–1940*. Urbana: University of Illinois Press.

Benton, James S. 1993. "Self and Society in Popular Social Criticism 1920–1980."
    Symbolic Interaction 16 (2): 145–70.

Berger, Michael L. 1979. *The Devil Wagon in God's Country: The Automobile and Social
    Change in Rural America, 1883–1939*. Hamden, CT: Archon Books.

Berkhoffer, Robert F. Jr. 1995. *Beyond the Great Story: History as Text and Discourse*.
    Cambridge, MA: Harvard University Press.

Berlin, Ira. 1998. *Many Thousands Gone: The First Two Centuries of Slavery in North
    America*. Cambridge, MA: Harvard University Press.

Berrol, Selma Cantor. 1995. *Growing Up American: Immigrant Children in America
    Then and Now*. New York: Twayne.

Berthoff, Rowland. 1971. *An Unsettled People*. New York: Harper & Row.

Best, Joel. 2001. *Damned Lies and Statistics: Untangling Numbers from the Media, Politi-
    cians, and Activists*. Berkeley: University of California Press.

———. 2001. "Social Progress and Social Problems: Toward a Sociology of Gloom."
    Sociological Quarterly 42 (Winter): 1–12.

Bianchi, Suzanne, John P. Robinson, and Melissa A. Milkie. 2006. *Changing Rhythms
    of American Family Life*. New York: Russell Sage Foundation.

Bigler, Monica, Greg J. Neimeyer, and Elliott Brown. 2001. "The Divided Self
    Revisited: Effects of Self-Concept Clarity and Self-Concept Differentiation on
    Psychological Adjustment." *Journal of Social and Clinical Psychology* 20 (3): 396–415.

Binford, Henry C. 1985. *The First Suburbs: Residential Communities on the Boston Pe-
    riphery 1815–1860*. Chicago: University of Chicago Press.

Binswanger, Mathias. 2006. "Why Does Income Growth Fail to Make Us Happier?
    Searching for the Treadmills Behind the Paradox of Happiness." *Journal of Socio-
    Economics* 35: 366–81.

Birch, Eugenie L. 2005. "Who Lives Downtown." Living Cities Census Series.

Washington DC: The Brookings Institution, November. http://www.brookings
.edu/metro/pubs/20051115_birch.htm.

Bishop, George. 1999. "Americans' Belief in God." *POQ* 63 (Fall): 421–34.

Bissell, Linda Auwers. 1973. "Family, Friends and Neighbors: Social Interaction in
Seventeenth-Century Windsor, Connecticut." PhD diss., Brandeis University.

Biswas-Diener, Robert, Ed Diener, and Maya Tamir. 2006. "The Psychology of Subjective Well-being." *Daedalus* 133 (Spring): 18–26.

Bjorklund, Diane. 1998. *Interpreting the Self: Two Hundred Years of American Autobiography*. Chicago: University of Chicago Press.

Blackwell, Marilyn S. 2001. "Surrogate Ministers: Women, Revivalism, and Mater-
nal Associations in Vermont." *Vermont History* 69 (Suppl.): 66–78.

Blais, Andre. 2006. "What Affects Voter Turnout?" *Annual Review of Political Science* 9:111–25.

Blakely, Edward J., and Mary Gail Snyder. 1997. *Fortress America: Gated Communities
in the United States*. Washington DC: Brookings Institution Press.

Blanchflower, David G., and Andrew J. Oswald. 2000. "Well-Being Over Time in
Britain and the USA." Working paper 7487. Cambridge, MA: NBER.

Blanke, David. 2000. *Sowing the American Dream: How Consumer Culture Took Root in
the Rural Midwest*. Athens: Ohio University Press.

Blassingame, John W. 1979. *The Slave Community. Revised and Enlarged Edition*. New
York: Oxford University Press.

Blauvelt, Martha Tomhave. 2002. "The Work of the Heart: Emotion in the 1805–35
Diary of Sarah Connell Ayer." *JSH* 35 (Spring): 577–92.

Blendon, Robert J., and others. 1999. "The 60s and the 90s." *Brookings Review*
(Spring): 14–17.

Bloch, Marc. 1961. *The Historian's Craft. Translated from the French by Peter Putnam*.
New York: Knopf.

———. 1966. *French Rural History*. Trans. J. Sandheimer. Berkeley: University of California Press.

Bloch, Ruth H. 2003. "Changing Conceptions of Sexuality and Romance in
Eighteenth-Century America." *WMQ* 3rd Ser., 60 (January): 13–42.

Block, James E. 2002. *A Nation of Agents: The American Path to a Modern Self and
Society*. Cambridge, MA: Harvard University Press.

Block, Sharon. 2003. "Bringing Rapes to Court." *Common-Place* 3 (April). http://
www.common-place.org/vol-03/no-03/block/.

Bloomquist, Leonard, Duane Williams, and Jeffrey C. Bridger. 2002. "Sublette,
Kansas: Persistence and Change in Haskell County." In Luloff and Krannich
2002, 23–43.

Blue, Frederick. J. 1995. "The Poet and the Reformer: Longfellow, Sumner, and the
Bonds of Male Friendship, 1837–1874." *JER* 15 (Summer): 273–97.

Bluestone, Daniel M. 1991. "'The Pushcart Evil': Peddlers, Merchants, and New
York City's Streets, 1890–1940." *JUH* 18 (November): 68–92.

Blum, Jerome. 1971. "The European Village as Community: Origins and Functions."
Agricultural History 45 (July): 157–78.

Blumin, Stuart M. 1973. "Residential Mobility Within the Nineteenth-Century City." In Davis and Haller 1973, 37–52.

——. 1976. *The Urban Threshold: Growth and Change in a Nineteenth-Century American Community*. Chicago: University of Chicago Press.

——. 1989. *The Emergence of the Middle Class: Social Experience in the American City, 1760–1900*. New York: Cambridge University Press.

Blumstein, Alfred, and Joel Wallman, eds. 2000. *The Crime Drop in America*. New York: Cambridge University Press.

Board of Governors of the Federal Reserve System. 2009. "Flow of Funds Accounts of the United States, Coded Tables for Z.1. Release." Washington DC: Federal Reserve System, March 12.

Boase, Jeffrey, and Barry Wellman. 2006. "Personal Relationships: On and Off the Internet." In *The Cambridge Handbook of Personal Relationships*, ed. Anita L. Vangelisti and Dan Perlman, 709–26. New York: Cambridge University Press.

Bock, Kenneth. 1980. *Human Nature and History: A Response to Sociobiology*. New York: Columbia University Press.

Bodnar, John E. 1985. *The Transplanted: A History of Immigrants in Urban America*. Bloomington: Indiana University Press.

Bodnar, John E., Roger Simon, and Michael P. Weber. 1982. *Lives of Their Own: Blacks, Italians, and Poles in Pittsburgh, 1900–1960*. Urbana: University of Illinois Press.

Bok, Edward. 1921. "Where America Fell Short with Me." Excerpt from *The Americanization of Edward Bok* in *The Flavor of the Past*. Vol. 1. ed. Leland D. Baldwin, 78–81. New York: Van Norstrand Reinhold, 1968.

Bolin, Winifred D. Wandersee. 1978. "The Economics of Middle-Income Family Life: Working Women During the Great Depression." *JAH* 65 (June): 60–74.

Bonnell, Victoria, and Lynn Hunt, eds. 1999. *Beyond the Cultural Turn: New Directions in the Study of Culture and Society*. Berkeley: University of California Press.

Bonomi, Patricia U., and Peter R. Eisenstadt. 1982. "Church Adherence in Eighteenth-Century British American Colonies." *WMQ* 3rd Ser., 39 (April): 245–86.

Boorstin, Daniel J. 1973. *The Americans: The Democratic Experience*. New York: Random House.

Borchert, James. 1980. *Alley Life in Washington: Family, Community, Religion, and Folk life, 1850–1970*. Urbana: University of Illinois Press.

Boudon, Raymond. 1983. "Why Theories of Social Change Fail: Methodological Thoughts." *POQ* 47 (Summer): 143–60.

Bourdieu, Pierre. 1984. *Distinction: A Social Critique of the Judgment of Taste*. Trans. Richard Nice. Cambridge, MA: Harvard University Press.

Bourke, Paul F., and Donald A. DeBats. 1977. "Identifiable Voting in Nineteenth-Century America: Toward a Comparison of Britain and the United States Before The Secret Ballot." *Perspectives in American History* 9:257–88.

Bowden, M. J. 1992. "The Invention of American Tradition." *Journal of Historical Geography* 18:3–26.

Boydston, Jeanne. 1997. "The Woman Who Wasn't There: Women's Market Labor and the Transition to Capitalism in the United States." In Gilje 1997, 23–47.

Boyer, Paul S. 1978. *Urban Masses and Moral Order in America, 1820–1920*. Cambridge, MA: Harvard University Press.

Boyer, Paul S., and Stephen Nissenbaum. 1974. *Salem Possessed: The Social Origins of Witchcraft*. Cambridge, MA: Harvard University Press.

Bradburn, Norman M. 1969. *The Structure of Psychological Well-Being*. Chicago: Aldine.

Brady, Henry E., Kay Lehman Schlozman, Sidney Verba, and Laurel Elms. 1998. "Who Bowls: Class, Race, and Changing Participatory Equality." Paper presented to the American Political Science Association, Boston.

Braverman, Harry. 1974. *Labor and Monopoly Capital: The Degradation of Work in the Twentieth Century*. New York: Monthly Review Press.

Breen, T. H. 1975. "Persistent Localism: English Social Change and the Shaping of New England Institutions." *WMQ* 32 (January): 3–28.

———. 1988. "'Baubles of Britain': The American and Consumer Revolutions of the Eighteenth Century." *Past and Present* 119:73–104.

———. 1993. "The Meaning of Things: Interpreting the Consumer Economy in the Eighteenth Century." In Brewer and Porter 1993, 249–60.

———. 1993. "Narrative of Commercial Life: Consumption, Ideology, and Community on the Eve of the American Revolution." *WMQ* 3rd Ser., 50 (July): 471–501.

Breen, T. H., and Stephen Foster. 1973. "The Puritans' Greatest Achievement: A Study of Social Cohesion in Seventeenth-Century Massachusetts." *JAH* 60 (June): 5–22.

Brehm, John, and Wendy Rahn. 1997. "Individual Level Evidence for the Causes and Consequences of Social Capital." *American Journal of Political Science* 41 (July): 999–1023.

Brewer, John, and Roy Porter, eds. 1993. *Consumption and the World of Goods*. New York: Routledge.

Brewer, Marilynn B., and Wendi Gardner. 1996. "Who Is This 'We'? Levels of Collective Identity and Self Representations." *JPSP* 71 (1): 83–93.

Briggs, Xavier de Souza. 2007. "'Some of My Best Friends Are . . .': Interracial Friendships, Class, and Segregation in America." *City & Community* 6 (December): 263–90.

Brinkley, Alan. 1990. "Prosperity, Depression, and War, 1920–1945." In Foner 1990, 119–41.

Brock, William R. 1988. *Welfare, Democracy, and the New Deal*. New York: Cambridge University Press.

Bronner, Simon J. 1989. *Consuming Visions: Accumulation and Display of Goods in America, 1880–1920*. New York: W. W. Norton.

———. 1989. "Reading Consumer Culture." In Bronner 1989, 13–53.

Brooke, John L. 1996. Review of *Innerworldly Individualism*, by Adam B. Seligman. *AHR* 101 (April): 556–57.

Brooks, Clem, and Simon Cheng. 2001. "Declining Government Confidence and Policy Preferences in the U.S.: Devolution, Regime Effects, or Symbolic Change." *SF* 79 (June): 1343–75.

Brown, Clair. 1994. *American Standards of Living, 1918–1988*. Cambridge, MA: Blackwell.

Brown, M. Craig, and Barbara D. Warner. 1992. "Immigrants, Urban Politics, and Policing in 1900." *ASR* 57 (June): 293–305.

Brown, Richard D. 1974. "The Emergence of Urban Society in Rural Massachusetts, 1760–1820." *JAH* 61 (June): 29–51.

———. 1975. "Modernization: A Victorian Climax." *AQ* 27 (December): 533–48.

———. 1976. *Modernization: The Transformation of American Life, 1600–1865*. New York: Hill & Wang.

———. 1989. *Knowledge is Power: The Diffusion of Information in Early America, 1700–1865*. New York: Oxford University Press.

Browne, Irene. 1995. "The Baby Boom and Trends in Poverty, 1967–1987." *SF* 73 (March): 1071–95.

Bruce, Steve, ed. 1992. *Religion and Modernization: Sociologists and Historians Debate the Secularization Thesis*. Oxford: Clarendon Press.

Bruce, Dickson D. Jr. 1974. *And They All Sang Hallelujah: Plain-Folk Camp-Meeting Religion, 1800–1845*. Knoxville: University of Tennessee Press.

Bruchey, Stuart. 1990. *Enterprise: The Dynamic Economy of a Free People*. Cambridge, MA: Harvard University Press.

Bruckner, Elke, and Karin Knaup. 1989. "Networks and Social Support in Comparative Perspective." Paper prepared for the European Conference on Social Network Analysis, Groningen, Netherlands.

Bruegel, Martin. 1995. "'Time that Can be Relied Upon': The Evolution of Time Consciousness in the Mid-Hudson Valley, 1790–1860." *JSH* 28 (Spring): 547–64.

———. 1996. "Unrest: Manorial Society and the Market in the Hudson Valley, 1780–1850." *JAH* 82 (March): 1393–1425.

———. 2006. "The Social Relations of Farming in the Early American Republic: A Microhistorical Approach." *JER* 26 (Winter): 523–55.

Brumberg, Paula. 1984. "'Ruined' Girls: Changing Community Responses to Illegitimacy in Upstate New York, 1890–1920." *JSH* 18 (Winter): 247–72.

Brunner, E. de Schweinitz, and J. K. Kolb. 1933. *Rural Social Trends*. New York: McGraw-Hill.

Bryant, W. Keith, and Catherine D. Zick. 1996. "Are We Investing Less in the Next Generation? Historical Trends in Time Spent Caring for Children." *Journal of Family and Economic Issues* 17 (Winter): 365–92.

Bryce, James. 1914. *The American Commonwealth*. Vol. 2. Repr., Indianapolis: Liberty Fund, 1995.

Buchmann, Claudia, and Thomas A. DiPrete. 2006. "The Growing Female Advantage in College Completion: The Role of Family Background and Academic Achievement." *ASR* 71 (August): 515–41.

Buchmann, Marlis, and Manuel Eisner. 1997. "The Transition from the Utilitarian to the Expressive Self: 1900–1992." *Poetics* 25 (November): 157–75.

Buhle, Mary Jo. 1993. "Feminist Approaches to Social History." In Cayton, Gorn, and Williams 1993, 319–33.

Burden, Barry C. 2000. "Voter Turnout and the National Election Studies." *Political Analysis* 8 (4): 389–98.

Bureau of Business Research. 1928. "The Automobile and the Village Merchant." Bulletin No. 19, College of Commerce and Business Administration. Champaign: University of Illinois.

Burham, Walter Dean. 2007. "Triumphs and Travails in the Study of American Voting Participation Rates, 1788–2006." *Journal of The Historical Society* 7 (December): 505–19.

Burnham, John C. 1973. "The Progressive Era Revolution in American Attitudes Toward Sex." *JAH* 59 (4): 885–908.

———. 1996. "Why Did Infants and Toddlers Die: Shifts in Americans' Ideas of Responsibility for Accidents—From Blaming Mom to Engineering." *JSH* 29 (Summer): 817–37.

Burrows, Edwin G., and Mike Wallace. 1999. *Gotham: A History of New York City to 1898*. New York: Oxford University Press.

Burstein, Alan N. 1981. "Immigrants and Residential Mobility: The Irish and Germans in Philadelphia, 1850–1880." In Hershberg 1981, 174–203.

Burstein, Andrew. 2002. "The Political Character of Sympathy." *JER* 21 (4): 601–32.

Bushman, Richard Lyman. 1998. "Markets and Composite Farms in Early America." *WMQ* 3rd Ser., 55 (July): 351–74.

———. 1967. *From Puritan to Yankee*. Cambridge, MA: Harvard University Press.

———. 1981. "Family Security in the Transition from Farm to City, 1750–1850." *Journal of Family History* 6 (Fall): 238–56.

———. 1993. *The Refinement of America: Persons, Houses, Cities*. New York: Vintage.

———. 1994. "Shopping and Advertising in Colonial America." In Carson, Hoffman, and Albert 1994, 233–52.

Butler, Jon. 1979. "Magic, Astrology, and the Early American Religious Heritage, 1600–1760." *AHR* 84 (April): 317–46.

———. 1990. *Awash in a Sea of Faith: Christianizing the American People*. Cambridge, MA: Harvard University Press.

———. 1997. "Protestant Success in the New American City, 1870–1920." In Stout and Hart 1997, 296–333.

———. 2000. *Becoming America: The Revolution Before 1776*. Cambridge, MA: Harvard University Press.

———. 2008. "Religion in Colonial America." In *Religion in American Life: A Short History*, Jon Butler, Grant Wacker, and Randall Balmer, 1–154. Updated ed. New York: Oxford University Press.

Calder, Lendol Glen. 1999. *Financing the American Dream: A Cultural History of Consumer Credit*. Princeton, NJ: Princeton University Press.

Calhoun, Craig. 1992. "The Infrastructure of Modernity." In Haferkamp and Smelser 1992, 205–36.

———. 1998. "Community without Propinquity Revisited: Communications Technology and the Transformation of the Urban Public Sphere." *Sociological Inquiry* 68:373–97.

Calhoun, Robert M. 1991."Religion and Individualism in Early America." In Curry and Goodheart 1991, 44–65.

Calvert, Karin. 1994. "The Function of Fashion in Eighteenth-Century America." In Carson, Hoffman, and Albert 1994, 252–83.

Campbell, Ballard C. 1996. "Federalism, State Action, and 'Critical Episodes' in the Growth of American Government." *SSH* 16 (Winter): 561–78.

Campbell, Colin. 1995. "The Sociology of Consumption." In Miller 1995, 96–126. New York: Routledge.

———. 2004. "I Shop therefore I Know that I Am." In Ekstrom and Brembeck 2004, 27–44.

Campbell, Karen. 1990. "Networks Past: A 1939 Bloomington Neighborhood." *SF* 69 (September): 139–55.

Campos, Paul, Abigail Saguy, Paul Ernsberger, Eric Oliver, and Glenn Gaesser. 2006. "The Epidemiology of Overweight and Obesity: Public Health Crisis or Moral Panic?" *International Journal of Epidemiology* 35 (1): 55–60.

Cantril, Albert H., and Susan Davis Cantril. 1999. *Reading Mixed Signals: Ambivalence in American Public Opinion About Government*. Washington DC: Woodrow Wilson Center.

Cantril, Hadley. 1965. *The Pattern of Human Concerns*. New Brunswick, NJ: Rutgers University Press.

Caplow, Theodore. 1982. "Christmas Gifts and Kin Networks." *ASR* 47 (June): 383–92.

———. 1984. "Rule Enforcement Without Visible Means: Christmas Gift Giving in Middletown." *AJS* 89 (May): 1306–1323.

Caplow, Theodore, Howard M. Bahr, and Vaughn A. Call. 2004. "The Middletown Replications: 75 Years of Change in Adolescent Attitudes, 1924–1999." *POQ* 68 (Summer): 287–313.

Caplow, Theodore, Howard M. Bahr, and Bruce A. Chadwick. 1983. *All Faithful People: Change and Continuity in Middletown's Religion*. Minneapolis: University of Minnesota Press.

Caplow, Theodore, Howard M. Bahr, John Modell, and Bruce A. Chadwick. 1991. *Recent Social Trends in the United States 1960–1990*. Ottawa: McGill-Queen's University Press.

Caplow, Theodore, Louis Hicks, and Ben J. Wattenberg. 2001. *The First Measured Century: An Illustrated Guide to Trends in America, 1900–2000*. Washington DC: AEI Press.

Caplow, Theodore et al. 1982. *Middletown Families: Fifty Years of Change and Continuity*. Minneapolis: University of Minnesota Press.

Caren, Neal. 2007. "Big City, Big Turnout? Electoral Participation in American Cities." *Journal of Urban Affairs* 29 (February): 31–46.

Carnes, Mark. 1993. "The Rise and Consolidation of Bourgeois Culture." In Cayton, Gorn, and Williams 1993, 605–20.

Carr, Lois Green, and Lorena S. Walsh. 1977. "The Planter's Wife: The Experience of White Women in Seventeenth-Century Maryland." *WMQ* 3rd Ser., 34 (October): 542–71.

———. 1988. "The Standard of Living in the Colonial Chesapeake." *WMQ* 3rd Ser., 45 (January): 135–59.

Carroll, Joseph. 2002. "Teens' Knowledge of World History Slipping." Gallup poll. March 5. http://www.gallup.com/poll/5785/Teens-Knowledge-World-History-Slipping.aspx.

———. 2005. "Americans Inventory Their Gadgets." Gallup News Service. http://www.gallup.com/poll/20593/Americans-Inventory-Their-Gadgets.aspx.

———. 2005. "Who Supports Marijuana Legalization?" Gallup poll, November 1, http://institution.gallup.com/content/default.aspx?ci=19561.

———. 2006. "Family Time Eclipses TV as Favorite Way to Spend an Evening." Gallup News Service. March 20.http://www.gallup.com/ poll/21856/Family-Time-Eclipses-Favorite-Way-Spend-Evening.aspx.

Carroll, Michael P. 2004. "Upstart Theories and Early American Religiosity: A Reassessment." *Religion* 34:129–43.

Carson, Cary. 1994. "The Consumer Revolution in Colonial British America: Why Demand?" In Carson, Hoffman, and Albert 1994, 483–696.

Carson, Cary, Ronald Hoffman, and Peter J. Albert, eds. 1994. *Of Consuming Interests: The Style of Life in the Eighteenth Century*. Charlottesville: University Press of Virginia.

Carter, Susan B. 1988. "The Changing Importance of Lifetime Jobs, 1892–1978." *Industrial Relations* 27 (Fall): 287–300.

Carter, Susan B., Scott Sigmund Gartner, Michael R. Haines, Alan L. Olmstead, Richard Sutch, and Gavin Wright, eds. 2006. *Historical Statistics of the United States, Earliest Times to the Present: Millennial Edition*. New York: Cambridge University Press, online ed., http://hsus.cambridge.org/HSUSWeb/index.do.

Carter, Susan B., and Elizabeth Savoca. 1990. "Labor Mobility and Lengthy Jobs in Nineteenth- Century America." *JEH* 50 (March): 1–16.

Carter, Susan B., and Richard Sutch. 1996. "Myth of the Industrial Scrapheap: A Revisionist View of Turn-of-the-Century American Retirement." *JEH* 56 (March): 5–38.

Carwardine, Richard. 2006. *Lincoln: A Life of Purpose and Power*. New York: Knopf.

Cashin, Joan E. 2000. "Households, Kinfolk, and Absent Teenagers: The Demographic Transition in the Old South." *Journal of Family History* 25 (2): 141–57.

Castells, Manuel. 1996. *The Rise of Network Society*. Cambridge, MA: Blackwell.

Cayton, Mary Kupiec. 1989. *Emerson's Emergence: Self and Society in the Transformation of New England, 1800–1845*. Chapel Hill: University of North Carolina Press.

Cayton, Mary Kupiec, Elliott J. Gorn, and Peter W. Williams, eds. 1993. *Encyclopedia of American Social History*. 3 vols. New York: Scribners.

Centerwall, Brandon S. 1993. "Television and Violent Crime." *Public Interest* 111 (Spring): 56–72.

Cerulo, Karen A. 1984. "Television, Magazine Covers, and the Shared Symbolic Environment: 1948–1970." *ASR* 49 (August): 566–70.

Chafe, William. 1972. *The American Woman: Her Changing Social, Economic, and Political Roles, 1920–1970*.New York: Oxford University Press.

Chambers, Clarke A. 1963. *Seedtime of Reform*. Minneapolis: University of Minnesota Press.

Chanda, Areendam, Lee A. Craig, and Julianne Treme. 2008. "Convergence (And Divergence) in the Biological Standard of Living in the USA, 1820–1900." *Cliometrica* 2 (April): 19–48.

Chandler, Mary G. 1854. *The Elements of Character*. 2nd ed. Boston: Crosby, Nichols, and Company.

Channing, William Ellery. 1838. *Self-Culture*. Boston: Outton and Wentworth. Online ed., http://www.americanunitarian.org/selfculture.htm.

Chappell, Edward A. 1994. "Housing a Nation: The Transformation of Living Standards in Early America." In Carson, Hoffman, and Albert 1994, 167–232.

Charles, Kerwin Kofi, Erik Hurst, and Nikolai Roussanov. 2008. "Conspicuous Consumption and Race." Working paper 13392. Cambridge, MA: NBER.

Chaves, Mark. 1994. "Secularization as Declining Religious Authority." *SF* 72 (March): 749–74.

Chaves, Mark, and Shawna Anderson. Forthcoming. "Continuity and Change in American Religion, 1972–2006." In *Social Trends in the United States, 1972–2006: Evidence from the General Social Survey*, ed. Peter V. Marsden. Princeton, NJ: Princeton University Press.

Chaves, Mark, and David E. Cann. 1992. "Regulation, Pluralism, and Religious Market Structure." *Rationality and Society* 4 (July): 272–90.

Cherlin, Andrew J. 1983. "Changing Family and Household: Contemporary Lessons from Historical Research." *ARS* 9 (1983): 51–66.

———. 1992. *Marriage, Divorce, Remarriage*. Rev. and expanded ed. Cambridge, MA.: Harvard University Press.

———. 2004. "The Deinstitutionalization of American Marriage." *Journal of Marriage and Family* 66 (November): 848–61.

———. 2009. *The Marriage-Go-Round: The State of Marriage and the Family in America Today*. New York: Knopf.

Cherlin, Andrew J., and Frank F. Furstenberg. 1986. *The New American Grandparent*. New York: Basic Books.

Chernev, Alexander. 2003. "Product Assortment and Individual Decision Processes." *JPSP* 85 (July): 151–62.

Chesterfield, Earl of [Philip Stanhope]. 1746–47. *Chesterfield's Letters to His Son* . Project Gutenberg. http://www.gutenberg.org/dirs/3/3/6/3361/3361.txt.

Chevan, Albert. 1989. "The Growth of Home Ownership: 1940–1980." *DEM* 26 (May): 249–66.

Ching, Pamela L. Y. H., Walter C. Willett, Eric B. Rimm, et al. 1996. "Activity Level and Risk of Overweight in Male Health Professionals." *American Journal of Public Health* 86 (January): 25–30.

Chiricos, Ted, Kathy Padgett, and Marc Gertz. 2000. "Fear, TV News, and the Reality of Crime." *Criminology* 38 (August): 755–86.

Chudacoff, Howard P. 1982. "Success and Security: The Meaning of Social Mobility in America." *Reviews in American History* 10 (December): 101–12.

———. 1989. *How Old Are You? Age Consciousness in American Culture*. Princeton, NJ: Princeton University Press.

———. 1999. *The Age of the Bachelor: Creating an American Subculture*. Princeton, NJ: Princeton University Press.

Chudacoff, Howard, and Judith E. Smith. 2000. *The Evolution of American Urban Society*. 5th ed. Upper Saddle River, NJ: Prentice-Hall.

Clark, Christopher. 1996. "Rural America and the Transition to Capitalism." *JER* 16 (Summer): 223–36.

———. 1996. "The Consequences of the Market Revolution in the American North." In Stokes and Conway 1996, 23–42.

Clark, Clifford Edward Jr. 1986. *The American Family Home, 1800–1960*. Chapel Hill: University of North Carolina Press.

Clark, Elizabeth B. 1995. "'The Sacred Rights of the Weak': Pain, Sympathy, and the Culture of Individual Rights in Antebellum America." *JAH* 82 (September): 463–93.

Clarke, Frances. 2007. "So Lonesome I Could Die: Nostalgia and Debates Over Emotional Control in the Civil War North." *JSH* 41(Winter): 253–82.

Clausen, John A. 1995. *American Lives: Looking Back at Children of the Depression*. Berkeley: University of California Press.

Clawson, Mary Ann. 1993. "Fraternal Organizations." In Cayton, Gorn, and Williams 1993, 1657–66.

Clemen, Rudolf A. 1960. "Shall I Not Take Mine Ease in Mine Inn." *American Heritage Magazine* 11 (June). http://www.americanheritage.com/articles/magazine/ah/1960/4/1960_4_60.shtml.

Clemens, Paul G. E. 2005. "The Consumer Culture of the Middle Atlantic, 1760–1820." *WMQ* 62(October): 577–624.

Clement, Elizabeth Alice. 2006. *Love for Sale: Courting, Treating, and Prostitution in New York City, 1900–1945*. Chapel Hill: University of North Carolina Press.

Clough, S.B., and L. Quimby. 1983. "Peacham, Vermont." *Vermont History* 51:5–28.

Clunas, Craig. 1999. "Modernity Global and Local: Consumption and the Rise of the West." *AHR* 104 (December): 1497–1512.

Cmiel, Kenneth. 1990. *Democratic Eloquence: The Fight over Popular Speech in Nineteenth-Century America*. New York: William Morrow.

Coclanis, Peter A., and John Komlos. 1995. "Nutrition and Economic Development in Post-Reconstruction South Carolina." *SSH* 19 (Spring): 91–115.

Cohen, Charles L. 1997. "The Post-Puritan Paradigm of Early American Religious History." *WMQ* 3rd Ser., 54 (October): 695–722.

Cohen, Daniel A. 1990. "The Murder of Maria Bickford: Fashion, Passion, and the Birth of a Consumer Culture." *American Studies* 31 (2): 5–30.

———. 1993. *Pillars of Salt, Monuments of Grace: New England Crime Literature and the Origins of American Popular Culture, 1674–1860*. New York: Oxford University Press.

Cohen, Dov, and Richard E. Nisbett. 1997. "Field Experiments Examining the Culture of Honor: The Role of Institutions in Perpetuating Norms About Violence." *Personality and Social Psychology Bulletin* 23 (November): 1188–99.

Cohen, Ira, and Ann Elder. 1989. "Major Cities and Disease Crises: A Comparative Perspective." *SSH* 13 (Spring): 25–63.

Cohen, Joel B., and Dipankar Chakravarti. 1990. "Consumer Psychology." *Annual Review of Psychology* 41:243–88.

Cohen, Lawrence E., and Kennth C. Land. 1987. "Age Structure and Crime: Symmetry versus Asymmetry and the Projection of Crime Rates through the 1990s." *ASR* 52 (April): 170–83.

Cohen, Lizabeth. 1980. "Embellishing a Life of Labor: An Interpretation of the Material Culture of American Working-Class Homes, 1885–1915." *Journal of American Culture* 3 (Winter):752–75.

———. 1989. "Encountering Mass Culture at the Grass Roots: The Experience of Chicago Workers in the 1920s." *AQ* 41 (March): 6–33.

———. 2003. *A Consumer's Republic: The Politics of Mass Consumption in Postwar America*. New York: Knopf.

Cohen, Patricia. 1982. *A Calculating People*. Chicago: University of Chicago Press.

Cohen, Stephen, and Arnold Eisen. 2000. *The Jew Within: Self, Family, and Community in America*. Bloomington: Indiana University Press.

Cohn, D'Vera. 2008. "Baby Boomers: The Gloomiest Generation." Pew Research Center, June 25. http://pewresearch.org/pubs/880/baby-boomers-the-gloomiest-generation.

Cohn, D'Vera, and Rich Morin. 2008. "American Mobility: Who Moves? Who Stays Put? Where's Home?" Pew Research Center, http://pewsocialtrends.org/pubs/721/movers-and-stayers.

Collier, James Lincoln. 1991. *The Rise of Selfishness in America*. New York: Oxford University Press.

Collier, Jane Fishburne. 1997. *From Duty to Desire: Remaking Families in a Spanish Village*. Princeton, NJ: Princeton University Press.

Collins, Randall. 1983. "Upheavals in Biological Theories Undermine Sociobiology." In *Sociological Theory*, ed. Randall Collins, 306–18. San Francisco: Jossey-Bass.

Collins, Robert M. 1988. "In Retrospect: David Potter's People of Plenty' and the Recycling of Consensus History." *Reviews in American History* 16 (June): 321–35.

Commager, Henry Steele. 1950. *The American Mind: An Interpretation of American Thought and Character Since the 1880s*. New Haven, CT: Yale University Press.

Comstock, George, Steven Chaffee, Nathan Katzman, Maxwell McCombs, and Donald Roberts. 1978. *Television and Human Behavior*. New York: Columbia University Press.

Comstock, George, and Haejung Paik. 1994. "The Effects of Television Violence on Antisocial Behavior: A Meta-Analysis." *Communication Research* 21 (4): 516–46.

Congressional Budget Office. 2007. "Trends in Earnings Variability Over the Past 20 Years." Washington DC: Congressional Budget Office, April.

Conrad, Cecilia A. 1996. "Where Have All the Majors Gone? Comment." *Journal of Economic Education* 27 (Fall): 376–78.

Conroy, David W. 1995. *In Public Houses: Drink and the Revolution of Authority in Colonial Massachusetts*. Chapel Hill: University of North Carolina Press.

Consumers Union. 1937. *CU Buying Guide 1937*. New York: Consumers Union of U.S.

Conzen, Kathleen Neils. 1976. *Immigrant Milwaukee*. Cambridge, MA: Harvard University Press.

——. 1980. "Community Studies, Urban History, and American Local History." In *The Past Before Us*, ed. Michael Kammen, 270–91. Ithaca, NY: Cornell University Press.

Conzen, Kathleen Neils, Harry S. Stout, E. Brooks Holifield, and Michael Zuckerman. 1996. "Forum: The Place of Religion in Urban and Community Studies." *Religion and American Culture* 6 (Summer): 107–30.

Cook, Daniel Thomas, 1995. "The Mother as Consumer: Insights from the Children's Wear Industry, 1917–1929." *Sociological Quarterly* 36 (Summer): 505–22.

Cook, Shelburne F. 1973. "The Significance of Disease in the Extinction of the New England Indians." *Human Biology* 45 (September): 485–508.

——. 1973. "Interracial Warfare and Population Decline Among the New England Indians." *Ethno History* 20 (Winter): 1–24.

Cook, Timothy E., and Paul Gronke. 2005. "The Skeptical American: Revisiting the Meanings of Trust in Government and Confidence in Institutions." *Journal of Politics* 67 (August): 784–803.

Cookingham, Mary E. 1984. "Working after Childbearing in Modern America." *JIH* 14 (Spring): 773–92.

Coontz, Stephanie. 1992. *The Way We Never Were: American Families and the Nostalgia Trap*. New York: Basic Books.

——. 1998. *The Social Origins of Private Life*. New York: Verso Press.

——. 2001. "The Challenge of Family History." *Magazine of History* 15 (Summer): 28–30.

Cordelian, W. 1990. "Television and Children." *Communication Research Trends* 10 (3): 1–20.

Coser, Rose. 1991. *In Defense of Modernity: Role Complexity and Individual Autonomy*. Palo Alto, CA: Stanford University Press.

Costa, Dora. 1993. "Height, Wealth, and Disease among Native-Born in the Rural, Antebellum North." *SSH* 17 (Fall): 355–83.

——. 1997. "Displacing the Family: Union Army Pensions and Elderly Living Arrangements." *Journal of Political Economy* 105 (December): 1269–92.

——. 1997. "A House of Her Own: Old Age Assistance and the Living Arrangements of Older Nonmarried Women." Working paper 6217. Cambridge, MA: NBER.

——. 1998. "Unequal at Birth: A Long-Term Comparison of Income and Birth Weight." *JEH* 58 (December): 987–1009.

——. 1999. "American Living Standards: Evidence from Recreational Expenditures." Working paper 7148. Cambridge, MA: NBER .

——. 2000. "The Wage and Length of the Workday: From the 1890s to 1991." *Journal of Labor Economics* 18 (January): 156–81.

——. 2000. "Understanding the Twentieth-Century Decline in Chronic Conditions Among Older Men." *DEM* 37 (February): 53–72.

Costa, Dora, and Matthew E. Kahn. 2003. "Civic Engagement and Community Heterogeneity: An Economist's Perspective." *Perspectives on Politics* 1 (March): 103–11.

———. 2003. "The Rising Price of Non-Market Goods." *AER* 93 (May): 227–32.

———. 2003. "Understanding the American Decline in Social Capital, 1952–1998." *Kyklos* 56 (February): 17–46.

———. 2008. *Heroes and Cowards: The Social Face of War*. Princeton, NJ: Princeton University Press.

Costa, Dora, and Richard F. Steckel. 1997. "Long-Term Trends in Health, Welfare, and Economic Growth in the United States." In Steckel and Floud 1997, 47–89.

Costello, E. Jane, Debra L. Foley, and Adrian Angold. 2006. "10-year Research Update Review: The Epidemiology of Child and Adolescent Psychiatric Disorders. II: Developmental Epidemiology." *Journal of the American Academy of Child and Adolescent Psychiatry* 45(January): 8–26.

Cott, Nancy F. 1978. "Divorce and the Changing Status of Women in Eighteenth-Century Massachusetts." In Gordon 1978, 115–39.

———. 1978. "Passionlessness: An Interpretation of Victorian Sexual Ideology, 1790–1850." *Signs* 4 (Winter): 219–36.

———. 2000. *Public Vows: A History of Marriage and the Nation*. Cambridge, MA: Harvard University Press.

Countryman, Edward. 1988. "American Liberalism and the Problem of American Socialism." In *Why Is There No Socialism in the United States?* ed. Jean Heffer and Jeanine Rovet, 87–100. Paris: Éditions de L'École des Hautes Études en Sciences Sociales.

Courtwright, David T. 1983. "The Hidden Epidemic: Opiate Addiction and Cocaine Use in the South, 1860–1920." *Journal of Southern History* 49 (February): 57–72.

———. 2001. *Dark Paradise: A History of Opiate Addiction in America*. Cambridge, MA: Harvard University Press.

Couvares, Francis G. 1983. "The Triumph of Commerce: Class Culture and Mass Culture in Pittsburgh." In *Working-Class America*, ed. M. H. Frisch and D. J. Walkowitz, 123–52. Urbana: University of Illinois Press.

Cowan, Ruth Schwartz. 1979. "From Virginia Dare to Virginia Slims: Women and Technology in American Life." In *Dynamos and Virgins Revisited*, ed. M. M. Trescott, 30–44 (Metuchen, NJ: Scarecrow Press, 1979).

———. 1983. *More Work for Mother*. New York: Basic Books.

Cowan, Ruth Schwartz, Mark H. Rose, and Marsha S. Rose. 1985. "Clean Homes and Large Utility Bills, 1900–1940." *Marriage and Family Review* 9 (Fall): 53–66.

Cowles, Julia. 1931. *The Diaries of Julia Cowles: A Connecticut Record, 1797–1803*. Ed. Anna Roosevelt Cowles and Laura Hadley Moseley. New Haven, CT: Yale University Press.

Cox, W. Michael, and Richard Alm. 1997. "Time Well Spent: The Declining Real Cost of Living in America." Annual Report of the Federal Reserve Bank of Dallas.

Craig, Lee A., Barry Goodwin, and Thomas Rennes. 2004. "The Effect of Mechanical Refrigeration on Nutrition in the United States." *SSH* 28 (Summer): 325–36.

Craig, Steve. 2006. "'The More They Listen, the More They Buy': Radio and the Modernizing of Rural America, 1930–1939." *Agricultural History* 80 (1): 1–16.

Crane, Elaine Forman. 1997. "'I Have Suffer'd Much Today': The Defining force of Pain in Early America." In Hoffman, Sobel, and Teute 1997, 370–403.

Craven, Wayne. 1986. "The Development of American Character in a Land of Opportunity." In *Colonial American Portraiture: The Economic, Religious, Social, Cultural, Philosophical, Scientific and Aesthetic Foundations*, 257–68. New York: Cambridge University Press.

Crenson, Matthew A., and Benjamin Ginsberg. 2002. *Downsizing Democracy: How America Sidelined Its Citizens and Privatized Its Public*. Baltimore: Johns Hopkins University Press.

Criblez, Adam. 2004. "Tavernocracy: Tavern Culture in Ohio's Western Reserve." *Northeast Ohio Journal of History* 22 (Summer): 60–83.

Crocker, Jennifer, and Lora E. Park. "The Costly Pursuit of Self-Esteem." *Psychological Bulletin* 130:392–414.

Cross, Gary. 1993. *Time and Money: The Making of Consumer Culture*. London: Routledge.

———. 1997. *Kids' Stuff: Toys and the Changing World of American Childhood*. Cambridge, MA: Harvard University Press.

———. 2000. *An All-Consuming Century: Why Commercialism Won in Modern America*. New York: Columbia University Press.

———. 2004. *The Cute and the Cool: Wondrous Innocence and Modern American Children's Culture*. New York: Oxford University Press.

———. 2005. "The Cute Child and Modern American Parenting." In *American Behavioral History*, ed. Peter Stearns, 19–41. New York: New York University Press.

Crowe, Patricia Ward. 1978. "Good Fences Make Good Neighbors: Social Networks at Three Levels of Urbanization in Tirol, Austria." PhD diss., Stanford University.

———. 1981. "Community Size and Social Relationships: A Comparison of Urban and Rural Social Patterns in Tirol." *Anthropological Quarterly* 54 (October): 210–29.

Crowley, John E. 1999. "The Sensibility of Comfort." *AHR* 99 (June): 749–82.

———. 2001. *Invention of Comfort : Sensibilities and Design in Early Modern Britain and Early America*. Baltimore: Johns Hopkins University Press.

Csikszentmihalyi, Mihaly, and Eugene Rochberg-Halton. 1981. *The Meaning of Things: Domestic Symbols and the Self*. New York: Cambridge University Press.

Cullen, Jim. 1996. *The Art of Democracy*. New York: Monthly Review Press.

Curley, M. Louise, and Edmond D. Villani. 1980. "The Personal Savings Rate: Is It Really Low?" *Journal of Retail Banking* 2 (June): 44–53.

Curry, Richard O., and Lawrence B. Goodheart, eds. 1991. *American Chameleon: Individualism in Trans-National Context*. Kent, OH: Kent State University Press.

———. 1991. "Individualism in Trans-National Context." In Curry and Goodheart 1991, 1–19.

Curry, Richard O., and Karl E. Valois. 1991. "The Emergence of an Individualistic Ethos in American Society." In Curry and Goodheart 1991, 20–43.

Curti, Merle. 1967. "The Changing Concept of 'Human Nature' in the Literature of American Advertising." *Business History Review* 41 (Winter): 335–57.

———. 1980. *Human Nature in American Thought: A History*. Madison: University of Wisconsin Press.

Curtis, James E., Edward G. Grabb, Douglas E. Baer. 1992. "Voluntary Association Membership in Fifteen Countries: A Comparative Analysis." *ASR* 57 (April): 139–52.

Curtis, James E., Ronald D. Lambert, Steven D. Brown, and Barry J. Kay. 1989. "Affiliating with Voluntary Association: Canadian-American Comparisons." *Canadian Journal of Sociology* 14 (2): 143–61.

Cutler, David M., and Edward L. Glaeser. 1997. "Are Ghettos Good or Bad?" *Quarterly Journal of Economics* 112 (August): 791–826.

Cutler, David M., Edward Glaeser, and Karen Norberg. 2001. "Explaining the Rise in Youth Suicide." Working paper W7713. Cambridge, MA: NBER.

Cutler, David M., Edward L. Glaeser, and Jesse M. Shapiro. 2003. "Why Have Americans Become More Obese?" Working paper 9446. Cambridge, MA: NBER.

Cutler, David M., Edward L. Glaeser, Jacob L. Vigdor. 1999. "The Rise and Decline of the American Ghetto." *Journal of Political Economy* 107 (3): 455–506.

Cutler, David M., and Lawrence F. Katz. 1992. "Rising Inequality? Changes in the Distribution of Income and Consumption in the 1980's." *AER* 82 (May): 546–51.

———, and Ellen Meara. 2001. "Changes in the Age Distribution of Mortality Over the 20th Century." Working paper 8556. Cambridge, MA: NBER.

———, and Grant Miller. 2005. "The Role of Public Health Improvements in Health Advances: the Twentieth-century United States." *DEM* 42 (February): 1–22.

Dalton, Russell J. 1988. *Citizen Politics in Western Democracies*. Chatham, NJ: Chatham House.

———. 2005. "The Social Transformation of Trust in Government." *International Review of Sociology* 15 (March): 133–54.

Danbom, David R. 1995. *Born in the Country: A History of Rural America*. Baltimore: John Hopkins University Press.

Danziger, Sheldon, and Peter Gottschalk. 1995. *America Unequal*. Cambridge, MA: Harvard University Press.

Danziger, Sheldon, and Cecilia Elena Rouse. 2007. "The Price of Independence: The Economics of Early Adulthood." In *The Price of Independence: The Economics of Early Adulthood,* 1–24. New York: Russell Sage Foundation.

Darity, William Jr., Jason Dietrich, and David K. Guilkey. 1997. "Racial and Ethnic Inequality in the United States: A Secular Perspective." *AER* 87, no. 2 (May): 301–6.

Darnton, Robert. 1995. "The Pursuit of Happiness." *Wilson Quarterly* 29 (Autumn): 42–53.

Darroch, A. Gordon. 1981. "Migrants in the Nineteenth Century: Fugitives or Families in Motion?" *Journal of Family History* 6 (Fall): 257–77.

Davenport, David Paul. 1985. "Duration of Residence in the 1855 Census of New York State." *Historical Methods* 18 (Winter): 5–12.

David, Paul A., and Warren C. Anderson. 1986. "Rudimentary Contraceptive Methods and American Transition to Marital Fertility Control, 1855–1915." In *Long-Term Forces in American Economic Growth*, ed. Stanley L. Engerman and R. E. Gallman, 307–90. Chicago: University of Chicago Press.

David, Paul A., and Peter Solar. 1977. "A Bicentenary Contribution to the History of the Cost of Living in America." *Research in Economic History* 2:1–80.

Davin, Eric Leif. 1993. "The Era of the Common Child: Egalitarian Death in Antebellum America." *Mid-America* 75 (April-July): 135–63.

Davis A. F., and M. H. Haller, eds., *The Peoples of Philadelphia*. Philadelphia: Temple University Press.

Davis, David Brion, ed. 1979. *Antebellum American Culture: An Interpretive Anthology*. Lexington, MA: D.C. Heath.

Davis, James A. 1996. "Patterns of Attitude Change in the USA:1972–1994." In *Understanding Change in Social Attitudes*, ed. Bridget Taylor and Katarina Thomson, 151–79. Aldershot, UK: Dartmouth.

———. 2004. "Did Growing Up in the 1960s Leave a Permanent Mark on Attitudes and Values?" *POQ* 68(2): 161–183.

Davis, Kenneth. 1990. *Don't Know Much About History*. New York: Avon.

Davis, Ronald L. 1976. "Sentimental Songs in Antebellum America." *Southwest Review* 6 (Winter): 50–65.

Dawley, Alan. 1976. *Class and Community: The Industrial Revolution in Lynn*. Cambridge, MA: Harvard University Press.

Day, Jennifer Cheeseman, Alex Janus, and Jessica Davis. 2005. "Computer and Internet Use in the United States: 2003." *Current Population Reports* P23–208. Washington DC: U.S. Bureau of the Census.

Deaton, Angus. 2008."Income, Health, and Well-Being around the World: Evidence from the Gallup World Poll." *JEP* 22 (Spring): 53–72.

Deetz, James. 1977. *In Small Things Forgotten: The Archeology of Early American Life*. Garden City, NY: Doubleday.

Degler, Carl N. 1980. *At Odds: Women and the Family in America from the Revolution to the Present*. New York: Oxford University Press.

Dekker, Paul. 2003. "Generalised Social Trust: Meanings and Political Correlates." Paper presented to the 19th IPSA World Congress, Durban, South Africa.

Delli Carpini, Michael X., and Scott Keeter. 1991. "Stability and Change in the U.S. Public's Knowledge of Politics." *POQ* 55 (Winter): 583–612.

D'Emilio, John, and Estelle B. Freedman. 1988. *Intimate Matters: A History of Sexuality in America*. New York: Harper & Row.

Demos, John. 1986. *Past, Present, and Personal: The Family and the Life Course in American History*. New York: Oxford University Press.

———. 1986. "The Changing Faces of Fatherhood." In *Past, Present, and Personal*, 41–67. New York: Oxford University Press.

DePastino, Todd. 2003. *Citizen Hobo: How a Century of Homelessness Shaped America*. Chicago: University of Chicago Press.

De Vries, Jan. 1993. "Between Purchasing Power and the World of Goods: Understanding the Household Economy in Early Modern Europe." In Brewer and Porter 1993, 85–132.

———. 2002. Review of *Consumerism in World History*, by Peter N. Sterns. *JEH* 62 (June): 638–39.

Dey, Eric L., Alexander W. Astin, and William S. Korn. 1991. *The American Freshman: Twenty-Five Year Trends, 1966–1990*. Los Angeles: Higher Education Research Institute.

Di Tella, Rafael, and Robert MacCulloch. 2005. "Gross National Happiness as an Answer to the Easterlin Paradox?" Unpublished paper, Harvard Business School.

———. 2006. "Some Uses of Happiness Data in Economics." *JEP* 20 (Winter): 25–46.

Di Tella, Rafael, Robert J. MacCulloch, and Andrew J. Oswald. 2003. "The Macroeconomics of Happiness." *Review of Economics and Statistics* 85 (November): 809–27.

Dickson, Charles Ellis. 1986. "Prosperity Rides on Rubber Tires: The Impact of the Automobile on Minot during the 1920's." *North Dakota Historical Quarterly* 53:14–23.

Diener, Ed, and Eunkook Mark Suh. 1999. "National Differences in Subjective Well-Being." In Kahneman, Diener, and Schwartz 1999, 434–50.

———, eds. 2000. *Culture and Subjective Well-Being*. Cambridge, MA: MIT Press.

Dierks, Konstantin. 2006. "Letter Writing, Stationery Supplies, and Consumer Modernity in the Eighteenth-Century Atlantic World." *Early American Literature* 41 (3): 473–94.

DiGirolamo, Vincent. 2002. "Newsboy Funerals: Tales of Sorrow and Solidarity in Urban America." *JSH* 36 (Fall): 5–30.

DiMaggio, Paul. 1982. "Cultural Entrepreneurship in Nineteenth-Century Boston: The Creation of an Organizational Base for High Culture in America." *Media, Culture & Society* 4:33–50.

DiMaggio, Paul, Eszter Hargittai, W. Russell Neuman, and John P. Robinson. 2001. "Social Implications of the Internet." *ARS* 27: 307–36.

DiMaggio, Paul, and Toqir Mukhtar. 2004. "Arts Participation as Cultural Capital in the United States, 1982–2002: Signs of Decline?" *Poetics* 32 (2): 169–94.

Dixon, Jo, and Alan J. Lizotte. 1987. "Gun Ownership and the 'Southern Subculture of Violence.'" *AJS* 93 (September): 383–405.

Doerflinger, Thomas M. 1988. "Farmers and Dry Goods in the Philadelphia Market Area, 1750–1800." In Hoffman et al. 1988, 166–95.

Dolan, Jay P. 1996. "The Search for an American Catholicism." *Catholic Historical Review* 82 (April): 169–86.

Domina, Thurston. 2006. "Brain Drain and Brain Gain: Rising Educational Segregation in the United States, 1940–2000." *City & Community* 5 (December): 387–407.

Donald, David Herbert. 1995. *Lincoln*. New York: Simon & Schuster.

Donaldson, Scott. 1969. *The Suburban Myth*. New York: Columbia University Press.

Doucet, Michael J., and John C. Weaver. 1985. "Material Culture and the North American House: The Era of the Common Man, 1870–1920." *JAH* 72 (December): 560–87.

Douglas, Ann. 1974. "Heaven Our Home: Consolation Literature in the Northern United States." *AQ* 36 (December): 496–515.

Douglas, Mary, and Baron Isherwood. 1979/1996. *The World of Goods: Towards and Anthropology of Consumption*. London: Routledge.

Dowling, Harry F. 1977. *Fighting Infection: Conquests of the Twentieth Century*. Cambridge, MA: Harvard University Press.

Downes, Thomas A., and Jeffrey E. Zabel. 2002. "The Impact of School Characteristics on House Prices: Chicago 1987–1991." *Journal of Urban Economics* 52 (July): 1–25.

Doyle, Don Harrison. 1977. "The Social Functions of Voluntary Associations in a Nineteenth-Century American Town." *SSH* 1 (Spring): 333–55.

———. 1977. "Social Theory and New Communities in Nineteenth-Century America." *Western Historical Quarterly* 8 (April): 151–65.

———. 1983. *The Social Order of a Frontier Community: Jacksonville, Illinois, 1825–70*. Urbana: University of Illinois Press.

Drake, St. Clair, and Horace R. Cayton. 1945. *Black Metropolis: A Study of Negro Life in a Northern City*. New York: Harcourt, Brace and Company.

Dreiser, Theodore. 1900. *Sister Carrie*. Repr., Whitefish, MT: Kessinger Publishing, 2004.

Dublin, Thomas. 1979. *Women and Work: The Transformation of Work and Community in Lowell, Massachusetts, 1826–1860*. New York: Columbia University Press.

———. 1986. "Rural-Urban Migrants in Industrial New England: The Case of Lynn, Massachusetts, in the Mid-Nineteenth Century." *JAH* 73 (December, 1986): 623–44.

———. 1991. "Rural Putting-Out Work in Early Nineteenth-Century New England: Women and the Transition to Capitalism in the Countryside." *New England Quarterly* 64 (December): 531–73.

———. 1994. *Transforming Women's Work: New England Lives in the Industrial Revolution*. Ithaca, NY: Cornell University Press.

Duffield, George C. 1903. "An Iowa Settler's Homestead." *Annals of Iowa* 6 (October). http://iagenweb.org/history/annals/1903-Oct.htm.

———. 1904. "Frontier Church Going." *Annals of Iowa* 6 (January). http://iagenweb.org/history/annals/1904-Jan.htm.

Duis, Perry R. 1983. *The Saloon: Public Drinking in Chicago and Boston, 1880–1920*. Urbana: University of Illinois Press.

———. 1983. "Whose City? Public and Private Places in Nineteenth-Century Chicago." *Chicago History* 12 (Spring): 2–27.

Dulles, Foster Rhea. 1940. *America Learns to Play: A History of Popular Recreation, 1607–1940*. New York: D. Appleton-Century.

Dumenil, Lynn. 1995. *The Modern Temper: American Culture and Society in the 1920s*. New York: Hill & Wang.

Duncan, Greg J., and Ken R. Smith. 1989. "The Rising Affluence of the Elderly: How Far, How Fair, How Frail?" *ARS* 15:261–89.

Duncan, Otis Dudley. 2003. "Facile Reporting: The Supposed Decline in Biblical Literalism." *Public Perspectives* (May/June): 40–3.

Durkheim, Emile. 1893. *Division of Labor in Society*. Repr., New York: Free Press, 1984.

———. 1897. *Suicide*. Repr., Glencoe, IL: Free Press, 1951.

Dye, Jane Lawler, and Tallese D. Johnson, 2006. "A Child's Day: 2003." *Current Population Reports*, 70–109. Washington DC: U.S. Bureau of the Census.

Dye, Nancy Schrom, and Daniel Blake Smith. 1986. "Mother Love and Infant Death, 1750–1920." *JAH* 73 (September): 329–53.

Dynan, Karen E., Douglas W. Elmendorf, and Daniel E. Michel. 2007. "The Evolution of Household Income Volatility." Working paper, Brookings Institution.

Earle, Carville. 1993. "Rural Life in the South." In Cayton, Gorn, and Williams 1993, 1223–34.

Easterlin, Richard A. 1973. "Does Money Buy Happiness?" *Public Interest* 30 (Winter): 3–10.

———. 1998. *Growth Triumphant: The Twenty-First Century in Historical Perspective*. Ann Arbor: University of Michigan Press.

———. 2005. "Feeding the Illusion of Growth and Happiness: A Reply to Hagerty and Veenhoven." *Social Indicators Research* 74:429–43.

Easterlin, Richard A., and Eileen M. Crimmins. 1997. "American Youth Are Becoming More Materialistic." In *Citizen Politics in Post-Industrial Societies*, ed. Terry Nichols Clark and Michael Rempel, 67–83. Boulder, CO: Westview Press.

Eckberg, Douglas Lee. 1995. "Estimates of Early Twentieth-Century U.S. Homicide Rates: An Econometric Forecasting Approach." *DEM* 32 (February): 1–16.

———. 2001. "Stalking the Elusive Homicide." *SSH* 21 (Spring): 67–91.

Eckersley, Richard, and Keith Dear. 2002. "Cultural Correlates of Youth Suicide." *Social Science & Medicine* 55:1891–1904.

Edgell, Penny, Joseph Gerteis, and Douglas Hartmann. 2006. "Atheists as 'Other': Moral Boundaries and Cultural Membership in American Society." *ASR* 71 (April): 211–34.

Edin, Katherine, and Maria Kefalas. 2005. "Unmarried with Children." *Contexts* 4 (Spring): 16–22.

Edwards, Gary T. 1999. "Men of Subsistence and Men of Substance: Agricultural Lifestyles in Antebellum Madison County, Tennessee." *Agricultural History* 73 (Summer): 303–21.

Egan, Timothy. 2006. *The Worst Hard Time*. New York: Houghton Mifflin.

Ehrenhalt, Alan. 2000. "The Lost City: The Case for Social Authority." In *The Essential Civil Society Reader: The Classic Essays*, ed. Don E. Eberly, 239–55. Lanham, MD: Rowman & Littlefield.

Eibach, Richard P., Lisa K. Libby, and Thomas D. Gilovich. 2003. "When Change in the Self Is Mistaken for Change in the World." *Journal of Personality & Social Psychology* 84 (May): 917–31.

Eisener, Manuel. 2003. "Long-Term Historical Trends in Violent Crime." *Crime and Justice* 30:83–142.

Ekrich, A. Roger. 2005. *At Day's Close: Night in Times Past*. New York: Norton.

Ekström, Karin M., and Helene Brembeck, eds. 2004. *Elusive Consumption*. New York: Berg.

Eldridge, Larry D. 1996. "'Crazy Brained': Mental Illness in Colonial America." *Bulletin of the History of Medicine* 70:361–86.

Elias, Norbert. 1982. *The Civilizing Process: The History of Manners*. Trans. Edmund Jephcott. New York: Pantheon Books.

Eldridge, Larry D., ed. 1997. *Women and Freedom in Early America*. New York: New York University Press.

Ellis, Joseph J. 1995. "Money and That Man from Monticello." Reviews *in American History* 23 (December): 588–93.

Ellis, Richard E. 1996. "The Market Revolution and the Transformation of American Politics, 1801–1837." In Stokes and Conway 1996, 149–76.

Ellis, Richard E., Mary H. Blewett, Joel H. Silbey, Major L. Wilson, Harry L. Watson, Amy Bridges, and Charles Sellers. 1992. "A Symposium on Charles Sellers, *The Market Revolution: Jacksonian America, 1815–1846*." *JER* 12 (Winter): 445–76.

Ellison, Christopher G. 1991. "An Eye for an Eye? A Note on the Southern Subculture of Violence." *SF* 69 (June): 1223–39.

Ellwood, David T., and Christopher Jencks. 2001. "The Growing Differences in Family Structure: What Do We Know? Where Do We Look for Answers?" Unpublished paper, John F. Kennedy School of Government, Harvard University.

Emerson, Ralph Waldo. 1841. *Self-Reliance and Other Essays*. Repr., Menola, NY: Courier Dover, 1993.

Engerman, Stanley L., and Robert E. Gallman, eds. 2000. *The Cambridge Economic History of the United States*. Vol. 3. New York: Cambridge University Press.

Engle, Dabid M. 1984. "The Oven Bird's Song: Insiders, Outsiders, and Personal Injuries in an American Community." *Law & Society Review* 18 (4): 515–50.

Ensminger, Douglas. 1949. "Rural Neighborhoods and Communities." In *Rural Life in the United States*, ed. Carl C. Taylor et al., 55–77. New York: Alfred Knopf.

Erenberg, Lewis A. 1984. *Steppin' Out: New York Nightlife and the Transformation of American Culture, 1890–1930*. Chicago: University of Chicago Press.

Ernst, Joseph A. 1988. "The Political Economy of the Chesapeake Colonies, 1760–1775: A Study in Comparative History." In Hoffman et al. 1988, 196–243.

Erskine, Hazel Gaudet. 1964. "The Polls: Some Thoughts About Life and People." *POQ* 28 (Autumn): 517–28.

Espenshade, Thomas J. 1985. "Marriage Trends in America: Estimates, Implications, and Underlying Causes." *Population and Development Review* 11 (June): 193–243.

Estlund, Cynthia. 2005. "Working Together: Crossing Color Lines at Work." *Labor History* 46(1): 79–98.

Eustace, Nicole. 2008. *Passion is the Gale: Emotion, Power, and the Coming of the American Revolution*. Chapel Hill: University of North Carolina Press.

Evans, Ivor H. 1981. *Brewer's Dictionary of Phrase and Fable*, Centenary ed., rev. New York: Harper & Row.

Evans, J. Martin. 1976. *America: The View from Europe*. San Francisco: San Francisco Book Co.

Ewen, Stuart. 1976. *Captains of Consciousness: Advertising and the Social Roots of Consumer Culture*. New York: McGraw-Hill.

Ezzati, Majid, Ari B. Friedman, Sandeep C. Kulkarni, and Christopher J. L. Murray. 2008. "The Reversal of Fortunes: Trends in County Mortality and Cross-County Mortality Disparities in the United States." *PLoS Medicine* 5 (April): e66.

Families and Work Institute. 1999. The 1997 National Study of the Changing Workforce: Executive Summary. http://www.familiesandwork.org /site/research/ summary/1997nscwsumm.pdf.

Faragher, John Mack. 1986. *Sugar Creek: Life on the Illinois Prairie*. New Haven, CT: Yale University Press.

Farkas, Janice I., and Dennis P. Hogan. 1995. "The Demography of Intergenerational Relationships." In *Adult Intergenerational Relationships*, ed. Vern L. Bengston, K. Warner Schaie, and Linda M. Burton, 1–25. New York: Springer.

Farley, Reynolds. 1996. *The New American Reality: Who We Are, How We Got Here, Where We Are Going*. New York: Russell Sage Foundation.

Farley, Reynolds, Charlotte Steeh, Maria Krysan, Tara Jackson, and Keith Reeves. 1994. "Stereotypes and Segregation: Neighborhoods in the Detroit Area." *AJS* 100 (November): 750–80.

Fass, Paula S. 1977. *The Damned and the Beautiful: American Youth in the 1920's*. New York: Oxford University Press.

Faust, Drew Gilpin. 2001. "The Civil War Soldier and the Art of Dying." *Journal of Southern History* 67 (February): 3–38.

Featherstone, Mike. 1991. *Consumer Culture and Postmodernism*. Newbury Park, CA: Sage.

Feld, Scott L. 1981. "The Focused Organization of Social Ties." *AJS* 86 (March): 1015–35.

Feldberg, Michael. 1973. "Urbanization as a Cause of Violence: Philadelphia as a Test Case." In Davis and Haller 1973, 53–70.

Feller, Daniel. 1997. "The Market Revolution Ate My Homework." *Reviews in American History* 25.3:408–15.

Felson, Marcus. 1978. "Invidious Distinctions among Cars, Clothes and Suburbs." *POQ* 42 (Spring): 49–58.

Ferrall, Simon A. 1832. *A Ramble of Six Thousand Miles through the United States of America*. Online ed. Project Gutenberg. http://www.gutenberg.net.

Ferrie, Joseph P. 2005 "The End of American Exceptionalism? Mobility in the United States Since 1850." *JEP* 19 (Summer): 199–215.

Ferrie, Joseph P., and Werner Troesken. 2008. "Water and Chicago's Mortality Transition, 1850–1925." *Explorations in Economic History* 45 (January): 1–16.

Fields, Jason and Lynne M. Casper. 2001. "America's Families and Living Arrangements: March 2000." *Current Population Reports*, Report P, 20–537. Washington DC: U.S. Bureau of the Census.

Fields, Jill. 1999. "'Fighting the Corsetless Evil: Shaping Corsets and Culture, 1900–1930." *JSH* 33(2): 355–84.

Figlio, David N., and Maurice E. Lucas. 2004. "What's in a Grade? School Report Cards and the Housing Market." *AER* 94 (June): 591–604.

Fine, Gary Alan, and Brooke Harrington. 2004. "Tiny Publics: Small Groups and Civil Society." *Sociological Theory* 22 (3): 341–56.

Fine, Lisa M. 1990. *The Souls of the Skyscraper: Female Clerical Workers in Chicago, 1870–1930*. Philadelphia: Temple University Press.

Finke, Roger. 1990. "Religious Deregulation: Origins and Consequences." *Journal of Church and State* 32 (Summer 1990): 609–26.

Finke, Roger, and Rodney Stark. 1986. "Turning Pews into People: Estimating 19th Century Church Membership." *Journal for the Scientific Study of Religion* 25:180–92.

———. 1992. *The Churching of America, 1776–1990: Winners and Losers in Our Religious Economy*. New Brunswick, NJ: Rutgers University Press.

Fiorina, Morris. 2004. *Culture War? The Myth of a Polarized America*. New York: Pearson Longman.

Firebaugh, Glenn, and Brian Harley. 1991. "Trends in U.S. Church Attendance: Secularization and Revival, or Merely Lifecycle Effects." *Journal for the Scientific Study of Religion* 30 (December): 487–500.

Fischer, Claude S. 1980. "The Spread of Crime from City to Countryside, 1955 to 1975." *Rural Sociology* 45 (Fall): 416–34.

———. 1981. "The Public and Private Worlds of City Life." *ASR* 46 (June): 306–16.

———. 1982. *To Dwell Among Friends: Personal Networks in Town and City*. Chicago: University of Chicago Press.

———. 1984. *The Urban Experience*. 2nd ed. San Diego: Harcourt Brace Jovanovich.

———. 1988. "Finding the 'Lost' Community: Facts and Fictions." *Tikkun* 3 (November): 69–72.

———. 1988. "Gender and the Residential Telephone in North America, 1890–1940: Technologies of Sociability." *Sociological Forum* 3 (Summer): 211–33.

———. 1992. *America Calling: A Social History of the Telephone to 1940*. Berkeley: University of California Press.

———. 1994. "Changes in Leisure Activities in Three Towns, 1890–1940," *JSH* 27 (Spring): 453–76.

———. 1994. "In Search of the Plot: American Social History in the 1990s." *Contemporary Sociology* 23 (March): 226–30.

———. 1999. "Comment on 'Anxiety': Compensation in Social History." *JSH* 33 (Fall): 143–46.

———. 2000. "Just How Is It that Americans are Individualistic?" Paper presented to the American Sociological Association Meetings, Washington DC.

———. 2002. "Ever-More Rooted Americans." *City & Community* 1 (June): 175–94.

————. 2007. "What Wealth-Happiness Paradox? A Short Note on the American Case." *Journal of Happiness Studies* 9 (June): 219–26.

————. 2008. "Paradoxes of American Individualism." *Sociological Forum* 23 (June): 363–72.

————. 2009. "The 2004 GSS Finding of Shrunken Networks: An Artifact?" *ASR* 74 (August): 657–69.

Fischer, Claude S., and Glenn Carroll. 1988. "Telephone and Automobile Diffusion in the United States, 1902–1937." *AJS* 93 (March): 1153–78.

Fischer, Claude S., Kathleen Gerson, Robert Max Jackson, Lynn McCallister, and Ann Stueve, with Mark Baldassare. 1977. *Networks and Places: Personal Networks in Town and City*. New York: Free Press.

Fischer, Claude S., and Michael Hout. 2006. *Century of Difference: How America Changed in the Last One Hundred Years*. New York: Russell Sage Foundation.

————. 2006. "The Family in Trouble: Since When? For Whom?" In *The Family in Interdisciplinary Perspective*, ed. Steven M. Tipton and John Witte Jr., 120–42. Princeton, NJ: Princeton University Press.

Fischer, Claude S., Michael Hout, Martín Sánchez Jankowski, Samuel R. Lucas, Ann Swidler, and Kim Voss. 1996. *Inequality by Design: Cracking the Bell Curve Myth*. Princeton, NJ: Princeton University Press.

Fischer, Claude S., and Greggor Mattson. 2009. "Is America Fragmenting?" *ARS* 35:435–55.

Fischer, Claude S., Gretchen Stockmayer, Jon Stiles, and Michael Hout. 2004. "Distinguishing the Levels and Dimensions of U.S. Urban Segregation." *DEM* 41 (February): 37–59.

Fischer, David Hackett. 1989. *Albion's Seed: Four British Folkways in America*. New York: Oxford University Press.

————. 2004. *Washington's Crossing*. New York: Oxford University Press.

Fischer, Mary J., and Douglas S. Massey. 2004. "The Ecology of Racial Discrimination." *City & Community* 3 (September): 221–41.

Fisher, Gordon M. 1995. "Is There Such a Thing as an Absolute Poverty Line Over Time?" Poverty Measurement working papers. Washington DC: U.S. Bureau of the Census. http://www.census.gov/hhes/www/povmeas/papers/elastap4.html.

Fisher, Sydney George. 1967. *A Philadelphia Perspective: The Diary of Sidney George Fisher Covering the Years 1834–1871*. Ed. Nicholas B. Wainwright. Philadelphia: The Historical Society of Pennsylvania.

Fishman, Sylvia Barack. 2004. *Double or Nothing?: Jewish Families and Mixed Marriage*. Lebanon, NH : Brandeis University Press.

Fitch, Catherine A., and Steven Ruggles. 2000. "Historical Trends in Marriage Formation: The United States 1850–1990." In Waite 2000, 59–89.

Fitch, Catherine A., Ron Goeken, and Steven Ruggles. 2005. "The Rise of Cohabitation in the United States: New Historical Estimates." Working paper 2005-03, Minnesota Population Center, University of Minnesota.

Fitzgerald, Mary. 2005. "Greater Convenience But Not Greater Turnout: The Impact of Alternative Voting Methods on Electoral Participation in the United States." *American Politics Research* 33 (6): 842–67.

Flegal, K. M., M. D. Carroll, R. J. Kuczmarski, and C. L. Johnson. 1998. "Overweight and Obesity in the United States: Prevalence and Trends, 1960–1994." *International Journal of Obesity and Related Metabolic Disorders* 22 (January): 39–47.

Fleischner, Jennifer. 2004. *Mrs. Lincoln and Mrs. Keckly: The Remarkable Story of the Friendship Between a First Lady and a Former Slave*. New York: Broadway.

Fleming, Patricia. 1979. *Villagers and Strangers: An English Proletarian Village Over Four Centuries*. Cambridge, MA: Schenkman.

Fligstein, Neil. 1983. "The Transformation of Southern Agriculture and the Migration of Blacks and Whites, 1930- 1940." *International Migration Review* 17 (Summer): 268–90.

Fligstein, Neil, and Taek-Jin Shin. 2002. "The Shareholder Value Society: A Review of the Changes in Working Conditions and Inequality in the U.S. 1976–2000." Working paper, Survey Research Center, University of California, Berkeley.

Flink, James J. 1989. *The Automobile Age*. Cambridge, MA: MIT Press.

Florida, Richard. 2003. "Cities and the Creative Class." *City & Community* 2 (March): 3–19.

Flynn, James R. 1984. "The Mean IQ of Americans: Massive Gains 1932 to 1978." *Psychological Bulletin* 95 (1): 29–51.

———. 1987. "Massive IQ Gains in 14 Nations: What IQ Tests Really Measure." *Psychological Bulletin* 101 (2): 171–91.

———. 2007. *What is Intelligence? Beyond the Flynn Effect*. New York: Cambridge University Press.

Fogel, Robert William. 1986. "Nutrition and the Decline in Mortality since 1700: Some Preliminary Findings." In *Long-Term Factors in American Economic Growth*. ed. Stanley L. Engerman and Robert E. Gallman, 439–556. NBER Studies in Income and Wealth. Chicago: University of Chicago Press.

———. 2000. *The Fourth Great Awakening & The Future of Egalitarianism*. Chicago: University of Chicago Press.

———. 2004. *The Escape from Hunger and Premature Death, 1700–2100*. New York: Cambridge University Press.

Fogleman, Aaron S. 1998. "From Slaves, Convicts, and Servants to Free Passengers: The Transformation of Immigration in the Era of the American Revolution." *JAH* 85 (June): 43–76.

Folbre, Nancy. 1993. "Women's Informal Market Work in Massachusetts, 1875–1920." *SSH* 17 (Spring): 135–60.

Folbre, Nancy, Jayoung Yoon, Kade Finnoff, and Allison Sidle Fuligni. 2005. "By What Measure? Family Time Devoted to Children in the United States." *DEM* 42 (May): 373–90.

Fombonne, E. 1994. "Increased Rates of Depression: Update of Epidemiological Findings and Analytical Problems." *Acta Psychiatrica Scandinavica* 90:145–56.

Foner, Eric. 1988. *Reconstruction: America's Unfinished Revolution, 1863–1877*. New York: Harper & Row.

———, ed. 1990. *The New American History*. Philadelphia: Temple University Press.

———. 1994. "The Meaning of Freedom in the Age of Emancipation." *JAH* 81 (September): 435–60.

———. 1998. *The Story of American Freedom*. New York: Norton.

Foner, Eric, and John A. Garraty, eds. 1991. *The Reader's Companion to American History*. Boston: Houghton Mifflin.

Fost, Dan. 1996. "Farewell to the Lodge." *American Demographics* 18 (January): 40.

Formisano, Ronald P. 1974. "Deferential-Participant Politics: The Early Republic's Political Culture, 1789–1840." *American Political Science Review* 68 (June): 473–87.

———. 1999. "The 'Party Period' Revisited." *JAH* 86 (June):93–120.

Foster, George M. 1960–61. "Interpersonal Relations in Peasant Society." *Human Organization* 19: 74–84.

Foster, Mark S. 1981. *From Streetcar to Superhighway: American City Planners and Urban Transportation, 1900–1940*. Philadelphia: Temple University Press.

Foster, Thomas A. 1999. "Deficient Husbands: Manhood, Sexual Incapacity, and Male Marital Sexuality in Seventeenth- Century New England." *WMQ* 3rd Ser., 56 (October): 723–44.

Foucault, Michel, Luther H. Martin, Huck Gutman, and Patrick H. Hutton. 1988. *Technologies of the Self: A Seminar with Michel Foucault*. Amherst: University of Massachusetts Press.

Fourcade, Marion, and Kieran Healy. 2007. "Moral Views of Market Society." *ARS* 33: 285–311.

Fowler, Robert Booth. 1991.*The Dance with Community: The Contemporary Debate in American Political Thought*. Lawrence: University Press of Kansas.

Fox, Richard Wrightman. 1976. "The Intolerable Deviance of the Insane: Civil Commitment in San Francisco, 1906–1929." *American Journal of Legal History* 20 (April): 136–54.

Fox, Richard Wrightman, and T. J. Jackson Lears. 1983. Introduction to *The Culture of Consumption*, Richard Wrightman Fox and T. J. Jackson Lears, ix–xiii. New York: Pantheon.

Fox, Stephen R. 1984. *The Mirror Makers: A History of American Advertising and Its Creators*. New York: Morrow.

Fox-Genovese, Elizabeth, and Eugene D. Genovese. 1976. "The Political Crisis of Social History." *JSH* 10 (Winter): 205–20.

Foy, Jessica H., and Thomas J. Schlereth, eds. 1992. *American Home Life, 1880–1930: A Social History of Spaces and Services*. Knoxville: University of Tennessee Press.

Frank, Robert H. 1999. *Luxury Fever: Why Money Fails to Satisfy in an Era of Excess*. New York: Free Press.

Frank, Stephen. 1994. "Peasantry." In *Encyclopedia of Social History*, ed. Peter N. Stearns, 555–57. New York: Garland.

Franklin, Benjamin. 1909. *The Autobiography of Benjamin Franklin*. The Harvard Classics. New York: P. F. Collier. Online ed., Google Books, http://books.google .com/books?id=v9MNAAAAYAAJ.

Franklin, Mark N., Patrick Lyons, and Michael Marsh. 2004. "Generational Basis of Turnout Decline in Established Democracies." *Acta Politica* 39:115–51.

Fredman, L. E. 1967. "The Introduction of the Australian Ballot in the United States." *Australian Journal of Politics and History* 13 (April–December): 204–21.

Fredrickson, George M. 1981. *White Supremacy: A Comparative Study in American and South African History*. New York: Oxford University Press.

——. 1995. "From Exceptionalism to Variability: Recent Developments in Cross-National Comparative History." *JAH* 82 (September): 587–606.

——. 1998. "Nineteenth-Century American History." In Molho and Wood 1998, 164–83

Freeman, Ruth, and Patricia Klaus. 1984. "Blessed or Not? The New Spinster in England and the United States in the Late Nineteenth and Early Twentieth Century." *Journal of Family History* 9 (Winter): 394–414.

Freeman, Susan Tax. 1970. *Neighbors: The Social Contract in a Castilian Hamlet*. Chicago. University of Chicago Press.

Frey, Bruno S., and Alois Stutzer. 2002. *Happiness and Economics*. Princeton, NJ: Princeton University Press.

——. 2005. "Happiness Research: State and Prospects." *Review of Social Economy* 52 (June): 207–28.

Frey, William H. 1996. "Immigration, Internal Out-Movement, and Demographic Balkanization in America: New Evidence for the 1990s." Population Studies Center Report No. 96–364. Ann Arbor: University of Michigan.

Friedeburg, Robert von. 1995 "Social and Geographical Mobility in the Old World and New World Communities: Earls Colne, Ipswich and Springfield, 1635–1685." *JSH* 29 (Winter): 375–400.

Frieden, Karl. 1987. "Public Needs and Private Wants: Making Choices." *Dissent* (Summer): 317–25.

Friedman, Lawrence M. 1985. *Total Justice*. New York: Russell Sage Foundation.

——. 1990. *The Republic of Choice: Law, Authority, and Culture*. Cambridge, MA: Harvard University Press.

——. 1993. *Crime and Punishment in American History*. New York: Basic Books.

——. 2002. *Law in America: A Short History*. New York: Modern Library Chronicles (Random House).

——, and Robert V. Percival. 1976. "Who Sues for Divorce? From Fault through Fiction to Freedom." *Journal of Legal Studies* 5 (January): 61–82.

Friend, Craig T. 1997. "Merchants and Markethouses: Reflections on Moral Economy in Early Kentucky." *JER* 17 (Winter): 553–74.

Frombonne, E. 1994. "Increased Rates of Depression: Update of Epidemiological Findings and Analytical Problems." *Acta Psychiatrica Scandinavica* 90:145–56.

Fromm, Erich. 1941. *Escape from Freedom*. Repr., New York : Holt, Rinehart and Winston, 1964.

——. 1955. *The Sane Society*. New York: Fawcett Premier.

Frykman, Jonas, and Orvar Lofgren. 1987. *Culture Builders: A Historical Anthropology of Middle-Class Life*. Trans. Alan Crozier. New Brunswick, NJ: Rutgers University Press.

Fuchs, Victor R. 1983. *How We Live*. Cambridge, MA: Harvard University Press.

Fuller, Wayne E. 1964. *RFD*. Bloomington: Indiana University Press.

——. 1972. *The American Mail: Enlarger of the Common Life*. Chicago: University of Chicago Press.

Fullerton, Andrew S., and Michael Wallace. 2007. "Traversing the Flexible Turn: U.S. Workers' Perceptions of Job Security, 1977–2002." *Social Science Research* 36 (March): 201–21.

Furstenberg, Francois. 2003. "Beyond Freedom and Slavery: Autonomy, Virtue, and Resistance in Early American Political Discourse." *JAH* 89 (March): 1295–30.

Furstenberg, Frank F. Jr. 1966. "Industrialization and the American Family: A Look Backward." *ASR* 31 (June): 326–38.

——. 1990. "Divorce and the American Family." *ARS* 16: 379–403.

——. 1999. "Family Change and Family Diversity." In *Diversity and Its Discontents*, ed. Neil J. Smelser and Jeffrey C. Alexander, 147–65. Princeton, NJ: Princeton University Press.

Furstenberg, Frank F. Jr., Sheela Kennedy, Vonnie C. McLoyd, Rubén G. Rumbaut, and Richard A. Settersten. 2004. "Growing Up is Harder to Do." *Contexts* 3 (July): 33–41.

Gabin, Nancy F. 1993. "Women and Work." In Cayton, Gorn, and Williams 1993, 1541–56.

Gabler, Neal. 1988. *An Empire of Their Own: How the Jews Invented Hollywood*. New York: Doubleday.

Gaddy, Gary D. 1986. "Television's Impact on High School Achievement." *POQ* 50 (Fall): 340–59.

Galambos, Louis. 1983. "Technology, Political Economy, and Professionalization: Central Themes of the Organizational Synthesis." *Business History Review* 57 (Winter): 471–93.

Galen, Cranz. 1978. "Changing Roles of Urban Parks." *Landscape* 22 (Summer): 9–18.

Gallaher, Art Jr. 1961. *Plainville Fifteen Years Later*. New York: Columbia University Press.

Gallman, Robert E., and John Joseph Wallis, eds. 1992. *American Economic Growth and Standards of Living before the Civil War*. Chicago: University of Chicago Press.

——. 1992. Introduction to Gallman and Wallis 1992, 1–18.

Gallup, George Jr. 1985. "Religion in America: 50 Years: 1935–1985." The Gallup Report No. 286. Princeton, NJ: Princeton Religion Research Center.

——. 1998. *The Gallup Poll: Public Opinion 1997*. Wilmington, DE: Scholarly Resources, Inc.

——. 1999. "Americans Celebrate Easter." http://www.gallup.com/poll/releases/pr990402b.asp.

——. 2002. *The Gallup Poll: Public Opinion 2001*. Wilmington, DE: Scholarly Resources Inc.

——. 2003. "Catholics Trail Protestants in Church Attendance." Gallup poll, Region and Social Trends. http://www.gallup.com/poll/10138/Catholics-Trail-Protestants-Church-Attendance.aspx.

——. 2004. *The Gallup Poll: Public Opinion 2003*. Lanham, MD: Rowman & Littlefield.

Gallup, George Jr., and Jim Castelli. 1989. *The People's Religion: American Faith in the '90s*. New York: Macmillan.

Gallup, George Jr., and D. Michael Lindsay. 1999. *Surveying the Religious Landscape: Trends in U.S. Beliefs*. Harrisburg, PA: Morehouse Publishing.

Galston, William A., and Peter Levine. 1997. "America's Civic Condition: A Glance at the Evidence." *Brookings Review* 15 (Fall): 23–6.

Gamber, Wendy. 2005. "Away from Home: Middle-Class Boarders in the Nineteenth-Century City." *JUH* 31 (March): 289–305.

Gamm, Gerald H. 1989. *The Making of New Deal Democrats: Voting Behavior and Realignment in Boston, 1920–1940*. Chicago: University of Chicago Press.

Gamm, Gerald H., and Robert D. Putnam. 1999. "The Growth of Voluntary Associations in America, 1840–1940." *JIH* 29 (Spring): 511–57.

Gannett, Lewis. 2005. "'Overwhelming Evidence' of a Lincoln-Ann Rutledge Romance?: Reexamining Rutledge Family Reminiscences." *Journal of the Abraham Lincoln Association* 26 (Winter): 28–41.

Gans, Herbert J. 1962. "Urbanism and Suburbanism as Ways of Life." In *Human Behavior and Social Processes*, ed. A. M. Rose, 625–48. Boston: Houghton Mifflin.

———. 1962. *The Urban Villagers: Group and Class in the Life of Italian-Americans*. New York: Free Press of Glencoe.

———. 1967. *The Levittowners*. New York: Random House.

———. 1988. *Middle American Individualism: The Future of American Individualism*. New York: Free Press.

Gardner, J. B., and G. R. Adams, eds. 1983. *Ordinary People and Everyday Life*. Nashville, TN: American Association for State and Local History.

Garner, C. Alan. 1996. "Can Measures of Consumer Debt Reliably Predict an Economic Slowdown?" *Economic Review* 81 (4): 64–76.

Garrett, Thomas A. 2007. "The Rise in Personal Bankruptcies: The Eighth Federal Reserve District and Beyond." *Federal Reserve Bank of St. Louis Review* 89 (January/February): 15–37.

Gartner, Rosemary. 1990. "The Victims of Homicide: A Temporal and Cross-National Comparison." *ASR* 55 (February): 92–106.

Gartner, Rosemary, and Robert Nash Parker. 1990. "Cross-National Evidence on Homicide and the Age Structure of the Population." *SF* 69 (December): 351–71.

Garvan, Anthony N. B. 1967. "Effects of Technology on Domestic Life, 1830–1880." In *Technology in Western Civilization*. Vol.1, ed. Melvin Kranzberg and Carroll W. Pursell Jr., 546–59. New York: Oxford University Press.

Gatchel, Robert J. 2004. "Comorbidity of Chronic Pain and Mental Health Disorders: The Biopsychosocial Perspective." *American Psychologist* 59 (November): 795–805.

Gatson, Sarah N., and Amanda Zweerink. 2004. "Ethnography Online: 'Natives' Practising and Inscribing Community." *Qualitative Research* 4 (2): 179–200.

Gecas, Viktor. 1989. "The Social Psychology of Self-Efficacy." *ARS* 15:291–316.

Geertz, Clifford. 1983. *Local Knowledge*. New York: Basic Books.

General Social Survey [GSS]. 1972–2008. General Social Survey. Chicago: NORC at the University of Chicago. http://www.norc.org/GSS+Website/.

Gentzkow, Matthew. 2006. "Television and Voter Turnout." *Quarterly Journal of Economics* 121 (August): 931–72.

Ger, G., and Russell W. Belk. 1996. "Cross-Cultural Differences in Materialism." *Journal of Economic Psychology* 17 (February): 55–77.

Gerber, Larry G. 1997. "Shifting Perspectives on American Exceptionalism: Recent Literature on American Labor Relations and Labor Politics." *Journal of American Studies* 31:253–74.

Gergen, Kenneth J. 1998. "The Self: Death by Technology." *Echoes*. Post-Modernity Project, University of Virginia (Winter): 10–15.

———. 2000. *The Saturated Self: Dilemmas of Identity in Contemporary Life*. New York: Basic Books.

Gershuny, Jonathan. 2003. "Web Use and Net Nerds: A Neofunctionalist Analysis of the Impact of Information Technology in the Home." *SF* 82 (1): 141–68.

Gerson, Kathleen. 1985. *Hard Choices: How Women Decide about Work, Career, and Motherhood*. Berkeley. University of California Press.

Gerson, Kathleen, and Jerry Jacobs. 2004. "The Work-Home Crunch." *Contexts* 3 (Fall): 29–37.

Gibbons, Robert D., C. Hendricks Brown, Kwan Hur, Sue M. Marcus, Dulal K. Bhaumik, Joëlle A. Erkens, Ron M.C. Herings, and J. John Mann. 2007. "Early Evidence on the Effects of Regulators' Suicidality Warnings on SSRI Prescriptions and Suicide in Children and Adolescents." *American Journal of Psychiatry* 164 (September): 1356–63.

Gibson, Campbell, and Kay Jung. 2005. "Historical Census Statistics on Population Totals by Race, 1790 to 1990, and by Hispanic Origin, 1970 to 1990, for Large Cities and Other Urban Areas in the United States." Population Division working paper 76. Washington DC: U.S. Bureau of the Census. http://www.census.gov/population/www/documentation/twps0076.html.

Giddens, Anthony. 1990. *The Consequences of Modernity*. Palo Alto, CA: Stanford University Press.

———. 1991. *Modernity and Self-Identity: Self and Society in the Late Modern Age*. Palo Alto, CA: Stanford University Press.

Gidlow, Liette. 2002. "Delegitimizing Democracy: 'Civic Slackers,' the Cultural Turn, and the Possibilities of Politics." *JAH* 89 (December): 922–57.

Gienapp, William E. 1993. "The Antebellum Era." In Cayton, Gorn, and Williams 1993, 105–30.

Gilbert, Daniel. 2006. *Stumbling on Happiness*. New York: Knopf.

Gilekson, John S. Jr. 1986. *Middle-Class Providence, 1820–1940*. Princeton, NJ: Princeton University Press.

Gilens, Martin. 1996. "Race and Poverty in America: Public Misperceptions and the American News Media." *POQ* 60 (Winter): 515–41.

———. 1999. *Why Americans Hate Welfare : Race, Media, and the Politics of Antipoverty Policy*. Chicago : University of Chicago Press.

Gilfoyle, Timothy J. 1987. "The Urban Geography of Commercial Sex: Prostitution in New York City, 1790–1860." *JUH* 13 (August): 371–93.

———. 1997. "Strumpets and Misogynists: Brothel 'Riots' and the Transformation of Prostitution in Antebellum New York City." In *The Making of Urban America*, ed. Raymond A. Mohl, 37–51. 2nd ed. Wilmington, DE: Scholarly Resources.

Gilje, Paul A. 1997. "The Rise of Capitalism in the Early Republic." In Gilje 1997, 1–22.

———, ed. 1997. *Wages of Independence: Capitalism in the Early American Republic*. Madison, WI: Madison House.

Gillespie, Joanna Bowen. 1985. "'The Clear Leadings of Providence': Pious Memoirs and the Problems of Self-Realization for Women in the Early Nineteenth Century." *JER* 5 (Summer): 197–221.

Gillespie, Mark. 2000. "Merry Christmas? Not for Many Americans, Who Believe the Holiday Has Lost Its Focus." http://institution.gallup.com/content/default.aspx?ci=2206.

Gillis, A. R. 1989. "Crime and State Surveillance in Nineteenth-Century France." *AJS* 95 (September): 307–41.

Gillis, John R., ed. 1994. *Commemorations: The Politics of National Identity*. Princeton, NJ: Princeton University Press.

———. 1996. *A World of Their Own Making: Myth, Ritual and the Quest for Family Values*. New York: Basic Books.

———. 1996. "Making Time for Family: The Invention of Family Time(s) and the Reinvention of Family History." *Journal of Family History* 21 (January): 4–21.

Gjerde, Jon. 1986. "Conflict and Community: A Case Study of the Immigrant Church in the United States." *JSH* 19 (Summer): 681–97.

———. 1997. *The Minds of the West: Ethno-Cultural Evolution in the Rural Middle West, 1830–1917*. Chapel Hill: University of North Carolina Press.

Glaeser, Edward L., David I. Laibson, Jose A. Scheinkman, and Christine L. Soutter. 2000. "Measuring Trust." *Quarterly Journal of Economics* 115 (August): 811–46.

Glassner, Barry. 1999. *The Culture of Fear: Why Americans Are Afraid of the Wrong Things*. New York: Basic Books.

Glendon, Mary Ann. 1991. *Rights Talk: The Impoverishment of Political Discourse*. New York: Free Press.

Glenn, Norval D. 1987. "The Trend in 'No Religion' Respondents to U.S. National Surveys, Late 1950s to Early 1980s." *POQ* 51 (Fall): 293–314.

———. 1990. Review of *Religious Change in America*, by Andrew Greely. *POQ* 54 (Fall): 444–47.

———. 1994. "Television Watching, Newspaper Reading, and Cohort Differences in Verbal Ability." *Sociology of Education* 67 (July): 216–30.

Glenn, Susan A. 1990. *Daughters of the Shtetl: Life and Labor in the Immigrant Generation*. Ithaca, NY: Cornell University Press.

Glennie, Paul. 1995. "Consumption Within Historical Studies." In Miller 1995, 164–203.

Godbeer, Richard. 1992. *The Devil's Dominion: Magic and Religion in Early New England*. New York: Cambridge University Press.

———. 2002. *Sexual Revolution in Early America*. Baltimore: Johns Hopkins University Press.

Goldin, Claudia. 1979. "Household and Market Production of Families in a Late Nineteenth Century American City." *Explorations in Economic History* 16:111–31.

———. 1980. "War." In *Encyclopedia of American Economic History*. Vol. 3. ed. Glenn
Porter, 935–57. New York: Scribner.

———. 1983. "Lifecycle Labor Force Participation of American Women, 1900–
1980." Paper presented to the *SSH* Association, Washington DC.

———. 2000. "Labor Markets in the Twentieth Century." In Engerman and Gallman 2000, 549–623.

———. 2006. "The Quiet Revolution That Transformed Women's Employment, Education, and Family." *AER* 96 (May): 1–20.

Goldin, Claudia, and Lawrence Katz. 2002. "The Power of the Pill: Oral Contra-
ceptives and Women's Career and Marriage Decisions." *Journal of Political Economy* 110 (4):730–70.

Goldscheider, Calvin, and Frances K. Goldscheider. 1987. "Moving Out and Marriage: What do Young Adults Expect?" *ASR* 52 (April): 278–85.

Goldscheider, Frances K., and Calvin Goldscheider. 1994. "Leaving and Returning
Home in 20th Century America." *Population Bulletin* 48 (March).

Goldscheider, Frances K., and Leora Lawton. 1998. "Family Experiences and the
Erosion of Support for Intergenerational Residence." *Journal of Marriage and the
Family* 60 (August): 623–32.

Goldscheider, Frances K., and Linda J. Waite. 1991. *New Families, No Families? The
Transformation of the American Home*. Berkeley: University of California Press.

Goldstein, Joshua R. 1999. "Kinship Networks That Cross Racial Lines: The Exception or the Rule?" *DEM* 36 (August): 399–408.

———. 1999. "The Leveling of Divorce in the United States." *DEM* 36 (August):
409–14.

Goldstein, Joshua R., and Catherine T. Kenny. 2001. "Marriage Delayed or Marriage Forgone? New Cohort Forecasts of First Marriage for U.S. Women." *ASR*
66 (August): 506–19.

Goodheart, Lawrence B. 1995. "The Concept of Insanity: Women Patients at the
Hartford Retreat for the Insane, 1824–1865." *Connecticut History* 36 (1): 31–47.

Gordon, David M., Richard Edwards, and Michael Reich. 1982. *Segmented Work,
Divided Workers: The Historical Transformation of Labor in the United States*. New
York: Cambridge University Press.

Gordon, Jean, and Jan McArthur. 1985. "American Women and Domestic Consumption, 1800–1920: Four Interpretive Themes." *Journal of American Culture* 8
(Fall 1985): 35–47.

Gordon, Michael, ed., *The American Family in Social-Historical Perspective*. 2nd ed.
New York: St. Martin's.

Gordon, Steven L. 1981. "The Sociology of Sentiments and Emotions." In *Social Psychology: Sociological Perspectives*, ed. Morris Rosenberg and Ralph H. Turner, 562–
92. New York: Basic Books.

Gorn, Elliott J. 1985. "'Gouge and Bite, Pull Hair and Scratch': The Social Significance of Fighting in the Southern Backcountry." *AHR* 90 (February): 18–43.

———. 1987. "'Good-Bye Boys, I Die a True American': Homicide, Nativism, and
Working-Class Culture in Antebellum New York City." *JAH* 74 (September):
388–410.

Gorski, Philip S. 2000. "Historicizing the Secularization Debate: Church, State, and Society in Late Medieval and Early Modern Europe, ca. 1300–1700." *ASR* 65 (February):135–67.

Gottdiener, Mark. 2000. "Approaches to Consumption: Classical and Contemporary Perspectives." In *New Forms of Consumption: Consumers, Culture, and Commodification*, ed. Mark Gottdiener, 3–31. New York: Rowman & Littlefield.

Gould, J. D. 1980. "European Inter-Continental Emigration. The Road Home: Return Migration from the U.S.A." *Journal of European Economic History* 9 (Spring): 41–112.

Graebner, William. 1980. "The Unstable World of Benjamin Spock: Social Engineering in a Democratic Culture, 1917–1950." *JAH* 67 (December): 612–29.

Graefe, Deborah Roempke, and Daniel T. Lichter. 1999. "Life Course Transitions of American Children: Parental Cohabitation, Marriage, and Single Motherhood." *DEM* 36 (May): 205–17.

Graff, Harvey J. 1987. *The Legacies of Literacy: Continuities and Contradictions in Western Culture and Society*. Bloomington: Indiana University Press.

———. 1995. *Conflicting Paths: Growing Up in America*. Cambridge, MA: Harvard University Press.

Grandin, Elaine, and Eugen Lupri. 1997. "Intimate Violence in Canada and the United States: A Cross-National Comparison." *Journal of Family Violence* 12 (December): 417–43.

Grasso, Christopher. 2008. "Deist Monster: On Religious Common Sense in the Wake of the American Revolution." *JAH* 95 (June): 43–68.

Gratton, Brian. 1996. "The Poverty of Impoverishment Theory: The Economic Well-Being of the Elderly, 1890–1950." *JEH* 56 (March): 39–59.

Gratton, Brian, and Frances M. Rotondo. 1991. "Industrialization, the Family Economy, and the Economic Status of the American Elderly." *SSH* 15 (Fall): 337–62.

Gray, Mark, and Miki Caul. 2000. "Declining Voter Turnout in Advanced Industrialized Democracies." *Comparative Political Studies* 33 (November):1091–1122.

Greeley, Andrew M. 1989. *Religious Change in America*. Cambridge, MA: Harvard University Press.

———. 1991."American Exceptionalism: The Religious Phenomenon." In Shafer 1991, 94–115.

———. 1997. "The Other Civic America." *American Prospect* 32 (May–June): 68–73.

Greeley, Andrew M., and Michael Hout. 1999. "Americans' Increasing Belief in Life After Death: Religious Competition and Acculturation." *ASR* 64: 813–15.

Green, Gary Paul. 2002. "Community Change in Harmony, Georgia, 1943–1993." In Luloff and Krannich 2002, 71–93.

Green, Harvey. 1992. *The Uncertainty of Everyday Life, 1915–1945*. New York: HarperCollins.

———. 1983. *The Light of the Home: An Intimate View of Lives of Women in Victorian America*. New York: Pantheon.

Green, Richard K., and Susan M. Wachter. 2005. "The American Mortgage in Historical and International Context." *JEP* 19 (Fall): 93–114.

Greene, Jack P. 1976. "Society, Ideology, and Politics: An Analysis of the Political

Culture of Mid-Eighteenth-Century Virginia." In *Society, Freedom, and Conscience: The American Revolution in Virginia, Massachusetts, and New York*, ed. Richard M. Jellison, 14–76. New York: W. W. Norton.

———. 1988. *Pursuits of Happiness: The Social Development of Early Modern British Colonies and the Formation of American Culture*. Chapel Hill: University of North Carolina Press.

———. 1993. *The Intellectual Construction of America: Exceptionalism and Identity from 1492 to 1800*. Chapel Hill: University of North Carolina Press.

———. 1999. "Social and Cultural Capital in Colonial British America: A Case Study." *JIH* 29 (Winter):491–509.

Greene, Jack P., and J. R. Pole, eds. 1984. *Colonial British America: Essays in the New History of the Early Modern Era*. Baltimore: Johns Hopkins University Press.

———. 1984. "Reconstructing British-American Colonial History: An Introduction." In Greene and Pole 1984, 1–17.

Greenfield, Patricia. 1998. "The Cultural Evolution of IQ." In *The Rising Curve: Long-Term Gains in IQ and Related Measures*, ed. U. Neisser, 81–124. Washington DC: American Psychological Association.

Greenstein, Robert, and Chad Stone. 2007. "Addressing Longstanding Gaps in Unemployment Insurance Coverage." Report, Center on Budget and Policy Priorities, August 7. http://www.cbpp.org/cms/?fa=view&id=517.

Greenstone, J. David. 1986."Political Culture and American Political Development: Liberty, Union, and the Liberal Bipolarity." *Studies in American Political Development* 1:1–49.

Greer, Scott. 1962. *The Urban View: Life and Politics in Metropolitan America*. New York: Oxford University Press.

Gregson, Mary Eschelbach. 1997. "Population Dynamics in Rural Missouri, 1860–1880." *SSH* 21 (Spring): 85–110.

Greven, Philip J. Jr. 1970. *Four Generations: Population, Land, and Family in Colonial Andover, Massachusetts*. Ithaca, NY: Cornell University Press.

Grew, Raymond. 1980. "More on Modernization." *JSH* 14 (Fall): 179–87.

Grier, Katherine C. 1992. "The Decline of the Memory Palace: The Parlor after 1890." In Foy and Schlereth 1992, 49–74.

———. 2006. *Pets in America: A History*. Chapel Hill: University of North Carolina Press.

Griswold, Robert L. 1982. *Family and Divorce in California, 1850–1890*. Albany: State University of New York Press.

———. 1986. "Law, Sex, Cruelty, and Divorce in Victorian America." *AQ* 38 (Winter): 721–45.

———. 1991. "Divorce." In *The Reader's Companion to American History*, ed. Eric Foner and John A. Garraty, 287–89. New York: Houghton Mifflin.

Griswold, Wendy. 1981. "American Character and the American Novel: An Expansion of Reflection Theory in the Sociology of Literature." *AJS* 86 (January): 740–65.

Grob, Gerald N. 1983. *Mental Illness and American Society, 1875–1940*. Princeton, NJ: Princeton University Press.

Gronke, Paul, Eva Galanes-Rosenbaum, Peter A. Miller, and Daniel Toffey. 2008. "Convenience Voting." *Annual Review of Political Science* 11:437–55.

Gross, Robert A. 1976. *The Minutemen and Their World*. New York: Hill & Wang.

Grossberg, Michael. 1985. *Governing the Hearth: Law and Family in Nineteenth-Century America*. Chapel Hill: University of North Carolina Press.

Grover, Kathryn, ed. 1992. *Hard at Play: Leisure in America, 1840–1940*. Amherst: University of Massachusetts Press.

Grubb, Farley. 2006. "Babes in Bondage? Debt Shifting by German Immigrants in Early America." *JIH* 37 (1): 1–34.

Gruber, Jonathan, and Daniel M. Hungerman. 2007. "Faith-Based Charity and Crowd-Out during the Great Depression." *Journal of Public Economics* 91 (June): 1043–69.

Grunebaum, M. F., S. P. Ellis, S. Li, M. A. Oquendo, and J. J. Mann. 2004. "Antidepressants and Suicide Risk in the United States, 1985–1999." *Journal of Clinical Psychiatry* 65: 1456–62.

Guelzo, Allen C. 1999. *Abraham Lincoln: Redeemer President*. Grand Rapids, MI: William B. Eerdmans.

Guest, Avery M., Jane K. Cover, Ross L. Matsuda, and Charis E. Kobrin. 2006. "Neighborhood Context and Neighboring Ties." *City & Community* 5 (4): 363–85.

Guest, Avery M., and Stewart E. Tolnay. 1983. "Children's Roles and Fertility." *SSH* 7 (Autumn): 355–80.

Guest, Avery M., and Susan K. Wierzbicki. 1999. "Social Ties at the Neighborhood Level: Two Decades of GSS Evidence." *Urban Affairs Review* 35 (September): 92–111.

Gurr, Ted Robert. 1989. "Historical Trends in Violent Crime: Europe and the United States." In Gurr 1989, 21–54.

———, ed. 1989. *Violence in America*. Vol. 1. *The History of Crime*. Newbury Park, CA: Sage.

Gusfield, Joseph R. 1967. "Tradition and Modernity: Misplaced Polarities in the Study of Social Change." *AJS* 72 (January):351–62.

Gutmann, Myron P., Sara M. Pullum-Pinon, and Thomas W. Pullum. 2002. "Three Eras of Young Adult Home Leaving in Twentieth-Century America." *JSH* 35 (Spring): 533–76.

Hacker, J. David. 2001. "The Human Cost of War: White Population in the United States, 1850–1880." *Journal of Economic Literature* 61 (June): 486–89.

———. 2008. "Economic, Demographic, and Anthropometric Correlates of First Marriage in the Mid-Nineteenth-Century United States." *SSH* 32 (Fall): 307–45.

Hacker, Jacob S. 2006. *The Great Risk Shift*. New York: Oxford University Press.

———. 2007. "Trends in the Transitory Variance of Family Income, 1969–2004." Presentation, Brookings Institution.

Hadaway, C. Kirk, Penny Long Marler, and Mark Chaves. 1993."What the Polls Don't Show: A Closer Look at U.S. Church Attendance." *ASR* 58 (December): 741–52.

Haferkamp, Hans, and Neil Smelser, eds. 1992. *Social Change and Modernity*. Berkeley: University of California Press.

Hagerty, Michael R. 2000. "Social Comparisons of Income in One's Community: Evidence from National Surveys of Income and Happiness." *JPSP* 78 (April): 764–71.

——. 2003. "Was Life Better in the 'Good Old Days'? Intertemporal Judgments of Life Satisfaction." *Journal of Happiness Studies* 4 (June): 115–39.

Hagerty, Michael R., and Ruut Veenhoven. 2003 "Wealth and Happiness Revisited: Growing National Income Does Go with Greater Happiness." *Social Indicators Research* 64:1–27.

Hahn, Steven. 1985. "The 'Unmaking' of Southern Yeomanry: The Transformation of the Georgia Upcountry, 1860–1890." In Hahn and Prude 1985, 179–203.

Hahn, Steve, and Jonathan Prude, eds. 1985. *The Countryside in the Age of Capitalist Transformation*. Chapel Hill: University of North Carolina Press.

Haines, Michael R. 1996. "Long-Term Marriage Patterns in the United States from Colonial Times to the Present." *History of the Family* 1 (1): 15–39.

——. 2005. "Fertility and Mortality in the United States." EH.Net Encyclopedia of Economic and Business History, ed. Robert Whaples. http://eh.net/encyclopedia/article/haines.demography.

——. 2006. "Marriage and Divorce Rates: 1920–1995." Table Ae507–513 in Carter et al. 2006.

Haines, Michael R., Lee A. Craig, and Thomas Weiss. 2003. "The Short and the Dead: Nutrition, Mortality, and the 'Antebellum Puzzle' in the United States." *JEH* 63 (June): 382–413.

Haines, Michael R., and Avery M. Guest. 2008. "Fertility in New York State in the Pre–Civil War Era." *DEM* 45 (May): 345–61.

Hall, Patricia Kelly, and Steven Ruggles. 2004. "'Restless in the Midst of Their Prosperity': New Evidence on the Internal Migration of Americans, 1850–2000." *JAH* 91 (December): 829–46.

Halle, David. 1984. *America's Working Man: Work, Home, and Politics among Blue-collar Property Owners*. Chicago: University of Chicago Press, 1984.

——. 1987. "The Family Photograph." *Art Journal* 46 (Autumn): 217–25.

Halman, Loek. 1996. "Individualism in Individualized Society? Results from the European Values Surveys." *International Journal of Comparative Sociology* 37 (December): 195–214.

Halttunen, Karen. 1982. *Confidence Men and Painted Women: A Study of Middle-Class Culture in America, 1830–1870*. New Haven, CT: Yale University Press.

——. 1995. "Humanitarianism and the Pornography of Pain in Anglo-American Culture." *AHR* 100 (April):303–34.

Hamilton, Richard F. 1991. "Work and Leisure: On the Reporting of Poll Results." *POQ* 55 (Fall 1991): 347–56.

Hampton, Keith, and Barry Wellman. 2001. "Long Distance Community in the Network Society: Contact and Support beyond Neville." *American Behavioral Scientist* 45 (November): 476–95.

Handlin, David P. 1979. *The American Home: Architecture and Society, 1815–1915*. Boston: Little-Brown.

Handlin, Oscar, and Lilian Handlin, eds. 1997. *From the Outer World*. Cambridge, MA: Harvard University Press.

Handy, Robert T. 1960. "The American Religious Depression, 1925–1935." *Church History* 29 (March): 3–16.

Hannigan, John A., ed. 2005. "Trend Report on the Postmodern City." *Current Sociology* 43(1). Special issue.

Hannon, Joan Underhill. 1984. "The Generosity of Antebellum Poor Relief." *JEH* 44 (September): 810–21.

Hansen, Karen V. 1992. "'Our Eyes Behold Each Other': Masculinity and Intimate Friendship in Antebellum New England." In *Men's Friendships*, ed. Peter M. Nardi, 35–58. Newbury Park, CA: Sage.

——. 1994. *A Very Social Time: Crafting Community in Antebellum New England*. Berkeley: University of California Press.

Hardin, Russell. 2001. "Solving the Problem of Trust." In *Trust in Society*, ed. Karen Cook, 3–39. New York: Russell Sage Foundation.

Harding, David J., and Christopher Jencks. 2003. "Changing Attitudes toward Premarital Sex." *POQ* 67(Summer): 211–27.

Hareven, Tamara K. 1978. "Historical Changes in the Life Course and the Family: Policy Implications." In *Major Social Issues: A Multidisciplinary View*, ed. J. M. Yinger and S. J. Cutler, 338–45. New York: Free Press.

——. 1982. *Family Time and Industrial Time*. New York: Cambridge University Press.

——. 1991. "The History of the Family and the Complexity of Social Change." *AHR* 96 (February, 1991): 95–124.

——. 1994. "Aging and Generational Relations: A Historical and Life Course Perspective." *ARS* 20:437–61.

Hareven, Tamara K., and Randolph Langenbach. 1978. *Amoskeag: Life and Work in an American Factory-City*. New York: Pantheon.

Hareven, Tamara K., and Peter Uhlenberg. 1995. "Transition to Widowhood and Family Support Systems in the Twentieth Century, Northeastern United States." In *Aging in the Past: Demography, Society, and Old Age*, ed. David I. Kertzer and Peter Laslett, 273–99. Berkeley: University of California Press.

Harper, Douglas. 2002. "Changing Works: Eliciting Accounts of Past and Present Dairy Farming." *Contexts* 1 (Spring): 52–8.

Harris, Richard. 1990. "Working-Class Home Ownership in the American Metropolis." *JUH* 17 (November): 46–69.

——. 1994. "The Flexible House: The Housing Backlog and the Persistence of Lodging, 1891–1951." *SSH* 18 (Spring): 31–53.

Hart, Hornell. 1933. "Changing Social Attitudes and Interests." In President's Research Committee on Social Trends, *Recent Social Trends in the United States*. Vol. 1, 382–442. New York: McGraw-Hill.

Hartog, Henrik. 2000. *Man and Wife in America: A History*. Cambridge, MA: Harvard University Press.

Haskell, Thomas L. 1985. "Capitalism and the Origins of the Humanitarian Sensibility, Part 1." *AHR* 90 (April):339–61.

———. 1985. "Capitalism and the Origins of the Humanitarian Sensibility, Part 2."
   AHR 90 (June):547–66.

Hatch, Nathan O. 1989. *The Democratization of American Christianity*. New Haven,
   CT: Yale University Press.

Hawke, David Freeman. 1988. *Everyday Life in Early America*. New York: Harper &
   Row.

Hawley, Amos, and Basil G. Zimmer. 1970. *The Metropolitan Community*. Newbury
   Park, CA: Sage.

Hayes, Edmund. 1983. "Mercy Otis Warren versus Lord Chesterfield, 1779." *WMQ*
   40 (October): 616–21.

Hays, Samuel P. 1992. "On the Meaning and Analysis of Change in History." In *Theory, Method and Practice in Social and Cultural History*, ed. Peter Karsten and John
   Modell, 33–56. New York: New York University Press.

Heath, Linda, and Kevin Gilbert. 1996. "Mass Media and Fear of Crime." *American
   Behavioral Scientist* 39 (February): 378–96.

Heberle, Rudolf. 1960. "The Normative Element in Neighborhood Relations." *Pacific Sociological Review* 3 (Spring): 3–11.

Heckelman, Jac C. 1995. "The Effect of the Secret Ballot on Voter Turnout Rates."
   Public Choice 82 (January): 107–24.

———. 2000. "Revisiting the Relationship Between Secret Ballots and Turnout A
   New Test of Two Legal-Institutional Theories." *American Politics Quarterly* 28
   (April): 194–215.

Heer, Clarence. 1933. "Taxation and Public Finance." In President's Research Committee on Social Trends, *Recent Social Trends in the United States*. Vol. 1, 1331–90.
   New York: McGraw-Hill.

Heinze, Andrew R. 1990. *Adapting to Abundance: Jewish Immigrants, Mass Consumption, and the Search for American Identity*. New York: Columbia University Press.

———. 2003. "Schizophrenia Americana: Aliens, Alienists and the 'Personality Shift'
   of Twentieth-Century Culture." *AQ* 55 (2): 227–56.

Helliwell, John F. 2003. "How's Life? Combining Individual and National Variables
   to Explain Subjective Well-Being." *Economic Modelling* 20:331–60.

Hemphill, C. Dallett. 1996. "The Middle Class Rising in Revolutionary America:
   The Evidence from Manners." *SSH* 30 (Winter): 317–44.

———. 1998. "Class, Gender, and the Regulation of Emotional Expression in Revo-
   lutionary-Era Conduct Literature." In Stearns and Lewis 1998, 33–51.

———. 1999. *Bowing to Necessities: A History of Manners in America, 1620–1860*. New
   York: Oxford University Press.

Henkin, David M. 2006. *The Postal Age: The Emergence of Modern Communications in
   Nineteenth-Century America*. Chicago: University of Chicago Press.

Henretta, James A. 1977. "'Modernization:' Toward a False Synthesis." *Reviews in
   American History* 5 (December): 455–52.

———. 1978. "Families and Farms: Mentalité in Pre-Industrial America." *WMQ* 35
   (January): 3–32.

———. 1979. "Social History as Lived and Written: Structure, Problematic, and Action." *AHR* 84 (December): 1293–1322.

——. 1980. "Reply [to "Comment" by Lemon]." *WMQ* 3rd Ser., 37 (October): 696–700.

——. 1984. "Wealth and Social Structure." In Greene and Pole 1984, 262–89.

——. 1991. *The Origins of American Capitalism*. Boston: Northeastern University Press.

——. 1992. "The Slow Triumph of Liberal Individualism: Law and Politics in New York, 1780–1860." In Curry and Goodheart 1991, 87–106.

——. 1998. "The 'Market' in the Early Republic." *JER* 18 (Summer): 289–304.

Henrich, Joseph, Robert Boyd, Samuel Bowles, Colin Camerer, Ernst Fehr, Herbert Gintis, Richard McElreath. 2001. "In Search of Homo Economicus: Behavioral Experiments in 15 Small-Scale Societies." *AER* 91 (May): 73–78.

Herberg, Will. 1955. *Protestant Catholic Jew: An Essay in American Religious Sociology*. Repr. Chicago: University of Chicago Press, 1983.

Herndon, Ruth Wallis. 1997. "Women of 'No Particular Home': Town Leaders and Female Transients in Rhode Island, 1750–1800." In Eldridge 1997, 269–89.

——. 2001. *Unwelcome Americans: Living on the Margin in Early New England*. Philadelphia: University of Pennsylvania Press.

——. 2004. "'Who Died an Expence to This Town': Poor Relief in Eighteenth-Century Rhode Island." In Smith 2004, 135–62.

Herring, Cedric. 2002. "Is Job Discrimination Dead?" *Contexts* 1 (Summer):13–18.

Hershberg, Theodore, ed. 1981. *Philadelphia: Work, Space, Family and Group Experience in the 19th Century*. New York: Oxford University Press.

Hershberg, Theodore, Dale Light Jr., Harold E. Cox, and Richard R. Greenfield. 1981. "The 'Journey to Work': An Empirical Investigation of Work, Residence, and Transportation, Philadelphia, 1850 and 1880." In Hershberg 1981, 128–73.

Hessinger, Rodney. 1996. "Problems and Promises: Colonial American Child Rearing and Modernization Theory." *Journal of Family History* 21 (April):125–43.

Hetherington, Marc J. 1998. "The Political Relevance of Political Trust." *American Political Science Review* 92 (December): 791–808.

——. 1999. "The Effect of Political Trust on the Presidential Vote, 1968–96." *American Political Science Review* 93 (June): 311–26.

Hewitt, John P. 1989. *Dilemmas of the American Self*. Philadelphia: Temple University Press.

Hexter, J. H. 1971. *Doing History*. Bloomington: Indiana University Press.

Hickman, Timothy A. 2004. "'Mania Americana': Narcotic Addiction and Modernity in the United States, 1870–1920." *JAH* 90 (March): 1269–94.

Higher Education Research Institute. 2000. "Most of the Nation's College Freshmen Embrace The Internet as an Educational Tool, UCLA Study Finds." News Release, January 25, University of California, Los Angeles. http://www.gseis.ucla.edu/heri/.

——. 2006. "The American Freshman: National Norms for Fall 2006." Graduate School of Education & Information Studies, University of California, Los Angeles. http://www.gseis.ucla.edu/heri/.

Hiltzheimer, Jacob. 1893. *Extracts from the Diary of Jacob Hilzheimer of Philadelphia, 1765–1798*. Ed. Jacob Cox Parsons. Philadelphia: Wm. F. Fell & Co.

Hine, Robert V. 1980. *Community on the American Frontier: Separate But Not Alone*. Norman: Oklahoma University Press.

Hipple, Steven. 2004. "Self-Employment in the United States: An Update." *Monthly Labor Review* 127 (July): 13–23.

Hirschhorn, Norbert. 2003. "Mary Lincoln's 'Suicide Attempt': A Physician Reconsiders the Evidence." *Lincoln Herald* 104 (3): 94–98.

Hirschman, Charles. 1994. "Why Fertility Changes." *ARS* 20:203–33.

Hirschman, Elizabeth C. and Morris Holbrook. 1982. "Hedonic Consumption: Emerging Concepts, Methods, and Propositions." *Journal of Marketing* 46 (Summer): 92–101.

Hobsbawm, Eric, and Terence Ranger, eds. 1983. *The Invention of Tradition*. New York: Cambridge University Press.

Hochschild, Arlie Russell. 1979. "Emotion Work, Feeling Rules, and Social Structure." *AJS* 85 (November): 551–75.

———1983. *The Managed Heart : Commercialization of Human Feeling*. Berkeley: University of California Press.

———. 1989. *The Second Shift : Working Parents and the Revolution at Home*. New York: Viking.

———. 1997. *The Time Bind: When Work Becomes Home and Home Becomes Work*. New York: Metropolitan Books.

Hodson, Randy. 2004. "Work Life and Social Fulfillment: Does Social Affiliation at Work Reflect a Carrot or a Stick?" *Social Science Quarterly* 85:221–39.

Hoffert, Sylvia D. 1987. "'A Very Peculiar Sorrow': Attitudes Toward Infant Death in the Urban Northeast, 1800–1860." *AQ* 39 (Winter): 601–16.

Hofferth, Sandra L., Joan R. Kahn, and Wendy Baldwin. 1987. "Premarital Sexual Activity Among American Teenage Women Over the Past Three Decades." *Family Planning Perspectives* 19 (March): 46–53.

Hofferth, Sandra L., and John F. Sandberg. 2001. "Changes in American Children's Time, 1981–1997." In *Children at the Millennium: Where Have We Come From, Where are We Going? Advances in Life Course Research*, ed. T. Owens and S. Hofferth, 193–229. New York: Elsevier Science.

Hoffman, Ronald, John J. McCusker, Russell R. Menard, and Peter J. Albert, eds. *The Economy of Early America: The Revolutionary Period, 1763–1790*. Charlottesville: University Press of Virginia.

Hoffman, Ronald, Mechal Sobel, and Fredrika Teute, eds. 1997. *Through a Glass Darkly: Reflections on Personal Identity in Early America*. Chapel Hill: University of North Carolina Press.

Hofstadter, Richard. 1965 . *Social Darwinism in American Thought*. Rev. ed. Boston : Beacon Press.

Hoge, Dean R., and Jann L. Hoge, 1992. "The Return of the Fifties?: Values Trends at the University of Michigan, 1952 to 1989." *Sociological Quarterly* 32 (4):611–23.

Hoge, Dean R., Benton Johnson, and Donald A. Luidens. 1995. "Types of Denominational Switching among Protestant Young Adults." *Journal for the Scientific Study of Religion* 34(June): 253–59.

Holberg, Eric O. 2002. "Irwin, Iowa: Persistence and Change in Shelby County." In Luloff and Krannich 2002, 45–70.

Holcombe, Randall G., and Donald J. Lacombe. 2001. "The Growth of Local Government in the United States from 1820 to 1870." *JEH* 61:184–89.

Holifield, E. Brooks. 1993. "Peace, Conflict, and Ritual in Puritan Congregations." *JIH* 23 (Winter):551–70.

———. 1994. "Toward a History of American Congregations." In *American Congregations*. Vol. 2. *New Perspectives in the Study of Congregations*, ed. James P. Wind and James M. Lewis, 23–53. Chicago: University of Chicago Press.

Holinger, Paul C. 1987. *Violent Deaths in the United States: An Epidemiological Study of Suicide, Homicide, and Accidents*. New York: Guilford.

Holinger, Paul C., Danile Offer, James T. Barter, and Carl C. Bell. 1994. *Suicide and Homicide among Adolescents*. New York: Guilford.

Hollinger, Franz, and Max Haller. 1990. "Kinship and Social Networks in Modern Societies: A Cross-Cultural Comparison Among Seven Nations." *European Sociological Review* 6 (September): 103–24.

Holmes, Amy E. 1990. "'Such is the Price We Pay:' American Widows and the Civil War Pension System." In Vinovskis 1990, 171–95.

Holt, Michael F. 1999. "The Primacy of Party Reasserted." *JAH* 86 (June):151–57.

Hood, Clifton. 1996. "Changing Perceptions of Public Space on the New York Rapid Transit System." *JUH* 22 (March): 308–31.

Hoover, Herbert. 1928. *American Individualism*. Garden City, NY: Doubleday, Doran, & Company.

Horn, Margo. 1984. "The Moral Message of Child Guidance 1925–45." *JSH* 18 (Fall): 25–36.

Horwitz, Allan V., and Jerome C. Wakefield. 2005. "The Age of Depression." *Public Interest* 158 (Winter): 39–58.

———. 2006. "The Epidemic in Mental Illness: Clinical Fact or Survey Artifact?" *Contexts* 5 (Winter): 19–23.

———. 2007. *The Loss of Sadness: How Psychiatry Transformed Normal Sorrow Into Depressive Disorder*. New York: Oxford University Press.

Horowitz, Daniel. 1985. *The Morality of Spending: Attitudes toward the Consumer Society in America, 1875–1940*. Baltimore: Johns Hopkins University Press.

———. 2004. *The Anxieties of Affluence: Critiques of American Consumer Culture, 1939–1979*. Amherst: University of Massachusetts Press.

Horwitz, Morton J. 1977. *The Transformation of American Law, 1780–1860*. Cambridge, MA: Harvard University Press.

Hout, Michael. 2006. "Money and Morale: Growing Inequality Affects How Americans View Themselves and Others." Working paper, Survey Research Center, University of California, Berkeley.

———. 2008. "How Class Works: Objective and Subjective Aspects of Class Since the 1970s." In *Social Class: How Does It Work*, ed. Annette Lareau and Dalton Conley, 25–64. New York: Russell Sage Foundation.

Hout, Michael, and Claude S. Fischer. 2002. "Explaining the Rise of Americans with No Religious Preference: Politics and Generation." *ASR* 67 (April): 165–90.

Hout, Michael, and Andrew M. Greeley. 1987. "The Center Doesn't Hold: Church Attendance in the United States, 1940–1984." *ASR* 52 (June): 325–45.

Hout, Michael, and Caroline Hanley. 2003. "The Overworked American Family: Trends and Nontrends in Working Hours, 1968–2001." Working paper, Survey Research Center, University of California, Berkeley.

Howard, Vicki. 2003. "A 'Real Man's Ring': Gender and the Invention of Tradition." *JSH* 36 (Summer): 837–56.

Howe, Daniel Walker. 1997. *Making the American Self: Jonathan Edwards to Abraham Lincoln*. Cambridge, MA: Harvard University Press.

———. 1997. "Protestantism, Voluntarism, and Personal Identity in Antebellum America." In Stout and Hart 1997, 206–35.

———. 2007. *What Hath God Wrought: The Transformation of America, 1815–1848*. New York: Oxford University Press.

Howe, Irving. 1976. *World of Our Fathers*. New York: Harcourt Brace Jovanovich.

Hoy, Suellen. 1995. *Chasing Dirt: The American Pursuit of Cleanliness*. New York: Oxford University Press.

Huberman, Michael, and Chris Minns. 2007. "The Times They Are Not Changin': Days and Hours of Work in Old and New Worlds, 1870–2000." *Explorations in Economic History* 44 (October): 538–67.

Hudson, John C. 1985. *Plains Country Towns*. Minneapolis: University of Minnesota Press.

Hughes, H. Stuart. 1982. "Contemporary Historiography: Progress, Paradigms, and the Regression Toward Positivism." In Almond, Chodorow, and Pearce 1982, 240–51.

Hunt, Alan. 1999. "Anxiety and Social Explanation: Some Anxieties About Anxiety." *JSH* 32 (Spring):509–28.

Hunter, Albert. 1975. "The Loss of Community: An Empirical Test Through Replication." *ASR* 40 (October):537–52.

———. 1985. "Private, Parochial and Public Social Orders: The Problem of Crime and Incivility in Urban Communities." In *The Challenge of Social Control*, ed. Gerald Suttles and Mayer E. Zald, 230–42. Norwood, NJ: Ablex.

Hunter, James Davidson, and Carl Bowman. 1996. "The State of Disunion." Vol. 2. Ivy, VA: In Media Res Educational Foundation.

Hurt, R. Douglas. 1985–6. "REA: A New Deal for Farmers." *Timeline* (December): 32–47.

———. 1993. "Rural Life in the West." In Cayton, Gorn, and Williams 1993, 1235–49.

Hurtado, Sylvia, and John H. Pryor. 2006. "The American Freshman: National Norms for Fall 2005." Cooperative Institutional Research Program, Higher Education Research Institute, Graduate School of Education & Information Studies, University of California, Los Angeles. http://www.gseis.ucla.edu/heri/PDFs/ResearchBrief05.PDF.

Huston, James L. 1998. *Securing the Fruits of Labor: The American Concept of Wealth Distribution, 1765–1900*. Baton Rouge: Louisiana State University Press.

Hyman, Herbert, and Charles Wright. 1971. "Trends in Voluntary Association Memberships of American Adults: Replications Based on Secondary Analysis of National Sample Surveys." *ASR* 36 (April): 191–206.

Iggers, Georg G. 1982. "The Idea of Progress in Historiography and Social Thought Since the Enlightenment." In Almond, Chodorow, and Pearce 1982, 41–66.

Igo, Sarah E. 2007. *The Averaged American: Surveys, Citizens, and the Making of a Mass Public*. Cambridge, MA: Harvard University Press.

Inglehart, Ronald. 1990. *Culture Shift in Advanced Industrial Society*. Princeton, NJ: Princeton University Press.

———. 1997. *Modernization and Postmodernization: Cultural, Economic, and Political Change in 43 Societies*. Princeton, NJ: Princeton University Press.

———. 1997. "Postmaterialist Values and the Erosion of Institutional Authority." In Nye, Zelikow, and King 1997, 217–36.

———. 2000. "Globalization and Postmodern Values." *Washington Quarterly* 23 (Winter): 215–17.

Inglehart, Ronald, Roberto Foa, Christopher Peterson, and Christian Welzel. 2008. "Development, Freedom, and Rising Happiness: A Global Perspective (1981–2007)." *Perspectives on Psychological Science* 3 (4): 264–85.

Inglehart, Ronald, and Christian Welzel. 2005. *Modernization, Cultural Change, and Democracy: The Human Development Sequence*. New York: Cambridge University Press.

Ingram, Rick E. 1990. "Self-Focused Attention in Clinical Disorders: Review and a Conceptual Model." *Psychological Bulletin* 107 (March): 156–76.

Inkeles, Alex, and David H. Smith. 1974. *Becoming Modern: Individual Change in Six Developing Countries*. Cambridge, MA: Harvard University Press.

Innes, Stephen. 1983. *Labor in a New Land: Economy and Society in Seventeenth-Century Springfield*. Princeton, NJ: Princeton University Press.

———. 1988. "Fulfilling John Smith's Vision: Work and Labor in Early America." In *Work and Labor in Early America*, 3–48. Chapel Hill: University of North Carolina Press.

Interrante, Joseph. 1979. "'You Can't Go to Town in a Bathtub': Automobile Movement and the Reorganization of Rural American Space." *Radical History Review* 21 (Fall): 151–68.

Isaac, Rhys. 1971. "Order and Growth, Authority and Meaning in Colonial New England." *AHR* 76 (June): 728–37.

———. 1974. "Evangelical Revolt: The Nature of the Baptists' Challenge to the Traditional Order in Virginia, 1765–1775." *WMQ* 3rd Ser., 31 (July): 345–68.

———. 1997. "Stories and Constructions of Identity: Folk Tellings and Diary Inscriptions in Revolutionary Virginia." In Hoffman, Sobel, and Teute 1997, 206–37.

Isaacs, Stephen L., and Steven A. Schroeder. 2001. "Where the Public Good Prevailed: Lessons from Success Stories in Health." *American Prospect* (4 June): 26–30.

Ito, Mizuko, Sonja Baumer, Matteo Bittanti, et al. 2008. "Living and Learning with New Media: Summary of Findings from the Digital Youth Project." John D. and

Catherine T. MacArthur Foundation Reports on Digital Media and Learning. http://digitalyouth.ischool.berkeley.edu/files/report/digitalyouth-WhitePaper .pdf.

Iyengar, Sheena S., and Mark R. Lepper. 2000. "When Choice is Demotivating: Can One Desire Too Much of a Good Thing?" *JPSP* 79(6): 995–1006.

———. 2002. "Choice and Its Consequences: On the Costs and Benefits of Self-Determination. In *Self and Motivation*, ed. Abraham Tesser, Dierderik A. Stapel, and Joanne V. Wood, 71–96. Washington DC: American Psychological Association.

Iyengar, Sheena S., and Wei Jiang. 2005. "The Psychological Costs of Ever Increasing Choice: A Fallback to the Sure Bet." Unpublished paper, Columbia Business School.

Iyengar, Sheena S., Rachael E. Wells, and Barry Schwartz. 2006. "Doing Better but Feeling Worse: Looking for the 'Best' Job Undermines Satisfaction." *Psychological Science* 17 (February): 143–50.

Jabour, Anya. 2000. "Male Friendship and Masculinity in the Early National South: William Wirt and His Friends." *JER* 20(1): 83–111.

Jackson, Kenneth T. 1985. *Crabgrass Frontier: The Suburbanization of the United States*. New York: Oxford University Press.

Jacobs, Eva, and Stephanie Shipp. 1990. "How Family Spending Has Changed in the U.S." *Monthly Labor Review* 113 (March): 20–28.

Jacobs, Jane. 1961. *The Death and Life of Great American Cities*. New York: Random House.

Jacobs, Jerry A. 1998. "Measuring Time at Work." *Monthly Labor Review* (December): 42–53.

Jacobs, Jerry A., and Kathleen Gerson. 1998. "Who Are the Overworked Americans?" *Review of Social Economy* 56 (Winter): 442–59.

———. 2001. "Overworked Individuals or Overworked Families? Explaining Trends in Work, Leisure, and Family Time." *Work and Occupations* 28 (February): 40–63.

Jacobs, Meg. 1999. "'Democracy's Third Estate:' New Deal Politics and the Construction of a 'Consuming Public.'" *International Labor and Working-Class History* 55:27–51.

Jacobson, Lisa. 1997. "Revitalizing the American Home: Children's Leisure and the Revolution of Play, 1920–1940." *JSH* 30 (Spring): 581–96.

Jacoby, Sanford M., and Sunil Sharma. 1992. "Employment Duration and Industrial Labor Mobility in the United States, 1880–1980." *JEH* 52 (March): 161–79.

Jacques, Jeffrey. 1998. "Changing Marital and Family Patterns: A Test of the Post-Modern Perspective." *Sociological Perspectives* 41 (2):381–413.

Jaffee, David. 1991. "Peddlers of Progress and the Transformation of the Rural North, 1760–1860." *JAH* 78 (September, 1991): 511–35.

———. 2003. "The Ebenezers Devotion: Pre- and Post-Revolutionary Consumption in Rural Connecticut." *New England Quarterly* 76 (June): 239–64.

James, William. 1890. *The Principles of Psychology*. New York: Macmillan.

Janowitz, Morris. 1967. *The Community Press in the Urban Setting: The Social Elements of Urbanism*. Chicago: University of Chicago Press.

——. 1976. *Social Control of the Welfare State*. Chicago: University of Chicago Press.

——. 1978. *The Last Half-Century: Societal Change and Politics in America*. Chicago: University of Chicago Press.

Jargowsky, Paul A. 1994. "Ghetto Poverty among Blacks in the 1980s." *Journal of Policy Analysis and Management* 13 (2): 288–310.

——. 1997. *Poverty and Place: Ghettos, Barrios, and the American City*. New York: Russell Sage Foundation.

——. 2003. "Stunning Progress, Hidden Problems: The Dramatic Decline of Concentrated Poverty in the 1990s." Living Cities Census Series Report. Washington DC: Brookings Institution:

Jary, David, and Julia Jary. 1991. *The HarperCollins Dictionary of Sociology*. New York: HarperCollins.

Jencks, Christopher. 1991. "Is Violent Crime Increasing?" *American Prospect* 1 (Winter): 98–109.

Jenkins, Jeffery A., Eric Schickler, and Jamie L. Carson. 2004. "Constituency Cleavages and Congressional Parties: Measuring Homogeneity and Polarization, 1857–1913." *SSH* 28 (Winter): 537–73.

Jennings, M. Kent. 1996. "Political Knowledge Over Time and Across Generations." *POQ* 60 (Summer): 228–52.

——. 1998. "Political Trust and the Roots of Devolution." In *Trust and Governance*, ed. Valerie Braithwaite and Margaret Levi, 218–46. New York: Russell Sage Foundation.

Jennings, M. Kent, and Laura Stoker. 2004. "Social Trust and Civic Engagement across Time and Generations." *Acta Politica* 39 (December): 342–79.

Jensen, Gary F. 2001. "The Invention of Television as a Cause of Homicide: The Reification of a Spurious Relationship." *Homicide Studies* 5 (May): 114–30.

Jensen, Richard. 1979. "The Lynds Revisited." *Indiana Magazine of History* 75 (December): 303–19.

——. 1989. "The Causes and Cures of Unemployment in the Great Depression." *JIH* 19 (Spring 1989): 553–83.

Jimenez, Mary Ann. 1986. "Madness in Early American History: Insanity in Massachusetts from 1700 to 1820." *JSH* 20(Fall):25–44.

Joas, Hans. 1993. "Communitarianism: A German Perspective." Distinguished Lecture Series 6, Institute for Advanced Study. Repr., Bloomington: Indiana University.

Johanson, H. E., and G. V. Fuguist. 1973. "Changing Retail Activity in Wisconsin Villages: 1939–1954–1970." *Rural Sociology* 38: 207–18.

John, Richard R. 1990. "Taking Sabbatarianism Seriously: The Postal System, the Sabbath, and the Transformation of American Political Culture." *JER* 10 (Winter): 517–65.

——. 1993. "Communications and Information Processing." In Cayton, Gorn, and Williams 1993, 2349–62.

Johnson, Claudia D. 1975. "That Guilty Third Tier: Prostitution in Nineteenth-Century American Theaters." *AQ* 27 (December): 575–84.

Johnson, Curtis D. 1995. "Supply-Side or Demand-Side Revivalism?: Evaluating the Social Influences on New York State Evangelism in the 1830s." *SSH* 19 (Spring): 1–30.

Johnson, Paul. 1978. *A Shopkeeper's Millennium: Society and Revivals in Rochester, New York, 1815–1837.* New York: Hill & Wang.

———. 1993. "Market Revolution." In Cayton, Gorn, and Williams 1993, 545–60.

Johnson, Robert A., and Dean Gerstein. 1998. "Initiation of Use of Alcohol, Cigarettes, Marijuana, Cocaine, and Other Substances in US Birth Cohorts since 1919." *American Journal of Public Health* 88 (January): 27–33.

Johnson, Tallese, and Jane Dye. 2005. "Indicators of Marriage and Fertility in the United States from the American Community Survey: 2000 to 2003." Population Division. Washington DC: United States Bureau of the Census. http://www.census.gov/population/www/socdemo/fertility/mar-fert-slides.html.

Johnson-Hanks, Jennifer. 2005. "When the Future Decides." *Current Anthropology* 46 (June): 363–85.

Johnston, L. D., P. M. O'Malley, J. G. Bachman, and J. E. Schulenberg. 2006. "Demographic Subgroup Trends for Various Licit and Illicit Drugs, 1975–2005." Monitoring the Future Occasional Paper 63. Ann Arbor, MI: Institute for Social Research. http://monitoringthefuture.org.

Jones, Douglas Lamar. 1984. "The Strolling Poor: Transiency in Eighteenth-Century Massachusetts." In Monkkonen 1984, 21–55.

Jones, James B. Jr. 1994. "Selected Aspects of Drug Abuse in Nineteenth- and Early Twentieth-Century Tennessee History, ca. 1830–1920." *West Tennessee Historical Society Papers* 48:1–23.

Jones, Jeffrey M. 2005. "U.S. Catholics' Reactions to Pope Benedict XVI More Positive Than Negative." Gallup Online, http://www.gallup.com.

———. 2002. "Public Divided on Benefits of Living Together Before Marriage." Gallup News Service, August 16. http://www.gallup.com/15955/US-Catholics-Reactions-Pope-Benedict-XVI-More-Positive-Than-Negative.aspx.

Joselit, Jenna Weissman. 1994. *The Wonders of America: Reinventing Jewish Culture, 1880–1950.* New York: Hill & Wang.

Judt, Tony. 1979. "A Clown in Regal Purple: Social History and the Historians." *History Workshop* 7 (Spring): 66–94.

Juster, Susan M., and Ellen Hartigan-O'Conner. 2002. "The 'Angel Delusion' of 1806–1811: Frustration and Fantasy in Northern New England." *JER* 22 (Fall): 375–404.

Juster, Susan M., and Maris A. Vinovskis. 1987. "Changing Perspectives on the American Family in the Past." *ARS* 13:193–216.

Kacapyr, Elia. 1997. "Are We Having Fun Yet?" *American Demographics*. October. Online ed. http://www.demographics.com/publications.

Kagan, Jerome. 2007. *What is Emotion? History, Measures and Meanings.* New Haven, CT: Yale University Press.

Kahneman, Daniel. 2003. "A Perspective on Judgment and Choice: Mapping Bounded Rationality." *American Psychologist* 58 (September): 697–720.

Kahneman, Daniel, Ed Diener, and Norbert Schwartz, eds. 1999. *Well-Being: The Foundation of Hedonistic Psychology*. New York: Russell Sage Foundation.

Kahneman, Daniel, and Alan B. Krueger. 2006. "Developments in the Measurement of Subjective Well-Being." *JEP* 20 (Winter): 3–24.

Kahneman, Daniel, Alan B. Krueger, David Schkade, Norbert Schwarz, Arthur A. Stone. 2006. "Would You Be Happier If You Were Richer? A Focusing Illusion." *Science* 312 (30 June): 1908–10.

Kahneman, Daniel, and Richard H. Thaler. 2006. "Anomalies: Utility Maximization and Experienced Utility." *JEP* 20 (Winter): 221–34.

Kaiser Family Foundation. 1996. "Why Don't Americans Trust the Government?" The *Washington Post*/Kaiser Family Foundation/Harvard University Survey Project. http://www.kff.org/kaiserpolls/1110-governs.cfm.

———. 2000. "Attitudes toward Government." NPR/Kaiser Family Foundation/Kennedy School Poll. http://www.kff.org/kaiserpolls/3036-index.cfm.

Kalberg, Stephen. 2009. "Max Weber's Analysis of the Unique American Civic Sphere." *Journal of Classical Sociology* 9 (1): 117–41.

Kalleberg, Arne L. 2009. "Precarious Work, Insecure Workers: Employment Relations in Transition." *ASR* 74 (February): 1–22.

Kalmijn, Matthijs. 1991. "Shifting Boundaries: Trends in Religious and Educational Homogamy." *ASR* 56 (December): 786–800.

Kamensky, Jane. 1997. *Governing the Tongue: The Politics of Speech in Early New England*. New York and Oxford: Oxford University Press.

———. 2008. "Salem Obsessed; Or, Plus Ça Change: An Introduction." *WMQ* 3rd Ser. 65 (July): 391–400.

Kammen, Michael. 1991. *Mystic Chords of Memory: The Transformation of Tradition in American Culture*. New York: Random House.

———. 1993. "The Problem of American Exceptionalism: A Reconsideration." *AQ* 45 (March): 1–43.

Kaplan, Michael. 1995. "New York City Tavern Violence and the Creation of a Working-Class Male Identity." *JER* 15 (4): 591–617.

Karp, Jeffrey. 1995. "Explaining Public Support for Legislative Term Limits." *POQ* 59 (Fall): 373–91.

Karr, Ronald Dale. 1989. "Brookline Rejects Annexation, 1873." In *Suburbia Re-Examined*, ed. Barbara M. Kelley, 103–10. New York: Greenwood Press.

Kasarda, John D., and Morris Janowitz. 1974. "Community Attachment in Mass Society." *ASR* 39 (June): 328–39.

Kasen, Stephanie, Patricia Cohen, Henian Chen, and Dorothy Castille. 2003. "Depression in Adult Women: Age Changes and Cohort Effects." *American Journal of Public Health* 93:2061–66.

Kasser, Tim, and Allen D. Kanner, eds. 2003. *Psychology and Consumer Culture: The Struggle for a Good Life in a Materialistic World*. Washington DC: American Psychological Association.

Kasson, John F. 1978. *Amusing the Million: Coney Island at the Turn of the Century*. New York: Hill & Wang.

———. 1990. *Rudeness & Civility: Manners in Nineteenth-Century Urban America*. New York: Hill & Wang.

Katz, James E., Ronald E. Rice, and Philip Aspen. 2001. "The Internet, 1995–2000: Access, Civic Involvement, and Social Interaction." *American Behavioral Scientist* 45 (November): 405–19.

Katz, Michael B. 1986. *In the Shadow of the Poorhouse*. New York: Basic Books.

Katz, Michael B., and Mark J. Stern. 2006. *One Nation Divisible: What America Was and What It is Becoming*. New York: Russell Sage Foundation.

Katzman, David. 1978. *Seven Days a Week: Women and Domestic Service in Industrializing America*. New York: Oxford University Press.

Kaufman, Jason. 2002. *For the Common Good? American Civil Life and the Golden Age of Fraternity*. New York: Oxford University Press.

———. 2002. "The Political Economy of Interdenominational Competition in Late-Nineteenth-Century American Cities." *JUH* 28 (May):445–65.

Kaufman, Jason, and David Weintraub. 2004. "Social-Capital Formation and American Fraternal Association: New Empirical Evidence." *JIH* 35 (Summer): 1–36.

Kazal, Russell. 1995. "Revisiting Assimilation: The Rise, Fall, and Reappraisal of a Concept in American Ethnic History." *AHR* 100 (April): 437–71.

Keegan, John. 1993. *A History of Warfare*. New York: Knopf.

Kefalas, Maria. 2003. *Working-Class Heroes: Protecting Home, Community, and Nation in a Chicago Neighborhood*. Berkeley: University of California Press.

Keller, Suzanne. 1968. *The Urban Neighborhood: A Sociological Perspective*. New York: Random House.

Kelley, Harold H., and John W. Thibaut. 1978. *Interpersonal Relations: A Theory of Interdependence*. New York: Wiley.

Kelley, Mary. 1979. "The Sentimentalists: Promise and Betrayal in the Home." *Signs* 4 (Spring): 434–46.

———. 2001. "Beyond the Boundaries." *JER* 21 (Spring):73–78.

Kellogg, Susan. 1990. "Exploring Diversity in Middle-Class Families: The Symbolism of American Ethnic Identity." *SSH* 14 (Spring): 27–41.

Kellstedt, Lyman A., John C. Green, James L. Guth, and Corwin E. Smidt. 1993. "Religious Traditions and Religious Commitments in the USA." Paper presented to 32nd International Conference of the International Society for the Sociology of Religion, Budapest.

Kelly, Catherine E. 1999. "'Well Bred Country People': Sociability, Social Networks, and the Creation of a Provincial Middle Class, 1820–1860." *JER* 19 (Autumn): 451–79.

Kelly, Timothy, and Joseph Kelly. 1998. "Our Lady of Perpetual Help, Gender Roles, and the Decline of Devotional Catholicism." *JSH* 32 (Fall): 5–27.

Kemp, Thomas R. 1990. "Community and War: The Civil War Experience of Two New Hampshire Towns." In Vinovskis 1990, 31–77.

Kennedy, David M. 1999. *Freedom from Fear: The American People in Depression and War, 1929–1945*. New York: Oxford University Press.

Kennedy, J. C. et al. 1914. *Wages and Family Budgets in the Chicago Stock-Yards District.* Chicago: University of Chicago Press.

Kennickell, Arthur B., Martha Starr-McCluer, and Anika E. Sundén. 1997. "Family Finances in the U.S.: Recent Evidence from the Survey of Consumer Finances." *Federal Reserve Bulletin* (January): 10–24.

Keppel, Kenneth G., Jeffrey N. Pearcy, and Diane K. Wagener. 2002. "Trends in Racial and Ethnic-Specific Rates for the Health Status Indicators: United States, 1990–98." Healthy People Statistical Notes No. 23. Hyattsville, MD: National Center for Health Statistics (January).

Kerber, Linda K. 1988. "Separate Spheres, Female Worlds, Woman's Place: The Rhetoric of Women's History." *JAH* 75 (June): 9–39.

——. 1991. "Can a Woman be an Individual? The Discourse of Self-Reliance." In Curry and Goodheart 1991, 151–66.

Kessler Ronald C., Patricia Berglund, Guilherme Borges, Matthew Nock, Philip S. Wang. 2005. "Trends in Suicide Ideation, Plans, Gestures, and Attempts in the United States, 1990–1992 to 2001–2003." *Journal of the American Medical Association* 293 (May 25): 2487–95.

Kessler, Ronald C., Patricia Berglund, Olga Demler, Robert Jin, Kathleen R. Merikangas, Ellen E. Walters. 2005. "Lifetime Prevalence and Age-of-Onset Distributions of DSM-IV Disorders in the National Comorbidity Survey Replication." *Archives of General Psychiatry* 62:593–602.

Kessler, Ronald C., G. Borges, and E. E. Walters. 1999. "Prevalence of and Risk Factors for Lifetime Suicide Attempts in the National Comorbidity Survey." *Archives of General Psychiatry* 56:617–26.

Kessler, Ronald C., O. Demler, R. G. Frank, M. Olfson, H. A. Pincus, E. E. Walters, P. Wang, K. B. Wells, and A. M. Zaslavsky. 2005. "Prevalence and Treatment of Mental Disorders, 1990 to 2003." *New England Journal of Medicine* 352 (June): 2515–23.

Kessler-Harris, Alice. 1990. "Social History." In Foner 1990, 163–84.

Kett, Joseph F. 1978. "The Stages of Life, 1790–1840." In Gordon 1978, 166–91.

Keyssar, Alexander. 1986. *Out of Work: The First Century of Unemployment in Massachusetts.* New York: Cambridge University Press.

——. 1991. "Poverty." In Foner and Garraty 1991, 858–61.

Kiesling, L. Lynne, and Margo, Robert A. 1997. "Explaining the Rise in Antebellum Pauperism, 1850–1860: New Evidence." *Quarterly Review of Economics and Finance* 37 (2): 405–17.

King, David C. 1997. "The Polarization of American Parties and Mistrust of Government." In Nye, Zelikow, and King 1997, 155–78.

Kingsdale, Jon M. 1973. "The 'Poor Man's Club': Social Functions of the Urban Working-Class Saloon." *AQ* 25 (October): 472–92.

Kinsella, Kevin G. 1992. "Changes in Life Expectancy, 1900-1990." *American Journal of Clinical Nutrition* 55:1196S–1202S.

Kirby, Jack Temple. 1987. *Rural World Lost: The American South 1920–1960.* Baton Rouge: Louisiana State University Press.

Kish, Andrew. 2006. "Perspectives on Recent Trends in Consumer Debt." Discussion paper. Payment Cards Center, Federal Reserve Bank of Philadelphia.

Kitayama, Shinobu, and Hazel Rose Markus, eds. 1994. *Emotion and Culture: Studies of Mutual Influence*. Washington DC: American Psychological Association.

Klein, Herbert S. 2004. *A Population History of the United States*. New York: Cambridge University Press.

Kleinberg, S. J. 1989. *The Shadow of the Mills: Working-Class Families in Pittsburgh, 1870–1907*. Pittsburgh: University of Pittsburgh Press.

Klepp, Susan E. 1994. "Lost, Hidden, Obstructed, and Repressed: Contraceptive and Abortive Technology in the Early Delaware Valley." In *Early American Technology: Making and Doing Things from the Colonial Era to 1850*, ed. Judith A. McGaw, 68–113. Chapel Hill: University of North Carolina Press.

———. 1998. "Revolutionary Bodies: Women and the Fertility Transition in the Mid-Atlantic Region,1760–1820." *JAH* 85(December): 910–45.

Kleppner, Paul. 1982. *Who Voted? The Dynamics of Electoral Turnout, 1870–1980*. New York: Praeger.

———. 1987. *Continuity and Change in Electoral Politics, 1893–1928*. New York: Greenwood Press.

Klerman, Gerald L., Philip W. Lavori, John Rice, Theodore Reich, Jean Endicott, Nancy C. Andreasen, Martin B. Keller, and Robert M. A. Hirschfield. 1985. "Birth-Cohort Trends in Rates of Major Depressive Disorder among Relatives of Patients with Affective Disorder." *Archives of General Psychiatry* 42 (July): 689–93.

Kline, Ronald R. 2000. *Consumers in the Country: Technology and Social Change in Rural America*. Baltimore: Johns Hopkins University Press.

Kling, David W. 1993. *A Field of Divine Wonders: The New Divinity and Village Revivals in Northwestern Connecticut, 1792–1822*. University Park: Pennsylvania State University Press.

Knights, Peter R. 1971. *The Plain People of Boston, 1830-1860: A Study in City Growth*. New York: Oxford University Press.

———. 1991. *Yankee Destinies: The Lives of Ordinary Nineteenth-Century Bostonians*. Chapel Hill: University of North Carolina Press.

Kobrin, Frances E. 1976. "The Primary Individual and the Family: Changes in Living Arrangements in the United States since 1940." *Journal of Marriage and the Family* 38 (May): 233–39.

———. 1978. "The Fall in Household Size and the Rise of the Primary Individual in the United States." In Gordon 1978, 69–81.

Koehlinger, Amy. 2004. "'Let Us Live for Those Who Love Us': Faith, Family, and the Contours of Manhood Among the Knights of Columbus in Late Nineteenth-Century Connecticut." *JSH* 38(Winter): 455–69.

Koerselman, Gary. 1972. "The Quest for Community in Rural Iowa: Neighborhood Life in Early Middleburg History." *Annals of Iowa* 41 (Summer): 1006–20.

Kohn, Melvin L. 1969. *Class and Conformity: A Study in Values*. Homewood, IL: Dorsey Press.

Kohn, Melvin L., and Carmi Schooler. 1969. "Class, Occupation, and Orientation." *ASR* 34 (October): 659–78.

———. 1973. "Occupational Experience and Psychological Functioning: An Assessment of Reciprocal Effects." *ASR* 38 (February): 97–118.

Kolb, J. H., and R. A. Polson. 1933. "Trends in Town-Country Relations." Research Bulletin No. 117. Madison: University of Wisconsin Agricultural Cooperative Station.

Kolchin, Peter. 1993. *American Slavery: 1619–1877*. New York: Hill & Wang.

Kolp, John G. 1992. "The Dynamics of Electoral Competition in Pre-Revolutionary Virginia." *WMQ* 3rd. Ser., 49 (October): 652–74.

Komarovsky, Mirriam. 1967. *Blue-Collar Marriage*. New York: Vintage.

Komlos, John. 1987. "The Height and Weight of West Point Cadets: Dietary Change in Antebellum America." *JEH* 47 (December): 897–927.

———, ed. 1994. *Stature, Living Standard, and Economic Development: Essays in Anthropometric History*. Chicago: University of Chicago Press.

———. 1995. *The Biological Standard of Living in Europe and America, 1700–1900*. Brookfield, VT: Ashgate

———. 1998. "Shrinking in a Growing Economy: The Mystery of Physical Stature During the Industrial Revolution." *JEH* 58 (September): 779–802.

Komlos, John, and Benjamin E. Lauderdale. 2007. "Underperformance in Affluence: The Remarkable Relative Decline in U.S. Heights in the Second Half of the 20th Century." *Social Science Quarterly* 88 (June): 283–305.

Kornblum, William. 1974. *Blue Collar Community*. Chicago: University of Chicago Press.

Kornbluth, Mark Lawrence. 2000. *Why America Stopped Voting: The Decline of Participatory Democracy and the Emergence of Modern American Politics*. New York: New York University Press.

Kosmin, Barry A., and Ariela Keysar. 2009. "American Religious Identification Survey." Summary Report, Hartford, CT: Trinity College, March. http://www.americanreligionsurvey-aris.org.

Köszegi, Botond, and Matthew Rabin. 2008. "Choices, Situations, and Happiness." *Journal of Public Economics* 92:1821–32.

Kotchemidova, Christina. 2005. "From Good Cheer to 'Drive-By Smiling': A Social History of Cheerfulness." *JSH* 39 (Fall): 5–37.

Kramarow, Ellen A. 1995. "The Elderly Who Live Alone in the United States: Historical Perspectives on Household Change." *DEM* 32 (August): 335–52.

Krieger, Nancy, David H. Rehkopf, Jarvis T. Chen, Pamela D. Waterman, Enrico Marcelli, and Malinda Kennedy. 2008. "The Fall and Rise of US Inequities in Premature Mortality: 1960–2002." *PLoS Medicine* 5 (February): e46.

Krueger, Dirk, and Fabrizio Perri. 2002. "Does Income Inequality Lead to Consumption Inequality?: Evidence and Theory." Working paper 9202. Cambridge, MA: NBER.

Kubey, Robert and Mihaly Csikszentmihalyi. 1990. *Television and the Quality of Life: How Viewing Shapes Everyday Experience*. Hillsdale, NJ: Lawrence Erlbaum.

Kulik, Gary. 1985. "Dams, Fish, and Farmers: Defense of Public Rights in Eighteenth-Century Rhode Island." In Hahn and Prude 1985, 25–50.

Kulikoff, Allan. 1989. "The Transition to Capitalism in Rural America." *WMQ* 3rd Ser., 46 (January): 120–44.

———. 2000. *From British Peasants to Colonial American Farmers*. Chapel Hill: University of North Carolina Press.

Kushner, Howard I. 1984. "Immigrant Suicide in the United States: Toward A Psycho-Social History." *JSH* 18(Fall): 3–28.

———. 1989. *Self-Destruction in the Promised Land: A Psychocultural Biology of American Suicide*. New Brunswick, NJ: Rutgers University Press.

———. 1993. "Suicide, Gender, and the Fear of Modernity in Nineteenth-Century Medical and Social Thought." *JSH* 26 (Spring): 461–90.

Laband, David N., and Deborah Hendry Heinbuch. 1987. *Blue Laws: The History, Economics, and Politics of Sunday-Closing Laws*. Lexington, MA: Lexington Books.

Lacey, Barbara E. 1988. "The World of Hannah Heaton: The Autobiography of an Eighteenth-Century Connecticut Farm Woman." *WMQ* 3rd Ser., 45 (April): 280–304.

———. 1991. "Gender, Piety, and Secularization in Connecticut Religion." *JSH* 24 (Summer): 799–821.

Ladd, Everett Carll. 1999. *The Ladd Report*. New York: Free Press.

———, and Karlyn Bowman. 1998. *Attitudes Toward Economic Inequality*. Washington DC: American Enterprise Institute.

Laird, Pamela Walker. 1998. *Advertising Progress: American Business and the Rise of Consumer Marketing*. Baltimore: Johns Hopkins University Press.

Lakdawalla, Darius, Jay Bhattacharya, and Dana Goldman. 2001. "Are the Young Becoming More Disabled?" Working paper 8247. Cambridge, MA: NBER.

Lamont, Michèle, and Virág Molnár. 2001. "How Blacks Use Consumption to Shape their Collective Identity: Evidence from Marketing Specialists." *Journal of Consumer Culture* 1 (1): 31–45.

Lamoreaux, Naomi R. 2003. "Rethinking the Transition to Capitalism in the Early American Northeast." *JAH* 90 (September): 437–61.

Landale, Nancy E., and Avery Guest. 1986. "Ideology and Sexuality Among Victorian Women." *SSH* 10 (Summer): 147–70.

Lands, LeeAnn. 2008. "Be a Patriot, Buy a Home: Re-Imagining Home Owners and Home Ownership in Early 20th Century Atlanta." *JSH* 41 (Summer): 943–66.

Lane, Robert E. 1965. "The Politics of Consensus in an Age of Affluence." *American Political Science Review* 59 (December): 874–95.

———. 1966. "The Decline of Politics and Ideology in a Knowledgeable Society." *ASR* 31 (October): 649–62.

———. 2000. *The Loss of Happiness in Market Democracies*. New Haven, CT: Yale University Press.

Lane, Roger. 1979. *Violent Death in the City: Suicide, Accident, and Murder in Nineteenth-Century Philadelphia*. Cambridge, MA: Harvard University Press.

———. 1986. *Roots of Violence in Black Philadelphia*. Cambridge, MA: Harvard University Press.

———. 1989. "On the Social Meaning of Homicide Trends in the United States, 1850–1875." In Gurr 1989, 55–79.

———. 1997. *Murder in America: A History*. Columbus, OH: Columbus University Press.

Lansing, K. J. 2005. "Spendthrift Nation." Federal Reserve Bank of San Francisco Economic Letter No. 2005-30. http://www.frbsf.org/publications/economics/letter/2005/el2005-30.html.

Lantz, Herman R., Margaret Britton, Raymond Schmitt, and Eloise C. Snyder. 1968. "Pre-Industrial Patterns in the Colonial Family in America: A Content Analysis of Colonial Magazines." *ASR* 33 (June): 413–26.

Lareau, Annette. 2002. "Invisible Inequality: Social Class and Childrearing in Black Families and White Families." *ASR* 67 (October): 747–76.

———. 2003. *Unequal Childhoods: Class, Race, and Family Life*. Berkeley: University of California Press.

Larkin, Jack. 1988. *The Reshaping of Everyday Life, 1790–1840*. New York: Harper & Row.

———. 1993. "Rural Life in the North." In Cayton, Gorn, and Williams 1993, 1209–21.

Larson, Carl F. W. 1987. "A History of the Automobile in North Dakota to 1911." *North Dakota History* 54 (4): 3–24.

Larson, John Lauritz. 1993. "Business Culture." In Cayton, Gorn, and Williams 1993, 347–58.

———. 1993. "Transportation and Mobility." In Cayton, Gorn, and Williams 1993, 2337–48.

Larson, O. F., and T.B. Jones. 1976. "The Unpublished Data from Roosevelt's Commission on Country Life." *Agricultural History* 50 (October): 583–99.

Lasch, Christopher. 1977. *Haven in a Heartless World: The Family Besieged*. New York: Basic Books.

———. 1993. "The Culture of Consumption." In Cayton, Gorn, and Williams 1993, 1381–90.

Laslett, Barbara. 1973. "The Family as a Public and Private Institution." *Journal of Marriage and the Family* 35 (August): 480–92.

Lassonde, Stephen. 1996. "Learning and Earning: Schooling, Juvenile Employment, and the Early Life Course in Late Nineteenth-Century New Haven." *JSH* 29 (Summer): 839–70.

Latner, Richard. 2008. "The Long and Short of Salem Witchcraft: Chronology and Collective Violence in 1692." *JSH* 42 (Fall): 137–56.

Laumann, Edward, John H. Gagnon, Robert T. Michael, and Stuart Michaels. 1994. *The Social Organization of Sexuality: Sexual Practices in the United States*. Chicago: University of Chicago Press.

Laurie, Bruce. 1980. *Working People of Philadelphia, 1800–1850*. Philadelphia: Temple University Press.

Lawson-Peebles, Robert. 1993. "America as Interpreted by Foreign Observers." In Cayton, Gorn, and Williams 1993, 269–79.

Layard, Richard. 2005. *Happiness: Lessons from a New Science*. New York: Penguin.

Leach, William R. 1984. "Transformations in a Culture of Consumption: Women and Department Stores, 1890–1925." *JAH* 71 (September): 319–42.

——. 1993. *Land of Desire: Merchants, Power, and the Rise of a New American Culture*. New York: Random House.

Lears, T. J. Jackson. 1981. *No Place of Grace: Antimodernism and the Transformation of American Culture*. New York: Pantheon.

——. 1983. "From Salvation to Self-Realization: Advertising and the Therapeutic Roots of the Consumer Culture, 1880–1930." In *The Culture of Consumption*, Richard Wrightman Fox and T. J. Jackson Lears, 3–38. New York: Pantheon.

——. 1989. "Beyond Veblen." In Bronner 1989, 73–98.

——. 1994. *Fables of Abundance: A Cultural History of Advertising in America*. New York: Basic Books.

Lebergott, Stanley. 1971. "Changes in Unemployment 1800–1960." In *The Reinterpretation of American Economic History*, ed. Robert W. Fogel and Stanley L. Engerman, 73–83. Rev. ed. New York: Harper & Row.

——. 1976. *The American Economy: Income, Wealth, and Want*. Princeton, NJ: Princeton University Press.

——. 1984. *The Americans: An Economic Record*. New York: W. W. Norton.

——. 1993. *Pursuing Happiness: American Consumers in the Twentieth Century*. Princeton, NJ: Princeton University Press.

——. 1996. *Consumer Expenditures: New Measures and Old Motives*. Princeton, NJ: Princeton University Press.

Lederman, Gary. 1996. *The Sacred Remains: American Attitudes Toward Death, 1799–1883*. New Haven, CT: Yale University Press.

Lee, Barrett A., R.S. Oropesa, Barbara J. Metch, and Avery M. Guest. 1984. "Testing the Decline-of-Community Thesis: Neighborhood Organizations in Seattle, 1929 and 1979." *AJS* 89 (March): 1161–88.

Lee, Shayne. 2007. "Prosperity Theology: T. O. Jakes and the Gospel of the Almighty Dollar." *Cross Currents* 57 (Summer): 227–36.

Lefcourt, Herbert M. 1992. "Durability and Impact of the Locus of Control Construct." *Psychological Bulletin* 112 (3): 411–14.

Lehman, Darrin R., Chi-yue Chiu, and Mark Schaller. 2004. "Psychology and Culture." *Annual Review of Psychology* 55 (February): 689–714.

Leibowitz, Arleen, and Jacob Alex Klerman. 1995. "Explaining Changes in Married Mothers' Employment Over Time." *DEM* 32 (August):365–78.

Lemon, James T. 1976. *The Best Poor Man's Country: A Geographical Study of Early Southeastern Pennsylvania*. New York: Norton.

——. 1980. "Comment on James A. Henretta's 'Families and Farms: Mentalité in Pre-Industrial America'." *WMQ* 3rd Ser., 37 (October): 688–96.

——. 1984. "Spatial Order: Households in Local Communities and Regions." In Greene and Pole 1984, 86–122.

Lender, Mark Edward, and James Kirby Martin. 1987. *Drinking in America*. Rev. ed. New York: Free Press.

Levenstein, Harvey A. 1988. *Revolution at the Table: The Transformation of the American Diet*. New York: Oxford University Press.

Levi, Margaret, and Laura Stoker. 2000. "Political Trust and Trustworthiness." *Annual Review of Political Science* 3:475–507.

Levine, Daniel. 1988. *Poverty and Society: The Growth of the American Welfare State in International Comparison*. New Brunswick, NJ: Rutgers University Press.

Levine, Larry W. 1988. *Highbrow, Lowbrow: The Emergence of Cultural Hierarchy in America*. Cambridge, MA: Harvard University Press.

Levinson, David M. and Ajay Kumar. 1994. "The Rational Locator: Why Travel Times Have Remained Stable." *Journal of the American Planning Association* 60 (Summer): 319–33.

Levitt, Peggy. 2004. "Salsa and Ketchup: Transnational Migrants Straddle Two Worlds." *Contexts* 3 (Spring): 20–26.

Levy, Barry. 1982. "The Birth of the 'Modern Family' in Early America: Quaker and Anglican Families in the Delaware Valley, Pennsylvania, 1681–1750." In Zuckerman 1982, 26–54.

Levy, Frank. 1998. *The New Dollars and Dreams*. New York: Russell Sage Foundation.

Lewis, Jan. 1987. "The Republican Wife: Virtue and Seduction in the Early Republic." *WMQ* 3rd Ser., 44 (October): 689–721.

———. 1989. "Mother's Love: The Construction of an Emotion in Nineteenth-Century America." In Barnes and Stearns 1989, 209–29.

Lewis, Oscar. 1965. "Further Observations on the Folk-Urban Continuum and Urbanization." In *The Study of Urbanization*, ed. P. M. Hauser and L. F. Schnore, 491–503. New York: Wiley.

Licht, Walter. 1992. *Getting Work: Philadelphia, 1840–1950*. Cambridge, MA: Harvard University Press.

———. 1995. *Industrializing America: The Nineteenth Century*. Baltimore: Johns Hopkins University Press.

Lichter, Daniel T., Diane K. McLaughlin, George Kephart, and David J. Landry. 1992. "Race and the Retreat From Marriage: A Shortage of Marriageable Men?" *ASR* 57 (December): 781–99.

Lieberman, Robert C. 1995. "Race, Institutions, and the Administration of Social Policy." *SSH* 19 (Winter): 511–42.

Lieberson, Stanley. 1963. *Ethnic Patterns in American Cities*. New York: Free Press.

Lieberson, Stanley, Guy Dalto, and Mary Ellen Johnston. 1975. "The Course of Mother-Tongue Diversity in Nations." *AJS* 81 (July): 34–61.

Lieberson, Stanley, and Mary Waters. 1988. *From Many Strands: Ethnic and Racial Groups in Contemporary America*. New York: Russell Sage Foundation.

Light, Ivan. 1977. "The Ethnic Vice Industry, 1880–1944." *ASR* 42 (June): 464–79.

Light, Paul C. 2000. "Government's Greatest Achievements of the Past Half Century." *Reform Watch* 2, Washington DC: Brookings Institution.

Liker, Jeffrey K., and Glen H. Elder Jr. 1983. "Economic Hardship and Marital Relations in the 1930s." *ASR* 48 (June): 343–59.

Lindberg, Laura Duberstein, Scott Boggess, Laura Porter, and Sean Williams. 2000. *Teen Risk-Taking: A Statistical Portrait*. Washington DC: The Urban Institute.

Lindert, Peter H. 2000. "Three Centuries of Inequality in Britain and America."

Handbook of Income Distribution. Vol. 1, ed. Anthony B. Atkinson and Francois Bourguignon, 170–216. New York: Elsevier.

Lindman, Janet Moore. 1997. "Wise Virgins and Pious Mothers: Spiritual Community Among Baptist Women of the Delaware Valley." In Eldgridge 1997, 127–44.

Lindsey, Brink. 2007. *The Age of Abundance: How Prosperity Transformed America's Politics and Culture*. New York: HarperCollins.

Linz, Werner Mark. 1996. "A Religious Country Reflected in its Publishing Industry." *Logos* 7 (1): 6–11.

Lipset, Seymour Martin. 1963. *The First New Nation: The United States in Historical and Comparative Perspective*. Repr., New York: Norton, 1979.

———. 1995. "Malaise and Resiliency in America." *Journal of Democracy* 6 (July):4–18.

———. 1996. *American Exceptionalism: A Two-Edged Sword*. New York: W. W. Norton.

Lipset, Seymour Martin, and William Schneider. 1983. *The Confidence Gap*. New York: The Free Press.

Lipset, Seymour Martin, and Gary Marks. 2000. *It Didn't Happen Here: Why Socialism Failed in the United States*. New York: Norton.

Liska, Allen E. and Baccaglini, William. 1990. "Feeling Safe by Comparison: Crime in the Newspapers." *Social Problems* 37 (3): 360–74.

List, John A., and Jason F. Shrogen. 1998. "The Deadweight Loss of Christmas: Comment." *AER* 88 (December): 1350–55.

Literary Digest. 1912. "Fallacies as to the High Cost of Living." 44 (February 24): 400–2.

Lockridge, Kenneth A. 1970. *A New England Town: The First Hundred Years*. New York: W. W. Norton.

———. 1985. Afterward to *A New England Town: The First Hundred Years*. Expanded ed. New York: W. W. Norton.

———. 1997. "Colonial Self-Fashioning: Paradoxes and Pathologies in the Construction of Genteel Identity in Eighteenth-Century America." In Hoffman, Sobel, and Teute 1997, 274–339.

Loewen, James W. 1995. *Lies My Teacher Told Me: Everything Your American History Textbook Got Wrong*. New York: Simon & Schuster.

Loewenstein, George. 2001. "The Creative Destruction of Decision Research." *JCR* 28 (December): 499–505.

Loewenstein, George, Ted O'Donoghue, and Matthew Rabin. 2003. "Projection Bias in Predicting Future Utility." *Quarterly Journal of Economics* 118 (November): 1209–48.

Lofland, Lyn. 1989. "Social Life in the Public Realm: A Review." *Journal of Contemporary Ethnography* 17 (January): 453–82.

Logan, John R., and Harvey L. Molotch. 1987. *Urban Fortunes: The Political Economy of Place*. Berkeley: University of California Press.

Logan, John R., Brian J. Stults, and Reynolds Farley. 2004. "Segregation of Minorities in the Metropolis: Two Decades of Change." *DEM* 41 (February): 1–22.

Long, Larry. 1988. *Migration and Residential Mobility in the United States*. New York: Russell Sage Foundation.

———. 1991. "Residential Mobility Differences Among Developed Countries." *International Regional Science Review* 14 (2): 133–47.

———. 1992. "International Perspectives on the Residential Mobility of America's Children." *Journal of Marriage and the Family* 54 (November): 861–69.

Lovell, Margaretta M. 1998. "Copley and the Case of the Blue Dress." *Yale Journal of Criticism* 11 (Spring): 53–68.

Low, Setha M. 2001. "The Edge and the Center: Gated Communities and the Discourse of Urban Fear." *American Anthropologist* 103 (March): 45–58.

Lowenthal, Leo. 1944 "Biographies in Popular Magazines." Repr. in *American Social Patterns*, ed. William Petersen, 63–118. Garden City, NY: Doubleday Anchor, 1956.

Lucas, Richard E. 2005. "Time Does Not Heal All Wounds. A Longitudinal Study of Reaction and Adaptation to Divorce." *Psychological Science* 16 (12): 945–50.

Lucas, Richard E., and Andrew E. Clark. 2006. "Do People Really Adapt to Marriage?" *Journal of Happiness Studies* 7 (November): 405–26.

Lucas, Richard E., Andrew E. Clark, Yannis Georgellis, and Ed Diener. 2004. "Unemployment Alters the Set Point for Life Satisfaction." *Psychological Science* 15 (1): 8–13.

Luchins, Abraham S. 1993. "Social Control Doctrines of Mental Illness and the Medical Profession in Nineteenth-Century America." *Journal of the History of the Behavioral Sciences* 29 (January): 29–47.

Luker, Kristin. 1984. *Abortion and the Politics of Motherhood*. Berkeley: University of California Press.

Lukes, Steven. 1971. "The Meanings of 'Individualism.'" *Journal of the History of Ideas* 32 (January-March): 45–66.

Luloff, A. E., and R. S. Krannich, eds. 2002. *Persistence and Change in Rural Communities: A 50-Year Follow-Up to Six Classic Studies*. New York: CABI Publishing.

Lundberg, George A., Mirra Komarovsky, and Mary Alice McInerny. 1934. *Leisure: A Suburban Study*. New York: Columbia University Press.

Lunt, Peter. 1995. "Psychological Approaches to Consumption." In Miller 1995, 238–63.

Luria, Daniel D. 1976. "Wealth, Capital, and Power: The Social Meaning of Home Ownership." *JIH* 7 (Autumn): 261–82.

Lynd, Robert S. 1933. "The People as Consumers." In *President's Research Committee on Social Trends, Recent Social Trends in the United States*. Vol. 1, 857–911. New York: McGraw-Hill.

Lynd, Robert S., and Helen Merrill Lynd. 1928. *Middletown*. New York: Harcourt Brace.

———. 1937. *Middletown in Transition: A Study in Cultural Conflicts*. New York : Harcourt, Brace and World.

Lyons, Clare A. 2006. *Sex Among the Rabble: An Intimate History of Gender & Power in the Age of Revolution, Philadelphia, 1730–1830*. Chapel Hill: University of North Carolina Press.

Lyons, Linda. 2002. "Kids and Divorce." Gallup Tuesday Briefing, March 5. http://www.gallup.com/poll/5419/Kids-Divorce.aspx.

Lyons, William, and Robert Alexander. 2000. "A Tale of Two Electorates: Generational Replacement and the Decline of Voting in Presidential Elections." *Journal of Politics* 62 (November): 1014–34.

Lystad, Mary. 1984. *At Home in America: As Seen Through Its Books for Children*. Cambridge, MA: Shenkman Publishing Co.

Lystra, Karen. 1989. *Searching the Heart: Women, Men, and Romantic Love in Nineteenth-Century America*. New York: Oxford University Press.

MacCulloch, Diarmaid. 2003. *The Reformation*. New York: Viking.

MacLeish, Kenneth, and Kimball Young. 1942. "Culture of a Contemporary Rural Community: Landaff, New Hampshire." *Rural Life Studies* 3. Washington DC: USDA Bureau of Agricultural Economics.

Madison, James H. 1986. "Reformers and the Rural Church, 1900–1950." *JAH* 73 (December): 645–68.

Madsen, Richard. 1991. "Contentless Consensus." In *America at Century's End*, ed. Alan Wolfe, 440–61. Berkeley: University of California Press.

———. 2009. "The Archipelago of Faith: Religious Individualism and Faith Community in America Today." *AJS* 114 (March): 1263–1301.

Magnússon, Sigurdur Gylfi. 2003. "The Singularization of History: Social History and Microhistory within the Postmodern State of Knowledge." *JSH* 36 (Spring): 701–35.

Maier, Pauline. 1997. *American Scripture: Making the Declaration of Independence*. New York: Vintage.

Maimon, David, and Danielle C. Kuhl. 2008. "Social Control and Youth Suicidality: Situating Durkheim's Ideas in a Multilevel Framework." *ASR* 73 (December): 921–43.

Main, Gloria L. 1988. "The Standard of Living in Southern New England, 1640–1773." *WMQ* 3rd Ser., 45 (January): 124–34.

———. 2001. *Peoples of a Spacious Land: Families and Cultures in Colonial New England*. Cambridge, MA: Harvard University Press.

———. 2006. "Rocking the Cradle: Downsizing the New England Family." *JIH* 37 (Summer): 35–58.

Main, Gloria L., and Jackson T. Main. 1999. "The Red Queen in New England?" *WMQ* 3rd Ser., 56 (January): 121–54.

Main, Jackson T. 1971. "Note: Trends in Wealth Concentration Before 1860." *JEH* 31 (June): 445–47.

Maki, Dean M. 2000. "The Growth of Consumer Credit and the Household Debt Service Burden." Dean M. Maki Finance and Economics Discussion Series 2000–12, Board of Governors of the Federal Reserve System. http://www.federalreserve.gov/pubs/feds/2000/200012/200012pap.pdf.

Maloney, Thomas N., and Scott Alan Carson. 2008. "Living Standards in Black and White: Evidence from the Heights of Ohio Prison Inmates, 1829–1913." *Economics & Human Biology* 6 (July): 237–51.

Mandell, Lewis. 1990. *The Credit Card Industry: A History*. Boston: Twayne.

Mann, Bruce H. 1980. "Rationality, Legal Change, and Community in Connecticut, 1690–1760." *Law and Society Review* 14:187–221.

——. 2002. *Republic of Debtors: Bankruptcy in the Age of American Independence*. Cambridge, MA: Harvard University Press.

Mannion, Caolin, and Terersa Brannick. 1995. "Materialism and Its Measurement." *Irish Business and Administrative Research* 16:1–16.

Mansbridge, Jane. 1997. "Social and Cultural Causes of Dissatisfaction with U.S. Government." In Nye, Zelikow, and King 1997, 133–54.

Manuel, Frank, and Fritzie Manuel. 1979. *Utopian Thought in the Modern Western World*. Cambridge, MA: Harvard University Press.

Marchand, Roland. 1985. *Advertising the American Dream: Making Way for Modernity, 1920–1940*. Berkeley: University of California Press.

Mare, Robert D. 1991. "Five Decades of Educational Assortative Mating." *ASR* 56 (February): 15–32.

Margo, Robert A. 1992. "Wages and Prices during the Antebellum Period: A Survey and New Evidence." In Gallman and Wallis 1992, 173–216.

——. 1999. "The History of Wage Inequality in America, 1820 to 1970." Working Paper 286, Jerome Levy Institute of Bard College.

Morin, Rich, and Paul Taylor. 2009. "Luxury or Necessity? The Public Makes a U-Turn." Pew Research Center, on-line, http://pewsocialtrends.org/pubs/733/luxury-necessity-recession-era-reevaluations.

Marks, Stephen R. 1994. "Intimacy in the Public Realm: The Case of Coworkers." *SF* 72 (March): 843–58.

Markus, Hazel Rose, and Shinobu Kitayama. 1991. "Culture and the Self: Implications for Cognition, Emotion, and Motivation." *Psychological Review* 98: 224–53.

——. 2003. "Culture, Self, and the Reality of the Social." *Psychological Inquiry* 14 (3–4): 277–83.

Marsh, Margaret. 1988. "Suburban Men and Masculine Domesticity, 1870–1915." *AQ* 40 (June): 165–86.

——. 1989. "From Separation to Togetherness: The Social Construction of Domestic Space in American Suburbs,1840–1915." *JAH* 76 (September): 506–27.

Martin, Ann Smart. 1993. "Makers, Buyers, and Users: Consumerism as a Material Culture Framework." *Winterthur Portfolio* 28 (Summer): 141–57.

——. 1995. "Common People and the Local Store: Consumerism in the Rural Virginia Backcountry." In *Common People and Their Material World: Free Men and Women in the Chesapeake, 1700–1830*, ed. David Harvey and Gregory Brown, 39–53. Williamsburg, VA: Colonial Williamsburg Foundation.

Martin, John Levi. 1996. "Structuring the Sexual Revolution." *Theory and Society* 25 (February): 105–51.

——. 1999. "The Myth of the Consumption-Oriented Economy and the Rise of the Desiring Subject." *Theory and Society* 28: 425–53.

Martin, Scott C. 1995. *Killing Time: Leisure and Culture in Southwestern Pennsylvania, 1800–1850*. Pittsburgh: University of Pittsburgh Press.

Martin, Steven P. 2006. "Trends in Marital Dissolution by Women's Education in the United States." *Demographic Research* 15 (December): 537–60. http://www.demographic-research.org/Volumes/V0l15/20/.

Marty, Martin E. 1982. "The Idea of Progress in Twentieth-Century Theology." In Almond, Chodorow, and Pearce 1982, 482–500.

———. 1984. *Pilgrims in Their Own Land: 500 Years of Religion in America*. New York: Penguin.

Marx, Leo. 1964. *The Machine in the Garden; Technology and the Pastoral Ideal in America*. New York : Oxford University Press.

Massey, Douglas S., and Nancy Denton. 1993. *American Apartheid: Segregation and the Making of the Underclass*. Cambridge, MA: Harvard University Press.

Matt, Susan J. 1998. "Frocks, Finery, and Feelings: Rural and Urban Women's Envy, 1890–1930." In Stearns and Lewis 1998, 377–97.

———. 2002. "Children's Envy and the Emergence of the Modern Consumer Ethic." *JSH* 36 (Winter): 283–302.

———. 2003. *Keeping up with the Joneses: Envy in American Consumer Society, 1890–1930*. Philadelphia: University of Pennsylvania Press.

———. 2007. "You Can't Go Home Again: Homesickness and Nostalgia in U.S. History." *JAH* 94 (September): 469–97.

Matthaei, Julie A. 1982. *An Economic History of Women in America*. New York: Schocken Books.

Matthews, Glenna. 1987. *"Just a Housewife": The Rise and Fall of Domesticity in America*. New York: Oxford University Press.

May, Dean L. 1994. *Three Frontiers: Family, Land, and Society in the American West, 1850–1970*. New York: Cambridge University Press.

May, Elaine Tyler. 1978. "The Pressure to Provide: Class, Consumerism, and Divorce in Urban America, 1880–1920." *JSH* 12 (Winter): 179–93.

———. 1980. *Great Expectations: Marriage and Divorce in Post-Victorian America*. Chicago: University of Chicago Press.

Mayfield, Loomis. 1993. "Voting Fraud in Early Twentieth-Century Pittsburgh." *JIH* 24 (Summer): 59–84.

McBee, Randy D. 1999. "'He Likes Women More than He Likes Drink and That Is Quite Unusual': Working-Class Social Clubs, Male Culture, and Heterosocial Relations in the United States, 1920s–1930s." *Gender & History* 11 (1): 84–112.

McCall, Laura, and Donald Yacovone, eds. 1998. *A Shared Experience: Men, Women, and the History of Gender*. New York: New York University Press.

McCall, Patricia L., and Kenneth C. Land. 1994. "Trends in White Male Adolescent, Young-Adult, and Elderly Suicide: Are There Common Underlying Structural Factors?" *Social Science Research* 23 (March): 57–81.

McCandless, Peter. 1996. *Moonlight, Magnolias, & Madness: Insanity in South Carolina from the Colonial Period to the Progressive Era*. Chapel Hill: University of North Carolina Press.

McClenahan, Bessie Averne. 1929. *The Changing Urban Neighborhood, from Neighbor to Nigh-Dweller*. Social Science Series, 1. Los Angeles: University of Southern California Studies.

McClintock, Megan. 1996. "Civil War Pensions and the Reconstruction of Families." *JAH* 83 (September): 456–80.

McCloskey, Deirdre N. 1990. *If You're So Smart: The Narrative of Economic Expertise*. Chicago: University of Chicago Press.

———. 1996. "The Economics of Choice." In *Economics and the Historian*, Thomas G. Rawski, Susan B. Carter, Jon S. Cohen, Stephen Cullenberg, Peter H. Lindert, Donald N. McCloskey, Hugh Rockoff, and Richard Sutch, 122–58. Berkeley: University of California Press.

McCormick, Richard L. 1979. "The Party Period and Public Policy: An Exploratory Hypothesis." *JAH* 66 (September): 279–98.

———. 1990. "Public Life in Industrial America, 1877–1917." In Foner 1990, 93–117.

McCracken, Grant. 1990. *Culture and Consumption*. Bloomington: Indiana University Press.

McCrae, Robert R., and Antonio Terracciano. 2006. "National Character and Personality." *Current Directions in Psychological Science* 15 (4): 156–61.

McCrossen, Alexis. 2000. *Holy Day, Holiday: The American Sunday*. Ithaca, NY: Cornell University Press.

McDaniel, Patricia A. 2003. *Shrinking Violets and Caspar Milquetoasts: Shyness, Power and Intimacy in the United Sates, 1950–1995*. New York: New York University Press.

McDermott, Stacy Pratt. 2002. "Love and Justice: Marital Dissolution in Antebellum Illinois, from the Casebook of A. Lincoln, Divorce Lawyer." *Illinois Heritage* 5 (6): 6–8, 16.

McDonagh, Edward C. 1950. "Television and the Family." *Sociology and Social Research* 35 (November): 113–22.

McDonald, Michael P., and Samuel Popkin. 2001. "The Myth of the Vanishing Voter." *American Political Science Review* 95 (December): 963–74.

McDonnell, Michael A. 1998. "Popular Mobilization and Political Culture in Revolutionary Virginia: The Failure of the Minutemen and the Revolution from Below." *JAH* 85 (December): 946–81.

McDougall, Walter A. 1995. "Whose History? Whose Standards?" *Commentary* 99 (May): 36–44.

McFadden, Daniel. 2001. "Economic Choices." *AER* 91 (June): 351–78.

———. 2006. "Free Markets and Fettered Consumers." *AER* 96 (March): 5–29.

McGarry, Kathleen, and Robert F Schoeni. 2000. "Social Security, Economic Growth, and the Rise in Elderly Widows' Independence in the Twentieth Century." *DEM* 37 (2): 221–36.

McGee, Micki. 2005. *Self-Help, Inc.: Makeover Culture in American Life*. New York: Oxford University Press.

McGerr, Michael. 1991. "The Price of the 'New Transnational History.'" *AHR* 96 (October): 1056–67.

McGovern, Charles. 1998. "Consumption and Citizenship in the United States." In *Getting and Spending: European and American Consumers in the Twentieth Century*, ed. Susan Strasser, Charles McGovern, and Matthias Judt, 37–58. Cambridge: Cambridge University Press.

———. 2004. "Consumption." In *A Companion to 20th-Century America*, ed. Stephen J. Whitfield, 336–57. Malden, MA: Blackwell.

McLanahan, Sara S. 1994. "The Consequences of Single Motherhood." *American Prospect* 18 (Summer): 48–58.

———. 2002. "Life without Father: What Happens to the Children?" *Contexts* 1 (Spring): 35–44.

———. 2004. "Diverging Destinies: How Children Are Faring Under the Second Demographic Transition." *DEM* 41 (November): 607–27.

McLanahan, Sara S., and Gary Sandefur. 1994. *Growing up with a Single Parent: What Hurts, What Helps.* Cambridge, MA: Harvard University Press.

McMahon, Darrin M. 2004. "From the Happiness of Virtue to the Virtue of Happiness: 400 B.C.–A.D. 1780." *Daedalus* 133 (Spring): 5–18.

McMahon, Sarah. 1985. "A Comfortable Subsistence: The Changing Composition of Diet in Rural New England, 1620–1840." *WMQ* 3rd Ser., 2 (January): 26–65.

McMurrer, Daniel P., and Amy B. Chasanov. 1995. "Trends in Unemployment Insurance Benefits." *Monthly Labor Review* 118 (September): 30–39. ·

McMurry, Sally. 1988. *Families and Farmhouses in Nineteenth-Century America: Vernacular Design and Social Change.* New York: Oxford University Press.

McPherson, Miller, Lynn Smith-Lovin, and Matthew E. Brashears. 2006. "Social Isolation in America: Changes in Core Discussion Networks over Two Decades." *ASR* 71 (June): 353–75.

McWilliams, James E. 2006. "Marketing Middle-Class Morality." *Reviews in American History* 34 (2): 162–68.

Mead, Deirdre. 2003. "The Community's Pulse." *The Responsive Community* 13 (Summer): 78–79.

Meeker, E. 1972. "The Improving Health of the United States, 1850–1915." *Explorations in Economic History* 9 (Summer): 353–73.

Mellon, James. 2001. *Bullwhip Days: The Slaves Remember.* New York: Grove.

Melosi, Martin C. 2000. *The Sanitary City: Urban Infrastructure in America from Colonial Times to the Present.* Baltimore: Johns Hopkins University Press.

Melvoin, Richard I. 1984. "Communalism in Frontier Deerfield." In *Early Settlement in the Connecticut Valley*, ed. Stephen C. Innes, Richard I. Melvoin, and Peter A. Thomas, 36–61. Deerfield, MA: Historic Deerfield, Inc.

Menagahan, Elizabeth G. 1989. "Role Changes and Psychological Well-Being." *SF* 67 (March): 693–714.

Menard, Scott, and David Huizinga. 1989. "Age, Period, and Cohort Size Effects on Self-Reported Alcohol, Marijuana, and Polydrug Use: Results from the National Youth Survey." *Social Science Research* 18 (2): 174–94.

Merish, Lori. 1993. "'The Hand of Refined Taste' in the Frontier Landscape: Caroline Kirkland's 'A New Home, Who'll Follow?' and the Feminization of American Consumerism." *AQ* 45 (December): 485–523.

———. 1996. "Sentimental Consumption: Harriet Beecher Stowe and the Aesthetics of Middle-Class Ownership." *American Literary History* 8 (Spring): 1–33.

Merrill, Michael. 1995. "Putting 'Capitalism' in its Place: A Review of Recent Literature." *WMQ* 3rd Ser., 52 (April): 315–26.

Mesquita, Batja, Nico H. Frijda, and Klaus R. Scherer. 1997. "Culture and Emotion." In *Handbook of Cross-Cultural Psychology.* Vol. 2, *Basic Processes and Human*

Development, ed. John W. Berry, Pierre R. Dasen, and T. S. Sarawathi, 255–97. 2nd ed. Boston: Allyn and Bacon.

Mettler, Suzanne. 2002. "Bringing the State Back in to Civic Engagement: Policy Feedback Effects of the G.I. Bill for World War II Veterans." *American Political Science Review* 96 (June): 351–65.

Meyerowitz, Joanne. 1987. "Women and Migration: Autonomous Female Migrants to Chicago, 1880–1930." *JUH* 13 (February): 147–68.

———. 1988. *Women Adrift: Independent Wage Earners in Chicago, 1880–1930*. Chicago: University of Chicago Press.

———. 1993. "Beyond the Feminine Mystique: A Reassessment of Postwar Mass Culture, 1946–1958." *JAH* 79 (March): 1455–82.

Meyrowitz, Joshua. 1985. *No Sense of Place: The Impact of Electronic Media on Social Behavior*. New York: Oxford University Press.

Mezulis, Amy H., Lyn Y. Abramson, Janet S. Hyde, and Benjamin L. Hankin. 2004. "Is There a Universal Positivity Bias in Attributions? A Meta-Analytic Review of Individual, Developmental, and Cultural Differences in the Self-Serving Attributional Bias." *Psychological Bulletin* 130 (September): 711–47.

Michael, Robert T., Victor R. Fuchs, and Sharon R. Scott. 1980. "Changes in the Propensity to Live Alone, 1950-1976." *DEM* 17 (February 1980): 39–56.

Michelson, William M. 1977. *Environmental Choice, Human Behavior, and Residential Satisfaction*. New York : Oxford University Press.

Miethe, Terance D., Michael Hughes, and David McDowall. 1991. "Social Change and Crime Rates: An Evaluation of Alternative Theoretical Approaches." *SF* 70 (September): 165–85.

Miller, Alan S., and Tomoko Mitamura. 2003. "Are Surveys on Trust Trustworthy?" *Social Psychology Quarterly* 66 (March): 62–70.

Miller, Christopher L., and George R. Hamell. 1986. "A New Perspective on Indian-White Contact: Cultural Symbols and Colonial Trade." *JAH* 73 (September): 311–28.

Miller, Daniel. 1987. *Material Culture and Mass Consumption*. New York: Oxford University Press.

———, ed. 1995. *Acknowledging Consumption: A Review of New Studies*. London: Routledge.

———. 2001. "The Poverty of Morality." *Journal of Consumer Culture* 1 (2): 225–43.

Miller, Jacquelyn C. 1996. "An 'Uncommon Tranquility of Mind': Emotional Self-Control and the Construction of a Middle-Class Identity in Eighteenth-Century Philadelphia." *JSH* 30 (Fall): 129–48.

Miller, Jon D., Eugenie C. Scott, and Shinji Okamoto. 2006. "Public Acceptance of Evolution." *Science* 313 (August 11): 765–66.

Miller, Perry. 1939. *The New England Mind: The Seventeenth Century*. Repr., Cambridge, MA: Harvard University Press, 1954.

Miller, Richard Lawrence. 2004. "What Is Hell to One like Me . . . ?" *American Heritage* 55 (4): 50–54.

Mills, C. Wright. 1959. *The Power Elite*. New York: Oxford University Press.

Mintz, Steven. 1993. "Life Stages." In Cayton, Gorn, and Williams 1993, 2011–22.

———. 2004. *Huck's Raft: A History of American Children*. Cambridge, MA: Harvard University Press.

Mintz, Steven, and Susan Kellogg. 1988. *Domestic Revolutions: A Social History of American Family Life*. New York: Free Press.

Mirola, William A. 1999. "Shorter Hours and the Protestant Sabbath." *SSH* 23 (Fall): 395–433.

Mirowsky, John, and Catherine E. Ross. 2007. "Life Course Trajectories of Perceived Control and Their Relationship to Education." *AJS* 112 (March): 1339–82.

Mittal, Banwari. 1994. "Public Assessment of TV Advertising: Faint Praise and Harsh Criticism." *Journal of Advertising Research* 34 (January–February): 35–53.

Modell, John. 1979. "Changing Risks, Changing Adaptations: American Families in the Nineteenth and Twentieth Centuries." In *Kin and Communities: Families in America*, ed. A. J. Lichtman and J. R. Challenor, 119–44. Washington DC: Smithsonian Institution Press.

———. 1983. "Dating Becomes the Way of American Youth." In *Essays on the Family and Historical Change*, ed. Leslie Page Moch and Gary D. Stark, 91–126. College Station: Texas A & M University Press.

———. 1989. *Into One's Own: From Youth to Adulthood in the United States, 1920–1975*. Berkeley: University of California Press.

Modell, John, Frank F. Furstenberg Jr., and Theodore Hershberg. 1976. "Social Change and Transitions to Adulthood in Historical Perspective." *Journal of Family History* 1 (September): 7–31.

Modell, John, and Tamara K. Hareven. 1973. "Urbanization and the Malleable Household: An Examination of Boarding and Lodging in American Families." *Journal of Marriage and the Family* 35 (August): 467–79.

Moe, Edward O., and Carl C. Taylor. 1942. "Culture of a Contemporary Rural Community: Irwin, Iowa." *Rural Life Studies* 5. Washington DC: USDA: Bureau of Agricultural Economics.

Moehling, Carolyn M. 1999. "State Child Labor Laws and the Decline of Child Labor." *Explorations in Economic History* 36:72–106.

Moffatt, Michael. 1992. "Ethnographic Writing About American Culture." *Annual Review of Anthropology* 21:205–29.

Mokdad, Ali H., Mary K. Serdula, William H. Dietz, et al. 1999. "The Spread of the Obesity Epidemic in the United States, 1991–1998." *Journal of the American Medical Association* 282 (October 27): 1519–22.

Mokyr, Joel. 2000. "Why 'More Work for Mother'? Knowledge and Household Behavior, 1870–1945." *JEH* 60 (March): 1–41.

Molho, Anthony, and Gordon S. Wood, eds. *Imagined Histories: American Historians Interpret the Past*. Princeton, NJ: Princeton University Press.

Moline, Norman T. 1971. "Mobility and the Small Town, 1900–1930: Transportation Change in Oregon, Illinois." Research paper 132. University of Chicago Department of Geography.

Monkkonen, Eric H., ed 1984. *Walking to Work: Tramps in America, 1790–1935*. Lincoln: University of Nebraska Press.

———. 1988. *America Becomes Urban*. Berkeley: University of California Press.

————. 1990. "American State from the Bottom Up: Of Homicides and Courts."
    Law and Society Review 24 (2): 521–31.

————. 2001. *Murder in New York City*. Berkeley: University of California Press.

————. 2005. "Homicide in Los Angeles, 1827–2002." *JIH* 36 (Autumn): 167–83.

————. 2006. "Homicide: Explaining America's Exceptionalism." *AHR* 111 (February): 76–94.

Monti, Daniel J., Colleen Butler, Alexandra Curley, Kirsten Tilney, and Melissa F.
    Weiner. 2003. "Private Lives and Public Worlds: Changes in Americans' Social
    Ties and Civic Attachments in Late-20th Century." *City & Community* 2 (June):
    143–63.

Moore, David W. 2005. "Three in Four Americans Believe in Paranormal." Gallup
    News Service, June 16, http://gallup.com.poll/ poll/16915/Three-Four-
    Americans-Believe-Paranormal.aspx

Moore, Geoffrey H., and Janice Neipert Hedges. 1971. "Trends in Labor and Lei-
    sure." *Monthly Labor Review* 9 (February): 3–11.

Moore, Peter N. 2004. "Family Dynamics and the Great Revival: Religious Con-
    version in the South Carolina Piedmont." *Journal of Southern History* 70 (Febru-
    ary): 35–62.

Moore, R. Laurence. 1994. *Selling God: American Religion in the Marketplace of Cul-
    ture*. New York: Oxford University Press.

————. 2000. "Bible Reading and Nonsectarian Schooling: The Failure of Religious
    Instruction in Nineteenth-Century Public Education." *JAH* 86 (March):
    1581–99.

Moore, Sean T. 2002. "'Justifiable Homicide': Violence Against Women in Essex
    County, New York, 1799–1860." *JSH* 35 (Summer): 889–918.

Mor, Nilly, and Jennifer Winquist. 2002. "Self-Focused Attention and Negative
    Affect: A Meta-Analysis." *Psychological Bulletin* 128 (July): 638–62.

Moran, James E. 2003. "The Signal and the Noise: the Historical Epidemiology of
    Insanity in Antebellum New Jersey." *History of Psychiatry* 14 (3): 281–301.

Morawska, Eva. 1985. *For Bread with Butter: The Life-Worlds of East Central Europeans
    in Johnstown, Pennsylvania, 1890–1940*. New York: Cambridge University Press.

————. 1994. "In Defense of the Assimilation Model." *Journal of American Ethnic
    History* 13 (Winter): 75–87.

Morawska, Jill G. 1997. "Educating the Emotions: Academic Psychology, Textbooks,
    and the Psychology Industry, 1890–1940." In *Inventing the Psychological: Toward a
    Cultural History of Emotional Life in America*, ed. Joel Pfister and Nancy Schnog,
    217–44. New Haven, CT: Yale University Press.

More, Louise Bolard. 1907. *Wage-Earners' Budgets*. New York: Henry Holt.

Morin, Richard. 2008. "Feeling Guilty: Americans Say They Aren't Saving Enough."
    Pew Social & Demographic Trends Project, May 14, http://pewresearch.org/
    pubs/837/americans-not-saving-enough.

————. 2008. "Who Wants to Be Rich?" Pew Social & Demographic Trends Project,
    April 30, http://pewsocialtrends.org/pubs/713/who-wants-to-be-rich.

Morris, Richard J. 1997. "Social Change, Republican Rhetoric, and the American
    Revolution: The Case of Salem, Massachusetts." *JSH* 31 (Winter): 419–34.

Morse, H. N., and Edmund de S. Brunner. 1923. *The Town and Country Church in the United States*. New York: George H. Duran.

Moskowitz, Marina. 2004. *Standard of Living The Measure of the Middle Class in Modern America*. Baltimore: Johns Hopkins University Press.

Moss, David A. 2002. *When All Else Fails: Government as the Ultimate Risk Manager*. Cambridge, MA: Harvard University Press.

Muller, Peter O. 1981. *Contemporary Suburban America*. Englewood Cliffs, NJ: Prentice-Hall.

Murphy, John Allen. 1917. "How the Automobile has Changed the Buying Habits of Farmers." *Printers' Ink* 101 (November 29): 3–6, 98–101.

Murray, John E. 2004. "Bound by Charity: The Abandoned Children of Late Eighteenth-Century Charleston." In Smith 2004, 213–34.

Mutz, Diana C., and Jeffery J. Mondak. 2006. "The Workplace as a Context for Cross-Cutting Political Discourse." *Journal of Politics* 68 (February): 140–155.

Myers, Aimee, and Carole Shammas. 1997. "Housing Standards in the United States, 1790s–1990s." Paper presented to the Organization of American Historians, San Francisco.

Naki, Dean M., and Michael Palumbo. 2001. "Disentangling the Wealth Effect: A Cohort Analysis of Household Saving in the 1990s." Finance and Economics Discussion Series, Board of Governors of the Federal Reserve System, http://www.federalreserve.gov/pubs/feds/2001/200121/200121pap.pdf.

Nasaw, David. 1993. *Going Out: The Rise and Fall of Public Amusements*. New York: Basic Books.

Nash, Gary B. 1973. "The Transformation of Urban Politics 1700–1765." *JAH* 60 (December): 605–32.

———. 1979. *The Urban Crucible: Social Change, Political Consciousness, and the Origins of the American Revolution*. Cambridge, MA: Harvard University Press.

———. 1984. "Social Development." In Greene and Pole 1984, 233–61.

———. 1987. "The Social Evolution of Pre-industrial American Cities, 1700–1820: Reflections and New Directions." *JUH* 13 (February): 115–45.

———. 2004 "Poverty and Politics in Early American History." In Smith 2004, 1–40.

National Center for Health Statistics. 1999. *Health, United States, 1999, With Health and Aging Chartbook*. Washington DC: U.S. Government Printing Office.

———. 2006. *Health, United States, 2006*. Hyattsville, MD: NCHS.

———. 2007. *Health, United States, 2007*. Hyattsville, MD: NCHS.

National Office of Vital Statistics. 1947. *Vital Statistics Rates in the United States, 1900–1940*. Washington DC: U.S. Government Printing Office.

National Opinion Research Center. 1997. "Trendlets." *GSS News* 11 (August): 3.

Neely, Mark E. Jr. *The Boundaries of American Political Culture in the Civil War Era*. Chapel Hill: University of North Carolina Press.

Nelson, Bruce C. 1991. "Revival and Upheaval: Religion, Irreligion and Chicago's Working Class in 1886." *JSH* 25 (Winter): 233–53.

Neth, Mary. 1993. "Leisure and Generational Change: Farm Youths in the Midwest, 1910–1940." *Agricultural History* 67 (Spring): 163–84.

Newman, Simon P. 2004. "Dead Bodies: Poverty and Death in Early National Philadelphia." In Smith 2004, 63–92.

———. 2007. "One Nation under God: Making Historical Sense of Evangelical Protestantism in Contemporary American Politics." *Journal of American Studies* 41 (3):
581–97.

Newport, Frank. 1999. "Seven Out of Ten American Families Will Be Giving Out
Treats this Halloween." Gallup News Service, October 29, http://www.gallup
.com/ poll/releases/pr991029.asp.

Nickles, Shelley. 2002. "More is Better: Mass Consumption, Gender, and Class
Identity in Postwar America." *AQ* 54 (4): 581–622.

Nicolaides, Becky M. 2004. "The Neighborhood Politics of Class in a Working-
Class Suburb of Los Angeles, 1920–1940." *JUH* 30 (March): 428–51.

Nie, Norman H., Jane Junn, and Kenneth Stehlik-Barry. 1996. *Education and Democratic Citizenship in America*. Chicago: University of Chicago Press.

Nielsen Media Research. 2006. "Nielsen Media Research Reports Television's
Popularity Is Still Growing." News release, http://www.nielsenmedia.com/nc/
portal/ site/Public/menuitem.55dc65b4a7d5adff3f65936147a062a0/?vgnextoid=
4156527aacccd010VgnVCM100000ac0a260aRCRD.

Nisbet, Robert. 1969. *The Quest for Community*. New York: Oxford University Press.

———. 1980. *History of the Idea of Progress*. New York: Basic Books.

Nisbett, Richard E. 2003. *The Geography of Thought: How Asians and Westerners Think
Differently . . . and Why*. New York: Free Press.

Nisbett, Richard E., Kaiping Peng, Incheol Choi, and Ara Norenzayan. 2001. "Culture and Systems of Thought: Holistic Versus Analytic Cognition." *Psychological
Review* 108 (April): 291–310.

Nissenbaum, Stephen. 1996. *The Battle for Christmas*. New York: Vintage.

Nobles, Gregory H. 1989. "Breaking into the Backcountry: New Approaches to the
Early American Frontier, 1750–1800." *WMQ* 3rd Ser., 46 (October): 641–70.

Noll, Mark. 1993. "The American Revolution and Protestant Evangelicalism." *JIH*
23 (Winter): 615–38.

Nolte, P. 2004. "Modernization and Modernity in History." In Smelser and Baltes
2004, 9954–61.

Norris, Pippa. 1996. "Does Television Erode Social Capital? A Reply to Putnam."
PS: Political Science & Politics 29 (September): 474–81.

Norris, Pippa, and Ronald Inglehart. 2004. *Sacred and Secular: Religion and Politics
Worldwide*. New York: Cambridge University Press.

Norton, Mary Beth. 1984. "The Evolution of White Women's Experience in Early
America." *AHR* 89 (June): 593–619.

Novick, Peter. 1988. *That Noble Dream: The 'Objectivity Question' and the American Historical Profession*. Chicago: University of Chicago Press.

Nugent, Walter T. 1981. *Structures of American Social History*. Bloomington: Indiana
University Press.

Nye, Joseph S. Jr., Philip D. Zelikow, and David C. King, eds. 1997. *Why People Don't
Trust Government*. Cambridge, MA: Harvard University Press.

Nye, Joseph S. Jr., and Philip D. Zelikow. 1997. "Conclusions: Reflections, Conjectures, and Puzzles." In Nye, Zelikow, and King 1997, 253–81.

O'Brien, Robert M., and Jean Stockard. 2006. "A Common Explanation for the Changing Age Distributions of Suicide and Homicide in the United States, 1930 to 2000." *SF* 84 (March):1539–57.

O'Brien, Robert M., Jean Stockard, and Lynne Isaacson. 1999. "The Enduring Effects of Cohort Characteristics on Age-Specific Homicide Rates." *AJS* 104 (January): 1061–95.

O'Guinn, Thomas C., and L. J. Shrum, 1997. "The Role of Television in the Construction of Consumer Reality." *JCR* 23 (March): 278–94.

Odem, Mary. 1993. "Sexual Behavior and Morality." In Cayton, Gorn, and Williams 1993, 1961–81.

Oestreicher, Richard. 1988. "Urban Working-Class Political Behavior and Theories of American Electoral Politics, 1870–1940." *JAH* 74 (March):1257–86.

———. 1993. "Labor: The Jacksonian Era Through Reconstruction." In Cayton, Gorn, and Williams 1993, 1447–58.

———. 1994. "The Counted and the Uncounted: The Occupational Structure of Early American Cities." *JSH* 28 (Winter): 351–62.

Office of Applied Studies. 2006. "Results from the 2004 National Survey on Drug Use and Health: National Findings." Substance Abuse and Mental Health Services Administration, Department of Health and Human Services. http://oas .samhsa.gov/NSDUH/2k4NSDUH/2k4results/2k4results.htm#1.2.

Ogburn, William F. 1957. "How Technology Causes Social Change." In *Technology and Social Change*, ed. F. R. Allen et al, 12–26. New York: Appleton Century Crofts.

Oldenburg, Ray. 1999. *The Great Good Place*. New York: Marlowe.

Oliker, Stacey J. 1998. "The Modernisation of Friendship: Individualism, Intimacy, and Gender in the Nineteenth Century." In *Placing Friendship in Context*, ed. Rebecca G. Adams and Graham Allan, 18–42. Cambridge: Cambridge University Press.

Olivas, J. Richard. 2004. "'God Helps Those Who Help Themselves': Religious Explanations of Poverty in Colonial Massachusetts, 1630–1776." In Smith 2004, 262–88.

Oliver, J. Eric. 2003. "Mental Life and the Metropolis in Suburban America: The Psychological Correlates of Metropolitan Place Characteristics." *Urban Affairs Review* 39 (2): 228–53.

Olney, Martha L. 1991. *Buy Now, Pay Later: Advertising, Credit, and Consumer Durables in the 1920s*. Chapel Hill: University of North Carolina Press.

———. 1999. "Avoiding Default: the Role of Credit in the Consumption Collapse of 1930." *Quarterly Journal of Economics* 14 (1): 319–35.

Ono, Hiromi. 1999. "Historical Time and U.S. Marital Dissolution." *SF* 77 (March): 969–97.

Osborn, Matthew Warner. 2009. "A Detestable Shrine: Alcohol Abuse in Antebellum Philadelphia." *JER* 29 (Spring): 101–32.

Ossian, Lisa L. 2006. "Bandits, Mad Men, and Suicides: Fear, Anger, and Death in a Troubled Iowa Landscape, 1929–1933." *Agricultural History* 80 (June): 296–311.

Österberg, Eva. 1992. "Criminality, Social Control, and the Early Modern State: Evidence and Interpretations in Scandinavian History." *SSH* 16 (Spring): 67–98.

Osterud, Nancy Grey. 1991. *Bonds of Community: The Lives of Farm Women in Nineteenth-Century New York.* Ithaca, NY: Cornell University Press.

Ott, Jan. 2001. "Did the Market Depress Happiness in the US?" *Journal of Happiness Studies* 2:433–43.

Ouimet, Marc. 1999. "Crime in Canada and in the United States: A Comparative Analysis." *Canadian Review of Sociology and Anthropology* 36 (August): 389–408.

Ovadia, Seth. 2003. "Suggestions of the Postmodern Self: Value Changes in American High School Students, 1976–1996." *Sociological Perspectives* 46 (2): 239–56.

Owen, John D. 1986. *Working Lives: The American Work Force since 1920.* Lexington, MA: Lexington Books.

Ownby, Ted. 1999. *American Dreams in Mississippi: Consumers, Poverty, & Culture, 1830–1998.* Chapel Hill: University of North Carolina Press.

Oyserman, Daphna, Heather M. Coon, and Markus Kemmelmeier. 2002. "Rethinking Individualism and Collectivism: Evaluation of Theoretical Assumptions and Meta-Analyses." *Psychological Bulletin* 128 (1): 3–72.

Packard, Vance. 1957. *The Hidden Persuaders.* New York: McKay.

Pacek, Alexander, and Benjamin Radcliff. 2008. "Assessing the Welfare State: The Politics of Happiness." *Perspectives on Politics* 6 (June): 267–77.

Pagnini, Deanna L., and S. Philip Morgan. 1990. "Intermarriage and Social Distance among U.S. Immigrants at the Turn of the Century." *AJS* 96 (September): 405–32.

———. 1996. "Racial Differences in Marriage and Childbearing: Oral History Evidence from the South in the Early Twentieth Century." *AJS* 101 (May): 1694–1718.

Palen, J. John. 2008. *The Urban World.* 8th ed. Boulder, CO: Paradigm.

Pampel, Fred C. 1996. "Cohort Size and Age-Specific Suicide Rates: A Contingent Relationship." *DEM* 33 (August): 341–55.

Panagopoulus, Costas. 2006. "The Polls—Trends: Obesity." *POQ* 70 (Summer): 249–68.

Park, No-Yong. 1934. "Cultural Strains." In Handlin and Handlin 1997, 151–63.

Park, Robert E. 1916. "The City: Suggestions for Investigation of Human Behavior in the Urban Environment." In *Classic Essays on the Culture of Cities,* ed. Richard Sennett, 91–130. New York: Appleton-Century Crofts, 1969.

Parke, Ross D., and Peter N. Stearns. 1994. "Fathers and Child Rearing." In *Children in Time and Place: Developmental and Historical Insights,* ed. Glen H. Elder Jr., John Modell, and Ross D. Parke, 147–70. New York: Cambridge University Press.

Parker, Jonathan A. 1999. "Spendthrift in America? On Two Decades of Decline In the U.S. Saving Rate." Working paper 7238. Cambridge, MA: NBER.

Parkerson, Donald H. 1982. "How Mobile Were Nineteenth-Century Americans?" *Historical Methods* 15 (Summer): 99–109.

Parkerson, Donald H., and Jo Ann Parkerson. 1988. "'Fewer Children of Greater Spiritual Quality': Religion and the Decline of Fertility in Nineteenth- Century America." *SSH* 12 (Spring): 49–70.

Parnell, Allan M., Gray Swicegood, and Gillian Stevens. 1994. "Nonmarital Pregnancies and Marriage in the United States." *SF* 73 (September): 263–87.

Parrella, Anne. 1992. "Industrialization and Murder: Northern France, 1815–1904." *JIH* 22 (Spring): 627–54.

Parsons, Elaine Frantz. 2000. "Risky Business: The Uncertain Boundaries of Manhood in the Midwestern Saloon." *JSH* 34 (Winter): 283–308.

Parsons, Talcott. 1951. *The Social System*. New York: Free Press of Glencoe.

Pasley, Jeffrey L. 2004. "The Cheese and the Worlds: Popular Political Culture and Participatory Democracy in the Early American Republic." In Pasley, Robertson, and Waldsteicher 2004, 31–56.

Pasley, Jeffrey L., Andrew W. Robertson, and David Waldstreicher, eds. 2004. *Beyond the Founders: New Approaches to the Political History of the Early American Republic*. Chapel Hill: University of North Carolina Press.

Patten, Scott B. 2003. "Recall Bias and Major Depression Lifetime Prevalence." *Social Psychiatry and Psychiatric Epidemiology* 38:290–96.

Paxton, Pamela. 1999. "Is Social Capital Declining in the United States? A Multiple Indicator Assessment." *AJS* 105 (July): 88–127.

Pease, Jane H., and William H. Pease. 1990. *Ladies, Women, & Wenches: Choice and Constraint in Antebellum Charleston & Boston*. Chapel Hill: University of North Carolina Press.

Peck, M. Scott. 1978. *The Road Less Traveled: A New Psychology of Love, Traditional Values and Spiritual Growth*. New York: Simon & Schuster.

Pederson, Jane Marie. 1992. *Between Memory and Reality: Family and Community in Rural Wisconsin, 1870–1970*. Madison: University of Wisconsin Press.

Peel, Mark. 1986. "On the Margins: Lodgers and Boarders in Boston, 1860–1900." *JAH* 72 (March): 813–34.

Peiss, Kathy. 1986. *Cheap Amusements: Working Women and Leisure in Turn-of-the-Century New York*. Philadelphia: Temple University Press.

Peixotto, Jessica B. 1927. *Getting and Spending at the Professional Standard of Living*. New York: MacMillan.

Pennington, Jon C. 2004. "It's Not A Revolution But It Sure Looks Like One: A Statistical Accounting of the Post-Sixties Sexual Revolution." *Radical History* 83:104–16.

Percheski, Christine. 2008. "Opting Out? Cohort Differences in Professional Women's Employment Rates from 1960 to 2005." *ASR* 73 (June): 497–517.

Pergams, Oliver R. W., and Patricia A. Zaradic. 2008. "Evidence for a Fundamental and Pervasive Shift Away from Nature-Based Recreation." *Proceedings of the National Academy of Sciences USA* (February 4), http://www.pnas.org/content/105/7/2295.abstract.

Perkins, Elizabeth A. 1991. "The Consumer Frontier: Household Consumption in Early Kentucky." *JAH* 78 (September): 486–510.

Perry, Ralph Barton. 1949. "The American Cast of Mind." In Wilkinson 1992, 33–49.

Pescosolido, Bernice A., and Robert Mendelsohn. 1986. "Social Causation or Social Construction of Suicide? An Investigation into the Social Organization of Official Rates." *ASR* 51(February): 80–100.

Pescosolido, Bernice A., Jack K. Martin, Bruce G. Link, Saeko Kikuzawa, Giovanni Burgos, Ralph Swindle, and Jo Phelan. 2000. "Americans' Views of Mental Health and Illness at Century's End: Continuity and Change." Report, Indiana Consortium for Mental Health Services Research, Department of Sociology, Indiana University, Bloomington.

Petigny, Alan. 2004. "Illegitimacy, Postwar Psychology, and the Reperiodization of the Sexual Revolution." *JSH* 38 (Fall): 64–79.

Pew Forum on Religion & Public Life. 2008. "U.S. Religious Landscape Survey." http://www.pewforum.org/reports.

———. 2008. "Many Americans Say Other Faiths Can Lead to Eternal Life." http://pewresearch.org/pubs/1062/many-americans-say-other-faiths-can-lead-to-eternal-life.

———. 2009. "Faith in Flux: Changes in Religious Affiliation in the U.S.," April. Washington: Pew Forum. http://www.pewforum.org/docs/?DocID=409-40k.

Pew Research Center For The People & The Press. 2001. "Deconstructing Distrust: How Americans View Government." http://www.people-press.org/trustrpt.htm.

———. 2003. "Evenly Divided and Increasingly Polarized." Pew Research Center, November. http://people-press.org/reports/pdf/196.pdf.

———. 2003. "Views of a Changing World: June 2003." The Pew Global Attitudes Project. http://www.pewresearch.org/report/185/views-of-a-changing-world-2003.

———. 2007. "Motherhood Today: Tougher Challenges, Less Success." News release, Pew Research Center, May 2. http://pewsocialtrends.org/pubs/468/motherhood.

———. 2008. "Federal Government's Favorable Ratings Slump." Survey Reports. http://people-press.org/report/420/federal-governments-favorable-ratings-slump.

———. 2008. "Fewer Mothers Prefer Full-Time Work." A Social and Demographic Trends Report. http://pewresearch.org/pubs/536/working-women.

Phelan, Jo C., Bruce G. Link, Ann Stueve, and Bernice A. Pescosolido. 2000. "Public Conceptions of Mental Illness in 1950 and 1996: What Is Mental Illness and Is It to be Feared?" *Journal of Health and Social Behavior* 41 (June): 188–207.

Pfister, Joel. 1997. "On Conceptualizing the Cultural History of Emotional and Psychological Life in America." In Pfister and Schnog 1997, 17–61.

Pfister, Joel, and Nancy Schnog, eds. 1997. *Inventing the Psychological: Toward a Cultural History of Emotional Life in America*. New Haven, CT: Yale University Press.

Pierce, Albert. 1967. "The Economic Cycle and the Social Suicide Rate." *ASR* 32 (June): 457–62.

Piketty, Thomas, and Emmanuel Saez. 2006. "The Evolution of Top Incomes: A Historical and International Perspective." *AER* 96 (May): 200–5.

Pilarczyk, Ian C. 1997. "The Terrible Haystack Murder: The Moral Paradox of Hypocrisy, Prudery and Piety in Antebellum America." *American Journal of Legal History* 41 (January): 25–60.

Pleck, Elizabeth. 1999. "The Making of a Domestic Occasion: The History of Thanksgiving in the United States." *JSH* 32 (Summer): 773–89.

Plotnick, Robert D., Eugene Smolensky, Erik Evenhouse, and Siobhan Reilly. 2000. "The Twentieth-Century Record of Inequality and Poverty in the United States." In Engerman and Gallman 2000, 249–99.

Plutzer, Eric, and Michael Berkman. 2008. "Trends: Evolution, Creationism, and the Teaching of Human Origins in Schools." *POQ* 72 (3): 540–53.

Pole, J. R. 1980. *American Individualism and the Promise of Progress*. Oxford: Clarendon Press.

———. 1988. "Equality: An American Dilemma." In *America in Theory*, ed. Leslie Berlowitz, Denis Donoghue, and Louis Menand, 69–83. New York: Oxford University Press.

Pollay, Richard. 1985. "The Subsiding Sizzle: A Descriptive History of Print Advertising, 1900–1980." *Journal of Marketing* 49 (Summer): 24–37.

Portes, Alejandro, and Lingxin Hao. 1998. "Bilingualism and Language Loss in the Second Generation." Working paper 229, The Jerome Levy Economics Institute of Bard College, New York.

Potter, David M. 1954. *People of Plenty: Economic Abundance and the American Character*. Chicago: University of Chicago Press.

Potter, Jim. 1984. "Demographic Development and Family Structure." In Greene and Pole 1984, 123–57.

Pred, A. R. 1973. *Urban Growth and The Circulation of Information: The United States System of Cities, 1790–1840*. Cambridge, MA: Harvard University Press.

Prescott, Cynthia Culver. 2007. "'Why She Didn't Marry Him': Love, Power, and Marital Choice on the Far Western Frontier." *Western Historical Quarterly* 38 (Spring): 25–45.

Presser, Harriet. 2004. "The Economy That Never Sleeps." *Contexts* 3 (Spring): 42–49.

Presser, Stanley, and Linda Stinson. 1998. "Data Collection Mode And Social Desirability Bias in Self-Reported Religious Attendance." *ASR* 63 (February): 137–45.

Preston, Samuel H., and Michael R. Haines. 1991. *Fatal Years: Child Mortality in Late Nineteenth-Century America*. Princeton, NJ: Princeton University Press.

Prude, Jonathan. 1997. "Capitalism, Industrialization, and the Factory in Post-Revolutionary America." In Gilje 1997, 81–100.

Pruitt, Bettye Hobbs. 1984. "Self-Sufficiency and the Agricultural Economy of Eighteenth-Century Massachusetts." *WMQ* 3rd. Ser., 41 (July): 334–64.

Pugh, Allison. 2009. *Longing and Belonging: Parents, Children, and Consumer Culture*. Berkeley: University of California Press.

Putnam, Robert D. 1995. "Tuning In, Tuning Out: The Strange Disappearance of Social Capital in America." *PS: Political Science & Politics* 28 (December): 664–83.

———. 1996. "The Strange Disappearance of Civic America." *American Prospect* 7 (December): 34–48.

———. 2000. *Bowling Alone: The Collapse and Revival of American Community*. New York: Simon & Schuster.

———. 2002. "Bowling Together." *American Prospect* (February 11): 20–22.

———. 2007. "E Pluribus Unum: Diversity and Community in the Twenty-First Century." *Scandinavian Political Studies* 30 (2): 138–75.

Qian, Zhenchao, and Daniel T. Lichter. 2007. "Social Boundaries and Marital Assimilation: Interpreting Trends in Racial and Ethnic Intermarriage." *ASR* 72 (February): 68–94.

Quackenbush, Michelle, and Lorna Lutes Sylvester, eds. 1981. "Letter of Jacob Schramm in Indiana to Karl Zimmerman in Germany, 1842." *Indiana Magazine of History* 77 (3): 268–87.

Quadagno, Jill. 1994. *The Color of Welfare: How Racism Undermined the War on Poverty*. New York: Oxford University Press.

Quell, Carsten, Ben Veenhof, Barry Wellman, and Bernie Hogan. 2007. "Isolation, Cohesion or Transformation? How Canadians' Use of the Internet is Shaping Society." Draft paper, Statistics Canada Socio-Economic Conference 2007, Ottawa.

Qutb, Sayyid. 1949. "Fundamentalism." In Handlin and Handlin 1997, 209–31.

Rachels, David. 2007. "Julia Moore." *The Literary Encyclopedia*. http://www.litencyc.com/.

Rader, Benjamin G. 1994. *Baseball: A History of America's Game*. Urbana: University of Illinois Press.

Rae, John B. 1971. *The Road and the Car in American Life*. Cambridge, MA: MIT Press.

Rahn, Wendy M., and John E. Transue. 1998. "Social Trust and Value Change: The Decline of Social Capital in American Youth, 1976–1995." *Political Psychology* 19 (September): 545–65.

Rainer, Joseph T. 1997. "The Sharper Image: Yankee Peddlers, Southern Consumers, and the Market Revolution." In *Cultural Change and the Market Revolution in America, 1789–1860*, ed. Scott C. Martin, 89–110. New York: Rowman & Littlefield, 2005.

Rainwater, Lee. 1974. *What Money Buys: Inequality and the Social Meanings of Income*. New York: Basic Books.

Raley, R. Kelly. 2000. "Recent Trends and Differentials in Marriage and Cohabitation: The United States." In Waite 2000, 19–39.

Ratcliffe, Donald J. 1987. "Voter Turnout in Early Ohio." *JER* 7 (Autumn): 223–51.

Ravitch, Diane. 1974. *The Great School Wars: New York City, 1805–1973*. New York: Basic Books.

Ray, Marcella Ridlin. 1999. "Technological Change and Associational Life." In Skocpol and Fiorina 1999, 297–330.

Reddy, William M. 1997. "Against Constructionism: The Historical Ethnography of Emotions." *Current Anthropology* 38 (June): 327–52.

Reed, Joanna M. 2006. "Not Crossing the "Extra Line": How Cohabitors with Children View Their Unions." *Journal of Marriage and Family* 68 (December): 1117–31.

Rehn, Alf and David Sköld. 2005. "'I Love The Dough': Rap Lyrics as a Minor Economic Literature." *Culture and Organization* 11 (March): 17–31.

Reid, Gerald F. 1993. "The Seeds of Prosperity and Discord: The Political Economy of Community Polarization in Greenfield, Massachusetts, 1770–1820." *JSH* 27 (Winter): 359–74.

Rhoads, Steven E. 1985. *The Economist's View of the World: Government, Markets, & Public Policy*. New York: Cambridge University Press.

Rice, Kym S. 1983. *Early American Taverns: For the Entertainment of Friends and Strangers*. Chicago: Regnery Gateway.

Richards, Raymond. 1993. *Closing the Door to Destitution: The Shaping of the Social Security Acts of the United States and New Zealand*. University Park: Pennsylvania State University Press.

Richins, Marsha L. 2004. "The Material Values Scale: Measurement Properties and Development of a Short Form." *JCR* 31 (June): 209–19.

Rideout, Victoria J., Ulla G. Foehr, Donald F. Roberts, Mollyann Brodie. 1999. *Kids & Media @ the New Millennium*. Executive summary. Kaiser Family Foundation Report.

Riesman, David, with Nathan Glazer and Reuel Denney. 1949. *The Lonely Crowd*. Rev. ed. New Haven, CT: Yale University Press, 2001.

Riley, Glenda. 1991. *Divorce: An American Tradition*. New York: Oxford University Press.

Ripken, Cal Jr., and Mike Bryan. 1997. *The Only Way I Know*. New York: Viking.
———. 1999. *My Story*. Adapted by Dan Gutman. New York: Dial.

Rischin, Moses. 1962. *The Promised City: New York's Jews, 1870–1914*. Cambridge, MA: Harvard University Press.

Ritzer, George. 1999. *Enchanting a Disenchanted World: Revolutionizing the Means of Consumption*. Thousand Oaks, CA: Pine Forge Press.

Roberts, Robert E., Eun Sul Lee, and Catherine R. Roberts. 1991. "Changes in Prevalence of Depressive Symptoms in Alameda County: Age, Period, and Cohort Trends." *Journal of Aging & Health* 3 (February): 66–86.

Robertson, Andrew W. 2004. "Voting Rites and Voting Acts: Electioneering Ritual, 1790–1820." In Pasley, Robertson, and Waldsteicher 2004, 57–78.

Robinson, John P. 1978. "'Massification' and Democratization of the Leisure Class." *Annals of AAPSS* 435 (January): 206–25.

Robinson, John P., and Philip E. Converse. 1972. "Social Change Reflected in the Use of Time." In *The Human Meaning of Social Change*, ed. Angus Campbell and Philip E. Converse, 17–86. New York: Russell Sage.

Robinson, John P., and Geoffrey Godbey. 1996. "The Great American Slowdown." *American Demographics* (June) http://findarticles.com/p/articles/mi_m4021/is_n6_v18/ai_18352296/?tag=content;coll.

———. 2005. "Busyness as Usual." *Social Research* 72 (Summer): 407–26.

Robinson, John P., and Jos De Haan. 2008. "Information Technology and Family Time Displacement." Unpublished paper, Department of Sociology, University of Maryland.

Robinson, John P., and Steven Martin. 2008. "IT and Activity Displacement: Behavioral Evidence from the U.S. General Social Survey." Unpublished paper, Department of Sociology, University of Maryland.

Robinson, Robert V. 1993. "Economic Necessity and the Life Cycle in the Family Economy of Nineteenth-Century Indianapolis." *AJS* 99 (July): 49–74.

Robinson, Robert V., and Elton F. Jackson. 2001. "Is Trust in Others Declining in America? An Age-Period-Cohort Analysis." *Social Science Research* 30 (March): 117–45.

Rodgers, Daniel T. 1980. "Socializing Middle-Class Children: Institutions, Fables, and Work Values in Nineteenth-Century America." *JSH* 13 (Spring): 354–57.

———. 1998. "Exceptionalism." In Molho and Wood 1998, 21–40.

Roemer, Daniel, Kathleen H. Jamieson, and Nicole J. de Cocteau. 1998. "The Treatment of Persons of Color in Local Television News." *Communications Research* 25 (June): 286–305.

Rogers, Alma A. 1905. "The Women's Club Movement: Its Origin, Significance and Present Results." *The Arena* 34 (October): 347–50.

Rogers, Mark R. 1990. "Measuring the Personal Savings Rate." *Economic Review* 75 (July): 38–49.

Romer, Christina. 1986. "Spurious Volatility in Historical Unemployment Data." *Journal of Political Economy* 94 (February): 1–37.

———. 1999. "Changes in Business Cycles: Evidence and Explanations." *JEP* 13 (Spring): 23–44.

Romig, Kevin. 2005. "The Upper Sonoran Lifestyle: Gated Communities in Scottsdale, Arizona." *City & Community* 4 (March): 67–86.

Ronsvalle, John, and Sylvia Ronsvalle, 1996. "The End of Benevolence? Alarming Trends in Church Giving." *Christian Century*, October 23. http://findarticles.com/p/articles/mi_m1058/is_n30_v113/ai_18819026/.

Roof, Wade Clark. 1999. *Spiritual Marketplace: Baby Boomers and the Remaking of American Religion*. Princeton, NJ: Princeton University Press.

Roof, Wade Clark, and William McKinney. 1987. *American Mainline Religion*. New Brunswick, NJ: Rutgers University Press.

Rorabaugh, W. J. 1979. *The Alcoholic Republic: An American Tradition*. New York: Oxford University Press.

Rose, Richard. 1985. "National Pride in Cross-National Perspective." *International Social Science Journal* 37 (1): 85–96.

Rosenberg, Charles E. 1973. "Sexuality, Class, and Role in 19th-Century America." *AQ* 25 (May): 131–53.

———. 1984. "What It Was Like to be Sick in 1884." *American Heritage* 35 (October): 22–31.

Rosenberg, Morris. 1956. "Misanthropy and Political Ideology." *ASR* 21 (December): 690–95.

Rosenberg, Nathan. 1986. *How the West Grew Rich: the Economic Transformation of the Industrial World*. New York: Basic Books.

Rosenbloom, Joshua L., and William A. Sundstrom. 2003. "The Decline and Rise of Interstate Migration in the United States: Evidence from the IPUMS, 1850–1990." Working paper W9857. Cambridge, MA: NBER.

Rosenfeld, Michael J., and Byung-Soo Kim. 2005. "The Independence of Young Adults and the Rise of Interracial and Same Sex Unions." *ASR* 70 (August): 541–62.

Rosenfeld, Richard. 2002. "The Crime Decline in Context." *Contexts* 1 (Spring): 25–34.

Rosenstone, Steven J., and John Mark Hansen. 1993. *Mobilization, Participation, and Democracy in America*. New York: MacMillan.

Rosenthal, Edward C. 2005. *The Era of Choice: The Ability to Choose and Its Transformation of Contemporary Life*. Cambridge, MA: MIT Press.

Rosenwein, Barbara H. 2002. "Worrying about Emotions in History." *AHR* 107 (3): 821–45.

Rosenzweig, Roy. 1985. *Eight Hours for What We Will: Workers and Leisure in an Industrial City, 1870–1920*. New York: Cambridge University Press.

Rosenzweig, Roy, and David Thelen. 1998. *The Presence of the Past: Popular Uses of History in American Life*. New York: Columbia University Press.

Ross, Catherine E., and John Mirowsky. 2002. "Age and the Gender Gap in the Sense of Personal Control." *Social Psychology Quarterly* 65 (June): 125–45.

———. 2003. "Social Structure and Psychological Functioning: Distress, Perceived Control, and Trust." In *Handbook of Social Psychology*, ed. John Delamater, 411–47. New York: Kluwer Academic.

Ross, Dorothy. 1998. "The New and Newer Histories: Social Theory and Historiography in an American Key." In Molho and Wood 1998, 85–106.

Roth, Randolph. 2001. "Child Murder in New England." *SSH* 25 (Spring): 101–47.

Rothenberg, Winifred. 1992. *From Market-Places to a Market Economy: The Transformation of Rural Massachusetts, 1750–1850*. Chicago: University of Chicago Press.

Rothman, Ellen K. 1982. "Sex and Self-Control: Middle-Class Courtship in America, 1770–1870." *JSH* 15 (Spring): 409–25.

———. 1984. *Hands and Hearts: A History of Courtship in America*. New York: Basic Books.

Rotolo, Thomas. 1999. "Trends in Voluntary Association Participation." *Nonprofit and Voluntary Sector Quarterly* 28 (June): 199–212.

Rotolo, Thomas, and John Wilson. 2004. "What Happened to the 'Long Civic Generation'? Explaining Cohort Differences in Volunteerism." *SF* 82 (March): 1091–121.

Rotter, Julian B. 1967. "A New Scale for the Measurement of Interpersonal Trust." *Journal of Personality* 35 (4): 651–65.

———. 1971. "Generalized Expectancies for Interpersonal Trust." *American Psychologist* 26 (5): 443–53.

———. 1980. "Interpersonal Trust, Trustworthiness, and Gullibility." *American Psychologist* 35 (January): 1–7.

Rotundo, E. Anthony. 1989. "Romantic Friendship: Male Intimacy and Middle Class Youth in the Northern United States, 1800–1900." *JSH* 23 (Fall): 1–25.

Rucker, Derek D., and Adam D. Galinsky. 2008. "Desire to Acquire: Powerlessness and Compensatory Consumption." *JCR* 35 (August): 257–67.

Ruggles, Steven. 1988. "The Demography of the Unrelated Individual: 1900–1950." *DEM* 25 (November): 521–46.

———. 1994. "The Transformation of American Family Structure." *AHR* 99 (February): 103–28.

———. 1996. *Prolonged Connections: The Rise the Extended Family in Nineteenth-Century England and America.* Madison: University of Wisconsin Press.

———. 1997. "The Rise of Divorce and Separation in the United States, 1880–1990." *DEM* 34 (November): 455–66.

———. 2003. "Multigenerational Families in Nineteenth-Century America." *Continuity and Change* 18 (1): 139–65.

———. 2007. "The Decline of Intergenerational Coresidence in the United States, 1850–2000." *ASR* 72 (December): 964–89.

Rugh, Susan Sessions. 2002. "Civilizing the Countryside: Class, Gender, and Crime in Nineteenth-Century Rural Illinois." *Agricultural History* 76 (1): 58–81.

Runciman, W. G. 1966. *Relative Deprivation and Social Justice: A Study of Attitudes to Social Inequality in Twentieth-century England.* London: Routledge & K. Paul.

Russell, Cheryl. 1997. "What's Wrong with Kids?" *American Demographics* (November). http://www.highbeam.com/doc/1G1-19977802.html .

Rutman, Darrett B. 1986. "Assessing the Little Communities of Early America." *WMQ* 3rd Ser., 43 (April): 163–78.

———. 1994. "Community: A Sunny Little Dream." In *Small Worlds, Large Questions: Explorations in Early American Social History, 1600–1850*, 287–306. Charlottesville: University Press of Virginia.

Rutman, Darrett B., and Anita H. Rutman. 1984. *A Place in Time: Middlesex County, Virginia 1650–1750.* New York: W. W. Norton.

Ryan, Mary P. 1981. *Cradle of the Middle Class: The Family in Oneida County, New York, 1790–1865.* New York: Cambridge University Press.

———. 1990. *Women in Public: Between Banners and Ballots, 1825–1880.* Baltimore: Johns Hopkins University Press.

———. 1997. *Civic Wars: Democracy and Public Life in the American City during the Nineteenth Century.* Berkeley: University of California Press.

Rytina, Steven. 2000. "Is Occupational Mobility Declining in the U.S.?" *SF* 78(June): 1227–76.

Saad, Lydia. 2001. "Fear of Conventional Crime at Record Lows." Gallup News Service, October 22. http://www.gallup.com/poll/5002/Fear-Conventional-Crime-Record-Lows.aspx

———. 2001. "Americans' Mood: Has Sept. 11 Made a Difference?" Gallup News Service, December 17. http://www.gallup.com/poll/pollInsights/#GPV, accessed November 12, 2002.

———. 2002. "There's No Place Like Home to Spend an Evening, Say Most

Americans." Gallup News Service, January 10. http://www.gallup.com/poll/5164/
Theres-Place-Like-Home-Spend-Evening-Say-Most-Americans.aspx.

———. 2007. "Women Slightly More Likely to Prefer Working to Homemaking."
Gallup Poll. http://www.gallup.com/poll/28567/Women-Slightly-More-Likely-
Prefer-Working-Homemaking.aspx.

———. 2009. "Church-Going Among U.S. Catholics Slides to Tie Protestants." Gallup Poll, April 9. http://www.gallup.com/poll/117382/Church-Going-Among-
Catholics-Slides-Tie-Protestants.aspx.

Safera, D. J., and J. M. Zito. 2007. "Do Antidepressants Reduce Suicide Rates?" *Public Health* 121 (April): 274–77.

Sanchez, Thomas W., Robert E. Lang, and Dawn M. Dhavale. 2005. "Security versus Status? A First Look at the Census's Gated Community Data." *Journal of
Planning Education and Research* 24:281–91.

Sánchez-Jankowski, Martín. 1991. *Islands in the Street: Gangs and American Urban Society*. Berkeley: University of California Press.

———. 2008. *Cracks in the Pavement: Social Change and Resilience in Poor Neighborhoods*.
Berkeley: University of California Press.

Sandberg, John F., and Sandra L. Hofferth. 2001. "Changes in Children's Time With
Parents: United States, 1981–1997." *DEM* 38:423–36.

———. 2005. "Changes in Children's Time With Parents: A Correction." *DEM*
42:391–95.

Sarna, Jonathan. 2004. *American Judaism*. New Haven, CT: Yale University Press.

Sarson, Steven. 2009. "Yeoman Farmers in a Planters' Republic: Socioeconomic
Conditions and Relations in Early National Prince George's County, Maryland."
JER 29 (Spring): 63–99.

Sasaki, Masamichi and Tatsuzo Suzuki. 1987. "Changes in Religious Commitment
in the United States, Holland, and Japan." *AJS* 92 (March): 1055–76.

Sastry, Jaya, and Catherine E. Ross. 1998. "Asian Ethnicity and the Sense of Personal
Control." *Social Psychology Quarterly* 61 (2): 101–20.

Satcher, David. 2000. "Youth Violence: A Report of the Surgeon General." http://
www.surgeongeneral.gov/library/youthviolence/report.htm.

Sautter, Udo. 1991. *Three Cheers for the Unemployed: Government and Unemployment
before the New Deal*. New York: Cambridge University Press.

Sayer, Liana C., Suzanne M. Bianchi, and John P. Robinson. 2004. "Are Parents Investing Less in Children? Trends in Mothers' and Fathers' Time with Children."
AJS 110 (July): 1–43.

Schäfer M. L. 2002. "On the History of the Concept Neurasthenia and its Modern Variants." *Fortschritte der Neurolologie-Psychiatrie* (Stuttgart) 70 (November):
570–82.

Scharf, Virginia. 1991. *Taking the Wheel: Women and the Coming of the Motor Age*. New
York: Free Press.

Scherer, Klaus R., and Harald G. Wallbott. 1994. "Evidence for Universality and
Cultural Variation of Differential Emotion Response Patterning." *JPSP* 66 (February): 310–28.

Scherzer, Kenneth A. 1992. *The Unbounded Community: Neighborhood Life and Social Structure in New York City, 1830–1875*. Durham, NC: Duke University Press.

Schieman, Scott, and Gabriele Plickert. 2008. "How Knowledge is Power: Education and the Sense of Control Social Forces." *SF* 87 (September): 153–83.

Schlereth, Thomas J. 1989. "Country Stores, County Fairs, and Mail-Order Catalogues: Consumption in Rural America." In Bronner 1989, 339–75

———. 1991. *Victorian America: Transformations in Everyday Life, 1876–1915*. New York: Harper Perennial.

Schlesinger, Arthur M. 1947. *Learning How to Behave: A Historical Study of American Etiquette Books*. New York: MacMillan.

Schmidt, Fred, Elizabeth Skinner, Louis A. Ploch, and Richard S. Krannich. 2002. "Community Change and Persistence: Landaff, New Hampshire." In Luloff and Krannich 2002, 95–116.

Schmidt, Leigh Eric. 1991. "The Commercialization of the Calendar: American Holidays and the Culture of Consumption, 1870–1930." *JAH* 78 (December): 887–916.

———. 1995. *Consumer Rites: The Buying and Selling of American Holidays*. Princeton, NJ: Princeton University Press.

Schmidt, Stefanie R. 1999. "Long-Run Trends in Workers' Beliefs about Their Own Job Security: Evidence from the General Social Survey." *Journal of Labor Economics* 17 (4 pt. 2): S127–S141.

Schmitt, Peter J. 1969. *Back to Nature: The Arcadian Myth in Urban America*. New York: Oxford University Press.

———. 1992. "Grave Matters: American Cemeteries in Transition." *JUH* 18 (3): 338–45.

Schneider, John C. 1980. *Detroit and the Problem of Social Order, 1830–1880: A Geography of Crime, Riot, and Policing*. Lincoln: University of Nebraska Press.

———. 1984. "Skid Row as an Urban Neighborhood, 1880–1960." *Urbanism Past & Present* 9 (Winter):10–20.

———. 1987. "Homeless Men and Housing Policy in Urban America, 1850–1920." Paper presented to the Social Science History Association, New Orleans.

Schnittker, Jason. 2008. "Diagnosing Our National Disease: Trends in Income and Happiness, 1973 to 2004." *Social Psychology Quarterly* 71 (September): 257–80.

Schoeni, Robert F. 1998. "Reassessing the Decline in Parent-Child Old-Age Coresidence During the Twentieth Century." *DEM* 35 (August): 307–13.

Schoeni, Robert F., and Vladimir Canudas-Romo. 2006. "Timing Effects on Divorce: 20th Century Experience in the United States." *Journal of Marriage and Family* 68 (August): 749–58.

Schoeni, Robert F., and Karen E. Ross. 2005. "Material Assistance from Families During the Transition to Adulthood," In Setterson, Furstenberg, and Rumbaut 2005, 396–416.

Schor, Juliet B. 1991. *The Overworked American: The Unexpected Decline of Leisure*. New York: Basic Books.

———. 1998. *The Overspent American: Upscaling, Downshifting, and the New Consumer*. New York: Basic Books.

———. 2000. *Do Americans Shop Too Much?* Joshua Cohen and Joel Rogers, eds. Boston: Beacon Press.

Schradie, Jen. 2009. "The Digital Divide and the Web 2.0 Collide: The Digital Production Gap." Paper presented to the American Sociological Association, San Francisco, August.

Schudson, Michael. 1984. *Advertising: The Uneasy Persuasion*. New York: Basic Books.

———. 1991. "Delectable Materialism: Were the Critics of Consumer Culture Wrong All Along?" *American Prospect* 5 (Spring): 26–35.

———. 1993. "Journalism." In Cayton, Gorn, and Williams 1993, 1895–912.

———. 1998. *The Good Citizen: A History of American Civic Life*. New York: Free Press.

Schulz, Jeremy. 2006. "Vehicle of the Self: The Social and Cultural Work of the H2 Hummer." *Journal of Consumer Culture* 6 (1): 57–86.

Schuman, Howard, Charlotte Steeh, and Lawrence Bobo. 1985. *Racial Attitudes in America: Trends and Interpretations*. Cambridge, MA: Harvard University Press.

Schwartz, Barry, ed. 1976. *The Changing Face of the Suburbs*. Chicago: University of Chicago Press.

Schwartz, Barry. 2000. "Self-Determination: The Tyranny of Freedom." *American Psychologist* 55 (1): 79–88.

———. 2004. *The Paradox of Choice: Why More is Less*. New York: Ecco (HarperCollins).

Schwartz, Barry, Andrew Ward, John Monterosso, Sonja Lyubomirsky, Katherine White, and Darrin R. Lehman. 2002. "Maximizing Versus Satisficing: Happiness Is a Matter of Choice." *JPSP* 83 (5): 1178–97.

Schwartz, Christine R., and Robert D. Mare. 2005. "Trends in Educational Assortative Marriage From 1940 to 2003." *DEM* 42:621–46.

Schwartzberg, Beverly. 2004. "'Lots of Them Did That': Desertion, Bigamy, and Marital Fluidity in Late-Nineteenth-Century America." *JSH* 37 (Spring): 573–600.

Scott, Anne Firor. 1984. "On Seeing and Not Seeing: A Case of Historical Invisibility." *JAH* 71 (June): 7–21.

———. 1990. "Most Invisible of All: Black Women's Voluntary Associations." *Journal of Southern History* 56 (February): 3–23.

Scott, Sean A. 2008. "'Earth Has No Sorrow That Heaven Cannot Cure': Northern Civilian Perspectives on Death and Eternity During the Civil War." *JSH* 41 (Summer): 843–66.

Scranton, Philip. 1994. "Manufacturing Diversity: Production Systems, Markets, and an American Consumer Society, 1870–1930." *Technology and Culture* 15 (July): 476–505.

Seidman, Stuart N., and Ronald O. Rieder. 1994. "A Review of Sexual Behavior in the United States." *American Journal of Psychiatry* 151 (March): 330–41.

Seligman, Adam B. 1998. "Between Public and Private." *Society* 35 (March/April): 28–36.

———. 2000. *Modernity's Wager: Authority, the Self and Transcendence*. Princeton, NJ: Princeton University Press.

Sellers, Charles. 1991. *The Market Revolution: Jacksonian America, 1815–1846*. New York: Oxford University Press.

Settersten, Richard, Frank Furstenberg, and Ruben Rumbaut, eds. 2005. *On the Frontier of Adulthood: Theory, Research, and Public Policy*. Chicago: University of Chicago Press.

Seward, R. H. 1978. *The American Family: A Demographic History*. Newbury Park, CA: Sage.

Sewell, William H. Jr. 2001. "Whatever Happened to the 'Social' in Social History?" In *Schools of Thought: Twenty-Five Years of Interpretive Social Science*, ed. Joan W. Scott and Debra Keates, 209–26. Princeton, NJ: Princeton University Press.

Shafer, Byron E., ed. 1991. *Is America Different? A New Look at American Exceptionalism*. Oxford: Clarendon Press.

Shain, Barry Alan. 1994. *The Myth of American Individualism: The Protestant Origins of American Political Thought*. Princeton, NJ: Princeton University Press.

Shalhope, Robert E. 1991. "Individualism in the Early Republic." In Curry and Goodheart 1991, 66–86.

Shama, Simon. 1993. "Perishable Commodities: Dutch Still-Life Painting and the 'Empire of Things.'" In Brewer and Porter 1993, 478–88.

Shammas, Carole. 1980. "The Domestic Environment in Early Modern England and America." *JSH* 14 (Fall): 3–24.

———. 1989. "Explaining Past Changes in Consumption and Consumer Behavior." *Historical Methods* 22 (Spring): 61–67.

———. 1990. *The Pre-Industrial Consumer in England and America*. Oxford: Clarendon Press.

———. 1993. "Changes in English and Anglo-American Consumption from 1550 to 1800." In Brewer and Porter 1993, 177–205.

———. 1993. "A New Look at Long-Term Trends in Wealth Inequality in the United States." *AHR* 98 (April):412–31.

———. 2002. *A History of Household Governance in America*. Charlottesville: University Press of Virginia.

Shanahan, Michael J. 2000. "Pathways to Adulthood in Changing Societies: Variability and Mechanisms in Life Course Perspective." *ARS* 26:667–92.

Shannon, Gary W., and John D. Nystuen. 1972. "Marriage, Migration and the Measurement of Social Interaction." In *International Geography 1972*, ed. W. Peter Abrams and Frederick M. Helleiner, 491–95. Toronto: University of Toronto Press.

Shapiro, Robert Y., and John T. Young. 1989. "Public Opinion and the Welfare State: The United States in Comparative Perspective." *Political Science Quarterly* 104 (Spring): 59–89.

Sheldon, Kennin M., Richard M. Ryan, Laird J. Rawsthorne, and Barbara Ilardi. 1997. "Trait Self and True Self: Cross-Role Variation in the Big-Five Personality Traits and Its Relations with Psychological Authenticity and Subjective Well-Being." *JPSP* 73:1380–93.

Sheridan, Richard B. 1984. "The Domestic Economy." In Greene and Pole 1984, 43–85.

Sherkat, Darren E. 2001. "Tracking the Restructuring of American Religion: Religious Affiliation and Patterns of Religious Mobility, 1973–1998." *SF* 79 (June): 1459–93.

Sherkat, Darren E., and Christopher G. Ellison. 1999. "Recent Developments and Current Controversies in the Sociology of Religion." *ARS* 25:363–94.

Sherkat, Darren E., and John Wilson. 1995. "Preferences, Constraints, and Choices in Religious Markets: An Examination of Religious Switching and Apostasy." *SF* 73 (March): 993–1026.

Shi, David E. 1985. *The Simple Life: Plain Living and High Thinking in American Culture*. New York: Oxford University Press.

Shields, Stephanie A., and Beth B. Koster. 1989. "Emotional Stereotyping of Parents in Child Rearing Manuals, 1915–1980." *Social Psychology Quarterly* 52 (March): 44–55.

Shirley, Michael. 1991. "The Market and Community Culture in Antebellum Salem, North Carolina." *JER* 11 (Summer): 219–48.

Shove, Elizabeth. 2003. *Comfort, Cleanliness and Convenience: The Social Organization of Normality*. New York: Berg Publishers.

Shrum, L. J., Robert S. Wyer Jr., and Thomas C. O'Guinn. 1998. "The Effects of Television Consumption on Social Perceptions: The Use of Priming Procedures to Investigate Psychological Processes." *JCR* 24 (March): 447–58.

Shumway, David. 1998. "Something Old, Something New: Romance and Marital Advice in the 1920s." In Stearns and Lewis 1998, 305–18.

Shweder, Richard A., and Edmund J. Bourne. 1984. "Does the Concept of the Person Vary Crossculturally?" In *Culture Theory: Essays on Mind, Self, and Emotion*, ed. Richard A. Shweder and Robert A. LeVine, 158–99. New York: Cambridge University Press.

Sicherman, Barbara. 1976. "The Paradox of Prudence: Mental Health in the Gilded Age." *JAH* 62 (March): 890–912.

———. 2001. "'The Wicked Agency of Others': Community, Law, and Marital Conflict in Vermont, 1790–1830." *JER* 21 (Spring): 19–39.

Silver, Allan. 1990. "Friendship in Commercial Society: Eighteenth-Century Social Theory and Modern Sociology." *AJS* 95 (May): 1474–1504.

———. 1997. "'Two Different Sorts of Commerce'—Friendship and Strangership in Civil Society." In Weintraub and Kumar 1997, 43–74.

Simmel, Georg. 1908. "The Stranger." In *The Sociology of Georg Simmel*. Trans. Kurt H. Wolff. Glencoe, IL: Free Press, 1950.

———. 1922. *Conflict and the Web of Group Affiliations*. Trans. K. Wolff and R. Bendix. New York: Free Press, 1955.

———. 1971. *On Individuality and Social Forms: Selected Writings*. Ed. Donald N. Levine. Chicago: University of Chicago Press.

Simmons, James C. 2000. *Star-Spangled Eden*. New York: Carroll & Graf.

Simon, Gregory E., and Michael Vonkorff. 1995. "Recall of Psychiatric History in Cross-sectional Surveys: Implications for Epidemiologic Research." *Epidemiological Review* 17:221–27.

Simon, Gregory E., Michael Vonkorff, T. Bedirhan Ustun, Richard Gater, Oye

Gureje, and Norman Sartorius. 1995. "Is the Lifetime Risk of Depression Actually Increasing?" *Journal of Clinical Epidemiology* 48 (9): 1109–18.

Simon, Herbert A. 1957. *Models of Man: Social and Rational: Mathematical Essays on Rational Human Behavior in a Social Setting.* New York: Wiley.

Simon, Rita J., and Jean M. Landis. 1989. "Women's and Men's Attitudes About a Woman's Place and Role." *POQ* 53 (Summer): 265–76.

Singleton, Gregory H. 1976. "Protestant Voluntary Organizations and the Shaping of Victorian America." In *Victorian America*, ed. Daniel Walker Howe, 47–58. Philadelphia: University of Pennsylvania Press.

Skocpol, Theda. 1997. "The Tocqueville Problem: Civic Engagement in American Democracy." *SSH* 21 (Winter): 455–79.

———. 1999. "Associations Without Members." *American Prospect* 45 (July–August): 66–77.

———. 1999. "How Americans Became Civic." In Skocpol and Fiorina 1999, 27–80.

———. 2002. "United States: From Membership to Advocacy." In *Democracies in Flux: The Evolution of Social Capital in Contemporary Society*, ed. Robert D. Putnam, 103–36. New York: Oxford University Press.

———. 2004. "Voice and Inequality: The Transformation of American Civic Democracy." *Perspectives on Politics* 2 (1): 3–20.

Skocpol, Theda, and Morris P. Fiorina, eds. 1999. *Civic Engagement in American Democracy.* Washington DC: Brookings Institution Press.

Skocpol, Theda, Marshall Ganz, and Ziad Munson. 2000. "A Nation of Organizers: The Institutional Origins of Voluntarism in the United States." *American Political Science Review* 94 (September): 527–46.

Skocpol, Theda, and Jennifer Lynn Oser. 2004. "Organization Despite Adversity: The Origins and Development of African American Fraternal Associations." *SSH* 28 (Fall): 367–439.

Slater, Don. 1997. *Consumer Culture and Modernity.* Cambridge: Polity Press.

Slesnick, Daniel T. 2001. *Consumption and Social Welfare: Living Standards and their Distribution in the United States.* New York: Cambridge University Press.

Sloane, David Charles. 1991. *The Last Great Necessity: Cemeteries in American History.* Baltimore: Johns Hopkins University Press.

Smelser, Neil J., and Paul B. Baltes, eds. 2004. *International Encyclopedia of the Social & Behavioral Sciences.* New York: Elsevier.

Smith, Barbara Clark. 2005. "Beyond the Vote: The Limits of Deference in Colonial Politics." *Early American Studies* 3 (2): 341–62.

Smith, Billy G. 1981. "The Material Lives of Laboring Philadelphians, 1750 to 1800." *WMQ* 3rd Ser., 38 (April): 163–202.

———, ed. 2004. *Down and Out in Early America.* University Park: Pennsylvania State University Press.

Smith, Christian, ed. 2003. *The Secular Revolution: Power, Interests, and Conflict in the Secularization of American Public Life.* Berkeley: University of California Press.

———. 2003. "Introduction: Rethinking the Secularization of American Public Life." In Christian Smith 2003, 1–96.

———. 2007. "Getting a Life: The Challenge of Emerging Adulthood." *Books &*

Culture: A Christian Review (November). http://www.christianitytoday.com/bc/2007/novdec/2.10.html.

Smith, Daniel Scott. 1973. "Parental Power and Marriage Patterns: An Analysis of Historical Trends in Hingham, Massachusetts." *Journal of Marriage and the Family* 35 (August): 419–28.

———. 1978. "'Modernization' and American Social History." *SSH* 2 (Spring): 361–67.

———. 1978. "The Dating of the American Sexual Revolution." In Gordon 1978, 426–38.

———. 1983. "Differential Mortality in the United States before 1900." *JIH* 33 (Spring): 735–59.

———. 1987. "'Early' Fertility Decline in America: A Problem in Family History." *Journal of Family History* 12 (1–3): 73–84.

———. 1989. "'All in Some Degree Related to Each Other': A Demographic and Comparative Resolution of the Anomaly of New England Kinship." *AHR* 94 (February): 44–77.

———. 1994. "Female Householding in Late Eighteenth Century America and the Problem of Poverty." *JSH* 28:83–107.

———. 1996. "'The Number and Quality of Children': Education and Marital Fertility in Early Twentieth-Century Iowa." *SSH* 30 (Winter):367–92.

Smith, Daniel Scott, and J. David Hacker. 1996. "Cultural Demography: New England Deaths and the Puritan Perception of Risk." *JIH* 25 (Winter): 367–92.

Smith, Daniel Scott, and M. S. Hindus. 1975. "Premarital Pregnancy in America, 1640–1971." *JIH* 4 (Spring): 537–70.

Smith, Judith E. 1985. *Family Connections: A History of Italian and Jewish Immigrant Lives in Providence, Rhode Island, 1900–1940*. Albany: State University of New York Press.

Smith, Merril D. 1991. *Breaking the Bonds: Marital Discord in Pennsylvania, 1730–1830*. New York: New York University Press.

Smith, Page. 1969. "Anxiety and Despair in American History." *WMQ* 3rd Ser., 26 (July): 416–24.

Smith, Tom W. 1979. "Happiness: Time Trends, Seasonal Variations, Intersurvey Differences, and Other Mysteries." *Social Psychology Quarterly* 42 (March): 18–30.

———. 1988. "A Report: Nuclear Anxiety." *POQ* 52 (Winter): 557–75.

———. 1990. "The Sexual Revolution." *POQ* 54 (Fall): 415–35.

———. 1990." Social Inequality in Cross-national Perspective." In *Attitudes to Inequality and the Role of Government*, ed. Duane F. Alwin et al., 21–29. Rijswijk: Sociaal en Cultureel Planbureua; Alphen aan des Rijn: Samsom (Netherlands).

———. 1990. "Trends in Voluntary Group Membership: Comments on Baumgartner and Walker." *American Journal of Political Science* 34 (August): 646–61.

———. 1992. "Are Conservative Churches Growing?" *Review of Religious Research* 33 (June): 305–29.

———. 1997. "Factors Relating to Misanthropy in Contemporary American Society." *Social Science Research* 26 (June): 170–96.

———. 2000. "Changes in the Generation Gap, 1972–1998." GSS Social Change Report 43. National Opinion Research Center, Chicago.

———. 2003. "American Sexual Behavior: Trends, Socio-Demographic Differences, and Risk Behavior." GSS Topical Report 25, version 5.0. National Opinion Research Center, Chicago.

———. 2006. "The National Spiritual Transformation Study." *Journal for the Scientific Study of Religion* 45 (2): 283–96.

Smith, Tom W., and Seokho Kim. 2007. "Counting Religious Nones and Other Religious Measurement Issues: A Comparison of the Baylor Religion Survey and General Social Survey." GSS Methodological Report 110. National Opinion Research Center, Chicago.

Smith-Lovin, Lynn. 2007. "The Strength of Weak Identities: Social Structural Sources, Situation, and Emotional Experience." *Social Psychology Quarterly* 70 (June): 106–24.

Smith-Rosenberg, Carroll. 1975. "The Female World of Love and Ritual: Relations Between Women in Nineteenth-Century America." *Signs* 1 (Autumn): 1–29.

Smock, Pamela J. 2000. "Cohabitation in the United States." *ARS* 26:1–20.

Snibbe, Alana Conner, and Hazel Rose Markus. 2005. "You Can't Always Get What You Want: Educational Attainment, Agency, and Choice." *JPSP* 88 (April): 703–20.

Snow, Dean R., and Kim M. Lanphear. 1988. "European Contact and Indian Depopulation in the Northeast: The Timing of the First Epidemics." *Ethnohistory* 35 (Winter): 34–59.

Sobel, Mechal. 2000. *Teach Me Dreams: The Search for Self in the Revolutionary Era.* Princeton, NJ: Princeton University Press.

Solomon, Sheldon, Jeff Greenberg, and Thomas A. Pyszczynski. 2003. "Lethal Consumption: Death-Denying Materialism." In Kasser and Kanner 2003, 127–46.

Soltow, Lee. 1992. "Inequalities in the Standard of Living in the United States, 1798–1875." In Gallman and Wallis 1992, 121–71.

———. 1993. "Wealth and Income Distribution." In Cayton, Gorn, and Williams 1993, 1517–31.

Somers, Dale A. 1971. "The Leisure Revolution: Recreation in the American City, 1820–1920." *Journal of Popular Culture* 5 (Summer): 125–47.

Sommerville, C. John. 1998. "Secular Society/Religious Population: Our Tacit Rules for Using the Term 'Secularization.'" *Journal for the Scientific Study of Religion* 37 (June): 249–53.

Spencer, Liz, and Ray Pahl. 2006. *Rethinking Friendship: Hidden Solidarities Today.* Princeton, NJ: Princeton University Press.

Spenner, Kenneth I. 1983. "Temporal Change in the Skill Level of Work." *ASR* 48 (December): 824–37.

Spierenburg, Pieter. 2006. "Violence and Culture: Bloodshed in Two or Three Worlds." Paper presented to the Center for the Study of Law and Society, University of California, Berkeley.

Spillane, Joseph H. 2000. *Cocaine: From Medical Marvel to Modern Menace in the United States, 1884–1920.* Baltimore: Johns Hopkins University Press.

Spindler, George D., and Louise Spindler. 1983. "Anthropologists View American Culture." *Annual Review of Anthropology* 12:49–78.

Springer, Kristen W. 2007. "Research or Rhetoric? A Response to Wilcox and Nock." *Sociological Forum* 22 (March): 111–16.

Spurlock, John C., and Cynthia A. Magistro, 1998. *New and Improved: The Transformation of American Women's Emotional Culture*. New York: New York University Press.

Srole, Leo. 1980. "The Midtown Manhattan Longitudinal Study vs. The Mental Paradise Lost' Doctrine." *Archives of General Psychiatry* 37 (February): 209–26.

Staloff, Darren Marcus. 1999. "'Where Religion and Profit Jump Together': Commerce and Piety in Puritan New England." *Reviews in American History* 27:8–13.

Stanger-Ross, Jordan, Christina Collins, and Mark J. Stern. 2005. "Falling Far from the Tree: Transitions to Adulthood and the Social History of Twentieth-Century America." *SSH* 29 (Winter): 625–48.

Staples, Ruth, and June Warren Smith. 1954. "Attitudes of Grandmothers and Mothers Toward Child-Rearing Practices." *Child Development* 25 (June): 91–7.

Stark, Rodney. 1999. "Secularization, R.I.P." *Sociology of Religion* 60 (Fall): 259–73.

Stark, Rodney, and Roger Finke. 1988. "American Religion in 1776: A Statistical Portrait." *Sociological Analysis* 49 (1): 39–51.

Stave, Bruce Martin. 1966. "The New Deal, the Last Hurrah, and the Building of an Urban Political Machine: Pittsburgh Committeemen, a Case Study." *Pennsylvania History* 33 (4): 460–83.

Stearns, Carol Zisowitz, and Peter N. Stearns. 1986. *Anger: The Struggle for Emotional Control in America's History*. Chicago: University of Chicago Press.

Stearns, Peter N. 1980. "Modernization and Social History: Some Suggestions, and a Muted Cheer." *JSH* 14 (Fall): 189–209.

———. 1983. "The New Social History." In Gardner and Adams 1983, 3–22 .

———. 1984. "The Idea of Postindustrial Society: Some Problems." *JSH* 17 (Summer): 685–93.

———. 1989. "Suppressing Unpleasant Emotions: The Development of a Twentieth-Century American Style." In Barnes and Stearns 1989, 230–61.

———. 1993. "The Old Social History and the New." In Cayton, Gorn, and Williams 1993, 237–50.

———. 1993. "Girls, Boys, and Emotions: Redefinitions and Historical Change." *JAH* 80 (June): 36–74.

———. 1994. *American Cool: Constructing a Twentieth- Century Emotional Style*. New York: New York University Press.

———. 1997. "Stages of Consumerism: Recent Work on the Issues of Periodization." *Journal of Modern History* 69 (March): 102–17.

———. 1998. "Consumerism and Childhood: New Targets for American Emotions." In Stearns and Lewis 1998, 396–413.

———. 1999. *Battleground of Desire: The Struggle for Self- Control in Modern America*. New York: New York University Press.

———. 2001. *Consumerism in World History: The Global Transformation of Desire*. New York: Routledge.

———. 2003. *Anxious Parents: A History of Modern Childrearing in America*. New York: New York University Press.

———. 2006. "Fear and Contemporary History: A Review Essay." *JSH* 40 (Winter): 477–84.

———. 2007. *Revolutions in Sorrow: the American Experience of Death in Global Perspective*. Boulder, CO: Paradigm Publishers.

Stearns, Peter N., and Timothy Haggerty. 1991. "The Role of Fear: Transitions in American Emotional Standards for Children, 1850–1950." *AHR* 96 (February): 63–94.

Stearns, Peter N., and Jan Lewis, eds. 1998. *An Emotional History of the United States*. New York: New York University Press.

Stearns, Peter N., and Carol Z. Stearns. 1985. "Emotionology: Clarifying the History of Emotions and Emotional Standards." *AHR* 90 (October): 813–36.

Steckel, Richard H. 1994. "Heights and Health in the United States, 1710–1950." In Komlos 1994, 153–72 .

———. 1995. "Stature and the Standard of Living." *Journal of Economic Literature* 33 (December): 1903–40.

———. 1999. "Nutritional Status in the Colonial American Economy." *WMQ* 56 (January): 31–52.

———. 2009. "Heights and Human Welfare: Recent Developments and New Directions." *Explorations in Economic History* 46:1–23.

Steckel, Richard F., and Roderick Floud, eds. 1997. *Health and Welfare During Industrialization*. Chicago: University of Chicago Press.

———. 1997. Conclusions to Steckel and Floud 1997, 423–49.

Steckel, Richard H., and Carolyn M. Moehling. 2001. "Wealth Inequality Trends in Industrializing New England: New Evidence and Tests of Competing Hypotheses." *JEH* 61 (March): 160–83.

Steffensmeier, Darrell, Cathy Streifel, and Miles D. Harper. 1997. "Relative Cohort Size and Youth Crime in the United States, 1953–1984." *ASR* 52 (October): 702–10.

Steigerwald, David. 2006. "All Hail the Republic of Choice: Consumer History as Contemporary Thought." *JAH* 93 (September): 385–403.

Steinberg, Allen. 1986. "'The Spirit of Litigation:' Private Prosecution and Criminal Justice in Nineteenth Century Philadelphia." *JSH* 20 (Winter): 231–50.

Steiner, J. F. 1933. "Recreation and Leisure Time Activities." In *President's Research Committee on Recent Social Trends*. Vol. 2, 912–57.

Steinmetz, George, and Erik Olin Wright. 1989. "The Fall and Rise of the Petty Bourgeoisie: Changing Patterns of Self-Employment in the Postwar United States." *AJS* 94 (March): 973–1018.

Stevens, Ann Huff. 2001. "Changes in Earnings Instability and Job Loss." *Industrial and Labor Relations Review* 55 (October): 60–78.

Stevens, David A. 1990. "New Evidence on the Timing of Early Life Transitions: The United States 1900 to 1980." *Journal of Family History* 15 (2): 163–78.

Stevenson, Betsey, and Justin Wolfers. 2007. "Marriage and Divorce: Changes and Their Driving Forces." *JEP* 21 (Spring): 27–52.

———. 2008. "Economic Growth and Subjective Well-Being: Reassessing the Easterlin Paradox." Unpublished paper, University of Pennsylvania. http://ssrn.com/abstract=1121237.

Stewart, David W. 1992. "Speculations on the Future of Advertising Research." *Journal of Advertising* 21 (September): 1–19.

Stewart, James Brewer. 2001. "Civil War: Domestic Effects." In *Oxford Companion to American History*, ed. Paul Boyer, 132–33. New York: Oxford University Press.

Stock, Catherine McNicol. 1992. *Main Street in Crisis: The Great Depression and the Old Middle Class on the Northern Plains*. Chapel Hill: University of North Carolina Press.

Stockard, Jean, and Robert M. O'Brien. 2002. "Cohort Variations and Changes in Age-Specific Suicide Rates over Time: Explaining Variations in Youth Suicide." *SF* 81 (December): 605–42.

Stokes, Melvyn. 1996. Introduction to Stokes and Conway 1996, 1–20.

Stokes, Melvyn, and Stephen Conway, eds., *The Market Revolution in America: Social, Political, and Religious Expressions, 1800–1880*. Charlottesville : University Press of Virginia.

Stolle, Dietlind, and Marc Hooghe. 2004. "Review Article: Inaccurate, Exceptional, One-Sided or Irrelevant? The Debate about the Alleged Decline of Social Capital and Civic Engagement in Western Societies." *British Journal of Political Science* 35:149–67.

Stolle, Dietlind, Stuart Soroka, and Richard Johnston. 2008. "When Does Diversity Erode Trust? Neighborhood Diversity, Interpersonal Trust and the Mediating Effect of Social Interactions." *Political Studies* 56 (1): 57–75.

Stone, Lawrence. 1977. *Family, Sex, and Marriage in England, 1500–1800*. New York: Harper & Row.

Storpfer, Miles D. 1990. *Intelligence and Giftedness*. San Francisco: Jossey-Bass.

Story, Ronald. 1993. "Social Class." In Cayton, Gorn, and Williams 1993, 467–82.

———. 1996. "Artisans and Capitalist Development." *JER* 16 (Summer): 257–71.

Stout, Harry S., and D. G. Hart, eds. 1997. *New Directions in American Religious History*. New York Oxford University Press.

Stout, Harry S., and Robert M. Taylor Jr. 1997. "Studies of Religion in American Society: The State of the Art." In Stout and Hart 1997, 15–50.

Strasser, Susan. 1989. *Satisfaction Guaranteed: The Making of the American Mass Market*. New York: Pantheon.

———. 2002. "Making Consumption Conspicuous: Transgressive Topics Go Mainstream." *Technology and Culture* 43 (October): 755–70.

Strauss, Richard S., and Harold A. Pollack. 2002. "Epidemic Increase in Childhood Overweight, 1986–1998." *Journal of the American Medical Association* 286 (December 12): 2845–88.

Stump, Roger W. 1998. "The Effects of Geographical Variability on Protestant Church Membership Trends, 1980–1990." *Journal for the Scientific Study of Religion* 37 (December): 636–51.

Sullins, D. Paul. 1993. "Switching Close to Home: Volatility or Coherence in Protestant Affiliation Patterns?" *SF* 72 (December): 399–419.

Sullivan, Teresa A., Elizabeth Warren, and Jay Lawrence Westbrook. 2000. *The Fragile Middle Class: Americans in Debt*. New Haven, CT: Yale University Press.

Sunder, Marco. 2004. "The Height of Tennessee Convicts: Another Piece of the 'Antebellum Puzzle.'" *Economics & Human Biology* 2 (March): 75–86.

Sussman, Warren I. 1984. "Culture and Civilization in the Nineteen-Twenties." In Sussman 1984, 105–21.

———. 1984. *Culture as History*. New York: Pantheon.

———. 1984. "'Personality' and the Making of Twentieth-Century Culture." In Sussman 1984, 271–85.

Suttles, Gerald. 1972. *The Social Construction of Communities*. Chicago: University of Chicago Press.

Sutton, John R. 1991. "The Political Economy of Madness: The Expansion of the Asylum in Progressive America." *ASR* 56 (October): 665–78.

Swaan, Abram de. 1995. "Widening Circles of Social Identification: Emotional Concerns in Sociogenetic Perspective." *Theory, Culture, & Society* 12 (2): 25–39.

Swart, Koenraad. 1962. "'Individualism' in the Mid-Nineteenth Century." *Journal of the History of Ideas* 23 (January–March): 77–90.

Swatos, William H. Jr., and Kevin J. Christiano. 1999. "Secularization Theory: The Course of a Concept." *Sociology of Religion* 60 (Fall): 209–28.

Sweeney, Megan M. 2002. "Two Decades of Family Change: The Shifting Economic Foundations of Marriage." *ASR* 67 (February): 132–47.

Swendsen, Joel D., Kathleen R. Merikang, Glorisa J. Canino, Ronald C. Kessler, Maritza Rubio-Stipec, and Jules Angst. 1998. "The Comorbidity of Alcoholism with Anxiety and Depressive Disorders in Four Geographic Communities." *Comprehensive Psychiatry* 39 (July–August): 176–84.

Swidler, Ann. 1973. "The Concept of Rationality in the Work of Max Weber." *Sociological Inquiry* 43 (1): 35–42.

———. 1992. "Cultural Constructions of Modern Individualism." Paper presented to the American Sociological Association, Pittsburgh.

———. 1996. "Geertz's Ambiguous Legacy." *Contemporary Sociology* 25 (May): 299–302.

———. 2001. *Talk of Love: How Culture Matters*. Chicago: University of Chicago Press.

———. 2002. "Saving the Self: Endowment versus Depletion in American Institutions." In *Meaning and Modernity: Religion, Polity, and Self*, ed. Richard Madsen, William M. Sullivan, Ann Swidler, and Steven M. Tipton, 41–55. Berkeley: University of California Press.

Swiencicki, Mark A. 1998. "Consuming Brotherhood: Men's Culture, Style, and Recreation as Consumer Culture, 1880- 1930." *JSH* 31(Summer): 773–808.

Swindle, Ralph Jr., Kenneth Heller, Bernice Pescosolido, and Saeko Kikuzawa. 2000. "Responses to Nervous Breakdowns in America over a 40-year Period: Mental Health Policy Implications." *American Psychologist* 55 (July): 740–49.

Tangires, Helen. 2003. *Public Markets and Civic Culture in Nineteenth-Century America*. Baltimore: Johns Hopkins University Press.

Tarr, Joel A. 1984. "The Evolution of the Urban Infrastructure in the Nineteenth and Twentieth Centuries." In *Perspectives on Urban Infrastructure*, National Academy of Sciences, 4–66. Washington DC: National Academy Press.

———. 1984. "Water and Wastes: A Retrospective Assessment of Wastewater Technology, 1800–1932." *Technology and Culture* 25 (April): 226–63.

———. 1989. "Infrastructure and City-Building in the Nineteenth and Twentieth Centuries." In *City at the Point: Essays on the Social History of Pittsburgh*, ed. Samuel P. Hays, 213–62. Pittsburgh: University of Pittsburgh Press.

Tarr, Joel A., and Josef W. Konvitz. 1987. "Patterns in the Development of the Urban Infrastructure." In *American Urbanism: A Historical Review*, ed. Howard Gillette Jr. and Zane L. Miller, 195–236. New York: Greenwood Press.

Tarr, Joel A., and Mark Tebeau. 1996. "Managing Danger in the Home Environment, 1900–1940." *JSH* 29 (Summer): 797–816.

Taylor, Carl. 1923. "The Rise of the Rural Problem." *SF* 2 (November): 29–36.

Taylor, George Rogers. 1968. *The Transportation Revolution, 1815–1860*. New York: Harper Torchbooks.

Taylor, Paul, and Associates. 2008. "Inside the Middle Class: Bad Times Hit the Good Life." Pew Research Center, April 9. http://pewsocialtrends.org/assets/pdf/MC-Middle-class-report.pdf.

Teaford, Jon C. 1984. *The Unheralded Triumph: City Government in America, 1870–1900*. Baltimore: Johns Hopkins University Press.

Tedlow, Richard S. 1990. *New and Improved: The Story of Mass Marketing in America*. New York: Basic Books.

Teixeira, Ruy A. 1992. *The Disappearing American Voter*. Washington DC: Brookings Institution.

Temin, Peter. 1991."Free Land and Federalism: American Economic Exceptionalism." In Shafer 1991, 71–93.

Tenn, Steven. 2005. "An Alternative Measure of Relative Education to Explain Voter Turnout." *Journal of Politics* 67 (February): 271–82.

Thompson, Peter. 1999. *Rum Punch & Revolution: Taverngoing & Public Life in Eighteenth-Century Philadelphia*. Philadelphia: University of Pennsylvania Press.

Thompson, Roger. 1983. "'Holy Watchfulness' and Communal Conformism: The Functions of Defamation in Early New England Communities." *The New England Quarterly* 56 (December):504–22.

Thompson, Thomas C. 1985. "The Life Course and Labor of a Colonial Farmer." *Historical New Hampshire* 40 (3–4): 135–55.

Thomson, Irene Taviss. 1989. "The Transformation of the Social Bond: Images of Individualism in the 1920s Versus the 1970s." *SF* 67 (June): 851–70.

———. 1992. "Individualism and Conformity in the 1950s vs. the 1980s." *Sociological Forum* 7 (3): 497–516.

———. 2000. *In Conflict No Longer: Self and Society in Contemporary America*. New York: Rowman & Littlefield.

Thoreau, Henry David. 1854. *Walden, or, Life in the Woods*. Ed. Robert F. Sayre. Online repr., http://etext.lib.virginia.edu/toc/modeng/public/ThoWald.html, 1995.

Thornton, Arland. 1989. "Changing Attitudes Toward Family Issues in the United States." *Journal of Marriage and the Family* 51 (November): 873–93.

Thorp, Daniel B. 1996. "Taverns and Tavern Culture on the Southern Colonial

Frontier: Rowan County, North Carolina, 1753–1776." *Journal of Southern History* 62 (November): 661–88.

Tilly, Charles. 1984. *Big Structures, Large Processes, and Huge Comparisons*. New York: Russell Sage.

Tipps, Dean C. 1973. "Modernization Theory and the Comparative Study of Societies: A Critical Perspective." *Comparative Studies in Society and History* 15 (January): 199–226.

Tiryakian, Edward A. 1992. "Dialectics of Modernity: Reenchantment and Dedifferentiation as Counterprocesses." In Haferkamp and Smelser 1992, 78–96.

Tobey, Ronald C. 1996. *Technology as Freedom: The New Deal and the Electrical Modernization of the American Home*. Berkeley: University of California Press.

Tobey, Ronald C., Charles Wetherell, and Jay Brigham. 1990. "Moving Out and Settling In: Residential Mobility, Home Owning, and the Public Enframing of Citizenship, 1921–1950." *AHR* 95 (December): 1395–1423.

Tocqueville, Alexis de. 1836. *Democracy in America*. Ed. J. P. Mayer. Trans. George Lawrence. Garden City, NY: Doubleday, 1969.

Tomaskovic-Devey, Donald, Catherine Zimmer, Kevin Stainback, Corre Robinson, Tiffany Taylor, and Tricia McTague. 2006. "Documenting Desegregation: Segregation in American Workplaces by Race, Ethnicity, and Sex, 1966–2003." *ASR* 71 (August): 565–88.

Tönnies, Ferdinand. 1887. *Community and Society*. Trans. and ed. C. P. Loomis. New York: Harper Torchbooks, 1957.

Toulmin, Stephen, and Jane Goodfield. 1982. *The Discovery of Time*. Phoenix ed. Chicago: University of Chicago Press.

Trattner, Walter I. 1994. *From Poor Law to Welfare State: A History of Social Welfare in America*. 5th ed. New York: Free Press.

Tremblay, Carol Horton, and Davina C. Ling. 2005. "AIDS Education, Condom Demand, and the Sexual Activity of American Youth." *Health Economics* 14 (August): 851–67.

Triandis, Harry C. 1990. "Cross-Cultural Studies of Individualism and Collectivism." In *Nebraska Symposium on Motivation*, ed. J. Berman, 41–133. Lincoln: University of Nebraska Press.

Tropea, J. L. 1989. "Rational Capitalism and Municipal Government." *SSH* 13 (Summer): 137–58.

Trzesniewski, Kali H., and M. Brent Donnellan. In Press. "Rethinking 'Generation Me': A Study of Cohort Effects from 1976–2006." *Perspectives in Psychological Science*.

Trzesniewski, Kali H., M. Brent Donnellan, and Richard W. Robins. 2008. "Is 'Generation Me' Really More Narcissistic Than Previous Generations?" *Journal of Personality* 76 (August): 903–18.

Turcotte, Martin. 2007. "Time Spent with Family During a Typical Workday, 1986 to 2005 ." *Canadian Social Trends* Catalogue No. 11–008. Ottawa: Statistics Canada.

Turner, Bryan S. 1987. "A Note on Nostalgia." *Theory, Culture, and Society* 4 (February): 147–56.

Turner, Charles F., Maria A. Villarroel, James R. Chromy, Elizabeth Eggleston, and Susan M. Rogers. 2005. "Same-Gender Sex among U.S. Adults: Trends across the Twentieth Century and during the 1990s." *POQ* 69 (Fall): 439–62.

Turner, James. 1985. *Without God, Without Creed: The Origins of Unbelief in America.* Baltimore: Johns Hopkins University Press.

Turner, Ralph. 1976. "The Real Self: From Institution to Impulse." *AJS* 81 (March): 989–1016.

Twenge, Jean M. 2000. "The Age of Anxiety? Birth Cohort Change in Anxiety and Neuroticism, 1952–1993." *JPSP* 79 (6): 1007–21.

Twenge, Jean M., Sara Konrath, Joshua D. Foster, W. Keith Campbell, and Brad J. Bushman. 2008. "Egos Inflating Over Time: A Cross-Temporal Meta-Analysis of the Narcissistic Personality Inventory." *Journal of Personality* 76 (August): 875–902.

Twenge, Jean M., and Susan Nolen-Hoeksema. 2002. "Age, Gender, Race, Socio-economic Status, and Birth Cohort Differences on the Children's Depression Inventory: A Meta-Analysis." *Journal of Abnormal Psychology* 111 (4): 578–88.

Twenge, Jean M., Liqing Zhang, and Charles Im. 2004. "It's Beyond My Control: a Cross-Temporal Meta-analysis of Increasing Externality in Locus of Control, 1960–2002." *Personality and Social Psychology Review* 8:308–19.

Tyrell, Ian. 1991. "American Exceptionalism in the Age of International History." *AHR* 96 (October): 1031–55.

Uhlenberg, Peter. 1978. "Changing Configurations of the Life Course." In *Transitions*, ed. Tamara Hareven, 65–97. New York: Academic Press.

———. 1985. "Death and the Family." In *Growing Up in America: Children in Historical Perspective*, ed. N. Ray Hiner and Joseph M. Hawes, 243–54. Urbana: University of Illinois Press.

Ulrich, Laurel Thatcher. 1982. *Good Wives: Image and Reality in the Lives of Women in Northern New England 1650–1750*. New York: Alfred A. Knopf.

———. 1990. *A Midwife's Tale: The Life of Martha Ballard, Based on Her Diary, 1785–1812*. New York: Vintage.

Umberson, Debra, Kristi Williams, Daniel A. Powers, Meichu D. Chen, and Anna M. Campbell. 2005. "As Good as it Gets? A Life Course Perspective on Marital Quality." *SF* 84 (1): 493–511.

United Nations. 2001. *Compendium on Human Settlements Statistics*. Department of Economic and Social Affairs. http://unstats.un.org/unsd/demographic/sconcerns/housing/housing2.htm.

United States Bureau of the Census. 1972–2009. *Statistical Abstract* [Various Years]. Washington DC: U.S. Government Printing Office. http://www.census.gov/compendia/statab/.

———. 1975. *Historical Statistics of the United States, Colonial Times to 1970, Bicentennial Edition*. Two vols. Washington DC: U.S. Government Printing Office.

———. 1991. "Children's Well-Being: An International Comparison." Statistical Brief SB/91–1. Washington DC: U.S. Government Printing Office.

———. 2009. "Geographical Mobility/Migration." http://www.census.gov/population/www/socdemo/migrate.html.

———. 2009. "HINC-01. Selected Characteristics of Households, by Total Money Income in 2007." *Current Population Survey 2008 Annual Social and Economic Supplement.* http://pubdb3.census.gov/macro/032008/hhinc/new 01_001.htm.

United States Department of Labor, Bureau of Labor Statistics. 1924. "The Cost of Living in the United States." Bulletin No. 357. Washington DC: Government Printing Office.

———. 2005. Consumer Expenditure Survey. ftp://ftp.bls.gov/pub/special.requests/ ce/share/2005/age.txt.

———. 2006. "American Time Use: Table 1." http://www.bls.gov/news.release/atus .t12.htm.

United States Senate. 1909. *Report of the Country Life Commission.* 60th Cong., 2nd sess., Senate Document 705. Washington DC: U.S. Government Printing Office.

Uslaner, Eric M. 1998. "Social Capital, Television, and the 'Mean World': Trust, Optimism, and Civic Participation," *Political Psychology* 19 (September): 441–67.

———. 2002. *The Moral Foundations of Trust.* New York: Cambridge University Press.

———. 2008. "Does Diversity Drive Down Trust?" Unpublished paper, Department of Government and Politics University of Maryland–College Park. http://www .bsos.umd.edu/gvpt/uslaner.

Uslaner, Eric M., and Mitchell Brown. 2005. "Inequality, Trust, and Civic Engagement." *American Politics Research* 33 (6): 868–94.

Valelly, Richard M. 1990. "Vanishing Voters." *American Prospect* 1 (Spring): 140–50.

Valetta, Rob. 1999. "Recent Research on Job Stability and Security." *Economic Letter* 99–22, Federal Reserve Bank of San Francisco, July 23.

Vandal, Gilles. 2000. *Rethinking Southern Violence: Homicides in Post-Civil War Louisiana, 1866–1884.* Columbus: Ohio State University Press.

Varenne, Hervé. 1977. *Americans Together: Structural Diversity in a Midwestern Town.* New York: Teachers College Press.

———. 1978. "Is Dedham American? The Diagnosis of Things American." *Anthropological Quarterly* 51 (October): 231–45.

Varon, Elizabeth R. 1998. "Tippecanoe and the Ladies, Too: White Women and Party Politics in Antebellum Virginia." In McCall and Yacovone 1998, 141–75

Veenhof, Ben. 2006 "The Internet: Is It Changing the Way Canadians Spend Their Time?" Science, Innovation and Electronic Information Division (SIEID). Ottawa: Statistics Canada.

Veenhoven, Ruut. 1996. "Developments in Satisfaction-Research." *Social Indicators Research* 37 (January): 1–46.

———. 2005. "Is Life Getting Better? How Long and Happily Do People Live in Modern Society?" *European Psychologist* 10 (4): 330–43.

———. 2006. "Average Happiness in 95 Nations 1995–2005." World Database of Happiness, Rank Report 2006–1d. http://worlddatabaseofhappiness.eur.nl.

———. 2008. Correlational findings, World Database of Happiness. http:// worlddatabaseofhappiness.eur.nl.

Veenhoven, Ruut, and Michael Hagerty. 2006. "Rising Happiness in Nations 1946–2004: A Reply to Easterlin." *Social Indicators Research* 79 (December): 421–36.

Vere, James F. 2007. "'Having it All' No Longer: Fertility, Female Labor Supply, and the New Life Choices of Generation X." *DEM* 44 (November): 821–28.

Veroff, Joseph, Elizabeth Douvan, and Richard A. Kulka. 1981. *The Inner American: A Self-Portrait from 1957 to 1976.* New York: Basic Books.

Veroff, Joseph, Richard A. Kulka, and Elizabeth Douvan. 1981. *Mental Health in America: Patterns of Help-Seeking from 1957 to 1976.* New York: Basic Books.

Vickers, Daniel. 1990. "Competency and Competition: Economic Culture in Early America." *WMQ* 3rd Ser., 47 (January): 3–29.

Vinovskis, Maris, ed. 1979. *Studies in American Historical Demography.* New York: Academic Press, 1979.

———. 1983. "American Families in the Past." In Gardner and Adams 1983, 118–138.

———, ed. 1990. *Toward a Social History of the American Civil War: Exploratory Essays.* New York: Cambridge University Press.

———. 1993. "Death." In Cayton, Gorn, and Williams 1993, 2063–70.

Vohs, Kathleen D., Roy F. Baumeister, Brandon J. Schmeichel, Jean M. Twenge, Noelle M. Nelson, and Dianne M. Tice. 2008. "Making Choices Impairs Subsequent Self-Control: A Limited-Resource Account of Decision Making, Self-Regulation, and Active Initiative." *JPSP* 94 (5): 883–98.

Vohs, Kathleen D., and Ronald J. Faber. 2007. "Spent Resources: Self-Regulatory Resource Availability Affects Impulse Buying." *JCR* 33 (March). http://www.journals.uchicago.edu/doi/full/10.1086/510228.

Volz, Candace M. 1992. "The Modern Look of the Twentieth-Century House." In Foy and Schlereth 1992, 25–48.

Von Hoffman, Alexander. 1994. *Local Attachments: The Making of an American Neighborhood, 1850 to 1920.* Baltimore: Johns Hopkins University Press.

Voss, Kim. 1993. *The Making of American Exceptionalism: The Knights of Labor and Class Formation in the Nineteenth Century.* Ithaca, NY: Cornell University Press.

Vovelle, Michel. 1980. "A Century and One-Half of American Epitaphs (1660–1813): Toward the Study of Collective Attitudes about Death." *Comparative Studies in Society and History* 22 (October): 534–47.

Wade, Richard C. 1959. *The Urban Frontier: Pioneer Life in Early Pittsburgh, Cincinnati, Lexington, Louisville, and St. Louis.* Chicago: University of Chicago Press.

Wagner, Carol Christine. 1989. "Town Growth, Town Controversy: Underhill Meetinghouses to 1840." *Vermont History* 57 (Summer):162–79.

Wagner, Peter. 1994. *A Sociology of Modernity: Liberty and Discipline.* New York: Routledge.

———. 1999. "The Resistance that Modernity Constantly Provokes: Europe, America and Social Theory." *Thesis Eleven* 58 (August): 35–58.

———. 2004. "Modernity: History of the Concept." In Smelser and Baltes 2004, 9949–54.

———. 2004. "Self: History of the Concept." In Smelser and Baltes 2004, 13,833–37.

Waite, Linda J., ed. *The Ties That Bind: Perspectives on Marriage and Cohabitation.* New York: Aldine de Gruyter.

Waldfogel, Joel. 2002. "Gifts, Cash, and Stigma." *Economic Inquiry* 40 (July): 415–27.

Waldinger, Roger David. 1996. *Still the Promised City? African-Americans and New Immigrants in Postindustrial New York*. Cambridge, MA: Harvard University Press.

Walker, Mack. 1998. *German Home Towns: Community, State, and General Estate, 1648–1871*. Ithaca, NY: Cornell University Press.

Walker, Melissa. 2000. "Narrative Themes in Oral Histories of Farming Folk." *Agricultural History* 74:340–51.

Wall, Helena M. 1990. *Fierce Communion: Family and Community in Early in America*. Cambridge, MA: Harvard University Press.

Wallace, Anthony F. C. 1972. *Rockdale: The Growth of an American Village in the Early Industrial Revolution*. New York: W. W. Norton.

Walsh, Lorena. 1983. "Urban Amenities and Rural Sufficiency: Living Standards and Consumer Behavior in the Colonial Chesapeake, 1643–1777." *JEH* 43 (March): 109–17.

———. 1992. "Consumer Behavior, Diet, and the Standard of Living in Late Colonial and Early Antebellum America, 1770–1840." In Gallman and Wallis 1992, 217–64.

Walters, Pamela Barnhouse, and Carl M. Briggs. 1993. "The Family Economy, Child Labor, and Schooling: Evidence from the Early Twentieth-Century South." *ASR* 58 (April): 163–81.

Ward, Florence E. 1920. "The Farm Woman's Problem." Department of Agriculture Circular 148. Washington DC: U.S. Government Printing Office.

Warner, R. Stephen Jr. 1993. "Work in Progress Toward a New Paradigm for the Sociological Study of Religion in the United States." *AJS* 98 (March): 1044–93.

Warner, Sam Bass Jr. 1962. *Streetcar Suburbs: The Process of Growth in Boston, 1870–1900*. Cambridge, MA: Harvard University Press.

———. 1968. *The Private City: Philadelphia in Three Periods of Its Growth*. Philadelphia: University of Pennsylvania Press.

Warner, W. Lloyd. 1949. *Democracy in Jonesville: A Study in Quality and Inequality*. New York: Harper.

Warner, W. Lloyd, and Paul S. Lunt. 1941. *[Yankee City:] The Social Life of a Modern Community*. Rev. ed. New Haven, CT: Yale University Press, 1950.

Warren, John Robert and Elaine M. Hernandez. 2007. "Did Socioeconomic Inequalities in Morbidity and Mortality Change in the United States over the Course of the Twentieth Century?" *Journal of Health and Social Behavior* 48 (December): 335–51.

Warren, Rick. 2002. *The Purpose Driven Life: What on Earth Am I Here For?* Grand Rapids, MI: Zondervan.

Wartella, Ellen, and Sharon Mazzarella. 1990. "A Historical Comparison of Children's Use of Leisure Time." In *For Fun and Profit: The Transformation of Leisure into Consumption*, ed. Richard Butsch, 173–94. Philadelphia: Temple University Press.

Watkins, Susan Cotts. 1990. "From Local to National Communities: The Transformation of Demographic Regimes, 1870–1960." *Population and Development Review* 16 (June): 241–72.

Watkins, Susan Cotts, Jane A. Menken, and John Bongaarts. 1987. "Demographic Foundations of Family Change." *ASR* 52 (June): 346–58.

Watkinson, James D. 2001. "'Fit Objects of Charity': Community, Race, Faith, and Welfare in Antebellum Lancaster County, Virginia, 1817–1860." *JER* 21 (Spring): 41–70.

Watson, Harry L. 1996. "'The Common Rights of Mankind': Subsistence, Shad, and Commerce in the Early Republican South." *JAH* 83 (June): 13–43.

Way, Peter. 1993. "Evil Humors and Ardent Spirits: The Rough Culture of Canal Construction Laborers." *JAH* 79 (March): 1397–1428.

Weakliem, David L., and Casey Borch. 2006. "Alienation in the United States: Uniform or Group-Specific Change?" *Sociological Forum* 21 (September): 415–38.

Weaver, R. Kent, Robert Y. Shapiro, and Lawrence R. Jacobs. 1995. "The Polls—Trends: Welfare." *POQ* 59 (Winter): 606–27.

Weber, Eugen. 1976. *Peasants into Frenchmen: The Modernization of Rural France, 1870–1914*. Pal Alto, CA: Stanford University Press.

Weber Max. 1904–5. *The Protestant Ethic and the Spirit of Capitalism*. Trans. Talcott Parsons. Rev. ed. New York: Charles Scribner's Sons, 1958.

———. 1920–22. *Economy and Society: An Outline of Interpretive Sociology*. Ed. Guenther Roth and Claus Wittich. Rev. ed. Berkeley: University of California Press, 1968.

Weintraub, Jeff. 1997. "The Theory and Politics of the Public/Private Distinction." In Weintraub and Kumar 1997, 1–42.

Weintraub, Jeff, and Krishan Kumar, eds. 1997. *Public and Private in Thought and Practice: Perspectives on a Grand Dichotomy*. Chicago: University of Chicago Press.

Weiss, Jessica. 2000. *To Have and to Hold: Marriage, the Baby Boom & Social Change*. Chicago: University of Chicago Press.

Weiss, Marc A. 1987. "Planning Subdivisions: Community Builders and Urban Planners in the Early Twentieth Century." *Essays in Public Works History*. Chicago: Public Works Historical Society.

Weiss, Richard. 1988. *The American Myth of Success: From Horatio Alger to Norman Vincent Peale*. Illini ed. Urbana: University of Illinois Press.

Weissman, M. M., M. B. Bland, C. J. Canino, et al. 1992. "The Changing Rate of Major Depression: Cross-National Comparisons." *Journal of the American Medical Association* 268 (December 2): 3098–105.

Weller, Christian. 2006. "The Middle Class Falls Back." *Challenge* 49 (January): 16-43.

Weller, Christian, and Derek Douglas. 2007. "One Nation Under Debt." *Challenge* 50 (January/February): 54–75.

Wellman, Barry. 1979. "The Community Question: The Intimate Networks of East Yorkers." *AJS* 84 (March): 1201–31.

———. 2001. "Physical Place and Cyberplace: The Rise of Personalized Networking." *International Journal of Urban and Regional Research* 25 (June): 227–52.

———. 2004. "Connecting Communities: On and Offline." *Contexts* 3 (Fall): 22–28.

Wells, Brooke E, and Jean M. Twenge. 2005. "Changes in Young People's Sexual Behavior and Attitudes, 1943–1999: A Cross-Temporal Meta-Analysis." *Review of General Psychology* 9 (September): 249–61.

Wells, Robert V. 1975. "Family History and the Demographic Transition." *JSH* 9:1–19.

———. 1982. *Revolutions in Americans' Lives*. Westport, CT: Greenwood Press.

———. 1985. *Uncle Sam's Family: Issues in and Perspectives on American Demographic History*. Albany: State University of New York Press.

———. 1995. "The Mortality Transition in Schenectady, New York, 1880–1930." *SSH* 19 (Fall): 399–423.

———. 2000. *Facing the "King of Terrors": Death and Society in an American Community, 1750–1990*. New York: Cambridge University Press.

Welter, Barbara. 1966. "The Cult of True Womanhood: 1820–1860." *AQ* 18:151–74.

Welter, Rush. 1975. *The Mind of America: 1820–1860*. New York: Columbia University Press.

Wermuth, Thomas S. 1998. "New York Farmers and the Market Revolution: Economic Behavior in the Mid-Hudson Valley, 1780–1830." *JSH* 32 (Fall): 179–96.

West, James [C. Withers]. 1945. *Plainville, U.S.A*. New York: Columbia University Press.

Western, Bruce, and Katherine Beckett. 1999. "How Unregulated Is the U.S. Labor Market? The Penal System as a Labor Market Institution." *AJS* 104 (January): 1030–60.

Whaples, Robert. 2001. "Hours of Work in U.S. History." EH.Net Encyclopedia of Economic and Business History, ed. Robert Whaples. http://eh.net/encyclopedia/article/whaples.work.hours.us.

White, Hayden V. 1973. *Metahistory: The Historical Imagination in Nineteenth-Century Europe*. Baltimore: Johns Hopkins University Press.

———. 1987. *The Content of the Form: Narrative Discourse and Historical Representation*. Baltimore, MD: Johns Hopkins University Press.

———. 1987. "The Value of Narrativity in the Representation of Reality." In *The Content of the Form*, 1–25.

White, Kevin. 1998. "The New Man and Early Twentieth-Century Emotional Culture in the United States." In Stearns and Lewis 1998, 333–56.

White, Leonard D. 1933, "Public Administration." In *President's Research Committee on Social Trends, Recent Social Trends in the United States*. Vol. 1, 1391–1429. New York: McGraw-Hill.

White, Lynn, and John N. Edwards. 1990. "Emptying the Nest and Parental Well-Being: An Analysis of National Panel Data." *ASR* 55 (April): 235–42.

Wiebe, Robert H. 1967. *The Search for Order, 1877–1920*. New York: Hill & Wang.

———. 1995. *Self-Rule: A Cultural History of American Democracy*. Chicago: University of Chicago Press.

Wiener, Jonathan M. 1989. "Radical Historians and the Crisis in American History, 1959–1980." *JAH* 76 (September): 399–434.

———. 1995. "History Lesson." *New Republic* 212 (January 2): 9–12.

Wik, Reynold M. 1972. *Henry Ford and Grass-Roots America*. Ann Arbor: University of Michigan Press.

Wilcox, Brian, Joanne Cantor, Peter Dowrick, Dale Kunkel, Susan Linn, and Edward Palmer. 2004. "A Report of the APA Task Force on Advertising and

Children." American Psychological Association. http://www.apa.org/releases/childrenads_summary.pdf.

Wilcox, Brian, and Steven L. Nock. 2006. "What's Love Got to Do with It? Equality, Equity, Commitment and Women's Marital Quality." *SF* 84 (March): 1321–45.

Wilentz, Sean. 1984. *Chants Democratic: New York City and the Rise of the American Working Class, 1788–1850*. New York: Oxford University Press.

———. 1990. "Society, Politics, and the Market Revolution, 1815–1848." In Foner 1990, 51–71.

———. 1991. "Jacksonian Democracy." In Foner and Garraty 1991, 582–86.

Wilkie, Jacqueline. 1986. "Submerged Sensuality: Technology and Perceptions of Bathing." *JSH* 19 (Summer): 649–64.

Wilkinson, Kenneth. 1978. "Rural Community Change." In *Rural USA: Persistence and Change*, ed. Thomas R. Ford, 115–25. Ames: Iowa State University Press.

Wilkinson, Rupert. 1988. *The Pursuit of American Character*. New York: Harper & Row.

———. 1992. "On American Social Character." In Wilkinson 1992, 1–14.

———, ed. 1992. *American Social Character*. New York: HarperCollins.

Willey, Malcolm, and Stuart Rice. 1933. *Communication Agencies and Social Life*. New York: McGraw-Hill.

Williams, Peter W. 1993. "New England." In Cayton, Gorn, and Williams 1993, 905–26.

———. 1993. "Foodways." In Cayton, Gorn, and Williams 1993, 1331–44.

Williams, Raymond. 1973. *The City and the Country*. New York: Oxford University Press.

Williams, Rhys H., ed. 1997. *Cultural Wars in American Politics: Critical Reviews of a Popular Myth*. New York: Aldine de Gruyter.

Williams, Tannis MacBeth, ed. 1986. *The Impact of Television: A National Experiment in Three Communities*. Orlando, FL: Academic.

Williamson, Jefferey, and Peter H. Lindert. 1980. "Long-Term Trends in American Wealth Inequality." In *Modeling the Distribution and Intergenerational Transmission of Wealth*, ed. James D. Smith, 9–94. Chicago: University of Chicago Press.

Wills, Garry. 1992. *Lincoln at Gettysburg: The Words That Remade America*. New York: Simon & Schuster.

———. 1999. *A Necessary Evil: A History of American Mistrust of Government*. New York: Simon & Schuster.

Wilson, Edmund. 1962. *Patriotic Gore: Studies in the Literature of the American Civil War*. Repr., New York: Norton, 1994.

Wilson, James A., and Walter R. Gove. 1999. "The Intercohort Decline in Verbal Ability: Does It Exist?" *ASR* 64 (April): 253–66.

Wilson, Thomas C. 1996. "Cohort and Prejudice: Whites' Attitudes toward Blacks, Hispanics, Jews, and Asians." *POQ* 60 (Summer): 253–74.

Wilson, W. G. 1979. *The American Woman in Transition*. Westport, CT: Greenwood Press.

Wilson, Warren H. 1912. *The Evolution of the Country Community: A Study in Religious*

Sociology. Boston: Pilgrim Press. Online ed., Google Books, http://books.google
.com/books?id=7X9JAAAAIAAJ&printsec=frontcover&dq=The+Evolution+of+
the+Country+Community.

Wilson, William Julius. 1987. *The Truly Disadvantaged: The Inner City, the Underclass,
and Public Policy*. Chicago: University of Chicago Press.

Winesman, Albert L. 2005. "Religion in America: Who Has None?" Gallup poll,
December 6. http://www.gallup.com/poll/20329/Religion-America-Who-Has-
None.aspx.

Winkle, Kenneth J. 1988. *The Politics of Community: Migration and Politics in Antebellum Ohio*. New York: Cambridge University Press.

———. 1992. "The Voters of Lincoln's Springfield: Migration and Political Participation in an Antebellum City." *JSH* 25 (Spring): 595–611.

Winthrop, John. 1630. *A Modell of Christian Charity*. Repr., Boston: Collections of
the Massachusetts Historical Society, 3rd series, 1838, 7:31–48. Online ed., Ha-
nover Historical Texts Project, http://history.hanover.edu/texts/winthmod.html.

Wirth, Louis. 1928. *The Ghetto*. Chicago: University of Chicago Press.

———. 1938. "Urbanism as a Way of Life." *AJS* 44 (1): 3–24.

Witten, Marsha G. 1993. *All is Forgiven: The Secular Message in American Protestantism*. Princeton, NJ: Princeton University Press.

Wolf, Maryanne. 2007. *Proust and the Squid: The Story and Science of the Reading Brain*.
New York: Harper.

Wolf, Stephanie Grauman. 1976. *Urban Village: Population, Community, and Family
Structure in Germantown, Pennsylvania, 1683–1800*. Princeton, NJ: Princeton University Press.

———. 1994. *As Various as Their Land: The Everyday Lives of Eighteenth-Century Americans*. New York: Harper Perennial.

Wolfe, Alan. 1998. *One Nation, After All*. New York: Viking.

———. 2008. "Hedonic Man: The New Economics and the Pursuit of Happiness."
New Republic 238 (July 9): 47–55.

Wolfson, Adam. 1997. "Individualism: New and Old." *Public Interest* 126 (Winter):
75–88.

Woloson, Wendy A. 2007. "In Hock: Pawning in Early America." *JER* 27 (1): 35–81.

Wood, Gordon S. 1969. *The Creation of the American Republic, 1776–1787*. Repr., New
York : Norton, 1993.

———. 1982. "Conspiracy and the Paranoid Style: Causality and Deceit in the Eighteenth Century." *WMQ* 3rd Ser., 39 (July): 401–41.

———. 1991. "Republicanism." In Foner and Garraty 1991, 930–31.

———. 1994. "Inventing American Capitalism." *New York Review of Books* 41 (June
9): 44–50.

———. 1996. "The Enemy is Us: Democratic Capitalism in the Early Republic."
JER 16 (Summer): 294–308.

———. 1997. "Religion and the American Revolution." In Stout and Hart 1997, 173–
205.

———. 2003. *The American Revolution: A History*. New York: Modern Library.

Wood, Joseph S. 1982. "Village and Community in Early Colonial New England."
Journal of Historical Geography 8 (4) :333–46.

Wood, Michael R., and Louis A. Zurcher. 1988. *The Development of a Postmodern Self*.
New York: Greenwood Press.

Woodward, C. Vann. 1968. "The Comparability of American History." In *The Comparative Approach to American History*, ed. C. Vann Woodward, 3–17. Rev. ed. New
York: Oxford University Press, 1997.

———1991.*The Old World's New World*. New York: Oxford University Press.

Wouters, Cas. 1995. "Etiquette Books and Emotion Management in the 20th Century: Part One: The Integration of Social Classes." *JSH* 29 (Fall): 107–24.

———. 1995. "Etiquette Books and Emotion Management in the 20th Century: Part
Two: The Integration of the Sexes." *JSH* 29 (Winter): 325–40.

Wright, Gwendolyn. 1981. *Building the American Dream: A Social History of Housing in
America*. Cambridge, MA: MIT Press.

Wright, Robert E. 1997. "The First Phase of the Empire State's 'Triple Transition.'"
SSH 21 (Winter): 521–58.

Wu, Jialu. 1994. "How Severe was the Great Depression? Evidence from the Pittsburgh Region." In Komlos 1994, 129–52.

Wuthnow, Robert. 1988. *The Restructuring of American Religion: Society and Faith Since
World War II*. Princeton, NJ: Princeton University Press.

———. 1991. *Acts of Compassion: Caring for Others and Helping Ourselves*. Princeton,
NJ: Princeton University Press.

———. 1994. *Sharing the Journey: Support Groups and America's New Quest for Community*. New York: Free Press.

———. 1995. "A Good Life and a Good Society: The Debate Over Materialism." In
Rethinking Materialism: Perspectives on the Spiritual Dimension of Economic Behavior,
ed. Robert Wuthnow, 1–21. Grand Rapids, MI: William B. Erdmans.

———. 1996. *Christianity and Civil Society*. Valley Forge, PA: Trinity Press International.

———. 1996. *Poor Richard's Almanac: Recovering the American Dream Through the
Moral Dimension of Work, Business, and Family*. Princeton, NJ: Princeton University Press.

———. 1998. *Loose Connections: Joining Together in America's Fragmented Communities*.
Cambridge, MA: Harvard University Press.

———. 2002. "Bridging the Privileged and the Marginalized?" In *Democracies in Flux:
The Evolution of Social Capital in Contemporary Society*, ed. Robert D. Putnam, 59–
102. New York: Oxford University Press.

———. 2004. "Trust as an Aspect of Social Structure." In *Self, Social Structure, and
Beliefs*, ed. Jeffrey C. Alexander, Gary T. Marx, and Christine L. Williams, 143–68.
Berkeley: University of California Press.

———. 2006. *American Mythos: Why Our Best Efforts to Be a Better Nation Fall Short*.
Princeton, NJ: Princeton University Press.

———. 2007. "Myths about American Religion." Heritage Lecture 1049. Washington DC: Heritage Foundation.

Wylie, Laurence. 1964. *Village in the Vaucluse*. New York: Harper & Row.

Wynne, Waller. 1943. "Culture of a Contemporary Rural Community: Harmony, Georgia." *Rural Life Studies* 6. USDA: Washington DC: Bureau of Agricultural Economics.

Yacovone, Donald. 1998. "'Surpassing the Love of Women:' Victorian Manhood and the Language of Fraternal Love." In McCall and Yacovone 1998, 193–221.

Yang, Alan S. 1997. "The Polls—Trends: Attitudes Toward Homosexuality." *POQ* 61 (Fall): 477–507.

Yang, Yang. 2007. "Is Old Age Depressing? Growth Trajectories and Cohort Variations in Late-Life Depression." *Journal of Health and Social Behavior* 48 (March): 16–32.

———. 2008. "Social Inequalities in Happiness in the United States, 1972 to 2004: An Age-Period-Cohort Analysis." *ASR* 73 (April): 204–26.

Yang, Yang, and Kenneth C. Land. 2006. "A Mixed Models Approach to the Age-Period-Cohort Analysis of Repeated Cross-section Surveys, with an Application to Data on Trends in Verbal Test Scores." *Sociological Methodology* 36 (December): 75–97.

Yellin, Janet. 2006. "Economic Inequality in the United States." *Economic Letter of the Federal Reserve Bank of San Francisco* (December). http://www.frbsf.org/publications/economics/letter/2006/el2006-33-34.html.

Zahn, Margaret A. 1980. "Homicide in the Twentieth Century United States." In *History and Crime: Implications for Criminal Justice Policy*, ed. James A. Incardi and Charles E. Faupel, 111–31. Beverly Hills, CA: Sage.

Zakim, Michael. 2001. "Sartorial Ideologies: From Homespun to Ready-Made." *AHR* 106 (December):1553–86.

———. 2003. *Ready-Made Democracy: A History of Men's Dress in the American Republic, 1760–1860*. Chicago: University of Chicago Press.

Zanot, Eric J. 1984. "Public Attitudes Toward Advertising." *International Journal of Advertising* 3 (1): 3–15.

Zelizer, Viviana. 1979. *Morals and Markets: The Development of Life Insurance in the United States*. New York: Columbia University Press.

———.1985. *Pricing the Priceless Child: The Changing Social Value of Children*. Repr., Princeton, NJ: Princeton University Press, 1994.

———. 1994. *The Social Meaning of Money*. New York: Basic Books.

———. 2005. "Culture and Consumption." In *The Handbook of Economic Sociology*, ed. Neil J. Smelser and Richard Swedberg, 331–54. Princeton, NJ: Princeton University Press.

———. 2005. *The Purchase of Intimacy*. Princeton, NJ: Princeton University Press.

Zimmer, Basil G. 1983. "The Metropolitan Community: Changing Spatial Orientation of Residents." Paper presented at the Population Association of America Annual Meeting, Pittsburgh.

Zimmermann, Anke C., and Richard A. Easterlin. 2006 "Happily Ever After? Cohabitation, Marriage, Divorce, and Happiness in Germany." *Population and Development Review* 32 (September): 511–28.

Zimring, Franklin E. 2007. *The Great American Crime Decline*. New York: Oxford University Press.

Zopf, Paul E. Jr. 1992. *Mortality Patterns and Trends in the United States*. Westport, CT: Greenwood Press.

Zorbaugh, Harvey Warren. 1929. *The Gold Coast and the Slum: A Sociological Study of Chicago's Near North Side*. Chicago: University of Chicago Press.

Zuckerman, Michael. 1970. *Peaceable Kingdoms: New England Towns in the Eighteenth Century*. New York: W. W. Norton.

———. 1977. "The Fabrication of Identity in Early America." *WMQ* 34 (April): 183–214.

———. 1978. "Dreams that Men Dare to Dream: The Role of Ideas in Western Modernization." *SSH* 3 (Spring): 332–45.

———, ed. 1982. *Friends and Neighbors: Group Life in America's First Plural Society*. Philadelphia : Temple University Press.

———. 1982. "Introduction: Puritans, Cavaliers, and the Motley Middle." In Zuckerman 1982, 3–25.

———. 1997. "The Dodo and the Phoenix: A Fable of American Exceptionalism." In *American Exceptionalism?* ed. Rick Halpern and Jonathan Morris, 14–35. New York: St. Martin's Press.

———. 1998. "Tocqueville, Turner, and Turds: Four Stories of Manners in Early America." *JAH* 85 (June):13–42.

Zukin, Cliff, Scott Keeter, Molly Andolina, Krista Jenkins, and Michael X. Delli Carping. 2006. *A New Engagement? Political Participation, Civic Life, and the Changing American Citizen*. New York: Oxford University Press.

Zukin, Sharon. 2004. *Point of Purchase: How Shopping Changed American Culture*. New York: Routledge.

Zukin, Sharon, and Jennifer Smith Maguire. 2004. "Consumers and Consumption." *ARS* 30:173–97.

Zunz, Olivier. 1982. *The Changing Face of Inequality*. Chicago: University of Chicago Press.

———. 1985. "The Synthesis of Social Change: Reflections on American Social History." In *Reliving the Past: Worlds of Social History*, ed. Olivier Zunz, 53–114. Chapel Hill: University of North Carolina Press.

Index

Street Corner Society (Whyte), 148
Streetwise (Anderson), 306n117
strikes, 134, 189
structural differentiation, 249n15
sublimation, 196, 197
"Subsiding Sizzle, The" (Pollay), 276n44
substance abuse, 234–35
suburbs/suburbanization: in antebellum
    era, 124; gated communities, 306n118;
    nineteenth century growth of, 48;
    as retreat from public spaces, 172–
    73, 194; separation from urban areas,
    295n65; in twentieth century, 49, 70,
    146, 175–76, 263n72
subway, 161
success, 11, 90, 145, 283n75
Sucher, Kristen, 303n101
"Such Is the Price" (Holmes), 263n72
suffering, 221
suffrage, 154, 182, 183, 185, 186
suicide: depression and, 231–33; due
    to Dust Bowl, 50; on frontier, 33;
    during Great Depression, 51; Lin-
    coln's thoughts of, 230; rates, 341n83,
    342n85; relationship to mobility, 3–4
Sumner, Charles, 133
sumptuary laws, 62, 108
Sunday, Billy, 171
Sunday schools, 120, 201
supernatural, belief in, 209
Supreme Court: concerns over original-
    ism of, 241; invention of rights, 158;
    ruling on abortions, 190; ruling on af-
    firmative action, 190; ruling on mar-
    ried couples, 96, 139, 159; ruling on
    segregation, 190
Supremes, 227
Sussman, Warren I., 326n7, 338n64
Sutch, Richard, 292n44
Swidler, Ann, 98, 329n21
swimming pools, public, 170, 175
sympathy: cultivation of, 5, 9, 36, 195,
    218–22, 224, 242; group life and, 240;
    for poor, 4–5, 43; taught to children,
    224; in twentieth century, 229
Synthesis of Social Change (Zunz), 251n16

Talmadge, Eugene, 53
Tammany Hall political machine, 131
taverns: church services in, 153; closure
    of, 176; ethnic segregation of, 131;
    as parochial meeting place, 164–65,
    180; revolution plotted in, 131; Salem
    witch craft trials and, 165. See also
    bars; saloons
Teach Me Dreams (Sobel), 326n5
technology: control of world through,
    195; effect on human contact, 242;
    for farming, 26, 40, 50, 147; for house
    building, 63–64, 173; industrializa-
    tion and, 45, 247–48n6; living stan-
    dards and, 267n87; as lure to public
    spaces, 168; for mass production, 63;
    as means to affluence, 49; modern-
    ization theory and, 249n15
teenagers. See children; youth
teleological notions, 250n16
telephone service, 67, 69, 92, 144, 147,
    156, 175
television: advertising on, 76; advice
    shows, 196, 325–26n2; aggressiveness
    on, 228–29; as cause of depression,
    345n90; conspiracy trope in, 192; con-
    struction of collective memory, 6; ef-
    fect on American culture/character,
    12; effect on baby boomers, 244; ef-
    fect on political participation, 190;
    effect on violence, 35, 36, 260n47; ef-
    fects on watchers, 178; as entertain-
    ment, 154, 157; hours watched, 177,
    178, 318n36; mental disorders and,
    236; as necessity, 78, 92; paradox of,
    179; pervasiveness of, 70, 272n30; po-
    litical campaigning on, 190; purchases
    of, 67, 69; sex/violence on, 224–25,
    227, 338n64; social groups among fans
    of shows, 157; spread of sympathy
    through, 222; stay-at-home trend and,
    174, 175; subversion of public life, 177–
    78; universal ownership of, 49; visual
    education through, 210. See also media
temperance movement, 126, 130, 132,
    169, 221